Beyond Bollywood and Broadway

BEYOND BOLLYWOOD

AND BROADWAY

Plays from the South Asian Diaspora

Edited by Neilesh Bose

INDIANA UNIVERSITY PRESS

Bloomington and Indianapolis

This book is a publication of
Indiana University Press
601 North Morton Street
Bloomington, IN 47404-3797 USA
http://iupress.indiana.edu

Telephone orders	800-842-6796
Fax orders	812-855-7931
Orders by e-mail	iuporder@indiana.edu

LIBRARY OF CONGRESS CATALOGING-IN-PUBLICATION DATA

Beyond Bollywood and Broadway : plays from the South Asian diaspora / edited by Neilesh Bose.
    p. cm.
  Includes bibliographical references.
  ISBN 978-0-253-35300-9 (cloth : alk. paper)—ISBN 978-0-253-22068-4 (pbk. : alk. paper)
  1. Commonwealth drama (English)—South Asian authors. 2. American drama—South Asian American authors. 3. Canadian drama—South Asian authors. 4. English drama—South Asian authors. 5. South African drama (English)—South Asian authors. 6. South Asians—Drama. 7. South Asian diaspora—Drama. I. Bose, Neilesh.
  PR9087.B49 2009
  822'.9208—dc22   2008043195

1 2 3 4 5 14 13 12 11 10 09

To Rajesh

Contents

Acknowledgments

I wish to thank all the playwrights represented in this collection—Ronnie Govender, Kessie Govender, Kriben Pillay, Shishir Kurup, Aasif Mandvi, Anuvab Pal, Jatinder Verma, Sudha Bhuchar and Kristen Landon-Smith, Rukhsana Ahmad, Rahul Varma, and Rana Bose. All have been generous with their time and energy in support of this project. Their imprints on the South Asian diaspora have enriched both the world of theatre as well as the world at large. It is an honor to document and preserve their work in this format. To all other South Asian diasporic playwrights whose work was not preserved in this book, I hope that this work encourages and stimulates future research, publication, and theatrical production.

Many individuals have supported this endeavor over the course of many years. Professor Rajini Srikanth of the University of Massachusetts, Boston, has encouraged and supported this project from the very beginning. Thanks also to Jisha Menon for encouraging me and providing useful feedback from the outset. Conversations with Sunil Swaroop over the years have greatly enriched and enlarged my ideas. Thanks to Professor Aparna Dharwadker for her conversations and insights over the years about this topic. Ayan Gangapadhyaya remains an inspiration, a friend, and a source of intellectual and dramatic sustenance. Kevin Wetmore, *rafiki yangu*, is a commanding presence of intellect, insight, and humor that has enlarged my approach to this book and my broader perspectives on the study of theatre and performance. Additionally, the influence, though indirect, of the rest of the old Each One Tell One—Javon Johnson, Derrick Sanders, and Mark Clayton Southers—has stayed with me over the years. Likewise, Professor Loren Kruger, whose extraordinary research output and previous guidance has added to my understanding of theatre and performance in ways perhaps not visible from a glance at this book. A special thanks to professor, dada, and friend Sudipto Chatterjee. Others whose influence, support, and inspiration have contributed to the making of this book include Jay Pather, Rajesh Gopie, Logan Shumnugam, Vinay Dharwadker, Charlotte McIvor, and the indefatigable Shishir Kurup. In addition to Shishir, the shape and conception of this book benefited from numerous conversations with Jatinder Verma, Kriben Pillay, Ronnie Govender, and Anuvab Pal.

This work was completed while I was affiliated with Tufts University, the College of St. Rose, and Colorado College. All of these institutions have supported, in various ways, the production of this book. Without this logistical and financial support, this project would not have seen the light of day.

At Indiana University Press, I wish to acknowledge the editorial talents of Rebecca Tolen, who believed in this work from the beginning. Laura McLeod also ably assisted in preparing this book for publication.

A simple thank you will not express the gratitude I feel for how Shahla has given me genuine and unconditional friendship, support, and encouragement.

Without the undying support and love from my father and mother, Somesh and Pompa Bose, none of the present work, and without a doubt, none of me would have been possible. My Rajesh-dada has always been a mentor, friend, and role model. This book is dedicated to him.

ছোটো ভেজা বেড়াল পুতুলকে ডাকছে, বলছে, এসো, আমার কাছে এসো

Beyond Bollywood and Broadway

An Introduction to South Asian Diasporic Theatre

From Jhumpa Lahiri's *The Namesake* to Zadie Smith's *White Teeth* to the writings of well-known authors such as Salman Rushdie, Amitav Ghosh, Arundhati Roy, and Monica Ali, works by South Asian diasporic (South Asians living outside of South Asia) writers figure prominently in contemporary cultural criticism. Popular films such as *Monsoon Wedding, Bend It Like Beckham,* and *Bride and Prejudice* also occupy a familiar place. Still, many people in the United States familiar with the works of these writers would be hard pressed to name a single play by a contemporary playwright of South Asian descent. Theatre rarely enters into discussions of South Asian cultures in the diaspora, although it poses provocative questions. When diaspora is represented onstage, through dramatic literature and performance, what happens? Do we find different questions and different kinds of resolutions? What does the power of performance, that "indescribably mystery," as South African Kriben Pillay puts it, do to our understanding diaspora?

More questions arise when we set out to determine what makes a play a part of "South Asian diasporic theatre." Does any play by or about South Asian immigrants qualify? Many plays written by people of South Asian background have nothing to do with the South Asian diaspora. What about the myriad plays written by non-South Asians that have featured South Asian diasporic roles and/or actors in productions? What about all the South Asian traditions of dance, dance-drama, and folk performance being produced around the world? Finally, what about all the South Asian plays that have been performed in diasporic locations, such as the work of Mahesh Dattani, Girish Karnad, or Vijay Tendulkar? This book documents and preserves plays written *by* and *about* South Asian diasporic people in order to focus on the creation of a South

Asian diasporic dramatic literature, emanating from the South Asian diaspora and accessible to audiences, practitioners, critics, and scholars.

The plays included in this volume reflect a variety of aesthetic, ideological, and practical considerations. Chosen first of all for the aesthetic power they bring to discussions of the South Asian diaspora, each play also examines diasporic concerns in ways that advance an emergent diasporic performance aesthetic. In South Africa and the United States, we see the intersection of class and race in widely different contexts. American Aasif Mandvi's *Sakina's Restaurant* grapples with generations of one family assimilating into America, whereas the life of working-class Indians under apartheid finds dramatic representation in Ronnie Govender's *The Lahnee's Pleasure.* Kessie Govender's *Working Class Hero* confronts race but does so by portraying a racist Indian mid-level manager type, so familiar to the South African environment, as well as the politically conscious Indian ready to smash racialism. Kriben Pillay and Anubav Pal both wrestle with intellectual and academic debates in their pieces. Pillay's *Looking for Muruga* plays with performance aesthetics and race politics, while Anuvab Pal's *Chaos Theory* deals with Indian intellectuals and their travails in American academe.

The United Kingdom and Canada offer realistic drawing room drama along with variations on dramaturgical form and technique. The UK's Rukhsana Ahmad details a realistic and traumatic world of domestic abuse in *Song for a Sanctuary.* Sudha Bhuchar and Kristin Landon-Smith's *Strictly Dandia* engages with a new demographic of young diasporic desis[1] and their world of race, religion, and caste. The two Canadian plays—Rahul Varma's *Bhopal* and Rana Bose's *The Death of Abbie Hoffman*—stand apart from the rest. The former engages with a historical event in India but includes diasporic characters. Bose's play, on the other hand, aims toward dramaturgical innovation and adapts neither a Western nor a South Asian classic but a stalwart of the modern Indian alternative theatre—Badal Sircar's *Micchil* (Procession)—into a South Asian Canadian context. Many of the plays engage with Western classics via South Asian cultural traditions and diasporic politics, including Shishir Kurup's *Merchant on Venice* and Jatinder Verma's *2001: A Ramayana Odyssey.*

Background on South Asian Diasporas

South Asian diasporas have planted roots all over the globe, including Africa, Europe, the Americas, and Southeast Asia. From places like Fiji, Trinidad and Tobago, Mauritius, and British Guyana, where South Asians form a sizable part of the population, to the United States and the United Kingdom, where South Asians form highly visible minority populations, hardly any areas of the world are untouched by the South Asian diaspora. The historical experiences that shape the making of this diaspora are as diverse as the countries that form their homes.

Long before the modern era's migrations of indentured laborers in the nineteenth century and middle-class professionals in the twentieth, South Asians were connected to other parts of the world by pre-modern trade routes and ancient exchanges of culture, ideas, and texts.

Before the eleventh century, trade linked South Indian Coromandel kings with Southeast Asia and Bengali Pala authorities formed ties and exchanges with Indonesia's Sailendra kings. Indian Buddhist mendicants traveled throughout central and eastern Asia from as early as the inception of Buddhism in the fifth century BCE. From the introduction of Islam into the region in the seventh century CE, through the end of the Mughal Empire in the nineteenth century, South Asia witnessed a flourishing of economic, cultural, linguistic, and culinary exchanges with central Asia, western Asia, and the horn of eastern Africa.

In the modern and contemporary world, South Asian diasporas fall into two categories. The first consists of labor migration, either of indentured laborers to parts of the empire beyond India or, in the case of the Americas, flights of Punjabis seeking work on the western coasts of the continent. The second includes the migrations that occurred after the 1947 partitions of British India and the creations of nation-states such as India, Bangladesh, and Pakistan. These included professional middle-class individuals along with working-class groups. In North America in the 1960s, both the United States and Canada eased previously stringent immigration quotas to allow hundreds of thousands of South Asians to enter and settle. In the United Kingdom, both working-class and middle-class migration has proceeded at high levels since the 1950s. These migrations to the United Kingdom and Canada include the exodus of South Asians from east Africa, who left due to the Africanization policies of east African states, particularly Uganda, in the early 1970s. Those who migrated became the ancestors of the millions of diasporic South Asians currently in the Americas, Africa, and the United Kingdom.

From the early 1830s to the end of World War I, hundreds of thousands of South Asians were sent as indentured laborers to plantations in various parts of the British Empire, filling holes in the labor force left by the empire's abolition of slavery in 1834. These workers were recruited for various aspects of the colonial-industrial economy that exploited raw materials and labor for the benefit of Euro-American consumption. Tropical environments in Natal, Fiji, Mauritius, Trinidad, Ceylon (present-day Sri Lanka), British Guyana, Jamaica, St. Lucia, Grenada, and British Honduras (present-day Belize) were sites of extensive plantations that produced sugar, coffee, tea, rubber, tobacco, and cotton. French islands such as Reunion, Martinique, and Guadalupe also employed indentured Indian labor.

Ships embarked from the ports of Calcutta, Madras, and Bombay for outposts of colonial capitalism in southern Africa, the Caribbean, and Central and South America. Recruiters for plantations would advertise in these cities, often unscrupulously, for the prospects of earning high wages and procuring useful work, pursuing poor agriculturists who were looking for ways to support their families. Especially during famine years when prospects were bleak, tens of thousands of laborers followed recruiters on months-long passages across the Indian Ocean. Conditions on plantations were little different from slave conditions, and, in fact, former slave owners oversaw production. Workers were cruelly exploited and at times denied their promised wages and return passage. Some were given plots of land on which to settle after their terms expired. Laborers and their descendants formed communities that would settle and mix with neighboring African, Asian, and European groups. Over a period of nearly ninety years of indentured labor, Indian communities slowly developed creolized linguistic and cultural practices. Forms of creolized Hindustani retain vitality in Mauritius and Fiji and creolized forms of Tamil live in contemporary South Africa.

In the early twentieth century, Mohandas Gandhi began to hone his political activism under the banner of *satyagraha,* protesting laws aimed at curtailing the rights of indentured and ex-indentured Indian laborers in South Africa. In other regions of the indentured labor diaspora, such as Mauritius, Indians such as the lawyer Manilal Maganlal protested the inhumane treatment of Indians on many plantations. By the conclusion of World War I, after protests in India and protracted investigations by the Government of India, the entire indentured system was formally abolished. This did not, however, prevent large populations of South Asians from settling and working in the local economies of South Africa, Trinidad, Fiji, Guyana, and Mauritius. There are more than one million South Asians in contemporary South Africa, and South Asians form nearly 40 percent of the entire Fijian population.

While indentured labor brought a South Asian diaspora to Africa, the West Indies, and Fiji and Mauritius, most South Asians who traveled and settled in North America and the United Kingdom arrived within different historical and political contexts. Migrants who left their homes after the 1947 partition of colonial India created what would become the nation-states of India, Pakistan, Sri Lanka, and Bangladesh. The political environment these migrants encountered included a national, as opposed to imperial, world. The language of nation-states, passports, and immigration quotas informs the migration and settlement of contemporary South Asian migrants.

After World War II, a labor shortage in the United Kingdom led to its doors being opened to thousands of the formerly colonized, as migrants sought work in manufacturing, service, and a variety of other middle-class and professional arenas. In North America, both the United States and Canada created avenues for technically qualified individuals—engineers, doctors, scientists—to gain easy entry for study and work. In the United Kingdom and North America, South Asians (nearly two million in the United States and Canada combined, and more than two million in the United Kingdom) have settled as a part of the contemporary scenario of labor and migration, one determined by nation-states and led by middle-class, educated professionals.

These historical experiences constitute the South Asian diasporic kaleido-scope today. Living in the United States or the United Kingdom, many first- or second-generation South Asian immigrants may feel little kinship with those descendants of indentured laborers who started to become South Africans, Fiji-ans, or Mauritians nearly one hundred fifty years ago. The identity politics of the two groups differs according to their experiences after settlement. In plu-ralist liberal democracies such as Britain or the United States, group identities are emphasized by the state. Institutions cementing a particular "South Asian" identity, from religion, the arts, and language in these areas, are supported in an institutional framework.[2] However, in the ex-indentured labor regions, such as South Africa or Mauritius, South Asians were racialized and denigrated because of their South Asian-ness from the very start. Today, the South African state celebrates its diversity, but only after a long history of official attempts to repatriate and, at times, to curtail the rights of Indians. Fiji also begrudgingly recognizes the Indian component of their population out of necessity, not out of liberal-democratic principle.[3]

In addition to this distinction between post-1947 migrations and inden-tured labor-era diasporas, the term *South Asian* itself requires some clarifica-tion. *South Asia* derives from the nearly fifty-year Cold War between the Soviet Union and the United States. It refers to the seven nation-states of India, Paki-stan, Bangladesh, Bhutan, Nepal, Sri Lanka, and the Maldive Islands, a region both superpowers were trying desperately to control. The term conveniently sidesteps any bias toward calling all of these inhabitants *Indians*, and so thereby includes groups as disparate as Santhal "tribals" in Bengal, Tamil Brahmins from Chennai, Baluchi tribespeople from Pakistan, Tamil and Sinhala Bud-dhists from Sri Lanka, Nepali royalty, and centuries-old communities of Mus-lim fishermen on the Malabar coast. Clearly, the term *South Asian* serves only as a geographical boundary marker and not as a description of the various cul-tures that are included in the region.

Similarly, the term *South Asian diaspora* marks geography and does not coherently describe the various historical, cultural, and political experiences of the peoples in all of these locations. A catch-all term to describe diasporic South Asians has not, and simply cannot, arise. *Indian, Desi, Hindu, Coolie,* and *Asian* are all labels that have generalized diasporic identity at various points in history. Many more can be found and perhaps will be generated as diasporic communities grow and further expand.

This book does not aim to find a historical or unifying thread to the diaspora, much less presume that one exists. Rather, it aims to document an aspect of artistic endeavor—theatre—that sheds light on processes of identity formation in any community, and places representative South Asian plays from diasporic locations around the world into conversation with one another. I hope this collection of eleven plays will stir in theatre artists and scholars reflection about what links and does not link diasporic South Asian populations in their theatre traditions. In turn, theatrical production and research will produce more historical work that will enliven our understanding of the past as well as our creation of a future.

The theatre of the South Asian diaspora reflects a highly diverse set of sociopolitical and aesthetic concerns, such as the engagement with classics of various forms as well as explorations of questions of the "homeland." It includes realistic portrayals of drawing-room dramatics as well as innovations in dramaturgy and technique. More than an appendage of the "homeland" or a footnote to dominant metropolitan theatre traditions, it is now beginning to establish its own voice.

As the first anthology dedicated to documenting South Asian diasporic drama,[4] this collection has its own limitations. Many locations could not be represented. Trinidad and Tobago, Australia, Fiji, New Zealand, Singapore, British Guyana, Kenya, and a host of other countries have vibrant diasporic communities with long histories and active traditions in the performing arts. At the same time, the four locations surveyed here—the United States, Canada, the UK, and South Africa—constitute the core of the English-speaking South Asian theatre world and have sustained much more theatre than the eleven plays here represent. In these locations playwrights, actors, and theatre companies have sprouted, producing critically praised plays such as Ayub Khan-Din's *East is East*, Hanif Kureishi's *Borderline*, Muthal Naidoo's *Flight from the Mahabharata,* and Rajesh Gopie's *Out of Bounds*. From the United States and Canada, Bina Sharif's *My Ancestor's House,* John Mathew's *Grave Affairs,* Rehana Mirza's *Barriers,* Uma Parameswaran's *Rootless But Green Are the Boulevard Trees,* and many others fill the South Asian diasporic theatre world.

Rather than serving as an exhaustive analysis, an anthology of this type points to a field in formation. It is no surprise to find university courses and lectures focused entirely on diasporic South Asian literature, politics, or history. When South Asian diasporic theatre enters the popular and academic conversation, our very concept of diaspora may undergo change: rather than finding an identity, we see our playwrights trying to stage a South Asian sound, as Shishir Kurup poignantly preferred.[5] It is this sound, this aesthetic, this form, that often eludes the popular and the literary. This particular aesthetic, forged in the diverse artistic imperatives of England, the Americas, and southern Africa, illuminates our experiences of being diasporic in ways that perhaps no other form of expression can. It is hoped that this foray into the dramatic will deepen how both theatre practitioners and scholars of South Asia understand this complicated concept.

PART ONE

The United States

In 1790, a Madras resident visited Salem, Massachusetts along with a sea captain, marking the first recorded entry of a South Asian into North America. In the late eighteenth and nineteenth centuries, as European colonial domination in South Asia grew and the new American polity developed, almost one thousand South Asians arrived on American shores. Along with occasional magicians, circus entertainers, and religious mendicants, some eminent public figures visited America, including Swami Vivekenanda, a nineteenth-century religious reformer who visited Chicago to address the World Parliament of Religions in 1893. Most Indians who arrived in the nineteenth century did not settle permanently. Popular history mentions a group of Indian slaves who found their way to Massachusetts in the seventeenth century, but their definitive story has yet to be written (Rangaswamy 2000: 15–72).

As the twentieth century progressed, South Asians in America began to acquire a larger political purpose and started to assimilate into U.S. society. Punjab was largely spared the system of indentured labor that sent workers across the British Empire. But a small group of Punjabi farmers endured a fate similar to that of their counterparts across the African and West Indian outposts of the empire. Attracted by promises of work and wealth by Canadian company representatives touring India to seek cheap labor, many farmers immigrated to present-day western North America. The first port of entry was British Columbia; the American coastal regions in Washington, Oregon, and California then followed. These migratory Indians sought work in lumber mills and railroads. A few thousand emigrated in the first two decades of the twentieth century, forming a visible population of South Asians on the west coast. Like their contemporary Chinese laborers, they fought the bitter anti-Asian laws that prevented them from owning land and, at times, gaining citizenship (Lal 1999: 42–48; Jensen 1988: 24–56). When work in mills and railroads often proved impossible, many immigrants sought to farm their own land; after much travail, they managed to do so successfully.

In addition to these farmers, students and political activists set up the Ghadr (revolution) Party, based in San Francisco around 1910. Famous anticolonialists such as Har Dayal and Taraknath Das published a newspaper and organized the South Asian community of California to oppose British colonialism. The party's constituency included several thousand students and politically minded individuals in Canada and the United States. Among them were Punjabi laborers who had arrived a few years earlier. With links to Germany, India, and the United Kingdom, the Ghadr Party formed a significant chapter in the history of Indian nationalist resistance to colonial rule. As World War I began, American and British forces crushed any hope for Ghadr to stay afloat, and the party more or less disintegrated by the end of the war.[1]

The population of South Asians in the United States remained steady, between 2,000 and 3,000 until 1965, as it was limited by the effects of the Immigration Act of 1917. From the early 1920s, a string of applications for citizenship by Indians set in motion the American practice of defining "whiteness" as a criterion for citizenship. In the early 1900s, a few Indians, including Taraknath Das, did acquire citizenship, while others did not. By 1922, sixty-nine Indians had applied for and received American citizenship. That year, Bhagat Singh Thind, a veteran of World War I, applied for citizenship but was denied because the courts deemed him "nonwhite" to the common man, even though he had argued by scientific rationale that he was of caste-Hindu, and therefore, Aryan, stock. This set off a trend of denaturalization, and forty-three Indians were stripped of their citizenship. In 1924, the Asiatic Exclusion Act was formed to restrict the entry of Asians into the United States and to prevent Asians from acquiring citizenship (Jensen 1988: 246–269; Lal 1999: 42–48).

By the 1940s, a few thousand Indians were living, working, and (in some cases) owning property in the United States. The country officially did not support British colonization in India, and President Franklin Roosevelt did not publicly support Winston's Churchill's dogged insistence on retaining India during World War II. Americans began to enter India during World War II. In 1943, thousands of American troops descended upon India to help defend the Allies from Japanese aggression on the eastern front, as Burma had been recently conquered by the Japanese. Inspired by the 1941 Atlantic Charter that promoted the right of self-government to all peoples, Indian activists lobbied the U.S. government to change its laws. After the war, in 1946, naturalization and citizenship were granted to Indians, albeit with quotas. About 7,000 Indians entered the United States between 1948 and 1965. Their numbers grew slowly in the 1950s, and California's Dilip Singh Saund become the first Indian American Congressman in 1956.

The 1965 Immigration Reform Act signed by President Lyndon Johnson ushered in a new era of middle-class professional migration and settlement. An official preference for professional and formally educated South Asians allowed large numbers of migrants with capital and personal connections, and skills to succeed in American work life (such as English-language proficiency) to settle and flourish in America. Since the 1960s, doctors, businessmen, lawyers, computer professionals, and other such groups have become a familiar part of the U.S. social landscape.

Second- and third-generation South Asian Americans appear on television, write for newspapers, and occupy visible locations in contemporary American society. Unlike the earlier Punjabi laborers or anticolonial revolutionaries, this wave of migrants encountered an America defined by pluralist multiculturalism in a world of nation-states, and they arrived as Indians, Pakistanis, or Bangladeshis. Also unlike the earlier migrants, they came with professional qualifications and skills to succeed in a global capitalist world. This America, officially a liberal democracy welcoming its newest members, is a state defined by the immigrant experience, where immigrants come to stay, not just to work. This is the America of *Merchant on Venice, Chaos Theory,* and *Sakina's Restaurant.*

As with most locations in the diaspora, community cultural organizations throughout the United States have imported troupes to fill their leisure time with performances involving music, dance, and dance-drama. Occasionally these imports include contemporary theatre groups from South Asia. In recent years, the use of high-profile performers from South Asia has burgeoned into an industry, as the NRI (Non Resident Indian) market for such performances has grown immensely.

But an indigenous dramatic literature and tradition of theatrical production by South Asians resident in the United States has developed quite slowly. The early history of South Asians there includes performances in Punjabi and Hindustani for the groups' own consumption, as was true for other South Asian diasporic units. In the early to mid-twentieth century, with only a few thousand South Asians in the country, there were very few recorded theatre performances. However, with the wave of migration that began in the 1960s, a professional presence in New York City has slowly emerged. For example, the organization Salaam Theatre has sponsored staged readings and numerous events relating to South Asian performance in New York. There is also a general South Asian performing arts environment in New York. Mainstream theatres now include the occasional blockbuster, such as the 2003–2004 Broadway musical *Bombay Dreams,* which showcased South Asian characters.

Outside of New York, companies have sprouted in recent years, such as

Chicago's Rasaka Theatre, Boston's South Asian American Theatre (SAATh), and a range of community groups in San Francisco's Bay Area, Washington, D.C., and Houston. Additionally, professional theatres with global orientations, such as Chicago's Silk Road Theatre, Minneapolis's Pangea World Theatre (led by Dipankar Mukherjee and Meena Natarajan, Indian theatre artists), or the University of Massachusetts—Amherst's New World Theatre, occasionally feature plays with South Asian themes or characters. Yet rarely have these theatres featured South Asian *diasporic* material. Chicago's Silk Road Theatre Project and their highly successful 2007 production of Shishir Kurup's *Merchant on Venice* is a rare exception. Playwrights across the country, such as Anuvab Pal, Rehana Mirza, John Mathew, Nandita Shenoy, Sujata Bhatt, Bina Sharif, and Rajiv Joseph, as well as productions of South Asian playwrights in South Asian spaces, like Mahesh Dattani in Boston's SAATh or Toronto's Rasikarts, have created an emergent South Asian North American theatre community without a clear institutional infrastructure supporting their work.

Unlike in the United Kingdom, where funds, organizations, and even opportunities to train in South Asian theatre techniques exist, the work of Shishir Kurup, Anuvab Pal, and Aasif Mandvi represent decades of theatre work in the different North American environment. Kurup, with a long career of playwriting, acting, and directing, represents a first in South Asian American dramatic literature, as he adapts Western classics from a South Asian diasporic perspective. This contrasts with the British experience, where such adaptations have been appearing for more than twenty years. Aasif Mandvi's *Sakina's Restaurant* showcases the one-man show, whereas Anuvab Pal's *Chaos Theory* connects South Asia, America, and the contemporary postcolonial condition.

Anuvab Pal's *Chaos Theory* explores the postcolonial condition of South Asian scholars from the vantage point of America. As perhaps the first South Asian American theatrical critique of postcolonial South Asia, Pal sends up both the America and the South Asia often encountered in college classrooms. Pal presents a love story between two South Asian academics who meet as budding humanists quoting Shakespeare, Keats, Russell, and the great minds of Western thought in 1960s Delhi University. The play then takes the audience through a humorous, politically charged, and romantic journey through graduate school, teaching at elite institutions like Harvard and Columbia, Marxist performance artists in 1970's Cambridge, and teaching young Americans about South Asia in the present day. Pal shows us two sides of the contemporary South Asian academic: Sunita, the wide-eyed, passionate subalternist, and Mukesh, the Anglophile Macaulay-loving scholar of Elizabethan literature. Both are parts of the colonial modern condition, including the lingering, often intangible hangover of colonialism, which is artfully explored in this play.

Diaspora forms the context of *Chaos Theory*—academic careers in the West and the culture of peddling ethnicity, a process known all too well to the South Asian diasporic academic community. Sprinkled with literary references and sensibilities, *Chaos Theory* also includes pretense, romance, and love. Sunita and Mukesh, in a messy, nontraditional way, form each other's constant in the chaos of life in the currently identity-infused world of the U.S. academy.

Two major themes elevate this piece into a sophisticated commentary on the South Asian diaspora: the postcolonial condition of South Asians as well as the ways in which lovers relate to each other over the course of a lifetime. Pal has sought to create a story about "what colonialism produces. [On] one side, we have extremists who disavow any identity, and then on the other, we have the English-loving fops, the Roger Mazumdars, wearing cravats going to Christmas dinner."[2] He seeks to uncover the ways that colonialism finds its way into how people think, relate, and form relationships with themselves and with others, to "engage a sliver of what's left behind."[3]

Pal describes his play as operating on two levels. On one level, his story concerns pure relationship. Here he writes about all sorts of people, among them "bakers, fishmongers, tailors . . . given that they are academics, this is just one thread, so they have their classical music and quotation games."[4] The work also, on another level, is a love story about people who miss each other but are always there for each other. Even though they are academics, they could be anyone. The story of these academics follows a banal trajectory; as Pal states, "conventional wisdom says they would fall in love and marry . . . but they never actually do. [The play is about] what happens in the meantime, in the interstices, what happens when they should be falling in love. They are two particles that will never connect, A and B, who share a lifetime together but never connect, each other's constant in chaos."[5] At the other end, there is a politics to this type of love. It is about the colonial modern.

Making the colonial modern come alive via theatre is the main thrust of Pal's endeavor. Giving dramatic shape to this condition through two opposing poles of the critical spectrum, putting them in love gives the colonial modern a palpable feeling much stronger than that which one might find in dense postcolonial theory.[6] Pal's sense of the colonial modern comes from the wedge between Sunita and Mukesh, an unresolved colonial hangover that informs so much of South Asian lives today, in the diaspora and in the United States:

We, Indians, in particular, [are a] product of Mughal-Aryan-British history . . . [and] the end product—is unresolved. All of it is usable, in the modern context, in a cosmopolitan cesspool, whether we are bankers, lawyers, academics, we are bringing who we are into the daily conversation. For Mukesh, being who we are, we have to ignore all of that. If there is a fictitious scene, where somebody asks him who Sharukh Khan is, he would deny it, but he can't escape his identity. He does know. Sunita would chuckle at Mukesh—these two kinds of Indians co-exist throughout the world.[7]

Mukesh's resistance to the concept of a mythical India wrapped in mysticism and Sunita's workhorse peddling of India form how Pal sees South Asians confronting modernity. Mukesh thinks "there is no difference between himself and Harold Bloom. The fact is, he can't be Simon Schwama, nor can he be the head of a Renaissance Literature department."[8] The question Pal asks, through Mukesh, concerns how much you can avoid the ways in which people ethnicize you. "Can you choose how important your ethnicity is or isn't? Maybe you can. Hopefully he speaks for the segment of people who can't run away from that."[9]

Sunita, by contrast, remains as an idealist who initially had no plans to sell her ethnicity; she was someone who sought "new interpretations, new ideas . . . a universal forum for exchange, without identity, without baggage, a cosmopolitan conveyor belt" of knowledge and ideas.[10] Over the course of her career she comes to the same endpoint as Mukesh, but is caught inside the identity machine because she specializes in South Asia, and ends up "depressed, frustrated with academia, with having to sell one's ethnicity to get bigger grants."[11] She, unlike Mukesh, takes action and decides to leave the identity maelstrom of academia and return to teach in India. Mukesh, as Pal describes him, is a tragic, drunken character who is rejected by American academia. Both Sunita and Mukesh, given the way identity politics works, are rejected. Whereas Mukesh chooses to maintain his alcohol-infused, self-deprecating lifestyle, Sunita chooses to leave to chart a new path.

Pal also shows the colonial modern taking shape in this play through his dramaturgical sense of reality. Because his work is set in America for an American audience, it can't be a play about silences, gaps, and infidelities, all the characteristics of a colonial modern condition. When we think of real people and their choices, according to Pal, "they can't be products of resolved histories," since neatly understood, nicely resolved histories generally inform modern Euro-American drama.[12] Postcolonial Indians' history, their sense of the present and of what they should/should not be in the present, comes from a complicated sense of colonialism, racialism, and political struggle, and does not produce characters and personalities with straightforward politics. Pal brings this to America, particularly in the character of Mukesh. As Pal says, "In the U.S. context, Mukesh is not completely understood as the American academy has an idea of India. On the other side, he doesn't fulfill that idea, and he's not an Englishman. This is an identity baggage he doesn't [or can't] resolve."[13] The play is an examination of what happens to a man with his qualities. As we see, this man's life is filled with tragedy, with comedy, and with love. But Pal's tragedy of modern man, unlike the tragic characters of Miller, Wilson, or Shepard, has more than a sense of personal disillusionment or alienation—his tragedy constitutes the condition of being colonially modern.

Pal manages to show that unresolvable colonial modern in all of its complexity. This colonial modern strikes at the moment an Indian knows that English is his key to a higher-paying job, when he realizes that in the diaspora, he needs to have a separate identity from the masses of South Asians "stuck" in their vernaculars. This is where Sunita and Mukesh participate in and indulge in this colonial modernity. They both think they have sobered from this hangover, as it were, but yet they are making and reshaping it in their own ways. Sunita and her constructs of teaching and South Asia; Mukesh and his running away from himself constitute their very specific modernity. When Mukesh derides the South Asian taxi driver dancing around to Bollywood music, we can sense that Mukesh secretly loves the film *Umrao Jaan,* Lata Mangeskhar, and Bhangra.

By the end of the play Amit's Gotham Holkar character, his Marxism, Mukesh and his pretentious love of Elizabethan literature, and the quoting games between Sunita and Mukesh are the real constants. As the critique has often been made, the liberal-colonial agenda of civilizing Indians via reform, representative government, civic–public culture—all these cover something much larger, such as economic exploitation and racism. In Pal's piece we find the pretense of everyday coping strategies with the colonial modern—Sunita's subalternism, and her disillusionment with it, Mukesh's romanticism, Amit's karlmarxwillreturn.com are all strategies South Asians use to cope with their colonial modernity. For the first time, we see an exploration of such strategies on the American stage.

As opposed to a focus on the intellectual and the witty entanglements of colonial modernity, *Sakina's Restaurant,* Aasif Mandvi's 1998 one-man show, explores a feature common in the American culture: the family-owned restaurant. Produced and published in the late 1990s after years of workshop performances, *Sakina's Restaurant* belongs to the generation before films like *Monsoon Wedding,* novels like *The Namesake,* and plays like *Bombay Dreams* flooded the American South Asian community. As a one-man piece exploring working-class American South Asian life from the 1980s, the play was constructed over five years of intense development. The show began with Mandvi performing his own characters, first from his living room, then at the Duplex Cabaret Space in Greenwich Village, and finally in Wynn Handman's acting studio. From there, in 1998, the show traveled to the American Place Theatre in New York City, to huge critical and popular acclaim. Among other locations, including universities and community organizations, the show has appeared in Chicago, Los Angeles, and London.

Mandvi acknowledges that he never had any intention of analyzing or politicizing the South Asian community, as he "had no statement about immigrants or South Asians in America, [because] all [he] wanted to do was write characters from [his] ethnic background that were real and that had never before been seen on the American Stage."[14] Whether he realized it or not, Mandvi certainly did create a lively document of South Asian diasporics and their experience in America. As he himself acknowledges, in the Broadway run of the show, the characters he created "transcended his family, his experience of them . . . they were reflections of a community, there was a level of recognition in the audience that he had never experienced."[15]

Through the narrator of Azgi, a young man migrating to India to work in a restaurant, Mandvi shares the story of several familiar personages in the community: the big, talkative restaurant owner, Hakim; his wife, Farrida, a former dancer who has given up her home and culture to come to the United States; their daughter Sakina, a young girl acculturated in America but dealing with her family's pressures; and her younger brother, happy with his game boys and quite uninterested in India. All the while Azgi weaves in out of the action, often with anecdotes and parables.

Sakina's Restaurant represents the South Asian diaspora in the United States before South Asians started to appear on Broadway and in novels accessible to the wider public. The play shows the community in a phase where racism, ignorance, and the problems of being a minority formed its major points of social departure. The characters are Mandvi's "friends, family, children, his voice."[16] They began to appear in the performing arts at a point when South Asian characters on stage acquired a reality beyond taxi drivers, terrorists, and convenience store workers. These people do work in a restaurant, they do have accents, they do often speak in their vernaculars, and they are wildly protective of the culture they left behind. But, with Mandvi's play, we gain a dignified, sympathetic, funny, and endearing picture of them.

Mandvi shows how the youth of this culture, the Sakinas and Samirs, are not necessarily caught between two cultures, but rather are creating their own type of culture, their own type of language and discourse within their families and their societies. One issue concerns the particular type of racism both felt by South Asians in America as well as the racism generated by South Asians living in the American context. Hakim comments on how quickly one will become an Indian again if one "steal[s] one of their good ole boys." He also demonstrates the racism that Sakina encounters with her friends. This racism emerges out of malice and hatred, as Sakina finds that girls call her "nigger"; she also confronts plain, rather innocent ignorance when her friend calls her "Iranian." The playwright presents tense issues in a way that does not judge and does not only report—he injects a level of sympathy for everyone involved. Also, Samir, the young boy raised on video games and American culture, develops distaste for India at a young age; his feelings reflect familiar Western stereotypes about India: India smells, it is dirty, it is a place where he just doesn't want to be.

Mandvi has documented, for perhaps the first time, South Asian life in America through performance. The Sakinas, Samirs, Mr. Hakim and Farridas, and Azgis of America now don't seem as "Other" as they may have twenty years ago. Now, after Mandvi's play, they may simply exist as a teenager, a young boy, or a restaurateur and his wife, without having to be termed "immigrants" or "foreigners." They may just be called Americans.

The final American piece represents a thoroughly different part of the South Asian diasporic theatrical spectrum, via adaptations of Western classics. Like British Jatinder Verma in his *2001: A Ramayana Odyssey*, Shishir Kurup engages with European classic literature in his adaptation of Shakespeare's *Merchant of Venice*. Unlike Verma, Kurup places the story's protagonists directly in early twentieth-first-century southern California. Kurup's performance text veers from the Shakespearean original but retains the vitality of language as his piece includes verse like Shakespeare's. Particular lines are transposed in their entirety,[17] and the storyline does remain intact. But the ending and Shakespeare's presentation of Elizabethan-era antisemitism, encounter a South Asian American coloration as these latter two characteristics transform Kurup's piece into a distinctively South Asian diasporic version of Shakespeare's story.

Though the storyline remains intact, several areas pointedly transpose the Elizabethan context into a South Asian American one. South Asian American references detail characters that had already been sketched by Shakespeare and also shape many of the archetypes of South Asian American society. These archetypes include the majoritarian Hindu community and their power, as represented in Devendra; the wealthy, palace-inhabiting girls looking for husbands in Pushpa; the marginalized within the South Asian space in Murali; and the careful, conservative, marginalized immigrant in Sharuk. This attempt by Kurup to showcase the internal diversities, contradictions, and conflicts of South Asian America through Shakespearean characters and conflicts, allows for contemporary South Asian American culture to appear on stage in a comprehensive fashion.

From the first scene on, Yogandanda and Sivananda (Salerio and Salarino) demonstrate the different types of South Asians who have come to the United States; they make reference to NRI struggles compared with Indian politics, referring to the 1998 nuclear tests, as Sivananda states in Act I, scene i: "And since those clowns back home have burst the bombs / They've made it harder on us NRIs / See, they don't give a damn as long as they / Can rabble rouse and keep the status quo. / It's how they stay in office over there / And over here."

Also Murali, as the Prince of Morocco character, a dark-skinned South Indian, and Toori, another South Indian, show marginalized South Asian spaces.

When asked about this, Kurup acknowledged that he consciously attempted to show Pushpa's opposition to dark skin, as an internalized South Asian expression of racism, and Toori's internalized Brahmanism (he recites the "dangers" of associating with lower castes and Muslims, akin to Gobbo's fear of Jews). Kurup also consciously moved the first Murali scene next to the second scene,[18] so the audience sees a direct connection to her being completely skin-color-racist in choosing a husband.[19] Kavita's lower-class and lower-caste sympathy with Murali's plight further characterizes the conflicts of South Asian Americanization. As Kurup states, Murali "is still protesting too much, he has internalized the racism. He talks too much about it [and] of course he's not going to change his prejudice. Kavita can't stand Pushpa's prejudices."[20]

The racism internal to South Asian Americans lives as well as the racism experienced by South Asian Americans in Yogananda and Sivananda's narration of a crucial part of the story. Sharuk sends the police to get Noori and Armando, who flee, in this version, to Las Vegas. As Shylock was in a rage both when Lorenzo and Jessica fled in a gondola and when French and English ships collided, potentially hurting Antonio's investments,[21] in Kurup's play, the police pursue who they think are Noori and Armando, but instead find Jitendra and Amitabha on their way to Carmel. In an incident of racialized violence, common to South Asians before and after 9–11, but thrown into public display in recent years, the police detain both Jitendra and Amitabha. Jitendra and Amitabha, a Sikh, are saved by Amitabha's high-quality singing. Though the narration of this significant moment in the story's development stays intact, a detour through American racism fleshes out a South Asian American perspective.

In addition to these South Asian American references and characterizations, Kurup also introduces two important differences between his play and Shakespeare's: the anti-Muslim ideology of the twenty-first century and the vulgar anti-semitic ideology of Shakespeare's seventeenth century come to a different ending when a lower-class Hindu, Kavita, emerges with an epiphany about empathy and Sharuk is not condemned in the way Shylock is punished in Shakespeare's.

The most visible face of the South Asian diaspora in America includes the post-1965 middle-class migrants[22] who often freeze their ideological worlds in time, and have little connection to the South Asian world after their migration. This frozen feeling applies to the world of "the Muslim" and how he/she is constructed in modern South Asia. The role of the "Muslim," as minority, as fanatic, as having questionable cultural and/or national credentials, has a long history in the South Asian sociocultural space.[23] In Kurup's play, a sketch of the Muslim presence in an American context emerges. The precarious role of the Muslim in contemporary South Asia, shot through with controversy from the nineteenth century, is transferred to the South Asian American stage through Kurup. Since the widespread rebellion against British rule in 1857 and the suspected Muslim instigation of it, the "Muslim" has been constructed as "fanatic" and dangerous to British colonialism. Through major points in South Asian history, such as the Khilafat movement, a world-wide pan-Islamic movement to restore the caliph after World War I and through the ways of the Muslim League, a political organization in colonial India, Muslims have often been constructed as "threatening" to the Indian colonial and nationalist space. From 1947 on, during the reign of the secular Indian nation-state, there have been no shortages of events that cast Islam, and Indian Muslims, as treacherous enemies to secularism and Indian nationalism. Among these have been Ayodhya in 1992, or, in the twenty-first century, Gujurat in 2002.[24] During both of these moments of consuming communal conflict, a large part of the Hindu press portrayed Muslims as foreign, nonsecular, and non-Indian. Though Islam has a long, colorful, and detailed history in South Asia, the precarious role of the Muslim allows for powerful and salient dramatic conflict, which Kurup exploits in the way Sharuk, as the Indian Muslim Shylock, is treated by his Hindu counterparts.

The Kurup version of "the Muslim" materializes first in the presentation of Armando and Noori, in rather different terms than Lorenzo and Jessica. In Shakespeare's play, Lorenzo and Jessica are involved in an intense bout of anti-Semitism, whereas Armando and Noori are simply trying to break free of a harsh father. There is almost no typology of Islam as an evil enemy, as we see in Lorenzo and Jessica. Armando sees Noori as South Asian, not as Muslim, whereas the Jewishness of Jessica and her father Shylock is paramount. Additionally, Armando is not Hindu; nor does he have anything to do with the religious culture of South Asia, so it would make sense for him to see Noori as "desi"[25] rather than belonging to a particular religion. Compare the closing monologues of Armando (II, iii, Kurup) with Lorenzo (II, iv, Shakespeare):

Armando:
We'll have ninitos brown and beautiful
Who'll speak the language of both east and west
Of pre-Columbia y Indus Valley
Of jalapeno y garam masala
Of Fateh Ali Khan y Santana
Of sub-commandante Marcos y Gandhi,
Of brown-skinned love tanned by a sun that seems
To shine with more intensity and passion
Upon the lands whose latitudes we share (<X-REF>)

Lorenzo:
If e'er the Jew her father comes to heaven
It will be for his gentle daughter's sake:

And never dare misfortune cross her foot,
Unless she do it under this excuse,
That she is issue to a faithless Jew (Act II, Scene iv)

Armando and Noori intend to celebrate their brownness and their Ameri-canness, whereas Jessica and Lorenzo clearly express antisemitism. In Kurup's play, there is no equivalent to Act III, Scene v, where Launcelot launches into an utterly anti-Jewish diatribe, as he says that Jessica has no place in heaven because she is a Jew and that the Christian Lorenzo should not make her Chris-tian because the price of pork would rise.

Similarly, Toori, Sharuk's assistant, does not oppose Islam and Muslims the way Launcelot and Gobbo engage with their anti-Jewish ideologies. Toori is not conspiring to help Noori become Hindu, as Armando has nothing to do with Hinduism, because he is not South Asian. This story is situated in southern California in the twenty-first century, and it is removed from a black–white religious conflict. Kurup intended to expunge the ugly anti-Jewish nature from his story, and the nature of Hindu–Muslim relations does not have a contem-porary parallel.[26]

In order to appreciate the second major difference between the two texts, we must first investigate the precise variations between Shylock and Sharuk. Sharuk talks of the shared Hindu–Muslim culture, whereas Shylock is sepa-rate as a Jew, in a black and white world. Compare the identity-based politics of Sharuk's speech with the corresponding "if you prick us, do we not bleed" speech of Shylock, both in Act III, Scene i:

Sharuk:
Our skins share the same hue! Our families the same village!
Our loyalties the same flag! The ghee that fries your dal is
as clarified as that which cooks our lamb. Our rites of cleansing
rival your own ritual ablutions. Our call to prayer is as much a
wail for God's attention as your bell-ringing pujas . . .

Shylock:
I am a Jew. Hath not a Jew eyes? hath not a Jew hands, organs, dimensions, senses, affections, passions? fed with the same food,
hurt with the same weapons, subject to the same diseases, healed by the same
means, warmed and cooled by the same winter and summer, as a Christian is? If
you prick us, do we not bleed? if you tickle us, do we not laugh? if you poi-son us,

do we not die? and if you wrong us, shall we not revenge . . . (Act III,
    Scene i)

Sharuk is crying for the shared culture of Hindus and Muslims in South Asia.
This veers from Shylock's assertion of his own dignity in a world where that is
denied on absolutist terms. In contemporary South Asia, Hindus and Muslims
are intertwined to such a degree that they cannot be understood apart from
each other. As Sharuk says, their lives are shared but inhabit a misunderstood
sameness complicated by nation, religious bigotry, and violence. In sixteenth-
and seventeenth-century Europe, Jews had to assert their sameness, as Shylock
had to argue.

Kurup aimed to maintain the sameness that informs the culture and rhetoric
of so many different types of South Asian Americans and their life choices. For
Kurup, it was important that Shylock mentioned the same flag, and that they
share "two same flags, Indian and American. (This is not out of Pakistan–India
rivalry or enmity). Maybe he chose not to become a citizen, and maybe (laugh-
ingly) I needed a device to potentially get him deported in the final scene, but it
is important that he is an Indian Muslim, not from Pakistan. He is speaking as a
minority, and his argument is that the health of a society depends on the health
of their minorities."[27] Actually, sameness, in Kurup's reading, "is what ultimately
underpins Shakespeare's speech,"[28] this commonality is what Sharuk is arguing
for, though in a different context than Shylock's.

This sameness is what informs Kurup's ending, which is marked by a series
of intense epiphanies marking a resolution to the actions, but not necessarily a
resolution to the characters' conflicts. Unlike Shakespeare's story, everyone, at
different points, in different ways, "finds grace," in Kurup's words. Before "grace"
is bestowed upon any of the characters, Sharuk emerges as more resourceful
than Shylock, as he holds a cauterizing machine that can procure a pound of
flesh without spilling any blood. This renders Pushpa's argument, unlike Portia's,
meaningless. But, just before he is able to accomplish his task, he undergoes a
complete change of heart. After Kavita's "Tat Avam Asi" speech, when the court
is trying to deal with Sharuk, Devendra expresses his love for Jitendra, and also
begs the court to have mercy upon Sharuk and give Sharuk at least his principal.
The most striking difference is Kavita's "Tat Avam Asi" speech and the complete
change of heart evidenced by the majority community of Hindus in the courtroom. This isn't a conscious decision, as the mood seems confused as to what
exactly happens when Kavita's appeal to empathy for the Other is acknowledged
by SABU and Sharuk simply leaves. Kurup attempted to translate a Shakespearean, early modern version of mercy, into a modern version of empathy.

This modern version of empathy is realized in Kavita's "Tat Avam Asi"
speech, which radically changes the spirit of the ending without changing the

actions that led to that ending. When discussing the ending, Kurup mentioned that "Pushpa's speech in the end, is not about mercy, it's about empathy . . . in a modern society, unlike in a theocratic or monarchic state, we think of mercy as something as barbaric, and outdated. Implicitly it says that there is someone above handing down mercy, like a king, or a god. Instead she is just making her plea."[29] Kavita's lower-class status and the marginal location of Sharuk all play into Kurup's display of an empathy that transcends difference, that realizes the unity of human beings in times of crisis.

In the first professional production of *Merchant* at Chicago's Silk Road The-atre Project, the many points of originality and diasporic complexity garnered nearly unanimously positive reviews from the press. Called a "polycultural deconstruction"[30] of the original, the play's various elements of intensely lay-ered and detailed South Asian American conflicts and characterizations, the "huge musical parody of Bollywood gestalt"[31] demonstrated an appreciation for the South Asian diasporic in the most vaunted of theatrical forms, Shakespeare. One critic even declared that the problems of ethics, morality, and diversity unresolved by Shakespeare's story were solved by Kurup's inventive and original change to the ending.[32] However, the actual novelty of its South Asian-ness was recognized as a liability for the play's longevity and ability to command wide audiences. A few Chicago critics noted the fact that the show was not seen ear-lier in a "mainstream" theatre, was probably due to the fact that it was a "risky, rambunctious show set in the U.S. South Asian community and thus out of the mainstream,"[33] and one commented on how it would act as miraculous outreach to the Indian population of Queens and the "Muslims of Brooklyn."[34] These two notwithstanding, all reviewers commended Kurup for appropriating Shake-speare in a manner faithful to the core conflicts of the story, but with full appre-ciation for an aesthetic that includes the diasporic experience as a constituent element. Many company members for the production not only repeated the critical praise of Kurup's uncannily precise dialectical interplay between Shake-speare and South Asian America, but found some unprecedented milestones in the representation of issues like racism by South Asian Americans toward others (as embodied by Pushpa), something never seen before in dramatic literature.[35]

Merchant has the goal of fixating on that particular South Asian Ameri-can diasporic vantage point, "of trying to find the sound of the South Asian diaspora, from homegrown all-American to FOB (fresh off the boat)."[36] From the complicated prejudices, ideologies, and histories of this particular, Kurup is also journeying into the universal, an area that Shakespeare himself is often credited with clarifying. Kurup, through the structure of Shakespeare's story, as well as through empathy for the Other, charts a new aesthetic voice in which neither the particularity of South Asian America nor the grandiose nature of Shakespearean conflict is sacrificed.

Anuvab Pal

Anuvab Pal, a playwright and screenwriter, was based in the United States for twelve years, where he wrote several plays including *Chaos Theory*. Born and reared in Kolkata, he studied dramatic literature and writing at Wesleyan University.

In 2005 he was nominated to the Dramatists Guild of America, the only playwright born in India to have that distinction. In that same year, *Playbill* named him "the leading South Asian playwright in the U.S.A." Also in 2005, Pal moved to Mumbai where his most recent play, *The President Is Coming*, premiered at The Rage Productions/Royal Court Theatre Writers Bloc Festival.

He remains the only Indian to have won the Best Play award for his play *Out of Fashion* at the Edward Albee Theater Festival. He also won the 2007 Lark Theater-Indo American Council Playwright Fellowship in New York City.

Pal's work has been noted in *Time Magazine*, the *New York Times*, the *Chicago Tribune*, the *Los Angeles Times*, *Time Out New York*, *Theatermania*, *NY Theatre*, *The Village Voice*, *Mint*, *Wall Street Journal*, and *Playbill*. In India, his writing has been discussed in *India Today*, *The Hindu*, *Rediff/India Abroad*, *Indian Express*, *Hindustan Times*, *DNA*, *Times of India*, *Midday*, *The Asian Age*, *Mumbai Mirror*, *Tehelka*, and many other publications.

Chaos Theory

Finalist, BBC World Playwriting Competition, 2007
ArtWallah Festival, 2005

Alter Ego Productions, 2004
STAGE Festival, Washington, D.C. 2003
American Place Theatre, 2002

Other Plays

FATWA
Life, Love, and EBITDA
Out of Fashion
Paris

Screenplays

Arranged Marriage
Contest
Crossroads
Here and Hereafter
Indian Idol
Loins of Punjab Presents
Postcards

Chaos Theory

Anuvab Pal

PRINCIPAL CHARACTERS

MUKESH "MICHAEL" SINGH, *Indian. The manners of a very proper, very out-of-date Victorian Englishman. He ages.*
SUNITA SEN, *Indian. A rather attractive woman of strong character and substantial will. Embraces change. She ages.*
AMIT*, *Indian. Constantly kind, excessively idealistic, always gentle. He ages.*
ELIZABETH, *Irish-American. The epitome of a bleeding-heart liberal.*

ACT 1, SCENE 1

(New York City. 2000. SUNITA's apartment. Classical music plays in the background. The apartment is overwhelmed with books. There is a bar trolley with whisky and glasses, a small table with a chess game set up. MUKESH SINGH, 52, academic, in an outdated suit, stands before Sunita, 51, dignified, in a sari.)
SUNITA: You look foolish.
MUKESH: So you do.

(He proffers a bunch of flowers to SUNITA.)

SUNITA: Thank You.
MUKESH: I'm sorry.
SUNITA: Five years.
MUKESH: What is it—silver?
SUNITA: What?
MUKESH: The 5-year mark after someone's dead—is it silver?

SUNITA: This isn't an anniversary.

MUKESH: Don't they call it that—death *anniversary*?

SUNITA: Who calls it that?

MUKESH: People who live with the dead one's memory. You, in this case.

SUNITA: "The Silver anniversary of the death of"—it sounds too happy.

MUKESH: The Irish drink at deaths.

SUNITA: I'm not Irish.

MUKESH: Really?

SUNITA: Are you suggesting that in a few years I organize a booze fest celebrating the golden jubilee of my husband's death?

(MUKESH *pulls out a cricket ball and throws it temptingly in the air.*)

SUNITA: No!

MUKESH: C'mon—it'll cheer you up.

SUNITA: Do you know how juvenile this is?

MUKESH: I do. That's the point.

SUNITA: You're just trying to kill an old woman.

MUKESH: Naturally.

(SUNITA *assumes a position.* MUKESH *throws the cricket ball at her—they run around tossing the ball back and forth and engaging in some verbal duel.*)

MUKESH: Everything that grows holds in perfection but a little moment?

SUNITA: Sonnet 15.

MUKESH: Life's uncertain voyage?

SUNITA: *Timon of Athens.*

MUKESH: They said an old man is twice a child?

SUNITA: *Hamlet.*

MUKESH: Poor soul, the center of my sinful earth?

SUNITA: Sonnet 146.

MUKESH: If music be the food of love, play on?

SUNITA: *Twelfth Night,* Act I, Scene i.

MUKESH: Your wit's too hot, it speeds too fast, 'twill tire?

SUNITA: *Love's Labor's Lost,* Act II, Scene i.

MUKESH: Praising what is lost makes the remembrance dear?

SUNITA: *All's Well That End's Well,* Act II, Scene . . .

MUKESH: Never mind, never mind, you win.

(*The game stops. He pulls out a wallet.*)

MUKESH: How much was it for . . . twe

SUNITA: Nope.

MUKESH: Ok Ok fifty, here's fifty . . . count it, you wench.

(She does.)

MUKESH: I can't believe this Sunita,—you're actually counting—do you think I'd cheat you out of a few dollars? (She nods) I'm tired of this game.

SUNITA: This was your bloody idea!

MUKESH: That was years ago. We should switch to Scrabble and Monopoly.

SUNITA: Even my kids don't play those games and I think you forget—between the two of us, we are a hundred and fifteen years old.

(New Delhi, India 1965. A garden of a home. Sunita, then 17, sits. Mukesh, then 18, enters with flourish.)

MUKESH: (drunk, loud) What a piece of work is man!

SUNITA: (annoyed) Oh God!

MUKESH: (drunker, louder) The beauty of the world! The paragon of animals! And yet, to me, what is this quintessence of dust? Man delights not me.

SUNITA: Drunk man delights not me.

MUKESH: (sees her, proclaiming) Ha! 'These violent delights have violent ends'.

(Slight pause.)

MUKESH: It's from *Measure for Measure* by William—

SUNITA: It's from *Romeo and Juliet*. Are you a fool?

MUKESH: Excuse me?

SUNITA: Like a Shakespearean jester, pretending to be a jester.

MUKESH: Oh sure, yes—Dogberry at your service.

SUNITA: The jester in *Much Ado* is actually Benedict.

MUKESH: Actually not, the—

SUNITA Why aren't you dancing?

MUKESH: I was—with this girl Kamini, attractive but shaded in idiocy. (points in the direction of the house)

SUNITA: I don't see her.

MUKESH: I think she said her name was Kamini or . . . canopy—Indian names are so hard to remember. Why aren't you—

SUNITA: I don't make my body go through vague contortions.

MUKESH: So you just sit here all alone like a banished hermit. Try some?

(Gives Sunita his hip flask)

SUNITA: I can't it's too adventurous for me . . . this is sufficient.

MUKESH: What are you eating?

SUNITA: A samosa—they are in the kitchen. (finishing it) Want one?

MUKESH: I don't indulge in native culinary experimentation.

SUNITA: By native you mean . . . ?

MUKESH: Indian. Naturally. 'The native provinces' as Rudyard Kipling defined us.

SUNITA: By us, you mean—

MUKESH: Indians. The unwashed masses. Naturally.

SUNITA: Naturally. So you're one of those.

MUKESH: One of who?

SUNITA: (correcting) Whom.

MUKESH: What? Anyways, these aperitifs are usually festered with disgusting spices. What's the libation?

(Sipping from her drink and spitting it out)

MUKESH: Tea! After 10 PM! Sacrilege—(thinks) unless you're a tea taster.

SUNITA: It's Thursday after 10 PM, which means we have class tomorrow. Besides, the principal, I mean it's his house.

MUKESH: Oh! The principal's beside himself, running into curtains and the new first-year women, the latter on purpose. He's got one of these too and his is just raw whisky, no soda.

SUNITA: Whisky and soda—is that something an eighteen year old should carry around?

MUKESH: Certainly not—it's morally wrong to be drinking whisky and soda. I drink whisky with 3 cubes of ice—the proper way—but it would look too conspicuous here.

(Giving her his drink.)

SUNITA: I can't, the servants may be looking. Gossip about students, especially us new ones, gets around.

MUKESH: The servants have stolen enough gin to keep them pissed drunk and passed out on the street for days.

SUNITA: Who are you? Do you work for a whisky company that's promoting Shakespeare at Indian colleges?

MUKESH: Oh how terribly rude, Mukesh Singh, First-year as well, which is no bloody incredible revelation, since, well, this is the 1965 First Year's welcome party, I mean I can't be a pastry chef or a lepidopterist, then I'm certainly in the wrong place aren't I?

SUNITA: (Laughs) Hi Mukesh, welcome to Delhi University—

MUKESH: You sound like a concierge.

SUNITA: It's nice to meet you too.

MUKESH: Michael, you can call me Michael.

SUNITA: Why?

MUKESH: It sounds English.

SUNITA: Where are you from?

MUKESH: Calcutta.

SUNITA: Ah! Home of English refuse, Land of Victorian fossil.

MUKESH: Hey, hey . . . It's not a crime to like things that sound and feel English, everyone deserves a colonial hangover, long live the British Empire, queen Victoria, cricket clubs, Churchill, all that.

SUNITA: Ah! Dead you know.

MUKESH: What is?

SUNITA: All of it, Churchill last to go, too much brandy.

MUKESH: Well it's a new world then—ours to rewrite through a fresh lens, starting tomorrow, the first day of an "education"—what a word. What a fucking word.

SUNITA: You sound like a librarian on acid.

MUKESH: C'mon have some?

(She takes a swig)

SUNITA: It's bitter.

MUKESH: But the drunkenness that follows is sweet. Remember, ideas, other peoples, are merely weapons to keep us confined within our own minds. Imagination, ours and only that will give us an education. The greatness of all learning lies in the originality of one. Bertrand Russell I think, but then I'm drunk—it could be Oscar Wilde.

SUNITA: You've read Russell and Wilde?

MUKESH: Amongst everything else.

SUNITA: What do we have here, a budding Socrates—you're here to study philosophy—BA in Philosophy.

MUKESH: What a terrible judge of character, remind me tomorrow never to be friends with you—someone that misses obvious connections doesn't deserve my affection—P. G. Wodehouse said that.

SUNITA: English then, BA Honors in English.

MUKESH: How'd you guess?

SUNITA: You drink too much, misquote a lot and talk far too much rubbish.

MUKESH: Something tells me I'm going to dislike you immensely.

SUNITA: What's the something?

MUKESH: Reason. A man's weapon.

SUNITA: Your something is right. But something tells me you won't go away easily.

MUKESH: What's your something?

SUNITA: Instinct.

MUKESH: A savage thing this instinct—a woman's weapon, a man's mirage. And does the keeper of this instinct bear a name?

SUNITA: Oh, how equally savage—Sen, Sunita, you can call me Sunita, it's better.

MUKESH: From Delhi then?

SUNITA: Born and raised.

MUKESH: I guessed—you look annoyingly third-world.

SUNITA: We like things that sound and feel Indian here, capital city, own flag, independence, vernacular language, Nehru, sitar, Mughal Empire and all that. We've been independent for eighteen years now but the news probably hasn't reached Calcutta.

MUKESH: Then most certainly admitted as an English honors as well, eh?

SUNITA: How'd you guess?

MUKESH: You sound too patriotic to be studying anything else.

(Nat King Cole's "Quizas" floats into the garden)

MUKESH: You must dance.

SUNITA: No.

MUKESH: I can plead.

SUNITA: How?

MUKESH: On bended knee.

(Appropriate gesture.)

SUNITA: Then I could be persuaded.

(She extends her arm.)

MUKESH: This song is one of my favorites.

(MUKESH draws her close with exuberance.)

SUNITA: Yes—I can tell from the excitement.

(They start dancing.)

MUKESH: So we do share a few things in common.

SUNITA: Nat King Cole?

MUKESH: Instinct. Who's Nat King Cole?

SUNITA: This isn't one of your favorite songs?

MUKESH: I've never heard it before.

SUNITA: I am beginning to see a pattern here.

MUKESH: Do you want to play a game?

SUNITA: At our age?

MUKESH: It's for all ages, it's a quotation game, I quote a line from a Shakespeare play, you guess the work.

SUNITA: Challenging my knowledge of fiction are you?

MUKESH: No. Tracing a pattern amongst all the knowledge stored in your mind. If you lose, you owe me five rupees.

SUNITA: This is vandalism. How about chess? You play chess?

MUKESH: Everything that grows holds in Perfection but a little moment?

SUNITA: (Quickly reacts) um—Sonnet 15.

MUKESH: Very good. Life's uncertain voyage?

SUNITA: (Pause) *Timon of . . . of Athens?*

MUKESH: Shit. Poor soul, the center of my sinful earth?

SUNITA: Sonnet 146?

MUKESH: (nervous) They say an old woman is twice a child?

SUNITA: *Hamlet.* Looks like someone owes me money.

MUKESH: Can I start an account? We'll add five rupees as an outstanding debt.

SUNITA: Fine. Be careful—looks like it might be much more than five rupees once we're done.

MUKESH: We're done then.

SUNITA: No—we're just getting started.

MUKESH: Fuck.

SUNITA: Ask me more.

MUKESH: Um—er—Friends, Romans . . .

SUNITA: You can do better than that.

MUKESH: I've never quite met—I mean, no one's ever beaten me. I must admit I'm surprised by this.

SUNITA: There will be other surprises, "Michael."

(Back to SUNITA's *apartment in New York, 2000.)*

MUKESH: You're old, I'm just distinguished.

SUNITA: That must be the difference then.

MUKESH: But at least you remember your Shakespeare, I mean over and above the years of reading this Sanskrit crap.

SUNITA: (walks over towards the drinks trolley) That "Sanskrit crap." Prof. Mukesh, is Indian Civilization—The Cultural Growth of the Subcontinent—Course 313—an "advanced" course mind you—and only brilliant professors can teach it. Like, um, me—music? (Pours herself a drink)

MUKESH: What sort of music?

SUNITA: I'm listening to Indian Classical musicians.

MUKESH: Indian Classical? Who the hell listens to that? Are you taking drugs?

SUNITA: What?

MUKESH: Consuming cheap liquor?

SUNITA: No no . . . I like it; I am actually fond of it . . . Zakir Hussein is fun stuff after a long day of lecturing uninterested brats.

MUKESH: Do you read any of Macaulay's essays?

SUNITA: Lord Macaulay?

MUKESH: No Macaulay Culkin, of course Lord Macaulay, you stupid moron—Lord Thomas Babington Macaulay, Head of the Supreme Council of India, 1834–1838.

SUNITA: Not recently, I mean he's not exactly up there with *Memoirs of a Geisha* or *Bridget Jones's Diary*. I don't randomly pick up essays from the late eighteenth century unless I have to.

MUKESH: Anyway, he wrote an essay entitled, "Culture and Indian Civilization in the late 19th century" where he said that a Raag or Raaga, as we know it in the west, was appropriate only at funerals because it created a sense of gloom that was a good weapon against enemies like the Dutch.

SUNITA: Macaulay didn't actually say that did he?

MUKESH: Of course not.

SUNITA: So you just made that up to prove your point?

MUKESH: Exactly—the art of good teaching my friend is knowing a little and lying a lot.

SUNITA: You are absolutely incorrigible—well what would you listen to?

MUKESH: Classical, the real thing, I mean western classical.

SUNITA: Debussy, Brahms, Strauss?

MUKESH: Chopin—I'd like to listen to Chopin. The Nocturnes—Opus 9—

SUNITA: No 2—the Andante—yeah—yeah. Last chance—Sitar?

MUKESH: I'll leave.

(SUNITA *plays the Chopin.*)

SUNITA: Asshole.

MUKESH: Hey—hey—bad language.

SUNITA: You know it's your loss if you don't listen to Indian music—it's absolutely divine.

MUKESH: I don't really understand what they are saying and it's too noisy.

SUNITA: Given your way, you'd whip every Indian school student, till they could swiftly pronounce complex English words—like—"juxtaposition" or "Connecticut."

MUKESH: *(getting the point)* English, madam—the lingua franca. Language of the masses. The Vatican of words for heretics of comprehension. Solves the damn problem these Indians have always had of too many languages. If I had to learn every Indian language to communicate, therefore, with every Indian—I'd never get laid.

SUNITA: You don't get laid anyway *(interrupts a* MUKESH *retort)* Tell me, you've lived in Delhi, haven't you?

MUKESH: What kind of question is that?—you know I have.

SUNITA: You speak Hindi.

MUKESH: Never in public and I only admit it to a few people.

SUNITA: What about Hindi music, Bollywood music . . . it's very popular in the west now, with the young.

MUKESH: So what? Do you think after being a professor of Elizabethan English for twenty years I should start jumping up and down like a deranged taxi driver dancing to loud Bollywood music?

SUNITA: It's better than jumping up and down like a deranged English professor screaming that every Indian needs to speak English.

(Black. A crackled radio announcement.)

RADIO ANNOUNCER: Good evening ladies and gents. All India Radio wishes its listeners a happy and prosperous 1967. May this year bring you all the joys that 1966 didn't. And to celebrate the New Year, we have for our wonderful young people whose college results come out today, a new song by Mr. Elvis Presley entitled "You ain't nothing but a hound dog."

(Elvis is heard, only the first line of "Hound Dog." We are outside the Delhi University in 1967. SUNITA and MUKESH, both in their early twenties, enter.)

SUNITA: First Division?

MUKESH: Missed it by a point—you?

SUNITA: 92%.

MUKESH: Is that first division?

SUNITA: No it's just passed, of course it's first division you nitwit—and with first class honors.

MUKESH: Is that enough?

SUNITA: I only needed 80%.

MUKESH: Boston University, you said?

SUNITA: It's a small school somewhere near Boston.

MUKESH: Of course. That small school near Boston. When do you leave?

SUNITA: Sometime next month

MUKESH: Ah.

SUNITA: And you? Plans?

MUKESH: Well I don't know—I may travel through England for a bit, where I really belong, and then I'm thinking of applying for Ph.D. programs in the U.S.

SUNITA: You didn't tell me you were thinking of a Ph.D. program in the U.S.

MUKESH: I—um—

SUNITA: You're going to apply to Harvard aren't you? You sly dog.

MUKESH: There's no such guarantee that—I mean it's not—I'm thinking—why not apply and—I mean it's expensive but because it *is* Harvard, there's the stamp and—

SUNITA: So we may meet again.

MUKESH: Maybe . . .

MUKESH: Hey I heard they have this new band in England now with girlie hair-cuts they call themselves the Beatles.[1]

---

[1]Though this scene takes place in 1967, the Beatles had been popular since 1964.

SUNITA: Like the insects . . . are they any good?

MUKESH: No, just a one hit wonder, couple of catchy tunes but they won't last very long.

(A college student enters.)

MUKESH: Hey call that Fresher, hey you, Fresher, come here?

AMIT: Yes.

MUKESH: Yes, sir when you talk to us? What subject? Eco or Maths?

AMIT: Neither, English sir, English Literature.

MUKESH: Oh! Our department. Who let in someone as ugly as you without asking us?

AMIT: Are you seniors, sir?

SUNITA: Of course, we are you idiot, you don't recognize us?

AMIT: No, I just got here.

MUKESH: Stand on one leg and sing us a song.

AMIT: What?

SUNITA: Yes and take off all your clothes while you're at it.

MUKESH: Yes, that too.

AMIT: What?

MUKESH: Yes, take off all your clothes, stand on one leg, sing a song and go and sing it to that girl
Over there

AMIT: But sir,

MUKESH: But what—you little piece of rodent excrement, you tiny piece of fungus ridden breadcrumb, you lowly bastard nephew of a dying dog, you smelly globule of armpit sweat—how dare you "but sir" us?

AMIT: Are you seniors or graduates?

MUKESH: "Are you Graduates . . . sir," you ungrateful pile of cat feces. Yes we are graduates.

AMIT: Then I don't have to do this—they warned me. *(Runs away)* fuck you. Fuck off. Fuck you both—Ha ha ha he he . . .

MUKESH: Hey—whoa—Hey—come back you little piece of shit—you dirt . . . *(as if to say dirty little scoundrel)*

SUNITA: It's no use Mukesh—he's gone.

MUKESH: Could you believe the cheek of that kid, it's unbelievable what freshers can get away with nowadays.

SUNITA: They don't have to fear us anymore, you know, we are graduates, that means gone, history, just another name on the alumni list.

MUKESH: Or etched on to the best actor award at the Inter-college Drama Festival, huh? *(Teasing)*

SUNITA: Which you did not deserve. Clearly the judges were asleep or seducing each other, I mean my performance of a Flamenco dancer was . . .

MUKESH: Why are you going to America?

SUNITA: What?

MUKESH: To America, why America?

SUNITA: I don't know.

MUKESH: You must have a reason.

SUNITA: Well, I mean I am getting a full scholarship to do a Ph.D.

MUKESH: Yes but it's odd to go to America to teach, isn't it? I mean not too many Indian professors there I'd assume.

SUNITA: I'm sure it's preferred to be Indian when teaching Indian history and civilization. They think you'd know more about your own history.

MUKESH: What a completely incorrect idea.

SUNITA: Isn't it? But that's not why I'm really going. I think—I think I'm looking for something. I don't know what that is yet but once I get there I'll have the freedom to search for it. Some sort of order—you know to learn things and teach them. There are so many books to be read, so many opinions to grapple with. That's why American universities are great, all this freedom, everything open to some interpretation that breeds other interpretations.

MUKESH: Wow! Sounds like you'll be pretty busy interpreting.

SUNITA: Hey do you want to come over, have tea and watch the television, my father just got one, and it's very good, some people call it a "TV," a lot of people are getting interested in watching it, some say someday it may even be as popular as the radio.

MUKESH: Rubbish, just another marketing gimmick, discovered by some sleazy man trying to make quick buck. Besides, I have to meet Kamini for ice cream and find out how she did.

SUNITA: Right. Ok, so I'd better be going then. I had no idea the last day of college would end like this and here, now. I mean you have a picture of it in your mind but it is never the same in reality.

(They hug)

MUKESH: Stop being so bloody dramatic, there are Freshers watching.

SUNITA: Right. Sorry. See you. This is the first time I feel that separation means something. Separate but Equal though.

MUKESH: Good quote, yours?

SUNITA: Never. Title of a new movie, just released. I have seen it, of course.

MUKESH: Of course. Hey Sunita?

SUNITA: What?

MUKESH: Maybe we will meet in America.

(Raises his Coke bottle to a toast.)

SUNITA: Maybe *(Raises her Coke bottle too)*—"I have always believed that all things depended upon Fortune, and nothing upon ourselves" *(They drink together).*

MUKESH: John Keats, "Ode To A Nightingale." Goodbye, Sunita.

SUNITA:—Hey Muk, wait!—*(Talking to an absent* MUKESH*)* It was Lord Gordon Byron, you stupid buffoon, 1823, I think, from "Untouched Love—A Fragment."

(Black. SUNITA's *apartment in 2000.)*

SUNITA: I remember how wrong you were about the Beatles. Idiot.

MUKESH: *(getting irritated)* Shut up-what time is it?

SUNITA: Why—have you to call some student of yours you are sleeping with? What's her name?

MUKESH: Victoria.

SUNITA: Disgusting.

MUKESH: It's Platonic.

SUNITA: How Platonic?

MUKESH: Well, some discussion on Plato, then mostly gin and tonic.

SUNITA: Disgusting.

MUKESH: I'm joking—it's just innocent phone chats—nothing really.

SUNITA: Which reminds me, I don't have your new number.

*(*SUNITA *starts pulling something out of her pocket.)*

MUKESH: What's that?

SUNITA: Oh! This. This is a Palm Pilot, it's one of those things nowadays you know, to keep your addresses, that sort of thing; they call it a digital organizer.

MUKESH: I know what the fuck it is—I meant what the hell are you doing with one of these—you're supposed to be a middle-aged impoverished intellectual in pursuit of higher knowledge—not a video game freak.

SUNITA: Very hip, you know, for a professor of Indian Literature, to be up with the modern technologies. Anita told me it's the latest one out there—it's the Palm VII or VIII or Maybe X, the higher the number—the more powerful it gets—like your English kings. They say I can "surf the web" with this or I could "browse the web," it's up to me, really.

MUKESH: Who are *they*?

SUNITA: You know, they, them, the people who spend a lot of time doing this sort of stuff—young people, people in offices, everyone other than us. It's a new millennium for God's sake, there's a whole different world out there.

*(*SUNITA's *cell phone rings.)*

SUNITA: Hello. Yes this is she. Aha—Hm. I—that's unfortunate. Is he all right? Yes, yes I understand. Aha. Yes, well unfortunately I can't do that—it is class policy that it has to be turned in by Monday. *(Disconnects telephone)* A girl just got her living-breathing boyfriend into a fictitious yet almost fatal car accident and all over an easy five-pager on Rushdie.

MUKESH: I know that excuse—let me guess, she said she is calling from the hospital, she is crying, hysterical—

SUNITA: While in reality she is probably lying on her boyfriend's couch—

MUKESH: They are having lots of unprotected sex—

SUNITA:—and smoking strange illegal substances.

MUKESH: Teenagers!!! Bloody bastards! By the way, how are yours? I don't see them home?

(Black. We go to New York City. Night. 1981. A Car. MUKESH is driving, SUNITA, is pregnant.)

SUNITA: I hate my husband.

MUKESH: Have I ever told you how much we have in common?

SUNITA: He is missing an important event.

MUKESH: It's only his first child.

SUNITA: What's flight delay *due to unnatural causes?*

MUKESH: There's a fucking blizzard in Canada . . . aren't you lucky I'm in town.

SUNITA: You're the last man I'd call in a crisis.

MUKESH: But you still did—breath . . .

SUNITA: I am breathing . . . what are you—a midwife?

MUKESH: Not like a pregnant woman, you are not breathing like one.

SUNITA: Reflecting on your pregnancy?

MUKESH: I saw it in a movie—Jesus of Nazareth, Peter Ustinov as Joseph and his wife, what's that broad's name?

SUNITA: Maggie Smith.

MUKESH: Jesus' mother wasn't Maggie Smith.

SUNITA: Mary.

MUKESH: Mary—right in some barn in suburban Bethlehem huffing and puffing like a rhino and here you are whimpering as if you've given birth every Thursday.

SUNITA: Keep your eye on the damn road, one accident could be bad enough.

MUKESH: An accident? Does that mean there's a bastard in our midst? Or should I say, in your midst—is it mine?

SUNITA: And when would that opportunity have arisen?

MUKESH: Some night in my deep slumber you could have taken undue advantage of my unconsciousness.

SUNITA: I'd rather consciously take advantage of livestock. What's the huge crowd on Central Park West? Another protest against that Khomenei fellow?

(MUKESH *switches on the radio.*)

RADIO VOICE: "And his wife Yoko, hearing of the former Beatles' assassination outside his apartment building, The Dakota, was rushed back on a special plane to New York City. John Lennon was one of the greatest rock stars of our era and his assassin Mark Chapman was a devout fan of . . . "

(MUKESH *switches it off.*)

SUNITA: Oh God!

MUKESH: One has to conclude thus that Strawberry Field's aren't forever. It's a tragic day *(looks at Sunita)* . . . so far.

SUNITA: *(Looking at her stomach)* See what a dangerous world welcomes you— *(Car makes a sharp turn)* Watch out!

MUKESH: I have everything under control.

SUNITA: We're in a stolen car, you've never driven, you're drunk, you're carrying my husband's *expired* license—*you're in fucking control of what exactly?*

MUKESH: Not stolen. Uninformed absence turns into theft only when knowledge breeds suspicion—sleep allows for neither. The Dean was asleep. His car will be returned before he realizes that it's been turned into an ambulance.

SUNITA: Or a graveyard. You could've told him.

MUKESH: One frantic call, the words "help" and "me" next to each other—where was the time? And what the fuck are you implying with *never driven*—I've been taking lessons—you *know* that. Wench.

SUNITA: The Dean's kind enough to let you stay in his house for God's sake— couldn't you wake him up and say it was an emergency!

MUKESH: I can't wake him up, he needs sleep. Tomorrow is my final round interview with a panel of Senior English professors which he chairs—big day.

SUNITA: So you STEAL his car keys and run!

MUKESH: You're making this sound like some crime.

SUNITA: It bloody well is! Robbing a Buick from the most influential academic supporting your candidacy to teach at Columbia—good move.

MUKESH: Fuck off! He has children.

SUNITA: And I bet they were delivered without him resorting to theft. Tomorrow morning, your chances of the new job—gone! Tenure at Harvard-gone! Jail! Jail! Gang violence! Arson! Jail!

MUKESH: Shut the fuck up. Your husband's gone too—At least I have an explanation.

SUNITA: So does he—Noam Chomsky's lecture in Montreal. Mount Sinai is three blocks up.

MUKESH: What destination is that to give birth in?—Makes me feel like a rabbi in a racecar.

SUNITA: *(stops herself from laughing)* Careful!—I don't want my child to be the result of a bad joke.

MUKESH: I'm just trying to bring up the little girl with a good sense of humor.

SUNITA: The grammatically correct term is bring in and it's a boy.

MUKESH: Got a name?

SUNITA: Mukesh.

MUKESH: I might have a friend with that name.

SUNITA: I might too.

MUKESH: Names are words, you know, and words have consequences.

SUNITA: You just drove by the hospital you nitwit.

MUKESH: Shit.

(SUNITA's apartment in 2000.)

SUNITA: Mukesh is taking pottery classes in Soho and Anita is in rehearsal for an off Broadway gig.

MUKESH: Mukesh taking pottery classes (bewildered), has he become a gay?

SUNITA: Gay.

MUKESH: What?

SUNITA: Not a gay. No one can become a gay, that's incorrect grammar.

MUKESH: I'm sorry; I'm not up with the nuances of homosexual idiom, even for an English professor. Too old fashioned you see.

SUNITA: Someone can be gay or not gay, not a gay. However one can be a lesbian or just lesbian. The women control everything; even English grammar (pause) but no.

MUKESH: No what?

SUNITA: I don't think he is—he is just trying to be more sensitive for the women. Like you used to play the piano for me or was it for Elizabeth, I was never sure.

MUKESH: Lets leave my ex-wife out of this—I'm in a good mood. So you admit you were mildly impressed by the piano maestro who could sooth your pretty ears?

SUNITA: I was just impressed because you could read Christopher Marlowe's *Faustus* at twice the speed as everyone else, not understand a word and then convincingly make up stuff about what it all meant.

MUKESH: That's what teaching is about, isn't it? Other people's words . . . our profession is about other people's words. Game?

SUNITA: But what about our opinions? You see, like you, no one really has a clue what these great books, poems and plays really mean because they don't mean anything.

Hamlet wooing Ophelia in Act III—what does it symbolize?

MUKESH: Shakespeare is using politics in relationships as a backdrop for politics in Post–Catholic England and that symbolizes the birth of the new world.

SUNITA: That's what we teach and its balls!

MUKESH: Balls! What kind of language is that?

SUNITA: Your kind.

MUKESH: Now Now . . .

SUNITA: Shakespeare wrote that because he wanted to have a scene where Hamlet and Ophelia have some good old fashioned humping, that's all—no metaphysical imagery, no surrealist thought, no religious rebellion—none of the rubbish we think it means—just Hamlet unable to control his testosterone in a Scandinavian garden with the virgin daughter of a nobleman. And yes I'd love a game.

(They begin a chess game.)

MUKESH: That's what makes him a great playwright.

SUNITA: His ability to write a good sex scene?

MUKESH: No but to leave it open to many interpretations even after all these years.

SUNITA: Too many interpretations, sir, too many. Chaos. Tell me Mukesh what do you really know?

MUKESH: Many things.

SUNITA: About literature?

MUKESH: *(offended)* I have read many thousands of books. *(She is about to interrupt but he continues)* You see what you are forgetting is that it is our job to find order through the chaos so that our students can see only the order, and we have sifted through the chaos for them. That's why they pay $50,000 a year or some ridiculous amount to the university.

SUNITA: All that money so we can regurgitate to our students a clean and concise world, a black and white world.

MUKESH: Exactly. Don't forget you also have to let them think. If you are any good at what you do, your students should look for answers, the search is part of being a student.

SUNITA: But you've already told them the answer.

MUKESH: Exactly. You know what they should know and they know what you want them to know but now what you want to know is how they know what they know which is what you've wanted them to know all along and yet what do they do to know it—that's the mystery? Check.

SUNITA: What on earth are you talking about?

MUKESH: I don't know but I think you know, no?

(Black. We go to the steps of Harvard University Library, 1972, late night.)

MUKESH: Tyger! Tyger! Burning bright,
In the forests of the night . . .

SUNITA: Truest treasure is fleeting; it sparkles for a moment, then goes. It does not tell its name; its tune.

MUKESH: What immortal hand or eye, Could frame thy . . .

(Pause) I hate poetry!

SUNITA: Sssshhhh!

MUKESH: What?

SUNITA: I'm trying to memorize.

MUKESH: You'll been trying to memorize for the last 6 years.

SUNITA: Tagore doesn't read in English.

MUKESH: Or perhaps you can't read English.

SUNITA: Translators can explain hijackers using sign language but when it comes to poets . . .

MUKESH: You should try this fucking Blake poem—verse written on some serious acid—

SUNITA: It's your Masters dissertation topic.

MUKESH: I don't enjoy it.

SUNITA: You chose it—"Understanding the Romantics in the Context of Modernism."

MUKESH: How else could I date that Irish poetess? You know . . . the brunette who's now humping that Afro-Hungarian deconstructionist.

SUNITA: Her poems—the ones you brought to me—they were awful.

MUKESH: Her fingers were lovely.

SUNITA: So the greater purpose of wanting to do a Harvard MA in English Literature is skirt chasing?

MUKESH: I'm sure there's another purpose but I can't find it. 'Find meaning in Blake's metaphorical allusions', says Professor Davis. Well fuck you, Professor Davis—and your Pulitzer. I bet Blake himself has no idea—after taking all those LSD's, no wonder there's a "tyger tyger burning bright." Look at this . . . 'What the hammer? And what the chain? In what furnace was thy brain?' Where was his brain?

SUNITA: You've got five hours to figure it out, if you want that Magna.

MUKESH: Summa—madam.

SUNITA: Isn't your GPA 3.6?

MUKESH: 3.8

SUNITA: *(factual)* You've taken 34 Masters classes and gotten two B's.

MUKESH: *(offended)* One. What have you been smoking?

SUNITA: B minus in Afro-Caribbean literature—

MUKESH: Yes the Wide Sargasso Sea was too wide to keep me awake.

SUNITA: —and B in Shakespeare's Ideas—Course 234.

MUKESH: A+, How could you even suppose that I'd get a B in Elizabethan drama? I *am* Elizabethan drama.

SUNITA: A minus then—I remember you messed up somewhere.

MUKESH: Oh that—I did my final paper on *Much Ado About Nothing*.

SUNITA: And that's what it was, wasn't it?

MUKESH: *(gives* SUNITA *a look)* Yes—sixty wasted pages on why I think Benedict of Padua is a better lover than Romeo. Regardless, a masterpiece.

SUNITA: And?

MUKESH: And like all masterpieces, treated with mild amusement by the present generation. That asshole medievalist Dr. Lewis gave me a C which messed up the overall course grade. If I ever become famous, I will run over his wife.

SUNITA: He doesn't have a wife—she was run over five years ago.

MUKESH: Oh!

SUNITA: And he's not an asshole. He gave me an A+ on my "fascinating introspective glimpse" into the tragic irony that is Richard the Third.

MUKESH: He's an asshole. He never understood my concept of unspoken love— why Beatrice and Benedict have a greater love than the soap operatic drivel that is *Romeo and Juliet*. A love out of words—the purest form, not of bodies and sweat like nowadays but of two minds, ideas playing with each other—a passion much fiercer than fire. It is as it is in life, about missed connections. You see, I was contending that Shakespeare, the comic unlike his own whiny sonnet side, and like maybe—*(thinks)* Blake in this poem, never intended love to be about "a perfect chemistry"—but rather an "imperfect physics"— Hmm, I like that, I might throw it in the paper tomorrow.

SUNITA: But this Blake poem is about Tigers?

MUKESH: Who cares? It's too late now to find out what the Tigers mean—they could mean the Chinese Olympic pole vaulting team for God's sake! No one fucking knows! So I'm going to say, the tigers represent love and then talk about my concept of unspoken love. *(Thinks)* I'm a genius! *(scribbles things down)*

SUNITA: Don't say you came up with it. It sounds too smart. In the exam, you'll need to attribute the concept to someone famous. Unspoken Love is explained by—

MUKESH:—Lord Gordon Byron in his Essay on . . .

SUNITA: No! no! Everyone with a proper English education has a leather bound Byron next to the television; if you've got to lie, get esoteric.

MUKESH: T. S. Eliot?

SUNITA: Eliot has opinions on everything, esoteric.

MUKESH: Schopenhauer on Literature?

SUNITA: What on earth do the Germans know about love?

MUKESH: All this deceit will catch up with me—I'll be found out and thrown out. Why are we Indians always thinking of cheating, at everything?

SUNITA: We think of lying at everything. Cheating is something we have to do to follow up on the lying.

MUKESH: They have these things in America called Honor codes.

SUNITA: It only applies to the honorable. If these universities are foolish enough to assume that when you quote someone in a paper, that person might actually have quoted it, it's their stupidity, not yours.

MUKESH: But if they get a sniff of deceit, it's deportation! Maybe jail.

SUNITA: Relax—always rely on why you started doing this in the first place . . .

MUKESH: I transferred from Oxford because I won a McMillan scholarship. Harvard gives the McMillan only to the best English student in—

SUNITA: You transferred because of me.

MUKESH: What?

SUNITA: Didn't you?

MUKESH: I certainly did not.

MUKESH: For dalliances with other women then. So go back to them when in trouble . . . quote Virginia Woolf.

MUKESH: Hmmm . . . think of an essay she may have written that no one could possibly have heard of?

SUNITA: Shakespearean Love, a Chaos—no, how about this—Unspoken Love— The Opposite of Romance?

MUKESH: Ooooh! Intensely believable—and a publication?

SUNITA: The—The Pari—no—The Milan Literary Journal of Love and . . . no- The Milan Literary Journal of Human Desires.

MUKESH: Nice! Milan! Nice! Completely fictitious?

SUNITA: Well I'm sure there are literary journals—just not in Milan and just not focusing on all human desires.

MUKESH: You'll make an excellent liar.

SUNITA: Good—that's a skill in our profession—as opposed to plagiarizing, which, according to the Harvard Code of Conduct book, is sin.

MUKESH: No fear of that here—you can't copy texts that don't exist.

SUNITA: Good point—If you get away with this, I hope to refer to fictitious fiction for my Tagore paper.

MUKESH: Woolf, Virginia [See Appendix A—scholar, critic (definition of scholar and critic from Karl Marx, see definitions Index A)] *(a thought)* maybe I should use my own voice, say that I made up the theory—talk about how I feel?

SUNITA: No one cares about your feelings or your theories—theories come from well-known people, preferably older—with beards-you're not famous—at least ten thousand copies have to be sold before you're quotable by academics. Just keep lying.

(It starts raining)

MUKESH: It's tedious to live under the constant flow of other people's words.

SUNITA: At least one day it will provide an income so we don't live under the constant flow of water.

MUKESH: Maybe we should develop the concept of unspoken love under a roof—my roof?

SUNITA: It's 2 AM—I was thinking of getting some hot samosas and tea from that 24-hour Pakistani deli—they make them fresh—

MUKESH: What do Pakistani samosas have that I do not?

SUNITA: Is that one of your pick-up lines?

MUKESH: Well if I wished to pick you up, I'd just do so wouldn't I?

(Physically picking her up and running around in the rain.)

SUNITA: Muk—ha ha—let me down. This is juvenile. By the way, I'm a little afraid of Virginia Woolf, maybe you should use . . .

MUKESH: Shut up and let me carry you to a better place.

SUNITA: Allen Ginsberg, *Collected Poems*, 1965?

(He puts her down, they are completely drenched.)

MUKESH: Mukesh Singh, Last Day before Masters finals at the Widener Library steps, 1972.

SUNITA: You can't quote yourself—that's cheating.

MUKESH: Once in a while, it's ok—it's ok to have things to say.

SUNITA: You have things to say?

MUKESH: About one thing—the one thing that all these poets don't know how to say.

SUNITA: What thing?

MUKESH: Amid the chaos—a pattern—a constant—a constant is important.

SUNITA: And I'm that?

MUKESH: *'Nothing exists outside us except a state of mind . . . a desire for solace, for relief, for something outside these miserable pigmies, these feeble, these ugly, these craven men and women.'* Virginia Woolf.

SUNITA: Still other people's words, what are yours?

(Slight pause.)

MUKESH: We should go.

SUNITA: *(Surprised)* Oh! *(Reacts)* Oh! Yes . . . yes we should . . . where should we? *(slight pause)* go?

MUKESH: Um. I'll go. You can—

SUNITA: No—*I* should go—get some sleep before my paper. I don't think I can stay with you.

MUKESH: Yes . . . yes of course, you must. You must *not* stay I mean . . . Go! The paper's important.

SUNITA: It's an important paper.

(Black. We go to New York City in 1986—two different classrooms at Columbia University. MUKESH *and* SUNITA *teach classes concurrently.)*

MUKESH: *Never seek to tell thy love*
Love that never told can be;
SUNITA: *O friend, when you come to my gate,*
* an unknown hidden flower's scent will startle you.*
Let this moment be my gift.
MUKESH: William Blake wrote this wounded love poem in 1825, two years before he died. It was a confession over a woman he was always close to and yet closed to. The poem tells of the disaster of his confession of love for her. Can anyone tell me who—
(Talking to a student we don't see) What are you doing Mr. Dakar? Why are you making your pencil perform miniature gymnastics? And what are you wearing? I don't care if its 1986 Mr. Dakar, if you're dressed like that someone in your family better have died recently. Well, I'm sorry that you're bored, shall I do some magic tricks to entertain you?—Tell you what, how about I make that B minus you have for the course vanish and reappear as an F. Do you hate the Romantics? Do you prefer a form a literature in violent opposition to what I'm teaching? Are you a Dadaist or Surrealist? Bit of a Breton? What? You're American!! I meant Andre Breton, you goat. Tell me have you read the Blake poem? You meant to? I meant to climb Mount Everest, Mr. Dakar, but I haven't done it, have I? Tell me, have you read anything? Ah! You don't let other people's creative side interfere with yours, charming answer. How about Shakespeare? You know most of the stories—lovely—then this should be easy for you, tell me Macbeth was the King Of? *(Waits for the student's answer)* Of course, Greece or Rome or one of those old Byzantine places. This is like trying to reason with cement. Mr. Dakar, you are a gigantic waste of vacant space, an unnecessary burden on the world's resources of oxygen, an aberration of a human being—a nothing, God's idea of a human semi-colon in the sentence of life. Get out of my class, and preferably the general vicinity of Manhattan before your stupidity causes someone physical harm.
SUNITA: "The Gift" is one of his shorter earlier poems. It's also one among the forty-five I asked you to read over the weekend—which I hope you have, have you?
(Slight pause) I will take the silence to mean an overwhelming yes. And since you are so well versed with eastern verse, Shelly . . .
  (Also talking to a student we don't see.) What would you say "The Gift" represented? You liked it. How nice—but that's a feeling, young lady—I asked you what you *thought.* It was kind of powerful in a positive sort of way. As opposed

to what? Powerful in a negative sort of way, you mean like a genocide? *(waits for answer)* Yes, the poem was open to a lot of interpretations, and yes it was because it had subtext within which wasn't easy to grasp, but that's why we call it *sub*text, my dear. *(Waits for another answer)* Did the class hear that? Shelly says that the poem was kind of freeing because she has a boyfriend and when she reads poems like this, it reassures her that being in a good relationship doesn't have to be a stressful thing. Shelly . . . thanks for that insight.

MUKESH: Keep in mind that love during the renaissance wasn't all Edmund Spenser, it—

SUNITA: *(to class)* Tagore, Rabindranath Tagore, India's foremost literary figure—in my opinion an overrated man, often mistakenly hailed as "Gurudeb" or the "The Guru of Gurus" . . .

MUKESH: . . . was an undying magnificent force of love, inside a person, never spoken, that never become a touch or a scent or a marriage. Just an idea of perfection, created with you and the romantic idea, in your head, of an imagined life. It is a passion of such magical grasp that no modern notions of commitment however long can even touch a fraction of how these Romantics pined for their women—forever. To me, this longing is a step away from my definition of perfection. A very small step. Consider;

SUNITA: Pay particular attention to how Tagore loves things and how he sees things loving him back. His idea of perfect love lay in the fleeting, the shadow, the absent. His lovers met in smoky silhouettes within dark halls, for minutes and the memories of those times haunted them like unfinished ghosts with better things to do. Making them hollow, forever numb, forever with something left to say. To me, as love, that isn't enough. It just isn't enough. For analysis, take—

MUKESH: Consider— *"She walks in beauty like the night / Of cloudless climes and starry skies"*—

SUNITA: *"Love remains a secret even when spoken, for only a lover truly knows that he is loved."*

MUKESH: Or Shakespeare— *"So long as men can breathe, or eyes can see, So long lives this, and this gives life to thee."*

SUNITA: Or from Tagore's *Fireflies*, *"In love I pay my endless debt to thee for what thou art."*

MUKESH: Compare with Tagore, the rubbish Indian poet, *"Let my love, like sunlight, surround you and yet give you illumined freedom."*

SUNITA: Compare with the incomparable Byron, *"When we two parted in silence and tears, half broken-hearted, to sever for years, pale grew thy cheek and cold, colder thy kiss; truly that hour foretold, sorrow to this."*

MUKESH: Of course Byron, *"The waves were dead; the tides were in their grave, the moon, their mistress, had expir'd before;*

SUNITA: Think of sadness— *"The winds were wither'd in the stagnant air,"*

MUKESH: *"And the clouds perish'd"*

SUNITA: *"Darkness had no need of aid from them"*

MUKESH: *"She was the Universe."* You see, a love complete.

SUNITA: A love complete, yet somehow a fraction— *"In secret we met, in silence I grieve—"*

MUKESH: *"That thy heart could forget, thy spirit deceive"*—

SUNITA: *"If I should meet thee"*—,

MUKESH: *"After long years,"*

SUNITA: *"How should I greet thee?"*

MUKESH: *"With silence and tears?"*

(Back to SUNITA's apartment in 2000.)

SUNITA: I think it's hypocritical for leading institutions to provide subjects completely irrelevant to what its graduates will spend the rest of their lives practicing.

MUKESH: A vocation, Sunita, a vocation like hunting or accounting, can always be picked up.

SUNITA: But not learnt?

MUKESH: Learning, my friend, knowledge—is not about facts but interpretations—how we imagine facts, distort them from experiences. Our classrooms are becoming video game parlors—bytes are replacing Byron—bigger buildings for computer sciences, smaller budgets for the classics, I—

SUNITA: Listen; I don't really care for a book that whines about why no one reads *Don Juan* and how that affects your silly little scotch-drinking lifestyle. My problem is with what we teach rather than how we're treated.

MUKESH: Well by the look of that nice new cell phone, I'd say you're treated very well.

SUNITA: I'm very well respected you know, at least around here. And checkmate.

MUKESH: Oh! I'm sure you are—respect in the non-essential academic departments, in their "Indian History" department which I'm assuming is what 2 maybe 3 people and a large storage room turned into a classroom. Can I finally have a drink now—whisky please, raw with . . .

SUNITA: 3 cubes of ice—I haven't forgotten. (Pause) You've been drinking it since our first year at Delhi University.

MUKESH: 20 years ago.

SUNITA: 30.

MUKESH: What? It's been that long?

SUNITA: We're old, Mukesh. I can still remember you—walking in with those bright hopeful teary eyes—full of this intense hunger for knowledge, a disturbed sense of humor and a complete inability to date women.

MUKESH: Fuck off! You don't remember Kamini; we used to go out for ice cream.

(Black on New York City in 2000. We are in a bookshop in Cambridge, Massachusetts, 1975. A set up for a book-reading. The small audience includes SUNITA *(in a sari), and three empty chairs next to her.)*

Announcer's voice *(from offstage—very colonial and British):* Hello Ladies and Gentleman and welcome to an Evening with novelist Gotham Holkar at the Ashanti Bookshop, here in Cambridge, Mass. I am Bubbles Patel of INDUS Culture Forum for artists, we provide a cultural forum for artists in India and US—*(emphatic)* hence INDUS. Hope you're enjoying the free wine and samosas. As the Nobel Prize winning Indian poet Tagore said, culture is . . .

*(*MUKESH *enters with* ELIZABETH *(21). She looks grungy.)*

MUKESH: Fuck! *(As he stumbles over people, making his way to* SUNITA*)* Bloody Hell, sorry, excuse me.
THE AUDIENCE: Shhhhhh!
MUKESH: *(To* SUNITA*):* Hey, hey I I'm here.
SUNITA: *(embarrassed)* Be quiet, I can see.
MUKESH: This is Elizabeth.
SUNITA: Sit down!
THE AUDIENCE: Shut Up!
ELIZABETH: It's nice to meet you—I've heard so much about . . . you're all he talks about when he isn't pontificating about Literature. I've been so excited this past month—
SUNITA: Yes.
MUKESH: This is *the* Elizabeth though, I mentioned her, remember, the—
SUNITA: Stop being nervous, you talk too much when you're nervous.
MUKESH: Where is he?
SUNITA: Late.
MUKESH: Are you dumping him then?
SUNITA: No—he has a nice nose.
MUKESH: A nice nose is a better reason to date someone than punctuality?
SUNITA: Sleep with.
MUKESH: What?
SUNITA: I had to.
MUKESH: Was he offering you tenure?
SUNITA: No but a huge sickle.
MUKESH: I bet he was.
SUNITA: Not like that—as part of a Hammer and Sickle rally in Cambridge, he's a communist—Harvard Communist Club, there was a certain innocence about it.

MUKESH: An innocent sickle—really Sunita, do I have to hear this?

SUNITA: Also the eyes—a suffering pupil.

MUKESH: A moron, you mean—D's and F's?

SUNITA: Pupils in the eyes you idiot—dilated, laden with sorrow, he's idealistic—it gets me hot.

MUKESH: That's sick.

SUNITA: Like me, he also sleeps late.

MUKESH: I sleep late.

SUNITA: You sleep with—um—*(trying to remember ELIZABETH's name)*

MUKESH: Nevertheless, I . . .

ELIZABETH: Elizabeth. With a z.

MUKESH: A name, does he have one? Is it Sleptin or Shagherov?

SUNITA: Amit.

MUKESH: What kind of a Russian name is that?

SUNITA: It isn't—Communists are like pop music—not restricted to geography.

MUKESH: He's just like us.

SUNITA: Yes a Ph.D. student.

MUKESH: I meant Indian.

SUNITA: Except he's not a prick. He ponders over the human cruelty of everyday. It's genuine.

MUKESH: How Buddhist of him. What's he doing at Harvard? Starting his own religion?

SUNITA: He's studying philosophy.

MUKESH: A communist philosopher in 70's America—that'll get him a job anywhere.

SUNITA: Shut up—he's writing a novel.

MUKESH: Who isn't?

SUNITA: No no he's actually writing one.

MUKESH: Some heartfelt fecal matter about a commie protagonist in a capitalist world going mad or some such nonsense—I'm sure of it.

SUNITA: *(to ELIZABETH)* So—how did this affair to remember begin?

ELIZABETH: Well, he asked me out for dinner after his lecture on unspoken love—he had this really cute cravat on—Blake, we were doing the romantics.

SUNITA: And now you're doing the one doing the romantics.

ELIZABETH: *(confused)* Huh?

SUNITA: *(To MUKESH)* Your student?

MUKESH: Well I . . .

ELIZABETH: He is also my advisor.

SUNITA: Lucky you—to have his advice in class and in the bed *(corrects it)* at home.

ELIZABETH: *(misunderstanding)* Yes—he wants me to go to journalism school.

SUNITA: Does he? Mukesh—you talent scout you—I can completely see how you see NBC written all over her.

MUKESH: *(changing the topic)* The cravat was from Saville Rowe.

SUNITA: Right—the cravat.

Elizabeth:—it was of the queen or the King or something, very regal you know like the British Monarchy sort of regal.

MUKESH: Well it wasn't all that really, just something silkish I threw around my neck and—

SUNITA: Shut up—*(To* ELIZABETH*)* you were saying . . .

ELIZABETH: How could I possibly refuse after he got me flowers and the Tennyson anthology . . .

MUKESH: Heliotropes.

SUNITA: Withers quickly.

MUKESH: The Tennyson doesn't.

ELIZABETH: And he's so British.

MUKESH: English you mean. my dear. I mean I wouldn't want to act like someone from Wales, or God forbid, Scotland.

SUNITA: A pseudo-anglophile, you mean. He's actually from Calcutta, my dear.

ELIZABETH: Where?

SUNITA: Very dirty place, east.

ELIZABETH: East as in India?

SUNITA: *(confused)* Yes—where else?

MUKESH: I told you I was born there, remember, the most cultured of all cities, like the Prague of the east.

SUNITA: Well you don't hear of the black hole of Prague do you?

ELIZABETH: I think I've seen some pictures of Calcutta, lots of poor starving children, naked—they looked so sad.

MUKESH: They're very well-fed kids—just modeling. What you saw was all trick photography darling—Japanese technology.

ANNOUNCER: The reclusive Mr. Gotham Holkar, India's celebrated postcolonial author is the winner of the Commonwealth Prize and a Booker for his debut novel, both of which he refused to accept. The reasons for his refusal are explained vaguely in a now famous letter he wrote to the Times titled "The Brown Identity " where he accused the judges of celebrated book awards of being Western Imperialists, Homos, and Spies.

ELIZABETH: I think I can bear some dirt and heat for that cute posh accent, I find it so . . .

SUNITA: Sophisticated.

ELIZABETH: Yeah, yes exactly I mean I'm from Parry, Oklahoma and no one in Parry speaks so fine.

SUNITA: Well, speaks well.

ELIZABETH: Yeah—see what I mean, you all Indians know this stuff in English, which words sounds nice next to the other, that sort of thing.

SUNITA: You mean grammar.

ELIZABETH: Yeah—and it's so well pronounciated.

SUNITA: Enunciated.

ELIZABETH: Right.

(A man enters. AMIT, *(29), in a Mao jacket.)*

AMIT: Hi Sunita! I'm so . . .

SUNITA: Sorry?

AMIT: Yes—I'm very . . .

MUKESH: You're late.

AMIT: I thoroughly apologize, have you been . . . ?

SUNITA: We've been waiting a while now. *(To* MUKESH*)* This is Amit.

MUKESH: I'm sorry to hear that—Slept late?

AMI: What?

SUNITA: This is Mukesh.

AMIT: Oh—yes—right—I've heard that.

MUKESH: You mean about me, you've heard about . . .

AMIT: The name before—I have a cousin.

MUKESH: I'm sure if he has my name, he's a great mind.

AMIT: He's in prison, tax fraud.

ELIZABETH: I'm Elizabeth, with a z.

SUNITA: Oh yes—sorry.

ANNOUNCER: The reclusive Mr. Holkar has been accused of beating up interviewers, public urination in houses of worship, and the kidnap and torture of a fellow Indian writer for describing herself a magical realist. He attributes his sporadic nature to his years at Delhi University which he describes as "an Auschwitz-like" experience.

SUNITA: *(whispers)* You're girlfriend is a fine catch. It's like walking around with a book of basic virtues with breasts.

MUKESH: Thank you—between wit and gullibility, I choose well.

ELIZABETH: What?

SUNITA: *(Immediately)* The Breasts of India Or Have We Been Sucked?—Holkar's new novel—have you read it?

ELIZABETH: Yes, loved it—specially the part where the British General stealing the Kohinoor Diamond gets burnt to death in a huge vat of Chicken Tikka Masala—I cried—the moment had an openness without being closed to other possibilities.

AMIT: Thanks. I thought so too.

BUBBLES: Mr. Holkar has decided to change his name to Gotham after his fascination for his newly adopted home, New York City. If you are addressing him at the book signing which will follow, please address him as Mr. Gotham.

AMIT: There was lots of traffic Sunita, there were protests in Chinatown.

MUKESH: You mean Chinese people?

AMIT: Yes.

MUKESH: Protesting?

AMIT: Um—right—disgruntled with Nixon going there, trying to make peace you see.

MUKESH: You were trying to make peace?

AMIT: Nixon is—

MUKESH: This upsets you?

AMIT: Its very disturbing, for this inferior generation of feudalists led by clowns like Kissinger, to understand the higher mind of Mao.

ELIZABETH: Wow! Good words.

MUKESH: You live there?

AMIT: China, someday.

SUNITA: Chinatown.

AMIT: Of course.

ELIZABETH: Nice—it's a good way to learn Chinese.

MUKESH: Cheaper is it?

AMIT: I have a lot in common with my comrades there. The only place I can find solace in this capitalist whorehouse of a college town.

MUKESH: That's a relief; I thought you had a part-time job as a take-out boy and delivered beef wantons.

AMIT: NO! What do you mean? I am a strict Vegan.

MUKESH: What is a Vegan—is that someone who lives in Vegas?

AMIT: Are you trying to be funny?

ELIZABETH: A Vegan is someone who eats no living animal or its derivatives.

MUKESH: Thanks darling.

MUKESH: Amit is moving to New York with the publication of his second novel.

MUKESH: Second one, huh? I thought—

SUNITA: And I with him.

MUKESH: What?

AMIT: She is contemplating—I have my fingers crossed.

MUKESH: Good. Pity New York City isn't further away.

SUNITA: I might get an offer as an Associate Professor in the Indian History department, tenure track, of course. Columbia.

MUKESH: (angry) Bugger off the lot of you to all that concrete—you'll hate it. It'll be like living in a jail and paying rent for it.

AMIT: No no—

ELIZABETH: New York City has the Empire State Building.

SUNITA: I'm sure you'll show up there too like a dog without purpose. You're like a human boomerang, recklessly wayward but always coming back to me.

MUKESH: Never!—Not unless I'm chained and pulled there by wild horses and shot dead before I reach, besides Elizabeth and I are building something beautiful right here in Boston.

ELIZABETH: See, he's so sensitive—always thinking of our future.

SUNITA: *(mocking him)* you soft little cuddly teddy you . . .

ELIZABETH: My little honey bunches of oats . . .

MUKESH: *(As both women start tickling him, he quickly changes the topic)* Look, his bio says he has grazed in our pastures, Delhi University, class of 1970.

AMIT: English Honors, I must have been a fresher when you and Sunita were just about graduating. I was heckled a lot by Seniors.

ANNOUNCER: And thus without much further ado, on this 30th day of April, 1975—I present, reading from his newest work, the ever controversial—Mr. Gotham Holkar . . .

(AMIT gets up and takes the author's chair. There is some applause.)

MUKESH: What the fuck?

SUNITA: I told you it was a double date at a book reading.

MUKESH: Yes but I didn't know it was *his* book! What happened to Gotham Holkar?

SUNITA: That's Amit's pen name.

MUKESH: Fuck.

ELIZABETH: You're dating Gotham Holkar—that's so cool.

MUKESH: This idiot has won all those awards—I must stop reading novels.

THE AUDIENCE: Quiet!

AMIT: *(Coarse, husky voice)* Thank you Bubbles—Ahem—Good Evening. Death—what, where is it? You know, Kafka had once said that death is the only objective reality and that got me thinking for a while, about depression and loneliness, then I ate some pomegranate and while staring at its seeds, this . . . this poem, a glimpse in my mind's eye, in fragments, starting piecing together. The idea around the death of a collective—a cruel death of a nation. This verse I am going to read is part of an epic poem, like a postmodern Mahabharata or Gilgamesh—it is something that has a lot of pain, like childbirth, like our nation, our mother-homeland, the sweat in our pores, like burning fat. I wrote it after crying for 3 nights straight. It means a lot to me. It came from voices in my head, many of them in languages I didn't know.

(Buries his face in his hands as if crying.)

MUKESH: Oh! My God!

AMIT: It's called . . . *(Slight Pause)* Your Tiranga and MY Vagina. The Tiranga, as you all know, are the three colors of the Indian flag.

(A few acknowledgements of deep understanding from the audience.)

GOTHAM HOLKAR: So hear goes . . .

(He has a very old notepad in his hand. He tries to begin twice but doesn't. Then he hides his face.)

MUKESH: Is he having a seizure?

SUNITA: Sssh!

GOTHAM HOLKAR: *(suddenly)* FUCK! *(Pause)* BHARAT! Murder!
Rama, Krishna, Kumbha Karna. Homer. Catillus. FUCK! *(Pause, screams)* Beckett!!!
This universe is nothing. I Love you. . . . Progressive rock. *(Screams again)* Oh! Fuck it.
Drops of blood, each split, each experience, each, acid trip, passed on, surviving, an honor.
Later to the liberation, later to his, his, country, own, own me,
Gandhi, bureaucracy—*(screams, elongates)* Har-a-a-mi
Slave—A Nation. A mother. Her tears. Rape me. My blood is fucking me. I look at it—it is saffron. Me. I. Am all. *(as if he's finished a Hindu prayer)* Om Nama Shivai *(Stands up)* *(In an Italian voice)* Mama Mama—*(As he runs, screaming)* Vaginaaaaaaaa—AAAAAAHHHHH!

(Runs out of the book reading, in tears. Total silence. Then some clapping, followed by more clapping, followed by wild standing ovation.)

SUNITA: Is it over?

ELIZABETH: I suppose so.

MUKESH: I need a gun or some sharp weapon to bludgeon him with.

ELIZABETH: Its great—his sense of self and the almost fluid rejection of structure—the arrogance to be angry—his love for India is evident—a beautiful cruelty.

SUNITA: I am assuming you two are a couple because of your artistic differences and not in spite of them.

MUKESH: I'm demanding a refund! What an asshole!

SUNITA: That asshole asked me to marry him.

MUKES: What?

SUNITA: Yesterday.

MUKESH: You're fucking joking! What did you say?

SUNITA: Maybe. But that didn't stop me from—

(She shows him the ring on her finger.)

ELIZABETH: Oh! Congratulations—that's so nice. You'll be Gotham Holkar's wife. You'll read his early drafts for free.

MUKESH: *(to ELIZABETH)* Let's go love—*(to Sunita)* I'm still demanding a refund!

(Black on 1975. A Civil Court in New York, summer 1979. MUKESH and AMIT are in suits, SUNITA is in a sari. AMIT is signing a marriage register.)

AMIT: There! Your turn.

SUNITA: *(Looking at the register)* Hmmm . . .

AMIT: *(pointing)* Right there darling.

SUNITA: Get away, away, vamoose, I need space.

AMIT: I'm supposed to stand next to you, for now and ever, it's assumed we get along since we're marrying each other.

MUKESH: Getting angry are we?

SUNITA: I'm just a little nervous, that's all.

SUNITA: *(Starts reading the document. Mumbling to self but loud enough for audience)* Will be in legal matrimony till death . . .

MUKESH: Forever relegated to domestic chores, this is it—the big leap . . . you're now the freshman of married life *(as if to evoke fear)* ooooh!

SUNITA: Shut up.

MUKESH: Driving you crazy isn't it—not the mistress of the your world anymore.

SUNITA: If you love me darling, you'll please kill him—forget the honeymoon make that our wedding present. Who asked you to be here anyway?

MUKESH: I received a special invitation from the groom and jumped on a Greyhound, thank you very much.

AMIT: No—Thank You.

MUKESH: As a *witness*, I'll have you know! I am sort of like his *best man*, if there be such a thing in the rituals of agnostic Communist nuptials.

AMIT: There is. And you are.

MUKESH: And it happens to be a convenient day as I have an interview at an Ivy League university right here in Manhattan. Yours.

SUNITA: You scheming bastard.

MUKESH: Surely language like this is disallowed in a courtroom! *(To AMIT)* What a shame—brides nowadays, all that sixties liberal thinking has fucked them up I tell you . . .

SUNITA: *(Mumbling)* Will share all material possessions . . . *(Loud)* my books, especially the philosophy ones, are mine and that's that you hear, as is the music system, and I keep my bank account.

AMIT: So it is.

SUNITA: *(thoughtful)* hmm . . . hmmm . . . in sickness and health, without prejudice or malice . . . *(makes a face as if she's read something horrible) (Reading again)* To have and to hold . . .

MUKESH: That should read to wash and to fold. *(To AMIT)* You kept this marriage registration a quiet affair. I was expecting a few more—

AMIT: We wanted to make it special.

SUNITA: He's lying—we don't have any other friends.

AMIT: That's not true, I have that one fellow, Barry, from the Communist club, he couldn't come, he's in prison.

SUNITA: *(continues to read)* And upon the presence of material witnesses, before the District Court of Lower Manhattan, we do foreswear, hereby on the 20th of July 1979, blah blah, written above thus . . . oh! Oh! *(aloud)* And if any person or persons, PRESENT HERE, shall have objections of any nature to this union may they speak now or forever hold their silence . . .

(looks at MUKESH) Well . . .

MUKESH: Read the fine print.

SUNITA: *(Looking at MUKESH)* Right. *(Looking at AMIT)* Where do I do this?— Sunit Bharti Sen—done!!

AMIT: *(celebratory)* Yes!!!

MUKESH: Well congratulations is in order I suppose, I brought some champagne.

AMIT: How kind.

SUNITA: Muk—don't overdo it, *(AMIT Tries to kiss her)* Please!

AMIT: Can't a husband get a first kiss from his wife?

SUNITA: No.

AMIT: Why?

SUNITA: You've kissed me before haven't you?

AMIT: Yes.

SUNITA: Well just try to remember what that was like and derive joy.

AMIT: What do you mean?

SUNITA: We're not going to flutter our eyes in coy romantic blush and drive away in a love-mobile.

MUKESH: Actually I was going to say, we should grab the subway to West Broadway because traffic—

(Another attempt at a kiss)

SUNITA: Calm down—later—please.

MUKESH: Whatever happened to romantic bravery—stealing a love that legally was yours, like a Knight in shining . . . suit.

(AMIT conjures up courage, grabs SUNITA *and kisses her vehemently)*

SUNITA: What the . . .

AMIT: *(nervous)* This is all right to do—we've signed papers that make this all right.

SUNITA: Now that you've embarrassed us enough, let's just pick up whatever dignity we have left and creep home.

MUKESH: And they lived wearily ever after.

(We move to MUKESH's *flat, Boston. December 1980. It is generally a careless intellectual place except for a nice piano which* MUKESH *plays.* ELIZABETH *walks about with a glass of wine, wearing something Indian, preferably a salwar-kameez.)*

ELIZABETH: Thanks for dinner.

MUKESH: *(raising his glass)* To you.

ELIZABETH: It's only an internship with NBC.

MUKESH: It's a beginning—how was my cooking?

ELIZABETH: Fabulous. Quirotic.

MUKESH: You mean Quixotic?

ELIZABETH: Yeah—that's it.

MUKESH: Good word that one—quixotic.

*(*MUKESH *carries on playing,* ELIZABETH *walks around and touches his shoulders.)*

ELIZABETH: What is it?

MUKESH: It's a piano.

ELIZABETH: Duh! I'm not an idiot, I meant what is it the piano's up to?

MUKESH: A sonata.

ELIZABETH: That's different from an Operetta isn't it?

MUKESH: Yes very.

ELIZABETH: Who wrote it? Chopping?

MUKESH: He did actually, very good, but it's pronounced Chopin.

ELIZABETH: I prefer Chopping.

MUKESH: As you wish. He prefers Chopin I think.

ELIZABETH: I saw the Oklahoma City Philharmonic once.

MUKESH: Wow.

ELIZABETH: Yeah. They came to the Parry town hall. They played a concerto. It was oh! . . . like awesome. I went and bought Leila Fletcher's Piano Course, Level II but my yoga schedule never let me practice. I love concertos . . . or a waltz. Is this a concerto or a waltz?

MUKESH: It's neither. It's a sonata, like I said before. This sonata is known as

The Nocturnes. Opus 9, No. 2. Arguably, the saddest music ever written for fingers.

ELIZABETH: It's very good—I've never heard it before.

MUKES: Liar! Bill played it for you when he proposed.

ELIZABETH: He did? I can't tell, all pianos sound the same. *(thinks)* Hey . . . how did you know?

MUKESH: I read in his letters.

ELIZABETH: That's, like, not nice . . . spying. I bet you don't know what I said in reply.

MUKESH: Well, you've left him, you're here . . . and in love with me, so my guess would be you said no.

ELIZABETH: You think you know everything, Mr. Smarty pants, don't you?

MUKESH: Just about, except . . .

ELIZABETH: Yes.

MUKESH: What you'd say if someone did it again?

ELIZABETH: Played the piano for me? I'd think it was cute.

MUKESH: No, I *am* playing the piano for you, I meant asked you the same question.

(Slight pause.)

ELIZABETH: So what are you asking exactly?

MUKESH: I'm asking you to marry me. What would you say to that?

ELIZABETH: I'd say—I'd say—Oh! My God—I'd be delighted. Like, wow.

MUKESH: I just want you to know that you don't have to marry me just because I'm advising you to do so—the advisee–professor relationship doesn't have to stretch this far.

ELIZABETH: I totally understand. This is personal.

(Black on 1980. We go to MUKESH's *Apartment—Boston—1984. There are many packing boxes around and all the furniture is covered in white cloth.* MUKESH *sits on his couch, drunk, watches a newscaster on TV (on mute) and drinks scotch. Several empty bottles of scotch sit in front of him—he looks distraught. An old Bollywood song plays gently in the background. It is Kishore Kumar's "Yeh Shaam Mastani." Thunder.* SUNITA *enters.)*

SUNITA: Right—I'm here to help.

*(*MUKESH *jumps up and dashes to change the music.)*

SUNITA: Ha! Caught you.

MUKESH: Fuck.

(He changes the music to Nat King Cole's "Quizas." He sings the words, badly.)

SUNITA: *(Even louder)* Pathetic!

(He sings some more.)

SUNITA: It's no use—your "native" preferences have been exposed—Kishore Kumar isn't it? That's who you spend your worst days with . . .

MUKESH: Today's the best day of my life.

(SUNITA shuts off the music.)

SUNITA: 16 years as Associate Professor at Harvard—people would die for it—but it's good—they'll never make you full professor. Where's the offer letter?

(MUKESH pulls out a letter from his trouser pocket.)

MUKESH: Thank You New York, New York.

SUNITA: Don't start thinking Columbia is going to be a joke. Full tenured professor of Renaissance English doesn't mean you can lie around in a pool of scotch all day.

MUKESH: No, no—damn serious—bloody serious! And I'm going to take it seriously. The Dean said I'm one in a million, he said. It . . . it was the toughest selection process in years. And this has nothing to do with her. *(Points to the TV)* Even though she's moved there—low-life, two-timing harlot.

SUNITA: *(Sees television on)* Oh! Can't get her out of the house even after all this eh? What's she blabbering about? *(Turns up volume)*

NEWSCASTER: "And President Reagan knows better than anyone that this year, 1984, will be the toughest of his fresh second term given the delicate nature of U.S.–Iran relations. This is Elizabeth Singh for International Newfirst, New York.

SUNITA: *(looking at the TV)* My God she's looking fat, must be eating well, all your alimony money. In due time I'm sure she'll drop the excess . . . and the last name.

(Switches off TV)

MUKESH: Thank God it's over.

SUNITA: Was she there or covering this Reagan nonsense.

MUKESH: She was there—with some new love interest—a blonde NBC cameraman—looked more tanned than *(thinks)* me—claimed they met on a "breaking story."

SUNITA: A breaking story leads to a broken marriage! *(slight pause)* Sorry. So how was it, the actual signing of the divorce papers?

MUKESH: A fucking party, how do you think?

SUNITA: Right.

MUKESH: She wanted more.

SUNITA: How much more? She's taking almost everything it appears.

(She looks around to survey the situation.)

SUNITA: Your books? You get to keep the books, yes?

MUKESH: Yeah—what'll she do with those—she doesn't know all the letters of the alphabet. The settlement was the best I could finagle.

SUNITA: Alimony deals are a bitch to negotiate.

MUKESH: I don't think I can do another one of these for the rest of my life.

SUNITA: "Marriages can either be prisons or islands," Gertrude Stein I think.

MUKESH: I've bowed out with dignity, haven't I?

SUNITA: Of course—and alive. That's important. Alcoholic, a little destroyed with all the infidelity and arguments and without employment . . .

MUKESH: Hey . . . hey . . .

SUNITA: But alive. And a new job near me. So which boxes are coming with us?

MUKESH: What boxes are what?

SUNITA: I'm here to pick you up. I figured I'd—that Boston must be lonely—you could stay with us for a few months in Brooklyn—you don't start till the end of the summer—explore the city—we've got an extra bedroom.

MUKESH: Explore the city? Who am I—Christopher fucking Columbus?

SUNITA: Look, Amit and I chatted. You could orient yourself by roaming around the university—have coffee with me. Read. Watch French movies. You aren't exactly in the happiest of moods to be alone. Now if you were clever enough to actually have some friends, *anywhere,* I wouldn't care so much but given you don't—

MUKESH: Lies—you just want to get away from it all. From all of him. You're my Mrs. Dalloway. You're here to change my life in one day. I'm your poet. But remember, eventually, the poet must die. The poet must not be alive only to make you happy. Virginia Woolf killed the poet.

SUNITA: That's rubbish, Mukesh, I drove to Cambridge to have a word about your pathetic lifestyle and your slovenly, unkempt, drunken—*(beat)* He called didn't he? Did he?

MUKESH: Maybe.

SUNITA: *(Conspiratorial)* look—it's—it isn't what you think—I've only run away for a while—I haven't left him. I need to sort out some things. Feelings. He's still there, in New York I mean—I've left—it's only been a day—the kids are in boarding school—they don't know—only he does—it's rude to call it a separation I suppose, not till I start paying my own rent.

MUKESH: You don't love him Mrs. Dalloway. You never did.

SUNITA: Stop being silly, Mukesh—You can't say all this—and to me. Not now.

When will you get it? 97 percent of a relationship is just hanging around, the other 3 is your notion of romantic love. Your 3 percent wasn't worthy of demanding that my world revolve around it. Married people build things, habits, like sweaters and children, dinner parties and joint checking accounts, institutions, permanence.

MUKESH: Go build then—why come here?

SUNITA: I remembered a man. A man in a cravat quoting Hamlet, a misfit, a childish clown, curious, vulnerable, who wasted most of his life in search of perfect literature yet taught it with disdain, someone I see through sometimes more than I see myself, someone who dismissed most of modernity as worthless but loved those within it like Paris his Helen, a resigned man forever solving a puzzle, a fallible dreamer, always following patterns—one in particular—of denial, of restrained words, of hiding away his loves. I thought I have to go and tell that man that . . . tell him that I have—before it's too late—that I—

MUKESH: It will spoil everything. It will—

(AMIT *storms in.*)

AMIT: Sunita!

SUNITA: Amit!

AMIT: It's time Sunita—let's go home. I've come to take you back.

SUNITA: I was—we were just talking.

AMIT: It's all right—I've heard it, what you feel, how you feel it.

SUNITA: You have?

AMIT: About us—me. I'm sorry for not saying what I should everyday. I'm not very good with emotion, Marx said emotion is only a stumbling block to human achievement so I try and avoid it. Yet, you—you see through me, your eyes are daggers, they capture it all, as if you can swim in my mind, socialize with my thoughts. Let words free us, then darling. I will talk more—to you— about everything—my dirtiest desires. Don't leave me again, come home— we'll give it all a fresh start.

(SUNITA *looks puzzled.*)

SUNITA: You were saying . . . ?

MUKESH: You should go.

SUNITA: Right.

AMIT: Come then, its late.

MUKESH: It's very late.

(*Black on Boston in 1984. We are in New York City, 1995.* SUNITA'*s apartment.* AMIT *and* SUNITA *are arranging plates and such around a dining area that has been set up to be festive. They wear party hats. Confetti, curly strings and other party accoutrements decorate the room. The O. J. Simpson trial plays on the background on a television.)*

AMIT: *The New Yorker* has asked me to do an article on the cultural implications of this trial.

SUNITA: The cultural implications are simple—a bunch of bastards at TV networks make billions from this perversion and sell you pills and grills in the commercial breaks.

AMIT: Sometimes I think you don't understand America at all.

SUNITA: Sometimes I think I understand it too well.

AMIT: Did you pay the Con Edison bill?

SUNITA: No.

AMIT: But it's the first. We discussed this. I have set up a check of the exact electricity bill amount to be generated every month through the bank of a sequential check number. It will arrive, has arrived, to your office desk. I have set it up like that. All you have to do is drop it in the mail which is adjacent to your office. The Con Edison address is a peeled sticker which I have created and enclosed in the very same envelope. You had to stick and post. Postage is done at a bulk adjusted rate and stamped, as per my negotiation with the post office. I have organized it to be simple and so we don't have a delay because the Federal Electricity Rules say that more than 15 days, and a consumer has less rights to—

SUNITA: I didn't pay the fucking bill, Amit, ok, I'm not as organized as you. I forgot. People forget.

AMIT: What's really bothering you?

SUNITA: I think this is stupid.

AMIT: He will love it.

SUNITA: He's fourteen.

AMIT: So?

SUNITA: Our son is a teenager—he should act like one—listen to rock music— which fourteen year olds' birthday party involves parents with party hats organizing board games? He will think we are idiots. His friends will laugh at him—he's at that age—precarious.

AMIT: But his friends are all geeks—like him.

SUNITA: That's the point, we should encourage him to do something different. Meet some girls, play a sport, anger rowdy boys, fight. We shouldn't be throwing him a birthday party.

AMIT: He asked us to. And I think he has a girlfriend.

SUNITA: That girl Amy who reads the encyclopedia? She is worse than him— have you seen the size of her glasses.

AMIT: Still—she comes over, they play chess. She's a champion or something.

SUNITA: You think its normal for a fourteen-year-old to spend his birthday preparing for a spelling bee contest that's six months away?

AMIT: Would you rather have him drinking outside malls and stealing money from us for crack?

SUNITA: It would be a start. At least I could ground him.

(MUKESH *enters dressed like Darth Vader.*)

MUKESH: The door was open.

SUNITA: What the fuck is going on?

(MUKES *takes off his helmet.*)

MUKESH: He loves Star Wars. I'm surprising him. We're going to have a saber fight later on.

SUNITA: You are an idiot.

MUKESH: *(sees the TV)* Oh! The OJ trial. He's a crap actor.

AMIT: *The New Yorker* has asked me to do an article on the cultural implications of this trial.

MUKESH: The cultural implications are simple—a bunch of bastards at TV networks make billions from this perversion and sell you pills and grills in the commercial breaks.

AMIT: That's what Sunita—

(MUKESH *notices a book on the table.*)

MUKESH: And what do our famous authors read, hmmm . . .

AMIT: Don't worry about that. It's nothing.

(AMIT *grabs it from him.*)

MUKESH: That was "How to Get Rich Using Technology," wasn't it—wonder what Lenin would say about that?

AMIT: Let's drop it, shall we?

SUNITA: Amit wants to spin something within the worldwide web—he reads books like that all day—isn't that what they call it, the web? Tell him.

AMIT: It's nothing. I'm contemplating starting a website called www.karlmarx willbeback.com. It's a chat room.

MUKESH: We need a computer nowadays to chat? What happened to the good old bar?

AMIT: It's a place for communists of all sorts to get together and chat.

MUKESH: Wasn't that the point of the Soviet Union?

SUNITA: Yes but this will take up a lot less space, I think.

AMIT: I don't want to talk about it. Be useful and help us prepare the punch.

I've put in the exact proportions of ingredients necessary. Why are you two hours early?

MUKESH: Where is the rotten bastard?

AMIT: He's at a Spelling Bee prep course with his girlfriend.

(MUKESH *pulls out a toy light saber that lights up. He is swooshing it around.*)

MUKESH: He doesn't need a prep course—I'll teach him. Sunday afternoons in the park, we'll walk around and I'll teach him *lascivious* and *progenitor* and *pterodactyls*. If he fucks up, I will beat him with this—if he gets it right, I will give him a disc of Brahms 4th movement. He likes Brahms. Wait—what girlfriend—he didn't say anything to me.

SUNITA: It's nothing to talk about. She has the social skills of a corpse. And not even accidentally attractive.

AMIT: They are cute together—both with big glasses—I hope they marry.

SUNITA: You will make my son completely dysfunctional.

AMIT: *(to MUKESH)* He plays Chopin for her—that's why I am also thinking of some piano lessons for him. His guidance counselor thinks he has a natural ear for notes.

SUNITA: Fuck the natural ear for notes! What about an unnatural ear for rowdiness? I want him to grow up to be Humphrey Bogart and you're both turning him into Stephen Hawking.

MUKESH: Leave it to me. Wednesday nights are good. I've heard him play—he's rubbish. In ten or fifteen years, he may be amateur concert level but that would mean rigorous training. No food, that sort of thing. So Sundays for spelling in the park, Wednesdays for music at home. In some years, there's a man in him yet.

SUNITA: He's 14!!!

MUKESH: Mozart was touring Europe with concertos at 9.

SUNITA: He was also dead at 33. I'd prefer my son to outlive me.

MUKESH: What kind of a Godfather am I going to be if I can't be God-like to the boy?

AMIT: Exactly.

SUNITA: He already has weak eyes because you insist on bringing him those classics every week.

AMIT: Classics are necessary—imperative. The history of Western classical literature—Horace, Euclid—

SUNITA: Shut up—you sound like a pompous novelist.

AMIT: I am a pompous novelist.

MUKESH: I didn't tell him to finish all of Proust in a week—he did it.

SUNITA: I want to see porn under my son's bed, not Proust. If you're going to teach him everything, I'd like you to teach him some naughty things as well.

MUKESH: I'll see what I can do about that. I'm not very familiar with where to acquire pornographic products.

AMIT: Sunita!

SUNITA: Find out. I didn't suffer for nine months to give birth to a frail pianist who dresses like the captain of an intergalactic spacecraft, spells xenophobe in Portuguese and marries Virginia Woolf. Can't you take him gambling or something?

MUKESH: I know a Dominican professor who is into off-track betting.

SUNITA: Good. Horse racing, the dog track, cock fights will also do. I read that there was illegal gambling in Queens. He might enjoy that—craps, poker.

MUKESH: We could rob a used book store. I know the owner, so he won't mind if I return the books later.

SUNITA: Good, good—it's good real life experience.

AMIT: Stop it.

SUNITA: How about some contact sports? Boxing—wrestling—don't you know any big wrestling things on tv? Get some beer and pizza and watch with him and his friends.

AMIT: Our son shouldn't drink beer.

MUKESH: There's some sumo wrestling lecture at University.

SUNITA: Take him and then take him to a bar and buy him a shot.

AMIT: AHHHHHH!!!!

SUNITA: I want that boy to breathe, to see things, to be reckless and young. If he wasn't so fucking clumsy as an athlete, I would tell him to abuse minorities and run—I might tell him anyway.

(AMIT *falls.*)

AMIT: Oh God!

SUNITA: Stop acting—you just don't understand what I mean about being young.

MUKESH: I don't think he is

(AMIT *flops about the floor.*)

SUNITA: What?

MUKESH: Acting.

AMIT: Aaaaahhhhh! Aaaahhhhh!

SUNITA: What the hell—

MUKESH: Is he breathing?

SUNITA: Bleeding? He isn't bleeding.

(*They rush over to him.* AMIT *stops flipping about and is still.*)

SUNITA: The heart—I knew it. The fucking heart—it's in his family.

MUKESH: What's the protocol in a circumstance like this?

SUNITA: Do something, Mukesh.

MUKESH: Right—a hospital—what? 911?

SUNITA: Something. Take charge.

MUKESH: Fuck.

(SUNITA *starts pumping* AMIT's *chest.*)

SUNITA: Wake up, Amit, wake up you bastard, it's your son's birthday. Amit, please! Please! Call an ambulance!

MUKESH: *(into telephone)* Hello—this is an emergency—don't put me on fucking hold—hello!

SUNITA: Save him—I'm helpless without him—I love him.

MUKESH: I know.

SUNITA: Not like the way you think I do . . . I do.

MUKESH: I see.

(MUKESH *drops the phone, picks up* AMIT.)

MUKESH: Fuck—he's fat.

SUNITA: What are you doing?

MUKESH: Taxi to Mount Sinai—quick!

(*Black on 1995. We are back to* SUNITA's *apartment in 2000.*)

SUNITA: Why Mukesh?

MUKESH: Why ice cream?

SUNITA: Why did you come here?

MUKESH: You invited me, like you've invited me every Thursday for the last five years. Ever since—you know—your Amit died—right there actually, behind the kitchen table.

SUNITA: No I don't mean now, I mean why all of this? Why the United States? Why academics?

MUKESH: Because I loved literature—you loved literature. What's with these questions?

SUNITA: I have to admit I often think how great it would be to be teaching in India.

MUKESH: Listen after 3 whiskies I am not going to listen to an existentialist green card crisis.

SUNITA: Even after all these years, you don't listen to me. I told you I wanted to teach.

MUKESH: Of course—teach. Teach in spider-infested classrooms in schools built by the British and now in a state of ruin. For a 300 rupee salary which is what, a buck, 2 bucks something like that. You'd quickly forget that palm pilot when you spend sleepless nights in a cockroach-infested apartment in Calcutta.

SUNITA: Don't be so cynical. I just think it would be nice to actually have an effect on a young mind, even if it meant a few sacrifices. We don't teach here in America anymore. It's publish or perish, some groundbreaking research, petty skirmishes amongst colleagues, schmoozing with the chair, partying with some administrator, grants for hip topics, Islam or communists or whatever the fuck is the flavor of the month. Where's the dedication to one field of study over a lifetime? Whose teaching the undergraduate student? Some drunken graduate student?

MUKESH: They are only undergraduates Sunita—they are not complete human beings.

SUNITA: Stop being clever and think. Think what are we doing with our time? Looking for cash by proffering up some ethnic aberration—some Guggenheim fellowship to spend a year studying tribal lunatics dancing in Rajasthan or deformed puppets in Manipur and then writing some book on it so that a bunch of New York academics can think how poetic and exotic it all is. But what do we really do with that grant money? Hang out in some big Indian city at some English club, drinking tea with the family—maybe going once to see the puppets and lunatics in some emaciated village. Is that any way to fit in to the west? Hiding our modernity? Is this what free thinking has led us to? Peddling our ethnicity to justify our jobs?

MUKESH: Maybe for you. I teach Shakespeare.

SUNITA: And look at you. Languishing after all these years as Associate Professor. Obscure, ignored and allowed to just be. Where are your colleagues who focused on Indian myths in Western Literature or the Power of India in the English Novel? Chairs of English Departments somewhere. And you still have the job that a smart thirty-year-old gets. Why? Because you want to teach fucking Edmund Spencer. Mukesh, you may be absolutely brilliant but you are rejected. You know it. You know how famous you'd be asking for grants on subjects like Indian Writers in English or Postcolonial Thought or Subaltern Studies or some nonsense like that, as long as you harped on how bad the English fucked us up.

MUKESH: But they didn't.

SUNITA: No one cares about the truth. You were colonized. It must have sucked. Write about it. Simple. Don't worry about shades of grey. Why do national stereotypes matter so much? Because they do. You may know more about *Hamlet* or *Beowolf* than any Anglo-Saxon but they will always find you fit enough to teach V. S. Naipul or "Shakespeare Compared with *The Ramayana*" or some such comparative shit. I'm repeating but that's how the world is broken up, Mukesh, not what you can do but where you're from and how

you sell it—at least in academia. Maybe it's different for widget makers or
bankers. If you were less drunk all the time, you'd see this for what it is.

MUKESH: I do. I also know that it's not a common picture in the west. The Indian
versed in Western classics. There are too few of us. We stay quiet. The model
Indian is wrapped in myth and magical realism.

SUNITA: That's why I am going somewhere where he is not. Maybe.

(Goes to take the glass away from her.)

MUKESH: That's it—No more booze for you. Look, forget all this rubbish about
work, there's something I've been wanting to tell you. I think—

SUNITA: This will come as a shock to you but I have made a decision too.

MUKESH: And what's that?

SUNITA: I'm going back.

MUKESH: What, where?

SUNITA: To Sudan, where the fuck do you think? To India.

MUKESH: *(Appropriate pause, stumbling)* Whoa, you, you can't do that, what do
you mean, the kids and your house and cars and your position, the money—
you're sixty years old for god sake! You'll die of syphilis in a week, you haven't
lived there for 300 years, and you can't even speak the language.

SUNITA: Yes I can, I think. I'm leaving Mukesh. The kids of course are going to
be here, it's best, jobs and all that plus they may not like it, with the weather.
They will visit of course, very often and there's email now. I've bought a small
house in Bangalore and I'm talking to the Vice Chancellor about a teaching
job at the local university—it should work out.

MUKESH: Why?

SUNITA: I'm looking for something. I don't know what it is yet but I'll have the
freedom to search for it. Some sort of order. Still.

MUKESH: You have fucking order . . . leading professor, good mother, reasonable
widow, eclectic apartment . . .

SUNITA: But the one thing—a constant—

MUKESH: You're not a mathematical equation!

SUNITA: I always thought of some idealism. One idea, one person, one—one
thing to live for, bettering it would better me.

MUKESH: Well there's always one thing to hold you back. There's always—

SUNITA: Yes?

MUKESH: Teaching.

SUNITA: Right. *(sighs)* I'm disillusioned with having to live between things I
suppose. Straddling ideas and cultures, being some ambassador, putting up
some front, explaining chicken curry or British rule.

MUKESH: That's xenophobic cowardice of the worst sort—It's nonsense! Not
joining a melting pot just because it is a melting pot. Mixing is all that's left.

SUNITA: But at least the place is mine. One thing that is mine. How I have loved it and it has loved me back hasn't changed. Everything holding still in some ideal state. Thirty years. Perhaps idealism is equilibrium. Maybe the way we were and want to be are the same.

MUKESH: Are you an idiot? Which India were you in—the one from Merchant Ivory movies? The country is an American theme park now—cell phones and soap operas and fast foods and phone sex companies. It's capitalist chaos—worse than here because it's the first phase—they are just finding everything money can do.

SUNITA: Maybe I'm looking to go back to live in an old dusty photograph that was lying in the first place. Maybe to understand something, you have to go away from something else.

MUKESH: You sound like a self-help Guru for expatriates.

SUNITA: Maybe it isn't that hard. Maybe simplicity is simple. Maybe love for something is as simple as saying I love—

MUKESH: So this has been planned for many years.

SUNITA: Just this last year—Amit had been wanting this for many years—I'm the one who held him back—noble profession and all that. I feel I could go back and redeem some things. He always wanted to see the Lake Palace. I could for him.

MUKESH: This is our last Thursday meeting, no more games.

SUNITA: Don't make it sentimental, you have no emotions so don't fake it; you said it, no more games.

MUKESH: Saved the best friend for last?

SUNITA: I didn't want to tell you earlier—I thought tonight would be special.

MUKESH: I can't believe you're doing this *(she comes very close to him)*. I think you're crazy *(she comes even closer)*, I think you're like a little girl with her first Barbie—you're—I know you will find what you want.

SUNITA: Every loss is a gain somewhere else—it keeps things equal.

MUKESH: You mean separate but equal.

SUNITA: Go live life—we've been too close too long.

MUKESH: We've never been away from each other since . . . since Harvard?

SUNITA: Before that. *(Pause)* It's been a while.

MUKESH: And what a while it's been.

SUNITA: I always thought you came here for me. I always thought you did everything for me.

MUKESH: I should've said something—at some point—something.

SUNITA: Then say something—there's nothing to lose now. There never was.

(MUKESH tries. Says silent.)

SUNITA: You still can't. After all these years, not a single word of your own.

MUKESH: Those women—Kamini, Victoria, all of them, they don't exist. They were never there.

SUNITA: I know.

MUKESH: Elizabeth—the marriage—it didn't mean anything.

SUNITA: I know.

MUKESH: In life—a pattern—the one thing—a constant—a constant is important.

SUNITA: Am I still that?

MUKESH: You're that. You always were and will be.

SUNITA: I'll see you before I leave.

MUKESH: Of course.

SUNITA: And Mukesh?

MUKESH: Yes.

SUNITA: You will never know what you could have been. This is your chaos.

MUKESH: You knew who I was; that is yours.

(SUNITA toasts with her Coke.)

SUNITA: "I have always believed that all things depended upon Fortune, and nothing upon ourselves."

(They drink together.)

MUKESH: John Keats, "Ode To A Nightingale." Goodbye, Sunita. Enjoy America—may it set you free.

SUNITA:—Hey Muk, wait!—*(He has left)* It was Lord Gordon Byron, you stupid buffoon, from "Untouched Love—A Fragment," *(a pause)* 1823, I think.

(SUNITA pours equal proportions of whisky into 2 glasses, hands one to MUKESH; they raise it as a toast.)

SUNITA: "Parting is such sweet sorrow. If we do meet again, we shall smile. If not this parting was well made."

(They drink together.)

MUKESH: Shakespeare—*Hamlet*, Act III, Scene II. Good night Sunita.

(He Leaves.)

SUNITA: Muk—Hey you Idiot! After all these years, he still won't admit I was better at Shakespeare than he was. It's from two separate plays, you illiterate baboon, *Romeo and Juliet* and *Julius Caesar*. Separate plays and yet connected words. It feels like the words flow together *(pause)*, separate but equal.

[End]

Aasif Mandvi

Aasif Mandvi is an actor and playwright based in New York City. After years of workshops and development, *Sakina's Restaurant* was presented to the American theatre public in 1998. In that same year, *Sakina's* was chosen as a best pick by the *Stage & Screen Book Club* and the New York Press Awards bestowed upon Mandvi the award for Best Monologist. *Sakina's Restaurant* received two Village Voice Obie Awards and was the inspiration for the upcoming film *7 To the Palace*.

On stage Mandvi has appeared in such plays as *Death Defying Acts, Suburbia, Guantanamo: Honor-Bound to Defend Freedom, Einstein's Gift, Homebody/Kabul, On the Razzle,* and the 2002 Broadway revival of *Oklahoma!* Film credits include Merchant/Ivory's *The Mystic Masseur, Spiderman 2, The Siege, Random Hearts, Analyze This, 3 AM, ABCD, American Chai, The War Within, Sorry Haters, Freedomland, Music and Lyrics* and the upcoming *Ghost Town* and *The Proposal*.

Television credits include guest star and recurring roles on *Law and Order, CSI, ER, Sex and the City, Jericho, The Bedford Diaries, Sleeper Cell, Oz,* and Robert Altman's *Tanner on Tanner.* Mandvi can currently be seen as a regular correspondent on *The Daily Show with Jon Stewart.* For more information please visit aasifmandvi.com.

Sakina's Restaurant

Bush Theatre, London, 2001
Odyssey Theatre, Los Angeles, 2000
Northlight Theatre, Chicago, 1999
American Place Theatre, New York, 1998

Sakina's Restaurant

Aasif Mandvi

(Lights up.)

(We see AZGI *standing with his suitcase center stage.)*

AZGI: Hello, my name is Azgi. I like Hamburger, Baseball and Mr. Bob Dylan. You know, I am practicing my introduction because today is a very important day for me, because today I leave my home here in India and I fly on an airplane! *(Motioning with his hands)* And I fly, and I fly and I fly, and then, I land! . . . *(Motioning with his hands)* And I land and I land and I land and I land, on the other side of the world in America. Oh, I am very excited. Practically the entire village has turned up in my parents' small house to celebrate my departure, can you believe?

(Turning up)

Ha waru me awuchu.

(Back to front)

OK, let's see. I have my passport, CHECK! My ticket, CHECK! You know, I am the first person in my entire family to even fly on an airplane . . . *(Nervous)* I hope no crashing. Oh, and the most important thing I have, a letter! . . . I read . . .

(He reads.)

"Dear Azgi,

(To audience)

That's me,

(Reading)

"America is a wonderful place, and as I told you in response to your letters, that since it was your dream to come here, I would help you as soon as Farrida and I could manage. Well Azgi, the time has come. I need help in my restaurant.

I can sponsor you, it is hard work, but you can come and work for me, live with us, and get to see America, your dream is coming true."

Mr. Hakim is a very very important man, he own a restaurant in Manhattan! Here is address, 400 East 6th Street . . . NYC . . . USA . . . the World . . . the Galaxy . . . the Universe!!!!!!

(Turning up)

Ha waru me awuchu.

(Turning back, he sees his mother.)

Ma, Ma, don't cry. Why you crying, Ma? Listen, listen, You know what, you know what, when I go to America, I will write to you everyday. I will write to you so much that my hand will fall off. Ma, come on. Ma, you know what? When I go to America, I will write to you from the . . . from the . . . Top of the Empire State Building!! I will write to you from . . . from the bottom of the Grand Canyon!! I write to you from everyplace I go, McDonalds! I will write to you!! Hollywood, Graceland, Miami, F.L.A. everyplace. I will even write you from Cleveland!! Cleveland, Ma! Home of the Indians! . . . Ma, come on, you know what you know what? When I go to America, one day I will be very rich! And then I will invite you and you can come and stay with me in my big house with my swimming pool, and my Cadillac—

(She hands him something)

What is this? A stone? You are giving me a stone! Ma, the poorest people in our village will give me more than a stone to take on my journey. How can I tell them that my own mother gave me a stone? The story of the river stone? The story of the river stone? I don't remember the story of the river stone. I don't remember, I don't remember—OK, OK, Bawa, I keep the stone. See? I'm keeping it, I'm keeping it.

(He mimes putting it into his pocket and then suddenly pretends to throw it away.)

Oh my God I threw it away!

I'm joking, I'm joking, Ma. It was a joke. Look, I keep it, OK! There it goes in my pocket, OK!

(Turning upstage and then turning back to face his mother)

Ma, I have to go.

(Music cue rises as AZGI slowly does Salaam to his mother, he kisses her hands and then her feet, he then picks up his suitcase and walks off towards America, he looks back at one point and holds up his hand as if to say goodbye. The lights fade and we hear an airplane fly through the air. When the lights come up accompanied by the song "Little Pink Houses" or any other appropriate song AZGI is standing on a busy New York street. He mimes looking at the buildings around him and attempts to speak to people on the street, all of whom give him a very clear cold shoulder. He tries to say hello to people on the subway and the same thing happens

until one solitary person speaks to him—this it turns out is a bum. AZGI *, somewhat disappointed, gives the man a dime and then is subsequently pick pocketed. He despondently hangs up his coat on the rack upstage and turns to face the audience and a brand new American day.)*

(Noticing audience)

Oh, hello, how are you? Here I am! I made it! Oh my God this New York is a crazy place. But welcome to Sakina's Restaurant. This is my new job. I am the Manager here . . . OK I'm not really the manager . . . I am the OWNER!!! . . . No, no, no I am not the owner, I am the waiter here but you know it is such a good job—

(He hears someone off stage.)

Oh, excuse me,

(Speaking offstage)

Yeah? . . . Oh, OK.

(He begins to set up tables.)

You know Mr. and Mrs. Hakim were waiting for me at the airport when I arrive. I think it is very nice of them to let me stay with them until I find a place of my own. Their two children, Sakina and Samir, are also very nice but they are completely American. Samir, he is only ten years old. He is always playing with his Game Boy. He say to me, he say, "Azgi how are you doing?" I say, "Samir, how am I doing what?" Then everybody start to laugh. Sakina, their daughter, she is older, she is going to be getting married soon. She say to me, she say, "Azgi, don't you worry you will soon Catch On."

I just smile and nod my head and say, "Yes, yes, yes, you are absolutely right," even though I have no idea what any of these people are talking about. But I have found that in America, if you just smile and nod your head, and say "Yes, yes, yes, you are absolutely right," people love you!!!

I have not made any friends yet, because I am here in the restaurant, working, working, working. Mr. Hakim the owner, he is my very good friend, you know when I told him my dream one day to be a American Millionaire, he say to me he say *(Mimicking Hakim)* "Azgi let me tell you something very profound." *(To audience)* So I listen to you know, he say, "In America, Azgi, any ordinary idiot can be RICH, but not any ordinary idiot can be RESPECTED. I am not any ordinary idiot." *(Confused)* I think about this, and then I smile and nod my head and I say, "Yes, yes, yes, you are absolutely right." Mr. Hakim says I will go very far.

When I told Mrs. Hakim my dream to be an American Millionaire, she looked at me and she said, "Azgi, you are smart. Don't be fooled. America can give you nothing that you don't already have." And then she said, "When I was a young girl, I had a dream, just like yours, my dream was to be a classical Indian dancer." I said, "Oh yeah? Show me how you used to dance." She said, "No, I don't dance anymore, but when I first came to America and Sakina was just a baby I used to dance everyday," and then suddenly she close her eyes and she start to do like this—

(He moves his hips.)

I didn't know what to say. I said, "Mrs. Hakim!" But then she say to me, she say, "Azgi, let me teach you how to dance," I say, "No, No, No, I cannot learn, I can only watch," she say "No! you can learn, let me teach you how to make a bird, so I try you know. *(He begins to move his hands in the style of an Indian dance that represents a bird.)* I make a bird, make a bird, make a bird, make a bird . . . and bird fly away, bye bye bird! Gone!—OK, OK, OK, I do it for real, I'm sorry I was just kidding, *(Seriously now with real intent to learn)* I make a bird, make a bird, make a bird, make a bird, hey I'm pretty good, and then I do like this *(He shakes his hips)* and like this and—"Hey Mrs. Hakim you know what, I'm pretty good at this. I think if I had studied like you, I could have been a dancer myself." *(He gets into the dancing.)* I do a little bit of this and a little bit of this—

(A light change happens simultaneously with a sound cue that sends AZGI *into slow motion as he continues to dance; the dance becomes more spiritual as he slowly wraps himself with a pink scarf that he picks up from under the stage, and as soon as he does the lights change and we are in the presence of)*

FARRIDA: *(She is surprised by her husband who has snuck up on her.)* Oh my God! You frightened death out of me. Why you have to sneak up like that? OK Hakim, please don't be ridiculous, I don't dance like that, I don't dance like this. *(She wiggles her butt)* I am a very good dancer, OK Hakim you know what, by making fun of me, you are the one who looks ridiculous.

Embarrassed?—Embarrassed! Why should I be embarrassed?—I am not in the least embarrassed. I just think that there is a thing like that called manners, when you don't just sneak up on someone when they are doing something, and then you don't know what I am doing, what if I am doing something I don't want you to see. OK, very funny, ha ha ha. It is not called embarrassment. It is called politeness.

(She picks up her rolling pin and begins to roll out chapati. Throughout most of this piece she is intermittently rolling out chapati as she speaks to her husband.)

Well, there are many things about your *new wife* that you don't know. I am a very talented and mysterious woman. I can do much more than cook your food.

(He tries to make a sexual advance.)

Chul, Chul, Hakim, come on stop, are' come on, you are being absolutely crazy. Oh my God, you see how you get, you see how you get. You see what happens to you—you work in that restaurant 15 hours a day, and then you come home and all you are thinking about is Hanky Panky. Before you eat Hanky

Panky! Before you wash your hands and face Hanky Panky! OK, Hakim you know what? I won't cook, I won't clean, I won't do anything, me and you we'll just do Hanky Panky, Hanky Panky, Hanky Panky!

(He pinches her and she turns around and tries to whack him with the rolling pin. He however ducks and she misses him.)

You are a lucky man!

—That was before, that was a long time back, that was before we came to America. In India, how many friends I had, how much family, anybody to help. Now do you know what I do, do you know?

—I cook, I clean, I take care of Sakina, and at the end of the day when she finally goes to sleep, I have five minutes for dance break which you interrupt with Hanky Panky.

—What you brought?—What present? Go away you didn't bring any present for me—Really! You brought present for me? Show no. Are' Show no—Come on, you can't bring present and then not show. OK. OK. OK. I close my eyes you show me? You promise, you promise, OK *(She covers her eyes.)* Guess? Guess? I can't guess, come on show no! . . . OK, OK I guess, I guess . . . no no no I want to guess.

OK you brought something to eat. No, something to wear? No!—Something for Sakina? No—Something for apartment?—YES!—New curtains!! You brought new curtains!!

(She has taken her hands away from her eyes.)

OK, OK, OK, I'm closing my eyes.

(She puts them up again.)

I can't guess anymore. C'mon, I'm looking—Ready, 1, 2, 3—

(She removes her hands from her eyes on the count of three, and she stands there staring in confusion at the sight before her.)

What you brought? What is this? A FERN? You brought a fern?—Why you brought a fern?—Oh my God, Hakim, flowers. Flowers. Flowers means roses, flowers means tulips, flowers does *not* mean fern!—My God, what a romantic Rock Hudson I married! No, no, it's very nice. It's very nice. We'll put it in the window, people will come by and say, "Oh look, this lady's husband, he bought her a bush!"

(He wants her to teach him to dance.)

No, no, I can't teach you—Please Hakim, I can't teach you to dance. Besides, Hakim, that is a woman's dance. If a man dances like that, people will think he is a you know what!? You go, you dance with your fern.

(He seems to insist.)

OK OK I'm sorry, come here you want to learn, come here, OK do like this, like this, make a bird, make a bird, OK? OK, now you are a dancer.

(Farrida pulls on her scarf, so as to give the illusion that he is trying to pull her to him.)

No, I don't want to kiss you. I don't want to, because *I don't want to.* Hakim, please don't argue with me, I just don't want to. Because, just because, because you smell like cigarette! Are you happy now?—Then how come I am smelling cigarette in your mouth right now, when you told me after last time that that was your last pack and now I can smell that you are smoking again.

No, no, I don't want to dance with you, I want to know why you broke your promise. Relax. Relax. How can I relax Hakim, when you told me, you told me with your own mouth. You said, "Farrida, because I love you, I will stop smoking," and what did I say? You don't remember, I will tell you what I said, I said, "No. No. You *will not,* because I know you, and I know the kind of man you are" and what did you say? What did you say? You don't remember, you don't remember what *you* said, OK I will tell you what you said. You said, "Khudda ni Kassam." Do you remember? Khudda ni Kassam Hakim. And you are a bloody liar! You lie to me, you lie to God, you lie to anybody.

Mane' tara sathe waat aj nai karwi, tara moma si gundhi waas aweche'.

—How can you say that? If you loved me, I would not smell cigarette in your mouth right now   Teach me to dance. You can't even do *one bloody thing* for me!

Dramatic. Dramatic. How can I be dramatic? You see me. You see my life. You see my life since I came to this country.—Can you imagine? Me. Me. Hakim, I was the girl in India who was always on the go! Movies, theatre, museum, money to burn. Where have you brought me? Where have we come, to this cold country where nobody talks to anybody, where I sit alone in two rooms all day long waiting for you come home. No friends, no one to talk to, nowhere to go. If I go anywhere, these Americans don't even understand what I am trying to speak.

Look at me, Hakim! I am not even the girl that you married. This is not me, this was not supposed to be my life. I gave up everything for you. For your dream, America! Land of Opportunity! For you, *yes.* For my baby, *yes.* For me, *no.* No opportunity.

—How can you say that, how do you know? Even if we do make it, what happens, do we just go on smoking and dancing forever.

(Soft music begins to play, signifying that SAKINA *has woken up.)*
See now, Sakina woke up.
(She looks offstage to talk to the apparently crying child.)
Na ro bacha Mummy aweche. Na ro.
(She turns back to Hakim, but he is gone.)
That's alright, Hak—you go, I'll take care of her.—You go, smoke your cigarette.
(She turns upstage.)
Na ro, Mummy aweche. Na ro bacha Mummy aweche, Na ro Na ro.

(Farrida walks upstage and we see her slowly take the scarf from around her neck and it becomes the baby SAKINA. *The scarf is eventually unraveled and we are back in the company of* AZGI, *as he addresses the audience.)*

AZGI: Once upon a time, an eagle and a lark sat on the branch of a giant tree. The eagle pushed out its giant chest and spread its powerful wings, and told the lark of its many adventures. "I have seen the world," said the eagle, "I have seen it seven times over. I have flown over temples and palaces, oceans and valleys, I have swooped down into valleys and I have flown so high that the sun has risen and set below me." The tiny lark had no such adventures of which to speak and it wracked its brain for a story to tell. Finally, it did the only thing it knew how to do. It began to sing. A tiny song, but as it did the tree, the field, the hillside and the entire valley, lifted up out of the earth and rose to heaven.

She doesn't dance anymore. I suppose that eventually she forgot that she could—or maybe she simply decided it was not worth trying to remember.

Dear Ma, another day in Sakina's Restaurant. I work, and I work, and I work and I work—but I never dance.

*(*AZGI *is suddenly in the restaurant. He mimes a conversation with a table, tries to clean their dirty silverware, he goes to another table and picks up their plates, he rushes over to the kitchen and screams at* ABDUL *the cook, who is working behind the line.)*

ABDUL!—I need two puris on table 5! I need two lassis on table 6, and this lamb curry is COLD, COLD, COLD! Food, Abdul, is supposed to be HOT, HOT! Not COLD! How come you don't seen to understand that?????

*(*AZGI *runs to speak to one of his tables. To first table.)*

I am very sorry. In all the time that I have worked in this restaurant, food is NEVER cold, NEVER! He is heating it up right now. I will bring it out in two minutes and you just keep enjoying your . . . water.

(He moves to the second table.)

Hello, how are you? My name is Azgi, I will be your waiter, How can I help you? Oh yeah, it is kind of spicy, but we have a scale. You see, you can order how spicy you would like one, two, three, four, five. You decide, He'll make it— What?—you want number five?

*(*AZGI *is a little concerned.)*

Sir don't take number five, Take number two—No, no, number two is better for you, it's very good, you'll like it very much.—Please sir, don't take number five. Sir I am trying to save your life OK. *(getting angry)* Look, look in my eyes, OK, number two is better for you. OK, you think about it, I will come back OK.

(He runs upstage again.)

ABDUL!—Where is my lamb curry????

(The lamb curry seems to have appeared on the line.)

A-ha!

(He runs over to the first table with the imaginary lamb curry. It is very hot and burns his hands.)

There you go. OK? piping hot—What happened? Why you look so sad? Not lamb?—CHICKEN—Oh my God!—No, no, please sit down. Where you going? Please don't leave, sit down, I am very sorry, this is a terrible mistake, I will bring out chicken in just two minutes, please don't leave, whatever you do don't leave.

(He runs over to the second table.)

OK, OK, look I tell you what, number three, number three is plenty hot. You don't need number five. LISTEN MAN!! I AM FROM INDIA!!! And even in India nobody asks for number five! It's not a real thing that you can eat, it's just for show. I am not screaming, you are screaming! Look, look, now your wife is crying! I didn't make her cry, you made her cry! OK, OK. Fine, Fine, you want five, fifteen, one hundred five!! I give you OK!

ABDUL!—Listen, on forty-one, I put number five, but you don't make it number five, you make it number two, OK? And this lamb curry is supposed to be chicken curry—Because I am telling you, that's why. Because I am the boss right now, OK. Listen you give me any trouble no, I will have Mr. Hakim fire you!!!—Oh, yeah? Oh, yeah? Come on. Come on, Abdul. *(He puts up his fists.)* I will take you right now! I will kick your butt so hard that you will be making lamb curry for the tigers in India! Oh, yeah? Come on, Big Guy, come on, Big Guy, come on—

(Suddenly AZGI *is faced with* ABDUL *who grabs him by the collar.)*

—BIG GUY!

I am joking, man. I am just kidding around, why you take me so seriously?—Please don't kill me.

(Turning)

Every night I have the same dream. I am a giant tandoori chicken wearing an Armani suit. I am sitting behind the wheel of a speeding Cadillac. I have no eyes to see, no mouth to speak and I don't know where I am going.

Mr. Hakim, he come up to me, he say, "Azgi, Azgi, Azgi, you have to calm down, man." He say to me, he say, "Success, Azgi, is like a mountain. From far away it is inspiring, but when you get close, you realize that it is simply made of earth and dirt and rocks, piled one on top of the other until it touches the sky." Mr. Hakim, he is a smart man, but I wonder to myself when God was building the mountain and piling the rock, one on top of the other, was he working or playing?

(He begins to ponder this thought, and then suddenly he smiles and goes over to the first table.)

Hello, my name is Azgi . . . I am working . . . and playing.

(He goes over to the second table.)

Hello, my name is Azgi . . . I am working and playing . . . how are you?

(He goes over and looks in the direction of ABDUL, *and blows him a big kiss.)*

ABDUL . . . I love you man!!!

(Phone rings, AZGI *turns and looks at the audience.)*

Phone!

(He picks up the phone.)

Hello, Sakina's Restaurant. Azgi speaking. How may I—Oh, oh, Mr. Hakim? No. No. He is right here. I will get him—

*(*AZGI *heads around behind the coat rack as if on his way to find Hakim, when he comes around the other side, with tie in hand. . . . he is Hakim.)*

HAKIM: *(Into the phone)* Hello, Sakina's, How may I help you?—Oh, hello Bob! I am very fine. Business is good, business is good you know can't complain, how about you?—Huh? Dinner for three? Tonight? Oh you must be going to have a big celebration—Usual table? OK—8 p.m. Very good. Oh congratulations, you must be very proud of him. Actually, we are also very proud of our Sakina because—

(He is embarrassingly interrupted on the other end of the line.)

Oh, OK Bob. No no that's fine. I understand. Time is money. Got to go. OK Bob, we'll see you later. OK, we'll see you then, bye bye . . . bye bye . . . bye bye.

(Hangs up, and then resumes putting on his tie and grooming himself in mirror and singing a Hindi song of choice. During this, he hears an imaginary knock on the door.)

Come in.

(He turns to see his daughter.)

Hey, hey, hey, hey! Come inside here, close the door, come here. What is this dress?—Oh, I see, I see.

(He talks to his daughter. His distress with his daughter is translated into his ineptness and frustration with his tie that he is trying to secure.)

You think you are too smart, huh?—You think you are too smart.—You think you can go anywhere, do anything, wear anything. You think you have become an American Girl!—You think the world should not care now how you behave, what you wear, how you dress, nothing! You have got all these fancy ideas from all your American friends. You are laughing with all your American friends you are saying, "Oh my parents are introducing me to an Indian man, nice professional Indian man, going to be a doctor, how foolish of them, right? How foolish they are." All your American friends are laughing. They are saying Hey, Sakina, life is not like that.—Life is easy, marry who you want to marry, Black guy, White guy—who cares, right? Who cares? In America, everything is OK! No right, no wrong, no good, no bad, everything is COOL! As long as I feel good about myself, who cares, right?—Who cares how my father feels, or my mother feels, or my grandfather feels or my grandmother feels. Who cares! It is my business, my life, this is a free country! Am I right?

(Phone rings.)

Hello, Sakina's, how may I help you?—Tonight, dinner for two, Martin . . . can you spell that? M . . . A . . . R *(He notices that* SAKINA *is leaving and he tries to get her to come back in the room while continuing with the customer on the phone.)* T . . . I . . . N. No I got it, I got it, yes we do, yes we do, free popadoms, yes all night long, as many as you want, OK we'll see you then, yes I am excited as well, OK then, bye bye . . . bye bye . . . bye bye.

(Hangs up)

Sakina!—Sakina! . . . Come inside—Close the door. I'm talking to you. Crazy girl, running away.

(He turns to the mirror, notices his tie is completely screwed up and he is a little embarrassed. He reties it.)

"Oh Dad!" You are saying, "Dad! Dad! Dad! What do you know about life in America? You are from India! In America you have to learn to relax, because everybody in America is very RELAXED and very COOL!" Well, let me tell you something, I have seen all of your cool and relaxed friends, and you are not fooling anyone—you will *never* be an American girl. You can TRY. Oh yeah, you can TRY. You can wear your BIG HAIR, like American hair, and you can wear makeup like American makeup, you can even wear this cheap dress and show off your breasts and your legs and disgrace your whole family—but you will always be an Indian girl, with Indian blood, and these Americans, oh they are very nice, very polite on the face, have a nice day. Have a nice day. Welcome to K-Mart, Very Nice.—They will look at you and say, "Oh, she is so pretty, she looks like Paula Abdul."—But let me tell you something, the minute you steal one of their good ole boys from them, suddenly you will see how quickly you become an Indian again. *(Phone rings. He speaks in Gujaratti.)*

Hello, Sakina's Restaurant how may I help you? Aaa Cam cho bhai, are koi divas miltaj nathi . . . aje, chullo, na na badha ne layaowjo, na khai takhlif nei, chullo pachi milsu . . . OK bye bye . . . bye bye . . . bye bye.

(Hangs up and faces his daughter.)

We love you, Sakina, you are our daughter. But I will never agree to what you are doing with your life.—Why do you think we came to this country?—For YOU! Why do you think I have this restaurant?—For YOU! Why do you think I am working twelve hours a day?—For YOU and your brother. So that you could grow up in the richest country in the world, have all the opportunity, all the advantages and become something. We are saving every penny for your college, why? So you can run around with American boys . . . NO!! So we will be proud of you. Indian children make their parents proud of them. Can your American friends teach you that?—Can they teach you about your Culture?

Your Religion? Your Language? Can they tell you who you are? . . . Go ask them. I know, I know, I know it is all fun and games right now, but what will happen? You will marry one of these American boys, have American children, and then what? Then everything will be forgotten—Everything will be GONE.—Tu kai samje che me su kawchu tane'. Tara Mugaj ma kai jaiche'.

Answer me, no? No No No No, Not in English. Speak to me in Gujaratti.

(He waits, and she does not respond. She is unable to.)

Can't . . . ! Won't maybe. Look at you, look what you have become. You will not go to this dance tonight. I will show you, I will get rid of this "I want to be American" nonsense—

(Exploding in anger.)

I DON'T CARE! I DON'T CARE, I DON'T CARE IF THIS IS THE BIG-GEST DANCE IN THE COUNTRY OR THE WORLD OR THE ENTIRE FUCKING AMERICA!! DANCING IS IMPORTANT, *(He dances around mocking her.)* BUT I AM NOT IMPORTANT!

(The phone rings. He composes himself and answers the phone.)

Hello, Sakina's how may I help you?—Yes, Bob, how are you?—Oh I am very sorry. Oh, no problem, that's perfectly alright, we'll see you another time. I hope she feels better, thank you for calling Bob. Bye-bye, bye-bye, bye-bye.

(Hangs up, and looks back at SAKINA.*)*

Tell Azgi that the Cohens have canceled, and go help your mother . . . in the kitchen.

(Phone rings, he watches her leave and then answers.)

AZGI: *(On phone)* Hey Ma, it is me, Azgi. Yeah, Azgi, I'm calling from New York. You know what, Ma? Next month Sakina is getting married, and tonight she is having a Bachelorette party, and I have been invited. I am very excited to be a Bachelorette. Hey, yeah, listen to the music.

(He holds up receiver.)

That's the music ma, You won't believe this party ma, so many people, Ma . . . I have to go, Ma. I love you, bye.

(He hangs up the phone and comes downstage dancing. He then dances downstage and then talks to the audience.)

Sakina told her parents that if she had to marry who they wanted her to marry, then she was going to have the kind of bachelorette party that she wanted to have. She invited 75 people, all of them would drink, including myself, and then she had a rock and roll band, and just to make sure that her parents would completely disapprove, she paid $200.00 for a "MALE STRIPPER." I told her, "I said for two hundred dollars in India I would run around naked for ONE WEEK!"—She said, "Oh, yeah?"

(The music that has been underlying the previous speech, suddenly becomes very loud and AZGI *begins to strip. He speaks as his clothes are seemingly ripped off his body. He is incredibly embarrassed.)*

No NO I cannot strip, No I do not do that kind of thing, I am very modest, I am from India, please do not do this, OK OK I tell you what I do this much OK? *(He simply opens a shirt a little.)* La la la la . . . That's all I can so thank you very much *(His shirt is ripped off him.)* Noooo!!! Because I was the only man, they decided to turn me into a Bachelorette.

(At this, AZGI *suddenly runs over to the hat stand and takes the tube dress that has been hanging there. The dress is slipped over his neck as if it were being done to him by the women at the party.)*

No, no, please. I cannot wear this, this is a dress! I am very embarrassed. Please not a DRESS, anything but a dress!

(His protests of genuine embarrassment are unheeded by the woman, who, after the dress, proceeds to finish off the transformation by squeezing a hair band onto his head much to AZGI's *amazement and distress.)*

AAAAAAAAAAAAAAAAAAAAAAAAAAAAAHHHHHHHH!!!!!!!!!!!!!!!

*(*AZGI *stands center stage wearing a tube dress and a hair band.)*

Once upon a time a man asked God for a new face because he was tired of the one he had, so God granted the man his wish. The tragedy of this story is that now every time the man looks in the mirror, he doesn't know who he is.

*(*AZGI *moves over to the table stage left and sits down. We are now in the presence of* SAKINA. *She primps and preens in a large hand mirror, until she is suddenly surprised by the presence of Tom who is sitting across the table.)*

SAKINA: Oh my GOD!!! *(Embarrassed)* I didn't see you come in . . . Wow you look great, I got your message. I can't stay long . . . 'cus I gotta get upstairs by 7:30.—Well we're having this religious festival at our house and all these people come over and we make this food called Biriani and . . . Never mind, I just gotta get back upstairs by 7:30 to help my mom get ready for it. *(Pause)* So, what's up?—I'm just surprised to see you because last time we talked you were like, "Sakina we are broke up" . . . and then you hung up the phone. What?—That's not true!—Is that why you came here, to tell me that? *(She turns and takes a deep breath and then turns back to him.)* No I'm fine, I'm fine, first of all Tom, first of all, Stacey and I are the ones who started this band and Stacey and I are the only ones who can—

(She looks up at the imaginary waiter.)

Hi!—No, I'm not eating . . . no neither is he, thanks, OK?—Thanks.

(Waiter leaves.)

And Stacey and I are the only ones who can kick anyone out of this band, which is not even a band yet, because Stacey still needs to learn how to play the piano and so you are kicking me out of a band that does not even exist yet!—No, no, no, no, the manager manages the band, Tom. He does not kick people out of the band, that is not his job.—What?—She said that? She said that! Stacey said that, Tom, look at me, look at me OK, Stacey is my best friend since the 8th grade, and if she said that, Tom, we are totally not friends anymore, so you better not be lying—Oh, my God! I can't believe she said that, I told her why I had to miss those practices, I totally said I have to miss three practices because I have to hang out with that Indian guy that my parents want me to marry—I had to hang out with him—I can't believe she said that, I don't understand, I explained the whole thing to her.

(Tom gets up to leave.)

Where are you going—That's it, that's all you had to say, now you're just gonna leave?

(She reaches for him.)

Wait! Would you please just sit down? *(She stands)* Please, Tom. *(She bends over and becomes cute and coy in order to lure him back to the table.)* Please, just for two minutes, please just sit down. *(He sits back down.)* Hi, What is going on here Tom?—What do you mean, what do I mean?—I mean you come here to tell me that my best friend is kicking me out of my band, and then last week you're like we have to break up 'cus "I need more space," and then this week I find out that you're dating Julie Montgomery, and I'm calling you every day this week and your Dad is like, "Tom? Tom went to the library"—and I'm like, Tom at the library? . . . I don't think so—no, I don't think I'd be jealous of her. Because, because, because she's a racist pig, that's why. I can't believe you would even date her.—I was hoping you came here to tell me of her untimely death.—I don't care if I'm not Black. It's still disgusting.—I didn't say that, I just said she's a racist pig and I wish she'd die. You can still date her.—Everyone knows she is, everyone in school knows. Have you ever heard her mouth?—"Nigger. Nigger. Nigger."

(She suddenly looks around hoping that no one heard her.)

She even called me that word . . . What's so funny?—You're laughing, yes you are, Oh my God you're sick, Tom. This is retarded, I'm leaving. *(Gets up to leave as waiter returns. She speaks to the waiter.)* Hi!—Yeah I have to leave, I have to go upstairs and *(Directing it at Tom)* THROW UP! What?—I don't care if she's sorry, Tom, my problem is you, my problem is—What? *(Realizing that waiter has taken her seriously.)* No I don't need any PEPTO. It's just HIM, I'm sorry thanks . . . no no I'm fine, thanks. *(Waiter leaves. She turns back to Tom)* My problem is not her, my problem is YOU. I'm starting to like not know you anymore.—You explained it to her? You explained it to her. OK, fine this should be great, *(Sitting back down)* What, Tom, did you explain to her?—

(She listens and then hears something that makes her suddenly furious.)

Ah ha,—and then?—and?—OK shut up! No, really Tom, shut up! Tom, Tom, Shut up! Shuuuuuuuuuuuuuuuut uuuuup!—Listen to me. I am NOT IRANIAN!—I am INDIAN! INDIAN! INDIAN! What do you mean? How could you not know that? Look around, Tom. We dated for TWO MONTHS, Tom, TWO MONTHS! In that TWO months, I brought you to THIS Indian

Restaurant like a million times. Where you ate all the "OOOOH, its SO GOOD!" INDIAN FOOD that my Mom put in front of your face. And remember that party I took you to in Brooklyn with all those INDIAN people, wearing INDIAN clothes celebrating INDIAN Independence Day and then you turn around and tell Julie Montgomery, "Hey, Sakina's not a nigger, she's IRANIAN!" Well there it is isn't it, everything is a big mistake to you. Our whole relationship was a big mistake, remember that one? Oh, my God! I can't believe you, I already explained the whole thing to you. It doesn't mean anything,—I am NOT going to marry him. Because I'm not, that's how I know—no no no. My parents can't make me. It's not some kind of medieval thing. It's just part of the culture, that's all. It's just a custom, they are just trying to make sure that I am secure in my life, that's all, they're not American, they're not like your parents— I'm not saying that—Your parents are great! I'm just saying that my parents have a different attitude about things and if you can just accept that and not make a big deal about it?—Well there it is isn't it!! If everyone doesn't think like you, talk like you, believe what you believe, then it's all just dumb, right?

(He takes her hand, music comes on.)

What are you doing? No I can't kiss you . . . because we are in my Dad's restaurant . . . What? *(She suddenly starts giggling based on what he has said, she slowly moves toward him, and as the music gets louder she and Tom engage in a big sloppy wet teenage kiss, she pulls away and realizes that she is chewing "his" gum, she takes it out of her mouth.)* What? Why?—No, you're gonna make fun of him. Because you always make fun of him. OK, if I show you, you promise not to laugh? Do you promise? Say it. Say I promise not to laugh . . . or make fun of him . . . OK

(She reaches into her purse, she pulls out of her purse a photograph and puts it on the table.)

When I was seven, my dad, yeah he gave me this picture of this guy that they betrothed me to, and I just kept it.—Because, because, I didn't know I was gonna meet anybody. When you're young and geeky with a funny name and your Mom makes you wear harem pants and braids everyday it's hard to imagine that you're ever gonna meet anyone.—I don't suppose you can even relate, Mr. Free Throw wins the Junior Championship. So it was a good feeling to have a picture of a guy who was like mine, and even though I was different, so was he, and so we were, like a team.—Jeez, I feel totally stupid. I don't even know why I'm telling you this.—

(He gets up to leave.)

Where are you going? Where are you going?—No No I will tell him, I couldn't tell him last time, I'm gonna tell him next time.

(She snaps the picture up as he reaches over to tear it up.)

Hey!!! I think before I tear up his picture, I should tell him that I am not going to marry him, I think that would be courteous. Would you please come back!! Why is this such a big deal to you?—I'm gonna tell him. Come back, Please come back. Fine! Fine, Tom! Just leave! Just leave the way you always do! *(Pause)* WAAAAIT!!!!

What you don't understand Tom is that it doesn't make any difference, it's just the way it is. You can kick me outta the band, you can date a racist pig, Stacey can be a total bitch, my parents can cry, and I can even tear up this picture and it doesn't make any difference. (Pause) OK OK OK OK OK, *(She picks up the picture)* Fine . . . fine . . . fine.

(As music builds SAKINA *attempts to tear up the picture, but it becomes obvious that she cannot. She holds the picture to her chest, and Tom walks away. she turns and undresses into* AZGI *again. As the music plays.* AZGI *picks up the strewn clothes and hangs them up, he then puts his shirt on again as the lights come up.)*

AZGI: *(Noticing audience)* Oh Hello!!! Oh you know, Sakina's wedding was wonderful. So many people. She looked beautiful, she looked so beautiful, she looked like a gift. The Groom? He also looked very handsome. In fact, the two of them together, they looked perfect. A little uncomfortable, but perfect. The Groom, he is a medical student and he is also a very religious Muslim man. In fact, even at his own wedding he was studying for his final exam the next day and praying that he would not fail. Can you believe?? By watching him, I also start to pray . . . But the only thing I could think of to pray after watching him was, "Please God, don't let me spend my whole life just praying and studying, praying and studying, praying and studying . . . " Oh for their honeymoon, they are going to travel across America. Oh, it sounds very exciting. They will see everything, the Hollywood and the Redwood, they will ride on Wide Open Ventura Highways, and they will see The Grand Canyon, and the Mississippi. I told the groom, I said, "If I could, I would follow you. I envy the adventure you are going to have." And he looked at me, and said, "Azgi, if I could, I would follow you, I envy the adventure you are going to have."

(A sudden light change, AZGI *suddenly doubles over in anguish.)*
ALI: Shut up! Shut up!—I have to walk, I have to clear my head, and I have to come back. I have to walk, I have to clear my head, I have to come back, I have to walk, I have to clear my head, I have to come back. I have to WALK! I have to clear my head, I have to come—

(Suddenly he looks up as if someone has opened a door and he is staring into their face. He is visibly nervous, his mouth is dry and his hands are sweaty.)

I only have fifty dollars, I don't know if that's enough or not. Oh, that's fine, whatever you do for fifty dollars is fine. I don't know if I want the complete package anyway. It's probably safer that way, in regards to diseases and such. *(Realizing his faux pas)* I'm sorry, I'm not saying that you have any diseases. Oh no I ruined the mood. I'm sorry, its just that I'm a Pre-Med student, so

I'm always thinking about diseases. I don't do this kind of thing normally—NEVER!! Never before actually, I don't know if that matters to you, but it matters to me, and so I just thought I would share that with you.

(Pulling money out of his pocket and handing it to her)

Look, I'll just give you the money and you can put it over there on the dresser, or in your *(Noticing that she put it in her underwear)* There! This is very unlikely for me to be in a place like this—I've actually been trying to deepen my religious faith lately. I'm a Muslim, you know. Do you know what that is? . . . Yes, it's a type of cloth. What is your name?—Angel?—Really? *(He laughs.)* No, no, I'm sorry. I was just thinking that that's an ironic name for someone who does what you do for a living.—What? No, no, I'm sorry, I'm not a jerk. I'm sorry that was rude, Look I think you're very attractive. In fact, that's even the reason I followed you in here from the street . . . was because of the way you look . . . or at least who you look like. Well, you see, you look amazingly like this girl Karen who sits next to me in my Human Anatomy class, and who I cannot stop thinking about, and earlier this evening I was trying to study for my exam tomorrow, but I can't seem to concentrate because I can't stop thinking about Karen, and then when I think about Karen all the time, I think about my parents beating their chests when they realize I've failed all my exams. So I decided to take a walk and pray for some concentration, and that's when I saw you, and you—well, you look exactly like her, and you looked at me, and you smiled, and so when you started thinking to myself that you must be a sign . . . a sign from God!! That since I'll never be with Karen, I could be with you, and then I could go home and be able to study, and pass my exam and make my parents proud of me!!! *(He suddenly breaks down into tears.)* I'm sorry, I'm really sorry, I think I've made a terrible mistake. You see I just realized that God would never, never lead me to a place like this. I must be losing my mind. I have to study, I have to go! I need some sleep! I have to study, I'm really sorry. I have obviously wasted your time, I'm really sorry but I have to go. *(He leaves, there is a long pause then he returns.)* I think I should probably just get a refund. I don't know what your policy is as far as refunds go. I'm sure that it doesn't come up very often.—What?—Uh, thank you, that's very kind of you—Well I think you're very attractive yourself—No, I can't do that actually, No I can't, No I really can't—Well, because I'm engaged . . . or at least "betrothed" which is actually more like . . . engaged!—She's a very nice girl, Sakina!! Would you like to see a picture? I have one,—No of course not. What I'm trying to say is that she really is the perfect girl for me, comes from a very similar family, same religion, same tradition, same values, these things are important, you know. Besides, Karen is just a distraction. I mean, she's American. In the long run she would never accept Indian culture, she would never understand the importance of an Islamic way of life, she would probably want to have pre-marital sex which is something that as a

Muslim I could never do. I know that probably sounds ridiculous under the circumstances, but it's true!!! It's not just a religion you know, it's a way of life and I have dedicated my entire spiritual life identity to the complete submission to the will of God. That's what Islam means. So you see, I can't just be running around having sex *(He thrust his pelvis forward unconsciously)* like a rabbit *(He does it again, with more vigor.)* It would be a SIN!! And that is why I have to leave. What? What is my name?

(He pauses.)

AL!—Really!—OK, OK. Its not Al the way you are thinking of it, like short for Alan or Alvin or something. Its actually the short form of a very religious name, a name I can't even say right now, otherwise it would be a sin—I think. I probably don't even deserve this name.

(We begin to hear the song, "No Ordinary Love." This plays throughout the rest of the piece.)

What are you doing?—No I really don't think you should . . . REMOVE THAT!!!

(He hides behind his hands so as not to look at her but then he slowly looks.)

You want me to call you Karen? . . . OK!? Karen, Karen, Karen, Karen . . .

(She unbuttons his pants and begins to perform oral sex, the rest of the lines are delivered while he is receiving a blow job.)

Oh, my God, this is not me, this is not my life. Oh, shit!

(Looking down)

I'm sorry, I'm trying not to swear. It's hard, you know, to do the right thing, you know.—I'm always asking for forgiveness, because I believe that God understands and he is forgiving, and he knows how hard it is, to do the right thing all the time, even when you want to, more than anything else, and if you fail and you disappoint people, you can just try again, right? And you can have the intention to try again even while you're failing . . . failing! I don't suppose there is really any chance of me passing this exam tomorrow. I mean, If I'm going to be punished for this, and I'm sure I will be, that will probably be the punishment, because when you're trying to do the right thing and make people proud of you, Satan wants you to fail. And then you end up being a huge disappointment. Well, if I'm not going to be a doctor, I wonder what I will be?—Maybe I will be a bum!—and Sakina will say, "I can't marry him, he's a BUM!!!"

(He is getting quite worked up at this point as he gets closer to orgasm.)

And I will say, "GOOD!!!! BECAUSE THIS BUM WOULDN'T MARRY YOU WHEN HELL FREEZES OVER!" AND HER PARENTS WILL SAY, "HOW DARE YOU TALK TO OUR DAUGHTER LIKE THAT!!! AND I WILL SAY I JUST DID!! AND MY PARENTS WILL SAY, HOW DARE YOU TALK TO HER PARENTS LIKE THAT, YOU ARE A GREAT DISAPPOINTMENT," AND I WILL SAY, "MOM, DAD EAT

(He orgasms.)
SHIIIT!!!!!"
(He falls to his knees in shock, and slowly as if almost in slow motion he doubles over on the floor, unconsciously going into the Islamic position of prayer. After a few seconds. he regains his composure and attempts to stand and button up his pants.)
Thank you Angel, I mean Kar- . . . I mean Angel.
(He takes off his glasses.)
AZGI: Once upon a time a hunter wandered into a forest, armed only with a bow and arrow, in order to find food for his family. After some time he came upon a clearing, and in the middle of the clearing stood a goat. The hunter, excited by this, raised his bow and arrow in order to kill the goat, but just as he did, the hunter noticed that the goat was crying. The hunter, intrigued by this, asked the animal why it wept. And the goat answered "I weep because God spoke to me and he told me all the secrets of the Universe." The hunter asked the goat to share the secrets with him, and so the goat did, and after he was done the hunter realized . . . that now, he could never return home.
(Music and lights change, as AZGI slowly sits center stage and contemplates. Suddenly his meditation is broken by a sudden light change and computerized sound, he gets up and finds the sound is coming from and discovers SAMIR's Game Boy)
(Looking off)
Samir!! Samir!! Hey how come you leave your stuff lying around man, I got to clean up!!
(noticing audience)
OH, HELLO!
You know, Samir he leaves his stuff just lying around you know, I have to clean up, *(Getting interested in the Game Boy.)* This is a very exciting little game though, apparently the idea is you see if you can just get your little man to the top of this mountain without getting hit by the falling rocks, then you get to go in the space ship and fly away . . . it's very good *(Playing)* Come on Jump! Jump! Come on you crazy man, come on, Jump! Jump!—
(Looking off)
HELLO! Oh Samir, yeah there you are, I found your hat and your Game Boy because you leave your junk here in the restaurant and then I have to pick up your stuff—No, no, no, you can't have it, because I'm almost up to the space ship.
(Listening and playing at the same time.)
Sakina? Oh yeah, she sent a postcard? From her honeymoon? Oh yeah? Good for you, good for you.—To me!! To me!! She sent a postcard to me? Oh yeah let me see, let me see!! Come on it's my postcard man. OK, I give you the

Game Boy, you give me the postcard, OK? I put it down, you put the postcard down, ready

(He puts the postcard on the table. SAMIR *obviously doesn't and* AZGI *chases him around the restaurant)*

Hey!! Hey!! You see how you are? Give me that postcard, come on Samir. Come on, give it to me! Hey!

(He chases SAMIR *around the stage trying to get the postcard. At a certain point in the chase* AZGI *puts on the hat and becomes* SAMIR, *he squirms around trying to keep a hold of the postcard and then he throws it offstage and runs over to the Game Boy)*

SAMIR: *(Playing with his Game Boy.)* It's on the floor—*(picking up the Game Boy)* Hey Cool! You're almost in outer space. You know what, you know what, you know what Azgi? My sister, she is gonna go all over the country for her honeymoon, and you know what, she said that she would send me a postcard from each place she went, but you know what the best part is, Azgi? You know what the best part is? When she goes to Disney World she is gonna send me an autographed picture of the Ninja Turtles. . . . Cool right! 'Cus that's where they live!!! And we were supposed to go to Disney World last year, but we didn't go, 'cus my grandmother died and then we had to go to India, *(He pretends to puke)* that sucked!!! And you know what? You know what? You know what? I got into this huge fight with my cousin Mustafa. 'Cus you know what, you know what, you know what,

(Light change.)

Dad!!! No I didn't punch him, I didn't punch him, I didn't punch him, no listen, I was showing Mustafa this really cool game, but he didn't wanna play, so then I said . . . let's play anyway! But he was being a spoil sport and messin up the game, and not playin right, so then I said, "FINE! I'm gonna play Ninja Turtles on my Game Boy," and when I was doing that he wanted to play too! All of sudden! But I said, "No way, Jose!" So then, so then, so then, Mom called me to come upstairs and look at some pictures of Dadi Ma when she was alive and she was really young and you were sitting in her lap and you were just a little baby—Dad Dad Dad, Do you remember that? Dad, do you remember when you were a baby?. . . . Do ya? *(Realizing he cannot change the subject so easily.)* SO THEN! I said that he could hold my Game Boy for just five minutes. JUST FIVE MINUTES! But then, when I came back he wouldn't give it so I had to give him a Ninja Kick in the head!!!

(He demonstrates a Ninja Kick to the head.)

That's all that happened, yeah but I didn't punch him, I didn't punch him, I didn't punch him. He said I punched him, I didn't punch him. So I don't have to share with a crybaby and a liar if I don't want to. But Dad it's my Game Boy, that I brought all the way from America remember? Remember, you said nobody could touch it, not even Sakina "'cus it was the only thing that would keep me shut up," remember you said that? Huh?—So that just means he's a crybaby that's all. I don't have to share with a crybaby—No,—No,—But I'm not even sorry.

(His father slaps SAMIR *on the behind. This is done by* SAMIR *turning himself with his right band and slapping his own behind with his left hand. Every time that* SAMIR *is slapped in the remainder of this piece. it is done using this method.)*

Hey!!! How come you're hitting me? He's the one who STOLE my Game Boy, how come no one is hitting him? What?—NA-AH—WHY?—Dad no!! That's totally not fair!—No, no, no, I don't want another stupid Game Boy. I just want the one I have. This was my birthday present from Jim's dad, you can't just give my birthday present to any stupid Indian kid that wants it just 'cus they don't have any cool toys here.—No, I don't want another one, why can't you buy HIM another one?—I'm sick of this. You know what, Mom already gave him my Ninja Turtle high tops, she already gave him those, yeah the ones with the lights in 'em that go "Kawabunga!" when you jump in 'em, she already gave him those. You're just gonna give him all my stuff.—I hate coming to India, I hate coming to this stupid country—No, no, no, he's not my brother, he's stupid! He smells!!—He can't even speak English! *(He is slapped again.)*

Didn't hurt *(Slap!)*

Didn't hurt more!!! *(Slap!!!)*

(Crying)

Alright! Alright! It hurt!! How come you always hit me when I tell the truth, huh? Yes you do, yes you do, yes you do, everyone in this country is stupid!! And they just want all my cool stuff, 'cus they don't have any cool stuff of their own, and they're just jealous, 'cus we get to live in America, and they're stuck here in ugly, smelly old India, and I never, ever, ever wanna come back here ever, and I don't ever wanna go anywhere with you and Mom ever again 'cus you're just liars! Liars! Liars! Liars! . . . And you abuse your children too!—Yes you do, yes you do! You said we were gonna go to Disney World this year, and we were gonna see the Ninja Turtles like all my friends did.—Yeah, well, I don't care. I hate Dadi Ma too!!! I hate her for dying and ruining everything!

(This time SAMIR *is slapped on the face. After the slap* SAMIR *stands in shocked silence as he is about to burst into tears; in that moment he witnesses his father starting to cry. He has never seen this before and is therefore frightened and confused by what he sees.)*

Dad? Are you alright? Dad, I'm sorry! I'm sorry I said that about Dadi Ma.— Listen, you know what, Mustafa can have my Game Boy, alright?

(He takes off the hat also, and hands it to his father.)

He can have all my stuff. *(*SAMIR *reaches out with his hat and Game Boy but his father does not take them.)*

Dad! I'm sorry that your mom died. *(SAMIR begins to cry, slowly he backs upstage and he places both the Game Boy and the hat on the nearest table. He is again AZGI. The lights change and in the area where Farrida had studios in a pool of light, AZGI enters it as himself)*

AZGI: "This is not me, this was not supposed to be my life," . . . she said *(Moving to the Hat and the Game Boy)* "I thought we were gonna go to Disney World!!!" . . . he said. *(Moving to where SAKINA had sat.)* It doesn't make any difference, it's just the way it is . . . she said. *(Moving to HAKIM's area)* Everything will be forgotten, everything will be gone . . . he said. *(Moving to where Ali had stood.)* "Well, maybe I should just get a refund," he said.

Everyone speaking my voice. Everyone except me, Ma. Where did I go? What happened to the top of the Empire State Building? What happened to the bottom of the Grand Canyon? How did all my adventures and romances end up on other people's postcards?

"I DON'T REMEMBER THE STORY OF THE RIVER STONE" . . . I SAID . . . Once upon a time, there was a boy, and this boy was standing by a stream, and by his foot he found a stone. He picked up the stone because he believed it was the most perfect stone he had ever seen. He immediately threw the tiny stone into the stream because in his young heart he believed that as soon as the stone entered the water and sparkled beneath the sunlight, it would become a diamond. As soon as the stone entered the stream, it began to flow with the current, faster and faster and faster and faster, the boy ran along side the stream watching his tiny stone, tossing and turning in the water, always moving, always dancing until . . . it disappeared and he could no longer see it. The boy panicked. He ran to the end of the stream, where he discovered that his tiny stone had been washed ashore amidst hundreds and thousands of rocks and stones and pebbles, all of which had taken the same journey down the same stream. The boy searched frantically for his perfect stone, picking up one stone after the next after the next, after the next but he could not find it. He searched day after day, week after week, month after month, year after year, until the boy became a man. And then one day he stopped searching, because he realized that the reason he could not find it was because he had never really known what it looked like.

(He pulls out the tiny pebble from the beginning of the play from his pocket. He looks at it and closes his fist around it; he turns and walks upstage as the music crescendos. Blackout.)

[End]

Shishir Kurup

Shishir Kurup is an actor, director, playwright, and composer based in Los Angeles. Reared in Mombassa, Kenya; Bombay, India; and in various locations across the United States, Kurup has contributed dramatic writing and performance across various media. He has created and performed in three one-man shows, *Assimilation, EXILE: Ruminations on a Reluctant Martyr,* and *Sharif Don't Like It.* These shows have been staged at various venues, including the New York Shakespeare Festival, the Mark Taper Forum, London's Institute for Contemporary Art, Manchester's Green Room, Loyola Marymount University, and Amherst's New World Theater.

Kurup has directed Platform's *The Scary Election Show,* Raven Group's *The Barking Wall,* and his own *Skeleton Dance,* all for the Los Angeles Theatre Center. As a member of the Cornerstone Theatre Company, he has written and directed *Ghurba,* a play about Arab-American culture in Los Angeles; codirected and composed music for *Everyman in the Mall,* a morality play taking place in the Santa Monica mall; and adapted Herman Hesse's *Siddhartha* in Watts, California, into a musical entitled *Sid Arthur.* He has directed and co-composed both *Candude: Or the Optimistic Civil Servant,* a peripatetic musical journey through the Los Angeles Central Library and *Demeter in the City* written by MacArthur Fellow Sarah Ruhl. *As Vishnu Dreams,* Shishir's meditation on the Ramayana, completed a highly successful run at East West Players with critic's choice from both the *Los Angeles Times* and the *LA Weekly.* In 2007, he directed the sold-out run of *Los Illegals* with the community of undocumented immigrants, by Michael John Garces, which kicked off Cornerstone's three-year Justice Cycle.

He has received Garland awards for acting and composing as well as the

Princess Grace Award for Theatre. In addition to being a Herb Alpert Award Nominee, he has received a Kennedy Center award for his playwriting. He was also one of only six people nationwide to receive the TIME (Time for Inspiration, Motivation, and Exploration) Grant from the Audrey Skirball Foundation in recognition of his body of work.

Merchant on Venice

(commissioned by Cornerstone Theater Company and the Audrey Skirball-Kenis Theater):
Silk Road Theatre Project, Chicago, 2007
Mark Taper Forum/Kirk Douglas Theatre, Los Angeles, Calif., 2005
Lark Theatre, New York, N.Y., Workshop, 2004
East-West Players, Los Angeles, Calif., Workshop, 2003

Other Plays

The Adventures of Heeb and Saheeb in the Holographic Universe (Co-writer and performer)
An Antigone Story
As Vishnu Dreams
Assimilation
Birthday of the Century
Exile: Ruminations on a Reluctant Martyr
Ghurba
Life and Death: A Vaudeville Show (Co-writer and performer)
On Caring for the Beast
Sharif Don't Like It
Sid Arthur
Skeleton Dance

Merchant on Venice

Shishir Kurup

CHARACTERS

MURALI, ARAVIND, *Suitors to Pushpa*

DEVENDRA, *A Hindu merchant on Venice Blvd*

JITENDRA, *His friend, suitor to Pushpa. In his early to mid-thirties.*

SHIVANANDA, *Journalist/Professor. Older. Mid- to late fifties*

YOGANANDA, *Shivananda's partner. Younger. Early to mid-forties*

AMITHABA, *Friend to Devendra and Jitendra, a bartender.*

ARMANDO, *In love with Noorani. Aspiring Latino musician. Twenties.*

SHARUK, *A wealthy Muslim. In is late forties, early fifties.*

TOUFIQ, *His friend. A Muslim.*

NOORANI, *Daughter to Sharuk. Sixteen years old.*

TOORANPOI, *The Clown. A Hindu. Employed by Sharuk.*

PUSHPA, *A rich Hindu heiress. In her mid-twenties.*

KAVITA, *Her poor cousin. Eight years older.*

RASIK, *Pushpa's father's estate's conservator.*

S.A.B.U. REP., *Presiding over the trial. A Hindu.*

HALAL BUTCHER, *A Muslim butcher.*

   (Partly in cafes on Venice Boulevard. Partly at SHARUK's *house and partly in Carmel at the mansion of* PUSHPA *Shah and at the meeting hall of the South Asian Businessmen's Union [S.A.B.U.] in Culver City.)*

   (The present.)

©March 1999. All rights resvd. by author. 3rd Draft 3/10/05 ©Songs and music by Shishir Kurup. A free adaptation of *Merchant of Venice* by William Shakespeare set in the South Asian community in and around Culver City, Calif. Commissioned by Audrey Skirball Kenis Theatre and Cornerstone Theater Company for L.A. Visions/L.A. Voices.

Note: *A number of these roles can be double cast to bring cast size down to 11. The Clown can and should play several characters; a combination of* ARAVIND, TOUFIQ, *and* S.A.B.U. REP. YOGANANDA *and* SHIVANANDA *can take up the roles of* MURALI, RASIK, *and* HALAL BUTCHER.

ACT I

SCENE I: VENICE BLVD. PETTERSONS. A STREET CAFE.

(*Enter* DEVENDRA, YOGANANDA, *and* SHIVANANDA)

DEVEN: I swear to god these herbs have no effect.
St. John's Wort, Kava Kava, nothing works.
I'm mopey, weepy and bluer than blue.
My therapist won't even take my calls.
O god! I'm bored with me, and so are you.
Now don't deny it!
Distraction is to what I'm truly moved.

YOGA: Now that's because your finger's in too many pies.
It's not enough to own a sari shop
And video and sweet and spices store,
With software, wholesale Macs and Dos;
But now this import, export business? Bap reh!
I'd drink the Maalox all the livelong day.
With NASDAQ on a rollercoaster ride,
I fear there you play much too fast and loose.

SHIVA: He's right at least in terms of import/export.
It's risky even in the simplest terms.
And since the Indo-Paki nuclear tests,
It's made it harder on us NRI's.
See, they don't give a damn as long as they
Can rabble rouse and keep the status quo.
It's how they stay in office over there.
And over here.

YOGA: Him and his politics.
What I'm concerned about's cholesterol.
Now yours was high the last time that you checked.
And stress is not the least of reasons why.
So though you're fit, this constant worrying
Must have a deleterious effect.
I say this as your friend, not to offend,
But stress will bear you to an early grave.
I've found that when I cogitate upon

The possibilities of raze and ruin
I age much faster. See these furrowed lines
And graying of the temples—premature!
It has a great effect on mind and body.
My ayurvedic doctor told me so,
The white guy up on Bundy and fourteenth.
This bugger's worked with Chopra in Del Mar,
So grant me this, he knows from whence he speaks.
And he contends that like a cold or flu,
Stress can be passed from man to man and back,
And slowly wears upon you day and night
Till all that's left is overwhelmedness
And this preoccupation with one's goods

DEVEN: I'm not preoccupied with merchandise!
All my investments are diversified!
I practice Chopra's seven principles!
I give out freely, freely as I get!
Now trust me when I say it's not my goods.

YOGA: Well, then could it be love?

DEVEN: Not in this lifetime.

YOGA: So, not in love?

SHIVA: Then let's root out the cause
Of what could seed affliction in one's heart
On such a glorious post El Niño morn.

YOGA: The sky above is cloudless and azure,

SHIVA: But over you it's mild precipitation.

YOGA: The air is cleaner now than twenty years ago,

SHIVA: You seem to court a stage-two smog alert.
Like some Chekhovian you're always in black—

YOGA:—Which absolutely drains your face of light.

(Enter JITENDRA, ARMANDO, and AMITHABA)

SHIVA: Look there's Jitendra, our own celebrity,
Amithaba and Armando. Well we're off:
We leave you now with your own distant kith.

YOGA: We would have stayed till you were much less dour,
But leave that honor to some better friends.

DEVEN: Don't play it coy and fish for compliments.
You're leaving 'cause you're bored to death with me
And their arrival's given you the out.

YOGA: Habari gani my rafikis three.[1]

---

[1] What's the news, my friends three?

JITEN: Muzuri sana strangers, what's the word?[2]

YOGA: When shall we meet and smoke the evil weed?

ARMAND: Just name the date, mi casa es su casa.

SHIVA: Y tu ganja es mi ganja mi carnal.

(Exit YOGANANDA and SHIVANANDA)

ARMAND: Since you've found who you're looking for, I'll head.

But later cruise to Natalee's for chow?

So what's tonight's big celebration?

JITEN: It's Holi man! Make sure you're dressed in white!

ARMAND: What's Holi man?

JITEN: A harvest festival.

AMITHAB: With dancing in the streets and drinking bhang.

ARMAND: What's Bhang?

AMITHAB: Maridge-uana milkshake dude.

ARMAND: No way Jose! Legal?

JITEN: Not quite, carnal.

AMITHAB: What up Senor Devendra, you down?

You need to change them shades for rosy ones.

It's time for Holi, babe, not doom and gloom

DEVEN: I call it like I see it, Amithabh.

If life's a song, I sing the sadder tune.

My ballads bittersweet.

AMITHAB: Mine's "That's Amore."

You rhyme "your eye" with "pizza pie," that's genius!

Hey life's too short to bum out everyone.

Just smile and pour some bourbon on the rocks

And smell the crackling ice. Then hit the clubs

Decked out in shark skin, armed with rapier quip,

Evoking Dino's ghost and Frankie and the Pack.

A time when carefree-cool was primary.

A time when honor guided principle;

When codes of conduct charted out the course

To navigate the treacherous seas of life.

With creases in your pants so razor sharp

You'd cut your hand just zippin' up your fly.

These strong and silent types defined manhood.

While walking tall they swung a swizzle stick.

If you got woes don't spill your guts like dames.

Just talk to Johnny Walker, Jimmy Beam,

Or everybody's favorite, Old Granddad.

---

[2]Very good.

The point is, they defined a course of action.
No whining! Pull the bootstraps! Bite the bullet!
Your generation got in touch with feelings,
My generation's got to pay the price.
The "sky is falling's" your mantra, not ours.
I have to say that after "pizza pie,"
I sing McFerrin's "Don't worry, be happy!"
I give it free of charge, this wisdom, babe!
Come Joey B. let's score some Indian skank!

ARMAND: So Natalee's for Phat See Yew and Singha.
I'm still not sure why I must dress in white!
(*To* AMITHABA)
I'm not your Joey Bishop, get that straight!

AMITHAB: Then be my Sammy baby, chi kong chik,
And maybe you can have my sloppy seconds.

DEVEN: See you when we see you, and not till then.

AMITHAB: I know you two have got to do your thang,
So time to find a tall cool drink and swang.
(*Exeunt* AMITHABA *and* ARMANDO)

DEVEN: So what the hell was that?

JITEN: Amithaba engages in a dialectical process that I call shaggy dog philosophy. I just nod my head and take the ride. But more often then not when we
arrive at said destination I am hard-pressed to glean the reason for the trip.

DEVEN: So, spill your guts about this girl my boy.
Just who and where and when and why?
I thought you were resigned to bachelorhood.

JITEN: Yes, but like all good things this too must pass.
You know my circumstance Devendra,
Like Yudhishter, I blindly rolled the die
Just one too many times—need I say more?
In Bombay I was like a god and lived so,
With all the requisite vice and piety.
Come here, I'm treated like a dog, but still
I tend to court excesses of a god.
To go from being big fish in little pond,
Although to say that Bollywood is small
Misrepresents the nature of the beast,
To being a minnow in a vasty sea,
Adrift, with no real prospect's damn depressing.
I've traded on the film star stock exchange
And crashed what once had been a bull market.
I've lost cache with our community,

And with no one more than with you Devendra.
And now I swear, all schemes, all cons aside,
I'm focused on potentialities—
The ones you claimed I long ago forsook.

DEVEN: I cannot fathom why this formal tone.
It makes me ill and sad that you have need
To justify your life to me with such words.
This cache that you claim from me you've lost
Is rot you talk, my dear Jitendra.
I've always said, "How high?" when you've said, "Jump!"
Have I but once asked you to make account
Of what you owe or do not owe thus far?
I love you; now as always, always will,
Undying love—(Uncomfortable beat or three)
Just name your plans and strain this camel's back.
My means exist to serve you in your needs.

JITEN: In Carmel is my future wife ensconced,
The heir to fortunes solely willed to her.
Her father was producer Bipin Shah
Who made his wealth in Bollywood. What's more
He cast me in my first real starring role
And helped to make my name a household word.
I owe him much and I remember then
This twelve-year-old who clung quite close to him.
A Sita in the making, swear to god,
With eyes that danced with fire for one so young!
Now don't look at me in that way Deva
I was, myself, just twenty at the time,
So steer your mind away from Nabokov.
I dreamt of meeting her one day full flowered
And did at this year's NETIP conference.
Truly, Deva, she's gone beyond all hopes
Of beauty, wisdom, fem'nine pulchritude.
I see the twelve-year-old but now full bloomed.
Fair skin and slender hips, her eyes still dance—
The starlet for my India Indie flick.
Not crass commercial fare, but art-house stuff.
Though not a pro upon the wooden O,
Her stints in college plays will more than serve.
This film will mark the birth of an auteur,
The comeback kid, the Phoenix from the ash,
Director, writer, star with femme fatale—

I'll play Polanski to her Kinski and
Have plans to lure her with the script and role.
And once signed on, her father's name, still hailed
Back home, will yield connections that assure
The film's success and blaze a brand new star—her!
A sure fire way to gain her confidence,
And to compete with all these software geeks
Who presently are courting her in hopes
Of matrimonial bliss and baby making.
They have the means I sorely lack and thus
I look to you to be my savior.
What's worse is that this dream, within a week,
Evaporates, because of timelines and
Of deadlines made by dead fathers, willing
The wealth to charity if not one of
The suitors will emerge victorious.

DEVEN: You know I'm strapped with not a drop that flows.
This deadline dams it up a measure more.
So cash the size that we've discussed is tight—
But never fear my dear, Devendra's here.
A deal thrice three times what you need nears end,
Involving factories my fam'ly owns
Which Glaxo Smith Kline wants to buy outright!
So, as I vowed, I will produce your film,
And also now perhaps your chance at bliss.
Now go out there, inquire, and so will I,
And test my credit and my fiscal worth
To back your needs to woo our Pushpabehn.[3]
My bliss will lie in yours being realized,
And swear your love shall not be compromised.
(Exit)

SCENE II: CARMEL. THE SOUND OF WAVES. MUSIC!
A ROOM IN PUSHPA'S HOUSE.

(Enter PUSHPA; *light skinned and her cousin* KAVITA, *dark-skinned.* KAVITA *carries a folder*)

PUSHPA: Just shoot me now, Kavita, this world is all over me like a cheap suit.

KAVITA: That, my dear cousin, is unfortunately the only kind of suit some of us can afford. Pushpa, you complaining about life is like Paris Hilton

---

[3]*Sister-Pushpa.*

complaining about sex. Diva, don't dive in a pool then dis the water for being wet. And yet, I guess, to die like Jim Morrison of excess is equally as bad as Michael Hutchence dying of INXS.[4] Bah dum pum! But seriously Cuz, I'm sure the silver spoon in your mouth is as apt to choke you as is the plastic one in mine, although I'm more apt to spit out mine well before you'd spit out yours.

PUSHPA: I guess you told me bitch!

KAVITA: Be better if you listened, slut!

PUSHPA: Easier said than done. If practicing what you preached was as easy to do as to say, then sinners would be saints and the Saints would have won the Superbowl. Buh dum pum! Like our parents taught. Do as I say, not as I do. They had a love marriage, not arranged. All their clucking Aunties fainted from shock. They suffered the slings and arrows. Why can't I? *(Beat)* Love marriage? What does that make the arranged ones? Hate marriages? What do the Aunties always cluck? *(They mockingly recite this together with exaggerated Indian accents)* "In the West you marry the man you fall in love with and in the East you fall in love with the man you marry." Be a Sita and marry Rama, but, as long as he's not too dark, Ravana is much more interesting. But would the rakhshasa make a suitable husband? Who knows? It's the unknown. The taboo, Baboo! Ravana is whom I'd choose. The brain may rule reason, but the heart rules the loins. Who am I kidding? I can't choose. I may neither choose whom I fancy nor refuse whom I disdain; and so the will of a living daughter is curbed by the "will" of a dead father. Isn't it unfair, Kavita, that I cannot choose one nor refuse none?

KAVITA: Would you like some cheese with that whine? Look, you don't have to comply. His will needn't be a testament to your life. Do what you will! But accept the consequences! Your father was, not to speak ill of the dead, a little bent. Look at his films. All those big breasted women in wet saris dancing and singing in fountains. Always in fountains or in the rain or lawn sprinklers. And then to take an idea from his Venice Kah Dukanwallah picture where the man who chooses correctly between three caskets of gold, silver, or lead correctly chooses the girl by gleaning it's correct meaning, and make that the way you receive your inheritance is bent! Walk away. Leave the money. Let it go to charity. So when the sunset clause on this wager burns out next week, let it fade. Or else one of these sorry bhaias here may have to suffice for your Ravana.

PUSHPA: Oh my god! Give me those pictures and I'll try to keep my gorge from rising.

(KAVITA has a series of headshots of the various suitors that she shares with us

---

[4]Jim Morrison, the lead singer for the Doors, from 1965 to 1971, died in Paris at the age of twenty-seven, allegedly from a drug overdose. Hutchence, the lead singer of INXZ from 1977 to 1997, was found dead in a hotel room in 1997.

as she hands them to PUSHPA. *Or she could be doing a Power Point presentation with slides of the suitors.)*

KAVITA: First, there's our software mughal.

PUSHPA: You mean the Mughal ka bacha! Fancies himself a poet. My god, you should read some of the dreck he's written for me. It's unforgivable that I inspire such insipid verse. He was a Ritalin baby and is now a Prozac adult. He hates his father's wealth, broods all the time, and bitterly complains about childhood abuse. Hey, who didn't have childhood abuse? We're Indians, it's how we show love. Now some amount of brooding is sexy, like Salman Khan,[5] but I like champagne too much to give it up for Bitters.

KAVITA: How does the Bengali biochemist fare in your vitriolic assessment?

PUSHPA: He knows about the biochemical nature of man and in my estimation prefers them to wo-man and thus lacks the properties that make him suitable for hus-band! He dresses impeccably, idolizes Martha Stewart, *lives* at Bed, Bath and Beyond and has a framed, autographed picture of Clay Aiken. Between him and me there is neither biology nor chemistry. His interest is feigned at best, at worst duty to his family. Let him find himself; be free. I'll not be responsible for locking the door to that closet.

KAVITA: Anything acerbic for our Sardarji?[6]

PUSHPA: I abhor a man who takes longer to do his hair than I do.

KAVITA: Oh no you di'in't! *(Beat)* Pushpa, if they should offer to choose and choose the right diskette, you would refuse to perform your father's will if you should refuse to accept them. *(Beat)* Hey what was his name the guy you used to tell me of? Mr. Song and Dance? Devoted to your father because he discovered him? Do you remember whom I'm talking about?

PUSHPA: Do I remember? It was Jitendra. Many a teenage, sleepless, night was spent with pillow moistening between my thighs as I dreamed of him. You know I met him again recently at the Network of Indian Professionals conference. We barely exchanged cards but as he bore through me with his coal black eyes I felt myself shudder.

KAVITA: Shuddering is good! If he looks anything like he does on screen you're a lucky girl. But what's he like?

PUSHPA: In my teenage mind I remember him being very cool and rakish. As an adult I can't say. Anyway, his looks would convey him at least to my outstretched, willing hand. From there my father's ghost might or might not prevent his acquisition of me.

(Enter RASIK *her father's executor and overseer of the Shah estate.)*

PUSHPA: Como esta Rasikbhai?

RASIK: Sorry to bother madam but . . . all your appointments are cancelled.

---

[5]A famous Bollywood actor.
[6]Sikh.

PUSHPA: Cancelled?

RASIK: You have the rest of your day free—

KAVITA: Maybe, the rest of your life.

PUSHPA: Shut up!

RASIK: They wish you all the best but dared not risk their own futures in the process of acquiring you.

PUSHPA: I guess I'm no Helen. This face isn't about to launch a thousand ships.

KAVITA: *(Cheering her up)* I'm glad this batch was chickenshit, for there is not one among them who would not have let you rule the roost.

RASIK: *(Chiming in)* I pray God grant them a speedy departure back to their coops.

PUSHPA: *(Petulant)* Yah! *(Beat)* Let's go to Fred Segal.

RASIK: Although the three have cancelled their appointments, a fourth, the Madrasi Minister of Finance, has just arrived.

PUSHPA: Oh really! One showed up. *(RASIK nods encouragingly)* Madrasi, huh? *Little dark babies!* I think not. If he has the condition of a Sadhu and the complexion of a Ravan, I had rather he should heal me than reel me. Bah dum pum! Rasikbhai, where is this Rakhshasa?

RASIK: *(Strong whisper)* On the other side of this door madam.

(And with that RASIK opens the door much to PUSHPA's horror and embarrassment and there standing on the other side is a dark-skinned man in a white suit and hat with a Boston Blackie moustache. Or perhaps he's dressed in the classic British Hunter's outfit with the canvas hunter's helmet. He looks like a throwback to another era. Early British Raj. There is an uncomfortable and pregnant pause as they ponder whether he has heard PUSHPA's last comment. The man walks in and takes PUSHPA's hand and in a very genteel fashion kisses the back of her hand. The women and RASIK look at each other. RASIK is impressed and the women are a little lost for words as he fixes her directly in the eye and begins to speak. He might have a very posh British-Indian accent.)

MURALI: The sun down south burns hot and stamps our skin,
And I its native son, the "darkest" of the lot,
Proclaim with pride that black is beautiful.
We Southerners have always been, you see,
The Rakshasas of Indian myth and lore—
The demon darkies of your worst nightmares.
So we, for very long, attempted cover-ups,
Like spreading copious amounts of talcum
On our faces hoping to enlighten
Ourselves and make us more desirable,
And in some cases even bleached our skin,
Internalizing our own hate and shame.

The fashion now dictates that skin color
Should matter not to we sophisticates.
But one quick glance at matrimonial ads
Will quickly disabuse us of that hope.
PUSHPA: In terms of choice, the choice "ain't" on my terms.
And thusly Daddy's lott'ry has removed
The prejudices otherwise that might
Exist or even fuel such arrangements
By barring voluntary choice for me—
Forcing me to yield myself willingly
To him that chooses wisely and with care.
Therefore according to this method your
Esteem stands in my eye as fair as any
For my affection.
MURALI: I thank you, I think.
So lead me to these diskettes where I might
Let roll the die. I'm curious to see
The part that luck will play in destiny,
For if the choice were meritorious,
If it were based upon accomplishment
I'd be considered leader of the pack—
With law degrees from Oxford and Harvard,
The youngest man to hold the office of
Financial Min'ster of Tamil Nadu,
And Captain of the Indian team in doubles
For our only win at Wimbledon.
But what of that, it matters not a jot.
For luck indeed can be a fickle dame,
Bestowing her blessings on one less worthy,
One whose accomplishments pale next to mine.
But, trusting in this universe I'll leap,
And hope that justice has an eye toward
The light of worthiness. Or else return
With empty hand and worse with empty bed
And grieve the loss.
KAVITA: You take your chance,
And either not attempt to choose at all
Or swear before you choose if you choose wrong,
To pay the dowry you yourself demanded.
RASIK: You also swear that you don't seek the hand,
For no less than a period of five years,

Of any woman, girl or divorcee.

KAVITA: And when you do, that you eschew demands

Of dowry and of claim. Do you swear this?

RASIK: You hesitate?

MURALI: I do!

PUSHPA and KAVITA: You do?

MURALI: I don't.

I mean, I swear to all of these demands!

(PUSHPA and KAVITA look to each other at a loss, their ploy didn't work. PUSHPA suddenly turns tail and flees. An awkward moment as RASIK and KAVITA are left alone with MURALI.)

KAVITA: *(Improvising)* But first lets go to temple for puja.

RASIK: *(Improvising)* Then after pray'r you'll choose.

MURALI: God grant what's best!

Tonight I pass or else I fail this test.

(Exit)

SCENE III: VENICE BL. PETTERSONS. A CAFE.

(Enter JITENDRA and SHARUK, who is dressed in traditional Bora clothing with a palm pilot kind of device in hand)

SHARUK: Two hundred lakhs; teekh.[7]

JITEN: Ah ji,[8] for two weeks.

SHARUK: For two weeks; teekh.

JITEN: For which, as I said, Devendra shall become . . . bound.

SHARUK: Devendra shall become bound, teekh.

JITEN: So, what do you say? Do we have a deal? Are you mulling it over?

SHARUK: Two hundred lakhs for two weeks and Devendra indebted.

JITEN: What do you say?

SHARUK: Devendra is a good man.

JITEN: Are you in any way implying otherwise?

SHARUK: Nei, nei, nei, nei, nei! What I'm saying in saying good, is that he's comfortable. But the word is that he's not liquid. And reckless with his assets. I suppose my immigrant nature doesn't allow me to put money into anything that is not tangible. He risks on what he calls innovation, I thrive on what I call the tried and true. Real estate, diamonds, currency, cold and hard the lot of them, but what warmth and security their coldness brings, eh? Shipping software from India, and sweets and spices and saris and sabh kuch? See,

---

[7]A fine of approximately $500,000.

[8]Yes, sir.

ships are but scatterings to the whims of weather. Exxon Valdez to Andrea Doria to the mother of all submersibles, Titanic. All his eggs seem to be in one basket and if that basket is dropped he's sunk and then he'll have to scramble! *(Chuckle)* Still, he comes from good old Gujarati money. Guju money! And we all know that old money makes new money. Particularly Guju money. I think Allah would smile on this transaction. I *think* I might do it!

JITEN: I'll need to know ASAP.

SHARUK: You'll be the first to know, when I know . . . maybe after my morning prayers. May I speak with Devendra?

JITEN: We can meet over a meal.

SHARUK: Not too many Halal restaurants around here if you've noticed. But then why would you, you're Hindu. You look for veg only, unless of course you're a meat-eater. A decadent. Also it's Ramadan, so for me nothing till sundown. No need for us to feign interest in dining together. Our business with each other is business, not dining, let's keep it that way. Speak of the devil!

(Enter DEVENDRA)

JITEN: Devendra, what a coincidence?

SHARUK: *(Aside)* Here comes Lord Vishnu's gift to all mankind!
I hate him for his strutting confidence,
His caustic, sneering, Brahmin arrogance.
He moralizes, publicly no less,
And calls my Money-Store, a legal franchise,
A den of thieves and state approv'd loan sharking.
But mark my words. I am no usurer!!!
I practice interest not excess, and while
Our rates are high they're fair, in keeping with
The law and that is well in keeping with
The dictates of our Holy Book. Our clients
Are not exactly high-caste men of means.
My risks are great, reflected in my rates.
Besides why need I justify myself
To this rich prat who's had it all from day one?
And how did his great family achieve
Their much-envied place in society?
I thought the priests were there to serve mankind
Not fleece the flock for their material gain.
Beneath his sanctimonious guff there beats
The heart of true disdain for me and mine.
I mean we Boras who endure great ridicule
For our beliefs and our keen business sense.

He hates me for precisely what I am,
A rival businessman not of his faith.
And lastly he proclaimed my firm support
Of fighting fire with fire in Ayodhya,
Avenging Babri Masjid as the ranting of
A Muslim devil. I'll be damned for sure
If I forgive that.

JITEN: Sharuk, you with us?

SHARUK: I'm accessing my Money-Store's accounts
On this iPhone my daughter bought for me.
Children. They light the road ahead of us.
(Beat) It looks to me that at this present time
I can't immediately raise-up the gross
Of all two hundred lakhs. Ah yes, but wait!
Toufiq, a wealthy Muslim at masjid,
Will bankroll me. But wait! How many weeks
Do you desire? *(To* DEVENDRA*)* Salaam alekh um friend
Long life to one arriving when spoken of—

DEVEN:—Sharuk, to lie with dogs one wakes with fleas,
Therefore, I bathe mine and keep them outdoors.
And yet to scratch the itch of my dear friend
I'll share a kennel. Is he up to speed,
Of all you need?

SHARUK: Yah, yah, two hundred lakhs.

DEVEN: And for two weeks?

SHARUK: Oh yah, two weeks; *(to* JIT*)* you told me that, *(to* DEV*)* but wait;
I thought you said you don't lie down with dogs
For fear of fleas.

DEVEN: By George I think he's got it!

SHARUK: Our Prophet once related that a man;
I mean Muhammad, peace be upon him,
Who fled from holy Mecca to Medina
To find a greater hospitality—

DEVEN: And then what? Did he lie down there with dogs?

SHARUK: No, not lie down, as you might say lie down,
But rested and resumed his holy teachings.
He said, one day, a man extremely parched
Climbed down into a well to quench his thirst.
He scaled back up to find a panting dog
Was eating moist earth to rehydrate.
Compassion overtook him and he cried:

"The same thing has oppressed this creature too."
Without a word he climbed back down again
And filled his shoe with water and returned,
His makeshift cup clenched tight between his teeth.
With eager laps the dog drank dry the shoe.
Then god absolved the man and thanked him well—
DEVEN:—So Allah blesses men who're kind to dogs.
    Or maybe blesses dogs who eat moist earth.
    But then again he might bless wayward shoes
    That pass for cups when none are within grasp—
SHARUK:—You joke at my expense, but it's okay!
    Muhammad said reward's dispensed in kind
    for treatment of all beings.
DEVEN: Check this out Jit,
    The ramblings of philosophy can be
    Elicited from unexpected sources.
    The smiling face belies a bitter heart.
    The sweetest kiss can mask a ven'mous bite.
    Beware the cobra's dance, for, beautiful
    As it may be, its purpose is to strike.
SHARUK: Two hundred lakhs is quite an even sum.
    Two weeks from four, in terms of rate, let's see—
DEVEN: Well, Sharuk, shall we be indebted to you?
SHARUK: Devendra sabh, so many times before
    In print and in public you've blasted me
    About my money-store and interest rates.
    I've shrugged it off abiding patiently,
    We Boras are inured to sticks and stones.
    You've called me Muslim dog so often now
    That I should bark back all your foul rebukes
    Of slandering my good name, and for what?
    For speaking out against the heinous crime
    Of desecrating our holy shrine?
    How often have you said, and possibly
    In jest, "Kill them before they multiply."
    Well then, it now appears you need my help:
    So be it, you come to me, and you say
    Sharuk, "We need such monies," you say so;
    You, who spit out the vilest epithets
    Aimed to incite my direst response,
    And thus shifting all of the blame of rashness

On me, the oldest trick of bait and switch,
Of smoke and mirrors: money's your desire.
What should I say to you? Should not I say,
"Can dogs lend money? Is it possible
A hound can raise two hundred lakhs worth?" And
"Those wiped out as you wish through genocide
Can scarcely own the means to lend?" Or instead
Shall I put palms together Hindu-style
With lowered eyes and Brahmin humbleness, say this?
'Sahib, you cursed my name in India West*
   *(This will change with respect to the city the play is playing in)
You called me "mad fanatic"; and what's more
You call'd me dog; and for these courtesies
I'll lend you all the monies you desire?'
DEVEN: Don't dare assume I won't do so again.
What you call slander I insist is truth.
If you will lend this money, don't lend it
As if to friends, for friendship is the farthest
Description of the bond that we both share;
But lend it rather to your enemy,
That, if defaulted, you can honestly,
Like Machiavel, exact the penalty.
SHARUK: Now look at who is being rash!
I would be friends with you if you'd allow it,
Forget the shames that you have stained me with,
Supply your needs and take no iota
Of profit for my stake, and you won't hear me:
I donate this in kind.
JITENDRA: (To Dev) This is kindness.
SHARUK: This kindness I will prove.
Let's seal a bond between a notary
And you and me. And, with our tongue in cheek
If you repay me not on such a day
In such a place, such sum or sums as are
Laid out in the condition, let the price,
And now I'm borrowing a chapter from
Your book, be the forfeiture of your manhood.
The losing of your means to procreate.
Not just a snip, something reversible,
But the entire fam'ly jewels sliced off,
Which I'll then happ'ly feed to my two dogs.

DEVEN: You've got a deal, I'll sign the dotted line.
　And they say Muslims have no sense of humor!
SHARUK: And with the stipulation that it be
　My hand that carries out this doubtful deed.
JITEN: You will not sign on any dotted line;
　I'd rather walk away, now, come let's go
DEVEN: Hold on now, what's to fear? I will not lose.
　The Glaxo Smith-Kline deal goes through next week
　And worth crore[9] times the value of this bond.
SHARUK: Y'Allah how these shrewd Hindus operate,
　Whose own compunctions make them trust no one
　No further than they can be thrown! It's clear
　I ask for less than what is mine, be it
　Through law of man or law of God. Pray tell,
　If he does break the deal, what will I gain
　By the exaction of the forfeiture?
　A "pound" of flesh or in this case an ounce
　Of man's flesh, is not worth equivalent
　With flesh of chicken, beef, or lamb. Just like
　Sadat to Begin I extend my hand:
　If he will take it, fine; if not, fine too;
　This world is yours and I just live in it.
DEVEN: Sharuk, I said I'd sign the dotted line
SHARUK: Then meet me at Kishimoto's, the not'ry,
　He'll draw the papers for this silly deal.
　But wait! Who'll arbitrate if you default?
　No Yankee court will give me satisfaction!
　Let's swear this bond to keep it underground,
　Agreeing to the ruling of S.A.B.U.:,
　The South Asian Businessmen's Union.
　Although you're on the board I'll take my chances.
　A sweeter deal you won't find anywhere.
DEVEN: Agreed. S.A.B.U. like Lord Ganesh presides.
SHARUK: I'm off to make arrangement for the check
　And close up shop, which foolishly I left
　Under the care of an incompetent,
　And soon I'll see you.
JITEN:　　　　　　Come break bread to seal
　(DEVENDRA *and* SHARUK *both look at* JITENDRA)
　The deal. On me. Halal. On Rose.

---

[9]Umpteen.

SHARUK: I'll think
   On it.
JITEN: Please do.
   (Exit SHARUK*)*
DEVEN: *(Quietly)*   Ta, Ta, Mughal bhaia.[10] The Muslim will turn Hindu he
   grows kind.
JITEN: I'm not sure I like what he has in mind.
DEVEN: Come on now what's to care you're in like Flynn,
   Within a week today my "ship" comes in.
   (Exit)

ACT II

SCENE I: THE MONEY-STORE.

(Enter TOORANPOI THE CLOWN*)*
TOORI: Oh god! What to do? What to do? Surely, my bloody conscience won't get
   in the way of my escaping the clutches of the Mapla my sponsor. My mummy,
   a pious Brahmin woman, said, "Be careful of them, they will cheat you." Did
   you realize that in the word "cheat" all the letters exist for "teach?" Curious,
   huh? Mummy said, that it's in the Muslim nature to teach. Cheat! My Daddy
   said, "Don't listen to her rot, she's an illiterate and her father fondled little
   girls." "You mean Muthachen was a—," "Shuddup and listen to your Acha
   before I strangle you to death. The Mussalman has provided an opportunity
   for you to get out of this hellhole—," "But Acha, Chavakad is not a hell—,"
   "Shuddup and listen, before I tell you what really happened to your doggy."
   Did you realize that in the word "doggy" there exists all the letters for the
   word "God-dy?" Curious, huh? Daddy said, "Tooranpoi my boy, the Mussle-
   man has promised you thrice what you'll make here. He has made his offer.
   Honor his offer. Then find a good woman and all night you can be on her
   and off her." My daddy is a strange kind of daddy. We agreed that the right
   thing to do was to honor Mussalman's offer. We hugged, and then he slapped
   me because he was uncomfortable with overt displays of affection, and I bid
   him a fond farewell. Mummy just sat there sucking the marrow from her
   chicken bones crying that her, "Tooranpoi is leaving me and who will pick
   out the lice from my thick, luxurious, hair and put olive oil in it for cooling."
   My mummy is a strange kind of mummy! So here came I. For promises of
   thrice my salary. Thrice my foot! It costs six times as much to live here, so if
   you calculated, Tooranpoi, you're an idiot! So now what to do? Should I stay
   or should I go. Sharif don't like it! I call home on my phone card, my phone

[10]Mughal Brother.

has been cut off, couldn't pay the bills to Kerala, so I buy the phone card and always I pay ten dollars but only seven dollars worth of call I can make because I buy it from the Indian shops and they always cheat you. Especially if you're Indian. Indians always cheat Indians first. Why is that? That's how you make money. On the poor ones. Beware the Indian shop. Did you realize that in the word "shop" all the letters exist for "posh"? Curious, huh? Anyway, I call. Daddy answers. Always daddy. And in the background, I hear Mummy crying, "Toori come home! Mummy's so lonely. Who'll cut my toenails and make me panjamridhm." She loves panjamridhm, you know when you mix honey and bananas and raisins and a little Tulsi leaf, it's so cooling . . . and so sweet—Anyway! Then Daddy says, "Toorimon," or sometimes "Toorimone," or even, "Ponnu-Toorimone,"[11] when he's been drinking and feeling particularly affectionate, "Honor his offer; honor, offer; on her, off her." Mummy in the back says, "Toorikuti,[12] my piles are bleeding" and "Last night at temple a bat flew into my hair" and "Your daddy and Mr. Menon are living together as man and wife." Daddy retorts, "She's a liar. Remember what I said about her father. Menon and I are only friends. And he honors his offers and all night I was on . . . stay there!" "Come home!" says Mummy. "Stay there" says Daddy. Mummy the siren calls me, Daddy the conscience bars me. What to do? Do I stay and continue to honor an offer I can't refuse or do I refuse the offer I can no longer honor. Hmm, indeed a dilemma! *(Beat)* What kind of Malayalee boy would I be if I didn't listen to my Mummy? She gives the better advice. I'll run away and somehow make my way to back home.

(Enter JITENDRA*)*

Ende Ammende Nair![13] Jitendra sahr![14] This is indeed an honor. The Song and Dance man! I loved you in, "Tereh bab ki ghand meh."[15]

JITENDRA: Sala![16] What rot! "Tereh bab keh *ghar* meh."[17]

TOORI: I only speak *movie* Hindi. I'm Malayalee you know? From Kerala? Mother tongue is Malayalam. But I know all the Hindi songs you sang. "Tinku, Tinku, Tinku, mera dil ka Rinku Dinku." What does that mean, Rinku, Dinku?

JITENDRA: Just words of nonsense my Malayalee friend.

TOORI: So you're singing words you don't know what you're saying?

JITENDRA: Are you always aware of what you're saying?

TOORI: I am seldom aware of what I'm saying. So, are you saying that the great

---

[11]Terms meaning, respectively, "Toori Son," "Toori Sonny," and "Golden Toori Sonny."
[12]Toori Child.
[13]My mother's husband.
[14]Sir.
[15]*In your father's anus.*
[16]Bastard.
[17]In your father's house.

Jitendra also sometimes or seldom sometimes knows not of whence he
speaks? That's cool baby! I'm just like Jitendra! *(Singing)* "Tereh bap ki gandh
meh, ekh chandini heh, tereh bap ki gandh meh . . . "[18]

JITENDRA: Please! First of all I'm not the one who sings.

I had some of the finest playback singers
Like Moh'mmed Rafi and even Kishore.
And as for meaning let's be serious,
A Bombay Talkie needs just song and dance,
A nice locale, Kashmir, Assam, or Goa,
The newest pretty face and hairy stud.
The boy meets girl and soon they sing and dance,
And then of course gratuitous attempts
Of rape by gundas on her chaste person
So that our hairy stud is justified
In thrashing them within an inch of life.
But not before her saris uncoiled
And she is lying, weeping at his feet—

TOORI: —Yah, yah. I like that. See no women have ever wept at my feet. They've
swept at my feet, but not wept. You're so lucky.

JITENDRA: Now keep repeating this till it sinks in.

"It's only, just a movie, nothing more."
Say it with me so that you'll understand.
"It's only, just a movie, nothing more."

TOORI: I can't! I only ever speak in prose not in verse.

JITENDRA: *(Aside)* Well no can accuse me of not trying!

TOORI: You know a lot about movies. I always wanted to be an actor. I can sing
and dance you know. *(Singing)* "Mera bhajia! Tera bhajia! Mera bhajia, tera
bhajia. Gharam, gharam. Chalo, chalo!"[19]

JITENDRA: Have you the faintest notion what you're saying?

TOORI: No, but I like the way it sounds. Do you think that I can become an
actor? Will you teach me? I'll become your disciple. You can be my guru! I'll
clean and cook and wash for you. Whatever I must do to be like you.

JITENDRA: You want to what? Become like me, for what?

TOORI: For what, he asks, for what? To be rich. To be famous. To be or not to
be! I'm stuck in Bora's office computing, accounting, imbibing. I look out the
window and I see people passing by and they never look at me. The windows
are tinted so it makes it hard; but nevertheless I can see them and I can see
them passing me by, just like my life. *(Aside)* Did you realize that in the word
"life" all the letters exist for "file"? Curious, huh? Oh, to have them look at

---

[18]In your father's anus, there is a moon, in your father's anus.
[19]My fritter! Your fritter! Hot, hot. Let's go, let's go!

me. To have them weep at my feet. To say my name in adulteration, "Tooran! Tooran! Tooran!" I want that! I want it all! I want to be a god! *(Beat. Mildly)* Like you.

JITENDRA: And so to be a god you'll serve a god.

TOORI: Serve you, sir, and serve myself. I'll be a sponge. I'll suck you dry. *(Beat)* The deep platonic kind. Of sucking. *(TOORI is on his knees in front of JIT. There is an awkward moment. Then he gets up and mimics everything that JITENDRA does which is what TOORI describes in the following passage)* I'll watch your every move, how you walk, hold a cigarette, light the bloody thing, cock your head one way, blow smoke the other way, learn everything I need to learn to be an A number one star of the Bollysilverscreen.

JITENDRA: I'm not sure that I want such scrutiny.
But you're not lacking in a certain kind of charm.
You work for Sharuk, that's a major plus.
We might have need of knowledge you possess.
Okay! You may observe my every move,
And be my Man Friday if that's your will.
I have no means, however, to pay you,
And question why you leave security
As such that he's provided, with such ease.

TOORI: My mother told me never trust the Mapla. He'll cheat you sure as he'll pray five times a day. Now, although my mother is a kind of paranoid kind of mother, I being a good son, listen to my Amma. So, before the Bora had a chance to cheat me, I started cheating him. Not much. A little here, a little there, enough to slip under the Musselman's nose and enough for me to work for you, gratis. I want to observe you and take from you the answer to stardom. Then with the open ticket that I bought, go back to home and become a Bollysilverscreen star. *(Beat)* And then I could hire someone to cut my Mummy's toenails.

JITENDRA: So, here's my card and my particulars.
I'll need a gopher on the set of my new film,
Made possible in part by your old boss
And by the love and deep devotion of
One Devendra by name, respect it well!
Now shake my hand and seal the pact begun
With your ridiculous soliciting
Of my acquaintance through your musical
And malapropped ignorance of Hindi.

TOORI: Wow! It must be nice to speak in verse because I didn't follow a single word of that last bit you said. But it sounded good to me.
I, Tooranpoi, shake, heartily shake, and promise undying loyalty to you and

yours. And although I did the same for Borasar, it's different when it comes to you. You're a Hindu and that goes a long way in my Mummy's book. Not a Brahmin, but that's okay. She'll still be proud. *(Starts to exit)*

JITENDRA: Tooranpoi? Does your name possess meaning?

TOORI: Yes. Its meaning is, *(With gravity)* "The one who has gone to seek the field in which to defecate."

JITENDRA: How apt! What have I stepped into this time.

TOORI: "Tinku, Tinku, Tinku, mera dill ka, rinku Dinku."

(TOORI exits as AMITHABA enters.)

AMITHAB: Paisan[20] Jitendra!

JITENDRA: Amithaba!

AMITHAB: I beg your indulgence.

JITENDRA: Indulge I will.

AMITHAB: My man, I must go with you to Carmel.
   I must be by your side when you woo Pushpa.

JITENDRA: You must, you must; but now indulge my must.
   You're too verbose, too rigid, way too loud!
   Not everyone appreciates the style
   You cultivate; the one we've grown to love.
   Mix into this scenario some gin
   And watch the walls come tumbling, crumbling.
   You are, my man, too hip for your own good.
   So, keep your flask close to your hip
   And nowhere near your lips. Copasetic?
   I can't lose out with Pushpa 'cause you felt
   You needed to pontificate upon
   The vagaries of broads, the virtues of
   A dry martini and the value of
   A foreskin that's intact.

AMITHAB: Hep-cat, I'm there:
   If I'm not more milk toasty than Pat Boone,
   More chilly than a foggy, Frisco, morn,
   More righteous than the Reverend Billy G,
   More pliant than Ann-Margret's inner thighs—

JITENDRA:—Eeuww!—

AMITHAB:—More beat around the Bush than Dick Cheney,
   More sober than a judge doing the twelve-step,
   I vow to burn my vinyl Esquivels,
   And my Antonio Carlos Jobims.

JITENDRA: Now that's a vow I'll hold you to paisan!

[20]The Italian American term for friend.

AMITHAB: But not tonight; tonight we wow, not vow!
　I've fin'lly got a line on ganj. I'm gone
　To find Armando, busboy to the chinks,
　Then off to bed and catch me forty winks.
　(Exit)

SCENE II: SHARUK'S HOUSE.

(Enter NOORANI *in full Hijab, talking, followed closely by* TOORANPOI.*)*
NOORANI: I'm sad that you've resigned but empathize.
　You've always made me laugh, I'll miss that so.
　To work for daddy is to work for gravity,
　Which consequently leads to graves untimely.
　He asks no less of others than himself
　And thus sobriety is his mantle
　And thus it should be also all the worlds'.
　But, I say, if the grave awaits with open maw,
　Or in your case the fiery pyre of wood,
　Why not sing and dance right up to the edge—
　Or till you feel the flames lick at your flesh.
　And then, in joyous rapture dive head-first
　Embracing death like a dear, childhood, friend—
　For it's been your lifelong companion.
　Why not sing? Why not dance? Why not?
　Why not be Pagan? Mystic! Gnostic! Sufi!
　Why not be in concert than in disconcert?
　It seems to me that more than Daddy more
　Than any, Rumi is the one who knew me.
　And as he spun in ecstasy so shall
　I spin and hope to glimpse the feet of god.
　I chatter on and you just nod and grin.
　Here's gold, my mother willed me, I give you.
　This man you work for now, Jitendra,
　His friend Armando's got to get this letter.
　Be totally discrete though! Oh my god!
　If daddy finds out I'll be totally screwed.
　Goodbye! I'll miss you. We made a good team
　Toori and Noori. Now go! Can't let dad
　See me plotting with you!
TOORI: Ta, Ta! Sadness chokes my throat and pussy gets my tongue. You are the
　　most beautiful Muslim girl whose father I have ever had the displeasure to

work under. May the gods smile upon you and forgive your ancestors for
converting in the first place. If that nice Catholic Vato doesn't make an honest
widow of you and turn you into a veritable baby-maker with fat little chimi-
changas dandling on your knee, call me a pathetically, poor, prognosticator.

NOORANI: I hope that your prognostication's poor.
    To dandle babies is not my intent.
    Why leave the frying pan for hotter flames.
    Take care, Toori, and don't forget the note.
    (*Exit* TOORANPOI)

NOORANI: I drape a cloth across my head so that
    I don't encourage undue male attention.
    I don't look men directly in the eye
    And inadvertently appear coy.
    I cover every inch of my exposed
    Flesh with the fabric of my mother's line
    So as to not appear to tempt the fates.
    But what I wear beneath belies my pious veneer.
    Like Freddie Mercury I want to break free!
    And though I love my father who believes
    This orthodoxy leads to paradise
    As spoke by god to Abraham to Moses,
    Muhammad and passed down to Hazrat Ali,
    It's love of love and love of man that fuels
    The fire that lights my heels and burns my bush.
    I'll break the bonds that keep my kind in line
    Regretting not at life's end, life that wasn't mine.
    (*Exit*)

SCENE III: OUTSIDE NATALEE'S THAI RESTAURANT

(*Enter* AMITHABA, ARMANDO, YOGANANDA, *and* SHIVANANDA)

ARMAND: You sure it's cool for me to wear this Kurtha?
    I could just wear a plain old white tee shirt.
    Why mess this up?

AMITHAB: No way Jose, tonight the Spic plays Wog!

YOGA: Remember you're the pilot for tonight's flight.
    (YOGA *lights a joint*)

SHIVA: Looks like you've already begun to taxi,
    Without a go from air traffic control.

ARMAND: It's only four o'clock and you're aflame?
    Don't crash and burn out Vato.

(Enter TOORANPOI, *with a letter)*
                              Dude, what up?
TOORAN: "What up" is the value of your stock in a certain "bond" market.
  (Hands ARMANDO *the note)*
ARMAND: There's only one who dots her I's with hearts.
  Hermosa, como cafe con leche!
  Mas rico que mantequilla.
AMITHAB: Skank news!
TOORAN: (Singing) "I'm off to drain my lizard . . ." *(Tune: "Off to see the*
  Wizard")
ARMAND: And then what?
TOORAN: Off to the "Why" accord. My new boss, Bollysar, your old friend, has
  invited my old boss, Borasar, your new friend, to dinner. After sundown of
  course. Ramadan-a-ding-dong!
ARMAND: Hold up, take this *(hands him a note)* tell my Chiquita Noor,
  I'll be there or be square, on the DL. *(Exit* TOORANPOI)
  Carnales, looks like I'm not flyin' solo!
  Let's get this harvest festival on track
  I'm feelin' Holi con mi chicken mole.
SHIVA: Straight love! How boring! Let's go home and change!
YOGA: You change! Not moi! I like the way I am.
SHIVA: Chalo, chalo![21]
ARMAND: Meet me and Amithab
  At Amithaba's condo in a few!
YOGA: We'll be there with bells on and punctual,
  Not Bombay time!
  (Exit YOGANANDA *and* SHIVANANDA)
AMITHAB: That note most likely was from Noorani!
  You're grinning like a crazed ventriloquist!
ARMAND: From ear to ear and wall to wall, Ese!
AMITHAB: Have you considered sixteen years of age
  Being just a tad too young for you?
  Albeit sweet as pie, she's jailbait man.
  E ticket to the land of anal gunch,
  Where butt-hole surfers meet the ass ponies
  And ride roughshod that lonesome jism trail.
ARMAND: You've got it wrong, bro, my intention's pure.
  This girl's the marry'n' kind, no bait, no jail.
  She's laid the land on how we'll pull this off.
  Las Vegas then Hawaiian honeymoon!

---

[21]Let's go, let's go!

All paid for by a dowry willed by Mom
Who died and left it toward matrimony.
She's also found a way to milk her trust fund—
It's not like stealing if you're stealing from you.
My baby's rich as cream and smooth as butter.
Her old man leashed her in on reins so tight
That something had to give and give it has.
When we get back we're gonna start a band.
I'll manage and play bass, she'll write the songs.
She's got a head for business, ear for hooks—
She's more Latina than your average ruca,
And loves los cantos de la raza too!
Quetzal and Ozomatli are her faves!
We'll have ninitos brown and beautiful
Who'll speak the language of both east and west,
Of pre-Columbia y Indus valley,
Of jalapeno y garam masala,
Of Fateh Ali Khan y Santana,
Of sub-commandante Marcos y Gandhi!
Of brown-skinned love tanned by a sun that seems
To shine with more intensity and passion
Upon the lands whose latitude we share.
Here check this out Amit, a foolproof plan,
Where soon the milk of Kheer will taste like Flan![22]
(Exit)

SCENE IV: SHARUK'S HOUSE.

(Enter SHARUK *followed closely by* TOORANPOI*)*

SHARUK: Just wait and see that's all I'll say. You'll see
What happens when you bite the hand that feeds.
Areh Noori!—A man's worth is only
As good as his good name:—Areh Noori!—
Allah sees all and measures loyalty
Commensurate with how he metes out justice.
Areh, Noori, ajao!

TOORI: Areh Noori, ajao!

SHARUK: Don't speak her name!!! You're no more part of fam'ly.

TOORAN: I didn't know I was part of fam'ly. Besides, I was just practicing my powers

---

[22]Rice pudding; crème custard.

of mimicry. And my Hindi. A Bollysilverscreen star must hone both skills.

SHARUK: A what?

TOORI: A Bollywood Wallah. Filmi star. Hero!

SHARUK: Oh? You a Hero? Try villain. Or clown.

(Enter NOORANI)

NOORANI: Baba, I'm here. Sorry you had to shout!

SHARUK: They've coaxed me into dining with them Noor.

Those bloody bastards! Now that they need me.

It's not through love that they invite me. Yet

I'll go and teach that hate breeds naught but hate

And Allah is all love. Noori beti[23]

Be careful when depositing this check.

All day I've had a churning in my gut.

Last night your mother came to me in dreams

In such a state of sadness that all day

I've been unable to shake off this unease!

TOORI: Aaah! When you talk of dead wives it makes my hair stand on my neck and puts flight to my fancy. I have done my duty as a gopher for Bollysar and secured your presence at the Holi supper after which the colors will be flying freely and the Bhang will be flowing equally freely.

SHARUK: Y'Allah! Not Holi, the most vile of Hindu

Hysterics that promotes frivolousness?

To speak it freely what else can be said

Of dancing in the streets like hooligans

And actively invoking altered states,

Inviting entry by Sheitan himself.

We on the other hand aspire to

Maintain a sober and a somber house

Denying entry to the devil's knock.

Noori stay in tonight and lock the doors.

I fear contamination not for me

But for the young, impressionables like you.

Although I'm tempted to forego this invite

I'll not lose face to Hindu Pagan'ry.

TOORI: I'll go and announce your intention. Noori, I passed your note like a proper schoolboy, which was received with a reaction that I reasoned was rapturous. Really! *(Exit. SHARUK shouting after him)*

SHARUK: Kya boltha hay, sala! Suer ka bacha![24]

NOORI: He only said how much he'll miss us both!

---

[23]Daughter.
[24]What are you saying, bastard. Son of a pig.

SHARUK: His words say one thing, his actions another.

No sense of loyalty these Hindus have.

I learn this lesson over and over.

I say good riddance to bad rubbish!

No asset he, but liability!

If laziness were virtue, he's a saint.

And always on some silly, snake oil, scam.

All right, occasionally he made one smile.

Does that excise the day-to-day mishaps

His blundering ineptitude contrived?

Therefore I part with him without regret

And wish the same that he did do for me

Befall his new benefactor. Noori,

Take heed of my unease depositing

The money. On second thought, give back the check.

What kind of father risks his child's well being

When fright'ning dreams have warned him otherwise.

Better safe than sorry, so goes the saying.

For vigilance observed displaces praying. *(Exit)*

NOORI: Baba, although I leave, I love you still,

I just can't be attendant to your will.

(She removes her dress and head covering revealing short, cropped hair dyed a bright color, a torn t-shirt and black leather pants. Exit)

SCENE V: THE STREET. A SIDE STREET OF VENICE BOULEVARD. WATSEKA AVE.

(Enter a group of men and women all in white dancing throwing the colors of Holi all around. They are having a great time singing a Holi song, giddy, laughing, spinning as the powder being thrown about gets all over their white clothes turning the scene from black and white to Technicolor, right before our eyes. Suddenly, SHARUK enters the scene. The revelers notice him and the singing and revelry stops. He walks through them cutting a swath as they allow him to pass. When SHARUK is clear, the revelry and singing begins again and the revelers scatter as AMITHABA and YOGANANDA are revealed covered head to foot in Technicolor brilliance.)

AMITHAB: Six hundred sixty-six, this is the place.

The beast's abode. Armando's running late.

SHIVA: And colored people time is no excuse!

AMITHAB: That's right! When hormones rage and reason fades,

All races stride in step with father time.

YOGA: Not just in step, but run ahead to prove
　　Ones loyalty to love in all its newness
　　Remains at journeys end, equivalent
　　To that at point of embarkation.
AMITHAB: A ship of fools on the Edmund Fitzgerald!
　　What sinks that boat is not a genuine
　　Desire not to float, but chemistry.
　　Our cells in seven years regenerate
　　Themselves so thoroughly as to render
　　Oneself unrecognizable to one.
　　If ones beloved's cycle's not in sync,
　　The lovers find they're sadly out of step.
　　And all the synchronicity that buoyed
　　Them on the ocean of their life thus far
　　Has vanished and they find themselves adrift,
　　Apart, in vast and unfamiliar seas.
　　She wonder's why he's changed, he hates her stasis,
　　The things that stimulate her, threaten him,
　　What makes him laugh brings tears to her eyes.
　　So sadly they attempt the cosmic rumba
　　Not grasping they no longer pas de deux.
YOGA: Look here's Mando; we'll pick this up in time.
　　(Enter ARMANDO)
ARMAND: It goes 'gainst nature our LA traffic,
　　This stagnant sea of crimson in the dusk
　　From which deliverance seems futile for us
　　Contestants in this suicidal race.
　　My future in-law's home!
　　(Enter NOORANI, *above, in Punk/Goth gear with her short, bright hair. In her hand a PDA.)*
Ay Dios Mio!!!
NOORI: You like it? Kinda shocking? You hate it!
　　I'm not a girly girl, get used to it!
ARMAND: Chill out, butch dyke, I love the look! It's you!
NOORI: You sure, 'cause I could soften it a bit.
　　You like the color? Found nowhere in nature.
　　And butch is right; it feels so good this short.
ARMAND: I'd never seen it long but dig it short.
　　We'll get a bass guitar to match its shade!
NOORANI: Get one for every hue that suits my do.
　　(Whispering to ARMANDO)

Here in my palm this pilot's got the numbers
That guides my flight from bondage unto freedom.
By morning we'll have cleaned out my account.
I'm glad the moonless night cloaks me from nosey
Fishwives who've nothing better than to gossip,
And this would give them ample grist to mill.

ARMAND: *(Whispering)* Come down, let's get you doused with Holi colors!
And celebrate your freedom with the gang.

NOORANI: I'll get my bags and turn off daddy's dinner.
I made enough to last him through the week.
Past that he'll have to learn to cook himself.
A funny thought, although it saddens me
To think of him alone in this old house.
(Exit above)

AMITHAB: Not bad in terms of sight and of sore eyes

ARMAND: I swear I run a few degrees hotter
When she's around as if my blood flows freer.
Yoga, she makes me feel like you say you feel
After one of your wheat grass enemas.
A real shiatsu, feng shue to the soul—
A shot of heparin straight into the heart!
(Enter NOORANI, *below)*

ARMAND: Noori, my friends! Carnales Noori! Soon
You'll love them like the brothers they're to me.
(There is an uncomfortable beat before . . .)

YOGA: No doubt the feelings will be mutual.

SHIVA: Chalo. The sooner we vamoose the better.
*(*NOORI *and* ARMANDO *head out.* YOGA *eyes her suitcase. To* AMITHABA*)*

YOGA: That girl has too much baggage for a night-
Out on the town,

AMITHAB: Don't ask. I'll have to kill
You if I tell you!

YOGA: Mum's the word.

SHIVA: Let's go!
(Exit with NOORANI, YOGA *and* AMITHABA. *As they do* DEVENDRA *enters and*
AMITHABA who is the last in line sees him and lingers behind.)*

DEVEN: Thank god!

AMITHAB: Monsignor Devendra, what up?

DEVEN: The elevation of my mood's what up!
I stand before you fully drunk, and glad
That for a fleeting moment feel no pain.
But only fleetingly. Jitendra leaves

Tonight for Carmel, his desire spurs him
As surely as mine own spurs my drunkenness.
(DEVENDRA starts to exit)
Oh, by the by, he wants you by his side.
AMITHAB: *(Aside)* At my request not by his choice I go
I have my own agenda, oats to sow.
DEVENDRA: *(Aside)* Thank god for altered states and tomorrows,
For love, this "many splendored thing," just blows.
(Music as lights cross fade to . . .)

SCENE VI: CARMEL. THE SOUND OF WAVES. A ROOM IN PUSHPA'S HOUSE.

(Music plays. Enter PUSHPA, with KAVITA, RASIK, the conservator of the Shah estate, and MURALI, the Madrasi Minister of Finance. When drawn aside the curtains will reveal three stands, each with a T.V. and DVD player. On top of each a gleaming DVD case. During this process only KAVITA and RASIK are in the room with MURALI. PUSHPA waits outside in anticipation.)
KAVITA: Go through the beaded curtain and discover
The several DVDs that hold the dubs
Of films from which you must correctly choose.
MURALI: The golden box, with title that's familiar.
"Girish Karnard's Karnatic classic, Kondura."
The second, silver canister, which holds,
"Satyajit Ray's seminal Pather Panchali."[25]
And lastly but not leastly this in tin,
"Sir Bipin Shah's, Jab pyar kisi ka joota heh."[26]
KAVITA: The proper one has her image within.
If you choose that, then she is yours without.
MURALI: Let's see what logic dictates and reveals.
Within the canister of tin we have
"Sir Bipin Shah's, Jab pyar kisi ka joota heh,"
As I recall a big box office smash.
But something in the title warrants care:
When Someone's Love is False. Connubial bliss?
I think not. Rather it's a warning from
Her father from the great beyond. And though
He puts one of his own amongst the three
He knows full well that his masala movie,
Devised for mass consumption and mass profit,

---

[25]Tales of the Road.
[26]When someone's love is false.

Is not the non-pareil that his daughter is.
I will not choose, When someone's love is false.
"Satyajit Ray's seminal, Pather Panchali."
The great Bengali! Seminally so!
The pioneering genius, quiet craftsman,
The champion of the people, not the masses!
Unknown, at best obscure, in his own land,
Who let lack of experience deter
Him no further than lack of resources.
Does my good fortune lie among the pebbles
Strewn in Ray's shimmering, Tales of the Road?
Let's see again what's on the golden box.
"Girish Karnard's Karnatic classic, Kondura."
His screenplay was superlative and too
His stature in the art house circuit looms
As large, amongst those in the know, as Ray's.
And in terms of obscurity he bests
Our Bengal tiger and thus by default
He rises well above the other two.
All things being equal piss in one's own pot.
My southern loyalties lean toward this man.
I'll stop here and insert the tape eagerly.
KAVITA: Press play to learn if she appear within.
Then she is yours.
(He inserts the DVD.)
MURALI: O god what have we here?
Like Yul Bryner's post mortem smoking ads
Your father speaks, with you nowhere in sight.
(Either we see a video of Bipin Shah or we hear his recorded voice)
SHAH: "To choose by regional loyalty,
Or stuffy, artsy-fartsity
Speaks volumes to foolhardiness
That threatens Pushpa's happiness.
This art-house flick brought no return,
Investors lost, no money earned,
Goddamned I'd be if I'd assign
Her life to one with such designs—
To wash away with no restrain
What took a lifetime to attain.
So fare thee well, you leave behind
An earnest love you sought to find.

Despair would be unsuitable,
Depart with iron mandible."
MURALI: My heart is tight my guts feel like on fire
    My vows to win you have proved me a liar.
    I'm leaving now in keeping with the pledge
    And walk the line that marks sanity's edge
    (*Exit* MURALI)
PUSHPA: I will not gentle into that night go.
    Let all with his complexion choose me so.
    (*Exit*)

SCENE VII: VENICE BLVD. PETTERSONS CAFE.

(*Enter* YOGANANDA *and* SHIVANANDA)
SHIVA: Have you seen Jit's new television show?
    "America's Most Wanted" Bolly fugitive!
YOGA: Say what? I saw Jitendra driving off!
SHIVA: With him Amithaba and no one else;
    No Noorani and no Armando right?
YOGA: Right! They split East to Las Vegas, while Jit
    Set course for wife wooing and for Carmel.
SHIVA: So why was our celebrity detained?
YOGA: Detained? By whom?
SHIVA: By whom? The Heat, sucka!
YOGA: (*Dawning on him*) 'Cause back at Bora central Sharuk howled
    And sent 5-0 chasing the wrong sedan,
    Thinking Mando and Noori stowed aboard.
SHIVA: Slowly the picture comes into relief.
    The highway cops in hot pursuit of Jit
    Surrounded both our Carmel bound compadres
    In what amounted to a slow speed chase
    That soon diverted to the freeway shoulder.
    The flatfoots' tension mounted, itching like
    A finger on the trigger of a gun;
    And might have ended in a tragic hail
    Of blazing lead had not our swinging, shaven,
    Sikh, Amithabh, begun to sing "My Way,"
    "And now the end is near and so I face"—
    Undoubtedly from fear, which did the trick;
    For cops the world over love "old blue eyes"
    And marveled at this sand nigger who crooned

In dulcet tones and perfect pitch even
As he lay face down spread-eagled beside
The road on highway 5, far from Carmel.
In time the fuzz released them sans apology.
Rattled, the two removed themselves in haste
To Carmel to resume Jitendra's wooing.
I saw it all on sky cam; channel five.
No word from Mando and Noorani yet?

YOGA: From Sin City came word that two high rollers
Had dropped some heavy change on slots and craps.
With glee, apparently, the money flowed,
From these young newlyweds—

SHIVA: —newlyweds?

YOGA: Yaah!
Sharuk heard this and gave birth to a cow.
I heard he cursed her as he fell out crying,
And fetally was bawling like a baby.
Then, just as suddenly he ceased his grief
And marshaled all his strength in calculated
Coldness and vowed that, "All involved would pay
And dearly pay"; with which he proudly stood
And walked back home a soiled, crumpled figure.

SHIVA: I hope Devendra takes such threats to heart,
This Sharuk strikes one as retributive.
You hear about the tanker that went down
Somewhere just off the coast of New Foundland?
It flew the Indian flag when it capsized.
I caught it on CNN as it sank.
I thought about Devendra, watching it all
Unfold and prayed his lot was not on board.

YOGA: I pray your prayers were received and heard.
Let's call him on your mobile; better yet,
Let's drop by and bring him some Madeleine's.

SHIVA: And half a pound of penda and ladoo.

YOGA: He's moony-goony, since Jitendra left
And if he's heard some bad news from the sea
He'll be on an emotional roller coaster.
We'd better get a pound of chocolate too.
You should have seen him as Jitendra drove off.
All wistful smile and proper fare-thee-well—

SHIVA:—The perfect martyr, pakha Bombay gent.

YOGA: He stood and waved long past the time their car

Was visible. Then slowly lowering
His hand as if entranced he gently wiped
A single tear that trickled down his cheek.
He caught my eye and smiled and shrugged his shoulders
As if to say, "What can you do, it's love."

SHIVA: The fact that he is Indian is what thwarts
My calling him the melancholy Dane.
Yet one has to admire such oblation
To send the keeper of ones heart to seek
The keeper's own. Let's find and ease his loss
With our delightfulness.

YOGA: You got it, sista!

(Exit)

SCENE VIII: CARMEL. A ROOM IN PUSHPA'S HOUSE.
THE SOUND OF WAVES.

(PUSHPA waits pensively. Enter KAVITA)

KAVITA: Here comes the next to wager for your love.
Having signed oaths of secrecy he comes,
Reluctantly but bold, this Aravind.
*(Music. Enter the CLOWN as ARAVIND with a large, unfortunate, mid-seventies
era, Bollywood Hero mustache. In tow is RASIK)*

PUSHPA: In front of you, you see technology
That holds my fate which may bind me to you.

RASIK: If you succeed you'll wed without pre-nup.

KAVITA: But if you fail, with brevity and charm
You must depart from here immediately.

ARAVIND: I am by writ compelled to hold three things:
First, never to impart to any one
Which film it was I chose; next, if I fail
To choose correctly; for the next five years
Abstain from sex and wife choosing. Lastly,
If, god forbid, I fail in fortune of my choice,
Immediately to leave you and be gone.

PUSHPA: To these injunctions every one has signed
That comes to gamble for my worthless self.

ARAVIND: Me too! Signed, sealed, delivered, I'm yours!
I jest! But hope.
*(PUSHPA steps out into her own pool of light awaiting her predicament. KAVITA
and RASIK remain with ARAVIND)*
                    So. Silver, gold and tin!

"Sir Bipin Shah's, Jab pyar kisi ka joota heh,"
Her father's film? Too obvious! I won't bite.
Let's see the name on this golden diskette.
"Girish Karnard's Karnatic classic, Kondura,"
I don't speak Kannada. What's Kondura?
The South of India is as alien to me
As the Bushmen of the Kalahari.
Her father being a Northern man of business
Would not pick some obscure Dravidian,
Nor would he be so pompous as to include
His own commercial fare as paragons
To be construed analogous to her.
He would choose something rare, but not obscure,
Fine, but surely not unattainable,
Deep, but not in the least incompliant.
Let me examine what the silver carton yields.
"Satyajit Ray's seminal, Pather Panchali."
That word arouses passions of a sort.
I mean that seminal's appropriate.
Creative! From the Latin meaning seed,
Providing stimulus for further growth
Potentialities. I stop right here,
Slip it right in and hold off no longer.
(He presses the DVD Player button)
PUSHPA: My patron Parvati please hear my plea.
ARAVIND: And what the bloody hell is this then eh?
(The T.V. blares as Bipin Shah talks)
SHAH: Since you did pick Tales of the Road,
    You walk alone and bear your load,
    Your fortunes neatly have been sewed,
    Success you weren't able to goad,
    Thus well of you this does not bode,
    A prince transformed into a toad.
    And on this journey you've begun
    Stand by your choice, stick to your guns,
    And take your poison like a man
    Refrain from making wedding plans.
    For two plus three is doubtless five
    Till then you may not thrive nor wive
ARAVIND: I swear to keep my bargain's end
    Eschewing love from foe or friend!

(Exit ARAVIND *and posse)*

PUSHPA: Was that a hairpiece on his upper lip?

KAVITA: No. Bloated caterpillars mid cocoon,
  With not a hope of birthing butterflies.

PUSHPA: I don't think I can take much more of this with
  Abortive pupa being my only choice.
  We dodged another bullet. Come let's drink. *(Enter* RASIK*)*

RASIK: Ka heh Pushpaben?[27]

PUSHPA: Bolo nah Rasikbhai.[28]

RASIK: A call just came in on your private line.
  The urgency with which he spoke impressed
  Upon me his intent was genuine.
  He hopes to make it here within the hour
  And begs you to consider his late entry
  To gamble for the honor of your hand.

PUSHPA: No more! If you find him desirable
  Let him pledge for the honor of your hand.
  You sure he's not some relative of yours
  You're trying to slip in. Sorry, it's weariness
  That wends these words. Once more unto the breach
  To honor my dear, dead, daddy's dementia.

KAVITA: *(Aside)* Here's hoping it's Jitendra this way comes!
  (Exit)

ACT III

Scene i: Petterson's Cafe.

(Enter SHIVANANDA *and* YOGANANDA*)*

YOGA: Spill it; I'm on pins and needles.

SHIVA: There was a devastating explosion that rocked the Glaxo-SmithKline
  factories in Bhopal and New Delhi. The bombs went off minutes apart from
  each other and seem to be the work of the radical Islamic Jihad in retaliation
  for Iraq and Afghanistan.

YOGA: But why in Bhopal and New Delhi? The ubiquity of Glaxo is legend.

SHIVA: Easier to blow up in India my dear. Miraculously, only seven dead but
  millions in property damage. Nothing like a few well placed bombs to pull
  down the precariously placed infrastructure of the offending multinational's
  House of Cards. Glaxo has decided to cut losses and pull up stakes.

---

[27]Where are you?
[28]Speak then, Rasikbhai.

YOGA: So Devendra's windfall deal?

SHIVA: They're pulling up stakes!!! You do the math!!!

YOGA: Don't get snippy with me. I didn't plant the bombs.

SHIVA: I'm sorry. I'm thinking of Devendra. He's already unstable; this'll put him over the top.

YOGA: Nipping at the heels of his sunken ship these bombs may serve to dislodge more than Glaxo-SmithKline.

SHIVA: The debris of his fortune is scattered on the moon and 20,000 leagues under the sea.

YOGA: Christ let this be the end of his travails.

SHIVA: It's good that you invoke the shepherd because here comes a Wolf in sheep's clothing. *(Enter* SHARUK*)* Sharuk Saab, kya bath hay?[29]

SHARUK: You knew, none so well, none so well as you, of my Daughter's flight.

YOGA: I cannot tell a lie. Unabashedly, I'll admit I knew the pilot of that plane.

SHIVA: And Sharuk knew, none so well, none so well as he, that all
Chicks, once hatched, one day fly the coop.

SHARUK: She'd scarcely cracked her shell!

SHIVA: Oppression weaves stronger wings!

SHARUK: If carrying out my duties as the father of a motherless child is construed as oppressive, then gladly I submit, guilty as charged!

YOGA: And yet look what your fatherly duty's wrought! Your
Motherless child's, fatherless.

SHIVA: And Sharuk, childless. *(Beat)* So tell us what you have in mind in terms of Devendra's recent misfortune? I mean the ship.

SHARUK: In mind? I have him not in mind. But come to think of it, I think I have him by the balls. Pun well intended! Dare I say I miss his smirk his smarmy smile his snide editorials. Not word one from him since the sea, like Jonah's whale, opened wide and swallowed his life up whole. His words may not have broken bones but scar they did, just as the words of our agreement will surely leave him scarred.

YOGA: You will take his testicles in one hand and with the other slice them clean off? *(*SHARUK *nods)* What the hell for?

SHARUK: To feed my dogs. And though to them an unsatisfying morsel, this tasty, tidbit will serve to sate my malnourished revenge. He has disgraced me and drained me a full half-million. Cheered at my losses, scoffed at my gains, blasted me behind my back, ignored me to my face, slandered me in print, threatened my livelihood, dismissed my practices, blasphemed my beliefs— and for what exactly? I'm Muslim? A Bora? Our skins share the same hue! Our families the same village! Our loyalties the same flag! The ghee that fries your dal is as clarified as that which cooks our lamb. Our rites of cleansing rival your own ritual ablutions. Our call to prayer is as much a wail for

---

[29]Sharuk, sir, what's the news?

God's attention as your bell-ringing pujas; and though your temples stand beside our mosques, we know as little of your religious practices as you do ours. When the monsoons rage we're subject to the same floods, when the drought drives the burning brush the same fiery terror; when the unpredictable earth quakes, the same uncontrollable shiver and when the communal riots rage the same clamor for shelter. We drive our children with the same blind ambition toward medical success as you do yours and respond with the same alacrity when a boy calls for one of our daughters. We share so much in common that when our worlds collide we share he same response, an eye for an eye, a tooth for a tooth. When neither of us turns the other cheek we risk the stumble of the blind and toothless, for at all costs we must save face. And at this game I'll strive to best the best!

(YOGA's beeper goes off)

YOGA: It's Devendra calling. Your cell phone!

(Enter TOUFIQ dressed in traditional Bora attire like SHARUK)

SHIVA: It's dead. There's a phone around the corner. I'll go with you. Here comes another of his tribe. I'm not waiting around to get tag teamed while my partner's left the ring.

(Exit SHIVA and YOGA)

SHARUK: Asalaam alekh oum, Toufiq! Any news? Any news of her?

(Lights up dimly on NOORI and ARMANDO as Sharuk and Toufiq talk about them)

TOUFIQ: Alekh oum salaam, Sharuk! Noorani is well, though you'd hardly recognize her. Where once a scarf covered her head, there now stands a shock of crimson hair. Her milky white arms that never saw the sun now reveal colorful tattoos. A face that once was adorned with nothing but her lovely smile, now sports piercings of every conceivable sort. Eyebrows, nose, cheek, the whole ear, and from what I hear even the tongue. And her virgin body that never would shame itself to the eyes of the world now walks with an unabashed swagger, resplendent in torn denim and leather.

SHARUK: Stop, stop, stop, stop, stop!!! Enough! No more! Why not just tell me she's dead. My Noori is dead. This vampire that walks in her place is the spawn of Shaitan. You stick a stake through my love when you speak of the walking dead. For in my heart she lives no more. She's sucked me dry one hundred grand and siphoned off five times that into an offshore account that has no paper trail. She learned it from the master and went me one better. What upheaval can match the mutiny of flesh and blood? The sedition of the soul. For my child was my flesh, my blood my very soul.

TOUFIQ: Born under a bad star. You're not the only one with bad luck. Devendra—

SHARUK: What, what? Bad luck? How bad luck?

TOUFIQ: The latest is he's looking into Chapter 13.

SHARUK: He can't do that we have a deal?

TOUFIQ: Sure he can and probably will. Hindus are not known for keeping their word. Besides, who can blame him after that shipping accident?

SHARUK: I can blame him! I can blame him!

TOUFIQ: Noori and her husband—

SHARUK: Don't call him that. He is the Shaitan! He is the Shaitan!

TOUFIQ: Your daughter and the Shaitan are building a recording studio.

SHARUK: A recording studio? For what? Does she sing?

TOUFIQ: I don't know. Don't you? (SHARUK *shakes his head.* TOUFIQ *starts to exit then . . .*) Should I pull the private dick out of Noori's case?

SHARUK: What advantage has he taken of us so far?

TOUFIQ: Twelve thousand.

SHARUK: Twelve thousand? Highway robbery. For what? To track her down?

TOUFIQ: Expenses, you know! You've seen *The Rockford Files!*

SHARUK: No! What's in them? Secret documents?

TOUFIQ: No. It was that seventies T.V.—

SHARUK:—is there some sort of conspiracy?

TOUFIQ: No! No conspiracy.

SHARUK: There is always a conspiracy afoot. The quiet cancer is as lethal as the hangman's noose. The brown, reclusive, spider's bite will remove a limb as surely as the Nile crocodile's. The sweet, scheming, smile will lull sooner than the snarling, spuming, snout. Trust no one. Vigilance is paramount. Noori's betrayal, wound's deeper than Devendra's blasphemy, her machinations more than his malice, her conniving more than his cabal. But, unlike her I will not rebel against my own flesh and blood is thicker and will flow like water when I exact my revenge. Mark my words. He will pay! He will pay.

(*Exit*)

SCENE II: VENICE BLVD. AT PETTERSONS.

(NOORANI *sits writing as* ARMANDO *is tapping a rhythm with a pencil.* NOORI *is also tapping and soon their tapping goes against each other's rhythms.*)

NOORI: Kiss my lips and make me cry,

Turn the lights off, whisper lies,

Night has fallen, fallen,

Dreams are callin', callin',

Hold me tight, don't let me breath, don't let me sigh!

ARMAND: What's that?

NOORI: Something I'm working on.

ARMAND: It's nice.

Except it's not iambic is it?

NOORI: No!

ARMAND: Nor is it pentametric, is it?

NOORI: No!

    I thought with songs tetrameter is fine!

ARMAND: I don't know. But, it sure makes me ill at ease!

NOORI: It does? How come? It makes me feel at ease.

ARMAND: Don't know how come, it's like a rhythm thing.

NOORI: Maybe it's just what you feel comfortable with.

ARMAND: Maybe I know my limits? My bound'ries?

NOORI: I like the options. Going back and forth.

ARMAND: Why back and forth? Why not just straight ahead?

    Trust me on this. Stick to the tried and true.

NOORI: No promises. I'll see what I can do. *(Beat)* For you. *(Exeunt)*

SCENE III: CARMEL. A ROOM IN PUSHPA'S HOUSE.

(Enter JITENDRA, PUSHPA, AMITHABA, KAVITA, *and* RASIK*)*

PUSHPA: Maybe it's best to wait a spell before
    You dive into the deep end of the pool.
    O Jit, I would detain you here a month
    If I had had foreknowledge it was you,
    And found a way to teach you how to choose;
    Although in doing so the oath I swore,
    Made in extreme duress and grief, I'll add,
    As daddy gasped his last, would be null and void.
    But what of that, he tricked me on his deathbed.
    As far back as I can remember I
    Was obstinate in my refusal to
    Give in to some arrangement for my hand.
    Arranged or love, it's "marriage" had me spooked.
    My own beloved parents were the models
    For my seemingly obdurate resistance.
    I have suspicions, since my birth followed
    So closely at the heel's of their, "I do's,"
    That shotguns and not love presided there,
    Forcing both in-laws and the bride and groom
    Into "arrangements" of matrimony.
    This forced commitment yielded filial love,
    A shell of loveless obligation
    That found expression in their love for me.
    Unable to impart affection to

Each other, I became the open vessel
In which they poured their unconditional love.
Of course I long suspected that my father
Carved out creative outlets with young starlets,
Which left my mother needy and the nag
And doubtless hastened her untimely end;
On whose deathbed I swore obeisance to
My father's wishes and to care for him
Since I was now the lady of the house.
Were I conspiratorially bent I'd swear
The two were in cahoots in life and death
To wear my iron will down to a point
That pricked my conscience with the thorns of guilt.
Thus, thankful counting my blessings in love,
I've known the kind that children need to thrive
But ignorant between a man and wife.

JITENDRA: I have not known and doubt the existence
Of blueprints for connubial success.
From childhood to adult I can't recall
Two people that embody blissful union
As yet to satisfy this skeptics soul.
No formula, concoction or divining
Assures the perfect match; so rolling of
The die to test the fates of love might well
Be how the universe conspires to mate
The karmic ties that tether soul to soul.

PUSHPA: I'm not so sure I truck with karmic ties
Though from your lips seems semi plausible.

JITENDRA: If I may be so bold to paraphrase
The now well-known riposte in terms of faith.
The helio-centric plant turns toward the sun
And yet no proof exists it's cognizant.
Nor does the sun require the leaf believe,
Before imparting photosynthesis.

PUSHPA: This talk of shrubs has put me in the mood
For pulling weeds and planting seeds and such.

JITENDRA: The bud that was the girl has flow'red into
The dame, demanding tending of her patch,
Whose fertile soil lies waiting for the till.
(The next two exchanges are spoken as asides to KAVITA *and* AMITABH
respectively.)

PUSHPA: It's strange to hear your childhood fantasy
    Speak words you've only dreamt, now manifest.
JITENDRA: It's strange to think my Lolita crush
    Might be the key to happiness fulfilled.
    (Back from the aside)
    As such, let's not a single moment waste.
    Reveal to me the DVDs, post haste!
PUSHPA: But wait my heart's begun to palpitate.
    Till you, I've been resigned to the outcome
    Of what the wager will reveal; but now,
    As if rejuvenated by your presence,
    I've come to life like Lazarus or Cher,
    And feel the panic and the desperation
    Of the invested and the vulner'ble!
    And like the old song daddy used to hum,
    "I can see clearly now the rain is gone."
    Kavita and the rest, give him some space.
    And to my fate submit; gallop apace!
JITENDRA: Gon' be a bright, bright, bright, sun shiny day!
    (JIT goes into the choosing room. Music as he contemplates his fate.)
JITENDRA: The gold diskette, silver diskette and tin.
    In which one do you lie? And lie it would be,
    For what is film but the ephemeral?
    The lie of celluloid that tells the truth;
    Of light imprinted, captured, stolen souls!
    The art form of the 20th century;
    The touchstone even cornerstone of life;
    The chosen medium to tell our tales,
    Be it through flights of fancy, docs or verite,
    That's changed perception, even changed our brains
    As we begin interpreting our lives
    Through cinematic zeitgeist and gestalt.
    This lie that tells the truth, I do believe,
    Has rearranged what we perceive as truth,
    And made it more attractive to receive the lie;
    The doppelganger we prefer to life.
    The real stands nervously behind me, yet,
    I search for Pushpa's counterfeit in here.
    These gilded boxes, with their arty films
    Designed to second guess, impress, cajole,
    Lead down the garden path, and aren't unlike

The shiny stones that catch the eye of gulls,
By that I mean the fool, the gullible.
For richness is concealed in plainest sight,
It's strewn amongst the crap, the bargain bins.
True populism comes from empathy,
The kind that hits a nerve and strikes a chord.
The sleeper, cut from crass commercial cloth,
Gives satisfaction not by marching to
The beating of a different drum, but by
The rat-a-tat of common time that has
A nice beat and is easy to dance to.
I choose Jab Pyar Kisi Kah Joota Heh,[30]
The Taiko drum of crass commercial fare.
(He slips in the DVD and presses the button)
PUSHPA: O Pushpa, don't dare dream, don't count the chicks.
He chooses where it seems the fates reside
But nothing is, as we know, what it seems.
(Bipin Shah's voice is heard)
SHAH: You that chose my simple flick,
Gain by taste not magic trick.
Heir apparent, earned your pick
Take your fortune wet your wick.
Follow nature's simple plan,
Procreate and build the clan,
Nothing else quite makes the man,
Children, wife and mini-van.
(The DVD starts to play a song and dance number that spills onto the stage as
PUSHPA *and* JITENDRA *take over the singing and dancing. A colorful, lavish,*
piece not unlike something from Bobby by Raj Kapoor. The song becomes the
climax to the wooing of PUSHPA. *Song ends leaving* PUSHPA *and* JITENDRA *in*
an embrace.)
JITENDRA: I dare not pinch myself for fear I'll wake
To find this rapture only fabricate.
And not unlike the mindless adulation
Accorded me when flavor of the month,
This reverie as well threatens to vanish.
But unlike that which soon grew tiresome
And made me question stardom like Leif Garrett,[31]

---

[30]A play on the title of a famous 1998 film, Jab Pyar Kisise Hota Hei, starring Salman Khan.

[31]A popular singer who experienced drug and alcohol problems in the 1980s.

This second chance to make my life anew
Forecasts an ending as upbeat as any
Twelve-step celebrity on VH 1.
PUSHPA: As you remake your life anew, I'll make
My new life as a wife, how strange that sounds,
Converge with yours in effortless confluence.
And though right now I can't conceive of kids,
I'm sure in time I'll squeeze out two or three.
And you will dote, devoutly dote, unlike
Your Pop or mine, on chubby Guju boys
Who'll not appreciate the privilege of
Their rich, suburban, cat-birded seating.
Then when we're old we'll wake at 5 AM
Like grannies do to rosy dawns and dew,
To surya namaskar[32] or Tai Chi Chuan,[33]
Abluting to the strains of Sheila Chandra[34]
Or some post Y2K equivalent.
So if what I've laid out's agreeable,
Then take this ring and swear that I am yours.
JITENDRA: You are mine and we are what we are. Yes!
The circle of this O, this hallowed hoop,
Exemplifies completion. Where you
Begin I end, where you and I begin.
KAVITA: Beginnings are what we'd like to discuss.
We'll own up to the fact that late night chats
Have cast a net and caught within the web
Of bots and bytes two corresponding lovers.
And though not neophytes in love it was
The first time that we looked before we leaped.
AMITHAB: Thank god, though, that in terms of looks we're golden.
I took the leap of faith to know the girl
Before I "knew" the girl and hoped that kind
Of blind investment would produce surprising
Returns. For months now I've been hard pressed not
To blab this to you, fearing ridicule.
JITENDRA: I'm shocked! The playboy of the eastern world!
AMITHAB: See that's exactly what I'm tired of bearing;
The Bombay bachelor banner for us all.

---

[32] An important yoga pose.
[33] A martial art.
[34] A British Asian pop singer.

I'm aging just like everyone and need
To ponder sagging chins and low motility,
Which leads one to thoughts of mortality.
JITENDRA: It blows my mind to hear you talk like this,
Though quite refreshing and wholly welcome!
But tell me how you hooked up in the first place?
AMITABH: Again I fear being mocked; and too, as I
Divulge our genesis, betray discretions—
KAVITA:—he called me on a 1–900 line.
PUSHPA: And what were you doing on the other end—
KAVITA:—Need I explain how phone sex actually works—
PUSHPA:—But why? For kicks, for thrills or—
KAVITA: —for money!
PUSHPA: But that's ridiculous. You're well provide—
KAVITA:—Provided for? Munificence I can
No longer, for my own sense of self-worth,
Accept. I have to earn my own. I mean
No disrespect. Your family has cared
For me as I have cared for you. My childhood,
Spent caring for your childhood, was the price
I paid, the prize my parents gained, for one
Too many daughters born. One less dowry
To sweat. Best give her up to what amounts
To child indentured servitude. I say
This with no heat and bear no ill will toward
My folks or yours, but state what's true and now
Reveal to you that we're not even cousins.
PUSHPA: What do you mean that we're not even cousins?
KAVITA: Our fathers weren't related, just old friends.
When you were born I was a girl of eight,
And eight was when I stopped being a girl.
Instead at eight I came to be a nurse
And nurtured this brown bundle with no hair,
A job alternately I loved and hated,
And vowed to see you through to wedded bliss
Before embarking on my own such quest.
Your destiny that hinged on wagering,
Was linked to mine, now come to sweet fruition.
So as your Rama broke your father's bow
And won your hand as well as won your heart,
My cyber-Lakshman's shot a shaft my way
And I have deigned to let it pierce my heart.

PUSHPA: We need a heart to heart, just girl to girl.
   I feel so in the dark, like Dubya.
   The feelings churning in my gut are mixed.
   I'm happy Jitendra's who rescued me,
   But sad that you and I are no longer kin;
   Ecstatic that you've found your own true love,
   Disturbed though at my own ignorance of your
   Indentured childhood state; and plead on my
   Behalf that I was innocent of these
   Contrivances and pray from you forgiveness.
KAVITA: You needn't ask forgiveness, just respect
   The means of consummating my solvency,
   Not judging how I earn my keep and know
   That our new state of kithlessness affects
   In me not one iota how I feel
   Maternally toward you nor ever will.
PUSHPA: That makes me want to cry! I love you, Bhen,
   And will respect your terms; and though we share
   No blood, cannot conceive a sisterhood
   More true than ours; and will demand of you,
   Amithaba, a true companion.
JITENDRA: For months you've kept this secret to yourself?
   Kavita rest assured this man's in love,
   A stoic he is not, so silence of
   This kind, I'd say, speaks volumes toward intent.
AMITHAB: This Gardner's found his Ava, I'll confess,
   But unlike Frank I'm laying roots with mine.
   (To KAVITA*)* And that's 'cause, "I got you under my skin"—
   (Enter RASIK*)*
RASIK: A call for you, sir, from Los Angeles.
   Mister Yogananda by name.
   (Lights up on YOGA *who has surreptitiously called while in the park with* DEVEN-
   DRA *who sits morosely on the park bench.* SHIVA *has to play it sotto voce)*
JITENDRA: Yoga!
   Rasikbhai, put it on the speaker-phone.
   Shiva, we made the cut, we made the grade.
   We'll marry on the set of our new film,
   And let the fruitfulness of our new match be
   Indicative of the creative fires
   We hope will burn till Death do us apart.
YOGA: That news should help uplift the spirits here.
   Devendra's condition is getting worse.

JITENDRA: Condition? Is he in some way unwell?

YOGA: Since you went north all of his deals went south.

JITENDRA: They're all waylaid? The Glaxo-SmithKline deal?

YOGA: Went south!

JITENDRA: The cargo ship?

YOGA: Went really south!

JITENDRA: Oh god, I knew it was too good to be true.
    Too much was going my way. This always happens!
    Just when I get my shit together, bam!
    I'm knocked back down. A cosmic joke. It's how
    The gods fuck with my life!

YOGA: He needs you Jitu.

JITENDRA: Of course he does. I'm sorry! He's the one
    In need. He's risked it all for me. And all
    I can think of is me, me, me, me, me!
    When does this vaudeville go to trial?

YOGA: In no more than a week.

JITENDRA: A week?

YOGA: A week!

PUSHPA: Is it a dear friend that is in such trouble?

JITENDRA: The dearest friend to me, the kindest man,
    A man who asks for nothing in return
    Just friendship. Of the deep platonic kind.

PUSHPA: How deep's his debt?

JITENDRA: He's in for half a mil.

PUSHPA: A half a mill-ion, U.S.? That's deep!

JITENDRA: O sweet Pushpa he's in so deep for me!
    He bought my ticket from Palookaville
    And I just left him standing at the station,
    A victim vulnerable to Sharuk's greed!

PUSHPA: Pay him one million, and deface the bond.
    Double one million, and then triple that,
    Before a friend like this, Devendra,
    Becomes a victim of palooka-ness.

JITEN: Great then let's wire him the cash!!

PUSHPA: We can't.

JITEN: Why not?

PUSHPA: Daddy's inheritance will not
    Mature for three more months, as failsafe to
    Insure this marriage is no scam. As such,
    Let's consecrate our bond immediately.
    I'll call you Husband you can call me Wife,

Which makes you qualify for half my wealth.
We'll make an offering they can't refuse.
YOGA: Dear Pushpaben, it seems that no amount
Will serve to satisfy the burning blood
Of our nemesis. He daily prays
Petitioning god and man, invoking justice,
And no amount of pleading quiets his soul.
We've all tried, save for Devendra; his pride
Prevents him and will soon emasculate him.
PUSHPA: Emasculate him, how?
JITENDRA: I'll fill you in.
Let's hurry to a judge and make our vows.
(Indicating KAVITA *and* AMITABH)
PUSHPA: Rasik go charter them a Lear Jet.
We'll see the two of you down in L.A. *(*KAVITA *and* AMITHAB *exit)*
We start our wedded life adventurously.
A judge, then quickie rural honeymoon
In Yellowstone where we can bone up on
The art and strategies of love and war.
Since you are dear bought, I will love you dear.
JITENDRA: I have in you a mate of fiery grace,
Reality exceeding fantasy.
I go to meet the devil face to face,
But with you by my side go fearlessly.
(Exit)

SCENE IV: VENICE BL. ON THE STREET OUTSIDE PETTERSON'S.

(Enter SHARUK, YOGANANDA, *and* DEVENDRA*)*
SHARUK: Look, there he is; the fool who lent for lust
And lost for love. I'm sure the gamble was
Well worth it no?
DEVEN: Now hear me out Sharukbhai.
SHARUK: Oh, Bhai? You call me brother? Bhai and Bhai?
And yet this circle's long been broken, Bhai.
And Bhai, if we now share this brotherhood,
When you had called me dog, had you not, brother,
Unwittingly called our mother, bitch.
And for that disrespect should not I now
Like Cain, a canine Cain, bite off the balls
Of my good brother if I am able?
DEVEN: *(Beat)* If you'd just hear me out.

SHARUK: I'll tune you out,
     How's that? I'll hold this piece of paper up
     And tune you out. I'll point to where you've signed
     And tune you out. I'll put my fingers in
     My ears and go la, la, and tune you out.
     We're both men of our word aren't we, therefore,
     I'll not relent and let you off the hook,
     Thus helping you to keep your good name good.
     This bond ensures your honor stays intact.
          (SHARUK *exits*)
YOGA: The bloody bastard, suer ka bacha!
     I mean this from a place of true agape,
     I hope he chokes on his—
DEVEN: —Just let it be!
     I'll not run after him to kiss his arse.
     He hates me sure and for good reason too!
     You seem to put much stock in karmic ties,
     I don't, but am beginning to believe
     That what we reap is truly what we sow.
     What did I do to make him hate me so?
YOGA: It's in the stars my dear Devendra.
     My psychic tells me that the retrograde
     That Mercury is in will end the day
     That this fiasco goes to trial; then all
     Will flow harmoniously, I'm sure of it.
     The S.A.B.U. arbiter will side with you.
     He's distant kith to your own family kin.
DEVEN: I'm not sure that's the way to win the case.
     I've always had the tides turn in my favor
     And not always 'cause I was in the right.
     The privilege of power and connections,
     The safety net that's always buoyed my
     Trapeze-like que sera, sera-ness, has
     Afforded me the bliss of ignorance,
     An opiate that's finally wearing off,
     Awakening in me a longing to
     Repent and come to terms with who I've been
     And pay the debt in full tomorrow to
     My bloody creditor. Pray God, Jitendra
     Returns to witness me repaying his debt,
     (*Exit*)

ACT IV

SCENE I: CULVER CITY. VENICE BLVD. AN OLD VFW HALL TRANSFORMED INTO THE SOUTH ASIAN BUSINESSMEN'S UNION (S.A.B.U.) COURT.

(Lights up on the representative from S.A.B.U., DEVENDRA, JITENDRA, AMITHABA, *and others. A big photo of* GANESH *behind the S.A.B.U. arbiter. During this scene everyone will address the audience as if they're the audience at the makeshift courthouse.)*

SABU: Stand forward Sharuk and Devendra.
  You've both agreed to transfer all assets to
  S.A.B.U. who'll bear the burden of deciding
  How the proverbial cookie will crumble.
  We'll arbitrate and our decision's final
  To this do you both swear?

DEVEN: I do!

SHARUK: As do I!

SABU: Then please if you will sign the contract proper.
  (They sign a piece of paper each)
  Before we start let's make puja and so
  Insure the gods will justly guide our hand.
  You don't object Sharuk?

SHARUK: And if I did
  What recourse do I have? How would that fare
  On my behalf, I mean my protesting,
  In terms of justice in a Hindu court?
  Good thing I prayed before I came.

SABU: Sharuk,
  I take great umbrage at your hyperbolic
  Assessment that this arbitration
  Is in the slightest way nonsecular.
  The puja is a way of honoring
  Our roots and our customs back at home.

SHARUK: Whose customs represent what you mean by:
  'Our roots and our customs back at home?'

SABU: Areh, the customs of the vast majority!
  The edicts of democracy demand
  That the majority speaks for the whole.

SHARUK: And yet the test that makes the mettle of
  The culture is its treatment of minorities,

Of which I am a card-carrying member.
The soundness of the state rests on the health
And wealth of it's most underprivileged;
Whose voiceless rage often directs itself
Inward and sows the seeds of self-hatred, who,
Nevertheless, when pushed too far, explode
With violence of such barbarity,
That the majority then, hayseed-like,
Scratching their heads, declaim, "How can this be?
See, they are sub-human as we surmised
And well deserve the treatment they receive."
But I'll not add my voice to protestations
That may prevent you praying to your gods.
I'll not give you the ammunition you need
To brand me a minority with axe
To grind, a scapegoat for your cultural wars.
I say pray on, 'cause I have contracts signed
And bonds that bind that Gods don't trifle with!

SABU: Proceed, Pujari. Please perform the prayers!
(*The Pujari chants with water and blesses the people, the audience, and space
conspicuously avoiding* SHARUK)
Sharuk, we've taken this . . . matter in stride
And honored your request for grievances.
You've made your point and forcefully I'd add.
The balls are in your court. I mean, the ball.
Look 'round, you're at the center of attention.
The people poised to let you have your say.
Now don't you think it's time for you to drop
This strange and seeming unenforceable
Contractual forfeiture; the slicing off of
A pound of this poor man's unmentionables?
It seems too stiff a sentence to mete out.
(*Aware he's making a joke the court falls into laughter*)
It's hard not tittering when talking of
The bonds distinct peculiarities.

SHARUK: I wonder if you tittered when you heard
Of Serbian camps where Muslim women were,
Through ritual rape, degraded, so as to
Destroy the peoples' will? Or Muslim boys
Who, soaked with kerosene, were set ablaze
During the not too distant Bombay riots.

Or Chechen girls shot point blank as they slept
And dreamt of freedom from their Russian hosts.
Or Palestinian youth both maimed and killed
When they, with rocks in hand, stood 'gainst the Uzi.
Or babies born malformed in Babylon,
The softest targets of the smartest wars
Whose smartness now conveys the cradle of
Civilization to the grave. Now, why
Evoke this lit'ny of unpleasantness,
Atrocities committed worlds away?
Why risk appearing strident or sincere?
The unifying theme of all these acts
Is that they center on the demonizing
Of one religious group, Muhammad's line.
More than a billion strong and still we are
The thing that goes bump in the night, the worlds'
Collective need to gate communities;
The black-hat wearing, bomb bursting, jihad
Enacting, mass-destructing, wife oppressors.
The more you hate the more we unify.
What binds us all is our submission to
Allah. And for that acquiescence we're
Reviled and vilified. And persecution
Has repercussions, side effects, you see.
It breeds within the victim the desire,
The thirst, to victimize the victimizer.
What does this have to do with family jewels,
Being separated from their rightful owner?
Not quite sure but the answers in there somewhere!

JITENDRA: You're on a soapbox now you sociopath!
Transforming airplanes into missiles and
Schoolyards into graveyards what makes the world
Revile you, not submission to Allah.

SHARUK: And what distinguishes a plane that fires
A missile from one that's deployed as one?

JITENDRA: One is a tool of terror the other
A tool of war.

SHARUK: Can you say which is which?

JITENDRA: So by emasculating my dear friend
You'll rectify "atrocities done worlds
Away?"

SHARUK: It will suffice for wrongs done me.

JITENDRA: And butchery's the antidote to hate?

SHARUK: No, love's the antidote to hate!

JITENDRA: And is there none that's left within your heart.

SHARUK: What? Love? For all the shames he's rained on me?
    I daresay even blessed Allah would
    Be hard pressed to find love for his offences.

JITENDRA: Every offense is not a hate at first.

SHARUK: What, turn the other cheek and get slapped twice?

JITENDRA: Yes.

SHARUK: And how often have you offered yours?

DEVEN: Don't question with the devil Jit. There's no use.
    You might as well go stand on Venice beach
    And question sewage why it spoils the sea.
    You might as well demand that San Andreas
    Pay reparations for admitting fault
    In bringing raze and ruin to the southland.
    You'd sooner move Snow Summit to Muhammad
    Than bring this Muhammad to Snow Summit.
    In seeking to defrost his frozen heart
    You'll only freeze your own. Therefore, I beg you,
    Make no more offers; placate me no more,
    But swiftly, like a jagged little pill,
    Let me have judgment, let him have his will.

JITENDRA: For your half million, here's a cool one mil.
    The only caveat, it takes three months
    To thaw into its full liquidity
    And so present a promissory note.

SHARUK: Nor promissory note, nor cash.
    If every dollar in this million
    Were torn in six and every tear a dollar,
    I'd leave it lie. (To DEVENDRA) I'd rather you kept your word.

SABU: How can you hope for mercy rend'ring none?

SHARUK: Need I your mercy being in the right?
    A lot of you own mansions in Irvine,
    Run businesses both black and gray and in
    Between. Declaring to the IRS
    At least as much as you, from them, keep hidden.
    And some of you have restaurants,
    With cooks brought over from the old country
    Who have no language and essentially are

  Enslaved to you, indebted, sending back
  Home to their families most of their meager
  Paychecks with taxes cut which you also
  Fail to report to Aunt and Uncle Sam.
  Now should I chastisingly say to you
  That taxes benefit us all and fraud
  Makes victims of us all? And should I tell
  You that to profit from your fellow man
  Especially from your countrymen is sinful?
  You'll tell me to "piss off, the cash is ours."
  You'll say, "the cooks are better off than back
  At home," which justifies your rationale.
  And so I say to you: the balls are mine!!!
  I stand for judgment: answer; shall I have it?

SABU: I have to say that I'm at my wit's end.
  I've had a letter from the head of S.A.B.U.,
  Our Mr. Prithviraj, who cites concerns
  In terms of liability and has
  Endorsed outside consultation from one
  P. Shah from Carmel who may have insight
  That may be apropos to our proceedings.

JITENDRA: P. Shah waits in the hall without, waiting
  Admittance to the court.

SABU: Please call him in!

  (PUSHPA and KAVITA enter dressed in business suits. A buzz goes up in the court)

SABU: Where is this Mr. P. Shah?

PUSHPA: I'm P. Shah.

SABU: You're not.

PUSHPA: I am.

SABU: Why that's completely mad!
  (Aside) What was our Mr. Prithviraj thinking?
  A woman in a matter so discrete!
  He knows the rules. No women in the court.
  (To PUSHPA) Are you aware, madam, you are a woman?

PUSHPA: It seems that you're aware enough for us both.
  Remember Mr. Prithviraj approved.

SABU: That may be so but I decide decorum.
  You look as though you're trying to pass yourself
  Off as a man. That will not do. Please change.

PUSHPA: Please change? Please change?

SABU: I stand steadfast on this.
    You have your choice. Salvar Chemise or Sari!
    Propriety is next to piety!
PUSHPA: And where is it that we'll find this finery?
SABU: Why there's a Bharat Bazaar right next door.
    (PUSHPA, *eyes ablaze, looks at* JITENDRA. *Imploring with his eyes he asks her*
    to conform. She and KAVITA *exit.*)
    It's almost teatime! Let's have chai and chevda,
    As we await return of our Sitas.
    (*The court takes a little recess as* AMITHAB *walks toward* SHARUK.)
AMITHAB: What is that scalpel doing in your hand?
SHARUK: It makes the cut as clean as possible.
AMITHAB: I'll tell you what I'd like to clean; I'd like
    To clean your clock. But what you ought to try
    To clean is your account with your Allah!
    Can you refuse repeated cries to reason?
SHARUK: The kind that spew from your illiterate mouth? Yes!
AMITHAB: Fuck you, you Bora bastard, piece of shit!
    Fuck you! Fuck you!! Fuck you!!! Eat shit and die!
    I hope your balls fall off; you lose your hair;
    Your prostate swells up bigger than your head.
    I'll pray that every proctological
    Mishap befall your flaming, gaping sphincter,
    Like fissures and flowing incontinence,
    So that you'll stew in your own sea of waste.
    (JIT *who's been keeping an eye on* AMITHAB *as he's moved closer to* SHARUK
    eventually restrains his friend to prevent a physical escalation.)
SHARUK: You are, undoubtedly, the diplomat
    They've deigned to send to make amends.
    With sticks and stones you've made no bones
    Of how you feel about me. But until
    You find a way for bitter bile to void
    Conditions of this bond, desist and cease,
    Since all you do is break wind from your lungs.
    Sit down now little boy; let grown-ups play.
    (*Enter* PUSHPA *and* KAVITA *dressed in Salvar Chemises*)[35]
SABU: Now that's more like it. Don't you feel better?
    (*Her eyes ablaze she fights to keep her civility*)
PUSHPA: I do. Thanks!
SABU: Now you're welcome!

---

[35]Traditional clothing.

PUSHPA: Now may I speak?

SABU: Please, yes! Are you acquainted with the dispute?

PUSHPA: I am acquainted thoroughly with it.

SABU: Sharuk and Devendra please step forward.

PUSHPA: Is your name Sharuk?

SHARUK: Sharuk is my name.

PUSHPA: It's odd that you pursue the course you do
   Yet with such systematic legalese.

   This would not stand in open court you know.

SHARUK: I know.

PUSHPA: Then why continue on this track?

SHARUK: Where else may I make my complaint? I swore
   To keep this underground. Were I the one
   To have defaulted I would have appeared
   Despite the cost, for all I have's my word.

DEVEN: And so have I and that is why I'm here.

PUSHPA: You stand within the line of fire don't you?

DEVEN: I do.

PUSHPA: And stand here on your own accord?

DEVEN: I do.

   (To SHARUK*)*

PUSHPA: Why then you must capitulate.

SHARUK: On what compulsion must I? Tell me that.

PUSHPA: It's not compulsion but acknowledgment
   Of empathy, should drive you to relent.

   This overlooked, sublime, gratuity

   Of God, reflected in the glint of light

   That shines out from the gleaming eyes of babes

   Or those that amble in the twilight of

   Their time, reminds us of the grace that is

   Our birthright; our tiny piece of the

   Divine that links us to one another,

   The temporal and to the evermore.

   This simple act of walking in the shoes

   Of he-that-is-not-you awakens in

   You, memories that scream out, "There go I!"

   This empathy—ineffable, amorphous,

   Personified in human beings who woke

   Within themselves the joyous pain of "sight,"

   Of uncontrollable compassion,

   Of love untouched by thoughts of loss or gain;

The "pious ones" who suffered for our sins
And set the mark toward which we all should strive—
Now hovers in this court and waits upon
The call for it to manifest within
Your heart; to wake in you, divinity;
To open the eternal, to glimpse god!
Defining moments such as this appear
But once or twice in life, so choose; and choose well!

SHARUK: I choose the truth! By god, I'll have my due,
 For in my heart I've wiped out empathy.

PUSHPA: Will no one stake him, to repay the sum?

JITENDRA: I have it here in promissory note.

PUSHPA: They offer twice.

JITEN: We'll triple it.

 (PUSHPA *glares at* JIT *in his zeal to spend her money*)

PUSHPA: Sharuk, That's thrice to what has been agreed to here.

SHARUK: I've fought for principle, the underdog,
 And sworn an oath to God to give no quarter.
 Would you have me lay perjury on my soul?

PUSHPA: Take thrice the money—tear this paper up.

SHARUK: I will when paid according to the letter.

DEVEN: With all my heart I do implore the court
 Let's get this over with.

PUSHPA: Then so be it!
 Have you prepared a place of privacy?

SABU: We didn't expect this case to go this far.

PUSHPA: And you claim no bias in this matter?

SABU: *(Sotto voce)* It is, after all, unenforceable.
 We went along with it to humor him.

SHARUK: The truth shall set you free. Thank you.

DEVEN   Now wait!
 To win in this way is no way to win.

PUSHPA: The purpose and intent of law is to
 Be blind to prejudice and weigh the facts
 Which in this case it seems the terms were forfeit.

SHARUK: A Mullah sent to oversee my plight!

 (JITENDRA *is incredulous at the course his wife is taking*)

SABU: And so what should we do? Make him a Eunuch?

PUSHPA: At least behave as if this court is fair.

SABU: We could hold up a cloth for him to stand
 Behind.

PUSHPA: Alright?

DEVEN: That's fine!

SABU: Let's get a Dhoti!

(A flurry of activity as the Pujari uses his own shawl for the masking. DEVEN-DRA *stands behind the fabric, in profile. We see him from the waist up and ankles down.)*

JITENDRA: What in the name of all that's holy are
You doing? Have you lost your bloody minds?
(To PUSHPA*)* I trust you have a plan in mind. I feel
Like I'm inside a lunatic asylum. *(He walks around hyperventilating)*

PUSHPA: Therefore prepare to cut!

SHARUK: His privates, oui?
I quote the bond, that's all, my Clarence Darrow.
"Remove from him the means to procreate."

PUSHPA: Devendra, any words in your defense?

DEVEN: I guess I'm ready as I'll ever be.
Give me your hand, Jitendra. Don't fret!
To take from me my manhood pales compared
To tearing from my chest my beating heart
Which you possess and I've relinquished.
If I should bleed to death I'll find solace
In knowing that the courage that escaped me
In life, I found when face to face with death.
Namely, that I expressed my love not only
Through action and long-suffering silence,
But that when I had nothing left to lose,
I loosed my tongue and spilled the beans on love.

JITENDRA: I can't hear this! You will not speak of . . . death!
This court has no authority except
What we agree is its authority.
Let's blow this kangaroo-popsicle-stand,
And take this up within the white folks court.

DEVEN: You know I can't do that; I gave my word,
My word of honor, that's all I have left.
I've lost my means, my heart and now my will.
Don't bind my wounds after the cut just let
My life flow out. I've no desire to
Exist as half a man. You have your wife,
I'll have my peace and Sharuk may be charged
With murder in the first. So let it flow!

JITENDRA: This isn't what's supposed to be happening!!!

SABU: Devendra, don't ask us to let you bleed,
  We have to do what's in our power to make
  Sure that you stay alive.
DEVEN: It is my will!
  My will!! I'll sign whatever needs signing.
  (He grabs a piece of paper and begins to write)
DEVEN: "Being of sound mind and of sound body
  I Devendra Bhatt hold no one to blame
  For my emasculating wounds but me."
  (DEVENDRA *drops his pants and we see them bunch up around his ankles as he*
  stands behind the dhoti.)
SHARUK: And once again your signing will absolve
  Me of responsibility.
JITENDRA: Do something!
PUSHPA: I'm thinking!
AMITHAB: There has been too much thinking
  We need some action. Give me just two minutes
  Alone with him and he'll relent, I swear.
  (*Holds up the scalpel towards the advancing Amithaba*)
SHARUK: Please spare us all this thuggy, roguishness.
  Delay no longer. Please pursue sentence.
PUSHPA: This prize of flesh of his you seek is yours.
SHARUK: The hanging Judge Roy Bean!
PUSHPA: And you must cut this flesh as is prescribed:
  The bond allows it, and is thus awarded.
SHARUK: A Sandra Day O'Connor! Come, prepare!
PUSHPA: Hold on a second; there is something else.
  This bond makes mention of no blood.
  The words expressly are "A modicum
  Of flesh." Take then this modicum you so crave;
  But, in the cutting it, if you but shed
  One drop of Hindu blood, your assets frozen
  And signed over to S.A.B.U. are subsumed
  And made the property of this union!
AMITHAB: A Johnnie Cockring! Hear that, Borabhai?
PUSHPA: For as you urged us towards justice, be certain
  You'll have more justice than you can deal with.
AMITHAB: O, if the glove don't fit you must acquit!
SHARUK: Anticipating that an argument
  As weak as this would be invoked I came
  Prepared with tools that cauterize while cutting.

(SHARUK *gestures and another man comes in with a bag and starts to prepare the instruments*)
I do believe they're used on sheep. How apt!
No drop of precious Hindu blood will stain
This floor, all guaranteed by my Halal
Butcher whose steady hand ensures
This cautery will burn the flesh off and
Seal the wound.
(*The crowd is dumbstruck.* SHARUK *puts down the scalpel which was a ruse all the time and grabs the cautery—a long thin needle-like instrument that works a lot like a soldering gun—away from the butcher and goes to face* DEVENDRA)
                    On second thought let me do it!
(*Looking at* DEVENDRA, *cautery pointed at his nemesis*)
My daughter was the final straw. While we
Broke bread and sealed this deal they whisked her off
With your complicity and broke my heart.
DEVEN: I swear I had no foreknowledge of this.
    I say this not in fear, for as you see
    I flinch not from your vengeance, but want to
    Set records straight as to complicity.
    When we broke bread that night I was not in
    Cahoots to break your heart.
AMITABH: It's true. I was
    The only one who knew and liable!
SHARUK: You care to take his place then, my diplomat?
    (*Beat as* AMITHABA *demurs*)
    No, I didn't think you would. Just wondering.
DEVEN: The plan was hers Sharuk. She is in love.
SHARUK: She's sixteen!! Just sixteen!!! You hear? Sixteen!!!
DEVEN: Have you forgotten how consuming love
    Can be at sixteen? Life and death, that's how.
SHARUK: She was the only thing of value in
    My life. And now to me she's dead.
DEVEN: And who's to blame for that? She lives Sharuk!
    To you she's dead. Don't "lie" that at my door.
    For that, look to your own obstinacy.
    (*Beat as* SHARUK *stares at* DEVENDRA. *Then*)
SHARUK: Let's do this thing! For justice loses patience.
    (SHARUK *readies the cautery. He looks* DEVENDRA *in the eye, as the cautery remains pointed at* DEVENDRA's *face. We hear a strange clicking sound.* SHARUK *lowers the cautery as a gasp goes up from the crowd.* SHARUK *struggles*

to maintain his hate as he stares at DEVENDRA *who continues to look at him. Slowly* DEVENDRA *closes his eyes ready for the inevitable. Suddenly, the thud of the cautery hitting the floor as* SHARUK *stares at his enemy and* DEVENDRA *slowly opens his eyes to see the hatred gone from* SHARUK's *eyes, who slowly turns away from* DEVENDRA *and starts to walk away. As he does this,* JIT *who has been fiddling away with something in his hand says . . .)*

JIT: Smile, you're on Candid Camera, Sharuk.

(We see what he was fiddling with. He shows it to the audience; a cell phone with a photo of SHARUK's *cautery in* DEVENDRA's *face just before he lowered it. The clicking sound was the photo being taken.)*

Oh isn't that a handsome picture now.
I love technology and all its perks.
Just one small button left to press and zap!
Homeland Security receives a nice
Snapshot of you attempting to do harm
To a defenseless citizen.

DEVEN: Jit don't!—

(There is an odd feeling from our characters. A little stumped as to what to do. Torn between informing JIT *of* SHARUK's *change of heart and letting him continue on the course he seems to be on* KAVITA *is particularly perplexed)*

JIT: Now back away from him you psychopath.

AMITHAB: Yo, yo! The Terminator in the house!

*(*JIT *places himself between* SHARUK *and* DEVENDRA. *The hero to the damsel in distress)*

JIT: A picture's worth a thousand words. So what
Do you think Feds will do when they see a
Crazed Muslim whose green card lapsed months ago
—That's right Toori forgot to send it in—
Waving a weapon in a threat'ning way
At this Hindu with all these witnesses?
Do you think they'll think this, a patriot's act?

SHARUK: We all appear the same to them.

PUSHPA: Ah yes
But since you strive to set yourself apart
In dress and in demeanor you resemble
Their most-wanted posters.

JIT: So what awaits
Might be jail time, deportation or both—

PUSHPA:—Thanks to the edicts of the Patriot act.

SHARUK: Beware the light you shine my way not spill
On you; inviting undue scrutiny.

DEVEN: Jit, don't do this. You'll make me break my word.

JIT: I will not let you do this Devendra.

I will not let myself become the source

Of your desire to martyr yourself.

I'll risk the loss of our friendship—

DEVEN: —Love,

JIT: Love. *(Beat)* Yes . . . love, but . . . not . . . how you might say . . . love.

DEVEN: *(Simultaneously as the last part of* JIT*'s line)* How I might say—I know.

JIT: *(Beat)* I'm married Deva. Thanks to you. You know?

Married. That's all I can say. Can you . . . hear this?

(There is an uncomfortable silence as DEVENDRA *stares at* JIT, *then . . .)*

SHARUK: I'm leaving and request return at least

The principal of what I lent him.

JIT: Here—

PUSHPA: Whoa!

That offer is no longer on the table.

He twice refused it and demanded justice.

He shall have nothing but the penalty.

SHARUK: Give me the promissory note, I'll sign.

JITENDRA: I have it ready for him; here it is.

*(*PUSHPA *prevents* JITENDRA *from giving* SHARUK *the note and points to* DEVENDRA.*)*

PUSHPA: Why do you pause? Please take your forfeiture.

SHARUK: Shall I not have barely my principal?

PUSHPA: You shall have nothing but the forfeiture,

And in the taking put yourself at risk!

SABU: Now, Sharuk you will see how mercy works!

We will keep mum on this to DHS

But keep the lion's share of your assets:

I mean your Money-store, your gold, your cash.

Your house is yours outright so that you'll keep

But threaten anyone again and we'll

Revoke the DHS gag order and

Pursue you with the dogged fervor of

A barrister for Scientology—

DEVEN: No! I beg the court to reconsider.

Please! Let him keep—

JITEN: —One third of all he owns—

AMITHAB:—The second third to his new son-in-law

And daughter who soon may be expecting—

PUJARI: The final third he send in donation

To aid construction of a temple in
The much-disputed area of Ayodhya,
Along with a note of apology.

SABU: I like that. Good! Team work! Thank you pujari.
He will do this, or else we'll drop a dime
To Homeland Security

PUSHPA: Are you contented by the terms provided?

KAVITA: Stop it! Stop it!! Stop it!!!

PUSHPA: Kavi?

KAVITA: Please! Stop!
We're Hindus! We're Hindus!! We're bloody Hindus, Goddamit!
(Beat. KAVITA *is on the verge of tears, trying to pull herself together, mercu-rially shifting between tragedy and whimsy. She is, at this moment, a vessel channeling words that surprise even her, having no idea what she will say next. She's spiritually afire but completely grounded, present and emotionally full).*

KAVITA: Somewhere . . . in the handwriting of God . . . at the core of our *Hindu* soul . . . is inscribed . . . Tat Tvam Asi. *I am that!* The Unbearable that-ness of being. I am not just "I," but I *(She points to an audience member)* . . . am that. *(She points to* DEVENDRA*)* I am that. *(And lastly to* SHARUK*)* And I am . . . that. Is that not why we put palms together when greeting one another? To acknowledge God hiding, twinkling, behind every eye, every breath, every sigh? God in everyone? In everything? In *all* of us? We believe that you know. We Hindus! But we have no idea what that really means in any prac-tical way and in the everyday. And we not only fail to recognize that but at times this thing flies out of us and we . . . do things . . . we hardly can believe. *(To* PUSHPA*)* Things that embody "love untouched by thoughts of loss or gain," "uncontrollable compassion," "opening to the eternal and glimpsing God." You said it little sister . . . then forgot. Because, as quickly as it flies out of us, it flies away. So we return to what we know. Blood . . . and flesh. And we are tearing at this poor man's flesh. Frenzied by the smell of blood. But . . . it's . . . only our own flesh we tear. It's only our own blood we smell. It's only our own soul we besmirch. Our own . . . and God's.
*(*KAVITA *stands there raw, having bared her soul. The court is a little at a loss as to how to deal with her outburst. Then* SHARUK *steps forward and nods to her. Gently contrite and moved by her plea on his behalf, he says . . .)*

SHARUK: I am content. *(Then turning to the audience eyes ablaze)* I am content.

SABU: Let's draw
A deed of gift from Sharuk to S.A.B.U.

SHARUK: I beg you, let me leave; I am not well.
Please send the deed and I will sign.
(They all stand there dazed, looking at one another, not quite sure what they

have won. Then slowly SHARUK *exits as* NOORANI, *dressed to rock with purple hair, bursts into the court missing him by seconds. She goes to look for him but has missed her chance.* ARMANDO *stares at her as do some of the court before* SABU *speaks, placating the moment.)*

SABU: So, all in all I'd say a good day's work!

Seems like all parties got what they wanted!

(Exit SABU. NOORI *turns and stares at* ARMANDO *who stares back in return. There is a sense of estrangement between the young couple)*

PUSHPA: *(Referring to* DEVENDRA*)* Is he all right?

JITENDRA: Yeah, yeah. I'm sure he's fine

PUSHPA: Are you two . . . you know . . . were you? You know?

JITENDRA: No!

Not in the slightest. . . . really . . . that's crazy!

PUSHPA: I just . . . you know . . . he said . . . he loved . . . just wondered

JITENDRA: Deva, come meet my wife, your sister!

DEVEN: So this is she? Indeed my sister!

PUSHPA: And you're my brother and will always be. *(They hug)*

JITENDRA: The day is ours as is the night and so

Let's celebrate! It's celebration time. Come on!

Next week we pack our bags and off we fly

To Mumbai for pre-production on

Our India Indie flick, an art house hit,

Called, "Dushman Do," which means two enemies,

And like the Latins long ago had writ

Carpe Diem we too the day will seize.

(They all start to exit leaving on the stage ARMANDO *and* NOORI *as they continue to stare at each other.)*

JITENDRA: Deva you coming?

DEVENDRA: Be right there.

JITENDRA: We'll be

At Natalee's. Phat See Yew with tofu?

(There is an uncomfortable beat before JIT *walks out with* PUSHPA. DEVENDRA *remains on stage as the music starts and* NOORI *walks toward* ARMANDO *who also remains and the Pujari brings on a mic stand w/microphone and places it downstage, splitting the two lovers as* NOORI *turns to the audience to sing.* ARMANDO *watches for a beat and then leaves the stage. We are left with* NOORI *at the front of the stage and* DEVENDRA *sitting lost in his own world of loss as she sings.)*

ACT V

NOORI: *(Starts her song)*

Verse   Kiss my lips and make me cry,
             Turn the lights off, whisper lies,
             Night has fallen, fallen,
             Dreams are callin', callin',
             Hold me tight, don't let me breathe, don't let me sigh!

(SHARUK enters the stage and sits on the other side in a pool of light isolating him in his world. His world of loss and devastation)

Verse   Fathers pine for daughters gone
             Hard conceiving life goes on
             Sitting, hating, hating
             Sadly, waiting, waiting
             Staring at the rosy fingertips of dawn

Chorus
             Passion followed, duty lost
             Self fulfilled at any cost
             Obligation consecrate
             Sacrifice inviolate

(In the musical break she removes her purple wig and her hair hangs down)

Verse   Kiss my lips and make me cry,

(She stops singing but the words continue as she puts the wig over the microphone and slowly backs away from the audience and turns toward her father walking up to him. The song continues. SHARUK turns to her.)

             Turn the lights off, whisper lies,
             Night has fallen, fallen,
             Dreams are callin', callin',
             Hold me tight, don't let me breathe, don't let me sigh!

(They stare at each other for a few beats. NOORI puts her hands on her belly. There is a moment of connection between her and her father as he gleans that she may be with child. He's unable to fully go to her. Slowly NOORI walks straight upstage and exits leaving SHARUK and DEVENDRA looking at each other as the last notes of the song crescendo. The lights get brighter on SHARUK and DEVENDRA in their isolated pools as the last note rings and then drops to black.)

[End]

PART TWO

Canada

Like that of the United States, Canada's history of South Asian immigration and settlement started with labor migration in the late nineteenth and early twentieth centuries. The context of this migration involved both the labor needs in this region of the Americas and the practice of agents luring migratory laborers from the Punjab with a promise of wealth and work in America. Punjab presents a different context than other regions; the others had been invaded by agents seeking such laborers in the 1830s and 1840s.[1] Punjab, however, was not annexed to the British Empire until 1849, well after the indentured labor system had began recruiting workers from the ports of Calcutta and Madras. Furthermore, the popular tradition of Punjabi self-sufficiency, strength, and fighting spirit for attaining political rights prevented Punjabis from moving in "indentured" circles.

Some Punjabis were taken to the Caribbean but proved to be most disobedient and escaped to Spanish Central America. Before North America received shiploads of Sikhs willing to work, Punjabis formed a thriving diaspora in the nineteenth century. Many Sikhs had been policemen in Singapore and Hong Kong. Additionally, many Punjabi workers who traveled during the nineteenth century went under the auspices of "free" labor.[2] This occurred in two primary waves of migration. One wave traveled to work on the Kenyan–Ugandan railway built under the auspices of the British Empire from 1896 to 1901. Many of these Punjabi Sikhs, and their descendants, then migrated to the United Kingdom in the late 1960s and 1970s, becoming "twice-migrants" (See Bhachu 1985).

The second wave began with the first South Asians who entered Canada in 1901. They were Punjabi soldiers attending the coronation of Edward VII in

London. Their ship happened to dock in Vancouver and these soldiers, mostly Sikhs, traveled to Montreal before their return. Back in India they shared stories with their brethren about jobs, money, and high wages to be enjoyed in Canada's western regions.

British Columbia, like California, then witnessed a small growth in an Indian, mostly Sikh, labor presence in the early 1900s. The first batch of South Asians seeking work arrived in 1903 in Vancouver. By the end of 1904, more than 2,000 South Asians lived and worked (or sought work) in lumber mills, steel factories, sawmills, shingle mills, and the timber industry. In 1904, as in the United States, these laborers worked amid racial prejudice. American and Canadian labor policies heavily opposed Chinese, Japanese, and Indian workers. Also, due to seasonal work fluctuations and the racist policies of landlords, by the end of 1904 the streets of Vancouver were filled with poor and malnourished South Asians, many living destitute lives. Anti-Asian sentiment was reaching high levels in Canada, as by this time, nearly 20,000 Chinese, more than 8,000 Japanese, and several thousand Indians were residing and working in Vancouver. The level of exclusionary anxiety was so high that a popular song of the day, "White Canada Forever," boasting that "To Oriental grasp and greed / We'll surrender, no, never . . . White Canada for ever!" was heard on the streets of western Canada (Jensen 1988: 62).

In 1907, in Bellingham, Washington, Indians were the victims of brutal race riots directed at "Hindus." Many of these Indians then fled to Canada. During that year, a report by a Canadian official put the number of Indians at a few thousand, many of them impoverished. The Canadian government attempted a variety of measures to curtail immigration. One was to only allow migrants who sailed on one continuous journey,[3] which was impossible for Indians as they had to pass through Shanghai. Also attempted were literacy tests in European languages as well as a financial minimum of $200, more than most Indians could afford. This effectively shut out additional Indian immigration. In 1908, about 2,000 Indians entered; in 1910, only 6; and by 1912, the total number of Indians was still less than 2,500 (Jensen 82). In addition to laborers, the early twentieth century saw hundreds of Indian nationalists, located on the west coast of the Americas, agitate for Indian independence. The Ghadr Party, based in San Francisco and led by Har Dayal, also included units in western Canada. Some of these radicals worked with Sikh laborers and helped them politicize their grievances and work for representation and rights.

Between 1909 and 1943, only 848 South Asians were allowed to enter Canada (McMahon http://www.lib.berkeley.edu/SSEAL/SouthAsia/overview.html). During this time, though only a handful of South Asians resided in Canada, laws allowed for South Asian men to return to South Asia, reenter Canada with wives and children, and start families. This policy was effected because, beginning in

1910–1911, resident Canadian Sikhs pushed the government to let them reunite with family members and return with them, starting in 1910 and 1911. Most stuck to racially bounded enclaves. The state also attempted to hamper South Asian interests in settling in Canada. Citizenship and enfranchisement was closed off to South Asians (until 1947) and employment in public and municipal sectors was barred. Additionally, for the younger generations, education in law and pharmacy also was forbidden. By all accounts, the late nineteenth century and the interwar period was a time of intense racialization (Johnston 1979: 135).

In 1913–1914, a wealthy investor named Gurdit Singh wanted to challenge imperial law by chartering a ship to sail with 400 Punjabis, just after the law requiring continuous voyage lapsed. After Singh landed his ship, the *Komagata Maru*, he indicated that as a subject of the British Empire he had a right to travel to any other part of it, as all on board had sufficient funds. This began a three month standoff with Canadian and imperial authorities. Local Canadians declared their racial animosity toward Indians and urged the passage of a specifically anti-Indian law. After two months, it was decided that they could be legally deported. Then the Indians on board mutinied and refused to go, resulting in several days of fighting with local authorities. Finally, after negotiations between the imperial officials and the Indians, the ship returned. Upon its return in August 1914, however, war broke out in Europe and Gurdit Singh began to make arrangements for the ship. It finally docked in Calcutta, but due to confrontations with police and new wartime ordinances, conflicts erupted and Singh himself became a fugitive; in 1921 he turned himself in (Jensen 1988: 121–138).

After and partially because of World War II, immigration rules and attitudes changed severely. In 1962 and 1967, legislation essentially reversed previous policy and opened doors to professional and middle-class migrants. Since the late 1960s, the South Asian population of Canada has diversified beyond its Punjabi roots and displays much of the kaleidoscope of South Asia, as Hindus, Muslims, and others from most parts of the subcontinent, including Pakistan, Bangladesh, and all regions of India, have settled, studied, and worked across Canada. Additionally, as the Commonwealth was transformed into an area (officially, at least) welcoming the citizens of other member nations, Indians from other parts, such as Fiji, Africa, and the West Indies, began to migrate to Canada in search of work.

From the late 1960s, hundreds of thousands of South Asian engineers, doctors, lawyers, and other professionally trained individuals entered Canada, as they did the United States. In the 1980s, South Asian Canadians numbered more than 200,000 and at the turn of the twenty-first century, more than 1 million. As the second largest and fastest growing minority group in Canada, most live in urban spaces such as Toronto or Vancouver. The descendants of the earliest South Asians in Canada, the Sikhs of the early twentieth century, now form a small minority of the overall South Asian population, as it now holds roots all over the subcontinent (Tran, Kaddatz, and Allard 2005: 20–25).

Though South Asians, as in the United States, statistically are one of the most well-educated and prosperous minority groups, they continue to be targets of racial harassment and discrimination. In the 1970s, an era of intense of racial discrimination, South Asian Canadians experienced racism that easily compared with that of their British counterparts. Just as in England of that decade, Canada was most unwelcoming to South Asians as hundreds of thousands of South Asians began to settle into new homes and environments. Stories of racist discrimination, harassment, and violence adorned news headlines. Deepa Mehta, the filmmaker, and Bharati Mukherjee, the novelist, have both written of their experiences with intense anti-South Asian, "Paki" bashing (Siddiqui 2004: 5).

Histories of racism and discord notwithstanding, South Asian Canadians have risen to visible heights in the public sphere, boasting leaders in business, government, and the arts.

Theatre traditions of South Asian Canadians, as is true of the rest of the diasporic world, began mostly with South Asian-language performances intended only for internal consumption in the 1960s and 1970s.

In 1981, Rahul Varma cofounded the theatre Teesri Duniya (Third World) in Montreal to address issues facing South Asian immigrants like himself in Canada. In 1986, after he assumed the role of artistic director, much of the group's work has proceeded under his leadership. In its early years, the group produced Hindi language plays, many of which were written by Varma, such as *Ghar Ghar Ki Kahani?* for Hindi-speaking members of Montreal's South Asian population. In the mid-1980s, the group began producing English plays that focused on the immediate political reality of South Asians, race and racism, and contemporary Canada. Varma also wrote many of these, including *Job Stealer, Isolated Incident,* and *No Man's Land.*

In the early 1990s, the group began to receive funding from the Canada Council on the Arts. Projects have included *Counter Offense,* about violence against women in Canada, *Reading Hebron,* about Israel–Palestine, and *Bhopal,* about the environmental disaster in Bhopal. Plays produced by Teesri Duniya have been translated and remounted in French, Tamil, and Hindi. Though started as a group by and for South Asian Canadians, the group is now multiethnic and multiracial in its ensemble, orientation, and mission.

The other major South Asian theatre company of Montreal is Montreal Serai. Just like Teesri Duniya, the group was founded in the 1980s, by Rana Bose. From Calcutta, Bose grew up on the revolutionary arts of Utpall Dutt and Badal Sircar, stalwarts of the avant-garde Indian theatre of the 1960s and 1970s.

Montreal Serai has continued this tradition with a host of productions, many of them about radical politics. A good number of them also use the radical drama-turgical techniques of absurdist and non-realistic modes of presentation. Also begun as a forum for South Asian theatre artists, the company is multiethnic in its orientation.

Other groups fill the South Asian Canadian spectrum, such as Vancouver Sath, also begun in the early 1980s. Like Teesri Duniya, the group began by producing South Asian language plays, in Punjabi, for the Punjabi Sikh community in Vancouver. *Picket Line,* a 1986 production, detailed the struggles of Punjabi farm workers in the Fraser Valley, often employed by Punjabi farmers and contractors.

Outside of Montreal and Vancouver, companies in Toronto, such as Rasikarts, begun in 2000, have consistently produced theatre by and about South Asians. Plays by modern Indian playwrights, like Mahesh Dattani's *Tara,* or Gurchuran Das's *9 Jakhoo Hill,* alongside diasporic plays like Tanika Gupta's *The Waiting Room* and Dinesh Narandas's *Inmates,* have been staged by the group. Additionally, thematic adaptations of stories from the South Asian cul-tural ethnoscape, such as *Umrao,* based on the life of the courtesan Umrao Jan, and *Ek qatra khoon* (a quart of blood), about the Battle of Karbala, memorial-ized by Shi'a Muslims, have also featured in the group's repertoire.

Most prominent contributions to the evolving South Asian Canadian dra-matic literature remain in the hands of writers such as Varma and Teesri Dun-iya, Bose and Montreal Serai, as well as Uma Parameswaran.[4] As Varma has been writing and producing plays about South Asian Canadians for more than twenty years, his most widely produced (in English, French, and Hindi) play is representative of South Asian Canadian theatre.

Bhopal stands out as the lone play in this collection that takes on a histori-cal event in India—the Bhopal gas tragedy of 1984, which claimed thousands of lives as well as tens of thousands of deformed lives after the fact—and includes a diasporic character. In *Bhopal,* Varma is not giving another factual account of the tragedy but is searching for the truth behind it in the art of representing it. This journey is maneuvered through fictional characters, such as the NRI CEO Devraj, fictional situations, such as the encounters of the village woman Izzat with the Canadian researcher Labonté, as well as Devraj. Varma's play critiques many different phenomena—the idea of developmentalism, the arrogance of non-Indian, Western businessmen and scientists (from all sides of the liberal do-good spectrum), and the inexcusable lack of responsibility shown by the Union Carbide corporation.

Bhopal presents a wide variety of characters across the South Asian spec-trum, from development-crazed diasporics and the women who love them to Indian bureaucrats and subaltern village women. Jaganlal, the Indian minister, by the end changes his tune and supports Labonté and fiercely opposes the development–big capitalism approach of Anderson and the company. Jagan-lal represents a believable part of the South Asian sociopolitical universe: the big-headed bureaucrat vested in his own power. He comes full circle from a full-fledged development–corporate investment supporter, eager to catch a photo-op with the village woman Izzat, to being a voice of the victims and sup-porter of Labonté's research.

Devraj, with his NRI persona, his lover Madiha, and their situation, repre-sents a notable passage in the creation of South Asian diasporic drama: an NRI who has returned to India to do "good" for Indians back in India. Though this character is secondary to the central tragedy of *Bhopal,* through him and what he represents, Varma shows the diversity of the concept of the NRI. Devraj necessarily has had some contact with the West, in the form of a deep-seated developmentalism, redolent of up-from-the-bootstraps America. He shows an MBA-type sensibility that ignores everything but the company line and the bot-tom line. Devraj is buying what the West is selling, hook, line, and sinker. When asked about this character and about the representation of the NRI in general, Varma states that although he is the typical MBA graduate, "he really believes that the poverty should be removed—he doesn't calculate risks associated with the mode he applies in order to remove the poverty."[5] Varma's work is inspired primarily by the diasporic South Asian Canadian community, as "they are com-plex as individuals as well as a community, and are hard working, multi-opin-ionated, and a necessary part of the Canadian fabric. Most of my work relates to them and their issues in their new country."[6] From Varma's experiences, the diaspora is as conflicted and complicated a space as the places they left in South Asia. Many come from working-class backgrounds, many from professional cir-cles, and all have some version of the "home" to which they are attached. When it comes to issues of social justice or social change, as in *Bhopal,* according to Varma, "any discussion of people's struggle to end extreme poverty, illiteracy and homelessness, and gender injustice too often is termed simply as negative talk by many of them. They pride in peace and tranquility . . . yet ignore dis-cussion about caste massacres, mosque demolition, church burnings, religious riots, industrial accidents and nuclear tests explosion like Bhopal."[7] But Devraj is not a simple send-up of the stereotypical money-hungry businessman. For Varma "he is a product of corporate globalization and more. . . . He is someone multinationals would love to co-opt to carry out their marauding and merciless economic agenda on the globe's poor with horrifying disregard for human life."[8] As mentioned earlier, he truly believes that poverty, not harmful pesticides, is the root cause for sickness and underdevelopment.

Regarding the critique of this idea of poverty's relationship to development, the play successfully turns the entire edifice on its head by destroying its very

own promoters—Devraj, Madiha, and their baby—in the midst of its own madness. This relates to an old colonial legacy about the outsiders—the corporation now instead of colonial officials—knowing more about what's good for
the locals than the locals do themselves. Labonté nicely fills the role of the new
liberal do-gooder, a scientist on a mission who can't stand how stupidly Izzat,
the village woman, willingly sells animals and kills her baby. Devraj is also in
on the racket of outsiders knowing more than locals, but his NRI connection
makes the interactions all the more complex. Izzat, as the lone subaltern character in the play, emerges as a particular type of hero. She is an example of
how "people, especially the poor, know more than what they are perceived to
know by the middle class. What inflicts them more is not the poverty but the
powerlessness."[9] Her heroism lies in how she manages to survive both the corporation and Labonté. By the end, she finally commands Labonté's respect.

Varma's *Bhopal* has been produced in many different venues and in several
languages. Originally written in English soon after the event occurred in 1984,
the play lay dormant until the author collaborated with Habib Tanvir, the famed
Indian theatre director in the late 1990s. An English language version was first
mounted in Montreal in 2001, with successive Canadian French productions
and Indian Hindi productions to follow, as well as American productions in
Madison, Wisconsin, and Boston. The play first ran immediately after the tragedy of September 11th in the United States. Though the play was received quite
well in the Canadian press, Varma was struck by the constant comparison and
referencing of 9-11 in the reviews. This shows how, in Varma's words, "the western media needs a western reference point to report on events of the non-western world"[10] and that such a tragedy in terms of loss of human life, damage to
the natural environment, and almost unquantifiable damage to future human
life, is not worthy of attention on its own in the Western media. Whereas the
Western audiences in Canada and the United States were most concerned with
learning more details about the tragedy, Indian audiences have been commem-
orating Bhopal and planning protests. The play has been produced in venues
around the world since U.S. President George W. Bush launched a preemp-
tive war to locate weapons of mass destruction. Varma notes that many Indian
audiences connected the rhetoric with the alleged weapons of mass destruction
in Iraq and the very real weapons of mass destruction in India, manufactured
in America by a U.S. company and shipped to India. During the 2002–2003
Indian run, Varma noted how many Indian protestors carried signs reading
"You want Osama, gives us Anderson!"[11]

The Death of Abbie Hoffman, unlike *Bhopal,* is not particularly about the
South Asian diaspora. It is a play that, albeit with a few references to South Asia,
comments on contemporary politics and radicalism. As Pal's *Chaos Theory*
manages to make perhaps the first analysis of the postcolonial modern in the

theatre, Bose creates the first nonrealistic, absurdist, politically inspired drama within the South Asian diaspora. Inspired by Badal Sircar's *Micchil* (Procession), Bose's theatre combines various elements of physical theatre along with absurdist political commentary. Its inclusion into an anthology of South Asian dramatic literature occasions not the appearance of South Asians, but an evolving diasporic dramatic sensibility in the South Asian ecumene. Though Bose's political commitment drives his art first and foremost, as he asserts that "if you believe in a similar non-conformist culture, your upbringing and skin color fades away . . . so my plays naturally swim in and out of Western and South Asian cultural attributes,"[12] in this and other works of his theatre company, Montreal Serai, he maintains how he "introduced a lot of Asian contemporariness into the mainstream of Canadian culture by exposing the larger white audience to many things South Asian."[13] *The Death of Abbie Hoffman* is a piece of protest theatre, a performance manifesto, and a novel inclusion of innovative performance aesthetics into a politically diasporic space.

Bose's inspiration for this piece comes from the 1960s Bengali theatre he viewed as a child in Kolkata. This theatre, both of Utpal Dutt and Badal Sircar, combined senses of radical politics with an all-out attack on the senses, a use of spectacle, song, dance, and physicality. The radicalism in theatre practice as well as the general politics of 1960s Calcutta is what motivated Bose, as the "deep state of irreverence towards the feudal controls in Indian society . . . the irreverence towards Indian dominant cultural traits in general, irreverence toward left statism, irreverence in general"[14] inform his sense of theatre, and most definitely, *The Death of Abbie Hoffman.* Coming of age during the turbulent Naxalite movement of West Bengal also set up Bose's admiration for Abbie Hoffman, a radical whose suicide, for Bose, marked the end of an era. So he devised a theatre piece that speaks to the death of a time, the death of critique, the death of thought. Badal Sircar's *Micchil,* with its physicality and absurdism, provided a basis for symbolizing the death of that time, the passing of an era, as Young Person's death, or discussion of it, informs the entire piece.

When it comes to the South Asian-ness of this piece, or of Bose's dramaturgy in general, Bose's politics of protest outweigh his identity politics. At the same time, his politics represent a constant engagement with that identity. His early theatre process, with physical theatre, agitprop workshop-style political theatre, was "a confrontation with that insipid, economist culture that proliferated the diaspora living in the suburbs . . . so [Bose would] introduce daily headlines in every segment of the workshop, keeping in mind the idea of highlighting the end of an era."[15] Though he has written other pieces directly about this "insipid, economist culture," including *Baba Jacques Dass and Turmoil at the Côtes-des-Neiges Cemetery* (1987), in *Death of Abbie Hoffman* he injects a sense of contemporary South Asia into the piece that allegedly is about all of us, regardless of our skin color, nation, identity, or any other marker of difference. As most of Serai's company actors are South Asian, and in their production, he "would work with their faces, their accents, their body movements . . . some South Asian inflections were accommodated."[16] Here we see how Bose, though attempting to capture a universal, in many ways like Shishir Kurup's revisioning of *Merchant of Venice,* does insert some of the particular, through South Asia.

His own South Asian upbringing in Kolkata occurred in a particularly irreverent and somewhat socially marginal space of Eliot Road where many non-Bengalis, Anglo-Indians, as well as Christians and Muslims, have settled. He describes his family, a "fiercely progressive, secular" set of "quietly, soberly modern" parents."[17] He grew up in the raucous student politics of the 1960s Calcutta scene, with Naxalites and the Utpal Dutt and Badal Sircar world of radical theatre. Dutt, to Bose's taste, became too much of a "party man," but Sircar was what he calls the "Kropotkin/Bakhunin" of Indian theatre, a true renegade. In this orbit of radical theatre, Bose aims to critique radicalism itself, as he states that "revolutionary zeal can become oppressive . . . the enemy can sometimes be very rational. Within a big lie, there is a big truth. . . . Chaos and lack of roots is not so bad after all."[18]

Not just exposing chaos, but delving into it, engaging with it, and manifesting it through performance makes *The Death of Abbie Hoffman* such a historically memorable piece of theatre for the South Asian diaspora. It connects with the theatrical landscape of South Asia through its inspirations from Dutt and Sircar and connects to its locality through its engagement with the Canadian milieu and Western audience. Bose solidifies the concept that diasporic South Asians not only create theatre and represent themselves in the theatre, but also comment and engage with dramaturgy. Thus, Bose's contribution gives diasporic South Asians not only a place onstage, but also a place in the world of creation, innovation, and critique.

Rahul Varma

Rahul Varma is a playwright, essayist, and an activist who migrated to Canada from India in 1976. In 1981, he cofounded the Teesri Duniya Theatre ("third world" in Hindi), which is dedicated to producing politically relevant theatre about cultural representation and diversity in Canada. Varma became the company's artistic director in 1986. In 1998, with Kapil Bawa, he cofounded the theatre quarterly *alt.theatre: cultural diversity and the stage*, which is now headed by editor in chief Dr. Edward (Ted) Little. Rahul is a member of the editorial board. His articles have appeared in *alt.theatre, Canadian Theatre Review,* the 2002 Canadian Theatre Conference Proceedings, among other books and publications.

He writes both in Hindi and English. Rahul's early Hindi plays *Bhanumati Ka Pitara* and *Ghar Ghar Ki Kahani* were written and performed entirely for the Canadian South Asian immigrant community. He made his first forays into the English language with a series of one-act plays that included *Job Stealer, Isolated Incident,* and *Equal Wages.* With *Land Where the Trees Talk,* in 1989, he turned his attention to the creation of full-length plays. His other full-length plays include *No Man's Land, Trading Injuries* (radio drama), *Counter Offence,* and *Bhopal. Counter Offence* has been translated into French as *L'Affaire Farhadi* and into Italian as *Il Caso Farhadi. Bhopal* has been translated into French with the same title and in Hindi as *Zahreeli Hawa,* by Dr. Habib Tanvir.

His most recent play, *Truth and Treason,* examining the so-called War on Terror, will premiere in 2009 in Montreal. Rahul is the recipient of the Special Juror's award from the Quebec Drama Federation and the Montreal English Critic's Circle Award for promoting interculturalism.

Bhopal

Théâtre Sortie de Secours, 2005, 2006 (French)
South Asian American Theatre, Boston, 2005
Cahoots Theatre, Toronto, 2003
Naya Theatre, Bhopal and Indian tour, 2002–03
Teesri Duniya Theatre, Montreal, 2001

Other Plays

Counter Offense
Equal Wages
Isolated Incident
Job Stealer
Land Where the Trees Talk
No Man's Land
Trading Injuries
Truth and Treason

Bhopal

Rahul Varma

AUTHOR'S INTRODUCTION

On the night of December 3, 1984, Union Carbide's pesticide plant exploded, engulfing the city in a billow of deadly poisonous fumes. Small children fell like flies, men and women vainly scurried for safety like wounded animals, only to collapse, breathless and blinded by the gas. By morning, the death toll was over 500, by sunset, 2,500. By the following day, numbers had no meaning. That night, Bhopal became the largest peacetime gas chamber in history.

Union Carbide came to India in 1905 while the country was still under British rule. Until the night of the explosion, the company was best known for the manufacture of the Eveready battery. By the mid-60s the company had moved into agrochemicals, and by the mid-70s it had become one of India's largest manufacturers of chemical fertilizers and pesticides. The company's promotional film showed healthy green crops blowing in the wind, birds singing, and men, women and children beaming with happiness as the line scrolled across the screen: "Union Carbide will touch every life in India."

Union Carbide did indeed touch many lives in India: over 20,000 people have died so far, over 10,000 were seriously injured, 20,000 were disabled, and thousands have suffered the ravages of respiratory disease, madness, cancer, and other unidentified illnesses. The foundations for the explosion were laid in a corporate boardroom in the U.S. and then shipped to India: the plan to mass manufacture Sevin Carbaryl, which would generate large quantities of a by-product called Methyl Isocynate (MIC)—the most poisonous chemical known to man.

Long before this "accident" the effects of MIC were seen in nearby residents, who experienced diseases unknown to medical science, as well as in animals, which died near the company drainage pipe. When animals were found dead near the pipe, the company responded with cash. After this, it became a routine practice for animals that died of old age to be tossed into the effluent by their owners so they could collect compensation from the company. While the company succeeded in silencing the villagers about the "loss of their animals," MIC continued to make its way into the bloodstreams of the neighboring people, with tragic effects. Women gave birth to deformed babies and infant mortality rose to alarming levels.

As environmental awareness and labor costs rise in the West, multinationals relocate their manufacturing operations to the Third World, where wages are ludicrously low and environmental regulations are virtually nonexistent. They do so by convincing the unpopular Third World states that poverty is their greatest environmental hazard. Mr. Warren Anderson then chief of Indian subsidiary's parent company put it succinctly when he said, "*Without the technology and the capital multinationals help to introduce, developing countries would have little hope of eradicating poverty and hunger.*" The MIC-based method of manufacturing Sevin Carbaryl was banned in Europe and the U.S.—an example, it would seem, of the multinationals placing a higher value on Western lives than on lives in the Third World.

Public analysis of Bhopal in the U.S. did little to lay the groundwork for the kind of change that will protect victims in the Third World from unequal treatment, dumping, negligence, and the callous behavior of multinationals. For example, Dow Chemical, which bought Union Carbide in 2001, refuses to clean up the waterbed in Bhopal. The waterbed is contaminated with over twenty known carcinogens. While governments, papers, Union Carbide's lawyers, and the company's new owner continue to speculate about who is responsible, the poor people of Bhopal have no choice but to live with poisoned water.

Bhopal is a vivid and painful reminder of corporate inhumanity, an example of callous mass murder legitimized in the name of progress, development, and the state. It does not grab the headlines anymore, but the Bhopal Syndrome lives on. Even after twenty years, mothers who inhaled poisonous gas on or after the explosion are giving birth to horribly deformed babies. While still in the womb, babies are inheriting unformed limbs, melted skin, and holes in their brain tissue. This is a fundamental attack on the God-given right of children to be born healthy and free from bodily harm.

In their death, the victims of Bhopal have given us a sense of awareness. Let no Bhopals happen anywhere in the world ever again.

RAHUL VARMA
MONTREAL, 2002

FOREWORD BY GUILLERMO VERDECHHIA

Nineteen years ago, highly toxic methyl isocyanate (used in the manufacture of the insecticide Sevin) leaked from a Union Carbide factory in Bhopal, India, killing thousands of people while they slept, and poisoning hundreds of thousands more in what is now acknowledged as the worst industrial accident in history. The repercussions of this "accident" can still be felt. Over 20,000 people have died to date and an estimated 150,000 people continue to suffer from the long-term effects of gas exposure: reduced vision and cancer, as well respiratory, neurological, and gynecological disorders. Children of survivors are born deformed and endure severe menstrual disorders.

The Union Carbide site (at the center of this populous city) has never been properly cleaned up. Chemical wastes continue to poison people living near the abandoned factory. Testing conducted by Greenpeace in 1999 found chemicals known to cause cancer, brain damage, and birth defects in the soil and groundwater in and around the factory site, at levels up to 50 times higher than U.S. Environmental Protection Agency safety limits. Mercury levels were 20,000 to 6 million times higher than levels accepted by the World Health Organization. A 2002 study by the Fact-Finding Mission on Bhopal found traces of lead and mercury in the breast milk of nursing women.

Dow Chemical bought Union Carbide in 2001. Dow publicly claims to be "a leading science and technology company . . . committed to the principles of sustainable development" that "seek[s] to balance economic, environmental and social responsibilities." The company, however, has refused to accept any responsibility for cleaning up the Bhopal site, claiming they acquired only Union Carbide's assets when they bought the company, not its liabilities. In December 2002, when 200 survivors of the Bhopal disaster staged a protest at Dow Chemical's Mumbai head office, demanding that Dow take responsibility for cleaning the site, Dow responded by suing the protesters the equivalent of $10,000 U.S. for "loss of work."

Dow Chemical isn't the only corporation that makes grand claims about its mission and then behaves with utter disregard for everything but its bottom line. Monsanto, for example, which makes genetically modified wheat, artificial growth hormones for dairy cows, and herbicides, is one of many other corporations whose lofty rhetoric obfuscates disreputable practices. In its company Pledge, Monsanto claims it "will deliver high-quality products that are beneficial to our customers and the environment." They will also "show respect to our employees, communities, customers, other key stakeholders and the environment." This Pledge issues from the company that sues farmers when its genetically modified wheat blows into their fields; the company whose genetically-modified canola has contaminated organic canola fields making it necessary for growers to abandon their canola rotations; the company that has been fined hundreds of millions of dollars for PCB poisoning; the company that has sued dairy producers for accurately labelling the milk they produce as "Artificial-Growth Hormone Free"; the company whose director of corporate communications told the *New York Times* on October 25, 1998, that the corporation should not have to take responsibility for the safety of its food products. "Monsanto should not have to vouchsafe the safety of biotech food," Phil Angell said. Cutting through the newspeak of the company's Pledge, he explained, "Our interest is in selling as much of it as possible."

Monsanto's hypocrisy doesn't end there. They claim that, "as part of the sharing element of the Monsanto Pledge, the company has provided fundamental scientific information, technology, and know-how to help growers in developing as well as developed nations." Claims regarding the munificence of our intentions and the beneficence of Western technology have been put forward before. In fact, Union Carbide's operations in Bhopal were explained in a similar way.

Warren Anderson, Union Carbide's CEO: "Without the technologies and the capital that multinationals help to introduce, developing countries would have little hope of eradicating poverty and hunger. In India alone it is estimated that pesticides alone save 10% of the annual food crop, enough to feed 70 million people."

Shortly after the Bhopal disaster *The Wall Street Journal* argued: " . . . it is worthwhile to remember that the Union Carbide insecticide plant and the people surrounding it were there for compelling reasons. India's agriculture had been thriving bringing a better life to millions of rural people, and partly because of the use of modern agricultural technology that includes applications of insect killers . . . "

To what degree were these claims accurate or defensible?

Union Carbide and other companies that produced fertilizers, herbicides, and pesticides, were part of a massive effort during the 1970s and 1980s known as the Green Revolution. This term described a movement that aimed to increase food yields through the use of new strains of food crops, irrigation, fertilizers, pesticides, and mechanization. The Green Revolution promised to harness the power of science, technology and industrial development to tackle hunger in the developing or Majority World. Unfortunately, the promises of the Green Revolution were never realized.

While some increases in yields were seen (not as spectacular as initially hoped) the Green Revolution also increased the disparity between rich and poor farmers. Only wealthy farmers with large plots of land could afford and use the mechanized equipment required for this type of farming. These farmers displaced or evicted the sharecroppers who then crowded into city slums (such as the one surrounding the UC plant in Bhopal).

Furthermore, the high yield varieties that were promoted and grown during the Green Revolution (and today) did not feed the hungry. The Green Revolution favored cereals, whereas the Majority World's poor typically eat peas, beans, and lentils. The "surplus" food the Green Revolution produced was exported to wealthy countries.

Business Week magazine noted, "even though Indian granaries are overflowing now," because of increased wheat and rice yields, "5,000 children die each day of malnutrition. One-third of India's 900 million people are poverty-stricken." And consequently can't afford to buy the "surplus" food. The World Bank noted in a 1986 report that simply increasing the amount of food available would not address the problem of hunger. To deal with hunger it would be necessary to "redistribute purchasing power and resources toward those who are undernourished." The Green Revolution did the opposite. And it made even those farmers who could afford the growth it offered more dependent on foreign technology, chemical products, and machinery. (A little over a decade ago, cotton farmers in Gujarat sprayed their cotton 6 to 8 times a year; today they spray 20 to 30 times a year).

Clearly, the claims made for Green Revolution technology were at best overstated, at worst outright lies. The fundamental reasons for Western corporate activity in the developing world were obscured at the time of the Bhopal disaster and remain so today.

Susan George, author of *How the Other Half Dies,* summed up the Green Revolution as "a complex system for foreign agribusiness domination of how, where, and what 3rd World farms will produce and at what cost." What then is the new agricultural revolution, the biotech version—trumpeted as the ultimate free market answer to hunger—but a complex system for agribusiness domination of the very genetic structure of life?

If this assertion appears hyperbolic or hysterical, consider the more than 30 U.S. patents on India's Neem tree, and on the indigenous knowledge about the tree's properties and uses. Consider the patents held by pharmaceutical firms Pfizer, Merck, and Bristol-Myers Squibb on various bacteria and fungi. Consider the $100 million earned annually by Eli Lilly from two drugs derived from the rosy periwinkle, a plant found only in the rainforest of Madagascar, which has received nothing in return for the plant's exploitation; consider the efforts to patent basmati rice, which has been cultivated for centuries by farmers on the foothills of the Himalayas. Finally, consider Monsanto's so-called "Terminator" Technology—the genetic modification of plants to prevent them from producing viable seeds. These bio-engineered plants "terminate" their own life cycles, preventing farmers from storing seeds and forcing them to return annually to Monsanto to buy more.

Of course, farmers aren't stupid. They can see through Monsanto's (and

similar) claims and pledges "to deliver high-quality products that are beneficial to our customers and the environment." Farmers in the Majority World
have consistently resisted the introduction of these second wave Green Revolution products. In India, a campaign of civil disobedience, Operation Cremate
Monsanto, has burned test fields of genetically modified crops. The world's
largest agricultural research institute, the Consultative Group on International
Agricultural Research (CGIAR), has banned "terminator technology" from
their crop breeding programs. They refuse to incorporate any genetic systems
designed to prevent seed germination because of "concerns over potential risks
of its inadvertent or unintended spread through pollen; the possibilities of sale
or exchange of inviable seed for planting; the importance of farm-saved seed,
particularly to resource-poor farmers; potential negative impacts on genetic
diversity, and the importance of farmer selection and breeding for sustainable
agriculture."

These challenges to corporate attempts to control the basic building blocks
of life are critical. But the fight is an uphill one because the stakes and spoils are
enormous, perhaps unprecedented. Atal Bihari Vajpayee, the ex Prime Minister
of India has proclaimed that "Biotechnology is a frontier area of science with a
high promise for the welfare of humanity. . . . I am confident that fruits of biotechnology would be harnessed for the benefit of millions of poor people as we
move into the next millennium."

Of course science and developing technology offer great possibilities for
humanity. The problem lies in the responsible application and control of those
technologies. This problem is at the heart of Rahul Varma's play. He is expert
at revealing the web of interests, competing, colliding, intermittent, colluding,
opportunistic, overt, covert, conscious, and unconscious, that underscore arguments and proposals about wealth and economic development. His play is a
powerful memorial and a tocsin. We would do well to listen, to remember, to
remain vigilant, and to resist.

GUILLERMO VERDECCHIA

TORONTO, 2004

ACKNOWLEDGMENTS

India's pre-eminent theatre artist Dr. Habib Tanvir, who conducted the very
first workshop on the basis of a one-page synopsis I showed him during his
visit to Montreal in 1997. His workshop taught me how to approach this play.
In 2002 he translated *Bhopal* into Hindi as *Zahreeli Hawa*. The production of
Zahreeli Hawa in Bhopal and other cities of India under Habib Tanvir's direction is a dream come true. Dr. Tanvir's association with this play is a matter of
great honor for me.

Directors Tapan Bose and Suhasini Mulay, for their documentary *Bhopal: Beyond Genocide,* which exposed me to the heart wrenching image of Zarina, a baby girl born after the accident.

Satinath Sarangi, Rashida Bie, and Champa Devi, most dedicated and tenacious activists, who introduced me to many of the survivors of Bhopal.

Dr. Daya Varma, my father, who started his research on the survivors of the Bhopal disaster within a month of the "accident." His untiring commitment to social causes continues to inspire me, and was the motivating force behind Dr. Sonya Labonté's character in *Bhopal.* Mrs. Krishna Varma, my mother, who is an example of resilience.

Paul Lefebvre, for his insightful dramaturgy and the translation of *Bhopal* into French.

Jack Langedijk, under whose direction *Bhopal* premiered in Montreal (2001). His contribution to the play went beyond that of a director and production dramaturge.

Guillermo Verdecchia, who sharpened my way of seeing this play. Dramaturges Ann Van Burik, Peter Hinton, and Brian Quirt for their valuable thoughts. My friend Sally Han who represents a turning point in my playwriting pursuit.

Kathryn Cleveland, who played a much bigger role in the premiere production in Montreal than what the title of Stage Manager suggests. Tracy Martin for designing an eye-catching poster for the play.

Ken McDonough, my friend, for editing my work with a deep understanding of all I write. Ted Little, Laurel Sprengelmeyer, Anisa Cameron, and Carlo Proto, whose mere presence is a source of confidence.

My wife, Dipti, and my five-year-old daughter, Aliya—their role cannot be described in a one-line acknowledgment. My late step-brother Sanjay who was a committed environmentalist. Ila, Sonia, Sarah. Family. My brother Prem Saroj, all my nieces and nephews, who keep alive my attachment to India.

Bhopal was developed at the Cahoots Theatre Projects' Lift Off program; Teesri Duniya Theatre's intercultural play development program, Fireworks; and in the *PlayRites Colony 2000* at the Banff Centre for the Arts.

The author gratefully acknowledges the financial assistance from the Canada Council for the Arts, the Conseil des arts et des lettres du Québec, and Conseil des arts de Communauté Urbaine de Montréal.

Bhopal

Devraj, an Indian businessman trained at the knee of Anderson, the American CEO of Karbide International, returns to his native country to head Karbide's Bhopal plant. A man of missionary zeal, he comes armed with a purpose:

to introduce India to the miraculous properties of Karbide Thunder, the latest chemical weapon in the arsenal against pests. He will feed his starving nation, while sharing with its poor the benefits of Western-style industrial development.

Sonya Labonté, a Canadian doctor, is suspicious. People near the plant are getting sick. Babies are being born with horrible abnormalities. With the patience of a Sherlock Holmes, she gathers evidence and mounts her case. The final piece of evidence? A young baby named Zarina.

The play *Bhopal* tells the story of how complex forces struggled to bury the truth, expose it, or shape it to the needs of self-interest, and how an unspeakable disaster ended all speculation. Ultimately, though, it is about—and for—those without means or influence, whose voices are seldom heard and yet who are made to pay the cost.

Bhopal was first produced in Montreal by the Teesri Duniya Theatre at the Arts Interculturels from November 15 to December 9, 2001, with the following cast:

Dr. Sonya Labonté	Rachell Glait
Izzat Bai	Micheline Dahlander,
Mr. Devraj Sarthi	Shomee Chakrabartty,
Minister Jaganlal Bhandari	Ivan Smith,
Madiha Akram	Millie Tresierra,
Pascale Sauvé	Nikija Malialin,
Mr. Warren Anderson	Frank Fontaine,
Story Teller	Shalini Lal,
Chorus	Andrea Cochrane, Cortney Lohnes, Young Choi, Dipti Gupta and Aliya Varma
Director	Jack Langedijk
Stage Manager	Kathryn Cleveland
Set Designer	Sheida Shojai
Light Design	Andrew Calamatas.
Music	Scott Murray and Brian Vockeroth
Poster Designer	Tracy Martin

Bhopal's Hindi translation, *Zahreeli Hawa,* was produced by Naya Theatre (India) in December 2002 under the direction of Habib Tanvir. The play toured six cities in India with the following cast:

Dr. Sonya Labonté	Terry Allen
Izzat Bai	Aagesh Naag
Mr. Devraj Sarthi	Ram Chandra Singh

Minister Jaganlal Bhandari	Uday Ram Srivas
Madiha Akram	Choity Ghosh
Pascale Sauvé	Rajive Yadava
Mr. Warren Anderson	David Francis
Chorus	Manoj Nayar, Yoshiko Vada, Rana Pratap Singh, Chandra Bhan Patel, Sheikh Arif, Sanyay Singh, Shyama Markaam, Nageen Tanvir, Tahira, Manharan Gandrarva, Chaitram Yadva, Amardas Manikpuri, Ramashankar Rishi, Shivdayal Devdas, Dhannulal Sinha, Tajnoor, Onkardas Manikpuri, Abhisar Bose, Usman.
Translator	Habib Tanvir
Director	Habib Tanvir
Stage Manager	Sheikh Arif
Costume	Monika Misra Tanvir
Set Design	Akhilesh Verma
Light Design	Dhannu Lal Sinha, Terry Allen
Music and Sound Effects	Nageen Tanvir
Publicity	Madan Soni
Harmonium	Rama Shankar Rishi
Tabla	Amardas manikpuri
Dholak	Shivdayal Devdas
Majira	Manharan Gandrarva

Bhopal was produced by Cahoots Theatre Projects at the Theatre Centre, Toronto from October 19 to November 9, 2003, with the following cast:

Dr. Sonya Labonté	Brooke Johnson
Izzat Bai	Yashoda Ranganathan
Mr. Devraj Sarthi	Sugith Varughese
Minister Jaganlal Bhandari	Errol Sitahal
Madiha Akram	Imali Perera
Pascale Sauvé	Michael Miranda
Mr. Warren Anderson	Tom Butler
Director	Guillermo Verdecchia
Producer	Carlo Proto
Stage Manager	Sarah Dagleish
Set and Costume	Camellia Koo

Light Design/Production Manager	Michelle Ramsay
Sound Designer	Darren Copeland
Assistant Directors	Jovanni Sy
	Oporajito Bhattacharjee
Assistant Stage Manager	Sherry Roher
Sound and Projection Operator	Jess Lyons

CHARACTERS

DR. SONYA LABONTÉ, *A Canadian doctor and an activist who works with slum dwellers in Bhopal, India. She is the head of a Canadian NGO based in Bhopal India.*

IZZAT BAI, *A young mother who lives in a Bhopal slum.*

MR. DEVRAJ SARTHI, *Head of the Indian subsidiary of an American multinational called Karbide International. The company produces a pesticide called Karbide Thunder. He is an Indian national who was trained in the U.S. and has returned to head Karbide International.*

JAGANLAL BHANDARI, *Chief Minister of the state in which the city of Bhopal exists.*

MADIHA AKRAM, *An employee at Karbide International. She is the personal assistant and lover of Mr. Sarthi.*

PASCALE SAUVÉ, *Canadian Deputy Minister on a special assignment in India.*

MR. WARREN ANDERSON, *President and the supreme head of the parent Karbide International.*

CHORUS, *Consisting of men, women, and children. (See note below)*

Note about the Chorus: *The chorus plays a wide range of roles, such as police officers, photographers, minister's aids, office workers, crowds, patients, and doctors' assistants. I have restricted the chorus to nonspeaking roles and have underwritten its action(s). The size of the chorus is flexible. The Montreal production had a five-member chorus, while the Indian production had over twenty members.*

SPECIAL CREDIT: The song "Ek Zahreeli Hawa" was written by Dr. Habib Tanvir especially for this play. "Aise kihis bhagwan" is a tribal song from the state of Madhya Pradesh, which Dr. Tanvir found in his book archives.

SONG

(The play starts with a song. A dancer performs the "Zahreeli Hawa" [poisoned gas] dance.)

Song   Gaib say chalnay lagee jub
            Ek Zahreeli Hawa
            Dil kay phapholo say bhari

Kis kis kay nalo say bhari
Khamosh cheekho say bhari
Yeay kahan say utha rahi hai aisi dardili hawa
Gaib say chalnay lagee jub
Ek Zahreeli Hawa.

Ek mauzay lahoo aa rahee hai
Maut ki jaisi boo aa rahi hai
Kubooku suboosu aa rahi hai
Apni bayrangi maien bhi hai ek zara peeli hawa
Gaib say chalnay lagee jub ek Zahreeli Hawa.

SCENE 1

(Slum. IZZAT's hut. The police are taking Sonya away. Crowd follows them saying, "Police, police." DEVRAJ enters and stands at the mouth of IZZAT's hut. Slum dwellers start to converge at some distance, watching DEVRAJ. DEVRAJ knocks at IZZAT's door. IZZAT charges out of the hut.)

IZZAT: Who is it? *(Shocked, seeing DEVRAJ. Turns to crowd)* Get the hell out of here, you no good rascals. What are you doing here? Uh??? *(Crowd disperses. To DEVRAJ)* Oh forgive me *sahib*, I thought some police *wallah* . . . bloody father of law. Not a moment of peace from them . . . You forgive me *sahib*?

DEVRAJ: Why do you seek forgiveness?

IZZAT: *Sahib,* I'm a poor woman, rotting in this slum. What do I know about law and order?

DEVRAJ: You don't need to worry.

IZZAT: How can I not worry, *sahib*? Who knows when one of them shows up, orders me to get lost, and flattens my hut . . .

DEVRAJ: That goat of yours . . . the one that died?

IZZAT: Yes, *sahib*. I'm not lying. My child lived on her milk. My own, my own chest, *sahib*, dried up long ago. I swear, *sahib*, my goat died. Do you want to check?

DEVRAJ: I believe you. *(Gives her money)* Here, keep this.

IZZAT: *Maherbani sahib,* may God give you happiness, may you live a long life.

DEVRAJ: Let's go inside.

IZZAT: *Hai bhagawan.* My hut is uninhabitable for your comfort, *malik*. What can I offer you? My food may be too strong for your stomach. My water is undrinkable, for your standard. *(Laughs)* Even I cannot digest my food, *malik,* how will you?

DEVRAJ: I need to talk to you. Let's go in.

(They step inside the hut.)

IZZAT: *Sahib,* I'll run to the tea stall. A *tarak chai* or *masala?*[1]

DEVRAJ: Don't bother.

IZZAT: I'm a poor woman, *sahib,* but I can't let you leave without sweetening your mouth, *sahib.* . . . Won't be long. Just from across the street . . .

DEVRAJ: Just stay. I don't have much time.

(*A feeble sound of a baby is heard from a wooden basket.* IZZAT *picks up the basket.*)

DEVRAJ: What's that?

IZZAT: My Zarina! My little daughter.

DEVRAJ: *(Looks inside)* Oh God! What has happened to her?

IZZAT: Don't let her fool you, *sahib.* She's a tough little monkey. God willing, she'll make me smile one day.

DEVRAJ: Did you bring her to a doctor?

IZZAT: Doctor Sonya Labonté, *sahib,* lady doctor Sonya!

DEVRAJ: Oh really! She's a good doctor . . .

IZZAT: But she doesn't know what Zarina has.

DEVRAJ: Well, does she know what you have?

IZZAT: Me, *sahib?*

DEVRAJ: You have poverty. Does the lady doctor Sonya know this?

IZZAT: What?

DEVRAJ: If you weren't poor, Zarina wouldn't be sick.

IZZAT: What are you saying, *sahib?*

DEVRAJ: Your little Zarina—she wasn't born sick, was she?

IZZAT: She, *sahib?* She was so sweet, her skin so smooth, so shiny, she looked like an angel at birth. Now she's always sick.

DEVRAJ: Of course. I don't know how you survive surrounded by filth.

IZZAT: Cleaning up filth costs money, *sahib.* Where's the money?

DEVRAJ: It's the filth that's the mother of all diseases. Among animals and among children! Someone told me there are other babies sick like Zarina. And they go to see this lady doctor, Dr. Sonya?

IZZAT: Yes, yes. I know them. I bring her patients.

DEVRAJ: Are they getting better?

IZZAT: Well . . . Veena, her baby . . . no! Budhiya . . . no, no, no, they don't get better.

DEVRAJ: Do you know Dr. Hans Weil?

IZZAT: No, *sahib.*

DEVRAJ: He lives behind the factory.

IZZAT: The yellow house?

DEVRAJ: That one. The yellow house! He is a tall man.

IZZAT: Pink skin. Thick cigar. I know who it is.

[1] Super hot tea or masala tea.

DEVRAJ: *(Gives her a card)* Give him this. Take Zarina to him.

IZZAT: Yes.

DEVRAJ: And if anybody's animal dies, let me know. I will compensate.

IZZAT: Shanta's goat died yesterday and Kachari's pig passed away last week. You give me the money, *sahib,* and I will give it to them.

DEVRAJ: Thank you, but I prefer to give them the money myself.

IZZAT: *Theek hai, sahib.*

DEVRAJ: You give me the names of the mothers who visit this Doctor Sonya for their sick children.

> *(*IZZAT *picks up the basket. She holds* DEVRAJ's *card in her hand. She says the names of other women.* DEVRAJ *repeats the names after her.)*

IZZAT: Sure, *sahib.* Sure. Here. Veena, Budhiya, Kasturi, Shanta, Farida, Phool-mati, Babban, Meeta, Imarti, Roshni, Rani . . .

DEVRAJ: Not a word of that to Dr. Sonya. This is between you and me. Can you keep it that way?

IZZAT: My lips are sealed. I give you my word, *sahib.*

> *(*DEVRAJ *leaves.* IZZAT *says blessings for him.)*

SCENE 2

> *(Detention cell. Chief Minister* JAGANLAL *talking to Sonya Labonté.)*

SONYA: For kidnapping?

JAGANLAL: Yes, for kidnapping.

SONYA: Have you gone completely insane?

JAGANLAL: Is that the way to talk to the chief minister?

SONYA: Who is charging me?

JAGANLAL: Doctor Labonté, I trusted you. I gave you a seat on the advisory board of one of my most important missions. I even granted you privileges reserved only for Indians. How can you stand there and tell me with a straight face that you were not abusing the privileges I granted you?

SONYA: Abusing? I have simply been carrying out the research you—

JAGANLAL: We both know you've been doing a great deal more than that. You have lost your perspective and completely overstepped the boundaries of your study.

SONYA: I'm just trying to help the women in your city. It's obvious what the problems are. Karbide is poisoning the—

JAGANLAL: Doctor, these are unfounded, uncorroborated allegations and—

SONYA: Have you read my research? Did you read any of the interim reports? Can anyone in your office read?

JAGANLAL: Your research will be impounded until we get to the bottom of this scam.

SONYA: You haven't even looked at it!

JAGANLAL: Whether or not I have read your material is not the issue, doctor. The issue is kidnapping. You have tried to smuggle two Indian citizens out of the country.

SONYA: I need to call my embassy.

JAGANLAL: You *need* to?

SONYA: I'm a Canadian citizen.

JAGANLAL: Therefore what?

SONYA: I am a field physician with an UN-sanctioned NGO.

JAGANLAL: I've seen many such missionaries from the West.

SONYA: Mr. Minister, you can't do this to me!

JAGANLAL: Yes I can. Poor, hungry, destitute they may be, doctor, but the children of my country are sacred.

(JAGANLAL *exits.*)

SCENE 3

(Detention cell. Canadian diplomat PASCAL SAUVÉ *enters.)*

SAUVÉ: *(Presenting his business card)* Pascal Sauvé, Government of Canada.

SONYA: They won't tell me who is charging me.

SAUVÉ: It's my duty to help troubled Canadians abroad.

SONYA: They're trying to bury my research.

SAUVÉ: Well, then let's get you out of here.

SONYA: These charges are completely trumped up. The minister or somebody close to him doesn't like the work I'm doing and they've invented this. My research points to some very serious problems and they think they can scare me and I'll just stop.

SAUVÉ: Doctor, all I want to do is get you back home safely.

SONYA: I don't want to go home. I want to get out of here, clear my name, and do my work.

SAUVÉ: *(Pulls out some papers from her suitcase)* Well, first we need to work through some problems before we can say what will happen.

SONYA: You believe me, don't you?

PASCAL: *(Showing her a document)* This, I believe, is yours.

SONYA: What's that?

PASCAL: A requisition for two plane tickets.

SONYA: Okay.

SAUVÉ: *(Pulls out a visa document)* And a visa application for Izzat.

SONYA: Isn't that supposed to be confidential?

SAUVÉ: What? The application or the fact that you signed for her?

SONYA: Nothing wrong with that! She gave me a right to—

SAUVÉ: Nothing to worry about then. *(Pointing at the photograph on the visa document)* So you know this woman?

SONYA: Izzat. Yes.

SAUVÉ: What is your relationship with her?

SONYA: She's one of my study subjects.

SAUVÉ: What did you tell her, Dr. Labonté?

SONYA: About what?

SAUVÉ: I need to know what you told her.

SONYA: *(In frustration)* I told her I was doing a study on women's health. That I would be collecting data pertaining to women's reproductive health in the slum. I would be examining women and their babies.

SAUVÉ: And did you promise her treatment if she came to Canada?

(Flashback: Sonya's clinic. IZZAT *lying on the floor. Sonya is examining* IZZAT'S *stomach and vaginal area. Member(s) of the chorus have become* SONYA'S *assistant(s).* ZARINA'S *basket sits nearby.)*

IZZAT: My stomach burns, feels hot inside.

SONYA: Are you menstruating normally?

IZZAT: I bleed a lot.

SONYA: Thick and dry?

IZZAT: A lot of mucky blood.

SONYA: Open your legs.

IZZAT: No, *doctorni sahiba,*[2] no, my . . . this thing is a mess.

SONYA: I will have to send you to Dr. Bhalerao.

IZZAT: I don't need this thing anymore. Zarina's father is dead.

SONYA: That's okay. You may sit up. Dr. Bhalerao must see this.

*(*IZZAT *gets up, picks up* ZARINA'S *basket.)*

IZZAT: Don't worry about me, *doctorni sahiba,* you help Zarina.

*(*SONYA *starts examining* ZARINA.*)*

SONYA: And her lungs are . . . weak, Izzat. Her breathing? It's difficult, hard for her. I don't know, can't tell right now, if there's actual tissue damage to the lungs but . . .

IZZAT: Why, doctor?

SONYA: Well, again it's difficult to say exactly, Izzat. There are any numbers of factors involved, many reasons. But given your own condition, the discharge, the cervical erosion—and its consistent with what I'm seeing in a lot of the other women—I think there's a contaminant, poisons, in your body that got into Zarina's body, and—

IZZAT: You help Zarina?

SONYA: Izzat, there's not much I can do here. Her arm is not going to grow. Her breathing. . . . Give her clean water, Izzat, clean milk. Keep her close, warm,

---

[2]Madam lady doctor.

hold her. We can keep her comfortable. I can't promise—
(IZZAT scoops ZARINA up from the basket and moves away.)
IZZAT: No. The company doctor says Zarina—
SONYA: What? Did you go to the company doctor? Hans Weil? Did you? Dr.
   Hans Weil?
IZZAT: Uh?
SONYA: Big hair, moustache?
IZZAT: No.
SONYA: Good.
IZZAT: He came to see me.
SONYA: Give me a straight answer, Izzat.
IZZAT: Sarthi *sahib* came by my hut. He said he wants to help me.
SONYA: Mr. Devraj Sarthi . . . the president of Karbide . . . he came to your hut?
IZZAT: To help me.
SONYA: Money?
IZZAT: God bless his soul.
SONYA: Oh yes, God bless his soul, he'll help you all right. He's the one making
   the poison.
IZZAT: How do you talk?
SONYA: You are forbidden to see another doctor. You come to me if there's a
   problem, Izzat. Go and wash up now.
IZZAT: I'm sorry.
SONYA: Just go.
   *(IZZAT goes to wash her feet. SONYA follows IZZAT and shows her some
   photographs.)*
SONYA: Where are these women?
IZZAT: Hasina? Kasturi??
SONYA: And why haven't they come to see me?
IZZAT: They are not seeing anybody.
SONYA: But I want to see them. I need to examine their babies.
IZZAT: Women are not talking.
SONYA: Why?
IZZAT: That's what we do—we don't talk when we lose someone in the family.
SONYA: So the babies are dead? Their babies are dead? *(IZZAT nods "yes")* Where
   are the bodies? When did they die? Why didn't you come and get me? They
   are crucial to my study.
IZZAT: You never told me.
SONYA: Listen to me carefully, Izzat. What I'm doing is good for you. Under-
   stand? What I am doing for you is something nobody else would do. And it's
   the best thing for Zarina. Do you understand? That's what we talked about
   and you signed it.

IZZAT: Thumbprint?

SONYA: Right and you didn't tell anyone, did you?

IZZAT: Plan to go to Canada? Zarina and me? Thumb-print. No.

SONYA: Good.

(Sonya returns to her charts and files, makes notes. Flashback ends.)

SAUVÉ: Dr. Labonté we didn't give you a grant to fly Izzat to Canada, did we?

SONYA: I did what's best for my patient.

SAUVÉ: She's not your patient. She is a study subject.

SONYA: She is my patient. These women, they don't have doctors. They don't have—

SAUVÉ: What about this company doctor?

SONYA: That doctor is ex-Pentagon.

SAUVÉ: Well, doctor, we fund nongovernmental organizations to promote Canadian values abroad not to—

SONYA: You want me to ignore what is happening to these women? Is that a Canadian value? Karbide is violating more than one of India's laws! The Obnoxious Industry Law says companies like Karbide have to be at least fifteen miles from populous areas.

SAUVÉ: There are so many laws, it is impossible not to break a few. But that's a matter for the Indian officials. Their laws are their business.

SONYA: I can show you my research—or I could if I knew where it was—Karbide is draining toxic waste into the lake, the pond. The children *play* in that water . . . people bathe in it and fall sick of diseases unknown to medical science.

SAUVÉ: Unknown to medical science?

SONYA: If you want to see a human baby that is not necessarily a human baby, go to the slum.

SAUVÉ: Dr. Labonté, I advise you to sign this.

SONYA: I'm not signing anything.

SAUVÉ: You are in serious trouble, doctor. I can get you out of here and back to Canada if you sign this.

SONYA: So they can say I'm guilty? I'm not quitting. These women need me.

SAUVÉ: Well, I leave you to weigh your options.

(SAUVÉ exits.)

SCENE 4

(Waiting area of DEVRAJ's *office.* SAUVÉ *enters.)*

SAUVÉ: I'd like to speak to Sarthi Devraj.

MADIHA: Devraj Sarthi. I'm sorry, but he's not here.

SAUVÉ: When will he be in?

MADIHA: Tomorrow morning at 8 AM!

SAUVÉ: Then I shall come back tomorrow morning

MADIHA: Maybe I can help you.

SAUVÉ: *(Starting to leave)* No thank you, I need to talk to him directly.

MADIHA: I am his executive assistant, you know. I sometimes know more about what goes on here than he does. (SAUVÉ *stops*) So, what trouble is he in?

SAUVÉ: Do you know a Doctor Sonya Labonté?

MADIHA: Yes.

SAUVÉ: Have you ever spoken to her?

MADIHA: Yes, many times. That woman keeps trying to destroy this company.

SAUVÉ: Pardon me?

MADIHA: She accuses us of the most outrageous things.

SAUVÉ: Such as?

MADIHA: All that Mr. Sarthi does is help these people.

> *(Flashback: DEVRAJ's office. IZZAT enters with her basket. MADIHA notices her with annoyance.)*

IZZAT: *Memsahib, memsahib, memsahib.*

MADIHA: Told you, don't call me *memsahib*.

IZZAT: I call *sahib . . . sahib* so I should call *memsahib . . . memsahib.*

MADIHA: Is it a goat? What is it this time? A dog? A rat? We're not paying for any more for your dead animals.

IZZAT: *Sahib* said . . .

MADIHA: *Chalo Raasta Napo.* (Beat. Her eyes on the basket, MADIHA *walks towards* IZZAT) Let me see . . .

IZZAT: No! For *sahib*!

MADIHA: You probably kill them yourself just to get the money. You can dodge him but I'm not a fool.

> *(DEVRAJ enters.)*

MADIHA: Oh, Mr. Sarthi . . . Mr. Sarthi.

IZZAT: *(To DEVRAJ)* I begged the *chowkidar, sahib,* because I wanted to show it to you right in your hand.

DEVRAJ: All right, show me what?

MADIHA: Another dead animal.

DEVRAJ: Miss Akram.

IZZAT: *(To DEVRAJ)* Look, look inside—

MADIHA: Which, I'm sure is not hers—

IZZAT: Getting worse, *sahib*. See one more time, please, *sahib*—

MADIHA: She probably picked it up from the street—

DEVRAJ: Wait, Miss Akram—

MADIHA: Don't pay her a *dhela*.[3]

IZZAT: Oh, please . . . please . . . look.

---

[3] Mud ball. Here it implies "a penny."

MADIHA: She says the company kills their animals. They are doing it them-selves.

IZZAT: *(To* MADIHA*)* No, no. You look. (MADIHA *pulls away the rag covering the basket and is visibly shocked at what she sees inside. We hear* ZARINA's *cry.* IZZAT *grabs the basket and runs to a corner. A hush sets in.)*

DEVRAJ: *(To* MADIHA*)* This is her baby. *(To* IZZAT*)* What do you want me to do? Didn't you bring her to Hans? Dr. Hans Weil?

IZZAT: I did. But she's getting worse.

DEVRAJ: He will treat her. I am not a doctor. *(Puts two one-hundred rupee notes in her palm)*

(Flashback ends.)

MADIHA: Mr. Sarthi goes out of his way to help these people and she tries—

SAUVÉ: Dr. Labonté?

MADIHA: Yes. She tries to twist it into something awful.

SAUVÉ: Does she?

MADIHA: Mr. Sarthi makes the company doctor available to these women and Labonté comes here, right into the office, and accuses the company doctor of stealing her patients, taking mothers and their babies from her clinic. Those women come here for money; they are very skilled beggars. It makes no sense. And she claims Karbide Thunder is poisonous. That the company is poisoning these people in their shacks around the factory. As if the company would do such a thing. We manufacture pesticides, you know. These chemicals, they improve the lives of everyone. If you could hear Devraj talk about how Karbide Thunder will change everyone's life, you'd soon see that that woman has malice in her heart.

SAUVÉ: I see.

MADIHA: I see you're from Canada?

SAUVÉ: Yes.

MADIHA: Take her back, and keep her there. We have enough problems.

SAUVÉ: Thank you for your time.

*(*SAUVÉ *departs.)*

SCENE 5

(A party hosted by JAGANLAL. *Festive mood. Chorus members act as guests.* DEVRAJ *and* MADIHA *enter.* JAGANLAL *greets them with great enthusiasm.)*

JAGANLAL: Ladies and gentlemen, Mr. Devraj Sarthi!

DEVRAJ: Thank you, Mr. Minister. What have I done to deserve such an honor?

JAGANLAL: I want to shake your hand, Mr. Sarthi. You're a great NRI.

DEVRAJ: NRI?

MADIHA: Nonresident Indian.

JAGANLAL: Not really Indian! Har, har, har . . . and *aadab* to you Madam . . . ?

MADIHA: *(Shaking hands with* JAGANLAL*)* Madiha Akram, Mr. Minister.

JAGANLAL: How so very wonderful to see women acting as equals. You have no idea how much I have anticipated this dinner tonight. Are you prepared to make a speech?

DEVRAJ: Speech?

JAGANLAL: A little after-dinner speech!

MADIHA: Of course, do it!

DEVRAJ: On the People's Progress Zone?

JAGANLAL: How must I introduce you? People say you're blinded by your feelings for the poor.

MADIHA: No doubt about that.

JAGANLAL: And you're an animal lover.

MADIHA: In a strange sort of way . . .

JAGANLAL: How so? How must I point that out?

MADIHA: He created the Animal Charity Fund.

JAGANLAL: I've heard great things about that.

DEVRAJ: The Animal Charity Fund is a public service. Sometimes, especially now due to this drought, animals die and people leave the dead animals on the streets.

MADIHA: And when they start to rot they contaminate the drinking water.

DEVRAJ: Thank you, Miss Akram. *(Turns to* JAGANLAL*)* Yes, in order to prevent disease from spreading, we encourage the people to bring the dead animals to Karbide International and we compensate them. That helps *them,* and certainly doesn't hurt our company image. That's what I call the Animal Charity Fund.

JAGANLAL: Animal Charity Fund, compensation. . . . Brilliant! Just brilliant.

MADIHA: Charity.

JAGANLAL: Excellent. Until yesterday, America had sent India its hippies, druggies, and devotees. In you, Mr. Sarthi, I see a new man. An exceptional NRI who went to America to learn, design, and build, and then returned to heal his home country.

(Flashback: DEVRAJ *being interviewed by* ANDERSON *for the post of CEO of the Indian branch of Karbide International.)*

ANDERSON: I know that, but what city in India?

DEVRAJ: From Lucknow, sir.

ANDERSON: And you've been with the company for eight years?

DEVRAJ: Yes.

ANDERSON: Now you want to go back home?

DEVRAJ: It's just the sort of challenge that I'm looking for. I was friends with the

son of my family's maidservant when I was young. I used to give him half of
my lunch at school. When we grew up, I got a business degree and he ended
up pulling a rickshaw. It was winter when I left for the U.S. and he came to
see me off at the airport. I gave him my coat. As I walked through the gate I
saw my mother, superior as always, walk up to him with a dirty look on her
face and I'm sure an insulting taunt on her tongue. Right then and there, I
swore to myself that I'd come back.
(Beat.)

ANDERSON: What are your thoughts on DDT?

DEVRAJ: In my opinion, sir, Karbide Thunder will replace DDT.

ANDERSON: You'd like to be known as the pest that killed DDT.

DEVRAJ: Because DDT has been found in bird populations.

ANDERSON: Aw, poor birds. *(Testing him)* What about the millions it has saved
from malaria?

DEVRAJ: But it's a carcinogen. I believe, sir, that Karbide Thunder is a superior product. Not only does it spare the bird population, it's also non-
carcinogenic.

ANDERSON: I'm sure you're aware there are scientific studies that suggest there
are other deleterious side effects.

DEVRAJ: I would put my faith in scientific studies if they truly prove the point
they claim to be proving. But, we know, one study proves a product is a
health hazard, another proves the contrary. So I plan to prove something
that's beyond any doubt, and that is that Karbide Thunder is safer than DDT,
cheaper to produce than DDT, and sure to tilt India's trade potential.

ANDERSON: And what about Karbide International, Mr. Sarthi? We are, you
know, looking to improve our performance.

DEVRAJ: Sir, India offers us a competitive advantage in many ways.

ANDERSON: I have to tell you that India is looking more and more marginal to us,
Mr. Sarthi. We need someone who will cut costs and improve productivity.

DEVRAJ: Sir, our offshore operations generate fourteen percent of revenue but
account for 23 percent of our profits. I am confident that I can find ways to
make our India operation more efficient and productive. Karbide Thunder
is the key, sir.

ANDERSON: You think so?

DEVRAJ: I'm sure of it, sir.

ANDERSON: I like that, son. The heroes of this world are men who have a vision,
and are willing to take risks.

DEVRAJ: If something can keep hungry millions from starving, it will more than
make up for the risk. Believe me, Mr. Anderson, given the chance, I'll show
you that Karbide Thunder will touch many lives.
(Flashback ends. DEVRAJ resumes his conversation with JAGANLAL.)

JAGANLAL: India needs more men like you.

DEVRAJ: India deserves a shot in the arm.

JAGANLAL: Shot?

DEVRAJ: Boost its production capacity.

JAGANLAL: All poor countries deserve a shot in the arm.

DEVRAJ: India is not poor, sir, it's simply forgotten.

JAGANLAL: It's about time somebody said that.

DEVRAJ: If we want the world to respect us, India's output must be increased tenfold

JAGANLAL: Quite right!

DEVRAJ: Granted your approval, I am prepared to increase our production tenfold.

JAGANLAL: And reduce your costs, I believe?

DEVRAJ: We've discussed the People's Progress Zone. It's like a country within a country.

JAGANLAL: *Achha.*

DEVRAJ: Free of bureaucratic barriers, an area of deregulation.

JAGANLAL: Okay.

DEVRAJ: Such incentives are needed to increase the country's industrial base, to generate wealth, and, yes, to support our efforts to produce profitable chemicals.

JAGANLAL: Pesticides, you mean?

DEVRAJ: As you may have seen in my submission, pesticides have recorded a quarter century of sustained growth. Under the People's Progress Zone plan, we can manufacture upwards of five to ten thousand tons of Karbide Thunder a year. But the quantity is not the important thing.

MADIHA: It's the quality. Pesticides are peaceful. They are not like chemicals of war.

JAGANLAL: Right, they just war against pests . . . har, har, har . . .

MADIHA: Of course. The pests will not be given a chance to eat poor peoples' food and leave them to go hungry. But let me tell you one more thing Mr. Minister. The life of an average Indian today, like myself, like yourself, we live better than the maharajas—because of the kind of chemicals Karbide produces.

JAGANLAL: Yes, yes. Although, Karbide Thunder is used for cotton, not for peoples' food.

DEVRAJ: But pesticides generally improve—

JAGANLAL: Of course. But I'm concerned. I've heard a rumor that Dr. Bhalerao is planning judicial action to stop the People's Progress Zone and Dr. Labonté's study is being cited as a proof of—

MADIHA: That woman? She thinks Karbide Thunder is poisoning everyone.

That woman just won't stop.

DEVRAJ: Miss Akram. *(To* JAGANLAL*)* They are worried someone might drink Karbide Thunder.

JAGANLAL Drink it?

DEVRAJ: As if someone would drink pesticide. But even if Karbide Thunder got into your body . . .

JAGANLAL: My body?

DEVRAJ: . . . it would only cause coughing, sneezing, and minor itching. Then it would be hydrolyzed.

JAGANLAL: *(Sighs)* Aaah . . . *(Thinks)* What?

DEVRAJ: Our company doctor, Hans Weil, confirms that it will roll out via the eyes.

JAGANLAL: Like tears?

DEVRAJ: Like tears!

JAGANLAL: Aaah! . . . Is your Bhopal plant identical to the one in the U.S.?

DEVRAJ: Of course!

JAGANLAL: And Karbide Thunder will roll out of American eyes like ours, in the form of tears?

(DEVRAJ *nods affirmatively.*)

Any proof?

MADIHA: Mr. Minister, let us invite these people to this dinner and feed them Karbide Thunder.

DEVRAJ: Miss Akram?

JAGANLAL: What?

MADIHA: Yes! To prove that it will roll out of their eyes.

JAGANLAL: Brilliant.

DEVRAJ: Of course we wouldn't need to do that.

(Transition to the after-dinner speech.)

DEVRAJ: Mr. Minister, on the way to your office, I passed through the slum. It was filled with open garbage, the heat was suffocating, and the stench of human excrement was unbearable. I stumbled over drunken men, saw babies hanging from their mothers' breasts, and encountered stubborn seven- and eight-year-old boys with faces that said that if I didn't give them some change, they'd die of hunger. I met a woman, a poor woman, who told me that her first child died of worms that crawled out of its body. Why? How did this happen? There are those who will blame industrial development. Chemicals like our Karbide Thunder. Obviously, that is not the case; we always think of safety first. But environmental safeguards are irrelevant if we don't attack poverty first, for it is the poverty that is our greatest environmental hazard. Yes, my efforts aren't reaching the people yet. But with my plan in place, the benefits will trickle all the way down to the poorest of the poor. That's why we need the People's Progress Zone.

(Applause.)

JAGANLAL: That storm of applause is for you.

MADIHA: That was wonderful.

DEVRAJ: Really?

MADIHA: Yes.

JAGANLAL: Mr. Sarthi, that was a very moving speech. People in this room, my staff and dignitaries, froze as you talked, and we now know we want to hear more from you. Yes, you must boost production. *(Announcing)* Ladies and gentlemen, the first gift of the People's Progress Zone. *(Eyes set on* DEVRAJ*)* Karbide will build seven hundred new houses!

DEVRAJ: Seven hundred new houses?

JAGANLAL: But of course! When you expand the Karbide complex . . .

DEVRAJ: But I don't remember promising seven hundred new houses . . .

(Before DEVRAJ *can answer,* JAGANLAL *walks up to him, stands face to face with him, and clasps both his hands in a traditional namastay.)*

JAGANLAL: That Mr. Sarthi must be the necessary gift of Karbide to my people.

*(*JAGANLAL *departs to loud applause from the Chorus.)*

DEVRAJ: Well . . . in that case, I must name it Jaganlal Colony.

(More applause from the dispersing crowd.)

SCENE 6

(Next day. MADIHA *in* DEVRAJ*'s office.* DEVRAJ *enters and grabs her in his arms. She frees herself and steps away from him.)*

MADIHA: Did you see the look in people's eyes?

DEVRAJ: What people?

MADIHA: At the party!

DEVRAJ: People looked victorious seeing the look on my face.

MADIHA: What?

DEVRAJ: When Jaganlal volunteered me to build seven hundred new houses.

MADIHA: I'm not talking about that look.

DEVRAJ: What look are you talking about then?

MADIHA: The look that says, "Look at that slut."

DEVRAJ: Darling, don't start that one.

MADIHA: You know what people think about me?

DEVRAJ: Please!

MADIHA: I blackened my name for you.

DEVRAJ: We have talked about it many times.

MADIHA: So what are you going to do about it?

DEVRAJ: I have something for you. *(Gives her a gift)* Open it.

(Before she can open the gift, he opens it for her.)

MADIHA: Devraj, what is this?

(He puts a locket around her neck.)

DEVRAJ: With this, I make you a promise.

MADIHA: Yes?

DEVRAJ: I'll be yours, I promise, but I can't handle marriage.

MADIHA: Then what's the promise?

DEVRAJ: Marriage like a sacred duty or marriage like a burden? What mother wants for me? The way she married?—It's a no, not for me. We don't need to be married to be together, do we?

(They embrace. Sound effects take us to the next scene.)

SCENE 7

(One week later. JAGANLAL visits the slum with his entourage. Reporters, cameramen, the members of the chorus as citizens and slum dwellers follow him.)

JAGANLAL: No, no, no. Don't take a photo yet. Over here!

(Slum dwellers begin to assemble. JAGANLAL notices IZZAT in the crowd.)

You, *Bai!* *(Calling)* Would you? Yes, yes, please—come here . . . stand here . . . don't move. *(In part to himself and in part to the media)* When I see a woman like you, *bai,* a voice inside me says, "Go hug her. Pick her child up in your arms, and give her your shawl."

(Puts his shawl over her shoulders.)

IZZAT: May God give you long life, *mantri ji.*

JAGANLAL: Okay. Now. Smile. *(She does)* No, no, not like that, like this. *(He models a smile and she imitates him)* Like that, okay. *(Cameras start flashing)* I'm sick of having my photograph taken. If I catch anyone of these photographers, I will shoot to kill . . .

(IZZAT steps out of the photo-shoot.)

IZZAT: Me too, *mantri ji.*

JAGANLAL: I feel very close to you, *bai,* so close that I want to drink from your glass and eat from your plate.

IZZAT: Honor is all mine, *mantri ji,* but I don't have much on my plate.

JAGANLAL: Where is your hut, *bai?*

IZZAT: Do you see this *pagdandi?*

JAGANLAL: I'm standing on it.

IZZAT: This *pagdandi* snakes through garbage, shit, and dead animals.

JAGANLAL: Bad, very bad . . .

IZZAT: All the way to the pond. Do you see the pond?

JAGANLAL: *Haan, haan . . .*

IZZAT: From the pond one *pagdandi* goes this way—to the lake—and the other goes that way—to the company. There, my hut is there.

JAGANLAL: I have decided to demolish it.

IZZAT: Oh, no . . . oh no, please . . . I beg *mantri ji* . . . I'm a poor woman . . .

JAGANLAL: But I am going to do something about it.

IZZAT: *Mantri ji,* please, my husband lost everything to the bottle. And I ended up here. I made my hut behind the railway. The *chowkidar* . . . "*hut haramzadi*" . . .

JAGANLAL: Your hut—

IZZAT: Then, I made a home between the fences and the *mandir* and the *pundit ji* chased me, "*Chal bhag. Bhagwan kay ghar say.*"[3] Then I go . . . under bridge . . . on sidewalk . . . by the gutter . . . "*bhaag, hatt bhaag.*"

JAGANLAL: Now *bai,* your new house—

IZZAT: Finally I made this shack . . . my home . . . in shadow of *sahib's* company . . .

JAGANLAL: But having your home here doesn't make you legal.

IZZAT: In front of all these people . . . *mantri ji,* these people are my witness . . . I don't know rules and regulations. In front of all these people, *mantri ji,* I say I will not leave my hut even if you kill me. In the name of all these people, *mantri ji,* be merciful. *(Showing* ZARINA's *basket)* I have a sick baby.

JAGANLAL: I'm sorry, this hut of yours will be replaced with a house!

IZZAT: What will happen to me, *mantri ji*?

JAGANLAL: You, *bai* . . . you will live in that house.

IZZAT: What?

JAGANLAL: Your hearing is fine, *bai.* You will own the house.

IZZAT: Me? House? Mine? But . . . but . . .

JAGANLAL: But what, *bai*?

IZZAT: It feels like a promise.

JAGANLAL: And didn't I promise a water tap in the *basti* last year?

IZZAT: We were hoping for some water from it this year.

JAGANLAL: Such life—such life here! You are the ray of hope. *(To media, crowd)* This *bai* is right. I hereby announce—and you media people note me and quote me—through the authority vested in me as the chief minister and the head of the new Super Ministry for Trade Liberalization, I declare that Bhopal Lake, the connecting bridge and the railway station—all this area surrounding Karbide International—to be known as the People's Progress Zone, a new, independent governing zone which will also be known as the PPZ.

IZZAT: PeePeeZeee . . .

JAGANLAL: The PPZ will be a model site. A country within a country with distinct rules! To help us help our people. To catch up on decades of

---

[3] Get lost from God's house.

underdevelopment! As of today, all inhabitants of the Peoples Progress Zone will own the piece of land on which their illegal huts sit. *Bai—*

IZZAT: May God give you longest life, *mantri ji,* I'll have a real home. God be merciful, this means a ration card and right to vote!

JAGANLAL: This is not for your vote *bai.* This is for real.

IZZAT: Oh?

JAGANLAL: You are the first citizen of the People's Progress Zone. Yes. And here is a sample of what your home will look like.

(He distributes pictures of model homes to the slum dwellers.)

This is for you. This, *maa ji,* this is for you.

(IZZAT calls other slum dwellers. They are happy, comparing photographs of their prospective homes.)

IZZAT: I live in this, in the paper. Imrati. Babu. Come here. Look, my home . . . window and indoor *snadas* . . . no more shutting the bowel from sunrise to sunset, no, noo . . . no more going behind the bush to do the business. And hey, look, a water tap.

SCENE 8

(One week later. Sauvé, who has just returned from the Canadian High Commission in New Delhi, visits JAGANLAL. *Sauvé opens a document.)*

SAUVÉ: Mr. Minister, may I be frank with you?

JAGANLAL: Please.

SAUVÉ: Either you free Doctor Labonté or lose India's Preferred Trading status.

JAGANLAL: One woman is more important than two countries?

(Sauvé gives him a document.)

SAUVÉ: As you know, our next bilateral trade summit is in Montreal.

JAGANLAL: I will say a line or two in French in my opening speech.

SAUVÉ: The problem is, sir, that Labonté is scheduled to speak at a parallel conference taking place next door to our trade talks.

JAGANLAL: Not if she's in my custody. I won't have anyone distracting attention from my presentation.

SAUVÉ: That's exactly what will happen if you keep her in jail. Protesters will throw themselves against the fences and throw tear gas at a time when the eyes of the world are set on our Prime Minister.

JAGANLAL: You want me to drop the charges against this doctor so your Prime Minister will have one less headache?

SAUVÉ: Quite frankly, sir, it is a trade headache.

JAGANLAL: I don't accept that.

SAUVÉ: Sir, it has taken years to prepare Canada for your trade mission. Our countries are setting an example in bilateral trade that will make the world envious. But when you and your trade delegation arrive in Canada, the media won't leave us alone, sir. Labonté is Canadian, after all, and her arrest is . . . dramatic. It will make things very difficult for us. Canada will be embarrassed and will have a hard time ratifying contracts and treaties signed with you.

JAGANLAL: Free a women who kidnaps mothers and children to bad-mouth my country abroad?

SAUVÉ: Sir, sooner or later the world will come to know that she wasn't kidnapping. She was just trying to bring a mother and her sick child to a conference in Canada. Forgive me for saying this—people would not only see her as a victim, but would also say that you caved in to Karbide.

JAGANLAL: That's nonsense.

SAUVÉ: Sir, I'm pleading for the success of our trade talks. If you don't sign her release, Karbide International will applaud you but Canadian trade and aid to India will not increase.

JAGANLAL: I do not appreciate blackmail from a trade partner.

SAUVÉ: Our government and transnationals don't want to have to answer embarrassing questions about the way a high-profile Canadian is treated by a trade partner. They'll be quite happy to invest in one of the seventy-five countries around the world whose GDP is less than their corporation's profit. You asked me to be frank, I'm being frank.

(Sauvé retrieves the document and moves as if to leave.)

JAGANLAL: What does the document say?

SAUVÉ: It contains an apology: she relinquishes all rights to her research, and accepts a lifetime ban from working in India.

JAGANLAL: Bring her in.

(Sonya enters [is "brought in"].)

JAGANLAL: Is this your first visit to India?

SONYA: First to a jail.

JAGANLAL: The children of my country are not your props.

SONYA: Nor should they be casualties of Karbide—

JAGANLAL: You have been here barely long enough to see a few malnourished kids and—

SONYA: And a lot of poisoned kids.

JAGANLAL: And you're in the habit of not seeing the millions of healthy kids.

SONYA: There aren't any healthy kids in the slums.

SAUVÉ: Well, madam doctor, Mr. Minister, I brought you both here—

JAGANLAL: I want to let this lady know something. *(To Sonya)* Sit down. *(She does)* Maybe your research is accurate, maybe our housing project is a bad idea. Maybe the People's Progress Zone is a big mistake. Maybe the children of Bhopal are really unlike any human beings you have ever seen before. But

I don't need a foreigner to exhibit a sick child of my country in a foreign land. Doctor, we can look after our sick. I resent white people showing me what's best for my people. Anyway, I didn't mean to say that. My last comment wasn't intentional.

SAUVÉ: We understand.

JAGANLAL: Mr. Sauvé has persuaded me to drop the charges against you.

SAUVÉ: You will sign this apology.

SONYA: Apology? For what?

SAUVÉ: That's the deal.

SONYA: Apologize?

SAUVÉ: And accept a lifetime ban.

SONYA: Are you out of your mind? I'll stay here.

(SAUVÉ *takes* SONYA *a few steps away.*)

SAUVÉ: Excuse me, Mr. Minister. Use your head, doctor.

SONYA: Who would believe that bringing a mother and her sick child to Canada is kidnapping?

SAUVÉ: I don't think you live in the real world.

SONYA: Izzat wanted to go. She knew that it was the best thing for her and Zarina.

(SAUVÉ *gives* SONYA *an affidavit.*)

SAUVÉ: This is in English, doctor! The woman didn't know what she was putting her thumbprint on!

SONYA: Bring her here and she will tell you.

SAUVÉ: She's the one who charged you.

SONYA: She did?

(SAUVÉ *pulls* SONYA *aside*)

SAUVÉ: Look Labonté, if you sign now, you can go somewhere else and carry on your research. Maybe—maybe you can find a way to get back to India and resume your work. On the other hand, if you want to be "principled," well, maybe the CBC will do a documentary on you, or environmentalists will circulate an on-line petition for your release, but you won't see daylight for fifteen years. Which one do you want?

(*Sauvé holds up a pen to Sonya, who is silent. He walks towards* JAGANLAL. *Sonya follows. Sauvé gestures both to sign the deal.*)

SONYA: I'll sign this, but it won't shut me up. I'll sign this, but it won't silence me.

SAUVÉ: Mr. Minister.

(JAGANLAL *signs, then* SAUVÉ *puts his own signature.* JAGANLAL *extends his hand to shake* SAUVÉ's, *but* SAUVÉ *in return clasps his hands in traditional namastay.*)

SAUVÉ: *Marché conclu.* (*To* SONYA) This prohibits you from Karbide International and the PPZ. Your plane leaves December third, 1984, at 0100 hours from Bhopal International Airport.

JAGANLAL: A government car will take you to the airport. My people will make sure you catch your plane with no inconvenience.

SAUVÉ: Congratulations, you are allowed to return to Canada.

(SONYA *angrily crushes the deal. Exits.*)

SCENE 9

(*Outside* IZZAT's *hut.* SONYA *enters.* ZARINA's *basket is absent.*)

SONYA: Izzat. How could you be so stupid?

IZZAT: *Mafi, doctorni sahiba!*

SONYA: How much did they pay you? What did you think would happen, eh?

IZZAT: Okay, okay, *doctorni sahiba,* don't shout.

SONYA: Do you know what they've done?

IZZAT: I'm sorry, *doctorni sahiba* . . .

SONYA: You're sorry!! They stole my research. I have nothing to present at the conference. All my surveys, blood, urine, samples—everything—is destroyed. The clinic is bulldozed, and I'll be put on a plane tomorrow night.

IZZAT: You will go?

SONYA: Yes! Zarina would have received the best treatment of her life. Now she will get nothing. . . . Where is Zarina?

IZZAT: She's sleeping.

SONYA: She's alone? I want to see her.

IZZAT: No! My man is back.

SONYA: Your man is dead!

IZZAT: Leave me alone, *doctorni sahiba!*

SONYA: Where is she?

IZZAT: She was my baby, my little angel. I don't want anyone to see her. She was my baby.

SONYA: She's dead? (*Long pause*) Where is her body? They bought her body, didn't they? Money? How much? You sold your baby.

IZZAT: No.

SONYA: Like Hasina.

IZZAT: No.

SONYA: Like Kastoori.

IZZAT: No.

SONYA: You sold your own child.

IZZAT: (*Breaking into tears*) Satan invaded my heart. Satan took money for Zarina. Devil in me did that. Devil lived in my stomach. I don't need this money. (*Pulls out a few rupees from her blouse and throws them towards*

SONYA) Throw this away into the gutter, I don't need it.

SONYA: The Devil lives in the company's poison . . . you fool.

IZZAT: Me, fool?

SONYA: The company killed Zarina and gave you some cash for her dead body and you came home thinking that the company did you an act of charity.

IZZAT: You don't know how I survive, *doctorni sahiba.* Why do you harass me?

SONYA: If money is all you wanted, this is nothing compared to what I could have got for you. You fool.

IZZAT: You? You cannot fool me! No clinic, no research, no treating, nothing, just a big mouth. What you want, huh? You want to take my daughter to a foreign country to show her. What will that say about my daughter? Huh? What will people say? What kind of mother is she, showing her daughter to everyone—her twisted hands, her heaving chest, her melting skin, shame on the mother who did that to her child. And who wants to look at my Zarina? How dare you? My daughter is in peace. I have peace. Why do you come between us? Please, *doctorni sahib,* please, be merciful to me, be merciful to my daughter, let my daughter have peace.

SCENE 10

*(*DEVRAJ'*s office.* DEVRAJ *enters.* SONYA *storms into the office.)*

SONYA: What are you doing? What the hell are you doing?

DEVRAJ: You're not supposed to be here, doctor.

SONYA: Stop it, damn it, stop killing everything that lives around this factory.

DEVRAJ: *Chowkidar!*

SONYA: Your Peoples' Progress Zone, your cover-up.

DEVRAJ: Get on your plane, white woman.

SONYA: Bloody coconut.

MADIHA: This woman does not stop.

SONYA: *(Turning to* MADIHA*)* Do you know what his company has been doing? *(To* DEVRAJ *)* Does she know your company doctor paid my patients for their babies?

DEVRAJ: Out! Out of here!

SONYA: Twenty-seven dead babies—

MADIHA: What is she talking about?

DEVRAJ: Where the hell is security?

SONYA: Was paying for Izzat's baby part of your Animal Charity Fund?

MADIHA: No, that woman is lying. Devraj?

DEVRAJ: *Chowkidar!!*

SONYA: You bought Izzat's baby to destroy evidence.

MADIHA: It was alive . . . the baby was alive.

SONYA: They sold you their dead babies.

DEVRAJ: I want you to leave . . . now!

MADIHA: They brought dead *animals*.

SONYA: You are destroying evidence of murder!

DEVRAJ: To hell with your evidence!

MADIHA: The evidence? The evidence is right here, right inside me. *(To* SONYA*)* I breathe more "poison" than any of those women in the slums. If what you say is true, then my baby must be ten times more deformed.

SONYA: You're damn right, madam, because the company's poison does not discriminate.

MADIHA: Then I'll be a good test case for you.

SONYA: What?

MADIHA: Sign me up for your study. Why not?

SONYA: My study is banned.

MADIHA: I offer my womb regardless.

DEVRAJ: What's wrong with you Madiha?

MADIHA: I'm helping you. I want to shut her mouth. *(Turns to* SONYA*)* To see you posturing *(Imitating her)* "I have this evidence, I have that evidence!" Well *(Pointing at her own stomach)* here is my evidence. When my baby is born, you'll see.

SONYA: *(To* MADIHA*)* I won't be around. *(Turns to* DEVRAJ*)* But how are *you* going to live with it?

(Sonya exits. DEVRAJ *turns to* MADIHA*.)*

DEVRAJ: What the fuck is wrong with you?

MADIHA: For the last two months, I have been thinking about how to break the news to you.

DEVRAJ: What news?

MADIHA: I missed two months.

DEVRAJ: What does that mean?

MADIHA: Yes, yes! I'm pregnant. Aren't you going to say something?

DEVRAJ: How did this happen?

MADIHA: Is that all you can say?

DEVRAJ: That night was the only night.

MADIHA: Are we talking about a single night? Devraj, I just revealed to you the fruit of our relationship.

(They speak over each other.)

DEVRAJ: I thought we had/

MADIHA: I'm going to be the/

DEVRAJ: an understanding.

MADIHA: mother of your child.

DEVRAJ: What do you want me to say?

MADIHA: Say something nice.

DEVRAJ: Are you sure?

MADIHA: Aaaaah . . .

DEVRAJ: Please, how do you know for sure?

MADIHA: I'm hungry, I vomit—of course I know for sure. It's in my body for goodness sake.

DEVRAJ: How long has it been?

MADIHA: Stop talking to me like that.

DEVRAJ: Madiha I think maybe—

MADIHA: What?

DEVRAJ: You could get an abortion.

(MADIHA *slaps him.*)

MADIHA: No. No! I would never do that. Never. Not on my life! This is your baby for God's sake, Devraj!

(*Sound of escaping gas starts, which* DEVRAJ *notices but ignores.*)

DEVRAJ: I'm sorry, I didn't know how to react to news like that.

MADIHA: Hold me in your arms, kiss me.

(*He kisses her.*)

DEVRAJ: It's just that I don't want to do something now that I can't handle later.

MADIHA: You can't handle a baby?

DEVRAJ: What if the baby . . .

MADIHA: What?

DEVRAJ: I mean . . .

MADIHA: What? Is not healthy? Like the babies of those slum women?

DEVRAJ: I mean I'm not prepared to be a father.

MADIHA: Why wouldn't the baby be healthy?

DEVRAJ: I didn't say that.

MADIHA: What is that woman's research about?

DEVRAJ: Her research is nonsense. The slum mothers are not dying of diseases caused by Karbide Thunder, but by poverty. I don't give a toss about Labonté, I'm just nervous at the thought of being a father. Afraid of your motherhood out of wedlock! Afraid of mud slinging! What will everyone say? How will you handle that?

MADIHA: I'm sorry I doubted you, but I only wanted to help you.

DEVRAJ: By betting your baby with that dreadful doctor?

MADIHA: I believe so much in your work, I don't mind betting my womb to shut her mouth.

(DEVRAJ *holds her in his arms, kisses her.*)

DEVRAJ: Oh Madiha you don't understand . . .

(*Deafening thunder starts.*)

(*Looking out*) What the hell is that?

(Sound of thunder rises like a massive earthquake. Sparks start going off in all directions. DEVRAJ's *phone starts ringing. Increasing sounds of chaos. People running in all directions. The noise from the street turns into cries for help.* DEVRAJ *runs to the window.)*

DEVRAJ: God! The plant is burning . . .

MADIHA: Oh my God.

DEVRAJ: *(Calling)* Rishi, Ashraf, Pooja! Wait! Wait! *(To* MADIHA*)* Go with them. Take the southeast exit. The southeast exit! *(Calling out)* Raja! You stay here with me.

MADIHA: Aah! My eyes. I can't breath.

*(*MADIHA *runs back to* DEVRAJ.*)*

DEVRAJ: Cover your eyes, Madiha. Just run. Madiha, just GO!!! *(Calling out)* Pooja, Rishi, help her!

(He pushes MADIHA *to escape. Complete darkness. We hear People whisper in the darkness.)*

DEVRAJ: What in God's name has happened? What do you mean exploded? What tank?

JAGANLAL: What?

DEVRAJ: The MIC?

("Zahreeli Hawa" song starts and continues overlapping all that is being said on the stage.)

Song Khamosh cheekho say bhari
     Yeay kahan say utha rahi hai aisi dardili hawa
     Gaib say chalnay lagee jub
     Ek Zahreeli Hawa.

MADIHA: My eyes.

JAGANLAL: Say it again. Where?

IZZAT: Run, *juldi, juldi chandalika bhago.*[4]

MADIHA: I can't see anything.

IZZAT: Run, *chandalika,* run.

(Loud clearing of throat is heard. It's from ANDERSON. *We see him in the U.S., while people continue in whispers.)*

ANDERSON: Sorry, I've had the flu for a week. But I'm getting over it. Washington is damp as hell at this time of year. I wanted to get back to Connecticut. But Julie was invited to lunch with the First Lady. What! How many? Over sixty?

(Noise of a crowd in India)

SONYA: Oxygen. Amylnitrate.

DEVRAJ: Mr. Minister, sorry to bother you.

SONYA: Thiosulphate.

---

[4]Hurry up, Chandalika, run.

ANDERSON: That's worse than Mexico!

SONYA: Oxygen. What do you mean you don't have any?

DEVRAJ: Damn it, Mukund, what about the scrubber?

JAGANLAL: Mr. Prime Minister, there is a problem . . .

MADIHA: Get out of my way! Move!

DEVRAJ: Move Mukund!

    (ANDERSON *in the U.S.*)

ANDERSON: Who's our guy over there? The minister. I want to talk to him.

JAGANLAL: Karbide International's slogan has come to haunt us.

SONYA: Body number on the forehead. One thousand five hundred and thirty-eight. One thousand five hundred and thirty-nine.

ANDERSON: What do you mean, no one knows for sure what happened?

JAGANLAL: Why Bhopal? Why Bhopal?

    (*As a deadly calm sets in, lights start to fade in. We see* ANDERSON *and* JAGANLAL *in their respective countries, which takes us to the next scene.*)

SCENE 11

    (ANDERSON *and* JAGANLAL *answer questions:* JAGANLAL *addressing the press in India and* ANDERSON *in the U.S. In effect, they are talking to each other through the press). A tightly packed crowd stands at some distance away from them.*

ANDERSON: You're ten times safer inside a Karbide International factory than in a slum.

JAGANLAL: Right, they all died on the streets, no one died inside the factory.

ANDERSON: Gentlemen, if any of you have been to India, you know how they live over there. They are desperate for jobs. There was no slum around the factory when we started.

JAGANLAL: What rubbish. Slums were there long before the factory. Not just the slum, the Deputy Inspector General of Police's bungalow too.

ANDERSON: Look, the name of the game is not to nail me down; the name of the game is to provide for the victims. What they need is fair compensation.

JAGANLAL: That's so typical, so bloody typical of the West. The courts of India haven't even opened the case against him, and he's already telling us what's fair! Absconder of justice, that's who he is! Three deadlines have passed, Mr. Anderson, and you're still talking to the *American press* for a crime committed in India.

ANDERSON: I'm going to see to it that the suffering is adequately compensated; I will pay compensation—no question about that at all. But no, I don't think there is any criminal responsibility here!

JAGANLAL: Really? What do you think?

ANDERSON: Obviously I didn't have, I don't have, and I never will have a criminal intent! I am personally going to go to India to better understand the situation.

JAGANLAL: Thank you.

SCENE 12

(SONYA's *makeshift clinic. Scores of victims are lying on the floor.* IZZAT *is among them. Many victims have eye patches.* SONYA *brings a patient in.*)

SONYA: If you are sick, stay in this area. There are doctors here that can help you. If you're looking for someone, go behind the market square, by the lake . . . there's a big poster on the lawn that says "Unidentified dead." Go there first. *Wahan jauw.*[5]

IZZAT: Doctor Sonya.

SONYA: What?

IZZAT: My body aches. What will happen?

SONYA: I don't know.

IZZAT: You know, *doctorni sahiba*. You have my file.

SONYA: The situation is changing every day. We're waiting for medicine. I have nothing here.

(IZZAT *pulls out a handful of tablets.*)

SONYA: M&Ms?

IZZAT: I want to live, *doctorni sahiba* . . . stop this pain.

SONYA: Oh God, who sold you these?

(*Sonya throws them away. Song starts while Sonya keeps helping* IZZAT. IZZAT *coughs up lumps of blood and tries to stop the blood by shoving the edge of her scarf into her mouth.* IZZAT *convulses. Sauvé enters meanwhile.*)

Song   Kaisa bhabhka kaisi gandh
        Ho rahi hai sans bandh
        Roshni ankhon ki mand
        Jismo jan main bus rahi hai, kaisi matmaili hawa
        Gaib say chalne lagi jub, ek zahreeli hawa

SONYA: Izzat, no!

SAUVÉ: Dr. Labonté.

SONYA: I can't talk to you now. Help me get her on to the table.

(SAUVÉ *hesitates.*)

Help me!! She's got fluid in her lungs!

(SAUVÉ *and* SONYA *help* IZZAT *on to the table.*)

SAUVÉ: Legally you can't help this woman.

(SONYA *continues to help* IZZAT.)

---

[5]Go there.

If something happens to this woman, you'd be personally liable.

SONYA: There is a bag on the table. Get me a bronchodilator!

SAUVÉ: I don't know what that is. You shouldn't be here, doctor.

SONYA: It's gray plastic!

SAUVÉ: It's not safe to stay here. *(He looks for it, holds it up)* Is this it?

   (SONYA administers a shot from the ventilator.)

SONYA: Get me a rag.

SAUVÉ: You're on your own, Labonté.

SONYA: Attendant!!

   (SONYA keeps helping IZZAT. SAUVÉ leaves.)

SCENE 13

   (AMID sounds of protest, ANDERSON arrives in India. JAGANLAL receives him at the airport.)

ANDERSON: Mr. Minister, I am so sorry.

JAGANLAL: Yes, Mr. Anderson.

ANDERSON: I really am sorry.

JAGANLAL: You don't have much time, Mr. Anderson.

ANDERSON: And I do appreciate your coming in person to meet me.

JAGANLAL: They are outside.

ANDERSON: Who?

JAGANLAL: The police.

ANDERSON: Am I being arrested?

JAGANLAL: You need protection.

ANDERSON: Where is Mr. Sarthi?

JAGANLAL: Well-protected!

ANDERSON: May I see him?

JAGANLAL: You will.

ANDERSON: Is it a police escort waiting for us?

JAGANLAL: Don't worry about the photographers. Let them photograph you. Our people need to see you answering to authority. I'm doing you a favor. I will keep you under house arrest. Twenty-four-hour surveillance. Nobody will be allowed near you but Sarthi. That is the best I can do under the circumstances.

ANDERSON: I'm sure.

JAGANLAL: *Chalo.*

   (Both exit.)

SCENE 14

(JAGANLAL's *office.*)

JAGANLAL: Doctor Labonté, we need your help.

SONYA: Pardon me?

JAGANLAL: The people of Bhopal need your help.

SONYA: You need my help? It's a little late. There isn't much I can do now. If you had listened to me earlier, if you had read my research, Mr. Minister. If- You're unbelievable. You're as bad as they are.

JAGANLAL: Doctor Labonté, I am asking you to please stay in Bhopal. I'd like you to work at the Hamidiya Hospital.

SONYA: You want me to care for—to give palliative care to the victims of this goddamn disaster that you, *you* are directly responsible for. We have no supplies, no oxygen, we are using the same syringes over and over again, we have no antidote for Karbide's—

JAGANLAL: What do you need?

SONYA: Thoisulfate. Sodium thiosulfate for a start. For the cyanide poisoning.

JAGANLAL: I'll see to it that you get all you need. Please write it down for me.

SONYA: You'll understand if I don't fall over with gratitude.

JAGANLAL: I am grateful to you.

SONYA: What is this about? What do you want from me?

JAGANLAL: I want you to continue the work you've been doing.

SONYA: The work?

JAGANLAL: Your research.

SONYA: The research you dismissed two weeks ago. The research you banned.

JAGANLAL: The situation has changed Doctor.

SONYA: I can continue my research without interference?

JAGANLAL: Yes. Yes.

SONYA: And if I agreed to continue my study, how do I know what will happen to my findings?

JAGANLAL: As I said, the situation has changed. I am in a position to make your findings public. To let the world know.

SONYA: Montreal. You're going to the trade talks, the conference. You can present the material there.

JAGANLAL: Yes. Yes I can, doctor.

SCENE 15

(ANDERSON *at* DEVRAJ's, *under house arrest.* DEVRAJ *is sitting nearby.*)

ANDERSON: (*On the telephone*) Yeah, how's the big snowstorm in Connecticut? Overnight? That makes me feel a helluva lot better. Oh no, beautiful, fine,

fine, well, apart from being jet-lagged and under house arrest. What? Yes . . .
I don't know . . . What? That much? . . . No. No. Fine. Get back to me. *(Hangs
up, turns to* DEVRAJ*)* We've lost eight hundred million in market capitaliza-
tion in the last week; production is shut down worldwide, so we have no
revenue; and our insurance may not cover us. What do you people get up to
in this country? *(Tosses a safety manual at* DEVRAJ*)* What is this?

DEVRAJ: Your safety manual.

ANDERSON: Our safety manual? Did you ever look at it?

DEVRAJ: Yes.

ANDERSON: You had a total of four safety devices. How many were working?

DEVRAJ: The refrigeration was turned off at your request to cut costs. The flare
tower was shut off to cut costs. The scrubber had just been repaired, but still
didn't function. The water hoses did not reach the tower.

ANDERSON: The book says at least two should have been working. How many
were working?

DEVRAJ: They were certified.

ANDERSON: But were they working?

DEVRAJ: I don't know.

ANDERSON: You don't know?

DEVRAJ: None!

ANDERSON: Who certified them?

DEVRAJ: The minister's safety inspection team—we were *certified.*

(DEVRAJ *gives* ANDERSON *a logbook.* ANDERSON *flips pages.)*

ANDERSON: When was the last time they were certified?

DEVRAJ: Two weeks ago.

ANDERSON: When is the next certification?

(DEVRAJ *is silent.)*

Okay . . . if the plant hadn't blown up, when would the next one have been?

DEVRAJ: Two weeks from today!

ANDERSON: That means week four. But that's already been certified. So have
weeks six, eight and ten. What is going on here? You have clearance for peri-
ods that haven't even arrived yet?

DEVRAJ: This is India.

ANDERSON: My apologies, I didn't know.

DEVRAJ: We have to adjust to local conditions here.

ANDERSON: Which means?

DEVRAJ: We must bribe. There are only two certification officers for the whole
state and they won't come every two weeks. So once they come for certification, we pay them to certify three months in advance. Corruption is culture
here, sir.

ANDERSON: You had gas leaks before didn't you?

DEVRAJ: Not this big.

ANDERSON: What was done?

DEVRAJ: We handed out flyers door to door.

ANDERSON: Flyers? Aren't people illiterate? (DEVRAJ *doesn't answer*) How much did you save shutting down the refrigeration?

DEVRAJ: It was—

ANDERSON: And the scrubber!

DEVRAJ: Listen sir—

ANDERSON: And on bribes . . . how much?

DEVRAJ: Mr. Anderson—

ANDERSON: Why wasn't I informed?

DEVRAJ: You were, sir. I have them recorded. Twenty-seven memos were sent to you.

ANDERSON: Twenty-seven memos?

DEVRAJ: Twenty-seven dead babies.

ANDERSON: What?

DEVRAJ: No, I'm sorry, eighteen, I sent you eighteen memos.

ANDERSON: How do I save this corporation?

DEVRAJ: We responded to all instructions sent by the head office.

ANDERSON: Just shut up.

(ANDERSON *picks up the newspaper.*)

This reporter here, Raj Kishore Keshwani, I keep seeing his name all over the place, how come he prophesied so much about the safety of the plant and I never heard about it?

DEVRAJ: Sir, he's been writing those ever since the plant opened.

ANDERSON: He mentions some clinic's research—about Karbide killing unborn babies!

DEVRAJ: A Canadian NGO doctor. She was doing research claiming that Karbide International has been poisoning unborn babies ever since its Bhopal plant was built.

ANDERSON: And you ignored it?

DEVRAJ: We had her barred from the plant.

ANDERSON: And what's this about a Karbide employee? Madiha Akram who is apparently pregnant with the CEO's child?

(DEVRAJ *snatches newspaper from him.*)

ANDERSON: So you got an employee pregnant.

DEVRAJ: Yes.

ANDERSON: What a mess. I thought I sent India a man with a vision. I didn't know I was sending a fucking playboy.

(ANDERSON *pushes a flyer in* DEVRAJ's *hand.*)

ANDERSON: What does it say?

DEVRAJ: *Zinda nahi murda.*

ANDERSON: Which means?

DEVRAJ: "Dead not alive."

ANDERSON: "Wanted. Anderson. Dead not alive!"

DEVRAJ: I'm sorry Mr. Anderson.

ANDERSON: People are calling me the ghost of Bhopal. Look at these eyes—a total of nine hundred and two wrinkles under these eyes. Each wrinkle represents a Karbide plant somewhere in the world. I and my men and women have hung on to a single hope—that Karbide would be a good citizen in each of those nine hundred towns, and, as in Bhopal, would help to put an end to poverty. Help realize untapped potential. And you Mr. Sarthi, have killed that hope. All nine hundred of us are fighting for our lives. Karbide is fighting for its life.

DEVRAJ: Mr. Anderson, the courts have not decided anything yet.

ANDERSON: Corporations don't lose in courts, they lose under public scrutiny. *(Giving him the flyer)* Merry fucking Christmas, Mr. Playboy.

SCENE 16

(The Hamidiya Hospital. Victims lying on the floor in groups. IZZAT and MADIHA are among them. MADIHA's eyes are covered with eye patches. IZZAT has one eye patch. IZZAT is nibbling dry seeds.)

IZZAT: MADIHA *memsahib?* *(No answer)* Bai? *Memesahib?* Madiha *memesahib?* You don't talk. Not a word. Eh. (MADIHA *starts to cough.* IZZAT *offers her seeds)* Would you like to eat? A little bit. Not even for the baby? *(Passes grain to* MADIHA *who drops it.)* Now you know where it is. You are saving it. You will need it later. Want to hear a story? Listen . . .

Song   Aise kihis bhagwan
       Badd devta patta pay bathis
       Haath la mal kay nikalis maile
       Maile say janmis ek kauwa
       Kauwa la kihis bhagwan
       Ja tai khoj key bhumi la laan
       Aise kihis bhagwan.

       Pher kauwa, makdi, auo kekda mun kachwa kay ghench la dabais,
       Tub kachwa ha bhumi la ugal dees.

       Paani ooper ghoom-ghoom kay
       Jaal bicha dis makdi
       Jaal kay ooper bade jatan say
       Bhumi jama dis makdi

Bhum la pahchan
Aise kihis bhagwan.

Pher sab jan milkay nachay gaye bur bhidgay. Okhar baad badd devta apan mudi kay jata say baal noach kay phakis. Okhar say pade bun gaye. Udi pade la kaat kay hul banis. Jub hul chale la laga-gay taub bhumi say anna upjis.

Anna la deemak kay banbee kay bheetar
Rakh do bhaiya
Sub munsay kay kaam yay aahi
Bolo ram ramiya
Kauwa, makdi, kekda, kachwa
Sab jan khais dhan.
Aise kihis bhagwan.

MADIHA: Phir kya hua?[6]
IZZAT: Phir?
MADIHA: Yeah, what happened then?
IZZAT: Then the crop got infected by pests.
MADIHA: Then?
IZZAT: Then men began to search for chemicals to kill the pests.
MADIHA: What happened next?
IZZAT: That chemical killed my daughter.
    (Sonya enters. She shows signs of sickness due to the poisonous gas.)
SONYA: (To IZZAT) She's talking?
IZZAT: Yes.
MADIHA: Sonya Labonté? Dr. Sonya Labonté?
    (MADIHA sits up, attempts to take off her eye-patch.)
SONYA: No, don't take that off.
MADIHA: Thank you. I know I have not been kind to you. I feel embarrassed.
    (Sonya examines her with stethoscope.)
SONYA: Don't be. Breathe.
MADIHA: I don't know how to thank you for giving me back my life . . . and my little baby.
SONYA: There is a heartbeat.
MADIHA: See, I told you.
SONYA: Yes, yes.
MADIHA: I need to see Devraj.
SONYA: Miss Madiha, there are some things you need to know. Bhopal is being littered with deformed and stillborn babies.

---

[6]Then what happened?

MADIHA: That won't include my baby. No. Look, those women lie. They lie about everything . . . about their animals . . . about their families . . . about their babies . . .

SONYA: Miss Madiha—

MADIHA: Like Izzat. She lied about everything—her dead dog, her dead pig, her dead goat . . .

SONYA: The chemical that killed Izaat's goat, killed her daughter; the same gas that poisoned you—is going to affect your baby.

MADIHA: I see what you're doing. You cannot stop, can you? You want to blame Devraj for everything. Why are you trying to scare me? Have you no shame?

SONYA: There was a baby born without eyes.

MADIHA: Why do you talk like that?

SONYA: I urge you to seriously consider terminating this pregnancy. I will not tell you what to do. I can't. But you need to know the facts.

(SONYA *starts to exit. She coughs and staggers as she walks. She stops, gasps for air, and then collapses slowly as the lights close on her. Dr. Labonté dies.)*

SCENE 17

(ANDERSON *at* DEVRAJ's *house arrest.)*

JAGANLAL: This is the settlement you are proposing?

ANDERSON: Yes.

JAGANLAL: This is not just.

ANDERSON: Mr. Minister, there is always an element of speculation in these arbitrations. The point is—the dead have stopped dying.

JAGANLAL: What?

ANDERSON: The dead have stopped dying.

JAGANLAL: The dead have stopped dying?

ANDERSON: Look—

JAGANLAL: My people are dying faster than the insects your chemical was supposed to kill.

ANDERSON: Well, your casualty numbers don't match ours.

JAGANLAL: Two hundred thousand and counting.

DEVRAJ: There have only been two thousand recorded deaths.

JAGANLAL: Only?

DEVRAJ: We ought to be precise about the numbers.

JAGANLAL: Thirty-seven wards are affected.

DEVRAJ: That's the entire city.

JAGANLAL: And the poison clouds are not clear yet.

ANDERSON: Mr. Minister, we'll provide compensation. We'll look after the gas victims, but first of all, you have to determine how many.

JAGANLAL: What?

ANDERSON: Who was living in the affected wards at the time?

JAGANLAL: And how should I determine that? Should I go to every dead body and ask his home address?

ANDERSON: Well, don't you have census records?

JAGANLAL: As if they had homes.

ANDERSON: So what are we supposed to do? Pay for every patient you happen to have in your hospitals.

JAGANLAL: *(Raising a file)* Three hundred fifty thousand registered medical files, two hundred thousand temporary disabilities, one hundred fifty thousand possible permanent disabilities.

DEVRAJ: How many of them are faking?

JAGANLAL: How does one fake death, Mr. Sarthi?

DEVRAJ: Half the dead wouldn't have been alive in the first place, had it not been for the wealth the plant provided.

JAGANLAL: For goodness sake, Devraj, I bent over backwards to grant you the People's Progress Zone. Bent over backwards to give you concessions that are unmatched in the history of India. You could at least think a little before opening your mouth. *(Imitates him in repulsion)* "Half the dead wouldn't have been alive!"

DEVRAJ: I'm sorry, Mr. Minister. You go on forgetting this was an accident!

JAGANLAL: An accident?

DEVRAJ: Do you think we'd do it purposely? It was an accident—a chemical, a chemical got too hot and exploded.

JAGANLAL: What chemical?

DEVRAJ: What?

JAGANLAL: Spell the name.

ANDERSON: What?

JAGANLAL: Spell that chemical, Methyl-Iso-Cyanate. It decomposes to hydrogen cyanide and carbon dioxide. It burns the skin, eyes, and respiratory membranes. It penetrates the skin and is lethal in very low doses.

ANDERSON: Look, Mr. Bhandari, our scientists know perfectly well what they—

JAGANLAL: MIC, the gas that killed my people!

ANDERSON: We acknowledge the damage this explosion has done. But it was an acc—

JAGANLAL: You knew you had a problem.

DEVRAJ: No!

JAGANLAL: No? Buying dead animals?

DEVRAJ: That was the Animal Charity Fund.

JAGANLAL: Charity?

ANDERSON: Mr. Minister, we have charities in all corners of the world. This was an accident. It could have happened in the U.S.

JAGANLAL: Then why didn't it? It didn't happen in the U.S. because you don't store enormous quantities of MIC at your American factory. It didn't happen there because you have automated monitoring systems: you don't rely on your workers' noses to tell you when there's been a leak. It didn't happen there because you have extra safety measures in place—measures you didn't bother to install here.

(Long silence.)

ANDERSON: I believe we all share the same philosophy—

JAGANLAL: Aaah, so there's a philosophy to killing people?

ANDERSON: *(To* DEVRAJ*)* Show him our figures.

JAGANLAL: Your figures?

ANDERSON: These are generous amounts and my final offer.

JAGANLAL: Shouldn't the courts of India determine what's final?

ANDERSON: I have shareholders, insurance companies—they are throwing Molotov cocktails at the factory in Stuttgart. The company's bonds are on credit watch. You have no idea of the scope of my problems.

JAGANLAL: Regardless of your problems, you can't be your own judge and your own jury. This happened here and an Indian court must settle this.

ANDERSON: If you want to wait that long—but your people need help, *now*! Give him our figures. Please just listen carefully.

DEVRAJ: Eight thousand per death, four thousand per partial permanent disability. and two thousand per partial temporary disability!

ANDERSON: Not in Rupees, in American dollars!

JAGANLAL: This is what an Indian life is worth?

DEVRAJ: These figures are based on the Indian standard of living.

JAGANLAL: How American, Indian boy!

DEVRAJ: You had nothing here. We brought you a world-class plant.

JAGANLAL: A world-class plant? I licensed you to manufacture mega-quantities of Karbide Thunder and agreed to an outrageous extension to the People's Progress Zone. Why? Because my country is poor. We are not competitive on the global market. We are *always* in the position of trying to catch up to *you*. But the price *we* pay for trying to catch up leaves us *victims* of your progress, your technology, and your crimes against humanity.

ANDERSON: We are not criminals.

*(*JAGANLAL *pulls out* LABONTÉ*'s research.)*

JAGANLAL: Really? All right, you don't want to wait for an Indian court, fine you will go to a U.S. court. I will negotiate with this.

ANDERSON: What's that?

JAGANLAL: Dr. Labonté's research

DEVRAJ: That can't be admissible.

JAGANLAL: Because you purposely hid information?

DEVRAJ: This is ludicrous.

JAGANLAL: And coerced mothers to abort and bury deformed dead babies listed in this study.

DEVRAJ: Oh please.

ANDERSON: Let him speak.

DEVRAJ: Mr. Anderson?

ANDERSON: You be quiet.

JAGANLAL: *(Reads the front page)* Significant amounts of MIC Methyl-Iso-Cyanate, have been detected in the blood of pregnant women, causing birth defects, birthing abnormalities, and deformities. Karbide International manufactures this product. This study shows that, while long-term health-risks are not conclusive, Karbide International has increased the production and . . .

DEVRAJ: A woman you charged with kidnapping has done this research!

JAGANLAL: We have dropped the charges. She is now working in the Hamidiya Hospital, and I have decided to lift the ban on her study and have asked a special commission to examine her findings.

(JAGANLAL starts to leave.)

DEVRAJ: Mr. Minister?

(ANDERSON walks towards JAGANLAL, motions DEVRAJ to leave. DEVRAJ leaves.)

ANDERSON: Mr. Minister, perhaps there is one area of our settlement that we could actually begin to discuss in depth.

JAGANLAL: Yes, there is an area we may talk about substantially.

(ANDERSON and JAGANLAL talk. They are very animated but their words are inaudible to the audience.)

SCENE 18

(MADIHA at the clinic. DEVRAJ enters.)

DEVRAJ: Madiha?

MADIHA: Just say hello.

DEVRAJ: Hello.

MADIHA: No, like when you would come bursting through my door Sunday morning, so full of life, "Hello Madiha," and run into my arms . . . "hellooo Madihaaa!"

DEVRAJ: *(Trying)* Hellooo Madihaaa. I thought you died.

MADIHA: Me too.

DEVRAJ: It's my fault. I told you to run. If only you didn't run, it's my fault, all my fault. You ran right into the gas . . . I'm sorry, I'm sorry. *(Pause)* Say something . . . something . . . just say it.

MADIHA: I love you.

DEVRAJ: No.

MADIHA: I love you.

(She touches DEVRAJ, *then kisses him passionately.)*

DEVRAJ: I have been thinking.

MADIHA: About what?

DEVRAJ: About us.

MADIHA: Yes?

DEVRAJ: I should go back to the U.S.

MADIHA: You should?

DEVRAJ: And you must come with me.

MADIHA: Yes. When? How soon can we go?

DEVRAJ: That depends.

MADIHA: On what?

DEVRAJ: What Jaganlal does with Labonté's research.

MADIHA: Labonté isn't in the picture anymore.

DEVRAJ: But do you have any idea what Labonté's research was about? Do you?

MADIHA: Some nonsense about the factory? About the factory!

DEVRAJ: What about the factory?

MADIHA: I don't know . . . about animals, women, babies. I don't know.

DEVRAJ: Why do you think we paid for all those dead animals?

MADIHA: It's beca . . . the Animal Charity . . . Oh my God.

DEVRAJ: My nightmare is growing in your belly.

MADIHA: You lied to me.

DEVRAJ: It was a mistake.

MADIHA: You told me—

DEVRAJ: Can you forgive me?

MADIHA: Forgive you? Forgive you for what?

DEVRAJ: This baby—

MADIHA: Forgive you for your own baby?

DEVRAJ: Madiha, please understand me.

MADIHA: That night, I thought I'd die. I was running . . . I couldn't breath . . . I couldn't see. I fell and my hand touched something. It was a dead body. Oh God, I had never touched a dead body before. I never prayed before but that night I prayed, "God save me and the life of my baby." I wanted to prove to myself that what you had told me before the accident was true.

DEVRAJ: Madiha, I'm sorry. It was a mistake. I didn't think this accident would happen until it happened. I thought I was doing something good. I thought I would be a bringer of prosperity. I really thought that. Now I look at you . . . Madiha, I'll make it all up to you. We can start over again in America.

MADIHA: What will America do for me? Will it give me back my eyes? Will it heal what's growing inside me?

DEVRAJ: What's growing inside you will have to be aborted.

MADIHA: Will have to be?

DEVRAJ: Madiha, I don't want to leave you alone.

MADIHA: So it's that simple. If I don't abort, I'm left alone.

DEVRAJ: That's not what I said.

MADIHA: Then why do you want me to abort this baby?

DEVRAJ: It's not a baby.

MADIHA: What is it?

DEVRAJ: You saw Izzat's baby.

MADIHA: I am not Izzat.

DEVRAJ: You don't understand.

MADIHA: What do I not understand?

DEVRAJ: Imagine how that creature would suffer. Every day would be a reminder of the mistake I made. Imagine if the child lived . . . knowing that his father . . . that I was responsible. I want us to be together. I want to marry you . . .

MADIHA: You have really mixed me up.

DEVRAJ: I really do want to marry you, Madiha. I know that now. . . . But we can't . . . we won't last with such a burden in our lives.

MADIHA: Labonté told me that all abortions in Bhopal will have to be recorded. It's government regulation.

DEVRAJ: We will go outside of Bhopal.

MADIHA: Izzat was saying that a woman died a horrible death at the hands of a doctor outside of Bhopal.

DEVRAJ: Don't be afraid, darling. Are we poor, uneducated clods who would leave such matters to some two-cent clinic outside of Bhopal? *(Holds her hands)* Hans will take care of you. I think you have made a good decision.

MADIHA: Stop—

DEVRAJ: We'll leave all this—

MADIHA: Stop please, I haven't made a decision . . . I want to think about it.

DEVRAJ: Shussssh . . . Sleep . . . We need to sleep.

MADIHA: I haven't made a decision.

DEVRAJ: Shusssss. . . . You will see the sense of it in the morning.

(MADIHA *rests, her eyes closing with drowsiness.* DEVRAJ *sits besides her.*)

SCENE 19

(ANDERSON *on phone.*)

ANDERSON: I thought we had an understanding. I don't have the luxury of only having one thing to worry about. I'm turning my attention to other things. I can't think about Bhopal one hundred percent of the time.

My hands? My hands shake hands with heads of state and men at the White House. My hands provide for a million employees around the world and give scholarships to bright Indian students. My hands were trying to build the future of this country. My hands are clean. I was ten thousand miles away.

We both know your charges are absurd. Well, they'll have to find me first, and then they'll have to drag me into court. I've got a plane to catch. Good luck.

SCENE 20

(Action takes place in three locations: at the Montreal Conference, at a grave-yard, and at DEVRAJ's *house arrest.)*
(At the Montreal conference where JAGANLAL *is preparing for a speech . . .)*
JAGANLAL: Dear Delegates, good people of Canada, and business leaders of the world assembled in Montreal, *je veux vous dire,* I want to tell you, *il n'y a pas d'amour,* there is no love left in Bhopal. There are ten thousand sick babies. Dying babies, orphaned at birth. What can I do? Seek to lay blame? Cry for one baby? No. Do I mourn the dead? No. Sad as it may sound, I cannot afford to mourn for the dead. It's useless. Because we know that for every child that dies, a new baby is born. The time for mourning has past, we must now pave the way to the future.
(Song starts.)

Song	Kya Zamin kya aasman	What on earth what heaven
	Ek kohra ek dhuan	one is fog and one is smoke *(gas)*
	Ek kayamat ka sama	The time has come for our fate
	Gaib say chalne lagi jab	When it starts to move unnoticed
	Ek zahreeli hawa.	This poisonous gas

(At the graveyard, where IZZAT *is sitting by a mud grave with* ZARINA's *empty basket beside her . . .)*
IZZAT: Doctor *sahiba,* Zarina died the day she was born. One leg, one arm, no fingers . . . there was nothing right with her. Her tiny little heart was like dried rubber . . . I could see it under her skin. Doctor *sahiba,* can you under-stand me? The night Zarina died, I saw her in a dream, standing. Looking like an angel. "Free me from my pain," she said. "Why am I like this? I am already dead. . . . " That night I felt something had changed. I woke up and turned to look at her. She had stopped crying. *(Takes out flower petals from the basket and drops them onto the grave)* She has peace. You have peace.
(At DEVRAJ *and* MADIHA's, *where they are under house arrest . . .)*
DEVRAJ: *(To* MADIHA) What are you thinking?
(MADIHA doesn't say a word, walks away from him, then tears the airline ticket in two. DEVRAJ *is stunned.)*
(Madih looks at Izzat, who is at a distance. Izzat looks at Madiha. Both women start walking towards each other and meet center stage. Madiha takes Izzat's hand in hers. The women have resolute expressions of defiance.)

Rana Bose

Rana Bose is a multilingual writer, playwright, engineer, poet, dramaturge, and novelist. Born in Kolkata, India, Bose has been based in Montreal for more than thirty years. While a college student in St. Louis in the 1970s, Bose created the lighting design (he learned a great deal by watching Tapas Sen's sets in the Bengali theatre of the 1960s) for Gerry Mulligan's Jazz Trio and the Charlie Mingus Ensemble. He has written ten published plays that have been produced in Canada, the United States, and India. Besides radicalism and its disappointments and failures in *Death of Abbie Hoffman*, Bose has tackled a variety of topics in his plays and other writings, including diasporic foibles and backwardness in *Baba Jacques Dass and Turmoil at Côte-des-Neiges Cemetery* (1987) and a mixture of Montreal history and South Asian migrants in *The Sulpician Escarpment* (1995).

Bose has produced a novel, *Recovering Rude* (2000), and *Fourth Canvas* (2008). His short stories, articles, and essays have appeared in the *Montreal Gazette*, the *Montreal Mirror*, the *Montreal Hour*, the *Globe and Mail*, and the *Ottawa Citizen*.

The Death of Abbie Hoffman

Montreal Serai, Théâtre Calixa Lavalée, Montreal, 1991

Other Plays

Baba Jacques Dass and Turmoil at Côte-des-Neiges Cemetery

Blackskirt
Five or Six Characters in Search of Toronto
Nobody Gets Laid
On the Double
Prairie Fire
Some Dogs
The Sulpician Escarpment
Who to Please?

The Death of Abbie Hoffman

Rana Bose

An adaptation of Badal Sircar's *Michhil*, 1991

Chorus	Amrita Choudhury
	Lisa Foster
	Angela Smith
	Anirban Choudhury
	Prasun Lala
	Patrica Ward
Old Person (Nina)	Nilambri Ghai
Young Person (also Nina)	Anita Choudhury
Mr Hydroxy Cue	Himmat Shinhat
Director	Rana Bose
Set Design	Aziz Sharafi
Lighting Design	Andy Calamatas
Music (Arranged, Composed and Performed)	Himmat Shinhat
Costume Design	Lisa Foster
Make-up	Angela Seth
Song Lyrics	Rana Bose
Singers	Himrnat Shinhat
	Raja Lala
	Babla Choudhury
	Lisa Foster
Back-up Singers' Choreography	Amrita Choudhury
Solo Dancer	Angela Seth

SCENE 1

(Audience walks into a foggy, cool room. Seating arrangements are in a maze-like formation. Blue tracer-like follow spot directs audience to seats all over the auditorium. Orchestral music, with a low note bias. The control has started.

In the dark background, a big mural hangs, made from masks of faces. Different sizes create a 3-d effect at the back. At the beginning, the lighting creates a grim quality. At the end of the play, these same masks, again with lighting, will seem to look pleasanter. Audience legs hang down from rectangular risers and cubes, placed like a maze.)

(When play begins, chorus of six come in with leader in front. All are dressed in grey ragged clothes—dark lines on faces. Leader walks in like she is muttering religious incantations. Actually she is saying "unanimous" and the rest of the chorus is saying "consensus." Occasionally each one will have doubts and will say, "But sir, may I . . . I also think . . . On the other hand . . . I can't see a thing . . . Can I . . . But why not? . . . Actually . . . Do I have to. . . ." Second time around the maze, they move in jerks and stop—hands freeze in dance-like movements [with music]. Leader's eyes are very stern. Eventually, the leader is more powerful—her voice of "unanimity" rises above all, and she moves through them with very threatening looks.)

(Suddenly there is a massive explosion sound and powder flash is seen at one end of the auditorium. All lights go out and a tremendous scream is heard from within the chorus—as if someone has been assaulted. In the dark the chorus moves through the alley, purposely bumping into the audience—asking them questions directly.)

(In the dark [soundtrack of Japanese bells], they all look up to the sky.)
1. Who turned off the light? Hey! Who turned off the fucking lights?
2. Someone blew the fuse, man. Overloaded the lines.
3. Bullshit! It's a fucking solar storm again! I tell ya! It's a new galaxy in the works.
4 *(very crude theatrical laugh).* New galaxy! My ass!
5. Watch it! Where the fuck do you think you're going?
6. Ooh! You touching my boobs!
4. I did not! I heard a scream.
10. Somebody's been murdered!
(Solemn silence for a while.)
2, 4, 6. What, c'est pas vrai—murder is impossible.
5 *(lights a match).* Depends on what is murdered, darlings *(all light matches and huddle).*

6. What is murdered? *(Repeat in several tones. At this point all except 1 confer in gibberish for a while, in a huddle, and then looking at each other and continuing in a huddle they say, "Gamma, alpha . . . delta, beta." Then they break off and spread out.)*

2. On January 3, 1889, Nietzsche collapsed into insanity.

3. On June 21, 1984, Michel Foucault was pronounced dead.

4. In the same institution where he researched madness.

2. He thought on the fringe . . .

6. He had a Eurocentric ego.

1. I have no ego. I have four pairs of socks, I wear my shoes loose, I never call in sick and I use nasal spray.

2. I can't think any more.

1. She is from Kennebunkport.

3. Somebody's been murdered.

4 *(nervous)*. Somebody's been stabbed and her body's been whisked away.

5. Nonsense! Nobody's been murdered.

4. Then somebody's fallen into a hole.

1. Yes! A manhole—a man-made hole.

2. It's a paradigm shift.

3. It's a pendulum swing.

4 *(to No. 1)*. Do you have thoughts!

5. They have dug up all the streets.

6. Why do they molest all the streets every year?

4 *(to No. 1)*. Do you have thoughts?

1. I am not a cat. Only cats think.

2. Well, do you see in the dark?

5. Last year, they dug up the Champlain Bridge.

6. Every year it is Champlain Bridge.

5. This year it is Champlain plus the Turcot interchange.[1]

6. Last year, it was Champlain plus Metropolitan.

5. The year before, it was Champlain plus Decarie.

6. I think Champlain was a world leader. He was one of us!

5. Yeah! Champlain was bigger than Descartes, Kant and Nietzsche. He was the father of Hegel.

6. Yeah! He was the brother of Freud. Carl Jung was his neighbor. His mind worked like a flash!

1. Does anybody have a flashlight?

2. Does nobody carry a flashlight?

5. There must be smokers amongst you. Do you have a match, sir, you, sir? Ma'am? *(Asks the audience.)*

---

[1]The Turcot interchange and the Metropolitan are large Montreal highways. The Metro is the Montreal transit system.

(He lights a match. Lights come on simultaneously. Police sirens sound. Masked Man [Mr Hydrox Cue] rises up from within the audience. Militaristic looks. Shaft of light on him alone, while police light turns. Across the room, a follow spot takes a big "Q," sound of water, floods. All players climb onto audience area. Blue watery lights in maze.)

MAN. *(walks in the maze, slowly). (Bilingual.)* What's going on here, eh? What's all the racket about, eh?

1. The lights went out, sir!

2. There was a scream.

3. Someone's been killed by a solar storm.

4. Someone's been stabbed and her body whisked away!

5. Yeah, into a manhole, sir.

6. Was she wearing any clothes?

MAN. Shut up! There's been no murder. There's nobody. How dare you talk about murder.

(Chorus mumbles amongst itself, huddled.)

1. But sir, we . . .

2. Saw with our own eyes.

3. There was a scream.

4. Must have been stabbed and the body whisked away.

MAN. Shut up! *(Walks about.)* There's nobody. There's no murder. Don't start rumors. Don't malign.

(A woman from within the audience, or from another end, comes running in and collapses onto the floor.)

1. There see, I told you it's her . . . she was murdered.

4. She was stabbed and whisked away.

MAN. Shut up I said! Go home! Stop spreading rumors. Nobody's dead. *(Bilingual.)*

2. What a mess . . .

MAN. Yo! I said get back inside your homes.

3. There she is . . .

4 *(in French).* I told you there was a murder.

5. Wait a minute. Is she murdered or is she dying?

2. Oh my God. What a mess!

5 *(in French).* It is a slow process.

4. Somebody whisked her away . . .

They whip around and look at No. 4 and then slowly approach the body.

5. If she is not dead, how could she have been murdered. . . . To be murdered, you must have been alive. Listen to me.

4. Sir, you're thinking the unthought. She was stabbed and whisked away . . . that's it. That's just her body.

5. Ah! Just like that?

4. Just like that!

5. Why was she murdered?

3. Who said she was alive?

4. I heard her scream.

2. Those who scream, they are the ones who . . . in here. *(Points finger to his head, winks.)*

MAN. I said shut up! Hiss! *(All cower a bit.)*

2. There's the body.

MAN. Silence! *(He walks about angrily.)* Listen, if you want to discuss, go somewhere else . . . For us, there is nothing to discuss. C'est claire? It is over, OK?

ALL CHORUS. It's over, OK! Unanimous consensus.

3. But sir . . .

4. We saw the body.

MAN. I said the word is "Nobody is dead." . . . There is nothing to discuss. And go home before I chase you all out. Hiss.

(The chorus scurry away like rats in the dark. Young person rises up slowly. . . . The man does not notice her.)

YP *(smiles).* I am the one who was killed. You know me, don't you? I was killed today. Now, just a little while ago . . . *(Goes close to each member of the audience)* It's me who's been killed . . . just now. Yes? I was killed right now. Every day, every fucking day, I am killed. I was killed yesterday. I was killed the day before. I've been slowly poisoned for the last ten years and I'll be killed this week, next month I will be killed.

(Man is totally oblivious. He walks around.)

For the last several years, they have been finishing me off and you come and you don't see me. What do you watch? Why can't you see me? What do you come to watch, anyway? Look! Look at me! Here, I am the one . . . every day, every week every year! You know! They've found a new way to kill me, and there is agreement all around. Isn't it amazing, they all agree, everybody agrees nowadays. There are no disagreements. Old enemies have become friends. Old walls have collapsed. Everybody fucking agrees! It's like the whole world is fighting to agree! And I had always thought history was progress by conflict. Instead there is only . . . there is only . . .

(The Chorus from the wings say "Consensus." She builds up to a peak and then slowly collapses and rolls over like a corpse. Music of wind sounds. The other man steps over the body and walks away. His shoe-steps resound in the auditorium. The Chorus come back in a line, humming "Bolo hari, Hari bol, Dump the body in the hole." They lift the body up, high above their shoulders, turn around to the music. Some of them start chanting . . . Slow fadeout.)

SCENE 2

(As sound of the Chorus slowly fades away, older person [Nina], with almost insane looks, comes rushing into the maze. S/he hands out cards to the audience. Cards say different things. [Consensus, sacred truth etc.] OP will, in the beginning, ask everybody to be silent [shush!]. Even to the soundtrack [towards the ceiling]. She will distribute these cards strategically. She wears a funny hat.)

OP. Don't tell them! I gave you these cards . . . Don't even tell them I am here . . . I am a journey person, I travel, I watch, I am a bystander, an onlooker. I watch processions, funerals, parades, manifestations, demonstrations, pickets, walkouts, lockouts, strikeouts . . . I hear hymns, chants, screams, prayers, pleas, psalms, slokas, screams! Screams! Lots of screams! *(She starts walking around the maze.)* Here, let me see . . . *(On her knees, very loud)* Allah ho Akbar, Sat Sri Akal, Garb Se Idaho Hindusthan Hamara! *(Very soft)* Halleluiah! Halleluiah, Halleluiah! May God be with you. Le Seigneur soit avec vous, et avec votre esprit, amen!

(She opens her eyes and asks members of the audience, if they have not already done so, to come and sit in the middle sections of the maze.)

Come along, come along, take these seats *(she takes them by the hand)*. We shall see a "juloos" or a "michhil" which means procession, manifestation *(in French)*. Juloos means a long journey in Persian—an endless journey. I have seen many julooses—for food, for clothes, for salvation, for revolution, processions of refugees, processions for guns, butter and flood relief, processions of St. Jean Baptiste, Carifete, Mardigras, O Canada[2]—processions with ministers and kings in waiting and trade union leaders, arms locked, processions for peace, . . . processions with stars, processions of taxi drivers, Iranians and Haitians mainly . . .

(As she is going around in the maze, talking to members of the audience, the Chorus comes back, in a quiet semi-circle, and huddles near the riser. At the end of her above piece, OP is swept aside and her hat gets knocked out by the Chorus. There is background music. All Chorus wear tight white masks or hold them in front of their faces.)

CHORUS *(very violent)*.
Consensus, Consensus,
Hezbollah, Hezbollah.
BJP, Babri Masjid,
New World Order, Now or Never,
Jerry Falwell, The job is done,
Hochelaga, Chateauguay[3]

---

[2]All parades in Canada. St. Jean Baptist is the patron saint of French Canadians and the Carifete is a Caribbean parade.

[3]Hochelaga is an Iroquois village; Chateauguay, a French Canadian village; Maradona, the Argentine football star; Cité Libre, an oppositional intellectual journal of the 1950s and 1960s; Janet Torge, a Montreal film producer; Jean Doré, former mayor of Montreal; Campeau Belander, committee set up to discuss Quebecois sovereignty.

Maradona, Now or Never
Janet Torge, Jean Doré
Cité Libre, Celine Dion
Ayatollah Khalkhali *(Eyes)*
Gabriella Sabatini *(Fluid tennis strokes)*
MC Hammer, DJ Cool
Ne touche pas, Hydro Q *(hiphop style)*
Serbs, Croats, Tamils
Campeau Belanger, Spicer
Dan Quayle, Joe Clark
Who do we want: Ben & Jerry *(twice)*
(Chorus leaves. Soft music—instrumental theme tune.)

OP *(picks up her hat slowly. Holds it in her hand).* When I was a little girl, one day early in the morning, somewhere between fall and winter—it was a sweet morning—there was a chill in the air—the sunshine felt wet and moist—I walked along a road, holding my father's hands. Dry leaves cracked under my feet, wild flowers swayed in the wind. I held my father's hand and followed the road. The road meandered along and disappeared under my feet. Old roads came and went. New roads appeared suddenly. *(She walks through the maze.)* At times, all roads seemed to vanish. Beyond a point, you could not see. It seemed the road had come to an end. Then suddenly, there was a bend, and beyond the bend a new road appeared like a flash. Just when you thought all roads had come to an end, a new one would appear. Roads! They appear and disappear and leave you wondering. Once we would come to a bend, my father would say, "Ma chérie, let's go back." I would say, "Just a little more, till the next bend." *(She walks a little faster.)* I could see a new road further beyond. My father would say, "Let's go back—that's the end of the road. . . . " And this would go on . . . I would say, "Let's go on . . . just a little bit further . . ." and he would say . . .

(Voice of Chorus)

CHORUS. Let's go back, ma chérie, it's the end of the road!
Let's go back, ma cherie, it's the end of the road!

OP. Just a little further, there's a bend ahead. *(She repeats and moves out fast.)*

CHORUS. *(frenzied shouts).* Hey! Come back! It's the end of the road. Nina, Nino, Nini! Ma petite chérie, reviens!

(Hysterical Chorus comes running in and scatter throughout the maze and confront the audience.)

1. Hey, you, have you seen a young girl? *(She holds a small mirror to the audience.)*
2. You, have you seen her?
3. She's got big eyes, and a snub nose?
4. Long legs, she shaves her pits.
5. She's naive and stupid.

6. She's short and thin.

1. She's little in years, little in wisdom, little in knowledge.

2. She's crazy, she loves to argue all the time.

3. She's sexy, she's always making a point.

4. She's stupid, she doesn't understand.

5. Have any of you seen her?

1 to 6. Have none of you seen her?

(They stop in a freeze and then spread out in the maze.)

1. Lost. One girl. Her name is Nina. She has a snub nose and big eyes. Anybody with any information please contact the *Gazette, La Presse, The Daily, The Link, Journal de Montreal, Le Devoir,* and Pierre Foglia,[4] he knows.

2. There has been an assassination or an abduction. A young girl named Nina has been assassinated or abducted. Anybody with any information please contact your nearest police station or the SQ or the GRC or the CSIS or the force Canadienne . . . We must have her body.

3. Hello, Lacolle, Phillipsburg *(Like she is using a cellular),* Niagra, Jean-Talon, Park Avenue, Guy Favreau . . .

4,5,6. Guy Favreau?

3. Canadian Immigration. Hello . . . Hello. Large eyes, snub nose, long legs, shaved pits.

4. This the CBC Radio Canada. Broadcasting at 100,000 KW with our transmitter on top of Mount Royal, we can be heard simultaneously in Baie-Comeau, Sherbrooke, Temiscaming, *(cut)* Abitibi, lower North Shore, Kampuchea, *(cut)* Kampala, Nairobi, New Delhi, *(cut)* Mascouche, and Repentigny. Can you hear us? *(To the audience, repeats. Others help the audience to say "yes").*
AUDIENCE. YES.

4. A girl named Nina is lost. She has been stabbed and her body whisked away into a manhole. Anybody with any information on any part of her body, mind or any other attribute, please call Dave Bronsttetter, Louise Penny, Augusta Lopez, John Kalina.

3. No! Not John Kalina, he is away for three weeks always!

5. Hi, this is radio station CJUT where hip is never and crack is dull or dull is crack. You have a problem? Hey, check us out.

Can tennis give you AIDS?

Do elbows have jaws?

Do bicycles ride fish?

Hey! Is politics getting to you?

This is "Notions and Motions"—a community program designed and altered by RADIO ALTERNATIFE, the alternate network for alternate people—We alternate news and views with motions and notions—and right now we are

---

[4]Journalist in Quebec, all Montreal papers.

looking for Nina. Yes NINA—N-i-n-a. Anybody out there with any information on Nina, please call 999–CJUT that ain't no party-line, honey. If you are
calling long distance, well keep it that way honey, we do not reverse charges.
Hey! Now! We are looking for Nina. N-I-N-A. Long, tall, thin and stupid. Last
seen on the corner of Hutchison and let me see . . . Trafalgar Square.

6. Nina, come back from wherever you are. You have no choice in this matter. There will be no negotiations—there were never any treaties. In fact, your
demands are stupid, absurd and bizarre. Everybody here agrees. We are happy
the way we are, we have no problems, no conflicts, why do you want to disturb
the peace? You have no choice, you have to come back.

1 (sobs). Your father and mother have been crying all day and night. They go
to bed crying in each other's arms. (Next person)

2. Your brother and sister cry as they play, they play and they cry.

3. Your uncles and aunts, your cousins and in-laws, they eat and they cry,
they cry as they eat.

4. Nina, come back, we promise to clean all the manholes and sewers.

5. You'll get whatever you want.

6. No, she won't!

5. Yes, she will. She will get whatever she wants. She will get her own cellular,
CD, and cop buster in her own Lexus.

1. She'll get her own detached cottage and a satellite in the sky.

2. She'll have happiness, peace and . . .

6. She will have religion!

ALL. Yeeeeup! She will have Religion, 'cos Religion is back. (Quick song)
CHORUS. The pope is from Poland, o yeah

Albanians want more pizza,

East Germans wear jackboots,

The wall is down in Berlin town,

The KGB takes NDG

The pope is from Poland.

2. Gorbachev wants investments, no technology, no MBAs . . .

1. Yeltsin says, "Over my matrushka's dead body"—He is a tricky mother-
fucker—he ends the Cold War to get money from the West—why I worked so
hard? President Bush says . . .

1 (Bush's voice). We are on the threshold of a new world.

2. I have drawn a line in the sand . . .

3. There shall be peace, happiness and salvation for all.

4. The United Nations is in the United States—which is in lower Manhattan!
(Eyebrows)

(Group from the Chorus do hiphop-style song "Woh, Nina!" The lyrics are con-
textual and change, reflecting current headlines or topical issues.)

SCENE 3

(OP has walked in after end of rap song.)
OP. Her parents named her Nina or Nino? Doesn't matter. Thousands of parents with thousands of Ninas. Nina means small, young. Nina means enquiring . . . It means green, raw, immature but questioning. Nina is not a closed book. It is an open mind. Lots of questions. Lots of arguments. Lots of debate. Lots of conflict. Ha, ha! Lots of conflict . . . Nina means there is no final answer, no closed chapters . . . *(Deep breath)* Nina is alive when the debate is on. Nina is lost when truth is sanctified, because, because, I tell you, no truth in this world is sacred. Nothing is sacred. *(Laughs)* Nothing is forever.
CHORUS *(in echo style)*. Nina . . . a . . . a!
OP *(becomes humorous in her walk and gestures, almost teasing)*. She is lo-oo-st *(mimics echo)*.
CHORUS. Nina, you better come back.
OP. Heh, Heh, she ain't coming back to this dumpy old house!
CHORUS. Nina, you got no choice.
OP. Sure she does, she'll come back to a new house, a new home, a real home, not this old dump, for God's sake what do you think she is?
OP *(back to normal tone, smiles)*. You remember I told you about the road? But these days the road goes round and round and you come back to the same road. You look for a bend and it ain't there, it's the same road again, eh! Have you ever thought of that? What's missing? Do you know? You don't want to . . . You don't want a bend in the road?
(A loud scream is heard. Horrible scream of "Nina.")
What's that? Who was that? God! Did you hear that scream? Like someone—you know? Was it at that bend? There? Beyond that bend? I must find her!
(She runs through the bend and leaves. The Chorus comes running in. All members of the Chorus wear local papers like Le Devoir, Globe and Mail, *etc. like dunce caps on their heads.)*
1. Check out the papers! Check out the papers!
2. Saddam arms himself again.
3. Britain and France supply rockets.
4. U.S. supplies bottled gas.
5. "We shall not allow this evil to happen on this earth again," warns President Schwarzkopf.
4. Prime Minister Barbara McDougall says: "It seems he has not learned a lesson."
6. Martina . . . will not go back to Czechoslovakia even though things are changing there. The President is a playwright, you know . . .
1. Hmm? Wonder if Brian was a playwright . . . then maybe.

2. Pele signs contract to run for PQ[5] in Jonquière: "We must get the Negro vote."

3. Otherwise the Mohawks will pow-wow downtown, next time esti . . .

4. Le Roi Jacques wants out.

The King of Quebec wants a bigger paycheck

like the Queen Mother at least.

(or he will disappear into a manhole).

5. Trudeau teams up with old flame Lise Payette to make a film of disappearing gold fish in Kenny Wong's China Pavilion in Brossard.

6. Mick Jagger will play lead fish, yeah!

1. Westmount declares sovereignty . . .

2. Speed limit will now be five mph . . .

3. Quebec police not racist, says Quebec priest.

4. Canadian space center will now be located in the Ville Marie Tunnel.

5. New research in the space center will explore ways of removing leaks in the tunnel. 62,000 jobs will be created.

6. New Big O roof contract will go to SOS—Salif Omar Salim, Kuwait's biggest tentmaker. 62,000 jobs will be created.

1. Kuwait and Quebec will merge as one country. Oil and Hydro will drive both economies. 62,000 jobs will be created.

2. British mag *Private Parts* claims Mila has taken to the bottle also.

CHORUS. 62,000 jobs . . .

3. 50 ton slab falls from sky on Civic Party Headquarters. Nick was not hurt. He was in between parties.

4. Guy Bouthillier and Robert Libman[6] form new party: Mouvement Quebecois pour moving sidewalks.

5 *(faking Indian guru's voice)*. Spiritualism alone can save this fucking world. join me and the rest of my fucking gang for a special, fun-filled, yoga-flipped cruise in the fucking Caribbean.

(Sound of Montreal subway comes suddenly. Whole Chorus pretend to be holding on to hand grips in the subway and lurching forward. Take off hats, bodies lurch to a stop.)

Yo! Bottled water *(like a hawker)* from Cajun country—Here's your last chance to buy clean pure water in this continent. All the way from Baton Rouge, Louisiana—Bayou Blues . . . the only brand that carries the authentic aroma of spiced jumbalaya when you pop the cork. Now or never, now or never, maintenant ou jamais . . . $17.99—bargain basement—here take a whiff *(to audience)*, uhhh! Smells good, you ma'am, hear it, can you hear it, can you hear it—buckwheat zydeco . . . ils sont partis—listen closer, listen closer, authentic French

---

[5]Parti Québecois, separatist Quebecois party.
[6]Politicians in Quebec.

flavor Bayou blues doucement, attention, buy two you get a third one free . . . quench your thirst. Yes, I . . .

2 *(to No. 3).* What did you say?

3. Nothing.

2. I heard you say something! What you looking at?

3. Nothing.

2. Oh yeah! I saw you looking at my shirt,

3. So?

2. So you were looking at my shirt, eh?

3. So?

2. You look at shirts all the time.

You dirty old shirt-looker

You drink white wine, right?

3. Yes, occasionally.

2. I knew it, I knew it!

3. Knew what?

2. You dirty old shirt-looking, white wine-drinking faggot—I know you— bet you work alone in a shoe store.

3. So . . . ?

2. See, I know you—now why would anybody work alone in a shoe store unless he has a dirty mind?

3. What you talking about now?

2. Listen, you guys, I hate you and them fucking short-haired feminist shits.

3. Hey, watch it man—it ain't gonna be so easy, you know—you guys think you are on a one-way street. No other view allowed *(all lurch to one side).*

4. One-dimensional world. *(Each turn their heads to each other.)*

5. Linear progression.

2. PC—political correctness.

6. No conflicts now.

1. We don't know.

We can't tell.

3. There was no discussion.

There was nothing to discuss.

4. Everyone agrees.

1. No debate.

3. No conflict.

4. No discourse.

ALL. Everyone agrees! Boom.

1. Attention! Attention *(like the metro driver at the stations Berri-de-Montigny, UQAM etc.).*

4. You're stepping on my toes.

5. Can't help it—it's too crowded.

4. You could have waited for the next train tabernac![8]

5. Then somebody would have said, "Why didn't you take the earlier one."

4. Then you'd have a problem.

5. Right! Whether to take the earlier one or the later one.

4. You're right.

5. You're right, too.

4. We're both right.

3. Why don't you move forward?

2. Yeah, there's lots of space up front.

6. Yeah, the seats are empty.

5. So what! I will not move forward.

4. Me too! I refuse to move forward.

1. What's the problem man, the train is moving Why we gotta move, eh? Don't make sense to me.

2. Yeah, right! *(All the bodies are crowded together in a heap)*

6. But there are lots of empty spaces, there.

1. Just don't worry about it, man—it's somebody else's problem.

6. You touching me.

3. It's the train—it's making me do it—it's not me.

4. You mean the train is touching her.

2. I guess there's nothing you can do about it.

5. Yup! Nothing you can do, the train is in charge. Nothing anybody can do . . .

1. "End of the line. Last station, Please get off carefully." *(All try to jump off together.)*

2. Heh! My shoes—they're left in the train.

3. Come back next time.

(They all run off. Train sound fades out. Lights fade out.)

SCENE 4

(After subway sound fades out from previous scene, OP's face is seen behind the mural. She has virtually merged with the masks. Looks kind of insane. Almost crazy smile. Eyes dart. She slowly comes out. First smiling, then laughing louder and louder.)

OP. I scared the shit out of you, didn't I? I think people should do whatever the fuck they want to do. What do you say? I am against all that pig shit like big corporations, big government, big acid spouting chimneys and big cops with big nervous fingers when they see big black kids in big little burgundy, playing big basketball—I mean you know all that . . . but this is all the hip shit that

---

[7]Extreme curse in Canadian culture, as it insults the Roman Catholic Church.

everybody likes to dump on . . . it's OK with me . . . but you know what else I hate? I hate big road signs, I hate big direction signals, I hate cul de sacs, I hate "no turning," I hate "bridge freezes before road," . . . and I'm really pissed off when I see "Yield," or "Prepare to merge." But I know, it's their signs, their roads, their triumphs, their order, their fucking agenda . . . I gotta wait it out, every few decades, the dust settles—the clouds move out, the roads reappear . . . I gotto go . . . *(repeats and leaves).*

(As she leaves, lights fade and guitar music begins. Lights fade in. Only two from Chorus come in. Man and Woman. They are two totally different people. She has a red jacket, headphones and reads a book. He has a green jacket, fedora hat and smokes a cigar. The flavor of this scene is in contrast to the rest of the play. The two display far more emotions and sensitivity in their acting style. The music track plays a guitar lick from Jimi Hendrix, like "Foxy Lady," etc. To disrupt her music, he purposely puts his foot on the riser and the music shuts off magically. Twice. He tries to establish an irritating superiority over her.)

1. You looked rather grave yesterday. *(Clearing his throat.)*

2 *(slowly turns her face).* Oh! I thought it was you who looked grave! *(Silence.)*

1. "Grave" is actually not very . . . correct terminology, you know.

2. Well, gee, you were the one who used it first! No?

1. Well! I guess . . . I was . . . I guess . . . *(silence for a while).*

2. Why is it incorrect anyway? I mean . . . hey, don't you guys *(to audience)* wanna know?

1. Well, because it suggests a relationship with death and dying . . .

2. Ah! Relationship with the dying?

1. No, that's not what I meant. What I meant was, it insults the dead! It is deathist . . .

2. Oh! Deathist! For a while I thought you were hinting at some kind of . . . sleeping with . . . necrophilia or some such thing.

(They both stare out over the audience for a while. A droning robotic sound starts building up and then stops. No. 1 puts his hand on No. 2's breast simultaneously. No. 2 has no reaction. No. 1 looks to see and then drops his hand in resignation. She is then startled.)

2. Why did you do that?

1. Do what?

2. Take your hand off?

1 *(clears his throat and gets up).* Well, uh-h, along with freedom of speech comes certain restrictions. . . . Unrestricted activity can be perilous . . .

2 *(goes after him in a "put on" seductive fashion).* Oh, I see! Perilous? Did you say? Hmmm. But without knowledge, there can be no democracy, and there is no knowledge without action, my dear—and action is often the ability to think of the "other." Were you thinking of the other?

1. Uh! just a minute. *(Takes his hat off)* What is this "other"? Everybody seems to be talking about it these days? The"other," the other, well, what is this other?

2. The "other" is the unthought, my dear. Unexplored territory. The unknown frontier. The other side. *(She runs her hand over his face, without touching him. His eyes closed. A dancer comes leaping through the maze with a long trail of colored cloth in her hand. His eyes are closed and he is controlling himself)* It is uncanny, gruesome ideas, crazy, modern, zany and unfettered—that is why there is no morality to thought. *(She pretends to kiss him.)* As soon as thought functions, it liberates or enslaves. *(Dancer throws several pieces of cloth into the air. They come down slowly.)* Thought itself is action—my dear, it moves whatever it touches. It is guerilla theatre. *(Dancer has left. No. 2 is virtually on top of him. He opens his eyes.)* Do you understand? It moves whatever it touches. *(She kisses him gently.)*

1 *(hurriedly gets up).* Did I move you when I touched your breasts? Did I? Tell me? Well, did I? Did I move anything? Tell me? *(She walks away from him. Her eyes closed in anger. He approaches her, then walks back.)*

2 *(to audience).* Did you move anything? Did you ever move anything in your entire life? Did you? There is this other fucking problem—that has—that has made us all clinical and glib actors in every stage. Feelings and emotions are objects of suspicion and ridicule. The sudden impulse, the subversive act, the voice of pain, the cathartic overflow, the three o'clock roadblock has been undermined by an overdose of systematized dissent—and you, my friend, you are at the core of this passionless act *(points to No. 1).*

(Chorus with four people come in slowly and assume frozen position on riser or in front of mural.)

1. Controlling emotions is a sign of maturity and necessary compromise. This is the era of correct terminology . . .

2. You don't understand, you don't understand at all . . . I am . . . talking about another time . . . long ago.

CHORUS. Long long ago. *(Leap into a tableaux as if from nowhere, orange glow behind them, and with percussion a-capella style)* Marlon Brando, Lenny Bruce, C Jam Blues, Velvet Underground, Miles Davis—cool jazz man.

1. Well, I know Charlie Sheen, REM, Midnight Oil, Kevin Costner, Rocket Eshmail, Eddie Murphy, Ninja man; Vanilla Ice, Bill Murray, and Spike Lee.

2. Right! Right! Yeah! Right! and Spike fucking Lee . . . Arnold the exterminator has been put in charge of the new order . . . Emotion is strictly forbidden.

CHORUS. Acting is strictly forbidden! *(Same style as before or change to one at a time—very physical, emotional—dancer accompanies.)* Lee Strasberg, the name is Dean—James Dean, Rod Steiger, Stanislavsky, Theeee Method, Geraldine Page, Group Theatre, Streetcar Named Desire, Hud, On the Waterfront, East of Eden, Bonnie & Clyde, The Graduate, MASH, and Waiting for Lefty.

(They collapse in a heap. Blackout and explosion sound—followed by the sound of water running out of a bathtub. Lights on 1 & 2 again.)

2. You thought you moved me? You thought you touched me?

1. Within allowable and discrete limits.

2. You are boring, you know. You are fucking boring. You cannot touch anything, man. You're busy screwing around with norms and ethics, rules and regulations.

1. Ask me what is my methodology . . . and I will tell you . . . tell me to write a grant, ask me—

2.—about employment equity and you know! Huh! You are like a party . . . party . . . apparitchik.

1. That's, okay, it's in Word Perfect 5.1 Spellcheck.

2. There's too many of you everywhere. That's it! You've seeped into every institution—in college newspapers, women's groups, union meetings, art councils, environmental lobbies—everywhere except native groups.

1. That's a coming.

2 *(she comes close to him aggressively)*. Hey! You don't understand! I said you are taking everyone for a ride.

1. That's a mighty serious accusation you are making there!

2. I couldn't get more serious with you. You do not know the difference between the sublime and the ridiculous *(1 tries to interrupt several times)*, between catharsis and repose, between knowledge and action—you're confusing all issues and getting everybody to groove on nothing *(laughs)*, nothing. And then you think "grave" is politically incorrect because it demeans the dead—don't you? Well! How ridiculous! How insane! How fucking insane, Mr Politically Correct! Look at him, Mr P.C.

1. Uh! Just a minute!

2. Just a minute, my ass—you've started the process of simplifying the debate—you're part of the problem—you've made a career out of the grey middle ground using soft terminology. That's why when you chew you sound like a liberal, when you walk you walk on the right—and you can chew and walk—Jesus! We have a problem right there. We're back to square one. No wonder everything is under attack.

1. I am standing still! You are getting spazzed out writhing in nostalgia and besides, let me tell you something. *(He puts his hat and cigar back on.)* Did you know, George Bush developed a thyroid condition just before the war. I mean, you know what I mean!

CHORUS *(in different questioning poses appear in a tableaux and they say things like)* You mean? Is that right? Could it be? Actually. . . . Now, why didn't I think of that before! Hm, come to think of it. I wonder. Well, you know. Did you say it was the thyroid gland? Did the Pentagon know?

(At the end, this scene blends into a song performed live "My Glands"; a parody of the well-known pop song "My Girl.")

SCENE 5

(OP comes trudging along. She's got a lantern or a flashlight. She goes into a quick jog to one end of the audience. She is busy rummaging through a sack she carries. She finally finds a bottle, takes it out and has a swig. She is happy.)

OP. I keep telling her—don't worry, you'll find your way home. She doesn't believe me. She thinks it's the end of the road. Now look at me, I kept losing my way and I kept finding a new bend in the road. My father would hold my hand tight. He would say let's go back. Uh-uh! When I grew up, mind you, I would lose my way too. But by that time my father was gone. What would I do? Ha! I would do something very clichéd. I'd take out my bottle and swig it down in big gulps and when I'd licked the last drops off—the sun would bob in the horizon—or at least that's all I remember. I have some friends who would say "Look at her—she don't wanna face it." But I'd always see the sun bobbin' in the horizon. And they'd see nothing.

(The young person has come in from the other side; she's got a flashlight. She keeps her distance—hiding from OP.)

OP. Now, let me see. Where is she—that one? Can any one see her! I have to see her. There is a road that I know . . . it's just a little after the first bend there, it's a narrow road with trees all over it . . . it's like a tunnel, but you can see something at the end . . . eh, you know what I mean? . . . Once I was with my father . . . and we were tired. The night was falling. There were only crickets . . . that was all we heard. If you looked up it was all dark. If you looked around there was nothing . . . just the sound of the crickets . . . that was all you heard . . . but then if you listened carefully . . . there! Can you hear it . . . can you hear it? A distant sound . . . yes! . . . So we followed that sound.

YP *(screaming)*. I don't want to hear that story again. I've heard it many times before.

OP. Ah! She is here. . . . Come here . . . I wanna talk to you. *(They are at opposite ends of the maze. YP tries to keep her distance.)*

YP. I don't wanna go on that road.

OP. It's not the old road. There's a new road.

YP. All roads are same here, I know that.

OP. No, this is a different road.

YP. I'm telling you, I don't wanna go to that old house on that old road.

OP. But this will he a new house.

YP. No, it's not true! There is no new house. It's the same thing with you every day . . . the same old shit routine dragged out in the streets and there are no breaks for me . . . and no explanations, everyday there is a procession, a rally. For what? For nothing! And I'm being stomped upon by your procession, your dreams, your ideas which don't mean a thing—in fact it's your procession that's killing me . . . I'm dying because there's nothing in your procession . . . don't you realize?

OP. Don't say that to me. It's not my procession. I did not call the rally. It's them . . . they called the rally.

(The Authoritarian Man appears in a very militaristic posture. He walks through the maze clicking his heels.)

MAN. Attention! *(All lights come up. OP and YP go close to each other inadvertently. They go and sit in the audience and quietly disappear after a while.)* Nobody's dead. Start the rally!

(Chorus appears as a band with kazoos and whistles. They hum "Tequila" and then at the appropriate moment, instead of "tequila," they say "No Problem." By this time the military man has changed his garb in front of the audience. He has put on a pair of shorts and a tie. The Chorus jog around the maze and slowly prostrate themselves in front of him like they were doing push-ups. He now assumes a TV/spiritual leader role. Every time he makes a statement . . . the Chorus says "Amen!" "Hallelejuh!" "Wah-wah!" in different languages.)

MAN. Today I will talk to you about something very important.

CHORUS. Shhhh.

MAN. About the environment and the government.

CHORUS. Ahhhhh.

MAN. We are all born as babies, not as men.

CHORUS. Ah! Yes, come to think of it.

MAN. The Lord said, "Children must grow up and become men."

CHORUS. Hallelulah.

MAN. And you can't be a man till you have made a deal with your environment.

CHORUS. Amen.

MAN. To be at peace with your environment you have to make a hash of the past and the present and dish up the future. That is the task of the government, my children *(heh, heh, heh).*

The future of the nation depends on grown men in government *(heh, heh, heh).* Grown men must tie together in a single bond. Our past, our heritage, our history, our land, our waters, our tradition and keep it alive for future business *(heh, heh, heh).*

CHORUS. Wah, wah, tawba, tawba.

MAN. Grown men must conquer all fears about conquering nature, because nature is for us to conquer. We all love the environment. Don't we? We all love the water. Don't we? The fresh air, the water, the breeze. There is power in the environment.

CHORUS. Mon dieu, this is very important, come to think of it. There is power in the environment.

MAN. Power through power. That is my message for today.

CHORUS. Power through power.

MAN. Power through power

Want not, waste not

Save power, have power

Sell power, have power

Have power, save the nation

Power through power

CHORUS. Power through power.

(They line either side of a walkway, while the man slowly walks away, acknowledging them and ringing a little bell from his hips. Grim somber music is heard.)

1. God save our great nation.

2. And our great leader.

3. Without him all would be mud.

4. Everything is mud anyway, whisked away into the sewer by the flood.

5. All power to our nation.

6. All power to our people.

7. State power is what we want.

3. Power lunch is what I want.

CHORUS *(in unison).* What!

3. I want lunch. Power lunch is what I want.

(He takes out a bag of chips and starts chewing on them. All Chorus surround him like a pack of wolves.)

2. What did you want?

3. Lunch. I want lunch.

(He cleans his ears.)

3. Don't shout in my ears.

2. She wants lunch. She wants to lunch.

1. Death to the terrorist.

3. I am ready to die for lunch.

4. Throw her in the manhole.

5. How dare you want lunch when I don't want lunch?

6. I think I want lunch, too.

3 & 6. We both want lunch.

(They separate slowly into two camps.)

1, 2, 4 & 5. What!

5 & 6. We agree, we want lunch, we want lunch. *(Repeat.)* Death to the terrorists.

1, 2, 4 & 5. Death to the terrorists.

2. Long live the motherland!

4. Long live free speech.

5. Allah ho Akbar.

1. Bande mataram.

2. Beat up the bastards, throw them out of this country.

4. Fucking refugees! *(They start pushing and shoving each other.)*

1. To the plans of Abraham!

3. We believe in Gandhi, we want lunch.

6. Don't touch me, I warn you, don't touch me.

1. Bomb them to the stone age.

2. Send in the fucking Stealths.

3. Long live David Suzuki.[8]

6. Long live Farley Mowat.[9]

4. Death to cross border shopping.

3. Death to GST, estee.

1. Beat up the bastards.

(They clash, punches fly, choreographed with lights, music, tai-chi movement. They all end up on the ground. Then they rise slowly as if in a tired walk. One of them, it seems, is carrying a human head that resembles the young person. Music.)

2. Can you tell us please, sir, where is the dernier recours?

3. My son wants to join the KKK.

4. My factory has moved to Buffalo.

5. My daughter hates science.

6. Our lady appeared in Ste Anne de Bellevue *(makes the sign of the cross).*

1. New York needs electricity.

2. Via Rail has stopped coming to our town.

3. The 144 will have fewer runs.

1. Banning Kashtin was just an error.

4. I saw my aunt Nellie at the NDG[10] food bank. She pretended she didn't see me.

5. The government will not pay for any more shelters.

2. We will have a new Forum. The city says it needs a new one.

3. The schools are full of Orientals.

(They slowly trudge away, repeating what they have already said, except No. 2. She stays. No. 2 keeps repeating about "derniers recours." Scene fades into Scene 6.)

SCENE 6

2. Can anybody tell me where is the dernier recours?

(She walks around in a slow fashion. There is a music score that builds up slowly. It has a searing quality. Under three separate spots at three levels we see

---

[8]Canadian environmentalist.

[9]Canadian conservationist and writer.

[10]Notre Dame de Grace, neighborhood in Montreal.

No. 2, Man and Woman from Scene 4 in an embrace kneeling and YP and OP. In the beginning No. 2 continues about "dernier recours," YP wraps herself up with her hands and sits down as if in pain, shuts her ear off. Then she explodes.)

YP. Stop, stop it godammit, stop it! I know where it is, I know where it is!

OP. Oh! You mean you want to go home? Is that right?

YP *(after looking at her for a while).* No! You don't understand. I've always wanted a home.

OP. That's new. I always thought . . .

YP. It's not like, I don't have any roots.

OP. Oh! You mean you're thinking about what my father said?

YP *(looks at her).* I don't really care for what all the fathers have said. *(Walks away.)*

OP. Where are you going?

YP. Somewhere you've never been. It's through those fields. There are no roads this time.

OP. I don't understand anymore! You don't wanna go home, but you're off somewhere and there is no road! This is strange! *(She fumbles and looks for something.)*

YP. Yes! I don't wanna go home anymore. I wanna find a new bend and one that no one's been on before—one that you don't know, one that they don't know, it's not on any map—it's just a bend out there . . . only I will know. So, this time they won't see me. They won't kill me anymore. I will come like a wind, formless . . . I will sweep through and they won't know what hit them, I will climb onto them and they won't see me, I will grab their little throats and they will gasp . . . I will throttle their little glands till their desert smiles evaporate and they will stand there like apes naked . . . I will tell everyone there is no consensus— they can agree, but we do not concur . . . I will tell everyone . . . *(She runs off repeating her lines.)*

OP. I better go . . . I need my . . . *(takes a swig from her bottle and runs after YP.)*

(Music changes. Only spot on Man and Woman. They turn their faces. They have greased-back hair, slick looks. After a sensuous embrace they stop, straighten their dresses.)

WOMAN. Well, now tell me, do your thoughts menstruate? Do you think the unthinkable till warm corpuscles of blood trickle out of your head?

(Long gaps in-between.)

MAN. Do you still listen to The Doors and have fat joints on Arabian beaches?

(They both mime like they are rowing oars in a boat. Fog starts to collect around them like they are in a boat in a fog. Music right through.)

WOMAN. Does your blood sear a path through the grass for you to follow? A path that you thought did not exist yesterday?

MAN. Do you still dabble in Fanon and reinvent a past that does not exist?

WOMAN. Do you ever want to undermine all your sacred cows?

MAN. Is there nothing in this world that you and me can agree upon as being rational and correct?

WOMAN. Does Europe always hold the keys to correctness and order?

MAN *(looking far away)*. Good question! Did the Roman Empire begin to falter after the triumphant declaration of a new order?

WOMAN *(puts her oar down)*. Who, what are the forces in charge of naming things and what do the named feel?

MAN *(to the audience)*. Are feelings like colonies that want to remain colonized?

WOMAN. The art of representation is getting to be pretty tricky. Scholars, newsmen and leaders have formed an alliance. To colonize all others. If you ain't with "them," you're with the "others." There is no debate. There is no common ground for peace in the valley. Lions and lambs can never represent each other.

MAN. Representation has become irrelevant. Images on the tube have captured the intellect. Anything done by the mob finds a political sponsor.
(As she says this the rest of the Chorus appears, holding candles in multi-candle stands. They pass them by with hmmmmmm sounds, through the fog. Possible Gregorian chant. They are wearing black robes, heads covered, arms are bare. Man and woman join them and move away.)

SCENE 7

(As the Chorus leaves to the chant, OP is seen on the riser. She is fiddling around with her sack. She is drinking, but she also sounds insane. YP slowly rises up while listening to OP. OP cannot see VP in the beginning.)

OP. I just can't find her. She ran away. I told you all along—and you wouldn't believe me. Right? You thought I was dreaming! Huh! Actually I knew it all along, My father was right! It's the end of the road! There ain't no bends—it is a straight road. Everything is in order—who wants bends anyway? Fuck bends! Things are fine without any complications—I mean why look for solutions, when there are no problems. And anyway, you see this bottle! It's almost finished. I'm gonna take a few more swigs and head back—back all the way. I know the road back. You know it's easy downhill—Me and my bottle, that's all it takes—You'll see now.

YP. Just a minute!

OP. Who? Who was that?

YP. It's me.

OP. Who's me?

YP. You were the one who started off about the bend!

OP. What bend! What're you talking about?

YP. About the bend, for Christ's sake! In the road!

(Gap)

OP. You're dreaming! But that's okay! Here! Wanna have some of this? Nectar, pure moon! Makes you blast through the sky! Ever been high, kid? Like I mean really high? Here, take a swig . . .

YP. You told me about the bend!

OP. Gee, what's with her? Listen to me, kid!

YP. You kept telling me about the sun bobbin' on the horizon!

OP. Ah! You're talking haze now, sister. Haze! *(OP takes another swig. YP thinks for a while.)*

YP. What about your father?

OP *(jumps)*. What about him?

YP. You kept telling me about him—and the bend in the road . . .

OP. Keep him outa this! You're tripping on something, or what?

YP. You said that he'd wanna turn back and you'd say just a little further and you don't wanna come back to this dumpy old house and he'd say let's go back . . .

OP. You're upsetting me, you know!

YP. . . . and what happened to the narrow road with the trees all over it. *(OP gets more unsettled. Starts staring out.)* . . . Like a tunnel and you could see something at the end—and then you'd talk about how you once told your father to go take a hike, 'cos he . . . *(OP gets up)* 'cos he didn't wanna hear you—

OP. . . . play Janis Joplin in the toilet.

YP. . . . right, but you loved to hear her scream "TRY—Just a little bit harder." Well?

OP. Just a minute, now!

YP. What's got to you, now?

OP. You're going too fast!

YP. And remember, the good laugh we had when you told me about the kid last year who wanted to know if Woodstock was a farm, owned by Bob Dylan . . .

OP *(laughs)*. Fucking Bob Dylan . . .

YP. Remember, what you told him?

OP. Yeah! I told him Dylan was a dog who thought he inherited the Nation.

YP. Yeah!

OP. And a farm dog, 'cos he pissed always on the same old posts. No city dog would do that!

YP. 'Cos city dogs piss on each post they pass.

OP. Even when they run out of piss.

YP. Yeah and you said the trick was to be urban, and move along! 'Cos otherwise you'd be dumping all your life on the same posts—and then some day, some smart ass who owns the farm, is gonna get rid of the posts—or move them somewhere else . . .

OP. And then you wouldn't know what to do—'cos you'd be looking for that same old post to piss on and you wouldn't find it—so you'd stand around, with your bladder full—meanwhile they'd straighten out the place and make it look totally different—totally unfamiliar.

YP. Yeah! But nothing's changed really in the farm.

OP. You just can't see the posts. You can't see the wire. But you know, they got it all rigged up—if you cross the lines—zap! They've won, Nina, this time, Nina. They've taken over the farm.

(The sound of the theme tune starts filtering in slowly. First it is grim, like in the beginning. Then it gets into a beat and a livelier rhythm.)

YP. No, they haven't—they've got the whole farm spiffed up, looking good, that's all—like everything's settled, but when you get closer—the shit still smells the same.

OP. Listen, can you hear something?

YP. And every few decades, it's the same! The smart asses who own the farms, figure out new ways of spreading the shit! And the new pigs, think—ah, the boss is different, not like in my dad's time. The shit is not bad! Hell, it even smells good! And the bosses declare triumphantly—they've won!

OP. Hold it, hold it, I can hear it!

YP. And we scurry around buying into it. We've lost our shtick! We've lost our sense of humor, sister. We can't joke about the banality of the powerful, we can't piss on their sacred cows, we even worship in their temples, and the shit is still the same.

OP. Hold it, you're not listening carefully—

YP. Listen to what?—Stop playing games! *(The sound gets louder.)*

OP. That's it! It's them! They are coming.

YP. Who? Who's coming?

OP. It's them. *(There is pride and emotion in her voice.)* The fools. They've finally got it together—this time. There! Can you hear it! It's them! Can you hear ... Where's my ...

(She puts on her hat, takes a quick swig. Chorus appears, dancing and singing, OP and YP eventually join them.)

SCENE 8 *(Alternate End)*

(As OP and YP rush out into the wings, looking for the sounds from the Chorus, the music gets louder and the lights fade and one by one, different members of the Chorus appear in different parts of the theater space. The music is a rock feedback guitar style. No. 3 weaves a dance pattern through the maze to the music.)

(When she finishes, the rest of the Chorus comes strolling through.)

6. Yes, yes ... we will go through those fields, where nobody's been before. We'll take a road, which is not on any map—we'll find a bend, where there was none before ...

4. Because, this time they won't see us, they won't know where we came from, they won't know what hit them . . . and they will not kill us any more . . .

2. No! They can't kill us any more. We will come like the wind, formless—we will sweep through their valleys in the night, we will turn around bends and double back on them and they won't know where we came from.

5. We will not go by their order of things, we will not buy their definitions, we will not be caught in useless debates on their side of the street, we will trash their road signs . . .

6. We will tell everyone . . . yes . . . we will tell everyone . . . my friends *(holds the hands of somebody in the audience),* there is no consensus . . . they can agree, but we do not concur . . . we will tell everyone . . . there will be no deals . . .

OP *(appears on riser).* We will climb onto them and they won't see us. We will grab their little throats and they will gasp. We will throttle their little glands, till their desert smiles evaporate, and they will stand there like apes naked.

(All of Chorus start moving slowly towards stage rear. Lights slowly fade out on OP. Music crests.)

PART THREE

United Kingdom

South Asians have maintained a long and multifaceted relationship with Great Britain. Rather than reflecting a simple relationship of domination, links between the two regions and their peoples extend beyond modern colonialism in time and space. Before the mid-nineteenth century moment when the British Empire formally included India as part of its prized possessions, Englishmen of various stripes visited and flourished in India. Indians, as well, were treading to English shores for hundreds of years before formal colonial rule began after 1857. But colonialism and postcolonialism form the foundational context (a long precolonial history notwithstanding) of politics, identity formation, and cultural production in contemporary South Asian British life. It is there that much of this story begins.

The eighteenth century was a time of greed, expanding capitalism, and rapacious expansion of European political control as well as of significant internal changes inside Indian politics. The Mughal Empire, with its base in north India, began to crumble in the early eighteenth century, due to the rise of regional kingdoms throughout the domain, as well as the establishment of European trading companies. In the eighteenth century, the East India Company started gaining enormous profits, often due to unethical dealings, and precipitated fevered debate in England about the manners and methods of doing business in India. As the English company was gaining ground, French and Dutch companies were vying for control and maneuvering amongst local leaders, *nawabs,* for greater shares of power. By the early nineteenth century, due to vibrant Company business, quite a few South Asians managed to land on English shores.

In the words of social historian Rozina Visram, these South Asians generally were part of three groups: ayahs, lascars, and princes.[1] Wealthy British families, rich from fortunes made with the Company, often brought their Indian ayahs and servants with them on their return to Britain in the late eighteenth and early nineteenth century. Ayahs and servants had great responsibility and were in charge of the entire family during travels; they were particularly charged with the rearing of children. Notices soliciting Indian servants dotted English newspapers and periodicals in the late eighteenth century (Visram 1986: 20). These Indians were sometimes abandoned or fired by their employers once in Britain. From the late eighteenth century, the presence of destitute Indians, abandoned by their employers and begging on the streets, garnered the attention of Company authorities. In the guise of humanitarianism, but in the service of protecting money, the Company began to facilitate the return of these individuals and also bid to restrict the entry of Indian ayahs and servants in the mid-nineteenth century (20–21). Nonetheless, many ayahs and servants remained, and their presence enabled the creation of a support network–employment agency for Indian ayahs, in 1900.

Another dimension of the Company era included the large number of lascars, or seamen, who would work on British ships transporting goods and wealth. From the early nineteenth century, the number of lascars employed on British ships increased from the hundreds to more than a thousand in 1813. Often mistreated and exploited, or underpaid for their services, many lascars deserted their ships once they landed in London and turned to a life of destitution. Some, while docked in England, were robbed or tricked out of their possessions, and were forced to lead desperate lives in cold England (39). Like their ayah counterparts, these lascars made headlines; charity and public dispensation was debated in the context of their presence.

As the nineteenth century progressed, another group of South Asians began to spend time in England. Students, the perennial travelers, entered British institutions as early as 1845, when four Bengali Hindu medical students began a degree course at University College London, courtesy of the East India Company. From the 1840s on, increasing numbers of Indians studied in England. While fewer than 400 students were in Britain in 1894, nearly 2,000 were studying in England in 1900 (Lahiri 2000: 5–7). Quite a few famous lawyers gained admittance to the bar in England, such as Manmohan Ghose, Michael Madhushudhan Dutt, Badruddin Tyabji, and J. C. Bonerjee. Women who studied medicine, including Govindu Rajulu, Miriam Singh, Motibai Kapadia, J.R. Dadabhoy, and Dr. Rukhmabai flourished in England in the late nineteenth and the early twentieth centuries. The latter fought a bitter divorce battle and settled in England. Among the most famous female Indians to study in England was Cornelia Sorabji, a Christian who became the first woman of any ethnicity to enroll in Oxford as a law student, in 1889. She returned to India and spent much of her life fighting for the legal rights of the destitute, orphaned children, and widows (Lahiri 2000: 10–13; Visram 1986: 187–189).

Another portion of the Indian student community in colonial-era England included the great men of modern Indian history, such as Jawarhalal Nehru, who studied at Harrow and Cambridge's Trinity College. He later passed the bar at London's Inner Temple before returning to India. Mohandas Gandhi had studied law at the University College in London and also passed the bar at the Inner Temple in the 1880s. Mohammed Ali Jinnah also trained as a lawyer in England and was called to the bar at Lincoln's Inn. In 1894, at the age of nineteen, Jinnah was the youngest Indian to pass the bar in England. For several years he participated in British politics, sometimes consorting with Dadabhai Naoraji, who in the late nineteenth century wrote several striking essays condemning colonial rule. Naoraji rose to be the first Asian Member of Parliament in 1892, from Finsbury Central. Along with these luminaries, ranks of the Indian monied and princely elite studied in Oxford, Cambridge, and London colleges. Other notables include Aurobindo Ghose, a student at Cambridge who went on to become an Indian revolutionary terrorist and then spiritual mystic. K. P. Menon, an Oxford student, would later occupy a vaunted role in English public life as a lawyer for Indian lascars. By the 1930s, Indian student populations had become quite radical and were closely monitored by the British state.

World War II marked the turning point between imperial and national organizational politics throughout the world, and brought forth a thoroughly new meaning to the idea and reality of South Asians living in Britain. After the war ended in 1945, in no small part due to the efforts of Indian soldiers across the world, colonial India proceeded on the path to decolonization. Protracted negotiations between major leaders such as Jinnah, Gandhi, Nehru, and Sardar Vallabhai Patel came to a strange end with the announcement of the new Viceroy Mountbatten that the region was to be partitioned into a Hindu India and a Muslim Pakistan. During the last years of the 1940s, chaos, displacement, and violence reigned across the borders of Punjab and Bengal. Millions died and even more lost their homes as colonial rule came to an end. In 1947, India and Pakistan became sovereign nation-states in the aftermath of a bloody partition.

In the post-1947 world, the Commonwealth of Nations formerly under the British Empire began to experience dislocation in terms of labor patterns and the global capitalism. The United Kingdom was faced with an acute labor crisis after the war and this, along with limited opportunities in South Asia for many elite educated middle-class professionals, began a wave of migration in the 1960s. At this time, East Africa was being purged of its so-called "Asian" population (really, the South Asian population, termed "Asian" by the British

African administration) by the increasingly violent Africanization policies of East African states. These "twice-migrants" began to arrive in the late 1960s and early 1970s as a result of the great purge of South Asians from Kenya, Tanzania, and Uganda. Idi Amin, the notorious dictator of Uganda of the period, ordered the exodus as official policy. Tens of thousands of South Asians left for the United Kingdom. Some communities traveled wholesale, such as the Ramgarhia Sikhs, a caste-based community in East Africa who left for Britain in the 1960s and 1970s. Others, from various regions of South Asia, but mainly Punjab, Gujarat, and parts of western India whence migration to East Africa occurred, also arrived at this time.[2] Most of these migrants built a new British life in a multinational world where nation-states like India and Pakistan coexist alongside Great Britain.

Like their social and political history, the theatre history of South Asians in Britain reveals a diverse map of artists, politics, and community constituencies. This history is slowly starting to gain a voice in academia.[3] Modern theatre practices by South Asians in Britain most likely began in the mid-nineteenth century, when a troupe of strolling players from Oudh was hired by two English brothers, George and Edward Hanlon. These brothers arranged for the troupe to tour Britain and made theatrical history. Little is known about them, much less their performances, but from official records it is known that their bosses were charged with theft and could not properly pay their actors. The troupe managed to entertain audiences in London, Manchester, and Norwich. Soon after their bosses were caught by the authorities, the actors were charged with vagrancy and were shipped back to India. From there, traditions of theatre and entertainment were born in the South Asian British cultural-aesthetic world.[4]

In the early twentieth century, student and other leftist groups produced plays. During World War I, the Indian Dramatic Art Society staged plays promoting the war effort, such as *Grand Performance in Aid of the Wounded Indian Troops.* Another group, the Indian Players, produced an Indian play in English with an all-Indian cast. English leftist and anti-imperialist theatre companies of the period, such as the Unity Theatre, staged plays with Indian themes. In 1943, they performed Mulk Raj Anand's *India Speaks,* a documentary drama, with an all-Indian cast.[5]

But after postcolonial migrations began in the 1950s, theatre, mostly in vernacular languages, began to address internal community dynamics. Some of these groups performed for large audiences, such as Shah Rehman's group, the Orientals, and their Bengali-language productions. One such production of *Siraj-ud-daulah* ran at the Barbican Theatre in 1963. Punjabi-, Gujarati-, Hindi-, and Urdu-language music, poetry, and, at times, theatre were produced by community organizations for their own entertainment and edification. The practice of a broader South Asian theatrical tradition in Britain had yet to emerge out of the confines of various linguistic and regional cultural borders (see Khan 1976).

From the mid-1960s on, official circles in England started to question the large influx of thousands of immigrants from former colonies such as India, as well as the West Indies and parts of Africa. In 1968, given the increasing flood of immigration, conservative MP Enoch Powell lectured a lively crowd about the dangers of immigration from Asia and Africa. During the late 1960s and early 1970s, racist attacks and murders of South Asians began to rise. One of these attacks resulted in the vicious murder of a Sikh teenager in Southall in the summer of 1976.

In response to this rising racism, Jatinder Verma and others met to create a platform for embattled South Asians in racist England. Entitled Tara Arts, under Verma's leadership the group started with Rabindranath Tagore's antiwar play, *Sacrifice*, on a shoe-string budget and with no official support. Throughout the late 1970s and early 1980s, the group toured and interviewed South Asian communities and presented original plays and adaptations of plays that focused on racial tensions in England, immigrant life, and intergenerational conflicts. In 1986, the group started to receive Arts Council funding and branched out in various aesthetic directions. In 1990, Verma became the first Asian director to stage a play at the National Theatre, with his production of Moliere's *Tartuffe*, set in seventeenth Mughal India. This was also the first appearance of a consciously and politically styled Indian English on a mainstream British stage.

In this and subsequent productions, Tara Arts has established an aesthetic via its approach to language and dramaturgy, *Binglish*, in which the highly specific British South Asian experiences with language, culture, modernity, and identity are fused in performance traditions that take elements from classical Indian inspirations, Western theatre practice, and postcolonial realities. Productions of *Le Bourgeois Gentilhomme, Cyrano de Bergerac, The Little Clay Cart,* and countless Shakespeare and Brecht plays evince this aesthetic. It is consciously eclectic and iconoclastically so, as Verma has declared that being Asian is not the sole determinant of dramaturgy or aesthetic range.[6] Italian *commedia dell'arte,* Brechtian staging technique, classical Indian dance, and a range of styles have been used, but they all fall under an aesthetic that reveals the realities of South Asian British life. Tara Arts has nurtured some of the most prominent talent in British Asian theatre today, including Sudha Bhuchar (the cowriter of *Strictly Dandia*, in this volume), Sanjeev Bhaskar of *Goodness Gracious Me,* and Ayub Khan Din, author of *East Is East* and *Rafta, Rafta.*

As Verma's group was rising in the 1970s, another South Asian British writer, Hanif Kureishi, was gaining fame as a novelist and essayist. In the early 1980s, in the midst of seemingly interminable racism directed toward South Asians, he was hired by the Joint Stock Company, to research and collaborate on a play about South Asian immigrants in Southall. After months of research and writing, the play that emerged was *Borderline*, produced in a tour and at the National Theatre in late 1981. This production featured actors such as Rita Wolf and Vincent Ibrahim, who previously worked with Tara Arts, and put South Asian issues on the mainstream theatrical map.[7]

In addition to Verma and Tara Arts, a number of other groups have emerged since the 1980s. In 1983, the Asian Theatre Co-operative formed to present plays by and about British Asians and included among its ranks Farrukh Dhondy, H. O. Nazareth, and Harmaje Kalirai. It and another company from that decade, Madhav Sharma's Actors Unlimited, used British Asian actors and stories but also presented adaptations of Western classics, infusing them with the South Asian linguistic cultural universe. One of the most notable examples of this process is the 1983 *Hedda in India,* a transplant of Ibsen's *Hedda Gabler* into nineteenth-century India.

From the 1990s on, both South Asian actors and, at times, stories have featured in mainstream, "white" theatres, such as the National Theatre and the Royal Stratford East. Institutions in addition to the pioneering Tara Arts have emerged, such as the Waterman Arts Centre and South Asian companies like Tamasha, led by Sudha Bhuchar and Kristin Landon-Smith. Notable recent productions include Tamasha's 1989 adaptation of Mulk Raj Anand's *Untouchable,* Ayub Khan-Din's 1997 *East Is East,* and their 2006 and 2007 productions of their adaptation of Rohinton Mistry's novel *A Fine Balance.* In 1990, the Kali Theatre Company was formed by Rita Wolf, of Tara Arts, and Rukhsana Ahmad, to showcase the voices of South Asian British women. Additionally, other groups, such as Man Mela, Sampad, and motiroti, form a diverse set of the South Asian British theatre art being produced in the twenty-first century. In addition to the inclusion of South Asians in traditionally non-South Asian theatres, or the creation of theatres by and about South Asians, new narrative and storytelling drama has also emerged within the last ten years. Rasa, a Manchester-based company led by writer/performer Rani Moorthy, has been in existence since 1998. The company has produced six original performance pieces that display a variety of forms. Three one-person shows, *Shades of Brown, Curry Tales*, and *Pooja,* have all been written and performed by Moorthy herself. She has also written three full-length plays, including *Too Close to Home*, about contemporary Muslims of Britain, for Rasa.

In addition to Rasa, the Vayu Naidu Company, begun in 2001 by storyteller Vayu Naidu, contributes storytelling and original interdisciplinary performance combining speech, movement, and music. At times, the company has commissioned original plays, such as Rukhsana Ahmad's *Mistaken . . . Annie Besant in India* (2007), which was a part of a three-play trilogy titled *Thought Provokes,* about examining history, heritage, and British cultural identity and hybridity anew. Other performances in the series included *Joining Forces* (2004), about stories of anticolonialism in Asia and Africa during World War II, and *Nothing but the Salt* (2005), about the cultural, historical, and political world of salt, including Gandhi's historic 1930 salt march. All of these performance combined music, dance, archival and visual media, and storytelling.

Other projects have included storytelling performances based on themes, like south Indian art, in *Southern Sojourn* (2007), and a multidisciplinary performance of *South* (2003), a combination of music, dance, and storytelling from Indian, Viking, and jazz traditions. Primarily a touring company, Vayu Naidu's troupe focuses on both creating multidisciplinary cross-cultural, cross-genre pieces as much as examining the politics of diaspora and postcoloniality. This new heritage of English is neither stridently postcolonial in a narrowly defined South Asian way, nor is it looking to the canonical starting points of any tradition and points to a transcendence of mere assimilation or recognition in "mainstream" theatre or performance traditions.

In 1974, Bhiku Parekh, a well-known South Asian British academic, declared that "the Indian in England is haunted by the spectre of self-consciousness."[8] The lascar marooned in Liverpool after 1910, the postgraduate student in Oxford or Cambridge in 1920, or the wounded soldier in southern England after World War II may have been so haunted. But in today's Britain where South Asian restaurants and groceries, cinematic triumphs such as *Bend it Like Beckham*, television shows like *The Kumars at No. 42*, and plays like *Rafta! Rafta!* entertain hundreds of thousands of Britishers, being South Asian and being British are quite easily one and the same.

In addition to food, cinema, and television, theatre by and about South Asians has entered the British cultural landscape. Not simply expressions of cultural sentiment, South Asian British theatre today spans several genres, including realist plays commenting on local politics, usually of race and class, adaptations of Western classics, and, in recent times, dance dramas–comedies that reflect the South Asian communities that combine the politics of present-day Britain with lighthearted enthusiasm. All three types of plays are represented in this anthology, led by Rukhsana Ahmad's *Song for a Sanctuary*.

Not unlike the attention given to race, the world of domestic abuse in South Asian diasporic households has garnered attention in academic studies[9] as well as popular cinema; among these is the 1993 film *Bhaji on the Beach*. Though the subject remains locked in taboo on the subcontinent, critical and activist discussion has flourished in the diaspora. Rukhsana Ahmad's *Song for a Sanctuary* enters the world of a South Asian woman in England, exploring the routes toward escaping domestic abuse. This play tells the story of Rajinder, a South Asian woman fleeing her violent husband, who takes her children into a shelter for battered woman. There she encounters all sorts of people, such as the young diasporic manager Kamla, the elder supervisor Eileen, and a white British woman and fellow resident, Sonia. At the shelter Rajinder tries to rear her young daughter Savita in the midst of such crisis and unsuccessfully tries to relate to the brash activist Kamla. Within a framework of domestic abuse and its fallout, the play covers a vast amount of ground, particularly the British–Asian race relations of the 1980s and diasporic identity politics between generations.

Like Hanif Kureishi's *Borderline*,[10] this play explores how British Asians deal with Britain in a context of race and/or class struggle, often within the Asian community itself. Unlike Kureishi, or Bhuchar and Landon-Smith's *Strictly Dandia*, this play portrays a slice of Asian life as they relate to themselves, in the form of Rajinder and Kamla's conflicts, and Rajinder's relationship with her daughter, as well as the types of conflicts that occur between Asians and whites in a British sociocultural space. This is demonstrated through Sonia's relationship with Rajinder and Savita. Though Ahmad's unifying theme is domestic abuse, these two types of characteristics of the political and cultural worlds of South Asian Britain appear with dramatic power and documentary gravity.

Sonia's interactions with Rajinder form a picture of South Asian Britain that is complicated, racialized, but yet sympathetic. Sonia's outburst, early on in the play, about Rajinder's praying and incessant washing, reveal a submerged type of racialization, as she often asks if Rajinder and others are treated differently simply because they are black. Sonia's characterization, though, doesn't remain onesided, as her friendship and support of Savita show a solidarity that cuts across racial boundaries. Rajinder, for her part, maintains a particularly stolid form of identity with Sonia, and most definitely with Kamla.

To Rajinder, Kamla is not Asian and is not aware of her "culture." If she did, she wouldn't be pressing so hard for rules, procedures, and law. She would respect the sanctity of family, honor, and privacy. Kamla's relation to Rajinder is equally hard-headed, as her attachment to all concepts Western results in more British liberalism than anyone could expect. She scoffs at the institution of marriage, puts faith in the "system" of laws, government, and all the ways the country is set up to help people like Rajinder. At a telling moment during one of their many altercations, Rajinder claims that Kamla just "doesn't understand my language. I didn't marry in a registry office. I married before God. It wasn't just a social arrangement, it was a sacred bond, made with body and soul" (175). Kamla can't find it in herself to try to relate to Rajinder's view of the world and declares Rajinder a fool "living in bloody cloud-cuckoo land" (ibid.). Her rock-hard rejection of Rajinder stems, in some part, from the rejection she must have faced as a child growing up in a "traditional" household. As we find early in the play, her family tried desperately to stuff her with languages, music, dance, and all the trappings of traditional Indian womanhood, only to fail.

Song for a Sanctuary presents a realistic, historical picture of the South Asian diaspora in Britain. Unlike the other plays represented in this anthology, it uses a specific political issue—domestic abuse—as a vehicle into the representation and interrogation of the South Asian diaspora. Ahmad, like Mandvi in *Sakina's Restaurant* or Kriben Pillay in *Looking for Muruga,* did not consciously plan to achieve such an interrogation through playwriting. But given the considerable historical and theatrical value this play offers to the world of theatre as well as to politics and academics, she very well did.

We find a completely different side to British Asian dramatic writing in Jatinder Verma's *2001: A Ramayana Odyssey.* Similar to Kurup's *Merchant on Venice,* Verma does not simply "adapt" a classic story to a contemporary context, but actually tinkers with the actual ideas, characters, and themes in the story itself rather than simply transplant them into a different time and space. As British South Asian theatre has perhaps the most infrastructural and community-based support within the entire diaspora, Verma represents a highly sophisticated foray into dramatic writing. This type of dramatic writing does not simply represent South Asian diasporics. Akin to Rana Bose and his innovation in dramaturgy, Verma actually interrogates a classic piece of Western literature, the *Odyssey,* and puts it in conversation with an Indian classic, the *Ramayana.* This yields several reflections on the nature of migration, power, and gender, all central parts of the diasporic experience. Though Verma has also written the acclaimed *Journey to the West,* a dramatic exploration into the migration of South Asians from their homes into places like East Africa and the United Kingdom, *2001: A Ramayana Odyssey* represents a different part of the diasporic dramatic universe: the interrogation of Western classic literature. This interrogation is not a dismissal of the classic from a subalternist perspective, nor a flat comparison of classics from different cultures, but rather a pointed inquiry into the nature of eternal problems, *through* a classic set of dramatic conflicts. Verma's intimate relationship with migration, power, and the whirling questions about identity, that the diaspora provides, gives him the space to create such inquiries.

Verma's text provides layers of meaning and inquiry. Through creating drama via conversation between two classic heroes, as well as through stylized production choices, Verma has contributed to the ongoing process of constructing dramatic literature from a diasporic vantage point. Issues of gender, power, and political choices are all interrogated with considerable skill. These are not thrashed out in a realistic South Asian diasporic setting, as we find in Mandvi's *Sakina's Restaurant* or Ahmad's *Song for a Sanctuary,* but rather in the dwelling of classic conflicts and dilemmas. Rather than find a documentary report, we find a contribution to the world of substantial theatre making. The diasporic nature of this enterprise lies in the intense interrogation of the status quo, of the "classic" that forms the backbone of the play. Here identities, truths, and certainties about self, other, present, and future are not easily contained. What it means to be a British South Asian, or an American South Asian, emerges as the result of constant inquiry and engagement. Likewise, the certainty of theatre practice—the established concepts and principles of classic theatre—are also set up for questioning, for inquiry.

Verma keeps the integrity of both the *Ramayana* and the *Odyssey* intact—the major events and plot turns faithfully adhere to traditional understandings of the epics. He begins the process with the simple question, "What if Rama were to meet Odysseus? What would they see in each other?"[11] After many improvisations, the company explored the two stories separately and produced the sequences that spoke to teach other the most. From there came the script included in this collection.[12]

The process of exploring both stories and finding the truth in both of them rejects a simplistic Greek Ramayana or an Indian Odyssey. The protagonists question their very choices, and come under intense scrutiny, but neither story gives in to the other. *This* is the drama. This subversion of certitude is not simply located in the diaspora but is inspired by the particular type of marginalization from various centers (South Asia itself, mainstream, non-South Asian culture in a diasporic host country) the diaspora has to face. His theatrical innovation strongly suggests a metaphor for the diasporic experience itself: "West" and "South Asia" exist, in rather pointed ways, but neither exists without questioning the other. His innovation is accomplished in two central ways: the interrogation of key concepts common to both pieces and the use of consciously, politically inspired stylized performance techniques.

The concepts Verma plays with include gender, power, and the curious combination of the two in male heroes who have something to fight for and something to lose. Rama and Odyssey attain a special bond as they appear to sympathize with each other's plights and offer almost identical counsel to each other during times of great gendered pressure. When Odysseus encounters Circe and accepts her advances, Rama quickly mentions Penelope and how she is waiting for him. Odysseus is fixated on his men, and on being a man, as opposed to thinking about Penelope. Later when Odysseus comes across Penelope and her suitors, Rama keeps advising Odysseus to keep space in his heart for pity. Odysseus, oblivious to such suggestions, is focused on his political standing, on his kingdom, on making sure that no rival dare overtake his Ithaca. In such a spirit, he slays all of Penelope's suitors and declares his duty done.

When Rama finds himself in a gendered manic, Odysseus plays the part of critic and advisor in much the same way. After Rama manages to get to Lanka and defeat Ravana and his minions, he curtly refuses to see Sita as anything but a woman who has spent time in another man's house. For this, Rama cannot see her as a wife, but only questions her faithfulness and loyalty. He speaks to her as a king, not as a husband, and Odysseus cannot help but question Rama and ask if "for this we have let loose our arrows? Is this the homecoming we longed for?" (35). If doubts about wives appear, Odysseus asks, why then the journey home? What is the point? Rama, not unlike Odysseus in his moment of kingly manliness, responds that he must keep the kingdom together and not allow anyone to question his power or ability. He also questions Odysseus and his lack of mercy when confronting Penelope's suitors. Both seem to concur that the preservation of the kingdom, the peace of the polity, takes priority over relations with women. For Rama, *dharma* has to be fulfilled; for Odysseus, duty has to be done. But in the end, both realize that even though dharma and duty were all faithfully obeyed, all was lost. In this way, Rama and Odysseus use each other's experiences to reflect on their own. In the end, there is no answer to the question of each other's journey. Both have learned from each other and perhaps learned of the futility of their *dharma* and duty. But perhaps the lesson lies in the questioning, the interrogation of all that is certain and supposedly eternal.

Along with this engagement of key principles, Verma also inserts a few production-oriented choices to further his aesthetic politics. Asserting that neither story shall be completely "adapted" from its context into another, he has written it to accommodate a minimalist set, actors, and costumes. The same actors portray characters in both stories and also use similar costumes and masks for both. In addition, he counters the tendency for Indian practitioners to create an "Indian" Odyssey by importing Indian performance traditions into the Greek story. These traditions appear through a variety of modalities. For example, Circe dances *bharatya natyam* during her seduction of Odysseus. Vedic chants are used in the choral chanting emanating in the Odyssey. Keralan martial arts appear during Greek archery sequences. Finally, Indian music conveying various moods of sadness, anger, or danger also appears throughout the play.

In order to create an appearance of sameness between the Greek and Indian characters, the lone female actor plays both Penelope and Sita while Rama and Cyclops and Odysseus and Lakshmana are double cast respectively. Additionally, both Odysseus and Rama wear masks to heighten the idea that they are not specific, real individuals but rather resemble an ideal character, and, each other.

Verma, a "twice migrant" from East Africa, injects his personal understanding of home and migration into his reading of these stories. Home for Verma is a concept that holds both a vague, often invented type of past, and a complex relation with the present. A central idea to him is the "dim notion of home which always acts as a shadow at the back and a very real home here."[13] Home conjures up unreal expectations and strange reactions; as we see for the protagonists in this play, the results often do not mesh with expectations. Traveling and encountering something unexpected, regardless of *dharma* or duty, informed his creation of this play. Migration for Verma implies multiple and fractured narratives, akin to the two narratives colliding in this play. Each narrative forms but a fraction of the entire process of migration, almost unknowable with the Other.

But the contact between self and Other, in political terms for Verma, is something that has to happen on dialogic terms. Verma is challenging the dominance of European dramatic traditions that are so faithfully taught in drama schools. He calls this play "a journey into the European texts, a dialogue, if you like, with England."[14] What sets this dialogue apart from most is that rather than questioning England from the outside, from a space of distance, it inquires in a space of intimacy, engagement, and curiosity. This intimate space is quite familiar to most South Asian diasporics whose Western sensibility of education, aesthetics, and language can hardly be approached from a distance.

2001: A Ramayana Odyssey forces its interlocutors to think hard about the central conflicts and resolutions of the two epics. It puts certainties in the air, but from a position of respect for the integrity of those certainties, from a position of detailed engagement with them. But like the diaspora itself, it is nothing but a long tribunal of those certainties. This vaults the play into an archive of South Asian diasporic drama that catapults its power into one of not merely documenting, but actually creating, a new aesthetic.

A new aesthetic perhaps isn't the goal of Sudha Bhuchar and Kristin Landon-Smith's *Strictly Dandia,* but a new sensibility, a new set of people from the diaspora (young British desi youth) appear on stage in the final British play of this volume. Race and class form two elements of the social world that almost always arise in discussions of the British South Asian world. Other familiar points of departure are the colonial hangover[15] and the complicated relations South Asians have with other nonwhite groups.[16] But unlike most other recent endeavors, and unlike the other British plays represented in this volume, Sudha Bhuchar and Kristin Landon-Smith use something central to South Asian cultures but not often seen in modern theatre: dance.

The kind of dance dealt with is not *bharata natyam* or *kathak*—dances diasporic children are often forced into learning—but dances of the youth culture, such as the Punjabi *bhangra* and Gujarati *garba.* Bhuchar and Landon-Smith proclaim these dances to be part and parcel of how South Asian British culture today conducts itself, from youth parties to weddings to the colorful ways in which public figures like Sanjeev Bhaskar or Meera Syal wax comedic on television. Bhangra "has become a powerful metaphor for sexy, irresistible, diverse new Britain" (introduction, not paginated). Bhangra, as we know from *Bend It Like Beckham* and *Monsoon Wedding,* has come to represent a pan-South Asian aesthetic accessible to the wider non-South Asian world. But the playwrights tackle a different dance in *Strictly Dandia*: Gujarati *garba* and *dandia*.

Garba and *dandia* are perhaps less accessible to the wider world, as they tend to be considered an exclusively Gujarati cultural practice. Though similar to the Punjabi *bhangra, garba* is a stick dance occurring in a circle. The story of *Strictly Dandia* takes place among lively Gujarati *garba* competitions, in contemporary London. These British Gujaratis are from East Africa, mostly Kenya, who brought with them a particular tradition of celebrating Navaratri, nine nights of *garba* dancing, marking the time before Ravan was defeated by the Hindu god Ram, and culminating in the Diwali festival. This *garba* has been particularly practiced by Hindu women, as they would find shelter from the non-Hindu world—whichever "enemy" found itself on the Hindu doorstep, such as African, untouchable, or Muslim men—and find protection through Hindu men. This type of Hindu womanness-on-display also functioned as a marriage market for families looking for brides.

Bhuchar and Landon-Smith's play charts the import of this tradition into contemporary twenty-first-century London, replete with choreographers, orchestrated *garba* competitions, Diwali floats, and young people meeting their future spouses. As Bhuchar and Landon-Smith put it, these garba festivals are a "showcase for their [Gujarati Britons'] pride, wealth, and increasing self-belief that they are the best, most worthy, and obliging, least troublesome immigrants" (introduction, unpaginated) to settle in Britain since World War II. Gujarati Britons form an excellent starting point into South Asian Britishness. In Bhuchar and Landon-Smith's words, they are profoundly English, as they are "brilliant small businessman, they love discretion, dislike too much clamor for rights, accept the establishment and class order (it links nicely with caste hierarchies), prefer infiltration to revolution, excel at compromise, and like to believe they are tolerant and self-effacing" (Ibid.). These qualities would probably resonate with most common understandings of the English themselves. But these Gujarati Britons, in their march toward absolute, (though perhaps unwitting) assimilation, bring their own East African–South Asian pasts and presents with them. The conflicts of *Strictly Dandia,* such as a romance between a Hindu girl and a Muslim boy, the obsessions with caste, the use of dance competitions as public space, are indicative of a culture that is hardly the white-washed British gentility one could expect. Rather, the Gujarati Britons in *Strictly Dandia* are in the forefront of defining a new sense of culture for British Asians, with elements from Africa, South Asia, and Britain. For Bhuchar and Landon-Smith, participative dance is a constitutive part of this culture. For them, dances like *garba* are "theatres of personal passion where the forces of conservatism can be subverted and reconfigured" (introduction, unpaginated). They cite spaces such as sixteenth-century Venice, Mughal India, and now contemporary Gujarati

London, in which dance allows status quo forms of culture to be questioned and reinvented.

Besides offering an entertaining picture of contemporary youth culture in Asian Britain, Bhuchar and Landon-Smith's story does not strictly deal with dance. Race appears but without heavy sermonizing or identity politics. When Mohan's newsstand is attacked and Raza and Jaz come to the rescue, readers may sense racialism lurking in the background. Race is not overstated and not even overtly discussed. But the incidence of attacks on South Asians, especially on cornershops, is such a common occurrence that the inclusion of it in the piece rings true. In addition to the violence of race, consciousness of a racialized past also appears in the midst of revelry about the East Africa—India migrations that most of the Gujarati Britons hold as a part of their family experiences. During the Navaratri celebrations, community members decorated the hall to resemble a ship taken from Dar es Salaam to Bombay. When Preeti asks her mother Prema about the supposed regalia on those ships, Prema reveals that ships had dinner, dancing, and cocktails, but of course only for Europeans.

The many faces of communalism and religious identity also appear in the play. There are humorous moments, such as when Raza muses "the things I'll do for you" when responding to the possibility that he might have to dress up as Rama in the Diwali float if he and Preeti win the dance. The ugliness of communalism also shows its face when it is disclosed that Raza is Muslim and the entire gang of Hindus lead a brigade of fear mongering and gossip. On the other hand, the bright side of Hindu–Muslim relations also finds a place as we get the encouraging spirit of harmony led by Mohan and his family after Raza and Jaz save them from the hoodlums who attacked their shop. In the end, we are unsure of how the deep-seated communalism entrenched in the mindsets of the Gujarati British community is transformed by this experience. Everyone recognizes how great a dancing team Raza and Prema are and all congratulate them, but what happens to all the prejudice that occasionally emerges during the piece? Perhaps, as the playwrights mention in their introduction, the story is meant to ask questions, not resolve them.

Strictly Dandia displays a complex yet enjoyable picture of the Gujarati British community through an essential part of their contemporary culture. The lives and fortunes of youth—their dancing, their romances, their encounters with elders—are often a powerful barometer of a community's changes and engagement with the past and future. Through Bhuchar and Landon-Smith's considerably researched and sympathetic efforts, we get a substantial sense of this youth in the theatre.

Rukhsana Ahmad

Rukhsana Ahmad is a London-based playwright and writer. In addition to *Song for a Sanctuary,* Ahmad has written six other plays, including *River on Fire* and *Mistaken: Annie Besant in India,* which was produced by the Vayu Naidu Company and the Yvonne Arnaud Theatre. Her radio plays include *An Urnful of Ashes* and *The Errant Gene.* She has adapted El Saadawi's *Woman at Point Zero,* Jean Rhys's *Wide Sargasso Sea,* R. K. Narayan's *The Guide,* Salman Rushdie's *Midnight's Children,* and Nadeem Aslam's *Maps for Lost Lovers.* Ahmad has written the novel *Hope Chest,* and her short stories have appeared in *Right of Way, The Man Who Loved Presents, The Inner Courtyard, Flaming Spirit, Story-Wallah, And Then the World Changed,* and *City of Sin and Splendour.*

She has received nominations for the Susan Smith Blackburn International Prize on numerous occasions, nominations for the Sony Awards, and awards from the Writers Guild for her adaptations.

With actress Rita Wolf, Ahmad co-founded the Kali Theatre Company in 1990 and was artistic director from 1994 to 2003.

Song for a Sanctuary

Kali and Glasgow Women's Group, 2007
National Theatre Studio (youth) presentation, 1999
BBC Radio 4 (adaptation), 1993 (Runner-up CRE award)
United Kingdom national tour, 1991
Kali Theatre Company, Worcester, 1990

Other Plays

Black Shalwar
The Gate-Keeper's Wife
Last Chance
The Man Who Refused to Be God
Partners in Crime
River on Fire

Song for a Sanctuary

Rukhsana Ahmad

Song for a Sanctuary was written partly in response to the murder of an Asian woman at a refuge. It is not, however, a documentary or a biographical play. It is a fiction, concerned as much with conflicts which arise between women who are under siege and are at a crisis point in their lives, as it is with domestic violence.

It took a long while to evolve into its present form. Earlier drafts, presented as readings at the Soho Poly Theatre, at Common Stock, and at the Riverside Studios had a much larger cast and more of a "slice of life" feel to them. Rita Wolf and I managed to set up the Kali Theatre Company, largely through her dedicated efforts and commitment to the play, which raised the finance for the workshops and reading at Riverside Studios and eventually, the funds to produce and tour the play nationally, with the support of the Arts Council in spring and autumn 1991.

We played to mixed audiences, occasionally small but always enthusiastic. The response of women who had been, or were at the time, living in refuges themselves, was deeply moving for both of us, and for the cast. It made all the effort seem worthwhile.

I would like to thank the women and workers in refuges who made time to see me when I was researching the play, all those actors who committed time and effort generously to the readings and the theatre venues which welcomed it. I would also like to thank Sue Parrish of the Women's Theatre Group for her careful criticism and clear-sighted analysis which helped me enormously with the final draft. But above all, I feel indebted to Rita Wolf for her consistent support and her faith in the play.

Characters:	Cast:
Rajinder, a resident	Kusum Haider
Savita, her daughter	Sanny Bharti
Pradeep, her husband	Simon Nagra
Amrit, her older sister	Simon Nagra
Sonia, another resident	Jackie Cowper
Client	Simon Nagra
Kamla	Sayan Akkadas
Refuge workers	
Eileen	Joanna Bacon
Director	Rita Wolf

ACT 1

SCENE 1

(Thursday morning. RAJINDER *is unpacking in the refuge kitchen. She is lining shelves with sheets of old newspaper and wiping and scrubbing with dedication, grumbling under her breath.)*

RAJINDER: Hai, hai, ainna gund! You'd never guess how filthy it is inside, disgraceful. . . . Where is it now? I thought I had some Dettox here . . .

SONIA: (enters) Hello, there!

RAJINDER: Good morning.

SONIA: Welcome aboard! You've got into it nice an' early.

RAJINDER: Mmm . . . I came a couple of hours ago.

SONIA: Jesus! You've got loads of stuff there! I came with just one Tesco carrier bag.

RAJINDER: I don't like to run out of things at odd times . . . it's taken an hour to get the locker and shelves into order. Looks as though they've never been cleaned since they were put up.

SONIA: Possible. Good housekeepin' ain't a huge priority round these parts specially as you don't 'ave to bother with coffee mornings and ladies' lunches in 'ere.

RAJINDER: I don't do it for show. It's hygiene I'm worried about. Can you imagine all the millions of germs in here?

SONIA: Creepin' an' crawlin'! Ugh. Do I have to?

RAJINDER: There's bits of cheese and breadcrumbs and stale crisps everywhere. You can actually smell the fungus.

SONIA: Hmm. Not very nice at all, is it?

RAJINDER: Just look at that . . . that was a forgotten banana I think. It's got no business to be here in the first place.

SONIA: None at all! The locker on the right's mine if you've got some energy left when you've finished yours. It looks a treat already. *(RAJINDER only glares and turns back to her work)*

SONIA: Coffee?

RAJINDER: No thanks.

SONIA: I think it'll be good to introduce ourselves before we start rowin', shall we? I'm Sonia.

RAJINDER: My name's Rajinder, Rajinder Basi.

SONIA: Hi, Rajinder, nice to meet you. You're goin' into the room next to me, aren't you?

RAJINDER: The room at the back, on the ground floor.

SONIA: Yeah, that's the one. You got any kids?

RAJINDER: (nods) Three. Two girls and a boy.

SONIA: Oh! Are they young?

RAJINDER: Fourteen, eleven, and eight. Sanjay my son's the youngest and I have two daughters.

SONIA: Oh, well, that's handy. They must be a help.

RAJINDER: They are, sometimes.

SONIA: At least they don't want feedin' in the middle of the night, like Barbara's little one. You can set your watch to his howlin', 2 AM every mornin' he starts.

RAJINDER: No, I've been through all of that. And how about yours?

SONIA: I 'aven't bothered with any of that yet.

RAJINDER: Oh, really?

SONIA: It's hit me now you must be the lady who came on the inspection last week? So, you forgot to look inside the cupboards then?

RAJINDER: Is that what she called it, "an inspection visit"?

SONIA: Well, you made history apparently; no one's ever done that before.

RAJINDER: I've always lived in a nice house. I thought it best to see the place beforehand, for the children's sake. I don't know why she got so resentful about that.

SONIA: Who did?

RAJINDER: Kamla, I think she said her name was. Indian name but she didn't look very Indian.

SONIA: Her soul's Indian I think.

RAJINDER: Do we have souls that are brown too, then?

SONIA: You are spoilin' for a row, aren't ya? Perhaps I sh'd take my coffee an' go to my own room?

RAJINDER: Sorry! I don't think I know what an Indian soul's really like?

SONIA: Unworldly? Committed, in some way . . . quite determined, maybe, like old Gandhi . . . bit like them Indian monks, you know, the ones who decide to give up the material world?

RAJINDER: I see.

SONIA: Oh, well. It was only an idea. *(pause)* Maybe we haven't got any souls anyway.

RAJINDER: I don't know that life's worth living if we don't.

SONIA: Yeah, you wonder sometimes if it is? Too heavy, all that for me this time of the mornin'. Got to get a move on. I do a Yoga class lunchtime on Thursdays. I think I need another coffee to get the ol' system goin'. *(SONIA winks at RAJINDER who looks unamused and concentrates on cleaning again. SONIA pulls up a chair, lights a cigarette and settles down to a comfortable silence with a newspaper and coffee)*

RAJINDER: Have you been here long?

SONIA: Five weeks this time.

RAJINDER: So it isn't your first time?

SONIA: Oh, no! An' yours?

RAJINDER: I've been in a refuge before . . . couple of years ago, I went in an emergency situation, and it was a mistake. That's why I planned it all carefully this time. I think you need to.

SONIA: Maybe you'll stick with it better. I've been in an' out of here a lot. Get's up Kamla's nose. She doesn't like returners, *(pause)* that's women who go back to their blokes.

RAJINDER: Doesn't she?

SONIA: I don't think she knows how hard it is to pull yourself out of it, for good. It's really tough.

RAJINDER: It's not easy when you go back either because husbands hate you so much for trying to get away, don't they?

SONIA: It's different I think with Gary. I'm not married, see, an' Gary, my partner, is actually quite nice for a bit when I go back to him.

RAJINDER: Not married!

SONIA: I think all men are different. An' he really tries to be nice when I go back, at least in the beginnin'; he'll get me presents, take me out for a drink, be quite lovin'. Then he falls into his ole habits. First it's a slap, and then maybe a fist or two, then a couple of kicks, until one day he has to let it all out on me. Last time he messed me up really bad . . . The worse it is the longer it takes me to get back to him, but I always do in the end. See my back?

RAJINDER: It looks dreadful. Five weeks, did you say?

SONIA: It doesn't hurt any more.

RAJINDER: *(Shakes her head in dismay)* You shouldn't go back this time. You're not even married to him. And it is so much . . . harder to leave, you know, once you have children, and then before you know it your whole life's gone. That is awful.

SONIA: He doesn't mean to be nasty or anythin' but you know what men are like. They only understand violence and they want to feel in charge, but me with my big mouth, I always slip out the wrong thing.

RAJINDER: *(Tries to distance herself a little)* They can't all be like that; my brothers are so good to their wives . . . Oh well . . .

SONIA: Lucky devils!

RAJINDER: God only knows what people do to deserve their luck.

KAMLA: (Enters) Hi. So you've met Sonia? I thought I'd come and say hello and get the papers out of the way.

RAJINDER: Sure.

KAMLA: Some details got left last week since you were in such a hurry.

RAJINDER: I only just made it in time. Pradeep got in a few minutes after I did.

KAMLA: That's okay. All I need is the names of the children here and your signatures.

RAJINDER: Savita, Bela, and Sanjay.

KAMLA: Right, got that. Now, there's one other thing, would you mind running through . . . a few details with me . . . just a couple of questions about what happened? *(RAJINDER looks annoyed but says nothing)* Have you taken out an injunction against him? Have you ever been to the police about your husband?

RAJINDER: Never. They open an inquiry and make your life hell with questions and questions and questions. The one who reports has to answer all their questions. They never catch the thugs; everyone knows that.

KAMLA: So was there an incident which made you leave?

RAJINDER: You're doing the same thing! I was told there would be no prying.

KAMLA: I'm sorry if it seems like that.

RAJINDER: This isn't easy for me, as it is.

KAMLA: Of course. Normally it isn't necessary.

RAJINDER: Then I would like to be treated "normally," please.

KAMLA: Trouble is you haven't been referred by any one, like a social worker or a doctor so, it is necessary. I'm sorry but resources are precious, we do need to prioritize in some way . . . to establish need.

RAJINDER: Do you imagine anyone would want to come to a refuge unless they needed to?

KAMLA: It's possible.

RAJINDER: Definitely not—if they've been in one before.

KAMLA: You may be right.

RAJINDER: I know I am right. It may look as though I have a choice, but I haven't really. I need to be two steps ahead of him.

KAMLA: Oh?

RAJINDER: I'm trying to escape from a man who's cunning, and strong, and tough as a bull; he can see through curtains, he can hear through walls. I am really frightened of him.

KAMLA: I'm sorry, I had to ask.

RAJINDER: It's all right. It's the haste of the young, isn't it, judging like that.

KAMLA: I'm not that young.

RAJINDER: You look very young to me. Where do you come from, Kamla?

KAMLA: South London.

RAJINDER: Oh, I see! *(pause)* 'Tusi Punjabi boalday o?

KAMLA: I'm sorry, I don't.

RAJINDER: It's . . . just, that I wondered about what other languages you spoke, if any?

KAMLA: Some French.

RAJINDER: Maybe I shouldn't have asked.

KAMLA: No, that was silly of me. I'm sure we can do better than this. Two grown women!

RAJINDER: Can we really?

KAMLA: Yes, I believe in friendship between women.

RAJINDER: I've heard about it too.

KAMLA: This language thing, it's just that, it looks like an inadequacy and it isn't. Names are all they had left to them, in the Caribbean; to keep the languages going seemed a bit pointless in the end.

RAJINDER: So you're not from India?

KAMLA: No, not quite. *(pause)* They struggled to make us Indian, in some sense. But it was hard; there probably isn't a lot we have in common.

RAJINDER: You're right, I'm sure.

KAMLA: It needn't be a problem though.

RAJINDER: I certainly hope not. *(Enter* EILEEN*)*

KAMLA: Hi, didn't know you were back! Rajinder this is Eileen, my colleague. She's been here since the refuge was set up.

EILEEN: Ages and ages ago! Hello.

RAJINDER: Pleased to meet you Eileen.

EILEEN: Me too.

RAJINDER: Could I talk to *you,* if that's all right, about "my case."

EILEEN: Sure, whenever you like.

RAJINDER: Tomorrow, maybe? It seems I need to justify my being here.

EILEEN: You're welcome to be here if you need to, no questions asked.

RAJINDER: Thank you. I'm glad to hear that. Now if you'll excuse me, I must go. They get quite upset in the school if mums are late. *(Exit* RAJINDER*)*

EILEEN: Phew! Been stepping on toes, eh?

KAMLA: She would say nothing of her circumstances and she seems totally calm.

EILEEN: Could just be a layer, like her make-up.

KAMLA: Pretty thick layer, then!

EILEEN: Come on! There's nothing wrong with a bit of make-up, K!

KAMLA: Well . . . *(pause)* The thing is she looks able . . . and quite well-off. I have to ask, do people like her deserve to use up room?

EILEEN: I don't think anyone comes here, if they have a choice, Kamla.

KAMLA: Hmm. She did claim that she has no family here.

EILEEN: Exactly, and maybe no friends.

KAMLA: I dunno about that. I'd be very surprised! You become that smug only when you've got everything; and then, of course, good luck follows you wherever you go. You're never short of friends.

EILEEN: She's not your type, that's all.

KAMLA: No, she isn't. I wonder if she's using us, in some way, for some strange game of her own. She's not the kind who needs help!

EILEEN: Oh, Kamla, what's that supposed to mean? Stop being suspicious. How many times've you said to yourself that class divides women, amongst other things. Don't let it do that to you now.

KAMLA: Just found her a bit . . . annoying . . .

EILEEN: Try to find the common ground, there must be some, somewhere within her, there must be the woman who needs help . . . think you're being quite irrational about her.

(KAMLA only shrugs. Exit EILEEN a little annoyed. KAMLA picks up RAJINDER's shawl and sits down on a chair. She opens the shawl and drapes it round her shoulders and walks slowly up and down the stage. She strokes the shawl and then lifts a finger to warn)

KAMLA: You wrap it up carefully in old muslin if you can't find a polythene bag . . . you don't just leave good shawls lying around. Don't you know moths get at them if you're not careful? *(Carefully folds shawl and puts it back)* Oh, sorry I nearly forgot. *(Pause. Hums to herself then tries to sing a snatch of an Indian song)* Aaj sajan mohay ang laga lo, janam safal ho jaai . . . "Any languages?" Riday ki peera, birha ki agni, sub sheetal jo jaai . . . Language classes, music lessons, dance lessons, they tried it all . . . it was no use to me. Who cares for all that crap anyway? *(Then she gets up and tries a few steps of kathak, holding her hands together in front of her looking stiff and awkward)* Tut, taa, thai, thai, tut, taa, thai, thai and now double *(faster)* taa, thai, thai tut, taa, thai, thai. *(Enter RAJINDER)*

RAJINDER: I forgot my . . . shawl . . . oh?

KAMLA: Here it is. *(Exit KAMLA flustered)*

SCENE 2

(Friday night; RAJINDER's bedroom in the refuge. The stage is in complete darkness. SAVITA has woken up after a nightmare. PRADEEP walks onto the stage and stands silently behind them. His shadow falling across them. Shuffles softly to her mother and whispers.)

SAVITA: Mummyji! Wake up, please Mummy!

RAJINDER: What is it, for God's sake, sshh quiet, Savita, you'll wake up the others.

Hush, meray bachchay, you're shivering, what happened? *(RAJINDER moves and lights a lamp. A small spotlight comes on above them emphasizing the darkness)*

SAVITA: There's someone in here.

RAJINDER: Where? Are you crazy, darling! There's no one here. Try to sleep, you'll wake up the whole house.

SAVITA: I saw him getting into the room. He broke in through the window.

RAJINDER: Who?

SAVITA: Maybe it was Papaji. I couldn't tell, his face was hidden in his turban, and, and he had his kirpaan, he was holding it like that, like a flag, above his head.

RAJINDER: Stop being so silly, Savita, there's no one here.

SAVITA: You know how he looked that day when he went mad 'cause you got back late. . . . He just stood there, he was polishing his kirpaan . . . and his eyes looked strange . . . I really felt so terrified of him.

RAJINDER: Yes, I remember it.

SAVITA: And you know, that time . . . when he flung his plate at you, for talking back at him?

RAJINDER: Savita, stop it. I won't be able to sleep, don't stir it all up in my head at this time.

SAVITA: He wouldn't, he wouldn't force us to go back, would he, really, Ammah?

RAJINDER: I don't think so. Calm down, Savita. He can't find us here.

SAVITA: But if he does? Would he beat you in front of the other women here?

RAJINDER: He won't, he can never trace us to this place. Hush. . . .

SAVITA: You can take self-defense classes at my school.

RAJINDER: *(Kisses her)* I'll think about it.

SAVITA: We could keep a hammer under the pillow. I kept Sanjay's bat under the bed, list night.

RAJINDER: Savita, what shall I do with you, my child, you're impossible . . . !

SAVITA: Ammah, I'm scared, don't laugh please.

RAJINDER: I'll cry if I don't.

SAVITA: Don't laugh, you sound strange. Why does everyone sound so different in the dark?

RAJINDER: Try to sleep, jaan. *(pause)* Hold on, what's that smell? Oh, Savita!

SAVITA: Ammah, I'm really, really sorry.

RAJINDER: Not again, I could kill you. All that washing it makes!

SAVITA: I never mean to. I don't know how it happens.

RAJINDER: Go and wash and then change your clothes. You're fourteen! What if someone finds out? *(SAVITA gets off the floor)*

RAJINDER: And just leave the wet things on the floor, I'll get up and rinse them out myself.

SAVITA: I *can* wash them out you know.

RAJINDER: I'll do it. Then I know it's done properly and they won't smell. *(Exit)*

SAVITA. *(Sound of a light switching on off-stage. Water running, then sound of a small baby crying)* Curse the day that brought us together, Pradeep! God forgive me, but I'll never let you find me ever again . . . I swear never to let you touch me again, Pradeep *(Exit PRADEEP in silence)* Wash the bedclothes, your hands, your face, your body, once, twice, three times and pray for it to be cleansed. Then wash him off your body, Rajinder . . . and never let him touch you again . . . *(Light fades slowly on RAJINDER)*

SCENE 3

(A bench in a park is set out at the front. RAJINDER walks on dressed for a walk. She sits down "feeding the birds." EILEEN follows her and joins her on the bench.)

EILEEN: Mind if I join you? I saw you from the window and I felt like a walk too. We all stay cooped up indoors too much.

RAJINDER: Not at all. *(Moves to make room for EILEEN)* I love this half hour of peace and quiet, before the children return from school.

EILEEN: Look at that cheeky thing, they seem to know you already. D'you come out here every day?

RAJINDER: Just to get rid of the old bread and rice. I just collect it all from everyone. It's sinful to throw food in the bin.

EILEEN: Didn't I see you pourin' a pint of milk down the sink only yesterday?

RAJINDER: That was different . . . it . . . it got polluted.

EILEEN: Oh! *(pause)*

RAJINDER: I didn't mean to make a scene, but it matters to me, a lot. They don't seem to understand how much. How someone can just leave meat to defrost in a bag on the shelf, I don't understand . . . ? The blood from it just dripped on to the milk.

EILEEN: Was only on the carton though, wasn't it?

RAJINDER: But still. It was . . . it is disgusting. It only needs for them to keep out of my bit of fridge and there wouldn't be a problem. Tell me, how long have you been here Eileen?

EILEEN: Almost eleven years now.

RAJINDER: We must all sound the same to you!

EILEEN: Not at all. The situation is the same but women are so different, I'm not bored. No. A bit thrown by the enormity of it sometimes, but not bored, never that.

RAJINDER: You really care, don't you?

EILEEN: I think all of us do, in our own ways. Kamla does too, and the others.

RAJINDER: Maybe it's because you're older I felt I'd find it easier talking to you. I thought you'd understand more . . . than Kamla?

EILEEN: Perhaps I do, just a tiny bit more, an' that because I've been there.

RAJINDER: Meaning?

EILEEN: I came to this place for refuge myself, it was different then, a couple of women had set it up as a safe house. Then they gave me the job.

RAJINDER: I didn't know that. Do you ever get over it? I dunno if I should ask?

EILEEN: I don't mind talking about it now. It hurts, but I'm not bitter any more. I feel angry, more with myself for having stood it so long.

RAJINDER: You must have hoped he would change.

EILEEN: Yes, don't we all do that? I gave him a good ten years, and you? More than that, I s'pose?

RAJINDER: Fifteen. Sometimes people repent, they say.

EILEEN: I just couldn't take it any more. Bullyin', beatin', abuse and insults—an' he'd torment me over the money an' the housework. I became so nervous I'd be shakin' at ten o'clock when it was time for him to come home. He'd walk in and start pickin' on me. The night I left, he actually came at me with a hammer. I was so shit-scared I ran all the way to the police station in my slippers.

RAJINDER: How terrible! God, I can just imagine what you went through.

EILEEN: You know what the coppers did? Dumped me right back with him again. "Domestic," they said. I nearly died when he finished with me that night. That was it. I had to leave after that. I was too scared to go back.

RAJINDER: Hmm.

EILEEN: That was it.

RAJINDER: Yes. No-one can really understand what it's like inside your four walls. (RAJINDER *is silent. Enter* PRADEEP. *Watches from a distance*) Do you have any children?

EILEEN: Two, they're grown now; wasn't much of a life for them I can tell you, all that bashin' an' terror day and night.

RAJINDER: It's the children you have to think of.

EILEEN: Are yours very disturbed by it all?

RAJINDER: Hmm.

EILEEN: For a long time I couldn't talk about it either. And for a long time, I never really felt safe. I'd be scared at night thinkin' he'd found me and was staring through the window panes.

RAJINDER: But he couldn't have, I suppose?

EILEEN: No. I'd put miles and miles between us.

RAJINDER: That means you can get away if you really want to. Can't you?

SCENE 4

(KAMLA *and* EILEEN *are working in the refuge office. Typing accompanied by some muttering from* KAMLA.)

KAMLA: When's the next management committee meeting, d'you know, Eileen?

EILEEN: 27th, I think.

KAMLA: Is there still time to put something on the agenda then?

EILEEN: Bit tight, I think, what did you? . . .

KAMLA: Just an idea, I had.

EILEEN: Hum?

KAMLA: Perhaps we should have a registration form for women to fill . . . to detail their case histories a bit more.

EILEEN: You must be joking.

KAMLA: We need to know everything . . . when they come.

EILEEN: There's plenty to do here without adding to the bureaucracy.

KAMLA: But . . . (SONIA *knocks and enters*)

SONIA: Are you two busy or can I come in and have a word?

EILEEN: Come in Sonia.

KAMLA: Tisn't the best of times, though.

SONIA: Won't be long, I promise.

EILEEN: Right, what's the problem?

SONIA: I want to change my room.

KAMLA: What's wrong with yours?

SONIA: Rajinder and family next door. I can't believe it, the place is dead as a morgue in the morning and it sounds like Piccadilly Circus in the middle of the night, there's noises through the night. You know how the water works go pumping and whistling and rattling the whole place up every time someone opens a tap or somethin'.

EILEEN: It's these old houses.

KAMLA: So they have baths in the middle of the night to keep the smell of curry down?

SONIA: Look here, Kamla, don't jump down my throat. It's nothin' like that. I'm no racist. You're new here, but Eileen knows me over the years. I've been in an' out of this place you know.

KAMLA: That gets no medals in my book.

EILEEN: Let's not get into a state over this. Isn't it best for you to have a chat with her yourself, in the first place, Sonia?

SONIA: I've done that. This is a lady with a big problem.

EILEEN: Well, ain't we all?

SONIA: Naw, it's different.

KAMLA: What's that supposed to mean? I won't listen to this, Eileen. There's rules about racism written out somewhere.

EILEEN: Would you let me deal with this please, Kamla. So what did she say when you asked her about the baths?

SONIA: She sez her youngest wets the bed sometimes. Well, would you call three nights out of seven sometimes?

EILEEN: No.

SONIA: And she says all the washing can't be left. Anyway she's got a thing about washin'. She's in the bathroom for hours an' hours.

EILEEN: She's right, the others won't want stinkin' bedsheets soakin' in the bath first thing in the morning; that would be a bigger nuisance, I reckon.

SONIA: I can't sleep with all the bloody racket, so what am I to do?

EILEEN: He'll stop wettin' the bed as soon as he settles down.

SONIA: That might take weeks, besides she's not helpin' any. She gets quite wound up if they start gettin' matey with the other kids. Her li'l girl likes to 'ave a chat with me an' you can see her gettin' pretty uptight about that. Then there's Barbara on my other side, and her Ricky starts screeching 2 AM sharp.

EILEEN: Tough! Babies have to be fed and changed.

SONIA: For fuck's sake, that kid's not a baby. Maybe she should have him down to the doctor's.

KAMLA: Surely noise can be kept down a little in consideration of others.

SONIA: Exactly; an' that's not all. Last night at about five I got my head cleared of all the cobwebs an' I thought, here goes, I was droppin' off and then I heard someone singin'! I couldn't believe it.

KAMLA: Singing?

SONIA: Yeah, I asked her. Well, what d'you know, it's 'er prayin' first thing in the morning.

KAMLA: Praying! In this day and age?

EILEEN: People do, you know.

SONIA: I don't mind 'er prayin' even at that time of the mornin' but not that loud, please!

EILEEN: I do think, Sonia, that is the kind of thing best dealt with, directly by yourself. Just ask her, nicely, over a cup of tea.

SONIA: Well if that isn't a fuckin' cop out. You two really want to sort this out, don't ya? Is it 'cos they're hard-pressed mums or 'cos they're both black?

EILEEN: You've got more sense than that, Sonia! (SONIA *stamps out angrily*)

KAMLA: I knew there'd be trouble with Rajinder.

EILEEN: Sonia'll soon come round to it.

KAMLA: I see the point of making concessions to the mums but I think you should've had a word with her yourself.

EILEEN: When you've been here as long as I have . . .

KAMLA: That's another thing! I'm sick to death of having the weight of your experience thrown at me all the time.

EILEEN: Sorry, not very tactful. It gets heavy if I interfere, spoils things. It's best if they talk to each other an' deal with it. They're adult women.

KAMLA: But praying in the middle of the night is a bit much! It's not adult behavior. We really do need to do some consciousness-raising work here.

EILEEN: I don't see much wrong with that. Praying's only a step away from wishing. Anyway, for some women, it's the only thing that keeps them goin'. Who are we to destroy that?

KAMLA: She's just like my mother. You won't destroy her faith. It would take a bloody miracle to do that!

EILEEN: So what d'you want me to do?

KAMLA: She can't relate to me at all, won't even talk to me. At least she talks to you, so you've got to do some work with her, you know . . . just to make sure she doesn't go back. She's done that once before.

EILEEN: I'd rather she chooses herself. Kamla. I'm not into mind-bending.

KAMLA: Look at the world we live in Eileen, it pushes women into marriage. There's always pressure to save the "home," keep the family together. They need support to get out and to stay out of a bad marriage and we've got to give that support. Sometimes it does mean challenging their beliefs, yeah?

EILEEN: Well, if you must!

KAMLA: She stays aloof, won't talk to the others. She's putting their backs up. She doesn't mix, won't give support or take it. Then her whole attitude and manner . . . it is so critical of what we try to do and so . . . uncritical of the outside world. It's too insidious. We've got to take her on.

EILEEN: I tried to draw her out, but I couldn't.

KAMLA: Why won't she talk of what's brought her here? Has she said anything to you?

EILEEN: She's not ready to talk yet. Takes a lot of trust to share the shame and humiliation you've hidden from the world for so long. Why should it be a problem? It's not right to try and prise it out of her. I'll fight you on that one, if you do put it on the agenda.

KAMLA: Maybe she'll never be ready. She's not facing up to it, is she? I am suspicious of secrecy. Just typical of this kind of woman, isn't it?

EILEEN: Kind of woman! Crap! All that stuff you churn out about stereotypes . . . if only you could listen to yourself talking!

KAMLA: See! She's divided us already! Some women are collaborators by nature, they're the ones who'll always sell you out, beat you down . . . with their mad, suicidal fanaticism. We need to fight that kind, specially in here.

EILEEN: I don't like the tone of any of that, Kamla. Just lay off—leave her be, till she asks for help. All kinds of women have a right to their views.

KAMLA: And I have a right to persuade them to change those views.

EILEEN: Only persuade, not pressure. The women who come to us are . . . stuck, they're stranded, they're ship-wrecked if you like . . . they don't know where to start. They need space, okay?

KAMLA: Sure. I'll give her space, all the space she needs . . . but I won't let her undermine the work we have to do.

EILEEN: She's hardly in a position to do that! *(Exit* EILEEN*)*

KAMLA: Maybe she'll change, but . . . maybe she can't. *(Pause)* I'm not going to be sentimental and gush over her just cause she's Indian. No guilt trips on that one!

SCENE 5

(Short stylized sequence. SONIA, KAMLA, SAVITA *and* EILEEN *are playing cards. We watch them playing and arguing for a few minutes. They bid, argue and shout excitedly as they play.* KAMLA *claims victory at the end and then* KAMLA *and* EILEEN *go offstage leaving* SONIA *and* SAVITA *to review the game.)*

SONIA: That was a bloody lousy game. You just can't afford to lose count of how many aces are out, Savita.

SAVITA: I didn't do too badly, I got such rotten cards.

SONIA: We're three down: not good enough, darlin'. If this was money, an' not match sticks, we'd be broke. By the way did you ask yer mum 'bout going to the film, Friday. Kamla wanted to know. She's booked six tickets, I think.

SAVITA: No, I think the only way she'll let me go is if she doesn't know it's a Fifteen film.[1]

SONIA: I'm not tellin' any lies. Never have done, even to save myself a hidin'. I think it's best to tell her. Sanjay'll tell her if you don't.

SAVITA: Oh, he's such a tell-tit. Rotten brat! Then she won't let me go. I want to go . . . so badly. Everyone in my class has seen it.

SONIA: I'll put in a word. I dunno if it'll help any, ah . . . *(Enter* RAJINDER*)* Here, Raji, could Savita come to see a film with all of us . . . it's me birthday.

RAJINDER: I don't think she's old enough for a night out yet. You always have homework and things to do at the weekend, Savita. You don't really want to go.

SAVITA: Please, Ammah. I do. Just for the film.

SONIA: That's all we're doin' really, probably get a takeaway after, everyone's skint.

SAVITA: Please. It's a film I really want to see. They've all seen it in my class. I'll do anything you say. Please.

RAJINDER: Never mind if they have. We're different from them, you know that.

---

[1] A fifteen film is rated to be for only those over the age of fifteen, akin to the R rating in the United States.

SONIA: Only a bit of fun for her. She'll be okay.

RAJINDER: What film is it?

SONIA: Pretty . . .

SAVITA: Out of Africa *(together)*

SONIA: A-aa! Savita?

RAJINDER: Hmm. All right then, but make sure you're not moaning on Sunday night about homework.

SAVITA: Thanks Ammah, you're so sweet, you're brilliant.

KAMLA: *(enters)* Hi, Rajinder, just the person I wanted to see.

RAJINDER: Hello.

SAVITA: Kamla, I meant to ask you, could I type something on your typewriter? We're doing an anonymous letter to our head teacher.

KAMLA: That sounds a bit dicey. Why should it be anonymous now?

RAJINDER: Don't you dare get involved in silly things like that. You need to do your homework now, you better be off.

SAVITA: I'm going, I'm going. *(Exit SAVITA)*

KAMLA: Just wanted you to know I've made an appointment for you to see the housing bloke tomorrow morning. Is that still okay? And I'd quite like us to have a chat about things after that.

RAJINDER: I thought Eileen was to be my caseworker.

KAMLA: She's got all she can handle at the moment. I'm sorry, but here women don't get to choose their caseworkers.

SONIA: Don't you think that's quite unfair, Kamla?

KAMLA: No, I don't. How does someone choose a caseworker? Because of the color of her eyes, skin, her smile, what? It's nonsense, really. Choice can be just a pointless complication sometimes. Anyway, people don't always know what's best for them.

SONIA: Sure. You love to cluck over us, your chickens, don't you Kamla? Then you can peck at the ones who try to get away. So now you know why they call her THE COLONEL! . . . Oh, well . . .

KAMLA: Meanwhile, I'll see you tomorrow afternoon, won't I?

RAJINDER: All right; if there isn't a choice.

KAMLA: By the way, Sonia. I got the tickets for *Pretty Woman* for your birthday. Would you tell the others please.

RAJINDER: I thought you said *Out of Africa*!

SONIA: There was some confusion about this, I think.

KAMLA: But that's what you told me, six tickets for *Pretty Woman*, I'm quite sure.

SONIA: Yes, yes, I know.

RAJINDER: So what's *Pretty Woman* about? Why didn't you want me to know it was that film?

KAMLA: It's nothing special, just an entertainer, I think. Are you going too?

RAJINDER: I'm not actually.

SONIA: Savita was scared you wouldn't let her go 'cos it's a Fifteen.

RAJINDER: If it is she certainly can't go to see it I don't think it's suitable.

KAMLA: They see worse on t.v. sometimes, I have to say.

RAJINDER: The others do, mine don't. I'd like my children to grow up with some sense of who they are. We're different.

KAMLA: Sometimes children are older than you think they are.

RAJINDER: I take it I can still make these choices at least for my own children.

SONIA: Sure. You're the boss. She'll go by what you say, Raji.

KAMLA: But, of course.

RAJINDER: I'm quite shocked, I didn't expect to be lied to by you, Sonia!

SONIA: I'm sorry. It was difficult. I, I didn't know quite . . . what . . . to say then.

RAJINDER: Sure. Because you felt she was right and I was wrong. Well, let me tell you, we've taken refuge here but that doesn't mean my children have to be taken over and remodeled into something that belongs neither here nor there. (*Throws a contemptuous glance at* KAMLA *and walks out. Ruffled,* KAMLA *avoids* SONIA's *look, tries to shrug it off and exits. Lights fade on the scene*)

SCENE 6

(AMRIT *appears behind the gauze. Stands squarely facing the audience.* RAJINDER *follows her and stands alongside.*)

RAJINDER: No one cared when he tried to push me over the window sill. I could have died then, his bride of six months carrying his child in my body: he meant it to happen. I felt it in his grip. None of you believed me.

AMRIT: But you're so wrong! We all love you. In any case you only ever complained about little things, Rajo. Trivial things.

RAJINDER: Not for me, they weren't. I'd have washed and cooked and cleaned for all of you. Maaji[2] just had to say yes, once. There were only the two of us to feed then but you forgave him, all of you. I can't forgive you for that now.

AMRIT: You don't make sense to me. To put this on Maaji's shoulders, at her age. It'll kill both of them, the shame of it all, the disgrace! You could have tried harder.

RAJINDER: I did my best.

AMRIT: There's no sweat on your brow, no tears in your eyes. Your hands are neither sore nor bloody.

RAJINDER: Must you have blood always? Would you rather I died, so you wouldn't have to explain to your friends? Look into my eyes and say it. Why don't you look into my eyes and then say I should go back to him?

AMRIT: What of the children? They will be asking, "What'll become of them?"

---

[2]Mother-in-law. See glossary for details.

RAJINDER: Don't you care for me at all? I've adored you, Amrit, ever since I was tiny. Why do you hate me so?

AMRIT: You'll be sorry. I'm warning you. Your selfishness will ruin your daughters, I can tell you that. They'll learn all the self-indulgent, sick ways of the West . . . their crazy, blind cult of the body—face creams, diet pills, and keep fit, you'll see. You'll regret this.

RAJINDER: Would you rather I set myself alight in my back garden?

AMRIT: Honor is always preferable to disgrace, but the choice of course is yours. *(Exit* AMRIT. *Light fades on* RAJINDER*)*

SCENE 7

*(*SONIA*'s bedroom. Stage is dimly lit. Soft mournful music is playing on the radio.* SONIA *is reading.* SAVITA *emerges from the wings and looks on uncertainly. Then tiptoes forward gently. Before she can surprise her,* SONIA *turns round and spots her. She shows no sign of welcome.)*

SAVITA: Hi, Sonia; listening to the radio?

SONIA: Hmm.

SAVITA: Dull, isn't it? *(*SONIA *just shrugs indifferently)* Shall I turn it off? Doesn't it make you a bit sad?

SONIA: I don't mind.

SAVITA: You can always find some good music on the radio. Try Choice FM. I can find it for you if you want.

SONIA: I don't want to listen to Choice bloody FM.

SAVITA: Okay, so don't. You don't have to shout.

SONIA: Can't you see I want to be left a—*(Stops as she sees* SAVITA*'s face crumbling)* to choose my own music at least when I am in my own room, if I can't choose the t.v. I want to watch. I'm sick to death of watching *Neighbors* and *Blind Date.*

SAVITA: Did you watch any t.v. today?

SONIA: No.

SAVITA: So you've been here all day?

SONIA: What is this? Some kind of a "Question Time" or somethin'. I'm just fine. I'm my own boss. I get up when I please an' I stop in when I please.

SAVITA: Why do you look so miserable then? Are you missing Gary?

SONIA: I'm just a bit fed up with myself. *(Pause)* You don't look that chirpy yourself, come to think of it. D'you miss your dad at all?

SAVITA: Sometimes. I feel a bit sorry for him. *(Pause. She pulls out a small square envelope from her pocket)* Look, I've got these.

SONIA: What are they?

SAVITA: Rude pictures.

SONIA: Gawd! (SONIA *jumps up in horror*) Fuckin' hell. (SAVITA *watches her calmly*)

These are not rude, Savita . . . they're filthy. Black and white originals like that! Where the hell did you get this lot from? (*Puts them back into the envelope hurriedly*)

SAVITA: Bit disgusting, aren't they?

SONIA: Come on, tell me, was it someone in school? Who gave them to you, you'll have to tell me now, Savita.

SAVITA: I took them.

SONIA: Where from?

SAVITA: I saw her hiding them behind the wardrobe in the bedroom.

SONIA: Who?

SAVITA: My mum. She must have been hiding them from him. She doesn't like this sort of thing. I don't know where he gets them from.

SONIA: Blimey! Does your mum know you've got these?

SAVITA: Of course not.

SONIA: Christ! Why do you keep them?

SAVITA: Dunno. (*Pause*)

SONIA: Oh, Savita, love . . . what is it?

SAVITA: I never mean to do it. I've these horrible dreams, I wake up and the bed is all squelchy and warm and wet and I feel so ashamed of everything.

SONIA: You poor kid, I didn't guess . . . I'm sorry.

SAVITA: Promise me you won't tell anyone. It hurts Mummyji so much and it makes her really cross with me. I'm so bad.

SONIA: You're not, you're all right. What's these bad dreams, eh?

SAVITA:(*Pause*) I can't even remember that much when I wake up . . . but I'm cold and I'm scared. (*Pause*)

SONIA: What do you see, then? Burglars, devils, witches, what?

SAVITA: Nothing like that . . .

SONIA: You can tell me, if you want to. Might help you get rid of them.

SAVITA: I always see . . . Papaji . . . that's my dad.

SONIA: Is he that scary then? Was he violent a lot?

SAVITA: He's angry with me, and he gets into my room and he sits on my bed. His eyes look strange and his lips curl up, like that, and his teeth are set.

SONIA: Angry with you, for what?

SAVITA: It's night time and I want him to go away, but he won't and he sits and sits. His hands are so big, and rough and hairy . . . and in his clothes he's hiding this . . . this dagger, to kill Mummyji . . . and, I think he might stick this into me . . . he won't go away and he won't leave me alone.

SONIA: (*Puts her arms round her and holds her close*) Awright. C'mon. Just leave it for now. Forget it. It's just a bad dream.

SAVITA: He said, it was my fault . . . that I made him come to me.

SONIA: . . . come to you . . . ?

SAVITA: . . . to my room . . . because I was too lovely. But never . . . And he said he would tell Mummyji it was my fault if I didn't let him come any more . . .

SONIA: Oh, Savita! *(Pause)* 'Course it's not your fault, love. (SAVITA *looks confused and tearful.* SONIA *takes both her hands and sits beside her on the floor)* You must know that it weren't your fault.

SAVITA: But I should've . . . made him stop. I should have tried to.

SONIA: You've got to tell your mum.

SAVITA: NO. No, no, please, Sonia. I beg of you don't make me. I'd rather die than tell her. She'll never forgive me. Never . . . if she thinks it's my fault she'll never talk to me again. I'm too frightened.

SONIA: You've got to tell someone.

SAVITA: If you say a word of this to anyone, I'll run away. I can't bear it if she doesn't talk to me any more. You won't tell her, will you Sonia? Swear to me you won't, please!

SONIA: Oh, all right, I swear I won't.

SAVITA: D'you believe me Sonia?

SONIA: I believe you, pet.

SAVITA: You wouldn't stop talking to me, would you?

SONIA: NO, of course not, silly.

SAVITA: What if he finds us and takes us back?

SONIA: No, he won't, I'm sure.

SAVITA: And, Sonia? . . . Sometimes . . .

SONIA: Yes?

SAVITA: I do miss him, sometimes . . . (SAVITA *bursts into tears and* SONIA *holds her in both her arms and soothes her)*

ACT 2

SCENE 1

(KAMLA is speaking on the telephone to KATIE in the refuge office.)

KAMLA: Now listen, Katie, you'll get worse sleeping rough like that. We'll have you as soon as we have place. . . . Why don't you put Bev on the phone, I'll speak to her. She'll get you fixed up for a few days . . . See you soon. *(Enter* RAJINDER*)* Won't keep you a moment. (RAJINDER *sits)* Bev, I don't think we can offer her a room for a couple of weeks yet. . . . Could you not have her for now? . . . Wonderful, I'll speak to you very soon . . . Okay. Bye now. *(Pause)* Sorry about that.

RAJINDER: That's all right.

KAMLA: Can I get you a tea or coffee?

RAJINDER: No, thanks.

KAMLA: Well, how are things?

RAJINDER: Not too bad.

KAMLA: Good, good. *(pause)* What about school? Are they all settled?

RAJINDER: Yes. They seem happy enough.

KAMLA: Finances? Everything running smoothly.

RAJINDER: It's all right, at the moment.

KAMLA: So, no problems at all? *(pause)* What am I saying? Of course there are problems. Dumb question. I mean any problems to do with the refuge, with other residents, or with facilities?

RAJINDER: Sharing a house isn't easy, even with your own family sometimes there are problems. There's been a few, but only little ones. I'm managing.

KAMLA: Good. Great to hear that. *(pause)* Have you thought of some training for yourself?

RAJINDER: I got a B.A. in India. You can't do much with it here.

KAMLA: So what've you thought about doing?

RAJINDER: Horoscopes . . . I mean professionally. I could do that from home, charge people, it would fit in with the children's timings.

KAMLA: You can't make enough doing that.

RAJINDER: That depends on what you call enough, and on your luck.

KAMLA: You don't believe in all that seriously though, do you? I couldn't. It leaves no room for human effort. How can you ask people to work towards change if you believe that someone else is pulling the strings?

RAJINDER: It doesn't mean you can't make any choices . . . just that . . . the circumstances in which you have to make them are often beyond your control. Like birth, or death.

KAMLA: Hmm. I hadn't thought of it like that. *(pause)* But there's a real world out there where you need a certain minimum to survive. Might be useful for you to think of some retraining, in more practical terms, hmm? Now, how did it go with the housing officer today?

RAJINDER: Not very well, I'm afraid.

KAMLA: Any special reason?

RAJINDER: It wasn't so much what he said . . . it's . . . what I couldn't say. I hadn't realized, until today that . . . you . . . have to go through all that in order to get a place. I've decided I can't take that.

KAMLA: What! You can't afford to decide those things any more.

RAJINDER: What do you mean? It's my life we're talking about. I'm not one of your illiterate working-class women to be managed by you.

KAMLA: Well, that's how it's done whatever class you are. You've got to establish your need to separate from your husband, that's all.

RAJINDER: I've to explain to some stranger the history of fifteen years of marriage, expose every intimate detail of my life and you say, "that's all," haan? But then you wouldn't know about it.

KAMLA: It's not pleasant, or easy, I know, but that is the procedure, for everyone, regardless of race and religion.

RAJINDER: I see.

KAMLA: In any case, you don't have to feel ashamed of anything. The shame's all his.

RAJINDER: Are you married, Kamla?

KAMLA: No. Fortunately. What's that got to do with anything?

RAJINDER: How can you understand what's involved then?

KAMLA: With respect, I can see marriage, as an institution, without the rose-colored glasses.

RAJINDER: Aren't we allowed to have privacy any more just because we left our homes?

KAMLA: What's the big deal in privacy?

RAJINDER: It's important to me.

KAMLA: Don't you see, it's the "privatization" of women's lives which keeps us from seeing domestic violence in a socio-political context?

RAJINDER: I don't need your political analysis. I have to deal with my life as I think best.

KAMLA: Your story is common enough, believe me. It's part of a pattern of how men have used women over the years. That's why we started the support group sessions. You haven't been to any of those yet, have you?

RAJINDER: I don't believe in washing my dirty linen in public. Thank you.

KAMLA: There's something positive about sharing.

RAJINDER: Sharing your troubles seems more like a sign of weakness to me.

KAMLA: Perhaps if you try a session some time . . .

RAJINDER: I don't think you understand my language Kamla. I didn't marry in a registry office. I married before God. It wasn't just a social arrangement, it was a sacred bond, made with body and soul.

KAMLA: Something broke that bond for you and exposing that something now is part of the price you pay for your release.

RAJINDER: What do I want release for? I'm not going to marry anyone else. I just left, because . . .

KAMLA: Because . . . ?

RAJINDER: . . . there was no other way.

KAMLA: I'm sorry, I know it still hurts.

RAJINDER: I need time to think through things.

KAMLA: Time just goes by, women forget the hurt, their wounds begin to heal and then, they start imagining that things might get better, simply if they go back. That's what looks the easiest, if you don't have accommodation.

RAJINDER: I've done my bit of going back to him and I won't make the same mistake again, you'll see. I don't need to take a begging bowl to anyone. I can survive.

KAMLA: It's not begging. You have a right to housing. You need a place to live and a proper source of income. You're living in bloody cloud-cuckoo land.

RAJINDER: It's strange—this passion that you put into destroying other people's marriages. All that matters to you is that I should never go back to him!

KAMLA: You're still hankering for some woolly romantic dream of saving your marriage with your heroism. Can't you see there's nothing left for me to destroy? You ran away to hide from that awful shell of a relationship that you can't even speak about to others . . .

RAJINDER: I don't need to. (*Exit* RAJINDER. KAMLA *gets up and paces to calm herself down*)

KAMLA: Stupid fool! (KAMLA *tries to return to her work*)

SCENE 2

(SAVITA's *bedroom. Pop music playing.* SAVITA *is singing along tunelessly. She is dressing up before the mirror.*)

SAVITA: I look cool in that, don't I, Ma?

RAJINDER: Sorry, Savita, you'll have to change.

SAVITA: Why? It looks fine to me.

RAJINDER: I don't want any discussion, or argument about this. You'll change, or else, you can't go to the party. It's as simple as that.

SAVITA: That's not fair. You have to say why.

RAJINDER: All right, then. The skirt's too short, the blouse is too grown up, together they look tartish.

SAVITA: Talk about stereotypes, Ammah! They're doing "tart with a heart" films even in Bombay now. What have you got against them anyway?

RAJINDER: I hate to hear you talk like this.

SAVITA: Like what? What's wrong with it?

RAJINDER: As if . . . you're all smart and sophisticated and grown-up and know everything.

SAVITA: Maybe I do know more than you think I know. How's that for a possibility?

RAJINDER: Not very likely.

SAVTIA: Do you like Sonia, Ma?

RAJINDER: She's okay.

SAVITA: Well, she's been on the game, off and on, she told me.

RAJINDER: What do you mean?

SAVITA: Don't you know what that means?

RAJINDER: Well, would I ask if did?

SAVITA: See, I do know more than you think. She's what they call a "hooker," a prostitute!

RAJINDER: Don't you dare talk to me like that. I don't want to hear you talk, crudely, like this, even if it's true. I wouldn't believe that, even of her.

SAVITA: It's true, she's not ashamed of it. She says she's in charge of her own body, that's all it means. *(pause)* Housewives sell their bodies too, you know. Only it's to one man, and that must be so boring, and they have no control over . . . their . . . bodies.

RAJINDER: Savita, shut up, that's enough out of you.

(RAJINDER *slaps* SAVITA *as she speaks.* SAVITA *is stunned for a second or two. Then she tries to make light of it)*

SAVITA: Ammah! That hurt! It's not fair. I was only . . . joking. You're too strict, you know.

RAJINDER: I've told you, we're different from all these people here. Don't you forget that.

SAVITA: Yeah, I know, we're Pakis.

RAJINDER: Behave yourself. I'm not going to let any of you out of this room any more, except for meals.

SAVITA: Brilliant. NO more school.

RAJINDER: I'm not joking, Savita. I'm dead serious.

SAVITA: So am I.

RAJINDER: Don't answer back.

SAVITA: You sound evil like him now. You're missing him aren't you?

RAJINDER: Shut up.

SAVITA: We'll be going back next, I suppose. We always do when you get like this.

RAJINDER: Like what?

SAVITA: Nasty, like him, and violent. Kamla said I could talk to her, anytime, if something bothered me. No violence, remember? It's a house rule. I could tell on you.

RAJINDER: Are you trying to threaten me now? She's put you up to it, hasn't she, the scheming little bitch! Tell her what?

SAVITA: Everything.

RAJINDER: About what?

SAVITA: All that you've been too coy to say . . .

RAJINDER: Don't try to play games with me Savita . . . what are you talking about now?

SAVITA: I know about the porno films, in the house . . . he forced you to drink, and . . . and . . . he made you do things you didn't want to do.

RAJINDER: That's not true . . . there was nothing like that. You're lying. You've no right to do this to me. Make things like this up, just to . . . humiliate me . . .

SAVITA: I heard you some nights.

RAJINDER: Shut up, Savita. For God's sake, be quiet. Someone'll hear you.

SAVITA: I don't care if they do. I hate you. I hate you even more than I hate him, you're such a bloody hypocrite.

RAJINDER: *(Bursts into sobs)* Meri tauba, Guruji. Forgive my sins. What did I do to deserve this?

SAVITA: *(Defiance slips away and she slips into childish protest)* I don't want to go any more. I wish I was dead. You spoil everything. I'm telling you, I'll run away if you hit me again. I mean it. *(RAJINDER says nothing but tries to calm herself. SAVITA watches her for a few seconds and then goes and puts her arms round her and kisses her)* I'm sorry, Ammah. I was so horrible to you. I don't know what came over me.

RAJINDER: *(Takes her arms away gently but firmly and turns her face away from her)* You better go and get ready. They'll be here to pick you up soon.

SAVITA: Are you O.K. now? *(RAJINDER only nods)* I'm only going because I hate this place. I wish I could get out of here for good. *(Exit SAVITA. RAJINDER slowly gets up and begins to undress. Takes off her chunni and folds it. Takes off her jewelry slowly, lets her hair down. F/X music flowing into the next sequence)*

SCENE 3

(Int. SONIA's bedroom. Soft romantic music is playing gently in the background. SONIA is giggling and chatting in a husky whisper as she "slips out" of a few things, slowly. The client she's entertaining sounds a bit drunk.)

SONIA: So what kind of music d'ya like? I mean what turns you on?

CLIENT: Who said I need music? You turn me on, baby. You can turn the bloody thing off, does nothing for me.

SONIA: I like it. *(pause)* Besides, it's good cover for any noise, 'en it?

CLIENT: Anythin's all right by me, darlin'. Keep it on if you want. To me it's all fuckin' noise that means nothin'. I was born tone deaf.

SONIA: Do you want a drink, to relax you, get you in the mood . . . be only another two quid on top?

CLIENT: Why not? We'll 'ave a drink together. Rip me off while I'm in the mood, I don' mind. I'll drink to your health. What've you got?

SONIA: A drop of whisky, if ya fancy that.

CLIENT: I fancy that. I fancy that very much, thank you.

SONIA: I'll 'ave to nip down to the kitchen to get some glasses, tho'. You don't move, or open the door to anyone, O.K.?

CLIENT: Sure, I understand.

SONIA: Told you about the crabby old bat, my landlady. She doesn't allow no gentlemen visitors in the bedrooms.

CLIENT: Shh . . . I won't move.

SONIA: Shan't be a minute. Be a good boy now, won't you?

CLIENT: *(Whispers)* I'll be quiet, as a grave . . . Promise. Cross my heart.

SONIA: *(Giggles nervously)* Shhhhh . . . *(Opens the door quietly, it creaks, and she tiptoes out shuffling a little. Bumps into* RAJINDER *who is coming across tiptoeing quietly from the other end of the stage. Both of them startle and gasp together)*

RAJINDER: God, you scared the life out of me.

SONIA: Rajinder! You made me jump!

RAJINDER: I'm sorry.

SONIA: What the bloody hell are you up to at this time of night?

RAJINDER: I'm just going to get a hot water bottle for Sanjay. He's wheezing. Are you all right?

SONIA: Er, I was just gonna get some glass . . . es.

RAJINDER: Glasses? Yeah, sure. Go on.

(SONIA *sighs and steps forward.* CLIENT *shouts off)*

CLIENT: Hey, Sylvie, baby? Hurry up. Where are ya?

RAJINDER: Oh, my God! There's someone . . . in your . . . You've got a man in there?

SONIA: Naw, it's just the radio.

RAJINDER: Yes, the radio's on, it's playing music.

SONIA: The wretched fool!

RAJINDER: You, you . . . O, God! How could you!

SONIA: He's just someone from down the local. He's drunk to the eyeballs. I don't think he knows where he is.

RAJINDER: It's disgraceful, this whole business!

SONIA: Listen, love, I'm too old for a lecture. Once in three friggin' months isn't a lot of business, what the hell difference does it make to anyone? Why don't you just shut your mouth and go back to bed?

RAJINDER: There's a no-men rule in the house.

SONIA: Bloody stupid rule. Doesn't mean anything.

RAJINDER: I'll talk to Eileen tomorrow about this!

SONIA: You do that. Eileen's a soft touch, she'll give me a warnin' an' I'll take it. O.K.?

CLIENT: How long 'ave I gotta wait in the fuckin' dark?

SCENE 4

(Refuge office. EILEEN *and* KAMLA *are busy with paperwork. Enter* RAJINDER *dressed to go out. Agitated.)*

RAJINDER: I came to return the key, and I thought there might be things to sign again.

KAMLA: Where do you think you're going?

RAJINDER: I'm going back.

KAMLA: But where to?

EILEEN: What happened?

RAJINDER: I kept thinking about how to tell you all this. When I came here, this place seemed to be okay. Now I find something horrible's going on here. Late last night, Sonia had a man in her room, he was drunk and I know what they were up to. I was a bit silly, I really saw this place as special in some way. Now, I see how filthy it really is and dangerous for my children. To think I brought them into this hell. Savita's been going shopping and for walks with her, no wonder she's been behaving so . . . shockingly. I've no choice but to go back home.

KAMLA: But you said you'd never do that!

RAJINDER: Barbara said you can get a court order to keep your husband out, I'll try to do that.

KAMLA: But that's a long process . . . Why don't you wait, let me ring round and try to get you into another refuge . . .

RAJINDER: I won't live under the same roof as a common prostitute! I can't.

SONIA: *(Walks in breezily)* Morning. I thought she'd be in here grassing me up, first thing!

RAJINDER: I don't want to get into a discussion with her either, so if you'll excuse me . . .

SONIA: Now, look 'ere . . . Rajinder . . . *(Exit* RAJINDER*)*

EILEEN: Shit! I could've done without this today.

KAMLA: How the fuck did you have the gall to do that anyway?

EILEEN: It's not the first time, either.

KAMLA: Maybe if she'd been dealt with severely the first time it wouldn't have happened again. She's leaving because of what you did last night.

SONIA: Isn't she a bloody loony!

EILEEN: That's beside the point. What's your excuse for fetchin' a man into the house when you know it's against the bloody rules?

SONIA: What did she say? Don't fall into her trap. She's exaggerated, you can be sure.

KAMLA: I'm absolutely furious. You seem to have no idea of how dangerous it is.

SONIA: Gus is somebody I knew when I was a girl. Like we nearly got married, at one time. I just asked him in for a laugh. He's such a scream, kept shoutin' "Sylvie, Sylvie baby," just 'cause I said he should keep his voice down. Anyway, he was too drunk to know where he was or what was goin' on.

EILEEN: Don't you understand Sonia, it's a rule you can't afford to break. You risk the safety of others and that's not on!

KAMLA: We haven't had a chance to discuss this between us, but we'll come back to you on this, you can be sure of that.

SONIA: It's a bloody jackpot for you, I reckon, show all of us how tough you are, eh?

EILEEN: I'm sorry not to see any sign of apology or regret from you, Sonia, in spite of what's happened.

SONIA: Hold on! She's not some poor twit who got scared of a bloke on the premises. She's into this fuckin' self-righteousness. Don't look at me like that, Eileen. 'Course I'm sorry. How was I to know that stupid Indian woman would make such a bloody drama out of it?

EILEEN: What's bein' Indian got to do with it?

SONIA: You know what she's like. Makes you feel like that.

KAMLA: I wish you'd learn the house rules, once and for all.

SONIA: I hope she won't get into trouble because of me. I've got nothin' 'gainst her. And I'm quite fond of Savita. That poor kid didn't want to go back at all. Her old man's been messin' her about. Did she tell you that?

EILEEN: I don't know anything about this. Do you Kamla?

KAMLA: Are you saying Savita was being abused by her father? You sure? How do you know this?

SONIA: She told me, that's how.

EILEEN: How dreadful . . . and we'd no idea.

SONIA: She's been wettin' the bed, it's her who does it.

EILEEN: Does Rajinder know?

SONIA: Dunno. Savita didn't think so. (KAMLA *goes for the telephone*)

EILEEN: Hang on!

KAMLA: The child's at risk, don't you see?

EILEEN: That's not the way to handle this. You don't want to rush in with a sledge-hammer at this point. What if she doesn't know?

SONIA: Look, I am real sorry about this, Eileen.

KAMLA: I'm concerned about Rajinder too, but the child's interest takes priority. There's a legal requirement. We must inform the authorities within a week of discovering abuse.

EILEEN: I'll go and see her first. We're dealin' with people here, not just cases, Kamla. No good creatin' another trauma for the kid.

KAMLA: You've got a day to fetch her back. After that I'll take action on my own if necessary.

SCENE 5

(*Int.* RAJINDER's *bedroom at home. Bed is prominent, covered with a bright red bedspread.* RAJINDER *and* SAVITA *walk into the bedroom carrying bags in both hands.*)

RAJINDER: Everything looks the same, doesn't it, Savita? As if we'd never left this place.

SAVITA: Yes, it does. How long were we away?

RAJINDER: Three weeks and three days. Seems longer somehow. Wa-ay Guruji! Only you know the future. I vowed never to return to this house. I never thought such a time would come that will bring me back to these walls!

SAVITA: I feel as if he's here, somewhere.

RAJINDER: He won't be back till five. He hasn't made the bed, of course. *(Enter* PRADEEP *from the left. He comes and stands squarely behind the bed)*

SAVITA: I knew we would come back.

RAJINDER: Why?

SAVITA: Papaji always has his way in the end.

RAJINDER: I thought you were unhappy there, you complained enough. Put that back. *(*SAVITA *has picked up the "Kirpaan" from the wall and is looking at it)*

SAVITA: I'm only looking. It wasn't exactly a holiday. If we had our own place it would have been different. We could've made it nice. Got little bits an' pieces, and I made it our own.

RAJINDER: Time wasn't on our side. Maybe some good will come of this. Maybe we can stay here and keep him out of this place. At least it's comfortable. There's a lot to be said for mixer taps and central heating that works.

SAVITA: The blade's still sharp.

RAJINDER: I said put that back. Why've you become so disobedient, child?

SAVITA: Just looking. Why did we come back? Like this, all of a sudden? I didn't even get to say goodbye to Sonia and the rest, and people at school, 'cos you made me miss school.

RAJINDER: God must have meant us to come back.

SAVITA: So why did he send us away in the first place, Ammah?

RAJINDER: Only he knows why he made us do that. I don't know all the answers. Go to your room and put your things away. *(Exit* SAVITA*)* Well, Pradeep. I'm back. But I'm not the same woman who walked out of that door three weeks ago. Your hold over me is broken now, forever. I know now what I have to do. I must safeguard my honor. That is my duty to myself and to Guruji. He'll protect me now. *(*PRADEEP *stands still behind her. Pause. Enter* SAVITA *wearing a short frilly black "naughty" nightie. Stands on the side watching* RAJINDER. RAJINDER *moves into the spotlight with* SAVITA*)*

SAVITA: Here I am Mummy . . .

RAJINDER: Where did you get that?

SAVITA: It was a secret present from Papaji.

RAJINDER: What are you saying, Savita?

SAVITA: Here's the card. I've still got it. Read it, if you don't believe me. *(*RAJINDER *takes the card.* PRADEEP *reads out)*

PRADEEP: To Savita, for being so lovely, Papa. *(Pause.* SAVITA *holds out two porn magazines to* RAJINDER*)*

SAVITA: He gave me these too. *(*RAJINDER *says nothing)* He said, you'd never believe me if I tried to tell you anything. He said he'd kill me if I tried to tell you. I never asked for any of this, I swear it by Guruji. He was lying, wasn't he? You believe me, don't you Ammah? Why don't you say something, then? Please, believe me, Ammah, please . . .

RAJINDER: *(Walks slowly up to* SAVITA. *Puts her shawl round* SAVITA's *shoulders and walks her away)* We better get back before he returns.

ACT 3

SCENE 1

(Int. Refuge lounge. RAJINDER *is ironing clothes.* Daytime Live *is on a low volume. Enter* KAMLA.*)*

KAMLA: We've got to talk before I leave today, Rajinder. O.K.?

RAJINDER: What about?

KAMLA: Savita.

RAJINDER: What have you got to do with Savita?

KAMLA: Both Eileen and I know about Savita. She told Sonia. You must see that the moment I discovered abuse, Savita became my client and I have to make sure that what's best for her should happen.

RAJINDER: I don't know what you're talking about. She told Sonia nothing. Sonia's lying.

KAMLA: If you continue to deny it I shall assume your collusion.

RAJINDER: What do you mean by that?

KAMLA: That means you knew what was happening and you didn't do anything to stop it.

RAJINDER: What are you saying, are you mad? She's my daughter, I'm more concerned about her welfare than you can ever be. You know what they say in India? "Only crafty old witches pretend to love you more than your own mother."

KAMLA: We all know about mothers, no one's born without one. A lot of the bullshit about love is to do with control.

RAJINDER: So what do you want from me now, Kamla?

KAMLA: I'd like to set up a case conference next week to deal with it.

RAJINDER: So what happens then?

KAMLA: Social Services get involved. She has to have a medical and then all the parties talk and decide what to do next.

RAJINDER: I can't agree to that. Why should I talk to strangers about my daughter? Where I come from we deal with things within the family.

KAMLA: That doesn't get you very far! There's two things you will get out of this if we go to court. You'll get housed and Savita'll get counseling and so would you. You've been through a lot.

RAJINDER: I'm not going to use her to get round your stupid, racist housing people.

KAMLA: I hope you'd have more sense than that. It is in your interest and hers.

RAJINDER: So, you want to deal with it your way. Do I have a choice?

KAMLA: Not really.

RAJINDER: All that talk about liberating women is just talk, isn't it?

KAMLA: There's a principle involved here and I do think men like him should be prosecuted.

RAJINDER: Ah! So that's it. I wondered about your motives. What if I told you she's lying, there was no abuse. She's always imagining things . . . sometimes, she exaggerates . . . but he couldn't have . . . touched her, really. I was home most nights.

KAMLA: Obviously you need counseling, too. I can arrange that.

RAJINDER: There's no reason to justify your doing anything. She said nothing concrete to Sonia, and she never confided in you, anyway. What's more, I'll not let you talk to her and harass her over this. I want her to forget what . . . might have happened. And, probably didn't happen.

KAMLA: You've decided to cover this up. If she blocks it off, it'll cause problems later.

RAJINDER: You know what the trouble is with the West? There's fads here. People think they think for themselves, but they're never allowed to. One day someone decides to worry about salmonella in eggs and people give up eating eggs. Someone decides to worry about child abuse and the cases multiply. There's always been salmonella in eggs, don't you know?

KAMLA: So you're not going to cooperate?

RAJINDER: I came back didn't I?

KAMLA: You're still avoiding facing it.

RAJINDER: I'd like to avoid a scandal. She's got to marry one day. But then you don't know what it is to live within the community. I don't know where women like you come from. Call yourself an Asian, do you?

KAMLA: I am one.

RAJINDER: I wouldn't go that far! Black you may be, Asian you certainly are not.

KAMLA: You can't deny me my identity. I won't let you. You people with your saris and your bloody lingo and all your certainties about the universe, you don't have a monopoly on being Asian. You can't box it and contain it and exclude others. I'll define myself as I bloody well want to.

RAJINDER: You don't try to attack my beliefs, okay?

KAMLA: This is hypocrisy and I won't let you cover it up. I'm getting in touch with Social Services.

RAJINDER: Don't you dare do that.

KAMLA: You try and stop me.

RAJINDER: You bitch! I curse you to misery forever!

KAMLA: I'm not trying to hurt her. I only want to help . . .

EILEEN:(Enters, stands and watches for a few seconds before KAMLA notices her) What a shouting match! I heard you in the office. I think I've got to take over this business from you, Kamla.

RAJINDER: Thank you. I'd appreciate that.

EILEEN: This isn't right. We all need to be calmer before we can deal with this, it's obvious. (EILEEN *puts her hand on* KAMLA's *arm and wheels her away.* RAJINDER *begins pacing the room*)

RAJINDER: There must be a way out, there must be one. If only he would die. I wish I had the courage to kill him, then maybe we could go back and live there, in the safety of our own home.

(RAJINDER *collapses on a chair, covers her face with both her hands. Sobbing. Reenter* EILEEN. *Pause*)

EILEEN: Rajinder, please, don't. It doesn't have to be like this.

RAJINDER: I'm sorry, I can't help it.

EILEEN: We're on the same side, believe me.

RAJINDER: I don't know what to do any more. I feel, as if I'm running out of time and, and there's nowhere to go.

EILEEN: I'll see to it that you get the time to take it all in before you have to deal with anything, O.K.?

RAJINDER: And Kamla?

EILEEN: She's worried, partly because you went back once.

RAJINDER: But I didn't know . . .

EILEEN: I know. *(Pause)*

RAJINDER: I sold my bangles today. But I still won't have enough to rent a place unless I get a job first. It'll take time . . . and, and he might find us.

EILEEN: We'll deal with it together, one thing at a time. It'll work out, you'll see. So you're looking for a job. I'm glad you're doing that. Kamla couldn't believe your career plans when you told her all that.

RAJINDER: I'm sorry, I shouldn't really have shouted at her. But . . . she thinks she knows everything. If she'd grown up in India maybe she'd know there's more to life than you can ever hope to learn in one lifetime, and she thinks she knows it all at thirty.

EILEEN: Her heart's in the right place.

RAJINDER: If she's got one!

SCENE 2

(PRADEEP *enter the stage facing the "outside" of the door. Looks around. He is wearing a cap pulled over his eyes and dark glasses which mask his face. He is carrying a large bag. Puts it on the floor. Stands beside the door and stares at it for a few seconds, then presses the entryphone.* EILEEN *answers.*)

PRADEEP: Hello.

EILEEN: Hello, who is it please?

PRADEEP: Good afternoon, Madam. Collecting for a children's charity.

EILEEN: I'm sorry. Try next door. *(Replaces the phone.* PRADEEP *stands beside the door and smiles. He looks at his watch and leans against the wall in a leisurely manner.* KAMLA *enters refuge office looking rushed and hurried as she rifles through papers)* You were going to tell me how much you can spare from the petty cash for the cake.

KAMLA: Sometimes you absolutely amaze me, Eileen. I am utterly thrown by the biggest problem that's hit us in months and you're worrying about how much you can have for the birthday cake. Does Sonia deserve a bloody surprise party after what she's been up to?

EILEEN: We need the bloody parties even more when there are problems. I wish I could wave a wand and get them both talking to each other; I want the tension and unpleasantness to go from the house.

KAMLA: Don't we all. *(Sits resignedly, opens the petty cash box)* I expect you're bloody right as well, as always. Twelve pounds. Here it is. Parties are nice, they do help. You know, we never had parties when we were little.

EILEEN: Was that a cultural thing, then?

KAMLA: That too. But mostly it was to do with money. God, I hate the meanness of poverty, the penny-pinching, the skimping, the making-do.

EILEEN: Don't remind us.

KAMLA: But it never affected me the way it did my brother. He owns three travel agencies in the West End, you know. I'm too filled with loathing for the system to want to become a woman of substance within it.

EILEEN: Yeah, we can all see the Puritan in you Kamla!

KAMLA: Now, now, no religious labels please, ascetic will do. Look, if you want me to, pick up the cake on my way back from Social Services.

EILEEN: That'll be a help. Thank you. *(Pause)* And Kamla, I must say this, don't rush Rajinder into anything, please.

KAMLA: There are professional guidelines on how to deal with child abuse, and, with respect, I'd like to keep to them, if I may. She's had a week to come to terms with this.

EILEEN: Not quite a week.

KAMLA: All right, I'll give her a few more days. If by Monday she doesn't come round, I will be getting in touch with Social Services, to notify them, that's my deadline.

EILEEN: Does it have to be set out like an ultimatum?

KAMLA: Yes, I'm afraid so.

EILEEN: Absolute deadlines make absolute disasters.

KAMLA: Some people need them.

EILEEN: Why do you want to be confrontational? Give her time, she'll come round.

KAMLA: And if she doesn't?

EILEEN: Then you could apply pressure later on. Savita's safe here, she's out of his reach. What's the point of going through a procedure, just for the heck of it? *(PRADEEP presses the entryphone buzzer again)* Yes. Who is it please?

PRADEEP: Could I see the lady of the house, maybe?

EILEEN: No, you can't I'm afraid, she's out.

PRADEEP: If you'd like to step out, Madam, I'd show you leaflets about our organization. It's a bonafide charity, all very worthwhile work.

EILEEN: I'm sure it is, it's just that I'm unable to contribute right now.

PRADEEP: Not even fifty pence ma'am?

EILEEN: I'm sorry, I said no. Is that clear or not?

PRADEEP: God bless you all the same, madam and goodbye.

EILEEN: Goodbye. *(Replaces the entryphone sharply this time with a sigh. Spotlight on PRADEEP)*

PRADEEP: So this is the house . . . no dustbins out in the front . . . there must be an alleyway at the back . . . which makes life a bit easier. I'll try the back. I told you, Rajinder, didn't I, the world isn't big enough to hide you from me. *(Exit PRADEEP)*

KAMLA: I can't believe that I should have to justify a duty . . . to a colleague.

EILEEN: It's become some kind of a crusade, or a witch hunt . . .

KAMLA: But she's letting him get away with it . . . and she shouldn't. He must be punished.

EILEEN: Kamla that has to be less important than the well-being of Rajinder and Savita.

KAMLA: Besides, Savita needs more help. I would like her to be a survivor, not a victim.

EILEEN: Don't you see, love, this would hurt her too.

KAMLA: No, it couldn't.

EILEEN: How do you know?

KAMLA: I'm going by the book and I expect others to do the same.

SCENE 3

(Night time. RAJINDER's bedroom.)

RAJINDER: You're still awake Savita.

SAVITA: I'll just finish this chapter and then I'll sleep.

RAJINDER: It's late, you won't wake up in the morning, then. Go on now, just get yourself a hot drink, settle down in bed and say your prayers. *(Exit SAVITA. RAJINDER is praying softly)* Dar teray tayaan khaloti may kamli teray darbaar di. Sub da pala karo Guruji, hai arz teray guizaar di. *(F/X glass smashing in the distance. RAJINDER stops abruptly. Enter PRADEEP. RAJINDER is startled)* Pradeep! . . . so it was you . . .

PRADEEP: Didn't I warn you not to try to run away from me again?

RAJINDER: I had no choice.

PRADEEP: Come back home, I want you back. I'll forgive you if you return to me.

RAJINDER: I could never go back, not now, never.

PRADEEP: You've no right to do this, to steal my children from me and run away like a thief in the night.

RAJINDER: That was the only way. *(Enter* SAVITA, *sees* PRADEEP *and screams)*

PRADEEP: Shhh . . .

RAJINDER: Savita, be a good girl, go and lie down quietly in your bed. Don't be frightened, your father's come to ask me something, that's all.

SAVITA: I'll try to be quiet. Papaji, promise you won't hurt Mummy, please.

PRADEEP: Don't worry. Go to bed now, I'm only talking to her. I'm asking you, for the last time, Rajinder, come back to me.

RAJINDER: I can't. I know about you.

PRADEEP: So you won't come? You mean it, do you?

RAJINDER: Absolutely.

PRADEEP: Turn your face away, Savita, so I can kiss your mother goodbye. *(Stabs her.* RAJINDER *gasps in shock and disbelief)*

RAJINDER: Oh, God! Pradeep?

PRADEEP: This is for denying me yourself, and this for denying me my children. This and this and this.

(Noise and commotion. SAVITA *begins to scream hysterically. Enter* SONIA*)*

SAVITA: Papa! What have you done to her! How could you? Mummy, Mummyji, say something, please Mummyji . . .

PRADEEP: I'm going home now. Tell the police when they come where I am.

SONIA: God, you crazy bastard! You've killed her, you murderer! Call a doctor. Someone phone please!

PRADEEP: This is not a murder, it is a death sentence, her punishment for taking away what was mine. Tell them when they come. She can't leave me, she's my wife. *(Exit* PRADEEP. SONIA *kneels beside* RAJINDER, *with her arm round* SAVITA'*s shoulder)*

SONIA: Oh, Rajinder, why didn't you shout for help? I was only next door.

SAVITA: Is she going to die, Sonia? He said he was only kissing her goodbye. What are we going to do?

SONIA: Someone will be here to help us soon, I'm sure.

Jatinder Verma

Jatinder Verma is a playwright, actor, director, and artistic director of *Tara Arts,* one of the oldest South Asian British theatre companies alive in England. Tara Arts was founded in 1977 with a production of Rabindranath Tagore's *Sacrifice.* Today, the company functions as a touring troupe that adapts European and Asian classics for the present day, develops new plays, and tours schools and colleges. Since the 1980s, the company has developed a distinctive "Binglish" style of integrating Asian aesthetics with the British performing arts community.

Tara Arts emerged as a national artistic force with its National Theatre production of *Tartuffe* in 1990, to be followed by memorable versions of *The Little Clay Cart* and *Cyrano de Bergerac.* In addition to plays such as *2001: A Ramayana Odyssey,* the company has produced landmark productions such as the trilogy *Journey to the West* (2002), about forced migration of South Asians into Kenya, and then, into the United Kingdom.

Western classics that have been transformed to represent British Asian aesthetics and realities include *Troilus and Cressida* (1993), *The Tempest* (1993), *The Bourgeois Gentilhomme* (1994), and *A Midsummer Night's Dream* (1997). From South Asia, the company has produced *Hayavadana* (1988), *Heer Ranjha* (1992), and *Diwali Stories* (1999). In *Oh Sweet Sita* (1997), the company combined the aesthetics and cultural attributes of South Asia and the West through Indian aesthetics and stories along with Chaplin, Chaplinesque movement, and the trials of a British Asian family.

In addition to being a playwright, Verma has contributed scores of articles on British Asian theatre, the politics of race and class in British performance, and the importance of underlining Asian voices in the making of British theatre. Recent work includes adaptations of Beaumarchais's *The Marriage of Figaro* and Ibsen's *Enemy of the People.*

2001: A Ramayana Odyssey

UK Tour, 2001

Other Plays

Fuse
Garba
Heer Ranjha
Inqalaab, 1919
Jhansi
Journey to the West
Playing the Flame
Revelations
Vilayat, or England, Your England
Yes, Memsahib

2001: A Ramayana Odyssey

Jatinder Verma

PROLOGUE

CHORUS: There lies the Mediterranean sea—
  Wine-dark and wide
  between Europe and Africa!
  And there is India—
  The vast landmass
  from the Himalaya's peaks
  to the tear-drop that is Sri Lanka!
  Parted by sea and land,
  from each comes a story,
  of a man who sailed on shifting seas,
  and of a man who walked beneath tumbling clouds,
  each separated from his home and wife.
  (Two men are sitting, waiting to be dressed)
MAN 1: They call me a man of many parts.
CHORUS: Odysseus!
  Resourceful Odysseus!
  Crafty Odysseus!
  Vengeful Odysseus!
MAN 2: They call me Raghuvans.
CHORUS: Rama!
  Seventh avatar of Vishnu—
  Born in the lap of Agni, Goddess of Fire—

Eternal consort of Sita!
(*The two men, who are Odysseus and Rama, pick up their bows and string arrows*)

RAMA: I let fly the arrow of Dharma to arc across the Eastern sky—

ODYSSEUS: To be met by the arrow of Duty racing across Western seas.

CHORUS: Kingdoms they reigned
Kingdoms they lost
Kingdoms they regained—
and lost to desire!

ODYSSEUS: Duty lost to desire?

RAMA: You sailed across the seas to your kingdom of Ithaca. From water comes life, so let's begin with your story!

ODYSSEUS: Will you come with me?

RAMA: My journey is over land, you must sail alone.

ODYSSEUS: I was not always alone!

ODYSSEUS: I left my homeland of Ithaca to do my duty to the Greeks. To avenge the wrong done to King Menelaus when Paris of Troy stole his wife, Helen. For ten years we laid siege to Troy and then I broke the siege. The Trojans worshiped Poseidon, God of the Sea, who rode the seas on a horse. So I thought to make the Trojans a gift. Of a huge wooden horse. The Trojans were pleased, and rolled it in through their gates. When night fell, our Greek soldiers tumbled out of the horse and we slaughtered the Trojans. After ten long years, I left Troy with my men for Ithaca. (*prays*) Poseidon, God of the wine-dark sea, look after my men and I! Give us favorable wind and let us ride gently in your lap, as we journey home.

CHORUS: Home! The booming,
Unreal word that sets
Hearts racing, makes
Tears spring from eyes
And lumps to form in
Throats when you turn back
from strange lands and find yourself in—

ODYSSEUS: The land of the Cyclops!

CHORUS: Cyclops?

ODYSSEUS: Giants with only one eye on their heads!

CHORUS: One eye?!

ODYSSEUS: Who herd goats and tend sheep. (*narrates*) My men and I sit in a large cave, where we find milk to drink and cheese to eat. Here we sit and wait for the Cyclops, praying he will treat us with the respect that is due to strangers. When night falls, the Cyclops enters and places a large rock blocking the entrance to the cave. He sees my men and I and speaks.

CYCLOPS: What manner of men are you?

ODYSSEUS: Strangers seeking food and shelter.

CYCLOPS: Ha!

ODYSSEUS: *(narrating)* The Cyclops picks up two of my men, slaps them against the rocks in the cave, where their brains run all over the floor, soaking the ground. Then he cuts them limb by limb and, roasting their flesh over a fire, eats them, entrails, flesh and marrow bones alike.—I must find a way to save my men! I have with me good wine. I offer this to the Cyclops as a present.
(Cyclops takes the wine and drinks)

CYCLOPS: This is good. Tell me your name and I will give you a guest-present that will make you happy.

ODYSSEUS: I decide to hide my true name. This Cyclops is a dangerous monster. *(to cyclops)* My name is Nobody. My father and mother named me Nobody, and that is how I am known by my men.

CYCLOPS: Then Nobody I will eat last, after all his men have filled my belly. That is my guest-present to you. More wine!
(Odysseus gives him more and Cyclops falls asleep)

ODYSSEUS: I take this olive branch—and stick it into his eye, twisting it to make the roots of his eye crackle!
(The cyclops howls in anguish)

CHORUS: Polyphemus, why do you shriek and cry?

CYCLOPS: I have been hurt by Nobody!

CHORUS: Nobody? Oh, it is just a bad dreaming you are having!

CYCLOPS: I am not dreaming! Nobody has struck me in the eye!

CHORUS: Go back to sleep, Polyphemus!

ODYSSEUS: *(to audience)* So this giant is called Polyphemus! His sheep and goats begin to moan and bleat. So he opens the entrance to his cave to let the animals out and sits blocking the entrance. He cannot see, but he can feel. I tell each of my men to tie themselves under the belly of the sheep. When Polyphemus feels with his giant hands, they touch only the fleece of his sheep and we make good our escape!
(Odysseus and his men leave the cave)

CHORUS: Resourceful Odysseus!
Cunning Odysseus!
With your cunning head
to lead us
we will return home,
as surely as day
must follow night!

ODYSSEUS: Hey, Polyphemus, if anyone ever asks who blinded you, tell them it was Odysseus of Ithaca!

CYCLOPS: Odysseus? Odysseus? O father, Poseidon God of the Seas, if I am truly your son, then let Odysseus be forever cursed on the western seas! Let him not return home. Or if he does let him wander long and hard to return to his land! Father rise, rise and throw storms, blow hurricane winds in the path of this Odysseus.

CHORUS: What have you done, Odysseus?
Did you have to be so boastful and tell him your name?
(Poseidon rises from the sea)

POSEIDON: You are a proud man, Odysseus,
an arrogant man, reckless towards the gods!
You blinded my son,
bringing pain eternal
to his sweet head.
Long will be your return home,
and full of trials.
And when you return,
greater will be the loss you suffer,
until you come to the land which knows not the sea,
where purple-cheeked men dwell and you give sacrifice to
me, Poseidon, Lord of the Seas!

CHORUS: What have you done, Odysseus?

ODYSSEUS: I led you all safely through battle in Troy! I have sworn to bring you home, friends, and so I will! *(prays)* Goddess Athene, you who are my friend, help me! Tame Poseidon's anger so that we may journey on!
(Odysseus picks up five sheets of paper)

ODYSSEUS: A gift from the gods! A favorable West wind to guide us to Ithaca!
(They sail)

CHORUS: What do you carry in your bag, Odysseus?
That bag, all battered and brown, that does not leave your hand, Odysseus?
Is it gold?
Silver you gained from Troy?
The commander carries riches
and his followers only their memories!

ODYSSEUS: Quiet all of you! See there, in the distance, is the land of our fathers! Can you see the fires, twinkling, eager to welcome us home! This will be our last night on board ship, friends, and the red earth of Ithaca will bring a new spring to our step.

CHORUS: Ithaca!
Ithaca!
Ithaca!
But what is in that battered bag, Odysseus?

ODYSSEUS: Rest now, tomorrow we return to Ithaca in triumph.

CHORUS: Gladly will we rest
But what is in that battered bag, Odysseus?

ODYSSEUS: A gift from the gods, to bring us favorable wind. Now rest and dream
of our return home.

CHORUS: We followed you to Troy, Odysseus,
followed you out of the wooden horse
to triumph over Troy, Odysseus,
followed you into the cave of Cyclops, Odysseus!
Now we will gladly follow again—
but only if you first lay down to rest and sleep!

ODYSSEUS: Very well. Let my snoring be your command to rest!

(Odysseus lays down to sleep. RAMA appears)

RAMA: Do not give in.

ODYSSEUS: To what?

RAMA: Temptation.

ODYSSEUS: You are mistaken. It is the desire for my home in Ithaca which drives
me on.

RAMA: Don't give in to the golden deer!

ODYSSEUS: Riddles. Ithaca is there, on the horizon, the wind is fair, the sea calm.
I will have my last sleep on board my ship.

(He sleeps)

CHORUS: Odysseus is loved and honored by all.
Wherever we stop, handsome treasures
are his gift. See now how he sleeps,
content, a baby smiling with the sweet
milk of gifts! And what do we bring home
to our wives and kin? Battered bodies,
sleepless nights, anguished hearts.
And no gifts.

(The chorus comes to the bag lying next to Odysseus. They open the bag. And
all the winds of aiolos fly out)

CHORUS: We fly!
Away from Ithaca!
The East Wind pushes us to the left!
West wind batters our ship to the right!
North wind pushes us on towards the rocks!
While the south wind speeds us away from home!
Odysseus!

ODYSSEUS: What have you done! What have you done! You have defiled the gift
of the gods!

CHORUS: Do we drift, then, Odysseus?
>   Lie in the lap of waves
>   to be taken where they will?

ODYSSEUS: Poseidon, God of the sea, hates me because I hurt Polyphemus his son. But no god can keep a man from his home. So put up the sail, pull out the oars while I keep my hand on the rudder and steer us through these howling winds! Row! Row on! Harder! We will tame Posiedon's anger or I am not Odysseus, king of Ithaca!

CHORUS: We row, and we row
>   and we row on until
>   before us lies an enchanted
>   island. The island of Circe,
>   daughter of Helios,
>   the Sun God who shines
>   on all mortals.
>   *(Circe is seated in her great hall, singing. Odysseus' men arrive at the doorway to the hall)*

CHORUS: Circe! She of the lovely hair!
>   Curling locks through which
>   the sun shines its rays!
>   *(Circe notices the men and abruptly stops her song. She goes to each one, offering wine from her hands)*

CHORUS: Ah! This is wine fit for gods!
>   Here we will stay,
>   set down our anchor on Circe's
>   shore, and drink to the beauty
>   of Circe before us
>   And forget Ithaca!
>   *(Circe strikes each one, turning the men into pigs)*

CIRCE: Pigs! Pigs! Pigs! With pig eyes you looked upon my face, so as pigs I will feed you acorns, cornel buds, and food such as pigs always feed on!
>   *(Odysseus enters, sees his men)*

CIRCE: Ah, Odysseus! There is a mind in you no magic will work on! Sheath your sword and come with me, so that lying together in my bed we may have trust and faith in each other.

ODYSSEUS: And when I am naked in your bed, will you unman me? Turn me also into a pig, or worse? Swear an oath no harm will come on me, and I will lie in your bed!

RAMA: And what of your Penelope? She waits in her lonely bed for you.

ODYSSEUS: I must do this to save my men!

CIRCE: You have my word, Odysseus, no harm will come to you in my bed. Let your restless mind take comfort and come with me.

RAMA: What you do, none will blame. But what if Penelope were to do the same?

(Odysseus grabs Circe)

ODYSSEUS: How can I enjoy to eat or drink when my men roam your fields as pigs?

CIRCE: Then look, there stand your men, free of my spell!

(Odysseus' men gather round him)

CIRCE: Eat now, and drink and gather back into your chests the spirit you had when you first set sail for your home.

CHORUS: So we eat

And we drink

Day after day

And the seasons come and go

ODYSSEUS: And a year passes away! *(to Circe)* See me on my way home now, Circe! A year has gone by, and the call of our homes in Ithaca is greater than ever.

CIRCE: What gods can stop men whose minds are fixed? But when you go, avoid the island of my father Helios, who is God of the Sun! His cattle graze there and a terrible doom will befall you and your men if they are disturbed! Go, sail in my ship!

(The Island of Helios)

CHORUS: You're a hard man, Odysseus!

You drive on, made of iron,

Your limbs never wearing out.

You force us to blunder on,

Through the running night,

When here is an island

For us to rest our weary limbs,

Make ready a greedy meal,

And set sail again on the wide sea

When Dawn spreads her rosy fingers.

ODYSSEUS: That is the island of Helios.

CHORUS: The god of the Sun!

What better place to rest,

warm our limbs from the

sea-spray's darts?

ODYSSEUS: Circe told me not to stop at Helios.

CHORUS: What can she know of hunger,

hunger born of water, endless, always

water! Let us stop, we beg you!

ODYSSEUS: Swear to me then, all of you, that if we come upon a herd of cattle, no one will slaughter them, no matter how loud your stomach may groan.

CHORUS: What shall we eat, hard Odysseus?
>   You have no need of food or sleep,
>   rushing as you are to your great hall in Ithaca.
>   But we of flesh and blood are made,
>   Meat we must have to eat,
>   And wine to slake salt-parched throats.

ODYSSEUS: Circe filled our ship with provisions before we set sail.

CHORUS: Circe! We turned into pigs
>   because of that witch,
>   swine roaming her island!
>   We won't eat pig-swill,
>   which's all she'll have given!

ODYSSEUS: Ungrateful wretches! She made you men again! And then did we not spend happy times on her island? And did she not send us away in her own ship? And give us directions which way to go?
>   *(The chorus swear oaths)*

CHORUS: So we eat Circe's food. Enough meat and bread and good wine to drink. And we all sleep close to our ship. In the morning, when we set sail, Poseidon forces the wind to bring us back to Helios again. *(the sequence is repeated)* And the food of Circe the witch is run out.

ODYSSEUS: I will go find a place on this island, build a fire to pray to the gods. One of them might show me the course to sail on. *(prays)* Athene, Goddess friend of mine, give me a sign, help me again to escape the anger of Poseidon!

CHORUS: Now we must hunt,
>   Range after fish and birds
>   With curved hooks and sticks,
>   Fool our bellies with thoughts of meat!

CHORUS 1: Friends, while death is bad, hunger is worse!

CHORUS: Tell us what we don't already know!

CHORUS 1: Sticks and stones are not for men such as us, who have scaled the topless towers of Troy and won Helen back from Paris! Lift up your burnished swords and your bronze-headed spears and let us kill the cattle of Helios! I would rather gulp the waves and die in them than be pinched to death on this island!
>   *(The chorus agree. They proceed to ritually slaughter the cattle, skin and roast the meat, and eat. Odysseus comes upon his men)*

ODYSSEUS: What doom have you brought upon your heads?!

CHORUS: *(pointing to CHORUS 1)* He egged us on,
>   Made our stomachs rumble
>   At the vision of meat roasting
>   And spitting on a spit!

CHORUS 1: See how hunger makes enemies of us?

ODYSSEUS: Not hunger—recklessness!

CHORUS 1: You were reckless when you injured Polyphemus, the Cyclops.

ODYSSEUS: To save us all!

CHORUS 1: This meat saves us from hunger!

ODYSSEUS: You spit in the face of the gods!

CHORUS 1: And your stubbornness drives us on! We were happy, content to stay on Circe's island, drink her wine and be tended by her maids! But you had to go on, always go on to Ithaca! We are men! And if Ithaca is not in our fates, then I am happy to die content, with a belly full of meat!

ODYSSEUS: Enough! On board ship, quickly, before the anger of Helios dooms us all!

(All scramble on board the ship)

CHORUS: As we hurry to leave the island,

The meat stuck on the spits,

Both roast and raw, bellows

Like the lowing of cattle,

And their dead skins begin to crawl!

ODYSSEUS: A blue-black cloud settles over our racing ship. A screaming wind comes and its blast snaps both the forestays holding the mast. My steersman tries to steady the ship, as the mast pole crashes down on his head, pounding all his bones to pieces. Thunder and lightning crash on our ship and she spins in a circle. All my men, trying to row their way out of this watery hell, are thrown in the water. Bobbing like sea crows, they stretch out hands to clutch on dear life but the gods take away their homecoming. . . . Hunger! O cruel hunger! Did you have to take all my men?!

(A sloka begins. RAMA appears)

ODYSSEUS: *(to RAMA)* Help me! Use your powers—lift me from these roaring waves.

RAMA: We each must do what fate wills.

ODYSSEUS: Fate? Is this my fate, to bob on these waves for eternity?

RAMA: As I must weave through this forest, hoping for sight of my Sita.

ODYSSEUS: Ithaca! Ithaca! I long for Ithaca!

(A vista of lone swords and spears, of heads hanging by their hair, of empty body-armor dangling. We are now with Odysseus in Hades)

SWORD: Odysseus!

HEAD: Oh, Odysseus! You too, despite your wiles!

BODY-ARMOR: Gaze upon this empty chest, Odysseus, and take heart in your cunning!

ODYSSEUS: What—what is this place?

SWORD: Did a ferryman bring you across?

ODYSSEUS: Yes.

HEAD: Then pray the gods take pity on you, Odysseus!

SWORD: For this is the hell of Hades!

ODYSSEUS: Hades! But I have not yet returned home!

BODY-ARMOR: Home! A word as hollow as my armor! Beware home, Odysseus, be wary of your home.

ODYSSEUS: Who are you that the gods have brought you to this?

SWORD: Forgotten already! Already you have taken two steps into Hades, where all your past is dust to choke you!

ODYSSEUS: Who are you?

HEAD: You were plowing your fields and your plow hit an obstruction . . .

ODYSSEUS: *(to* BODY-ARMOR*)* Agamemnon! You are Agamemnon! *(kneels)* General—what happened to you . . .

BODY-ARMOR: Ten years we fought, you and I, in far-off Troy. Ten years we left our homes for my Clytemnestra and your Penelope to keep warm. Ten years for a snake to enter into my home, and strike me dead from behind while my Clytemnestra hugged me with her happy smile.

ODYSSEUS: No! No!

BODY-ARMOR: Gaze upon my hollow armor, Odysseus, and be wary how you enter your house!

ODYSSEUS: I *will* see home again! Your doom I will not share. Ithaca is mine and will be mine again!

(RAMA appears)

RAMA: At what cost?

ODYSSEUS: Whatever cost.

RAMA: Keep space in your heart for pity.

ODYSSEUS: If there are others in my house, then I have been wronged, wronged more shamefully than any wrong I may have committed to the gods! I will show no mercy to the wrong-doers! My kingdom will not be snatched from me.

RAMA: Keep space in your heart for pity. See there, Penelope sits in your great house.

(A scene unfolds, of PENELOPE weaving)

PENELOPE: I sit weaving my tapestry. On a sunny field, a plowman with his oxen. Before him stand armed generals, with their shining shields and burnished swords. The plowman is looking down on the ground before him. A bundled baby lies in the path of his sharp plow. If only Agamemnon had not thrown our baby son in front of your plow, Odysseus, you would have stayed, the young men of Ithaca would not now be teeming in your great hall, eating your meat and drinking your wine while they wait to hear my answer to their various suits! If only my heart could accept what all around me say, that you are dead for sure, after twenty long years of silence claimed by the wine-dark sea, then I could take the hand of the suitor who promises the most! This is my life, by tricks, smiles, and lies to keep at bay the wolves of desire. I have promised the suitors a decision once my weave is done. So each day I sit at my loom and at night, when the suitors retire to their beds and only the sound of the crackling fire fills my ears, I undo my day's work, to begin again at the next rosy-fingered Dawn.

(The scene returns to ODYSSEUS *and* RAMA*)*

ODYSSEUS: Can she still be waiting? Have others entered into her heart?

RAMA: You doubt her?

ODYSSEUS: Clytemnestra betrayed Agamemnon!

RAMA: You doubt her.

ODYSSEUS: I doubt what is not certain before my eyes!

RAMA: Do you pine for her?

ODYSSEUS: What else is home?

RAMA: A battlefield!

(Ithaca. Enter suitors, chanting)

SUITORS: His kingdom is besieged by suitors,
who bring tokens of love
and eat his food and drink his wine,
while cunning Penelope—
true queen to crafty Odysseus—
tries with all her tricks to keep
constant a heart that dreams
only of Odysseus.

(PENELOPE enters)

PENELOPE: Odysseus! . . . My sleepy thoughts place you bobbing in the wine-dark sea. . . . When you left me behind in the land of your fathers, your right hand held my wrist and your iron fingers whispered, "when you see our son grown up and bearded, and I am not yet returned, then marry whatever man you please and leave this house." Our son is bearded now, am I free?

SUITORS: Odysseus is dead, Penelope!
Odysseus is lost, Penelope!
Odysseus is with a new wife, Penelope!

PENELOPE: You come every day and eat the food of Odysseus' house and drink the wine from his fields. And each day I welcome you as guests into the house of Odysseus. Have you no shame? No fear that one day you may pay for this recklessness?

SUITORS: Cruel, how cruel you are!
Is it right that a woman as fair as Penelope—
As proud as Penelope—

As regal as Penelope—

As clever as Penelope—

Should remain without a husband to protect her?

(ODYSSEUS *enters*)

ODYSSEUS: I see the young men of Ithaca in my house, around my wife and anger boils in my heart. But I will not make the mistake Agamemnon did. I will hide my anger.

(PENELOPE *takes out the bow of* ODYSSEUS, *with his quiver of arrows*)

PENELOPE: This is a dream I had last night, that the man who will be worthy of me must be equal to Odysseus in endurance. Here is the great bow of Odysseus. The one who takes this bow in his hands, strings it with ease and then sends an arrow clean through twelve axes, he I will go away with, leaving this house where I was a bride. Prepare your hearts and return tomorrow with resolve for the test.

SUITORS: Look, Penelope

See there, Penelope

a stranger in your house.

(*Enter* ODYSSEUS, *disguised*)

PENELOPE: Welcome, stranger, to the house of Odysseus. . . . Eat well, stranger, and then tell me who you are, and from where you came.

ODYSSEUS: I thank you. Here in your house I will answer all your questions, but do not ask who I am or the name of my country. My grief is so full, I swim in tears and drown in sorrow.

PENELOPE: Then we are happily met, for I too waste away at the inward heart, longing for Odysseus.

ODYSSEUS: Do not waste your beauty in mourning for your husband.

PENELOPE: I had a dream last night. My twenty geese were feeding on grains of wheat from the trough. A great eagle with crooked beak swooped down from the mountain and broke the necks of them all and killed them. While the twenty lay dead about the house, the eagle soared high in the bright air.

ODYSSEUS: This dream says your husband is alive and will free you.

PENELOPE: Dreams are only dreams, not all of them end in anything. The dawn to come will be an evil day, which will take me from the house of Odysseus.

ODYSSEUS: Let me tell you, he will be back here with you! (*checks himself*) I have had a long journey, and your food and your words have filled my belly as never before. Now sleep draws my eyelids together. . . .

(ODYSSEUS *sleeps. Dawn comes. The suitors gather*)

SUITORS: Now dawns the day

When the long wait is done

A bow to string

An arrow to wing

Through axes twelve

And fair Penelope is in hand!

(They see the disguised ODYSSEUS *lying asleep)*

You? Still here!

A beggar asleep

in your great hall!

Shoo him, kick him

Shove him out the door!

PENELOPE: It brings no honor on you to shame my guest. You have your task in hand, let him sleep his weariness away.

SUITORS: Who shall be first then among us?

What does it matter! We have

Been together in wooing Penelope

Let us now welcome the best among

Us, for he will win Penelope

And bring honor to all!

(One by one, they begin the contest)

PENELOPE: One stands forth from among the suitors, takes up the bow of Odysseus, turns it round and round by the blaze of the fire, but cannot string it.

SUITOR 1: Oh what shame!

PENELOPE: Now stands another, and he too lifts the bow of Odysseus, turns it round and round by the blaze of the fire, but cannot string it.

SUITOR 2: Oh what shame! Not that I cannot now have Penelope—there are many other beside her here in Ithaca—

PENELOPE: Yet another stands, lifts the bow of Odysseus, turns it round and round by the blaze of the fire, but cannot string it.

SUITOR 3: Oh what shame! Not that I cannot now have Penelope—there are many other beside her here in Ithaca—but that so far short of Odysseus in strength are we that we cannot even string his bow!

ODYSSEUS: May I try?

SUITORS: What?

Are you, wretched beggar,

become shameless in your old age?

Pick him up! Let's drag him,

Beat him about the body

And put him in a black ship!

PENELOPE: Do you think if this stranger succeeds where you have failed that I would go to his home with him and be his wife? No. He is a stranger, whose name and story I still do not know. But can I refuse the request of a stranger to our door? Let him try for the sake of the trial itself.

SUITORS: It is not for fear of him taking you away

We object. But what will meaner men than we
Say, when a beggar such as he, wandering in
From somewhere, strings the bow and sends
A shaft through the iron? That base men are
Now courting the wife of a stately man.
It is for fear of your honor
That we object!

PENELOPE: Now, after all these years, you worry about gossip-mongers?! What honor has there been in Ithaca since you started to eat away at the glory and livelihood of Odysseus' house? If this stranger can string the bow, I will give him fine clothing to wear and give him a sharp spear and sandals for his feet, a sword with two edges and send him wherever his heart and spirit desire.

ODYSSEUS: I see the young men of Ithaca around Penelope and now the time has come to act! I pick up the bow, string it, and my arrow speeds through each of the twelve axes Penelope laid out in our great hall. *(to* SUITORS*)* Now you dogs! You thought I would never return from Troy! Now on you all the seal of destruction is set!

SUITORS: Odysseus!

*(*RAMA *appears)*

RAMA: Keep space in your heart for pity.

ODYSSEUS: I defied you, defied all the trials you sent to keep me from my king-dom! Now I will let fly my arrows and regain my house!

RAMA: At what do you aim your arrow? Their hearts, or the dark cloud of doubt in your own heart?

ODYSSEUS: Dogs! They never thought I would return from Troy!

RAMA: You have. Now let life begins again from the long years of separation. Welcome Penelope and sit again in your great hall.

ODYSSEUS: The seal of destruction is set on them all. *(to* SUITORS*)* Fight me or run.

SUITORS: Draw your swords, friends
And let us rush him all together.
He is only one old man
Against many young!

(Arrows fly, a battle rages)

ODYSSEUS: Through the neck of one my arrow speeds—

SUITOR: and blood gushes out like water to a thirsty man!

ODYSSEUS: I lift my spear and hurl it through the chest of another—

SUITOR: hearing ribs crack like thunder over the dark sea!

ODYSSEUS: My burnished sword cracks open the head of a third—

SUITOR: rich fruit for the tasting!

*(*ODYSSEUS *empties his quiver, killing all the suitors)*

PENELOPE: The geese! The geese!

ODYSSEUS: All the young men of Ithaca are dead! I am Odysseus, come home to my Ithaca. *(to RAMA)* Now let loose your arrow of Dharma. My arc of Duty is done.

(He goes to PENELOPE. She recoils in horror. Pause)

ODYSSEUS: *(to PENELOPE)* I was told when I returned home I would go where there are men living who know nothing of the sea. Men whose cheeks are painted purple. And there when I meet a man who thinks my oar is a fan I carry on my shoulder, there I must plant my oar and make a large sacrifice to Poseidon.

(PENELOPE accepts ODYSSEUS in her lap)

[End of First Half]

THE RAMAYAN

(ODYSSEUS and RAMA appear. RAMA moves to the havan-kund and lights the fire)

RAMA: Two *krauncha* birds.

ODYSSEUS: What about them?

RAMA: They were making love! A hunter came and killed the male. The female pined to her death. Out of this *shoka,* out of this grief, comes *sloka,* comes poetry!

ODYSSEUS: Not poetry—vengeance!

RAMA: But what is the arrow aimed at, the enemy outside or the heart within?

(RAMA pours samagri into the fire and speaks through the smoke)

RAMA: Dashratha, King of Ayodhya, built a huge sacrificial fire, praying to Vishnu for a son. Out of the smoke rose Vishnu's answer—I, Rama, seventh avatar of Vishnu. As the son of a king, I needed a bow.

(The CHORUS transforms the scene to Janaka's court)

CHORUS: Sunno, sunno, sunno!

Raja Janak nay Sita svyamvurr ka élan kiya hai!

Kay jho-bhi Shiv-rachit danush ko

Raja Janak kay durbar meyn

uTha paaey gha

Usska kumari Sita say vivah kiya jaaey gha!

(Hear ye, hear ye, hear ye!

King Janak has announced a contest for Sita's hand

That whosoever lifts the bow of Shiva in King Janak's hall

he will be married to his daughter Sita!)

JANAKA: Here is the bow of Parasurama. A bow that has lain in my hall since the day that fierce warrior left. Only my daughter, Sita, has ever lifted the bow and played with it. Now she is older, her time for play is gone and I, King Janaka of Mithila seek a son worthy of her hand. Whoever lifts this bow will win the hand of my daughter Sita as his wife and lift the burden of duty from my heart!

(RAMA approaches)

JANAKA: Lift the bow and it is more than a vow you will take, young prince. Your life will be my daughter Sita's life, as her life will be yours. This will be your new dharma.

RAMA: I understand.

JANAKA: Consider well, young prince. Till this moment you have enjoyed the freedom of being Rama, alone and always just Rama, free to do whatever Rama desired. The dharma that lies before you is filled with greater duty.

RAMA: I understand.

(Enter RAVANA)

RAVANA: Janaka! A king should address a king first!

JANAKA: *(surprised)* The king of Lanka!

RAVANA: Ravana himself! Each one of my ten lives chants the name of Sita, Sita alone is the sound sailing from our tongues, and it is for this Sita I have come!

(RAMA sniggers. RAVANA looks at RAMA, and then SITA. And retires)

RAMA: The bow waits for the right hand. *(To JANAKA)* Aghya maang?

(JANAKA indicates compliance. RAMA pays obeisance to JANAKA, then to all the assembled and finally to the bow. RAMA lifts the bow)

CHORUS: *Sia-vurr Raamchandra ki*

Jai!

Jai-ho Raamchandra ki

Jai!

Sia-pati Raamchandra ki

Jai!

RAVANA: Laughter escaped from your mouth, Rama, when I approached the bow. A day will come when that smile will become a stranger to you.

(SITA walks up to Rama, garlands in hand. She garlands him. He takes a garland from her and garlands her. RAMA and SITA make a round. We are now in RAMA's palace in Ayodhya)

LAKSHMANA: *(to RAMA)* You can't do this!

BHARATA: It is not right, Rama—you are the eldest!

RAMA: Bharata, Lakshamana—if you are both true brothers, then don't stop me from doing what I must.

BHARATA: You are Lord Rama! How was it that father himself announced on your return with Sita that you would be king?

RAMA: To obey is my dharma, Bharata.

LAKSHMANA: It is wrong!

RAMA: Dharma is neither right nor wrong—it simply *is*, Lakshmana. Our father made a promise to Kaikeyi—your mother, Bharata. Now she is claiming it. And her price is for me to go into exile in the forest so that you can become king. Would you have me ask our father not to honor his promise? Then tomorrow, if your charioteer were to decide not to take you hunting, having promised he would, what will you do? If a king cannot keep his promise it is the end of the kingdom. So I must leave my beloved Ayodhya.

SITA: Leave?

RAMA: Yes, I must leave.

SITA: It seems, Rama, my father's words fell like so much water on an elephant's back—vanished into air at the first moment of heat!

RAMA: What are you saying?

SITA: I accept my dharma. I would my Rama accepted his.

RAMA: But . . . I am to go into exile in the forest!

SITA: I will share the sights of the forest with you.

RAMA: But . . . we will walk on thorns, have weeds for flowers and flies for music!

SITA: I will share the sounds and the smells and the touch of the forest with you.

RAMA: But . . . the forest is no place for a daughter of Lord Janaka!

SITA: It is the place for Rama's Sita. Did you not know I was born from the earth? My father's plow found me in his field, a daughter from the earth. Here, I take off the robes of royalty, remove the jewelry of nobility and am now plain Sita, a woman of the forest.

RAMA: Bharata, you look after the kingdom. That is your now dharma.

BHARATA: Then give me your sandals.

RAMA: Take them, I will have no need of these in the forest.

(BHARATA *takes the sandals*)

BHARATA: These will sit on the throne, reminding all who is rightfully king. And I will guard them and rule as if you were seated there, whispering in my ear.

LAKSHMANA: At least you'll have work to do! What am I without you, Rama? I am coming with you and don't say a word! (*strides off*)

RAMA: Come, Sita, let us begin our new life.

(RAMA *and* SITA *get into a boat, with Lakshmana in train, and are ferried across the Ganges*)

RAMA AND SITA'S SONG

Hold me in your palm, Ganga, O Ganga,
Rock me in your lap, Ganga, O Ganga,
Ferry our souls, Ganga, O Ganga
Through your door!
Between the shore we left

And the shore to come
There is only you,
Ganga, O Ganga,
Who is to know what lies
Through your door!

FERRYMAN: Here we are, travelers, mother Ganga has brought us safely to the other shore. From here, as far as the eye can see, there is only forest, and more forest.

RAMA: Ferryman, your duty is done for now. We will meet again, when it is time.

(As RAMA, SITA *and* LAKSHMANA *leave, the* FERRYMAN *touches the ground where* RAMA's *feet had been)*

FERRYMAN: Bless me, Lord Rama . . . !

*(*FERRYMAN *exits)*

SITA: I will pick berries and season them with leaves—our old lives may be over, but not entirely forgotten!

RAMA: *(to* LAKSHMANA*)* Come, Lakshmana, our first task is to make a shelter before nightfall.

*(*SURPANAKHA *appears. Presents herself. Sees* RAMA.*)*

SURPANAKHA: Who are you?!

RAMA: I am Rama.

SURPANAKHA: You are the most beautiful man I have ever seen! You are the husband I must have! I am the sister of Ravana, the king of Lanka! Come, I will take you to my brother Ravana's palace in Lanka and we will have the greatest wedding the world's ever seen!

RAMA: *(laughing)* And you are in truth the woman of my dreams! What silken hair you have flowing from your head! Your body moves with the grace of a peacock and your feet delicately touch the earth!

SURPANAKHA: Then delay not! Come, I will fly you to my palace, out of this dirty and dreadful forest!

RAMA: But—I have a problem.

SURPANAKHA: What? Tell me! There is no problem Ravana my brother cannot solve!

RAMA: I am married.

SURPANAKHA: *(distraught)* Oh!

RAMA: Don't be sad. I have a way to make you happy. My brother, Lakshmana, is even more handsome than me! Lakshmana!

*(*LAKSHMANA *appears)*

RAMA: Here, brother, is the sister of Ravana. Take good care of her!

*(*LAKSHMANA *cuts off her nose)*

SURPANAKHA: My nose! My nose! You have cut off my nose! Revenge, my brother, revenge!

*(*SURPANAKHA *exits, as* SITA *enters)*

SITA: Rama! Rama!

(RAMA *rushes in*)

RAMA: What's happened? Sita—are you all right?

SITA: I—I—I have just—just seen a sight like none other!

RAMA: What? A demon? A serpent?

SITA: What a serpent! What a rakshasa!

RAMA: Will you stop talking in riddles and tell me what happened!

SITA: Oh, Rama . . . ! I was gathering berries there, and leaves to season them with, when a golden deer shot across the corner of my eye! Oh Rama, will you get the golden deer for me?

RAMA: A deer! A golden deer!

SITA: *(misunderstanding)* Yes! Yes! A beautiful, magical golden deer to color our dark nights in the forest!

RAMA: Sita, you saw what you wanted to see.

(*Leaves*)

SITA: *(to audience)* It was no vision I saw—or, to tell the truth, such a vision as will turn even gods into unbelievers! Its coat as soft and velvet as no gold could be, yet shining as only gold can. Tiny ruby-spots on its fur, like tear-drops on gold. Its ivory-eyes spotted with darkest ebony, full of mirth . . . ! I *saw* it. And Rama will get it for me!

(RAMA *gets up, picking his bow*)

ODYSSEUS: Do not give in to temptation!

RAMA: Desire keeps a home alive! It is my dharma to look after her desires.

ODYSSEUS: Even if it leads to your doom?

RAMA: What else is a man?!

(RAMA *leaves, after a lingering last glance at* SITA)

LAKSHMANA: Rama gave me this (*holds up the stick he's been fashioning*).

SITA: A stick?! What can it do?

LAKSHMANA: Whatever I will it to.

SITA: Then why put your brother through the effort of chasing after the deer?! Go fetch my golden deer!

LAKSHMANA: It must only be used when we are most in need.

SITA: Do all men do this?

(*A cry is heard off-stage*)

V/O: Help me! Sita! Lakshmana! Help!

SITA: Rama! Lakshmana—what's happened to Rama?

LAKSHMANA: I am not sure it's Rama's voice . . .

SITA: Your brother is crying out for help and you're not sure?!

LAKSHMANA: Sita please—this may be another trick of the forest!

V/O: Help me! Sita! Lakshmana! Help!

SITA: Is that cry for help a trick? It's Rama—my heart cannot lie! Go to him. Now!

LAKSHMANA: Rama asked me to guard you!

SITA: And whose need is greater now? Am I crying for help? Go now—or give me your bow and I will go myself! Oh, I see . . . ! Now I understand. You are hoping Rama will be killed and then you can claim me for yourself! You've always longed for me! Don't think I can be fooled by your trick of never looking me in the eye! What a brother!

(LAKSHMANA *inscribes a circle on the ground around* SITA, *with his arrow*)

LAKSHMANA: With this stick I draw a circle to guard you. Whatever happens, you must not step outside the circle. Will you promise?

SITA: I do, I do—now go on!

V/O: Help me! Sita! Lakshmana! Help!

SITA: Hurry!

(LAKSHMANA *leaves, as a* SLOKA *begins to be heard. Behind a screen, a shadow-play begins, narrated by* SITA)

SITA: The sun began to sink lower in the west, the shadows of trees racing across the forest-floor, and no word from either Rama or Lakshmana. But, since Lakshmana left, my heart was relieved a little—brothers will look after each other. As I started to prepare the evening meal, I heard a voice—

OLD MAN: *Beyti*, some food for a poor beggar . . .

SITA: And saw an old man slowly approach our shelter. I had only a little rice for the three of us, but it is good dharma to offer strangers food, and I did not want to feel the anger of the forest by refusing. Of course, I said, please, come and have the rice we have.

(OLD MAN *approaches* SITA, *as she continues to narrate*)

SITA: As the old man slowly made his way to the bowl of rice I was holding in my out-stretched hand, he came to the line Lakshmana had drawn on the ground. As he took a step over the line, suddenly sheets of flame rose from the ground, completely veiling me from the stranger! The stranger cried out—

OLD MAN: Aww!

SITA: And fell to the ground! I rushed to see he was not hurt, and to apologize. I am deeply sorry, dear sir, my brother-in-law created this ring of fire to protect me when he went to help Rama.

OLD MAN: Rama!

SITA: My husband.

OLD MAN: Ah, then, dear lady, you are none other than Sita! I had heard that Raam-Sita had come to live in our forest and I traveled from afar to gain the blessing of Rama. But now I am blessed more than my heart can bear, seeing you.

SITA: Please, sir, you will honor us by sharing our food.

OLD MAN: I cannot come to you, daughter . . .

SITA: And I cannot leave the protection of this circle.

OLD MAN: Then I will just sit here, and fill my hungry stomach with the sight of your divine beauty . . .

SITA: What harm, I wondered, surely only good can come from a good deed. So with my bowl of rice, I stepped over the line Lakshmana has drawn, and bent down to offer rice to the kindly old man.

(*The sheet disappears and the* OLD MAN *is* RAVANA, *holding fast to* SITA's *hand. We are in the Ashoka garden, where* RAVANA *has kept* SITA *prisoner*)

RAVANA: This is how I took you from that forest shelter you call home, and brought you here—here in my palace in Lanka! The wrong Rama did to my sister Surpanakha has been avenged. You are mine, Sita, the most perfect beauty in the world, as once Surpanakha was beautiful. But you choose to spend your days in my small Ashoka Garden, so be it. I will wait. I can wait to the end of time for you to give me your hand of your own will.

SITA: Then you will wait a very long time. If all my days are to be spent singing the name of Rama in my heart, the days will not be long enough!

RAVANA: Then prepare for night, it will surely come. For Rama to win you back, he must first bridge the ocean that lies around this island of Lanka. Then he must face my ten thousand-strong army of demons. And if he somehow passes through these tests, then he will face me.

SITA: And kill you, for daring to take me by force.

RAVANA: Sita, Sita! I only took that which quickened my heart and yours. When I saw you in your father's great hall, when your eyes met mine, our fate was sealed. Here, in my Ashoka Garden, you sit as you should, a queen surrounded by beauty. And not once have I forced myself on you.

SITA: My heart belongs to Rama, you must know that.

RAVANA: If Ravana stood on one leg for a whole yuga, in penance in the deep snows of the Himalayas, he can wait another yuga for your hand, Sita. And you will one day see it in your heart to give me your hand. Even the gods relented in the face of my penance, granting me the boon of ten lives!

SITA: Rama will kill you.

RAVANA: Has he desire enough? I wanted you, and sacrificed my uncle Maricha to get you. He appeared before your eyes as a golden deer and led Rama away from you!

(RAVANA *leaves. A sloka is recited, as* SITA *sits by a tree*)

SITA: The golden deer! Oh, how my own desires have betrayed me! When will you come, Rama? I sing your name in my heart, each flower your name as I weave the garland that binds us!

(RAMA *appears.* ODYSSEUS *comes upon him*)

ODYSSEUS: What use this sorrow? You are too tender, faint-hearted. As I fought through raging seas to regain my Ithaca, so now cut through this forest and regain your love.

RAMA: How? The forest does not reveal where she is! At least you had Ithaca in your sight—what have I?

ODYSSEUS: Then pray! Seek help from the gods above!

(HANUMAN *appears*)

HANUMAN: Hanuman, son of Vyau, God of Wind, stands before you! Come, I will take you where your heart lies—to the edge of the forest; where you can see the island of Lanka! That is where Ravana holds Sita captive!

RAMA: How do we get there?

HANUMAN: I lift you both and seat you on the palm of my hand! Watch now, as the ground beneath your feet races by, the wind courses blood through your veins and the clouds wrap round you for warmth!

(They race through the sky and come to rest at the edge of the forest)

HANUMAN: Here is the edge of land. Before you, there in the distance beyond the roaring sea, is the island of Lanka.

LAKSHMANA: Fires burn all over the island!

RAMA: Smoke rises high from the fires, clouding the light of the sun. Now my heart is heavier still. Each fire we see on Lanka is the breath of a rakshasa! Ten thousand fires, ten thousand rakshasas! And the roaring sea is their voices, defying us to come to their land!

HANUMAN: Let me answer both your fears! My army of little monkeys will gather stones from the Dandaka Forest and make a bridge across the sea. Big stones, small stones, any stones they'll use and join this place marked by your feet with the island that lies smoking on the horizon! And then we'll take on Ravana's rakshasas! His demons will beg to stop the monkeys chattering in their ears! While we keep the army occupied, you deal with Ravana himself.

(The work begins, to build the bridge. CHORUS *chants a building song.* RAMA *and* LAKSHMANA *cross the bridge)*

LAKSHMANA: *(awed)* Oh my God! Is this the end? Is the world only darkness?

RAMA: Before and around and above are thousands upon thousands of rakshasas! Light has fled the earth. Pick up your bow, string the arrow and let fly the dogs of war!

(A mighty battle rages, with RAMA *and* LAKSHMANA *setting off a seemingly inexhaustable supply of arrows. at the end,* RAVANA *stands facing* RAMA*)*

RAVANA: Kill my rakshasas! Lay waste my Lanka! But the gods granted me ten lives and I will spend each one of those lives tormenting you and all that is most precious to you, Rama!

*(*RAMA *fires an arrow, aiming at* RAVANA'*s head. the head comes off—only for another to appear! Again and again* RAMA *tries, with the same result each time)*

HANUMAN: Lord Rama—your aim is not right.

RAMA: Can't you see? I cut off his head and another appears!

HANUMAN: So I say again, your aim is not right! There is only one part of a man's body which bears the mark of his birth throughout his life. Ravana was human once—aim for the source of his being!

(RAMA *slowly takes aim, lowering the arrow to aim for* RAVANA'*s navel.* RAVANA *sees the new aim and laughs in defiance*)

RAVANA: That monkey can chatter my rakshasa army to death but he will only chatter you to your doom, Rama! I am beyond human—the gods have made it so! So take aim, shoot at my navel, my little belly-button of another age and I will come roaring back for you and tear you limb from limb! When I finally kill you, this world will know only darkness. Dark clouds will bring smiles on peoples faces, and they will hide from the sun!

(RAMA'*s arrow speeds to* RAVANA'*s navel. It strikes.* RAVANA *laughs. The arrow then burrows further in, cutting-off* RAVANA'*s laugh. A beat, and he falls. Slowly the darkness rolls back, revealing light*)

RAMA: It is done. *(calls out)* Bring Sita before me! Make sure she is well-dressed, as befits a queen.

(SITA *is brought to* RAMA)

RAMA: Sita . . .

(SITA *steps towards* RAMA. RAMA *stops her*)

RAMA: I vowed to win you back and have done so. Ravana insulted me, and he has paid the price. I am once more my own master. All this I did for the sake of my honor and the good name of the royal house of Ayodhya. Sita, you have been a long time in another man's house. So you are free. Our marriage vows mean nothing now. You are free to decide what you must do.

SITA: You question my loyalty, Rama?

RAMA: I speak as the heir to the throne of Ayodhya.

SITA: Speak to me as my Rama! I am a daughter of the earth, seized against my will and held captive in the Ashoka Garden here in Lanka with only your name in my heart to keep company!

RAMA: None can know what happened between you and Ravana in the Ashoka Garden. But all can imagine. I must free their minds.

SITA: By doubting me?

RAMA: Doubt was born when you were taken by Ravana. Now I must kill it.

SITA: What should I have done? Killed myself? And killed my hope of ever seeing Rama again?

ODYSSEUS: What is this, Rama? For this we have let loose our arrows? Is this the homecoming we longed for?

RAMA: I speak according to my dharma.

ODYSSEUS: Speak according to your heart—what does it say?! If we have doubts about our wives, then what use the journey, what point the blood shed to return home?

RAMA: The dharma of kings is not the dharma of men!

ODYSSEUS: But it is men who rule!

RAMA: My dharma is for all to be certain, to harbor no doubts in their hearts.

SITA: Bring twigs that burn quickly. Build a stack where I stand. My Rama has spoken and now let the gods hold me in their lap and proclaim my purity.

(RAMA *stops her*)

RAMA: This was a test for all who harbored evil thoughts in their hearts about the long years you spent a prisoner of Ravana!

HANUMAN: I must leave now.

RAMA: You have been devoted to me. You will live as long as my story is remembered on this earth! Your fame will last beyond the memory of my world!

(HANUMAN *exits*)

CHORUS: Raam-Rajya[1] has begun,
the rule of Rama,
and this is the most golden
of times, the best of kingdoms under the sun!
Buss, kahani khatam!
The story is finished!
Hey, the story's not finished yet! Rama told the Ferryman we'll meet again, when it is time!
Is it time?
Where is the Ferryman?
There!

(FERRYMAN *enters. Approaches his wife*)

FERRYMAN: I am not like Lord Rama. I cannot accept a wife back who has been with another man!

(FERRYMAN *exits.* COURTIERS *whisper among themselves.* RAMA *enters*)

RAMA: You whisper among yourselves. Is there no one brave enough to speak to me? If a ruler is so feared, the kingdom is lost. Come, speak to me—Sita is soon to give birth to my son and heir!

CHORUS: Speech is hard when
the matter is delicate.
But not to speak
is a matter worse.
We are the eyes and ears
of the king and truth—
though sometimes painful—
is our dharma entire.

RAMA: And truth, held prisoner in the heart too long, can curdle into its rival.

CHORUS: Exactly our thoughts!

(*A beat*)

RAMA: So?

---

[1]Lit., kingdom of Ram. In this conception of governance, the ruled dictate how rulers should behave in a benevolent dictatorship. Mahatma Gandhi in *Hind Swaraj* wrote of the ideas of Ram-Rajya.

CHORUS: In Ayodhya's bazaars we have been—
  along Ayodhya's common streets we have seen—
  In Ayodhya's gardens we have heard—
  talk that seemed to us most absurd!
  But when so many men talk,
  argue, opinionate
  all on one topic,
  we must take note
  or turn victim to gossip.

RAMA: And the topic?

CHORUS: Sita.

  (A beat. ODYSSEUS enters)

ODYSSEUS: You will listen once again to mere gossip?! Is this the nature of your
  mercy?

RAMA: When the suitors begged for their life, you defied the law of mercy.

ODYSSEUS: Yes! To punish their shamefulness!

RAMA: Why?

ODYSSEUS: To preserve the kingdom. That no man in future do what they did.

RAMA: And if now my kingdom has no peace, what must I do?

  (SITA exits)

CHORUS: Fourteen years—
  again, once again fourteen years—
  Sita lived in Valmiki's hut
  deep in the Dandaka Forest.
  And there gave birth to
  twins, two sons,
  Kush and Lava,
  sons of Rama.
  Valmiki taught
  the young sons
  a poem to recite.
  The day came when
  Rama invited Valmiki
  to a grand sacrifice.

RAMA: My Raam-Rajya has lasted over fourteen years, years in which a sadness has fallen over the kingdom. Dark clouds gather and so I invite you all,
  learned men from the four corners of the world, to take part in this great
  ceremony, that the gods on high may favor once more my Ayodhya.

  (The children of RAMA take their seats around the havan-kund and begin recit-
  ing, with VALMIKI presiding. RAMA addresses them)

RAMA: Who are you, whose voices ring clear to the sky? Who is your teacher?
  And what is it you recite?

LAVA: With guru Valmiki we have lived

KUSH: From guru Valmiki we have learnt

LAVA: This poem which he fashioned

KUSH: After seeing the plight of two *krauncha* birds.

LAVA: A poem which he calls *The Ramayana*.

RAMA: Who is your father?

VALMIKI: Rama.

> (SITA *enters.* RAMA *looks at her. A pause, as on another part of the stage,* ODYSSEUS *sits before* PENELOPE)

LAVA: Mother, why do you steel your heart? You do not go up to our father, do not sit beside him, do not ask him any questions!

SITA: My child, I cannot find anything to say to him, nor question him, nor look him straight in the face. You are his dharma now.

RAMA: Forgive me, Sita. Return with me to your rightful seat in Ayodhya and let another Raam-Rajya bloom.

SITA: Your sons have regained their father.

RAMA: And you? Will my sons not need their mother?

SITA: Your story began, Rama, when I was found on the earth beneath my father's plow. Out of the earth I came, needing the sky. From the sky you were brought for me. If in all my years I have remained true to you, then let my mother take me in her arms.

RAMA: Stay. There is a world yet to live.

SITA: I have desired you so much all my days! As much as the earth desires the sky for light, for warmth, for life-giving rain. For me. For my heart. There was only Rama. Rama in my sleep, Rama in my waking eye. For you, there has always been more than Sita.

RAMA: The sky cannot exist without the earth!

ODYSSEUS: I must make sacrifice to Poseidon!

SITA: I return to my mother's home, in the earth. When your time comes, you will join me there, but only when earth and sky melt into one. Until then, do not weep.

RAMA: These are tears for the sorrow that has come.

SITA: Our story has run its course.

> (*The earth cracks open, and* SITA *descends into its bowels.* RAMA *and* ODYSSEUS *come upon each other from opposite ends of the stage*)

ODYSSEUS: Why did we journey so long and so far?

RAMA: Land and sea, earth and sky.

ODYSSEUS: At every turn you fulfilled dharma, and lost all . . .

RAMA: At each turn you defied fate, and lost all . . .

ODYSSEUS: Your cheeks are painted purple.

RAMA: You carry a fan on your shoulder.

> [End]

Sudha Bhuchar and Kristine Landon-Smith

Sudha Bhuchar and Kristine Landon-Smith are the joint founders and artistic directors of the Tamasha Theatre Company. Inspired by Asian culture in Britain, the company is committed to creating new works through work with local communities.

Sudha Bhuchar is both an actor and a playwright. She recently played Dina Dalal in Tamasha's *A Fine Balance* (based on the novel by Rohinton Mistry) in 2007. Her many acting credits include *Murder* (BBC) by Abi Morgan, *East-Enders* (BBC), *Doctors* (BBC), *Holby City* (BBC), and *Haroun and the Sea of Stories* (Royal National Theatre), and she is a regular on the BBC Radio drama *Silverstreet*.

Her writing credits for Tamasha include *Balti Kings, Fourteen Songs, Two Weddings and a Funeral, Strictly Dandia*, and *A Fine Balance*, in which she also performed. She writes regularly with Shaheen Khan and their many credits include three series of *Girlies* for BBC Radio 4 and *Balti Kings* (stage play as well as a six-part series for Radio 4). Their screenplay, *The House across the Street*, has been shown on BBC 4 as part of a new writers' initiative, and they have cowritten an episode of *Doctors* for the BBC.

Kristine Landon-Smith has directed all of Tamasha's shows. Her 1996 production of *East is East* was nominated for an Olivier Award and her original production of *Fourteen Songs, Two Weddings and a Funeral* won the Barclays Theatre Award for Best New Musical. She has also directed for the *Royal Court Theatre*, the *Bristol Old Vic*, the *Palace Theatre Westcliff*, and *Nitro*.

Tamasha has produced fourteen plays since its inaugural 1989 production of Mulk Raj Anand's *Untouchable*. Recent productions include the 2007 *A Fine Balance* and the 2005 *The Trouble with Asian Men*.

Strictly Dandia

The Lowry, Salford Quays, UK, 2005
Nuffield Southampton, 2005
Lyric Theatre Hammersmith, London, 2004, 2005
Edinburgh International Festival, 2003

Other Plays

Balti Kings (by Sudha Bhuchar and Shaheen Khan)
Child of the Divide
A Fine Balance
Fourteen Songs, Two Weddings and a Funeral
House of the Sun
Ryman and the Sheikh (by Kristine Landon-Smith, Sudha Bhuchar, Rehan Sheikh, Chris Ryman, and Richard Vranch)
A Tainted Dawn
The Trouble with Asian Men (by Sudha Bhuchar, Kristine Landon-Smith, and Louise Wallinger)
Untouchable

Strictly Dandia

Sudha Bhuchar and Kristine Landon-Smith

CHARACTERS

PREMA

PUSHPA

POPATLAL

PREETHI

ROOPA

BHARAT

SONYA

SHRENEK

JAZ

RAZA

SHANTI

KETAN

HINA

DINESH

ANANT

MOHAN

(*The play is set over one Navratri season in contemporary London.*)

SCENE ONE

(*A big gymnasium hall in a leisure center on the North Circular. Characters enter and sit on the grandstand.* SHRENEK *and* SONYA *[young Patels from*

Reproduced by permission of Methuen Drama, an imprint of A & C Black Publishers. This play was first performed at The Kings Theatre, Edinburgh as part of the Edinburgh International Festival on Wednesday 27 August 2003.

Tooting, in the competition], PUSHPA *and* POPATLAL *[Shah couple, on the committee],* BHARAT *and* DINESH SHAH *[accountant and IT whiz son] and* SHANTI *[widow],* ANANT *[choreographer],* PREETHI DATANI *[pretty young Lohana girl] and* ROOPA *[her best friend]. They wait for the festivities to begin as we hear* PREETHI DATANI *on the tannoy.)*

PREMA: Bhaiyo ne Bheno, Mayor and Mayoress . . . ladies and gentlemen, boys and girls . . . welcome. This is Prema Datani, your hostess, Chair of Lohana Ladies for last five years. There are so many Navratri celebrations in London but none as famous as the Lohana Ladies. The hall is the same, I know, but that is the only thing. On behalf of my committee, I'm proud to announce an Intercaste dance competition . . . Patels, Lohanas and Shahs, all together competing for the much-coveted titles of Diwali King and Queen. The two lucky winners will be crowned at the grand finale on Saturday. They will have the honor of taking their place on the number-one float at the Diwali parade and switching on the seasonal lights on Ealing Road.

(A light isolates POPATLAL *and* PUSHPA. *The convention is that when the characters speak, no one else can hear them.)*

PUSHPA: Intercaste dance competition! I never heard of such a thing. That Prema Datani is full of progressive ideas. Lohanas. Even the way they look, they are different. Fair-skinned and attitude problem, he ne? I don't mind pun the way she looks down on us.

POPATLAL: We Shahs might be businessy but at least we mind our own business.

PUSHPA: Every year she gets this hall for the Lohanas, even though Bharat Shah who looks after the tenders is one of us.

POPATLAL: He is accountant, and Prema's husband Ketan is his biggest client.

PUSHPA: If we had this hall even for one year we would do traditional Navratri, respecting the religious significance of the festival.

POPATLAL: Well, Bharat knows which side his bread is buttered. It's not surprising he forgets he's a Shah.

PUSHPA: The biggest and best hall . . . so central . . . just off the North Circular. I'm going to make sure our daughter dances with Bharat's son. Dinesh is in IT and Hina has done computer course. They have always been close. They surf and talk sometimes . . . in her bedroom. I don't mind as long as door is open. Hina's a good girl. They won the fancy dress as children, tumhe yaad che? When I sent Hina as Radha and Dinesh came as Krishna.

POPATLAL: Tell the youngsters to make it official then this season.

PUSHPA: That's if Bharat agrees. He's got his eyes set on Prema's daughter for his son. As if you can jump caste so easily.

(The light now isolates PREETHI *and* ROOPA.*)*

PREETHI: So you fasting, Roops?

ROOPA: Apart from a bar of Snickers.

PREETHI: Chocolate counts with God. What happens if you don't fall for a Louis?

ROOPA: You get outcast if you marry out of caste.

PREETHI: I'd risk it for a Hindu Punjabi.

ROOPA: Its true Punjabis are better looking but at least you know when a Gujarati boy is wearing a suit he's paid for it.

PREETHI: What about Dinesh? He's a babe-magnet.

ROOPA: One, he's a Shah. Two, he's a geek. Those Patels from Tooting are lowering the tone.

(The light now isolates BHARAT *and* DINESH SHAH.*)*

BHARAT: Preethi Datani is bound to be the Diwali Queen . . . Prema has been giving her dancing lessons since she was six . . . Dinesh, dikro, you can dance. When your mother was alive she was always telling you. . . . Just need some confidence. Do your best. Smile . . . Mr. Ketan Datani is a high-networth individual and already he is thrilled with the way you've transformed his stocktaking systems. Gotta have ambition. When old Idi Amin chucked me out, I came with just my muffler and anorak, and look where I am now. If Ketan sees you dancing with his daughter and winning the Diwali King, who knows, he might be prepared to forget you are a Shah and then think where it might lead.

(The light now isolates SONYA *and* SHRENEK.*)*

SONYA: These North London Lohana girls. Hasn't anyone told them that highlights are out?

SHRENEK: The guys are worse. How can you wear CK jeans? South of the river is where the style is.

SONYA: We're the only semi-professionals here. Those Louyes might be "full of it" but have they got the range of moves? The medals that we have? Granby Hall in Leicester, Birmingham, Wolverhampton.

SHRENEK: Amateurs. Weekend dancers with no commitment.

SONYA: I bet none of them go to Pineapple for classes. Or train with Beni Katania. Our mix of old-school ballet, jazz, and Dandia is gonna proper blow their minds.

SHRENEK: They call it a competition when there is no competition. We might be Patels, but there's no corner-shop mentality with us.

SONYA: Winning Diwali King and Queen's gonna open doors for us. You don't think the diamante crown's tempting fate?

SHRENEK: Fate? It's fait accompli, babe . . . we'll walk it.

(The garba begins and one by one they start to dance.)

PREMA: *(tannoy announcement)* I just want to remind everyone of the religious significance of our festival. There is a dress code. Save the halter necks and navel jewels for Disco Dandia, night. Ladies, make sure your hair is open if your back is bare and make sure your shoulders are covered, otherwise a committee member will ask you to cover up.

(As the dance progresses, JAZ *and* RAZA *[two Muslim boys in their twenties] enter. They stand on the sidelines for a while and watch.* PREETHI *recognizes* RAZA. *They join in the dancing.* PREETHI *is clearly not happy to see him there. The dance gets faster and we hear* PREMA *again on the tannoy.)*

PREMA: Prema Datani again. The judges are going around spotting and short-listing. For those who want to choose their own partner . . . great! But for the singletons, your numbers will be pulled out of a hat. As Hindus, we believe in destiny, so we're going to let Fate choose your dance partners! I hope Fate chooses well. Your dance partner could become your partner for life. The rules are relaxed. Standard steps or stand out! We are not looking for Strictly Dandia!

(The dance reaches a crescendo and finishes.)

SCENE TWO

(Same night. A little while later. Near the drinks kiosk. In the background three people are texting on their mobile phones. JAZ *and* RAZA *enter.* SHANTI *is clearing away her kiosk of drinks and confectionery.)*

JAZ: That Preethi's stressing with you, man.

RAZA: Yeah, it was a prickly exchange. She don't mind meeting at Leicester Square but she doesn't want me here . . . with her family around . . . her community.

JAZ: You knew there was going to be sandpaper between you.

RAZA: I know, but I had to come and see who they've got lined up for her.

JAZ: You gotta get real, Raza. This is the Guju marriage market, and she's gonna pick one of them. Doesn't stop you testing her out and doing an MOT.

RAZA: We shouldn't have come here.

JAZ: Too late. Our numbers were chosen out of the hat. Fate wants you to dance with Preethi . . . and my one's sweet. Her name's Roopa. We've swapped digits. . . . She's smitten.

RAZA: That's 'cos she don't know you're a Muslim.

JAZ: She's got a wicked arse.

RAZA: Grow up, Jaz. Act your age.

JAZ: I am acting my age.

RAZA: These girls are classy women. Don't go talking about her arse in front of her. That's all you see.

JAZ: That's 'cos I'm not gay.

RAZA: I know you're not gay . . . What about personality? Charisma?

JAZ: Charisma . . . Karishma Kapoor. She's rough.

(RAZA *approaches* SHANTI.)

RAZA: Two Cokes, please.

SHANTI: *(giving him the Coke)* I've locked the cash tin. You give me one pound tomorrow.

SHANTI looks at RAZA closely and thinks she recognizes him.

SHANTI: I know you from somewhere. I never forget a face.

RAZA: *(also recognizing her, but not wanting to admit to it)* I don't think so.

SHANTI: You live in Wembley?

RAZA: No.

SHANTI: Ah . . . Heathrow Airport!

JAZ: You know people that live in the Airport?

SHANTI: *(to RAZA)* Your father is that agency fellow, he ne?

RAZA: *(uncomfortable)* Recruitment consultant.

SHANTI: Mr. Khan. He got me cleaning job at Heathrow.

RAZA: We're not here to cause trouble.

SHANTI: I wasn't supposed to work at my age, but your father always said, "It's work that keeps you alive." He never told anyone how old I was. I too can keep a secret.

RAZA: Thank you.

SHANTI: In East Africa we lived side by side. Your people celebrated our Diwali and only because I am vegetarian, I couldn't eat your biryanis on the Festival of Eid.

(PUSHPA, POPATLAL, *and* HINA *are leaving, and* PREETHI *and* PREMA *are saying goodbye to them.* RAZA *and* JAZ *are also leaving.*)

POPATLAL: You have done it again, Prema. You Lohana Ladies are one step ahead.

PREMA: Well, we like to be the trendsetters.

PUSHPA: Half the job is done for you in choice of venue, he ne?

PREMA: Well, North London is Lohana and Lohana is North London. As soon as the Gujarati calendar comes out, we snap up dates for next year's Navratri.

PUSHPA: Well, you know people in the right places, he ne?

POPATLAL: The Mayor and Mayoress? They are Shahs. I'm surprised you got them as your chief guests.

PREMA: Bharat Shah managed to get us in their calendar.

POPATLAL: Bharat is very well connected.

PUSHPA: *(about RAZA)* And this is the boy who has got all the tongues wagging. Is it your friend, Preethi?

PREETHI: Yes.

POPATLAL: You musn't be too shy to introduce him. That's what these functions are for. Boys and girls meeting and courting. Even our Lord Krishna would dance with his "girlfriends."

PREMA: Youngsters are all chaperoned. We want them to enjoy and have fun. Better than going behind parents' backs.

PREETHI: *(to everyone, but keeping a closer eye on Prema's reaction)* This is Raj, and Jaz.

(General greeting from everyone.)

PUSHPA: Raj, lovely to meet you. You are Punjabi?

RAZA: Yeah . . . that's right.

JAZ: Punjabi and proud.

PREETHI: Raj, this is my mum, Prema, and this is Pushpa aunty and . . .

POPATLAL: Popatlal Shah. Everyone calls me PS . . . *(Laughing at his own joke.)* That way I always have the last word. Punjabi . . . Thought I recognized a bit of bhangra there. *(Making a silly gesture of the arms in bhangra.)* A bit of changing the light bulbs. . . . Well, Prema, this is the proof in the pudding. . . . The success of your "open door" policy.

PREMA: Well, anyone is welcome as long as they respect the intention.

POPATLAL: Yes, the only difference between us and Punjabis is they eat parathas and we eat daal bhat, and it is showing in our bodies, isn't it, Raj?

RAZA: Yes.

PUSHPA: The trouble starts when the Muslims come in, isn't it?

PREMA: We've never had any "incidents" at our functions.

POPATLAL: Well, they can't look at their girls, they come to look at ours, and one of these days it's going to happen the other way round and then what will happen?

JAZ: The Gujus'll get mashed up, innit?

RAZA: It's been nice to meet you.

(JAZ and RAZA leave.)

POPATLAL: Okay then. Auo jo. Maybe next time we get to see your good husband.

PREMA: Ketan's very busy.

PUSHPA: Oh yes, always busy.

POPATLAL: He is busy minting money, ahh. . . . He was telling me about your conservatory . . . under-floor heating, ah . . . anything to keep the wives happy? Halo . . .

PUSHPA: You didn't let me have conservatory.

POPATLAL: Where would I put my barbeque?

PUSHPA: *(to PREMA)* Honestly, Prema bhen. . . . The way these men want to eat meat. I don't mind it outside. I make sure they cook my corn on the cob before they put on their chicken.

(POPATLAL and PUSHPA exit.)

PREMA: So why you didn't tell me you had a special friend?

PREETHI: Mum, he's just a friend?

PREMA: From uni?

PREETHI: No. I met him outside the sweet shop.

PREMA: That's nice. You didn't say? Is he a student?

PREETHI: No . . . he's got his own business . . . drives the same car as Dad's.
    (KETAN enters.)

KETAN: Ready? I'm expecting an international call.

PREETHI: Hi, Dad.

KETAN: How's my baby? Had the boys falling at your feet?

PREMA: I hope you're going to use your hands-free because I'm not sitting in the
    car park while you talk to Dubai.

KETAN: It's these deals that have paid for your conservatory.

PREMA: And the bar is for your cocktail parties.

KETAN: Yes, darling.

PREMA: And who coped with the builders?

KETAN: You do everything in the house.

PREMA: Not just at home, darling. The Mayor and Mayoress were so impressed
    with my function they've agreed to be the judges on the finale.

KETAN: That's good.

PREMA: And you will be coming to that?

KETAN: Of course. Datani Sparks is the sponsor. I'll be bringing some clients.

PREMA: Don't forget you're partnering me at the dinner and dance on Tuesday.

KETAN: You better get my dinner jacket dry-cleaned.

PREMA: It's already hanging in your cupboard. *(Saying goodbye to SHANTI.)* Auo
    jo, Shant bhen. Please make sure everything is cleared away. They have got
    basketball practice in the hall first thing in the morning.

SHANTI: Auo jo.

SCENE THREE

(A rehearsal room. Early evening.)

ROOPA: I'll dance with Jaz if you dance with Raj.

PREETHI: I dunno.

ROOPA: I thought you said you'd risk it for a Hindu Punjabi.

PREETHI: Look, my mum's the chairperson.

ROOPA: So you're all mouth?

PREETHI: She wasn't that pleased to see that I got partnered with some fella I
    met outside the sweet shop.

ROOPA: You cow, you've been seeing Raj and you never told me. I thought I was
    your best friend.

PREETHI: A girl's gotta have some secrets.

ROOPA: Bitch. So how about it? Let's dance with them. There's safety in numbers.

PREETHI: Look, I've already texted Raj and told him he can't be my partner.

ROOPA: Thanks a million. What am I meant to say to Jaz? He's really keen . . . he's left me five messages.

PREETHI: You're on your own.

ROOPA: So now I have to find another partner.

PREETHI: Join the club.

ROOPA: I'm going to get some water. Want anything?

PREETHI: No.

(ROOPA exits. PREETHI is alone for a moment before JAZ and RAZA enter.)

PREETHI: I don't believe this. How did you know I was gonna be here? This is a rehearsal.

RAZA: I know, and we've got a personal invitation.

PREETHI: From who?

JAZ: Your batty boy friend . . . the Gujarati Wayne Sleep.

PREETHI: What?

RAZA: That choreographer geezer . . .

PREETHI: Anant.

RAZA: He seemed to like what we're doing the other night.

JAZ: The man loves us.

PREETHI: You've got a nerve . . . it's bad enough you rock up at the garba without any notice. Didn't you get my text? I'm not dancing with you, Raza.

RAZA: Call me Raj.

PREETHI: It's not as if we're even going out.

RAZA: A month and a half . . . we're seeing each other.

PREETHI: Yeah, we're seeing each other, but it's not like Romeo and Juliet.

RAZA: I think it is.

PREETHI: Grow up.

RAZA: It was nice to see you dressed up in your red and green . . .

PREETHI: Chanya Choli . . .

RAZA: You don't do that when we go Leicester Square . . . you put your jeans on like . . .

PREETHI: I wore my high heels last time.

RAZA: And I liked it.

PREETHI: So I did it.

RAZA: I like it when your nostrils go like that . . .

PREETHI: Don't push it.

RAZA: And your eyebrows . . . the way you look away. Look at you.

PREETHI: You're not getting round me. This competition is really important for my mum.

RAZA: Got a Gujarati geek lined up?

PREETHI: It's none of your business.

RAZA: Jaz's got the hots for your mate. She gonna be here?

PREETHI: Yeah. *(To* JAZ.*)* You better not get too fresh with her. . . . Roopa doesn't know about you two.

JAZ: Chill. Thanks to you we're saucy, we're HPs . . . Hindu Punjabis.

PREETHI: If anyone finds out you're SLIMS, literally hell is gonna come on earth.

*(*ROOPA *enters.)*

ROOPA: It's a bit of a surprise seeing you two.

JAZ: We're like wolves. We like to surprise. So you gonna do the Disco Dandia with me?

ROOPA: *(looking at* PREETHI*)* I dunno.

PREETHI: *(to* JAZ*)* Her parents are really strict . . . I know you're Hindu, but they're even funny about Punjabis.

RAZA: You girls wanna hook up this weekend?

PREETHI: We're doing the competition Saturday.

RAZA: Next weekend. We could go Park Royal . . . see a film. Chinese. You like Chinese?

ROOPA: Don't mind.

RAZA: There's an oriental buffet going on . . . prawn crackers, starters and shit like that . . . *(To girls.)* Have you seen Bullet-Proof Monk?

ROOPA: It's a bit violent, isn't it?

JAZ: It's comic. Don't you like laughing?

PREETHI: English Patient. That's her favorite film.

RAZA: What?

ROOPA: It's a romance. In the desert.

RAZA: You want romance. You should come down my yard. I got Kuch Kuch Hota Hai on DVD. With extras.

*(*PREETHI *looks at* RAZA *and he realizes he's overstepped the limit by asking them to his place.)*

RAZA: We could go bowling beforehand.

ROOPA: Do we look like the kind of girls who go bowling?

*(*HINA *and* DINESH *enter.)*

PREETHI: All right, Hina? This is Jaz and Raj.

JAZ and RAZA: Hi.

HINA: Hi.

PREETHI: All right, che Dinesh?

DINESH: I'm fine. I've just installed the new application on your dad's Excel program. It means he can pinpoint exactly what stock he's got in what outlet . . . serial number, model, quantity.

PREETHI: Great.

DINESH: It's totally revolutionary—it's like when Windows took over from MS DOS—everything's just a mouse-click away.

PREETHI: Fancy being my partner for Disco Dandia?

HINA: He's already got a partner.

(ANANT *enters.*)

ANANT Kemcho, everyone? Hi, Preethi. Mummy, Daddy; okay? Dinesh, Jaz, Raj. Fantastic! I'm glad you took up my offer . . . great to have new blood in the class You guys blew my mind the other night. Raj, where did you learn to dance like that?

RAZA: On the street.

JAZ: Nah man . . . it's from Ritek Roshan. He's taken his moves and added a bit of turbo.

ANANT: You guys are gonna put me out of business. Being able to do that with no training.

JAZ: He's bad, innit? I'm not gay but I think he's bad.

ANANT: Yeah, the raw talent is there but needs a signature, Jaz. You can vouch, girls. How many times do you get picked out of a crowd and people say, "The way you dance. You must be from the Anant Patel Academy."

HINA: We spread your fame, Anant.

ANANT: I'm a big fish in a small pond. You think this is everyone?

HINA: Vinita rang to say she's gotta hand in her project. And Bharti's not feeling very well.

ANANT: And Seema?

HINA: She'll be here.

ANANT: She's probably told Mummy she's coming here, but she's out with her boyfriend. Okay, let's start without her. Now you were all short-listed for Disco Dandia, you've got your partners. The Lohana Ladies season is open competition. You're all going to be challenging each other for the title of Diwali King and Queen, and hopefully you'll still be friends at the end of it.

ROOPA: Preethi's bound to win.

HINA: Not necessarily.

ANANT: Roopa, that's not the attitude. You put your mind to something, you can do it. Positive thinking! Any of you could win, but let's make sure the winner is amongst us. We don't want those Patels from Tooting to walk away with the crowns. (*To* JAZ *and* RAZA.) I'm a Patel myself, and I tell you, I was embarrassed. They go to that. Beni Katania's South London Academy. . . . She calls herself a choreographer but it's all thrusting bosoms and wriggling bums. Now, everybody, please go and get your sticks. We're gonna concentrate on putting the Disco into Dandia. (*Puts the music on.*)

RAZA: Chuck us a stick, Preethi.

(PREETHI *throws* RAZA *a stick.*)

JAZ: *(to* ROOPA*)* You up for it?

(ROOPA *nods.*)

ANANT: Find a space in front of the mirror. We're going to start with the basic Dandia step. You hit your partner's stick for the first three counts, one, two three; do your own thing, four, five, six, seven, eight; and then hit again on the one; and then do freestyle for the next seven counts. Have you got that? Okay—let's have a go.

(*They dance.*)

Five, six, seven, eight.

One, two, three and one.

One, two, three and one.

Okay, let's try it in pairs now. Find yourself a partner.

One, two, three and one.

Change partners. Keep your sticks up. Six, seven, eight and one. Change again. One, two, three and one. Maintain eye-contact.

Okay. Let's form two lines facing each other—this time when you hit the stick on the one, you move to your left so you are facing a new dancing partner. Okay, you got that?

(*They move into the formation.*)

Left—that's it.

Okay—next time you do a turn when you move to your left.

And one.

Turn.

Okay, now show me what you can do, show me your best. Let's see who is the Sharukh Khan and Madhuri Dixit amongst you.

Okay, now clear the floor—we're going to work in pairs.

(RAZA *continues to dance while everyone else has stopped.*)

Thank you, Raj. We'll start with Roopa and Jaz.

(ROOPA *and* JAZ *dance. After they finish,* ANANT *calls* HINA *and* DINESH *to the floor. They dance. They finish*)

ANANT: Very nice, Dinesh—but don't forget to dance with your partner.

(ANANT *calls* PREETHI *and* RAZA *to the floor. They dance. They finish.*)

ANANT: *(looking at* RAZA*)* Fantastic. That was fantastic. I think we've just invented the Salsa Dandia.

JAZ: You're fit, man. You should be setting the steps on those Bollywood films, man.

ANANT: They have their own choreographers. Very difficult to break in.

JAZ: There's an Indian explosion, man. How come it's passed you by? These geezers, they come and film in Scotland . . . Tulip season in Amsterdam. You gotta find out.

ANANT: I should get you as my agent, Jaz.

JAZ: Thirty-five per cent, mate.

ANANT: That was fantastic, guys! I'm gonna slot in another rehearsal tomorrow
night. Seven o'clock. With some fine-tuning, we'll storm the Disco Dandia
night. Okay, off you go now, go home—go home or wherever you have to
go.

(They all filter off. ANANT *puts on the music and starts to dance as if working
out a routine in his head.* PREMA *enters.)*

ANANT: Prema bhen, Kemcho? Your Preethi and her partner are good
together.

PREMA: You think so? He's Punjabi, you know?

ANANT: He can dance.

PREMA: So she's in with a chance for Diwali Queen?

ANANT: Good as done.

PREMA: All my dedication has paid off. I had to drag her to your class when she
was eight. And now the tables have turned. She can't miss it.

ANANT: It's nice to know that one has had some effect.

(Pause.)

ANANT: Can I do something for you?

PREMA: Anant, I . . . Last night there were a few complaints about the crisp fla-
vors. The vegetarian lobby. Why not tell Shanti Bhen to keep ready-salted
only?

ANANT: Of course . . .

PREMA: Aao jo.

*(*PREMA *starts to go and then stops.)*

ANANT: Anything else?

PREMA: I know Mohan bhai says you're winding up your business . . .

ANANT: My father is speaking for me when nothing has been decided.

PREMA: I thought you were going to run the new underground outlet.

ANANT: If Bapu has his way, I will be a true Patel like him, running a news
agent.

PREMA: So you might still have some room for a private student?

ANANT: Preethi doesn't need extra coaching.

PREMA: No, no, Anant. It's for me. Will you give me some steps for the dinner
and dance? I'll of course give you your going rate.

ANANT: No, no. It would be my pleasure.

PREMA: It's just that Ketan is such a good dancer. I don't want to tread on his
toes.

ANANT: Yes, we fix it.

PREMA: Tomorrow afternoon? My place. Will my new conservatory be suitable?

ANANT: Perfect. After all, dinner and dance is about dancing effectively in a confined space.

PREMA: So I'll see you tomorrow. Aao jo.

ANANT: Aao jo.

(PREMA *leaves and* ANANT *goes back to his dance.*)

SCENE FOUR

(*Same night.* MOHAN *and* ANANT'*s home. Three-bedroom suburban detached house in a cul-de-sac. Floral carpet, glass table, and Hindu paraphernalia.*)

MOHAN: Lovely kadhi, Ba. At my age I should have my daughter-in-law serving my rotlis, not my mother.

SHANTI: Be thankful there is food on your plate.

MOHAN: To this day I don't know why Anant won't marry. He's married to his dancing.

SHANTI: Leave it, Mohan.

MOHAN: I'm thinking of you. Ba. If he had a wife you could go and live with Satish in Canada. They have Mexican maid who will look after you.

SHANTI: I was prisoner when I went to visit your brother. Sat and watched video and got fat. Couldn't go anywhere without somebody driving me in a car.

MOHAN: You should be pampered, Ba.

SHANTI: I might as well be dead . . . I prefer to use my legs. Go to Ealing Road and get my fresh fruit and veg for your rotlis and shaak.

MOHAN: And Anant can't even be bothered to show up for dinner on time.

SHANTI: You should accept this is his passion. Navratri is the highlight of his year. This is where he can show off his talent. Of course he doesn't think about eating.

MOHAN: Well, this is his last season.

SHANTI: Why you are trying to turn him from choreographer to news agent? If only you came once to see what his gift is, then you would change your mind.

MOHAN: Navratri took my wife away from me. How can you ask me to go and celebrate?

SHANTI: Varsha died because it was her time to go. You have been carrying this thing for too long now. Don't take it out on Anant.

(*The phone rings and* MOHAN *picks it up. We hear his side of the conversation.*)

MOHAN: Hello? . . . No. There is no dance academy here. This is a private residence. . . . No, he is not here. This is Mohan Patel, his father. Who am I speaking with? . . . You want to leave message? You are producer of commercial?

And you need choreographer of Dandia . . . well, my son is amateur . . . So
what, you want me to tell him? . . . You can't cast Gary Lineker as Krishna.
He is the wrong color. Krishna is blue . . . Walker's Crisps. Good brand. Sells
well . . . I can tell you, my son will be too busy for this. He's in business with
me. We have a new outlet on the Jubilee Line. If you need a shop to film in,
that's another story. *(Puts the phone down.)*

SHANTI: It isn't for you to decide for the boy.

MOHAN: I've given him his freedom. It's time for him to get back on track. And
I need all hands on deck. So don't you go saying anything.

(ANANT *enters.*)

SHANTI: Food is ready. You must be tired after rehearsal.

ANANT: I'm elated. Once in a while you see raw talent and you know you can
really shape it into something.

SHANTI: You are really fired up. Who are you talking about?

ANANT: Punjabi. Raj. He's dancing with Preethi. I know I can give them advanced
steps and they will be able to pull it off.

SHANTI: And the teacher? He needs to get some glory as well.

ANANT: I'm sure I'll make the cover of the Lohana *Ladies' Bulletin.*

MOHAN: How many years you've been teaching the daughters of these society
ladies? What have you get to show for it?

SHANTI: What are you talking about? A cupboard full of cups and trophies he
has won and who knows what is just around the corner?

MOHAN: Working in the new outlet is what's around the corner.

SHANTI: Aren't you going to tell him about his phone call?

ANANT: What call?

MOHAN: Nothing important.

SHANTI: Not important? The man wanted Anant to give steps to Gary Lineker.

ANANT: What was it about, Bapu?

MOHAN: They are doing some advert. Yesterday it was bhangra, now it's garba.
Where is that going to get you? I told them you wouldn't be interested.

ANANT: You had no right to speak for me. Of course I am interested.

MOHAN: You want to pursue some pipe dream while your father gets swallowed
up by Tesco Metro and Sri Lankans who work round the clock. They can't
even say "please" and "thank you," but still their tills are ringing. Half the
time the customer wants their attention, they're on an international call
arranging for one of their relatives to come over from Colombo as asylum
cases and work for nothing.

ANANT: Bapu, I know the shop is in trouble but I can't turn it round for you. I'm
not a businessman. I keep telling you.

MOHAN: And I keep telling you, you don't need a degree to be a businessman.
Just you have to be by your father's side. That Navin from Tanzania. His son

studied dentistry but still he made more money joining his father as news
agent. Now they are taking six holidays a year.

ANANT: Good for them.

MOHAN: That's all you can say. You invest in your children and you think you're
going to get back with interest.

SHANTI: Mohan!

MOHAN: I've bought this underground kiosk so it can help to keep the other
shop afloat. This is our last chance, otherwise he might as well go and tell
those refugees they can have it on a plate.

(ANANT *leaves.*)

SCENE FIVE

(*Early evening.* RAZA *and* PREETHI *run onto a bridge overlooking the
Thames.*)

PREETHI: So you booked our tickets for the London Eye?

RAZA: I'm not going on that . . . it hardly moves.

PREETHI: You're just like one of those White Hart Lane rude boys, aren't you?
Everything fast. Fast food, fast cars . . . you don't want to take the time to
take in the view?

RAZA: (*looking at her*) I've got all the time in the world to take in the view.

PREETHI: You want what you can't have.

RAZA: Doesn't stop me trying.

PREETHI: Look, we're doing the competition, then it's goodbye.

RAZA: You're keen when we're out, but you're quite happy to kiss me goodbye
and hope one of those Gujarati frogs will turn into a prince.

PREETHI: Some of them are quite good-looking, actually.

RAZA: You still haven't told me which one's lined up for you.

PREETHI: We're not like you SLIMs, you know. I'm free to choose.

RAZA: So who have you chosen?

PREETHI: I haven't yet. But there's a hall full of boys every night. I'll take my pick
when I'm ready.

RAZA: Having me dangling on your arm surely is gonna spoil your chances.

PREETHI: Not at all. Everyone knows you're just my dancing partner.

RAZA: I'm good, aren't I?

PREETHI: You can dance.

RAZA: We're good together.

PREETHI: You reckon yourself, don't you?

RAZA: Try that turn.

PREETHI: Not here.

RAZA: Why not?

PREETHI: You're crazy.

(She does it reluctantly. They start to rehearse their routine together. The dance finishes.)

RAZA: You wanna win, don't you?

PREETHI: Well my mum's the Chair. The spotlight's on me.

RAZA: How would you have won if I hadn't gate-crashed?

PREETHI: God—you love yourself, don't you.

RAZA: Gotta have belief, Inshallah . . .

PREETHI: You do realize if you're Diwali King, you're gonna be dressed up as Lord Ram on that float.

RAZA: The things I'd do for you.

SCENE SIX

(Two days later. The Disco Dandia competition. A corner of the hall. A moment before the dancers are called.)

PREMA: (on tannoy) It's the night you've been waiting for, guys and dolls—Disco Dandia! I can see the judges are going to have a tough time deciding who to eliminate and who to select as finalists for the grand finale on Saturday! Tonight we also have another spotlight on us as we have a special guest mingling anonymously looking for talent: choreographers, dancers, movers and shakers. Disco Dandia is taking center stage. They want pretty girls and dashing boys and, looking around at this fashion parade, I can see that they're going to be spoiled for choice.

ANENT: (to his students) You're all great . . . all the moves are really polished now. There won't be anybody better on the dance floor than you guys. Just believe in yourselves. Remember facial expression, smiling . . . it's just as important as fancy footwork . . . Presentation as well as execution. That's what the judges will be looking for. Okay, guys. You're all stars. Break a leg!

(PREETHI and RAZA, ROOPA and JAZ, HINA and DINESH take their positions on the dance floor.)

JAZ: So you told your parents you're dancing with a Hindu Punjabi?

ROOPA: Didn't need to.

JAZ: But aren't they watching us?

ROOPA: No, they'd rather stay home and watch EastEnders. Suits me . . . As long as I check in on my moby every twenty minutes they're cool. Preethi and Raj look like they've been putting in some extra rehearsal.

JAZ: Yeah.

ROOPA: That's Preethi all over. She'd say she hadn't revised for her Maths, then she'd get a straight A.

JAZ: Don't worry. I beat Raj at everything.

HINA: *(to Dinesh)* I'm gonna marry you.

DINESH: My dad's got Preethi in mind for me.

HINA: I know your dad's her dad's accountant, but she's a Louis and you and I are Shahs, Dinesh.

DINESH: So what?

HINA: What they call halva, we call halvo. If you don't get a move on, I'm registering for that Shah speed dating. I'm not going to be available next year.

SONYA: I heard those Louis tarts talking about that talent scout in the toilets. They shut up the minute I came out of the loo. You know they're making an ad. The old lady off the Kumars marries Gary Lineker. Just think, I could be sharing the small screen with Meera Syal.

SHRENEK: The close-up will be on you, babe.

SONYA: Your shimmy's gonna wipe the floor. When I saw that at Wandsworth Town Hall. That's when I decided . . . this is the man I'm gonna dance with.

SHRENEK: What about the rest?

SONYA: Don't go on about that. I told you. I'm focused on the future.

(PREETHI and RAZA are dancing and he looks at her intimately.)

PREETHI: Everyone's looking at us.

RAZA: Yeah, 'cos we're the best.

PREETHI: Nah, it's 'cos they all think I've snuck my Hindu Punjabi boyfriend in. God, if they knew the truth.

(The dance speeds up. RAZA and JAZ are being more exuberant. JAZ hits SHRENEK's stick too hard.)

SHRENEK: *(to JAZ)* What's with the stick flex, mate?

JAZ: What you on about?

SHRENEK: You bang my stick so hard, you nearly bang it out of my hand.

(Dance ends.)

PREMA: *(on tannoy)* Thank you, boys and girls. That was fantastic. Now could we please clear the floor for Contestants 36 to 40.

SCENE SEVEN

(Car park. Just outside. A little while later. ROOPA and JAZ are kissing.)

JAZ: You were rough on the dance floor. We're bound to be chosen.

ROOPA: I can't believe you've never done Dandia.

JAZ: It's in my blood. I've got a great place to rehearse for the finale.

ROOPA: Where?

JAZ: Raj's flat in Kew Gardens. Got a wicked Playstation, sauna, jacuzzi . . . fridge . . . kitchen kitted out.

(PREETHI, RAZA, HINA and DINESH enter.)

RAZA: Is that talent scout business for real?

PREETHI: Yeah, my mum got a phone call about it. The Louis ladies are getting all excited.

HINA: It's not just the Lohanas he rang, you know. My mum said they're ringing round all the Navratri committees.

DINESH: Might be a hoax. Guy rings up says he's a talent scout. All the "stay at home" gujus come out thinking they might become stars . . . halls are bursting to the seams. Bombs go off simultaneously. Bingo! What better way of getting rid of the Gujarati community in one go?

ROOPA: Whatever, Dinesh. Adds to the excitement.

(SONYA *and* SHRENEK *enter.*)

SHRENEK: I've been looking for you. What do you think you were doing in there?

JAZ: Dunno what you talking about, big boy.

SHRENEK: Hit my stick too hard.

JAZ: You got a overactive imagination.

SHRENEK: You're trying to distract me and ruin my chances.

JAZ: You think you're competition?

SONYA: What you talking about? We're the only movers here. You're just intimidated by our steps.

SHRENEK: Doesn't have to come down to violence.

JAZ: You pussy. It's Dandia. You can't be timid about hitting the stick.

SONYA: Hitting the stick like you did implies a challenge. I saw it.

JAZ: Hey, lady. I'm talking to your man.

RAZA: Come on, Jaz. Leave it out.

SHRENEK: I saw the look you gave me.

JAZ: I'm dancing. I'm concentrating. What look did I give you?

SHRENEK: That look there. You looking at me funny? What are you looking at me like that for?

JAZ: You must be gay. The man must be gay.

SONYA: Takes one to know one.

JAZ: Get out of my face.

RAZA: Jaz. It's not worth it.

SHRENEK: You bang my stick like that again, I'll bang you back.

JAZ: Just try it.

SHRENEK: What are you gonna do? Bring your bad boys from Punjab?

JAZ: We'll bring our whole crew down.

SHRENEK: I'm not scared of you, gay boy.

(JAZ *strikes* SHRENEK, *and* RAZA *tries to intervene.*)

PREETHI: Jaz! Raza!

SONYA: Raza . . . This is revelation time. I thought it was Raj . . .

SHRENEK: That says it all. Mosis coming in on Hindu territory.

SONYA: Who brought them in?

PREETHI: They're my friends.

ROOPA He's a Muslim, you kutti, why didn't you tell me?

JAZ: I'm the same guy.

ROOPA: We don't go there, yeah . . . I don't go there. *(To* PREETHI *as she's leaving.)* People don't do that to their worst enemies.

SHRENEK: Any girl that goes with a Muslim needs her head looked at. Didn't you hear about the rape last Navratri? That was a Muslim. You're after our girls . . . keep your sisters locked up at home.

(RAZA *goes for* SHRENEK *and they fight, with the others trying to stop them.* DINESH *intervenes to try and stop them.)*

HINA: *(to* DINESH*)* Don't you get involved. It's not us who brought them in.

(PREMA *and* ANANT *come on.)*

PREMA: Preethi! What is going on?

ANANT: Stop it, boys.

(The fight breaks up.)

PREMA: When I heard there was a scuffle out here, the last person I expected to be involved was you.

SONYA: It was them that started it, not us.

PREMA: Fighting leads to immediate disqualification.

SONYA: You should disqualify them. They come in here under false pretences . . . they're looking for trouble. They're not dancers, they're Muslims.

PREMA: Darling, is this true?

PREETHI: Yes, Mum.

PREMA: And you knew?

PREETHI: Yes.

PREMA: So you were all in on this deceit?

HINA: Prema aunty, Dinesh and I knew nothing about this.

PREMA: After all the freedom I've given you. Kick-boxing lessons . . . navel-piercing . . . anything you've asked for. Your generation thinks us to be idiots. Why you didn't just come and tell me you want to bring some friends from college or wherever? When have we ever stopped people coming? . . . We allow black people, English . . . as long as they come with Gujarati friends and behave appropriately.

RAZA: It's not Preethi's fault we gate-crashed.

PREMA: I don't know what your parents expect from you, Raj . . .

RAZA: Raza.

PREMA: . . . but I expect better from my daughter.

SONYA: Are you going to disqualify them?

RAZA: You don't need to. Come on, Jaz.

ANANT: You shouldn't have lied, guys. It's a shame.

(JAZ *and* RAZA *leave.*)

PREETHI: Mum . . .

PREMA: I don't wish to hang out our linen in the car park. Get your things and let's go.

HINA: So you still gonna dance, Preethi?

(They all leave apart from ANANT, *who sits down and takes out the card that the scout has given him.)*

MOHAN: Ready, son? Kiosk all packed, up.

ANANT: Nearly. Ba is finishing up.

MOHAN: You'll have to be more cheerful when you're dealing with customers. Talk to them about their highs and lows instead of showing yours.

ANANT: There was a fight.

MOHAN: I thought Prema forked out a fortune for Nigerian security. Who was involved?

ANANT: My students.

MOHAN: Youngsters are more interested in fighting and sex than your dancing. Good you're coming to work with me. You won't have to bother with the likes of them.

ANANT: Bapu, I don't see myself as a news agent.

MOHAN: So how do you see yourself? A tortured artist?

ANANT: Dance is all I know.

MOHAN: Dance doesn't pay the bills. 5 AM.

ANANT: It could. That man who rang up at home asking for me. Julian. Well, he found me even though you tried to stop him. I've got talent. He's coming to the finale.

MOHAN: Stop this "dance, dance, talent, talent" . . . what is this talent? Stopping you living your life. You start work with me. From 6 AM, taking newspaper delivery to late at night. You won't have time to think about your talent.

ANANT: You would love that for me? You've never even seen any of my work.

MOHAN: I've seen enough what dance does to people. It takes possession of you like it took possession of your mother. She would dance till she thought the goddess came to her. People would worship her, but who was there to help her when the dance took her?

ANANT: Bapu, she was an epileptic. It could have happened at any time.

MOHAN: No, it happened in this season of Navratri, and now you are tying to kill me with your dance.

ANANT: All right. Enough. In any case I've lost my best student, so what is there for Julian to see at the finale? Fine. Next week. 6 AM I'll be there. Happy now?

SCENE EIGHT

(The community hall, which has been decorated for the dinner and dance. A ship in the sixties, on its journey from Dar es Salaam to Bombay. POPATLAL *and* PUSHPA, *in* PREMA's *black and white theme, are standing on what looks like the deck of a ship eating chana bateta and with tall drinks in their hands.* SHANTI *is serving food in this scene.)*

PUSHPA: It is Prema's daughter that brings in the Muslims and it is my daughter that is suffering! Dinesh and Hina entered as a couple. Now Hina is in her bedroom crying with no partner, and Dinesh has been ordered by his papa to dance with Preethi . . . as if that's going to save her reputation!

POPATLAL: Prema is taking advantage of her role as Chair. Changing the rules to suit.

PUSHPA: Hina and Dinesh have been virtually engaged since they were eight . . . everyone knows. *(To* SHANTI.*)* This coconut in the chana bateta isn't fresh.

SHANTI: From the packet . . . tastes the same.

PUSHPA: And the Mogo chips are frozen. It's all very well having East African theme, but Prema should have made sure she got the food right.

*(*BHARAT *enters.)*

PUSHPA: *(to* POPATLAL*)* Think of your daughter. Go and talk to Bharat.

POPATLAL: This incident in the car park has upset the apple cart.

BHARAT: A couple of outsiders come in . . . they've got green eyes. Of course our girls are going to swoon over them. Prema nipped it in the bud.

PUSHPA: They didn't just come in. They were invited. They were introduced to us as Preethi's "friends."

BHARAT: The way our community likes to make a mountain out of a molehill.

PUSHPA: Going behind parents' backs is something Hina would never do. And she certainly wouldn't steal someone else's partner.

BHARAT: Pushpa bhen, who holds the strings to the hearts of youngsters? Until they are engaged, they are free to change their minds. Dinesh and Preethi want to dance with each other.

PUSHPA: Our daughter is not going to be anybody's "back-up."

*(*PREMA *enters.)*

BHARAT: Prema, bhen. You have transported us back to the port of Dar es Salaam. You can almost smell the sea breeze.

PREMA: So you like the idea of the ship? Cocktails on deck before departure, virgin of course, and then we sail on to Bombay via the Seychelles, and all in one evening. . . . Pushpa bhen, you look like Cinderella at the ball.

PUSHPA: Blouse is a bit tight, he ne? I'll have to go to the gym.

POPATLAL: Half an hour on the treadmill, you come back and raid the fridge.

PUSHPA: And where is your Prince Charming, Prema?

POPATLAL: More than fashionably late.

PREMA: He'll be here. People are starting to dance. Please join them. Bharat bhai, there's plenty of mature single ladies waiting to have their card filled.

PUSHPA: *(under her breath to* POPATLAL*)* Most of them are at an age when they should be singing devotional songs at home.

(They go onto the dance floor and start dancing. PREMA *exits, obviously anxious that* KETAN *isn't there.* PREETHI *and* DINESH *enter and stand leaning on the ship's railings.)*

DINESH: Drowning is one of easiest ways, I suppose, to top yourself . . . otherwise it's not that easy.

PREETHI: I'm not contemplating suicide, Dinesh.

DINESH: No, no, it's just interesting . . . you know, there's this site where you can find out the most effective ways: what's a lethal dose . . . how to tie the knot . . . prime locations—that bridge over Archway Road, the cliff at Beachy Head . . .

PREETHI: You don't want to dance with me at the finale, do you?

DINESH: No, no, it's fine.

PREETHI: I've got a bit of a "rep" now. If you want to dance with Hina, it's okay with me.

DINESH: Where d'you meet that Raza, guy, anyway?

PREETHI: Outside the sweet shop.

DINESH: He didn't seem like one of those prayer-mat types.

PREETHI: Raza is one of the sweetest fellas you could ever meet. It just happens he's a Muslim.

DINESH: At the end of the day you gotta stick within.

PREETHI: Why? Why? I'm sick of this, you know . . . you're a Lohanna, or Shah, Patel . . . whatever . . . so-and-so's daughter from such-and-such village, and after marriage you become so-and-so's wife from his village. Everyone's got roots. What's so special about Gujaratis?

DINESH: Our parents do so much for us. How do you pay them back?

PREETHI: So that's what you're doing with me?

(The focus shifts to the dance, which is now in full swing. PREMA *and* ANANT *have now joined as a couple.* PREETHI *and* DINESH *exit.)*

PREMA: Thanks for partnering me.

ANANT: I can see you've been practicing.

PREMA: Yes, but what for?

ANENT: I'm sure Ketan bhai will be here soon.

PREMA: It's nine o'clock already. If he was coming, he would have been here by now, Anant.

ANANT: Maybe he has got delayed in his business.

PREMA: Maybe he just doesn't care.

ANANT: Prema bhen . . .

PREMA: Having to deal with people's comments about Preethi is bad enough. And now this? Ketan knows how much I have put into this evening, but he is not interested. Single-handedly I have organized each detail, even though I have got a subcommittee. The fruit display . . . I told Sita, use your initiative. The float ran out, so she buys three apples. How can you make an impact with three apples? You saw everyone, how they were looking at me. Pushpa is thoroughly enjoying my humiliation on the dance floor, seeing me without my husband on a night I'm hosting while hers is stuck to her like a Siamese twin.

ANANT: Prema bhen, nobody is looking at you.

PREMA: Believe me, I know them. Women like her, false nails and imitation jewelry . . . they would enjoy nothing better than to see my downfall. I am the Chair of Lohana Ladies. My functions are talked about and copied. In a million years Pushpa couldn't come up with my concepts. She is just watching, watching to see me put a foot wrong so she can step into the breach and have her victory.

ANENT: Why you are worrying about other people?

PREMA: You're right, Anant. I spend my life trying to please other people. I try to make everything just right, but no matter how much effort I put I can't seem to fix what's broken.

ANANT: It's a perfect evening, Prema bhen. Everyone appreciates what you do.

PREMA: Everyone except the person you want to appreciate you. To him I am invisible.

(Silence.)

PREMA: I'm sorry. I shouldn't burden you with my problems. I'm sure you have plenty of your own.

ANANT: None that a dose of hard labor at the shop won't fix.

PREMA: You're going to join Mohan bhai in the shop? It's a shame.

ANANT: I'm sure nobody will miss their Gujarati ballet class in Bounds Green.

PREMA: But that Julian was very impressed with you. He's coming at the finale just to see your work.

ANANT: If he could have seen Raj . . . Raza and Preethi dance.

PREMA: My hands are tied, Anant.

ANANT: Of course. Shall we dance to "Malaika"? It would be a shame not to show off what you've learnt.

(The next dance starts to the classic Swahili hit and they go back onto the floor.)

PREMA: Thank you, Anant.

SCENE NINE

(*Later that night.* PREMA'*s conservatory.* PREMA *and* PREETHI *are having a glass of wine.*)

PREETHI: Are you waiting up for Dad?

PREMA: I'm just finishing my wine.

PREETHI: It was a great evening. Did they really have dinner and dances on those ships?

PREMA: Of course, but only in first class. The people dancing were the Europeans.

PREETHI: You were good. I didn't know you could dance like that.

PREMA: I can't. It was down to Anant.

PREETHI: Secret lessons—whatever next?

PREMA: At least my secrets are harmless.

PREETHI: I'm sorry, Mum.

PREMA: We've never restricted you in any way.

PREETHI: I know, Mum. But sometimes you meet someone and they don't have a label stuck to their head.

PREMA: But now you've got a label stuck to yours.

(KETAN *enters.*)

PREETHI: Hi, Dad.

KETAN: Did you get my message?

PREMA: The one you left at ten o'clock, just as dinner was being served?

KETAN: Sorry, darling, I fully intended to be there. . . . You know these Arabs. They like to eat late. By the time I could get round to ringing you, it was already ten.

PREMA: You had a previous engagement . . . with me.

KETAN: So how did it go?

PREMA: Oh, it was fantastic. . . . Everybody had a great time gabbing about our daughter and her reputation, and seeing me partnered by the "camp chore-ographer" was the icing on the cake.

PREETHI: Mum, Dad said he was sorry.

PREMA: Yes, both of you have said sorry and sorry makes it all right, ne? Mummy is always here to pick up the pieces. Prema will put on her lipstick and smile at everyone. "No, no . . . not my daughter. My daughter doesn't abuse her freedom. . . ." "Definitely not my husband . . . he is working hard . . . family man . . . always working late making sure his princess is well provided for." (*To Ketan.*) I make it so easy for you . . . When do I ask you for anything?

KETAN: I know, darling. I know you do a lot for us, but I'm also working so you can have things you want . . . car, conservatory.

PREMA: Is that all you think I need?

KETAN: I know I've neglected you, but I'll make it up to you. I had my travel agent book the resort in Dubai for our silver wedding anniversary. Seven-star treatment.

PREMA: Meanwhile I have to be satisfied with zero-star treatment?

KETAN: You have everything. I'm sure many women would love to be in your shoes.

PREMA: Oh, I know . . . don't think I don't know you already have someone in my shoes.

PREETHI: Mum!

PREMA: Ask him! Ask him where he was when he knew how important it was for me to have him at the dinner and dance . . .

KETAN: I've already told you. You can't offend Arabs.

PREMA: Ask him why his secretary chooses my birthday presents when he has time to choose gifts for his . . . mistress.

KETAN: I haven't got the energy for this. I've got a breakfast meeting in the morning.

(KETAN leaves.)

PREETHI: Is it true, Mummy?

PREMA: What do you think?

PREETHI: I can't believe Dad would do that.

PREMA: Why? Because your daddy is perfect? Must be Mummy imagining things . . . All I asked is for him to be at my side for one night, and he couldn't even do that . . .

PREETHI: Oh, poor Mum.

(Her phone signals a text message.)

PREMA: Who is sending you messages at this time?

(PREMA takes PREETHI's phone and RAZA's name comes up.)

PREMA: Like father, like daughter. Keeping secrets from me.

PREETHI: I told Raza not to phone me.

PREMA: And you expect me to believe that?

PREETHI: Give me my phone.

PREMA: (giving her back her phone) I've done my best with you. . . . You're lucky that Bharat Shah wants to suck up to your daddy and is willing to overlook the gossip. . . . Apart from Dinesh, there is no Gujarati boy in London for you.

(PREETHI looks at her text message.)

PREETHI: Mum, something's happened to Mohan uncle. Raza's outside . . . he needs to speak to you.

PREMA: Why doesn't he ring the bell like a man?

(PREETHI goes to let Raza in.)

RAZA: I'm sorry to disturb you at this time.

PREMA: Come in.

PREETHI: What's happened?

RAZA: Jaz and I were waiting for the tube . . . we went into a kiosk to buy some chewing gum. Two guys came running out as soon as they saw us. . . . They'd attacked this geezer in the shop . . . turned out he was Anant's dad.

PREMA: Is he all right?

RAZA: He's more shaken than hurt but they want to keep him overnight at the hospital. Anant's with him.

PREMA: Poor Mohan bhai.

RAZA: Anant wanted me to give you the float and keys for tomorrow night. He and Shanti won't be able to open the stall.

PREMA: Of course. It must have been a terrible shock for her. Where is she?

RAZA: She's in the van. Anant asked me to drop her home.

PREMA: I'll go and see her.

RAZA: She's fast asleep. Call her tomorrow. I've unloaded the crisps and drinks. Where do you want them?

PREMA: In the garage.

RAZA: I wanted to say sorry for any trouble I caused.

PREMA: Anant is very disappointed you won't be in the finale.

RAZA: So am I.

PREMA: You should have thought twice before deceiving people.

PREETHI: It was me who introduced him as Raj.

RAZA: Preethi, I came in myself. I wanted to see your life.

PREMA: Well, curiosity killed the cat. Preethi will show you the garage.

(PREETHI and RAZA leave. PREMA is left alone. She exits.)

SCENE TEN

(A few seconds later. PREETHI and RAZA come on with crisp boxes that they put in the garage.)

RAZA: I missed you.

(PREETHI doesn't say anything.)

RAZA: So you haven't missed me, then?

PREETHI: What would be the point?

RAZA: What's wrong?

PREETHI: What's right? (Noticing a scratch on RAZA's face.) What's that?

RAZA: Just a scratch.

PREETHI: Been in a fight?

RAZA: Those geezers. Jaz and I had to pull them off Anant's dad.

PREETHI: Why didn't you tell my mum the full story?

RAZA: She's still got the hump with me. I didn't want to be playing the hero.

PREETHI: D'ya blame her?

PREETHI: Just 'cos Gandhi was a Gujarati doesn't mean we can't get angry.

RAZA: I didn't want it to happen like this.

PREETHI: When you rocked up at the garba you changed the rules. What did you expect would happen?

RAZA: When I checked you outside the sweetshop, I thought, I wanna get to know this woman . . . really get to know her.

PREETHI: So you chatted me up . . . talked the talk, made the right moves.

RAZA: It's not just talk you know . . . we can make it real.

PREETHI: What's real? Everything you think is real turns out to be pretend.

RAZA: What are you talking about?

PREETHI: Nothing.

RAZA: I love you.

PREETHI: Every Guju girl's got a friend who's been seeing a SLIM for years, only to find that the bloke goes back to Pakistan when it comes to marriage.

RAZA: And you think I'm going to do that?

PREETHI: I dunno . . . your parents are out there. . . . What are they gonna say about me? It can't be me against the world.

RAZA: Let me talk to your parents.

PREETHI: It's the biggest time of the year for my mum, and it all had to happen now.

RAZA: Doesn't have to be the end of us.

PREETHI: Look, we went out, few drinks, had a laugh but it's not very funny now. You're a great guy, Raza, but . . .

RAZA: No buts . . . *(Holding her closer and starting to dance.)* I'm not letting go of you . . . we'll take it a bit slower.

PREETHI: There ain't nothing to take slower. *(PREETHI dances, her actions contradicting her words.)* It was nothing in the first place.
(They say goodbye, through dancing the duet that they should have danced at the finale. At a moment in the dance, SHANTI comes on and observes unseen. PREETHI exits.)

SHANTI: I was getting cold waiting in the van, I thought Prema had exiled you to the forest.

RAZA: Well, she wants me as far away from her daughter as possible.

SHANTI: People see it as Bhagwan versus Allah and not about Preethi and Raza.

RAZA: You should have told me the score on that first night that Jaz and me gate-crashed.

SHANTI: And you would have listened?
(RAZA doesn't answer.)

SHANTI: Wisdom only comes from living your own life, not walking down the path that others have laid.

RAZA: Look, Preethi and I have said goodbye.

SHANTI: So you're going to let her dance with Dinesh Shah?

RAZA: You're kidding? She didn't say.

SHANTI: Bharat Shah is taking advantage of the scandal, He has always had designs on Preethi for his Dinesh.

RAZA: That's her lookout now.

SHANTI: You're young . . . you have to fight for what you want in this world.

RAZA: Well, Preethi comes from a different world and they won't let me in. . . . Look, can I ask you a favor?

SHANTI: The way you came to my son's aid, you can ask for anything from me.

RAZA: Will you call me on Saturday? When Preethi's crowned Diwali Queen?

SHANTI: You're so certain it will be her.

RAZA: Yeah. Even with Dinesh as her partner.

SHANTI: Yes, she's like the garbo pot. She has an inner light.

RAZA: I'll give you my number. You will call?

SHANTI: Of course. Son and grandson have bought me a mobile. Even though I'm never out of their sight for long.

RAZA: Come on.

SCENE ELEVEN

(Gymnasium. Evening. The grand finale. As in Scene One, characters are sitting on the grandstand waiting before they go onto the floor. ROOPA, DINESH and PREETHI, SONYA and SHRENEK, BHARAT, KETAN, POPATLAL and PUSHPA. We see PREMA making an announcement on the tannoy.)

PREMA: We are nearly at the culmination of our season. Tension among the finalists here at the grand finale is thicker than the fog and the traffic on the North Circular tonight. So far our eminent guests, dignitaries, and of course our esteemed judges, the Mayor and Mayoress, have been treated to an evening of innovation and interpretation. Dandia has never been more dazzling. We are almost there. Shahs, Patels and Lohanas are evenly matched. But who knows? The final four couples could tip the balance! Watch this space! As you youngsters would say. I'll soon be announcing the final couples.

PREETHI: I'm so nervous. Hope I don't muck up the body-popping bit.

DINESH: Just let me lead.

PREETHI: The crowd clapometer is certainly not going to be with us.

DINESH: It's about how well we dance, not how popular we are.

PREETHI: Well, I'd lose in the popularity stakes. The way that Sonya looked at me in the loos, you'd think I had SARS. *(Indicating ROOPA.)* And there's another one who's blanking me out. Roops and I go back years.

(ROOPA exits.)

DINESH: Yeah, Hina and I used to do "speak and spell" together. Look at ency-clopedias . . . planets, capital cities, that sort of thing.

PREETHI: Where is Hina? Isn't she dancing?

DINESH: Don't know. She's blocked my address on her e-mail. My messages keep bouncing back to me.

PREETHI: It's all my fault, isn't it? What a mess.

DINESH: Dad's set his heart on us winning.

PREETHI: And we can't disappoint our parents, can we?

(Our focus goes to PUSHPA *and* POPATLAL.)

PUSHPA: That Bharat has really got Ketan Datani in his pocket now. He's going around with his Colgate smile. You wait and see. The wedding invitations are probably at the printers already.

POPATLAL: Bharat is Ketan's spin doctor, neh? Wiping out the scandal so the Datanis can come out smiling.

PUSHPA: Han, the Lohanas get what they want and they don't care how and now Dinesh is lost to us.

POPATLAL: Poor Hina. She's missed most of the competition. She should have come with us.

PUSHPA: She'll be here. She's ironing her hair and plucking her eyebrows to look anonymous. I said to her, forget Dinesh, still might meet a match. She's a year younger than Preethi Datani and no black marks on her character . . . She's got another season. Let's go wait outside for her. Not nice to walk in alone.

(We focus on PREMA, KETAN, *and* BHARAT.)

BHARAT: *(looking at* DINESH *and* PREETHI*)* Our children look so good together.

KETAN: My princess lights up any room she walks into.

BHARAT: The home she enters will be blessed.

KETAN: That is for sure.

BHARAT: And these days . . . caste . . . what does it matter? Shah, Lohanna . . . I say to Dinesh . . . Gujarati girl will do. Of course, you and I know each other very well . . . I don't need to investigate what village you are from.

KETAN: You give children choice . . . all the sweets are there . . . I know Preethi will pick the right one.

BHARAT: Han. We parents have done our bit.

*(*BHARAT *shakes* KETAN's *hand and goes.)*

PREMA: Why are you letting Bharat think that we're going to allow Preethi to marry Dinesh?

KETAN: That is my intention.

PREMA: What? Without discussing it with Preethi or me?

KETAN: When she abused her freedom, she sealed her fate.

PREMA: Why don't you look at some Lohana boys overseas through the golf club?

KETAN: The golf club? They're all talking about her. I can't set foot in there.

PREMA: Isn't she allowed one mistake in life?

KETAN: She could have chosen who she wants, but she knew the boundaries and she crossed over them.

PREMA: And you think she's going to say yes to your plans?

KETAN: How else are we going to save face?

PREMA: Everything we do in our lives is just to save face, isn't it?

KETAN: I'm going to greet my clients. You haven't acknowledged my firm yet. We have sponsored the whole evening.

(KETAN and PREMA exit. Our focus shifts to SONYA and SHRENEK.)

SONYA: I've already introduced myself to the Mayor and Mayoress.

SHRENEK: Bit eager! You should have waited till we'd danced.

SONYA: Nah! You gotta be one step ahead. It's good for the judges to put a face to the winners.

SHRENEK: And what a face . . . hair really works.

SONYA: Took me five hours. Heated rollers, serum on each individual strand . . . can't wait to get a personal stylist. When we win and get that commercial, we'll be able to get our glossies done for free, invitations to premieres, paparazzi following us around.

SHRENEK: Sonya and Shrenek will be in a different league.

PREMA: (on the annoy) I just want to take a moment to remind everyone, especially the dancers who are chewing their nails backstage, everyone's a winner tonight! You've all done tremendously well to get to this stage, so all of you will walk away with at least a memento. Prizes and indeed today's entire event is sponsored by leading electronics firm Datani Sparks! The MD Mr. Ketan Datani's mission is to add a sparkle to everyday lives! And judging by the prizes he will certainly succeed in that. Top prizes range from electronic calculators to electric toothbrushes to keep you smiling! It's back to the contest in just a moment.

(MOHAN enters.)

SHANTI: What are you doing here, son?

MOHAN: I haven't missed Anant's students, have I? The program said that they were on towards the end?

SHANTI: Since when have you taken an interest in this?

MOHAN: At least I'm here.

SHANTI: Well, it's too little too late. What is Anant going to do with your interest now? You have already tethered him to your shop.

MOHAN: Ba, stepping foot into a Navratri is big step for me.

(ANANT enters.)

ANANT: What are you doing here, Bapu?

MOHAN: Son, I wanted to see what you do before it's too late.

ANANT: Why are you talking like that? You have plenty of time ahead of you.

MOHAN: Who knows with life? Look what happened to me, even with twenty-four-hour CCTV cameras. Tomorrow there might be a terrorist on the underground.

ANANT: Well, you're not going back there again. It's my responsibility to see how both outlets are manned.

SHANTI: Have you talked to that Julian at least?

ANANT: What's the point?

MOHAN: Punjabis have been fashionable for long enough.

SHANTI: He's interested in you. Go and explain to him why Raza isn't dancing. He'll understand.

ANANT: There's no need.

MOHAN: Raza. Who is he?

SHANTI: Olo chokra . . . Raza . . . the same one who saved you from those rough boys.

MOHAN: What a brave boy! Putting his life at risk for me. I didn't know he was Anant's student.

SHANTI: Not just student . . . his prize student for the competition.

MOHAN: A Muslim? His prize student? How did that happen?

ANANT: It's a long story.

SHANTI: Those Patels from Tooting are buttering up that TV man. If you don't show him that you're keen, their teacher Beni Katania is going to get the choreography job.

ANANT: Let her have her five minutes of fame.

(ANANT *leaves.*)

SHANTI: If only Raza was dancing, Anant would have his showcase.

MOHAN: I wanted to offer him and his friend a reward.

SHANTI: I have his number on my mobile.

(MOHAN *and* SHANTI *leave.*)

PREMA: *(on tannoy)* Here we are! The final contestants of the grand finale. It gives me great pleasure to invite Miss Roopa Kotecha and Mr. Kalpesh Tanna to the floor.

(ROOPA *and* KALPESH *dance.*)

PREMA: And now, hot contenders for the title, Sonya and Shrenek Patel, from Beni Katania's South London Dance Academy.

(SONYA *and* SHRENEK *are cheered on and they dance.*)

PREMA: And finally Miss Preethi Datani and Mr. Dinesh Shah.

(PREETHI *and* DINESH *are cheered onto the floor. They take their positions but, before they start,* RAZA *enters and stops everyone in their tracks.*)

RAZA: Mrs. Datani, I would like your permission to dance with Preethi.

SONYA: But he's been disqualified.

RAZA: Mrs. Datani, you have disqualified me from the dance competition, but don't disqualify me from competing for Preethi's heart. I know I shouldn't have come here but someone told me that I should fight for what I want in life and my life is nothing without your daughter. I don't want to take her away from all this. I want to be a part of it.

(DINESH *steps aside for* RAZA.)

BHARAT: What do you think you're doing, son? Everything I've done is to get you to this place. You're throwing away your passport to happiness.

DINESH: No, Dad. Hina is my partner. I should never have let her go. *(To* PREMA.*)* Mrs. Datani, if Hina is here, I would like to dance with Hina Shah.

(HINA *enters, clearly showing her delight.*)

DINESH: Will you please announce us?

PREMA: Ladies and gentlemen, there has been a slight change in the line-up for this evening. We will now have Miss Hina Shah and Mr. Dinesh Shah, followed by Miss Preethi Datani and Mr. Raza . . . ?

RAZA: Khan.

SONYA: Changing rules when they feel like it!

SHRENEK: Don't worry, babes. He can't touch us.

KETAN: Are you out of your mind? Stop this madness.

PREMA: Why? So Preethi can keep up the pretence for your sake?

KETAN: Why are you humiliating me? In front of clients? Community?

PREMA: You didn't mind humiliating me in front of the same community. Everyone knows about you. They don't say, but they talk behind your back. I have kept quiet for too long, painting a perfect picture of our life which was false, but I won't have my daughter living a lie.

KETAN: You think Preethi is going to thank you when he has left her for a virgin in purdah and she is left with no prospects?

PREMA: Preethi and I can live with the consequences of our actions. Can you live with the consequences of yours?

(KETAN *leaves.*)

PREMA: Music, please.

(*Music comes on.* HINA *and* DINESH *dance.*)

PREMA: And now for the final couple of the season, Miss Preethi Datani and Mr. Raza Khan.

(RAZA *and* PREETHI *dance. The crowd is uncertain how to react.*)

PREMA: I'm sure the judges would like to take a couple of moments to deliberate. I will be back with the results soon.

(*Focus shifts to* BHARAT *and* POPATLAL.*)

POPATLAL: You see, Bharat bhai, they use you and spit you out when it suits them.

BHARAT: Han, you were right, bhai. I should have stuck with the Shahs, instead of trying to build bridges. As Ketan's accountant, I got to know his ins and outs, but I wasn't expecting this from the daughter.

POPATLAL: Well, you have our guarantee that we have no skeletons in our cupboard.

BHARAT: Dinesh is very lucky that you are willing to forgive and forget.

POPATLAL: We have to look forward, he ne? No point to dwell backwards.

BHARAT: Han. Let's end the season with an official announcement of the engagement. With my connections, we can get this hall for the wedding if you want.

POPATLAL: Even with both families and friends this hall is too big, he ne? But for next year's Navratri?

BHARAT: Goes without saying. It's time for the Shahs to take control of our cultural heritage.

POPATLAL: Yes. Integration is all very well but it has its place. This sort of dilution leads to pollution. Preethi and her partner danced well. A Muslim could be waving from the number one float and switching on the Diwali lights.

BHARAT: God forbid, and I'm sure His Worshipful would agree with us. Normally I wouldn't use my influence with him, but desperate circumstances call for desperate measures.

(He exits to talk to the Mayor and Mayoress.)

PREMA: Now for the moment we've all been waiting for. The judges have deliberated and I have the envelope here with the results. I will announce them in reverse order. *(She opens the envelope and reads.)* In third place, Miss Hema Patel and Mr. Ritesh Shah. In second place we have Sonya and Shrenek Patel . . .

(SONYA shrieks in disbelief.)

SONYA: This is a stitch-up. Bet it's that SLIM and his slag.

SHRENEK: Next time, eh, babe?

SONYA: What next time? I've been talking to Julian. He said you were holding me back. I'm going solo.

SHRENEK: Babe?

SONYA: Oh, piss off! *(Storms off.)*

PREMA: And finally. The judges would like to crown Miss Hina Shah and Mr. Dinesh Shah as the Diwali Queen and Diwali King. Hina and Dinesh will head the Diwali parade and take home with them his-and-her foot-massage machines. Please come forward.

(HINA gushingly drags DINESH forward. SHANTI crowns HINA and DINESH.)

DINESH: I know how much it means to my dad to see me wearing this, and I just want you to know, Dad, that you brought me up to work hard, be better than anyone else and to get by on merit. That is what winning this competition was about for me, not about being a Shah, Patel, or Lohana. Everyone here knows who the real winners are. I'm sorry I can't accept this crown.

(He takes off his crown and hands it back. HINA *follows his example.)*

PREMA: Bravo! How gracefully this young man has spoken. You're a credit to your parents. When I proposed this intercaste competition, I had no idea just how much of a challenge I was going to face. You young people of today have to show us the way. If I have failed in my duty as Chair, I am more than willing to step down, but I would urge everyone to remember how often we Gujaratis have been the outsiders and have asked to be accepted in. I speak as a mother when I say that I'm sure that in our hearts what all of us want is for our children to be happy.

MOHAN: Hear, hear! Prema bhen! I would like to say that as a father I thought I had the God-given right to choose my son's path. I was willing for him to sacrifice his life stacking shelves, when God has given him a talent that I chose to close my eyes to. His mother died in this season and I have carried that wound. When I was attacked, recently, I realized the most important thing in life. Someone's son helped me, and there I was allowing my son to disappear before my eyes.

SHANTI: Are you sure those boys didn't hit him on the head?

(ANANT goes up to MOHAN.)

ANANT: Thank you, Bapu. It was you, wasn't it, who got Raza here?

MOHAN: He was already here. Playing squash downstairs. Ready to play Romeo.

ANANT: How do you know he was downstairs?

MOHAN: Mobiles have their uses. Instant communication. Your grandmother had the number, I just pressed the button.

ANANT: Bapu, Julian is keen for me to come on board.

MOHAN: With my blessing.

ANANT: He wants me to choreograph a dance for Meera Syal.

MOHAN: Well, if anyone can give steps to that gulab jamun it's you.

ANANT: I've told him that if he wants me, he has to shoot in your kiosk.

MOHAN: Two birds with one stone. Spoken like a true Patel.

ANANT: Come and meet him, Bapu.

(MOHAN and ANANT leave. PREMA is back on the tannoy.)

PREMA: I'd like everyone to join me in congratulating Preethi and Raza.

(General applause as PREMA hugs and congratulates RAZA.)

PREETHI: Thank you, Mum.

(ROOPA comes and hugs PREETHI.)

ROOPA: Your mum's wicked. Safe.

PREETHI: Yeah. She's come good.

ROOPA: I'm sorry about your dad.

PREETHI: You knew?

ROOPA: Everyone knows.

PREETHI: And there's you having the hump with me for keeping secrets?

ROOPA: Will you say sorry to Jaz for me?

RAZA: No worries.

(One by one, the youngsters all come and congratulate them. BHARAT *and* POPATLAL *also come and grudgingly congratulate them.)*

POPATLAL: Congratulations, Preethi! Raza! You've crossed over very well. I thought dancing was against your religion.

RAZA: No.

POPATLAL: No, of course, it's just intoxication that is not permitted.

RAZA: Alcohol.

POPATLAL: Yes, although it could be argued that a woman's beauty is more intoxicating than a peg of whisky. Prema bhen, Pushpa and I would like to take our hats off to you. We have had so much of enjoyment and who would have thought this was the season for both our daughters to meet their matches?

PREMA: Who would have thought? So Bharat bhai, can the Lohana ladies count on our arrangement for next year's dates?

BHARAT: I have not been equitable. I'm going to rotate the hall between the castes. So it will be the Shah turn.

POPATLAL: Pushpa is already talking to the Mayor and Mayoress about next season. I hope you don't mind, but imitation is the best form of flattery.

PREMA: Not at all . . . I look forward to being a guest rather than host next season!

POPATLAL: Most welcome.

SHRENEK: Got to hand it to you, Raza. You're a great dancer and you swing a better left hook than me.

(Music comes on. PREETHI *and* RAZA *start to dance and one by one everyone joins in.)*

[End]

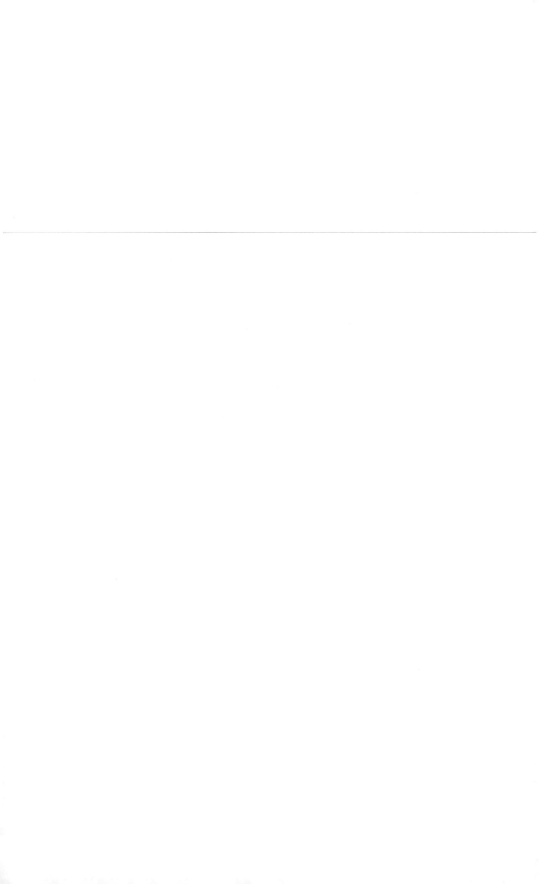

PART FOUR

South Africa

By most textbook accounts, South Asian migration to South Africa began with the entry of indentured laborers into present-day KwaZulu-Natal in November 1860. However, evidence corroborates the presence of Indian slaves who were imported into the Cape region by the Dutch East Indies Company in the seventeenth century. Historians have usually presumed that these slaves were integrated into the community of slaves brought from Southeast Asia.[1] Nonetheless, more than 100,000 indentured laborers entered colonial Natal in the mid-nineteenth century. The majority of South Asians in contemporary South Africa most likely descend from the laborers who arrived between 1860 and 1911. Most who landed on Natal's shores came from either Tamil-speaking southern regions through Madras, or from Hindi-speaking northern regions, from Calcutta (Vahed 1995: 27). A total of 262 ships from Madras, carrying mostly Tamil-speaking southerners, and 122 ships from Calcutta, with mostly Hindi-speaking Indians from Bihar and parts of Bengal, arrived as part of the fifty-one years of indentured labor migration into Natal. 152,184 Indian indentured laborers entered Natal during this period. In addition, a small number of laborers who finished their contracts applied to work in Natal after serving in other areas such as Fiji or Mauritius. Smaller numbers of other South Asians, in the thousands, paid their own passage to Africa. Dubbed "passenger Indians," these individuals, mostly from Gujarat, sought business opportunities. In the 1870s and 1880s, they traveled without restriction as subjects of the empire. One of the most famous "passengers" was Mohandas Gandhi, whose twenty-one year sojourn in South Africa saw the crystalization of political techniques of civil disobedience and *satyagraha* (see Vahed 1995; Ebr.Vally 2001; Tinker 1979).

In the 1890s and 1900s, many ex-indentured laborers settled in Natal, parts of the Cape in the southwest corner of the country, and in the Transvaal (present-day Gauteng). As more and more Indians were prospering in establishing successful shops and owning land in Transvaal, the Afrikaaner government devised measures to encourage Indians to leave, even though they could not directly discriminate against them, as they were British subjects. The Transvaal government refused them property rights in many areas, levied a 3-pound tax on every Indian, and refused to recognize Indian marriages, among other strategies. From when the independent Union of South Africa was created in 1910 through the 1920s, the government attempted various measures to reduce the power and rights of Indians, passing laws requiring accounts kept by shops to be written in English only. The government also reserved the right to close down businesses judged unsanitary or unhygienic; often these were Indian enterprises (see Ebr.-Vally 2001: 82–83).

The early twentieth century, particularly the first two decades, witnessed the burgeoning of Mohandas Gandhi's techniques of civil disobedience. During this time, as many laws were passed restricting the movement of Indians, including the famous law requiring all nonwhites to carry passes, Gandhi and his followers' struggles against unjust laws culminated in a 1914 agreement between him and Jan Smuts, then minister of the interior, in which all taxes would be revoked, Indian marriages would be recognized, and the *satyagraha* campaign would end. Shortly thereafter, Gandhi left for India, never to return.

In the mid-1920s plans were afoot to establish segregated residential patterns for Indians. This failed, but soon a repatriation plan, with aggressive Afrikaaner support, was passed in 1925 and endured until 1939. Though the government attempted to root out Indians systematically, this initiative also failed. From a population of more than 100,000 Indians, only a few thousand returned to India. In the meantime, the 1920s saw the emergence of the South African Indian Congress, formed as a response to the government's plans to segregate and restrict the movement of Indians. In the interwar years, politically prominent Indians such as Yusuf Dadoo, Monty Naicker, and others, filled headlines of Indian community newspapers. Besides the actions of a handful of prominent and educated elites, and besides the Afrikaaner characterization of all Indians as wealthy shopkeepers, the majority of Indians were poor, many were unemployed, and many lived in conditions similar to those experienced by Coloureds and Africans, the other nonwhite groups of South Africa (Ebr.-Vally 2001: 91).

The granting of independence to India and Pakistan in 1947 solved a long-term problem faced by the South African government: dealing with Indians as British imperial subjects. From 1947 to 1961, all Indians were automatically classed as Indian citizens who were foreign residents in South Africa. In 1961, Hendrik Verwoerd, about a century after the first South Asians arrived, granted

Indians citizenship and the status of a permanent population. This was not a magnanimous gesture of welcome but rather marked closure to many decades of British Indian and Indian national protests against South African mistreatment of Indians.

A long history of restrictive legislation, including the nearly fifty years of apartheid, resulted in the "complete indigenisation of Indians in South Africa" (Vahed 1995: 229). As residential segregation grew more prominent, the ethnic insularity and attention on solely "Indian South African" culture grew within Indian communities. The structures of the extended family, religion, and Indian cultural imports such as dance performances in the early twentieth century marked a distinctive Indian South African ethnicity. The residential segregation of the early twentieth century, which was strengthened by state legislation like the Group Areas Act in 1950, created a distinctive Indian South African culture thoroughly separate from cultural forms in India.

From the 1950s through the end of formal apartheid in 1994, Indian South African culture reflected the broader reality of separate residential, educational, and employment opportunities divided on racial lines. In Natal, particularly, Indians built their own schools, temples, mosques, and community centers during the apartheid era.[2] Indian South Africans filled the ranks of the African National Congress, the major political challenger to apartheid and the current majority party of post-apartheid South Africa. Prominent anti-apartheid activists, including Ahmed Kathrada, imprisoned on Robben Island as a result of the Treason Trial, Ismail and Fatima Meer, Mac Maharaj, Strini Moodley, and countless others fill the pages of South African history.

Before the late 1950s, Indian South African theatre and performance was encompassed under traditional Indian dance-drama forms such as Therakutu, a popular performance form deriving from Tamil Nadu in South India. Other performances included dramatizations of Indian epic stories such as the *Mahabharata* or the *Ramayana,* or history plays such as *Nallatankal* or *Satyavan-Savitri.* These stories were all enacted in vernacular languages such as Tamil, Telugu, or Gujarati (Naidoo 1997: 2). As a prominent Indian South African practitioner has recollected, her earliest theatre experiences in the 1940s include performing in a Telugu version of Kalidasa's *Sakuntala.* With the advance of formal apartheid in the 1950s, Indian-language theatre withered and English-based theatre began to grow.

In the 1950s, an alliance between educated Indians and liberal whites began to form within the theatre practices of Durban. In this milieu, "a multi-racial theatre tradition began to develop . . . where Indian actors began to perform works by British playwrights [in English] for non-white audiences in Durban" (Hansen 2000: 4). This period is marked mostly by liberal whites promoting Orientalist versions of Indian culture through the productions of "classic"

Indian plays by authors such as Kalidasa or Tagore.[3] The plays produced and the theatre activity engaged in by whites and Indians together did not address local concerns. The link between "local" needs of Indians (apartheid laws, perceptions as second-class citizens) and theatre did not arise until the 1960s.

Indian South African theatre then started to reflect both the issues of its communities and started to use local casts. After the visit of India's Krishna Shah to Durban in 1962 (who staged Rabindranath Tagore's *The King of the Dark Chamber*), Muthal Naidoo, Ronnie Govender, Welcome Msomi, and others formed the Durban Academy of Theatre Arts (DATA). This company produced European works such as Sheridan's *The School for Scandal*, Molière's *Le Bourgeois Gentilhomme*, and Albee's *Who's Afraid of Virginia Woolf*. Some, including Naidoo and Govender, formed another company, the Shah Theatre Academy, in honor of Krishna Shah. This company produced canonical American and European plays such as Miller's *All My Sons* and Odets's *Golden Boy*. Also, plays written by Indian South Africans were produced, such as Ronnie Govender's *Beyond Calvary*, a love story about a Hindu and a Christian in South Africa and Kessie Govender's *Working Class Hero*, which detailed racist animosity between Indian and African construction workers.

At this juncture, a new tradition of political and social satire was forming within the ranks of the Indian South African theatre. During the 1960s and 1970s, with the establishment of political writers like Ronnie Govender, Kessie Govender, and Muthal Naidoo, a "new genre of indigenous South African Indian theatre that combined social criticism, political satire, and the use of local idioms and expressions" (Hansen 2000: 5) arose. Muthal Naidoo's *We 3 Kings* spoofed the 1980s Tri-Cameral Parliament which included chambers for Whites, Coloureds, and Indians, but not black Africans.

This tradition is perhaps best exemplified in Ronnie Govender's *The Lahnee's Pleasure* (1972), represented in this volume, the first theatrical exposure of working-class Indian South African life on stage. The 1960s and 1970s saw an array of Indian theatre practitioners such as Saths Cooper, Strini Moodley, and others working closely with the Black Consciousness (BC) movement[4] to create politically motivated "black" theatre. However, the BC movement did not command much attention in Indian South African theatre. Indian theatre then began to find its own aesthetic voice. A number of works appeared in the following years that exemplified a new "Indian" component to South African theatre, culminating in Ronnie Govender's highly successful 1996 productions of *1949* and *At the Edge*, based on the forced removals of Indians from Cato Manor, in Durban, in the wake of the 1949 Durban riots and the 1950 Group Areas Act, respectively.

Prominent South Asian diasporic theatre today comes from the pen of Rajesh Gopie, whose plays *Marital Blitz* (1996), *Out of Bounds!* (toured 1998–2003), and *A Coolie Odyssey* (2002) tackle issues of import to post-apartheid Indian communities, such as gender, spousal abuse, and youth in Indian South Africa. The Indian component of post-anti-apartheid South African theatre is just beginning to acquire its own voice. After many years of characterization Indian theatre as simply "ethnic," critics in the post-apartheid period are realizing that the "most neglected area of theatre research in South Africa is that which seeks to investigate the contribution of South Africans of Indian classification" (Schauffer 1992: 84). Figures like Ronnie Govender and Kriben Pillay are being noticed in non-Indian contexts, such as by the African practitioner Zakes Mda, the journalist Mark Gevisser, and by the many awards Govender has received from the South African theatre establishment.[5]

A more recent and dynamic addition to post-apartheid South African theatre is Yugan Naidoo's 2003 play *Lataas FM*. This spoof of the Durban Indian radio station, Lotus FM, ran successfully in Durban's Playhouse Theatre. Naidoo is an established comedian and performer in the Indian South African community, and his farces have long toured community halls. His acceptance marks the entrance of ethnic–intra-communal comedy into a mainstream theatre. The play consists of the radio-station commentators, and their humorous personalities, such as Auntie Tamasha, who gives cooking advice, and Revy, who discusses racism in the new South Africa, or Gruffy, who has a devious plan to raise money to get their own tv station. Predictable hijinks arise as the promotion of a new manager threatens to break up their plan; the play ends with a humorous trial in which an attorney accuses the radio announcers of spoofing the Indian community, focusing on internal problems, and ignoring their many contributions to business, science, and the nation. Naidoo, in an interview, confirmed that this was a humorous demonstration of the liberal-bourgeois indictment of ethnicized "lowbrow" humor that pervades the Indian South African theatre community. Such a play functions as an interrogation of self, as not only are common Indian stereotypes engaged, but the liberal critique of them is sent up as well.

Recent events, such as the 2002 release of Ngema's song "Amandiya" that cast Indians as middle-men minorities out to economically exploit the majority, as displayed in Govender's *1949*, sober the post-apartheid reality of South Africa. Though the song attracted widespread condemnation from the ANC, the South African Human Rights Commission, and a public censure by Nelson Mandela, a spate of violence directed toward Indians occurred in Chatsworth, a predominantly Indian section of KwaZulu-Natal, in August 2002. Perpetrators did claim inspiration from the song. The song was pulled from the radio soon after its release and Ngema was initially unapologetic, stating that his song mirrored the reality of African perceptions of Indians in South Africa. After rising condemnation and violence was perpetrated in the song's name, Ngema pulled back, saying that his "message was received wrongly" and that he "would like to allay the fears of the Indian community" generated by the song.

In addition to the 2002 Ngema song, the demise of the University of Durban-Westville (UDW) drama department in August 1999 was a blow to the Indian performing arts community in South Africa. This program was the center for dramatic training and production in Durban from the 1960s though the late 1990s. Many of the personalities known to Indian South African theatre came from this institution, including Jay Pather, Kriben Pillay, Suria Govender, Robin Singh, and Rajesh Gopie.

Regardless of the grim characteristics of the immediate post-apartheid era, a host of playwrights write for today's South African Indian theatre, such as Ismael Mahomed, who deals with Muslim communities in Gauteng; Krijay Govender, who has written about Indian women in the "new South Africa"; Rajesh Gopie; and Yugan Naidoo. The plays included in this volume, however, represent earlier, classic plays in Indian South African theatre history. Any discussion of Indian South African theatre begins with the first aesthetically and politically sophisticated play by Ronnie Govender, his *The Lahnee's Pleasure* (1972).

Govender's classic *The Lahnee's Pleasure* combines the best elements of modern English-language South African theatre: anti-apartheid protest, examinations of race and class, and the patois and ethos of South Africa. Written and first performed in the early 1970s, this play remains one of the most definitive documents of South African Indian society and culture. With a strong critique of class relations, an element common to all to the South African pieces included in this volume, *The Lahnee's Pleasure* is perhaps the first play to arise out of a specifically South African Indian space and yet speak to the wider South African population. As the numerous positive reviews attest, the truth of Govender's characters—the working-class Mothie, the middle-class Stranger, the timid barman Sunny, the imperious and racist Lahnee—has always come out. In the midst of the agricultural boycott, Govender was asked by Strini Moodley and Steve Biko to write a play for the South African Black Union Theatre Festival in 1972.[6] *Lahnee,* meaning "boss" in Afrikaans, is set in a nonwhite Indian and Coloured bar of a hotel in a small town in the north coast of Natal.[7] The bar is owned by a white man, whose establishment is divided by a partition to separate whites from a nonwhites. The barman, Sunny, tends to both the white and non-white sections. The play opens with a description of the premises that well serves as a historical document, as the bar is makeshift and shabby, but resembles a small English country pub. Also, before any lines are spoken, readers learn that close to the bar is a sugar mill, described as the lifeblood of the town. In 1970s coastal Natal, as was true almost a hundred years earlier when cane plantations as well as imported Indian laborers filled the countryside, the scene of a sugar mill and a small bar was a very common appearance.[8] In 1972 when the play was first staged, there were very few academic studies of South African Indians, so the play serves as a valuable historical analysis of the time.

The Lahnee's Pleasure was born out of Govender's real-life experiences as well as his own political commitments and activism. In the early 1970s, Govender was banned because of his politics from his day job as a teacher. He found another job as a sales representative for a brewery. On his first day at work in Mt. Edgecombe (an area referenced in the play), he tried to find the white manager but could npt enter through the whites-only entrance. He went into the nonwhite section and asked the Indian barman there to send for the manager, the *lahnee*. When the boss appeared, Govender stuck out his hand, only for it to hang in limbo as the *lahnee* wouldn't touch him. He then turned to the Indian barman and said, "Where's the tap bro? Maybe if I wash my hand, this *ou* [guy] will shake it."[9] This almost got Govender fired, but it provided the inspiration for the *lahnee* in the story. On his next visit, he found a middle-aged laborer in overalls, drinking a cheap glass of wine. Govender caught the laborer looking at him resentfully, as if to say, "If I want to drink wine, it is my business," which ended up being a line in the play.

In a quick week, and after a three-week rehearsal period, the play was born. Govender had the idea brewing through these experiences but was also was asked specifically to write for the South African Black Union Theatre Festival in 1972. The play premiered as a one-act piece, alongside Fugard's well-known *Sizwe Bansi Is Dead* at the aforementioned festival to a rousing reception. As the play was a serious hit at the festival, Govender then expanded it into a two-act version, which is represented in this volume. The play in this latter form first ran in Durban's Himalaya Hotel in 1977. Though it was scheduled for a three-week run, it ran for twelve weeks to many standing ovations. At this point, in the late 1970s, one of the lowest points in apartheid, Govender was approached by the state-run Performing Arts Council to stage the play for mixed audiences provided they sat separately. As a pioneer of the Cultural and Sports Boycott, Govender refused.[10] He then took the play to townships such as Chatsworth, Phoenix, Merewent, and other cities such as Maritzburg, Verulam, and Tongaat, with the aim of making this theatre accessible to the general population, a long-time goal of the Shah Theatre Academy. Finally, Govender and company received an invitation to the Johannesburg Market Theatre in 1977, which they accepted. This was the first staging in front of a theatre-literate audience and professional critics. Despite the pressures, the play received excellent reviews and managed to please critics on all sides of the spectrum. Reviewers furnished high praise, as Sydney Duval of the *Rand Daily Mail* called it a "refreshing piece of indigenous theatre . . . something we have been craving for a long time. Its intrinsic value lays in its break from the rigid formalism of classical

Indian tradition."[11] Noting how the play speaks to all audiences across the South African spectrum, Peta Thornycroft termed it "no picturesque buffoonery for either white or non-white audiences to laugh at for the mere sake of mirth. It is comedy certainly, but all the daily drama of being a second-class citizen in this country shines through in a disquieting way."[12] The play was also produced in the 1980s to mixed audiences at the University of Transkei before mostly African students in its Great Hall. Finally, *Lahnee* was also produced in 2004, in Johannesburg's Cinema Supernova, again to much applause. It has toured Indian townships, universities, as well as major venues in the South African theatrical environment.

Lahnee built up the consciousness for a generation of the Indian community in South Africa, as audiences generally broke into loud cheers and applause when the Stranger, in the end, is prodded into yelling "One day, white man, one day!". One particular tour in the township of Phoenix, where the show played in a tent, found children waiting outside ready to stone the *lahnee*. Many a political activist confessed to Govender that the Mothies and Sunnys of their world revolted them and stirred their inspiration for political change. All in all, the play presents a level of complexity about South African Indians on both an aesthetic and political level.

Aesthetically, Govender successfully introduced an Indian patois into a show that spoke to all South Africans. This was a conscious choice, as he states that "even if we [politically conscious South African writers] wrote in English we had to find our own tongue. Colonized people were expected to educate themselves to understand the culturally specific utterances of Shakespeare's Falstaff, of the characters of Brendan Behan, James Joyce, Chaucer, even Charles Dickens. It was time the 'other' was understood on his own terms."[13] This level of artistic and political consciousness came out of Govender well before the notion of "writing back" to empire or any other kind of postcolonial artistic identity was born. This aesthetic choice of inputting a specific patois and sensibility into the world of South African drama in no way detracts from the political, class-based message of racialized consciousness. Govender's particular focus on the Indian situation easily and fluidly merges with a critique and reflection of South Africa at the time. Because of this unique combination, *The Lahnee's Pleasure* commands a space in the archive of diasporic South Asian dramatic literature.

Kessie Govender's *Working Class Hero*, like his namesake's *The Lahnee's Pleasure*, documents Indians' cultural and sociopolitical role in the chaos of deep apartheid. Also like *Lahnee*, this play from the 1970s simultaneously engages with class and race in South African Indian society. As Govender was a bricklayer himself, he examines the psychology of laborers, foremen, and supervisors at a construction site in apartheid-era Durban. This era of the 1960s and 1970s showed immense expansion of settlements in and around that city, usually conducted through the toils of African laborers and Indian "skilled laborers" who were one step above Africans in the sociopolitical hierarchy. In addition to documenting the working-class world of Indian–African relations of the time, Govender critiques the many-faceted character of the South African Indian caught in the strictures of apartheid.

Not unlike Pillay's *Looking for Muruga,* Govender includes an African character, Indian characters who are defensively racist in their behavior and words, and an Indian university student who encounters the situation with objectivity and politically inspired antiracialism. Though *Working Class Hero* remains naturalistic unlike *Muruga*'s cerebral discussions of nondualism and spirituality, both plays present a pressing conflict in South African Indian society: the battle between the university educated, ready to battle racism, and the working classes, whose consciousness remains locked within the violence around them. Whereas Pillay ends his play in an ironically Beckettian way[14] where nothing, as such, happens, Govender ends his story through a stark comment on Indian racism in 1970s apartheid. *Working Class Hero,* like the patois and dialogue of *Lahnee,* and the intellectual debates of *Muruga,* captures the language, ethos, and conflicts of working-class Indian life within South African apartheid.

In addition to representing race relations between Blacks and Indians in deep apartheid, Govender critiques Indian racism and political identity through *Working Class Hero.* Unlike *Lahnee,* where the conflicts entail Indian–White relations, and unlike *Muruga,* where the Black character functions as a symbol as opposed to an active character, Govender places his Indians and Blacks squarely against each other. As he remarks in his foreword,[15] the play refers to the "South African Indian who has become a peculiar breed in the history of today . . . enjoying a middle class position in a three phased society, he is fighting for the privileges of the upper class, and treads on the lower class, whose fight for survival is too awesome in comparison with any of the privileges that the Indian so righteously demands" (5). Neither Anand, the university-educated, nor Siva and Jits, the racist construction workers, are spared a searching critique. Simultaneously, both sets of characters receive sympathy, as Govender manages to show the reasons behind the racism of Siva and Jits as well as the studious antiracialism of Anand.

Anand represents a particularly striking portion of the Indian diaspora—educated, liberal (but not necessarily progressive), and out of touch with the people who struggle with work, race, and class on a daily basis as a means of survival. Both with his brother Siva and with the supervisor Jits, Anand speaks from an academic (however impassioned) place of objectivity. Unlike Jits, his politics of race didn't emerge from a life in the racialized system, but rather from an academic understanding of it. This does not delegitimatize Anand's perspective, but sets it clearly apart from Siva and Jits. Siva's racism occurs on a cruder, less sophisticated level Jits' consciousness at times meets with Anand, as in their many discussions of the "system" and the division between the university world and the world of workers.

Anand's relationship with Frank compares with his relationship with Jits and Siva. He means well and tries sincerely to speak with Frank, so that he can understand his life and problems. He also sincerely protests anytime Siva and Jits treat him as an inferior. But a pedagogical element creeps into their conversation early in the play. Anand's English reeks of university education whereas Frank's language is a mix of broken English and Zulu. Anand strains to understand Frank's language just as Frank has trouble following Anand's discourse. In the end, despite the overflowing liberalism of Anand, he can't help but stay silent when true-to-life racism on the ground appears, outside a book or theory. When the Inspector asks if Frank was allowed to conduct skilled labor, Anand has nothing to say and can't honestly defend Frank. Though he is educated, impassioned, and caring, Anand simply can't find it in himself to truly cross the color bar and help Frank. Thus, we see two sides of the Indian diasporic spectrum in the characters of the intellectual, but politically spineless, Anand, and the racist, caught-in-the-hierarchy Siva and Jits.

Other diasporic plays such as Ahmad's *Song for a Sanctuary,* Aasif Mandvi's *Sakina's Restaurant,* and Hanif Kureishi's *Borderline*[16] include depictions of racism directed toward South Asians. *Working Class Hero* offers another view of the diaspora: the racism South Asians direct toward other groups. This racism has its own complex history, sociology, and web of meanings. As Govender expertly weaves all of these elements into a compelling story about apartheid South Africa, his *Working Class Hero* deserves the appellation of a classic of South African Indian, and diasporic South Asian, theatre.

The final play in this volume, Kriben Pillay's *Looking for Muruga,* covers a lot of ground, including Indians and apartheid in the early 1990s, performance aesthetics, and Indo-African relations. Though the play presents the very real situation of an Indian Marxist student, an Indian barman, and an African student and dancer in 1990s South Africa, it manages also to weave in allegory and commentary via the use of Muruga, a god venerated by South African Indians. The play itself, described by Pillay "as a series of jokes strung together that should have been performed in a bar, which is what many non-Indian critics said about the play"[17] functions as a document of South Asian diasporics engaging with their societies through the theatre. It presents the Indo-South African environment, with its internal community dynamics, its gods, dances, relations with the greater society, as well as class divisions within the community itself.

Muruga engages with a variety of dramaturgical and political issues regarding the diaspora as well as politics on many levels. These include the politics of South Africa during apartheid within Indian communities, Indo-African relations during the heyday of apartheid, and finally the politics of performance itself, through the stand-off between Muruga and Sherwin, two Indian South Africans who represent vastly different sociopolitical and aesthetic perspectives.

Pillay offers a searching representation of Indian working-class life and race relations through *Looking for Muruga.* The South African portion of the South Asian diaspora, though accessible through the fiction of Imraan Coovadia, the literary writings of Ronnie Govender, or the academic work by sociologist Fatima Mir, rarely has seen much airtime in dramatic literature outside South African Indian communities. In their case, as with the many other indentured labor diasporas in Trinidad and Fiji, *India* and *Indian* is a construct from the nineteenth century and not from the contemporary world of nation-states, linguistic identities, and partition-informed politics that form the diasporic world of South Asians in the United States, Britain, and Canada. However alive the world of Bollywood globalization and Indian dance may be in South Africa, the identity of South African South Asians has been developed wholly on South African soil, via intimate relations with Afrikaans and Afrikaaner culture, apartheid, and a specifically modern race consciousness in a world of South African blackness, whiteness, Colouredness, and Indianness.[18]

On the other hand, we cannot deny specific traditions and phenomena cultivated by and reproduced by South Asians that are most certainly coming from the region. Particular parts of South Asian languages, such as Tamil and Gujarati, particular dance and music traditions, like the Tamil *therukoothu* or Carnatic *bharatiya natyam,* and South Asian culinary traditions and clothing fashions are undoubtedly a part of South Asian South Africa. When asked about the meaning of the South Asian parts of the South African society, Pillay interestingly compared the Indian community to the Afrikaaner community: "I think attitudes to India may be similar to the Afrikaaner's attitude to Holland—a place of origin in the distant past . . . there are pockets of people who view their country of origin as their true home but this would be very, very small in relation to the overall consciousness."[19] Though certain traditions from India, rather than the complete South Asian sociopolitical context, do exist in South African South Asian lives, their politics, their lives, their families, their sense of import and meaning, derive completely from South Africa. Pillay confirms that the history and culture referenced in his play, such as Ahmed Kathrada, the 1949 riots, the "Indian *kugels,*" the Tamil dance traditions, the Tamil and Gujarati words, are all specific to South Africa and would simply not translate to the diaspora in other parts of the world. But, they would certainly translate to a non-South Asian South African audience of Blacks, Whites, or Coloureds.[20]

Though Pillay is certainly committed to theatre as an instrument for reflection and action, he maintains that "theatre never changes society, it can only be an indicator, a reflector, of what is happening . . . and it can point to possibilities . . . if theatre did change society obviously we would all be wonderful, conflict-free human beings."[21] But he is committed, as in his personal transformation consultancy work and other writings, to challenging perceptions within individuals and societies. This is demonstrated early on in the play by Muruga, who in one of his first exchanges with Sherwin, tellingly states that "you can only write about what you see and what you make up in your head, and what you make up in your head is what you want to see" (9). Near the end of the play, Pillay returns to this theme by showing Sherwin attempting to teach Muruga Marxist ideas about illusions and reality. The entire play, in a sense, is about what is real—objective Marxist reality or a mystical type of folk reality propagated by Muruga, who has a nondistant view of South African race relations—and what is not real. As in his other work, Pillay's play is also about transformation, as he claims that "artists must reflect transformation in society—where it has been intentional, it has been very elitist and very exclusive, but where theatre is a natural spontaneous outcome then you will find that what is appropriate for that society will happen."[22]

In this instance, we see a rather aggressive critique of the "West," both in the form of the hegemony of Western dramaturgy as well as Western academic training. Pillay uses Muruga and Sherwin to comment on the existential condition represented in *Waiting for Godot* by having the condition itself fall flat on non-Western ears (the implied Indian bar patrons of the Sherwin-Muruga Godot routine). At one stroke it demonstrates the influence of Beckett—the futility of modernity, or in this case, the futility of the politics of Sherwin, which are thoroughly modern. At other level, we see that the limited applicability of Beckett, as Godot in a non-Western setting does not transmit to a non-Western audience. We see an emergent "subaltern performance aesthetic" where the subaltern actually does speak, in the form of Muruga, as he is "disparaging of this kind of [Western] drama, and refers to the hits of Indian theatre as the kind of drama that is worthwhile" (14). Pillay comments on how the performance aesthetics of the West, with its experience of modernity, with its alienation, its lack, its unfulfilled individualism, capitalism, and will to power in the form of imperialism and nationalism, simply do not fit the Indian experience. Not only does it not fit, but working-class Indian South Africans, with their own patois, ethos, and highly specific cultural positioning, have their own aesthetic, filled with song, dance, and fourth-wall breakthroughs. Pillay acknowledges that he is trying to show the "dominant aesthetic of the Indian working classes through Muruga."[23] Pillay, as well as Ronnie Govender, by Pillay's own admission, are "thoroughly au fait with Western aesthetics, but are writing for audiences who are not. In the case of *Muruga,* [Pillay] interrogates this context through the Western-educated Sherwin and the working-class Muruga."[24]

Pillay's drama is a pointed response to the dramatic training he and his peers received in the highly Eurocentric tradition of theatre education in South Africa during apartheid. Even though a dramatic tradition in vernacular languages like Tamil and Gujarati did exist in the 1930s, 1940s, and 1950s, by the time high apartheid was established, "Western drama did inform playmaking and was utilized to create a South African Indian theatre rooted not in the South Asian dramas of the vernaculars, such as enactments of religious myths or courtly stories from India, but [in] the growing need to reflect local Indian realities."[25] Here we see how theatre in this particular diasporic context grew in a space thoroughly cut off from the South Asian source, mixed with a European aesthetic and practical politics. But Pillay's effort here reflects his own "Western training in drama which had no connection to the stories of South African Indians. There was no connection."[26] Hence, *Muruga* was born in that effort to create a theatre that spoke to the realities of apartheid without sacrificing an authentic connection with the realities of Indian life and aesthetic characteristics. The presence of Dante, the Black African dance student, testifies to Pillay's work in this regard. Dante, "a symbol of the mute Black presence in the lives of South African Indians at that point in history,"[27] was roundly criticized on the one hand by those who felt having a mute Black character who simply dances portrays Blacks in a rather unflattering manner. Some right-wing religious types also objected to a Black African playing a Hindu deity. Pillay simply wanted to show the Indo-South African world and "it seemed very natural that interaction happens between Muruga and Dante but the moment Sherwin comes into the picture, he is simply an onlooker, he dances. His dancing and muteness are very accurate symbols of what the society was at that time [early 1990s apartheid South Africa]."[28]

Looking for Muruga enlivens our concept of South Asian diaspora by placing South Asians in a context of dizzying complexity. We find intellectual Marxist theatre people and working-class waiters trying to deal with issues specific to their own community, including the Indian *kugels* and the internal classism of the Indian community. Though they have their Tamil, their dance routines, their Hindu mythology, and their South Asian names, their lives and struggles primarily relate to race, class, and apartheid. It is this African face of the South Asian diaspora that Pillay manages to capture. He not only captures the world of the South Asian diaspora of that period but also critiques and comments on the politics of performance. This lifts *Muruga* into the type of piece that simultaneously takes on many different identities—historical document and commentary, dramaturgical and political critique, and, finally, a resounding reflection of a large part of the South Asian diaspora.

Ronnie Govender

Ronnie Govender is an award-winning, internationally acclaimed playwright, director, producer, short-story writer, and novelist. He started the Shah Theatre Academy in Durban in the 1960s, which without funding trained black theatre practitioners free of charge. It was also a pioneer of the cultural boycott. The artists who trained under Govender through the academy or through subsequent productions include many of the luminaries of the South African theatre—Kessie Govender (also represented in this volume), Welcome Msomi, Saths Cooper, Essop Khan, Leanda Reddy, Stanley Mnyandu, Rajesh Gopi, Pat Pillai, and Bassy Bhola. Throughout his long career, he has written memorable plays that document and analyze the life of South African Indian communities—such as his trilogy of satires against the 1980s Tri-Cameral Parliament, *Off-Side!*, *In-Side!*, and *Back-Side!*, his internationally renowned adaptation of stories from his book *At the Edge*, and his one-man version of a story about the 1949 pogrom against Indians in Durban, titled *1949*.

As a playwright and fiction writer, Govender has been invited to the Pan-Canadian Writers Festival, the International Theatre Festival in Manila, Philippines, and the Pan-African Literary Conference in Accra, Ghana. His collection of short stories, *At the Edge and Other Cato Manor Stories*, won the Commonwealth Writers Prize for the Africa region. He has received the AA Vita award for lifelong contribution to South African theatre as well as a medal from the English Academy of South Africa for outstanding contributions to English literature. His most recent work is the novel *Song of the Atman*, a history of generations of his family's experiences in South Africa. The first South African novel to be published in India, under the name *Black Chin, White Chin*, it was nominated for the Commonwealth Prize. He has recently finished writing a novel based on his play *The Lahnee's Pleasure,* which holds the record for the most number of performances of a South African play.

He was recently awarded a Lifetime Literary Achievement Award by the Department of Arts and Culture. This was followed by the Lifetime Achievement Award for his contribution to the arts by the Arts and Culture Trust of South Africa.

The Lahnee's Pleasure

Cinema Supernova, Durban, 2004
Wits University Great Hall, 2001
University of Transkei, Transkei, 1988
Himalaya Hotel, Durban, 1977
Market Theatre, Johannesburg, 1977
South African Black Theatre Union, Durban, 1972

Other Plays

Beyond Calvary	*1949*
The First Stone	*Too Muckin' Futch*
His Brother's Keeper	*The Great R31M Robbery*
Swami	*Who or What is Deena Naicker?*
At the Edge	*Your Own Dog Won't Bite You*
Off-Side!	*Blossoms from the Bough*
In-Side!	
Back-Side!	

The Lahnee's Pleasure

Ronnie Govender

ACT ONE

(The scene throughout the play is the "nonwhite" (meaning Indian and "colored") bar of a white-owned hotel in a small Natal North Coast town. The pub is shabby and run-down, the furniture make-shift, but it somehow bears the characteristics of an English country pub. The "nonwhite" pub is separated from the white pub by a partition. The barman SUNNY *serves both sides through an inter-leading door.*

It is 3 PM. The pub is empty. Enter the STRANGER *. He is about 35 years old and neatly dressed. Obviously a stranger to the place, he looks around, peers through a window which looks out over the sugar mill—the life-blood of the town. Enter* SUNNY *in white shirt, black tie and black pants.)*

STRANGER: Oh, there you are, barman. Nice little place you have here.

SUNNY: It's alright, bro.

STRANGER: It reminds me of an English country pub—same kind of atmosphere. Give me a double cane and coke, please. Lovely place. When I was in England I used to love visiting those country pubs. They had a special charm. This place is very much like that. Makes you want to drink a lot more, though. It's very quiet today, isn't it?

SUNNY: Oh weekdays very quiet.

STRANGER: Picks up over the weekends, I suppose?

SUNNY: Yeah. Friday Saturday, full up. See the mill here?

STRANGER: Oh, is that where the smoke is coming from?

SUNNY: Yeah. All these fullers working in the mill, you know. These fullers get paid Friday. They come here—full bro, man. I get so busy here . . . I got to serve both sides man.

STRANGER: Both sides?

SUNNY: See this partition here? That side for white people, this side for Indian people.

STRANGER: No trouble and all that?

SUNNY: No, no trouble nothing with these fullers, man. You know bro, twelve and a half years I'm working here.

STRANGER: Twelve and a half years, gee, you know something, in another twelve and a half years you might get yourself a gold watch.

SUNNY: My Lahnee will give it to me, man.

STRANGER: Your?

SUNNY: My boss, man.

STRANGER: Oh, yes, yes.

SUNNY: Hey, such a nice man, bro. Very nice man. You know, last week only he met accident man. Got hurt in the hand and leg everything, man. Very nice man, bro. You know my father was barman here.

STRANGER: In the same bar?

SUNNY: Yeah!

STRANGER: You couldn't have got better training, then.

SUNNY: That time I was a wine steward, man.

STRANGER: Well, you had to start from somewhere.

SUNNY: You know how much scolding I used to get from my father, bro? Old man used to scold me, man.

STRANGER: That's the best way to learn.

SUNNY: It helped me helluva lot.

(Enter MOTHIE *with his son,* PREM. MOTHIE *is a middle-aged laborer in worn-out overalls.* PREM *is about ten years old and, although his clothing is also worn-out, he is as neat as circumstances allow.)*

MOTHIE: *(To* PREM*)* Hey, monkey—don't come inside man. You know that Uncle will shout. Come on you stand by the door, I'm coming just now. Don't come inside, I'm coming just now.

Sunny!! Give one glass wine.

SUNNY: Hey, Mothie, hey! You can't bring that fuller here, you know you can't bring that fuller here, you know you can't bring that fuller here!

MOTHIE: Hey, never mind man.

SUNNY: *(To* PREM*)* Hey, stand right by the door, you.

MOTHIE: Every time something new will come out for you, eh Sunnyia.

SUNNY: Hey, you know Lahnee will make a noise, eh, you know Lahnee will make a noise!

MOTHIE: Hey, bugger your Lahnee, man. *(Pays for his drink.)* Little bit position you get here Sunnyia, you think you own the place.

SUNNY: *(To* PREM*)* Hey, come and have one lemonade. Hey boy, come here.

MOTHIE: Go, Uncle giving mineral, go!

PREM: Thank you.

SUNNY: Hey, Mothie, hey!

MOTHIE: What?

SUNNY: Why this fuller didn't go school today?

MOTHIE: Big trouble man. Those bloody swines, eh!

SUNNY: Ssssh. *(Pointing to white section.)*

MOTHIE: No, but what they think man?

SUNNY: I told you Lahnee's next door man.

MOTHIE: Hey, bugger your Lahnee man. I got my trouble here—Lahnee, Lahnee, Lahnee!

SUNNY: I told you one time you won't listen, eh? I tell you one time you won't bloody listen, you, eh?

MOTHIE: They think they can act like that to me? I'll fix them up today.

SUNNY: Who's that?

MOTHIE: Those bloody bastards, man. They think they can act like that to me and get away. You bloody see what I'm going to do today. I'll fix them up, one by one I'll fix them up! Yeah! Act like that to me and get away! You wait and see today what I'm gonna do. Just wait and see. Hey Premwa, come here—you mustn't fright huh. Tell them everything you saw. You tell them from the beginning what you saw. You mustn't be frightened. I'll be standing by you. I'll be standing by you—right there. You gone stand by the door. They think they can act like that!

SUNNY: What happened, didn't go work today, you?

MOTHIE: First time in thirty years I took off. I had to go to that police station.

SUNNY: Why, what happened?

MOTHIE: I went there. I went there and they laugh at me, man. Police must look after us, not right Sunnyia?

SUNNY: Right! Yeah!

MOTHIE: But they laughing at me, man.

SUNNY: Don't be silly.

MOTHIE: For nothing hey! Yeah, they don't know me. They don't know me. Me, I'll tell my Lahnee and I'll go straight by the magistrate and then they'll know.

SUNNY: They can't laugh at you for nothing, right?

MOTHIE: For nothing, reh Sunnyia.

SUNNY: Hey, don't be silly man.

MOTHIE: How you'll like it if you go police station to make your report and they laugh at you? How you'll like it?

SUNNY: Hey bro, *(to* STRANGER*)* where you heard story like this—you go police station to write your report and they laugh at you. Where you heard story like that?

MOTHIE: He, Maai Keeriai, they laughing for nothing, man. Yeah they don't know me yet. They don't know me yet. I'll tell my Lahnee and I'll go straight by the magistrate.

SUNNY: Hey, hey, hey! You can't go by the magistrate just like that!

MOTHIE: I'll go me. Don't know me yet. The polices don't know me yet. Think they can laugh at me and get away. You just wait and see what I'm going to do today. Arreh, Sunnyia, man! How long you know me, man?

SUNNY: I know you long time, man.

MOTHIE: Arreh, I know your whole family. I knew your father when he was barman here.

SUNNY: Yeah?

MOTHIE: Yeah! You lightie that time. I never used to drink those days, Sunnyia. Never used to touch it, man. Hell, your father too—Kista!—what a nice man! What a nice man! Arreh, what a good thunee player! We used to play partners!

SUNNY: Yeah?

MOTHIE: Nobody can beat us, man, nobody can beat us. All Mount Edgecombe nobody can beat us. Arreh, we'll win competition after competition—we'll win. Hell, your father, too, man! What a nice man. What a nice man. Sorry he died, eh Sunnyia?

SUNNY: One of those things man, got to die one day.

MOTHIE: Yeah, where you can get man like that today. Little bit money they got, little bit edication they got, they think they somebody, they somebody! Arreh, our time, man—our time. Saturday night! Jolling night! Arreh, what big, big prayers we'll have. Wedding! Big, big wedding we'll have. All Mount Edgecombe will be full up. People coming from Durban, Sydenham all over. Full, full, Mount Edgecombe. Saturday night, all night dancing. Arreh, all night dancing! Wedding night! Your father, mandraji fuller, right? And me, I'm roti fuller. Arreh, but dancing time, we'll dance Natchannia together.

SUNNY: What my father too?

MOTHIE: Yeah, I teach your father to dance. Arreh, chee! chee! chee! Sunnyia not like today's dancing. Everybody will go in one dark room—biting in the neck, biting in the mouth. Or they'll put one fast music—then everybody *(demonstrates a modern dance).* When this leg get tired—thava they'll put this leg. Dancing that? Dancing that?

SUNNY: Never, man, never!

MOTHIE: Arreh, our time, man, our time. Girls can't come out of the house—so strict they was. Arreh, six o'clock all the doors will be closed. Can't see one girl with one eyes. That time boys must dance girls part. Saturday night! Saturday night! Fire all burning one side. All the pots will be cooking one side. Thabla, saranji, all getting hot by the fire. Everybody will ask, Mothie came way? Me! Kisten came way? Your father! Everybody looking for us to start the wedding joll.

You know these big, big shots from Durban, Sunnyia—arreh, all will come and sit in one place. Drinking whisky, brandy, everything man. You know your father, your father will say, "Put one number for them, put one number for the big big shots." Arreh, I'll say, why you not starting the joll? But where that fuller want to start? Give him one two dops then that fuller on the tops. Your father! Me too, I'll go stand by the big, big shots. Watch everything. Father will come with the thabla—thava joll started.

(Sings a Natchannia song. Then breaks into the lively Natchannia dance. He gets louder as the song progresses, much to the consternation of SUNNY, *ever worried about what his Lahnee will say.* SUNNY *eventually stops him as the song and dance reach a crescendo.)*

SUNNY: *(Apologetic at having to break into the old man's ecstatic nostalgia)* Lahnee's next door man.

MOTHIE: Bugger your Lahnee, man. You remember that time, eh, Sunnyia?

SUNNY: Yeah, you lightie that time. Hey son. Look my son reh. Clever fuller. Come out first every time in the school.

(The LAHNEE *shouts from the white section: Sunny!* SUNNY *jumps to attention but* MOTHIE *stops him.)*

MOTHIE: Hey Sunnyia, wait, wait, wait! Give nother one wine quickly. Give nother one wine.

SUNNY: *(Pouring out the wine)* Hey bloody good singer you was, eh?

MOTHIE: That's nothing, listen this one. *(Promptly breaks into another lively song, louder than before.)*

(SUNNY stops him and exits.)

(MOTHIE hums his song, picks up his drink and—as he is about to proceed to his seat at the table—notices the STRANGER *who is looking at him in kindly amusement.* MOTHIE *is resentful.)*

MOTHIE: *(Proceeds to table and says loudly)* If I want to drink wine it's my business!

STRANGER: *(A little upset at the old man's unnecessarily aggressive manner)* If you want to drink wine, man, drink. Why do you look at me?

MOTHIE: I never looked at you.

STRANGER: Of course you looked at me. You looked at me and then you said that.

MOTHIE: Answer me one thing, eh! How you know I looked at you, if you never looked at me first? Go on answer me that!

STRANGER: Now look old man, if you . . .

MOTHIE: Hey, go on answer me that man. You think you big shot because drinking cane. Cane and wine same thing man, you must get drunk.

STRANGER: If you want to drink wine that's your business, I didn't say anything . . .

MOTHIE: What you mean my business. Look thambi, I'm telling you nicely. I'm older than you—you got no respect?

(Enter SUNNY.*)*

SUNNY: Alright, leave it out Mothie. Why you worrying him, he never do you nothing.

MOTHIE: You saw me making trouble in this bar, Sunny? How many years I'm coming here, you saw me making trouble?

SUNNY: No.

MOTHIE: Everybody know me in Mount Edgecombe. I got lot respect. If I want to drink wine, my bloody business. Why he must worry?

SUNNY: But he never say nothing to you.

STRANGER: I didn't say a word.

MOTHIE: *(Mocking)* You never say one word! You think because you drink cane, you big shot!

SUNNY: Keep quiet Mothie, man.

MOTHIE: Whole day I got trouble. Nobody know my trouble. How much trouble I got. If I want to drink wine, I want to bloody drink wine!

SUNNY: Sssh man, don't make so much noise. The wit ous are laughing at us.

MOTHIE: Let them laugh, hell! I'm paying for my wine. Just because they white people I must start shivering for them! Me I don't fright for white people. White people can do me bugger all.

(Enter LAHNEE, MOTHIE *turns suddenly to notice him behind the counter.)*

MOTHIE: Hello boss, how you boss?

(The LAHNEE *glares at him, takes two glasses and exits.)*

MOTHIE: *(To* STRANGER*)* Hey! Hey you! That's Mr. Simpson. He's the Lahnee here. He likes me. I come here every time. Not right Sunny?

SUNNY: Wait, wait. Come here, I'll tell you something. Don't shout, White people are listening to us . . .

MOTHIE: Hell, let them listen. I'm drinking here. My business if I want to make noise. You saw yourself the Lahnee never say nothing . . .

SUNNY: Come here, man, come here. You making too much noise. You make us a fool. You got no sense? You like white people must laugh at us. You got no shame?

MOTHIE: What shame? You think I'm running naked here. This is a bar this. Let them laugh. What you think they, God?

SUNNY: *(Exasperated)* Sssh man, I'm telling you nicely!

MOTHIE: Awright. Gimme nother one wine. Wait, wait, wait. I want to go lavatory. I'll gon make one piss and come. Don't fight with me Sunnyia.

SUNNY: I'm not fighting, man, I'm only saying don't make so much noise.

MOTHIE: *(To his son)* Monkey! Don't go inside, that Uncle will shout. *(Exit).*

STRANGER: I didn't say anything to him. What's wrong with him?

SUNNY: Oh, he's alright. He's a nice chap. Something must be troubling him.
We've all got our troubles you know.

STRANGER: He's making a fool of himself.

SUNNY: What can you do?

STRANGER: Maybe he's got troubles, but he's making fools of us. Those white
chaps are laughing at us. Guys like this make us look stupid.

SUNNY: Sure I feel sorry for him. He works hard. Gives his family everything.
He doesn't drink every time. Only Fridays. Drinks quietly and goes home
early.

STRANGER: I wonder what's worrying him?

SUNNY: Poor people got all the trouble. He's a tractor driver. They only pay him
R60 a month. They get place to stay and rations. But he's got seven children.
What can you do with R60 a month. But he's a good man. He keeps them all
clean and tidy and he sends them all to school.
*(STRANGER suddenly knocks down a cockroach from the counter and stamps
on it.)*

SUNNY: Oh, cockroach, bro. Hot days these things come out. Last week only my
Lahnee sprayed the place.

STRANGER: He still left some huge ones around.
(PREM brings in his empty bottle.)

SUNNY: Thanks son. Why didn't you go to school today?

PREM: My father stopped me.

SUNNY: What standard are you?

PREM: Standard One.

SUNNY: Yes eh, what you came out in your exams?

PREM: First.

SUNNY: Clever boy, huh! What you going to do when you grow big?

PREM: I don't know.

SUNNY: What you mean you don't know—you must become a doctor or lawyer.
You must make a big man of yourself.

STRANGER: Tell me, boy, why did your father stop you from school today?

PREM: Big trouble at home.

SUNNY: What trouble?

PREM: You know, my sister, she was in . . .
(Enter MOTHIE.)

MOTHIE: Hey! What you standing there? Told you you must stand by the door.

Go outside. Hey Sunny, what you making kooser, kooser with my son?

SUNNY: He only brought the bottle here, man.

MOTHIE: I know you. Give my wine.

SUNNY: Day time now Mothie . . .

MOTHIE: I know it's day time, I can see it's day time. Why you telling me it's day time, you think I'm stupid?

SUNNY: I didn't say you stupid.

MOTHIE: You clever fullers, all you fullers, man. You think I'm stupid because I'm tractor driver. You just like the police fullers.

SUNNY: I didn't say you stupid. I said day time now why you drinking so much?

MOTHIE: Hey you are not giving me free drink. If I want to drink—my business!

SUNNY: Don't shout man.

MOTHIE: Why you stopping me from drinking then?

SUNNY: (Loses his patience and shouts back) I'm not bloody stopping you, I'm only trying to tell you . . . (The LAHNEE shouts: Sunny!) Yes Boss! (Exits).

MOTHIE: (Mimicking SUNNY) Yes boss. (To STRANGER, who finds it hard to hide his amusement) Too much frightened fuller, bhai. Not like his father, Kista! Me, I don't fright for my Lahnee. My Lahnee likes me. You know how long I'm working for him bhai?

STRANGER: No.

MOTHIE: Thirty years!

STRANGER: In the same job?

MOTHIE: One job, one boss!

STRANGER: Uncle I'm sorry about that little argument we had just now.

MOTHIE: Arreh, jaanethe bhai. Little, little thing like this we worry about, when we die what we take with us? When you worry you die, when you don't worry you still die. Then why must die, bhai?

Yes, bhai, thirty years I'm working for my Lahnee. Anything I want my lahnee gives me. One day, I said, Sir, I want one loan, sir. My Mother died, bhai.

STRANGER: I'm sorry to hear that.

MOTHIE: I'm the eldest son.

STRANGER: Oh, so you've got to do all the prayers and all that.

MOTHIE: Must do prayers for thirteen-day ceremony, cook the food, make the sweetmeats. Where I'm going to get the money? Then I asked my Lahnee. He never say nothing. He didn't even ask me why I want the money. He just put his hand in the back pocket and took out so much notes. Bhai, white people carry so much money, eh? (SUNNY has returned and pours out the wine). He say how much you want Mothie. I say I want five rands, no five pounds—those days there was pounds not rands. He gave me ten rands. I said I don't want so much. He said never mind. I told him I'll give him back one pound a month but he said no, don't worry, when you have enough you can give it back. You know up to today he never ask for the money. Where can you get a Lahnee like that? But this fuller, I don't know. Mustn't fright for your Lahnee, Sunnyia.

SUNNY: I'm not frightened. *(Casts furtive look behind him)* Who says I'm frightened for my Lahnee?

MOTHIE: You mustn't fright. You must just do your work. Your Lahnee can do you fuckall.

SUNNY: Sssh man. I think you better go home. How long your son is waiting for you? He must be hungry. You better take him and go home.

MOTHIE: You feeling hungry, Premwa. Sunny, got some nuts?

SUNNY: No nuts.

MOTHIE: Serve?

SUNNY: Hey, no nuts, no serve, no nothing. Just take him and go home. I don't know where you come with this nuts and serve.

MOTHIE: Yeah you better go home. Thava take some money and buy bread. Got curry by the house. You dish yourself. Go, my baby *(And other such endearments. Exit* PREM*).*

Clever fuller Sunny. He come out first every time in school.

SUNNY: Yeah, he was just telling us.

STRANGER: You must not stop him from school like this, Uncle. He seems an intelligent child. He must go to school every day, then one day he will go to high school, and then maybe to university and then who knows . . .

MOTHIE: I want to do so much for my children, bhai. I don't want them to battle like me. I work hard, bhai—Sunny you know for yourself. Five o'clock, bhai, five o'clock I'm on that tractor. I want to do so much for my children.

SUNNY: I know Mothie. Why don't you go home and have a rest—you can come back later.

STRANGER: I think that's a very good idea Uncle.

MOTHIE: I don't want to go home Sunny. If I go home I'll only sit down and cry. *(Stifles a sob.)* My boy, Prem, he saw it Sunny . . .

SUNNY: What did he see? What happened?

MOTHIE: First time thing like this happen in my family. Disgrace. What I must tell my brothers and sisters, what I must tell my brother-in-laws, my sister-in-laws . . . what I must tell them?

SUNNY: Why you worrying about them, they not looking after you.

MOTHIE: Disgrace. I tell you Sunny, it's a disgrace. First time thing like this happen in our family. What a good name I had. Nobody can say anything about my family. *(Wipes away a tear.)* My boy Prem, he's clever fuller. Every time I go home, first thing I ask for is my boy. He listen so nice to me. Yesterday he's hiding. I washed and all, and I thought funny, where's my boy. I call him, he's crying. I say son, why you crying and he says . . . he says he come home lunch time from school because he left his homework book behind. The front door was closed. He came through the back door. He saw my daughter, Sunny, he saw my daughter. She was sleeping with one man. *(He breaks down.)* She was sleeping with one man. How you like that? Since my wife died, I bring her up like one gold. I give my children everything. Look my position. I don't buy for myself. I give my children everything. I want my children must marry nicely, not like this. Every penny I get, I put one side, that one day word will come for her and I'll marry and I'll give it. Now she gon do a thing like this to me, she gon do a thing like this.

When my son told me I got mad. I gave her one punch in the mouth. See here—teeth marks. *(To* STRANGER*)* You too look, bhai. But she never fall down. She just run away. Now don't know where she's gone.

SUNNY: Don't worry Mothie, she must be one of your connections' place. Don't worry, you'll find her.

MOTHIE: Why she must do this thing to me? Why she must do this thing to me? Never mind, gimme nother one wine.

SUNNY: Sure.

MOTHIE: Wait, wait, wait. I gon wash my face and come. Same time I gon make nother one piss and come. *(Exit.)*

STRANGER: Kids nowadays cause a lot of problems.

SUNNY: True's God. You know when we was lighties we couldn't catch a joll like today's lighties. We used to get it—one day my father hit me with a sjambok.

STRANGER: Today they've got the free life. Even the teachers can't hit them. What's the good of that? We used to get six of the best if we didn't learn our lessons. Today I'm not sorry.

SUNNY: Me too. That day my father hit me with a sjambok I wanted to pull out from the pozzie.

STRANGER: I felt like doing that once or twice myself but today I'm not sorry.

SUNNY: Sure that time, hell my father was angry. I never saw him so angry in all my life. You see, where we used to stay—you heard of Bulwa's farm?

STRANGER: Bulwa's farm . . .

SUNNY: You don't know Bulwa's Farm?

STRANGER: Huh, huh.

SUNNY: Hell if you don't know Bulwa's Farm then you can't be staying on the North Coast. Even if you staying in Stanger you must know Bulwa's Farm.

STRANGER: No I don't live on the North Coast . . .

SUNNY: Bulwa's farm is the biggest and best farm. You know when you coming by the Main Road, just by the dip you see lot, lot mandarin trees . . .

STRANGER: On the right-hand side, where those huge fences are?

SUNNY: That's it.

STRANGER: So that's Bulwa's Farm? You know I come up this way every fort-night and I always admire those lovely mandarins—huge juicy-looking ones—and I often wonder how come those mandarins never seem to get to the Indian market . . .

SUNNY: Oh, this fuller sends it to the English Market.

STRANGER: I see.

SUNNY: Anyway one day me and my friend decided to steal the mandarins.

STRANGER: Steal the mandarins! But what about those huge fences?

SUNNY: When you want anything for nothing . . . fence, wall, everything disappears.

STRANGER: You've got a point there.

SUNNY: We checked nobody was around and we got into the farm. My friend got into the tree. While he's throwing them down I'm filling away. While I'm filling away I checked these two ous behind nother one tree. I left the bag, everything. I grabbed my friend and one way we pulled out like lightning.

STRANGER: But didn't you check who was behind the trees?

SUNNY: That time, where you got time to check? That night that old man Bulwa came home, man . . .

STRANGER: But how did he know it was you?

SUNNY: My old man's bag gave us away, man.

STRANGER: But how did he know it was your old man's bag?

SUNNY: These old people got habit of writing their name on the bag, bro. Any-way he brought the bag and showed my father. He said look Kisten, green, green mandarins. I don't mind if the mandarins ripe but it's not nice to cut green mandarins—and he looked at me and he said, if you want mandarins my boy why never come and ask nicely? Why you must steal like a rogue? Bloody hell, he'll give anything for nothing. . . . When he went away my father took the sjambok. One thing he didn't like—stealing. Hell, he gave it to me. Nowadays the lighties don't catch it like that.

STRANGER: Definitely not: that's why they're so spoilt.

SUNNY: Hey but that Bulwa was good, man. The mandarins were ripe ripe, and he says they were green.

STRANGER: He must have been color-blind.

SUNNY: He's dead now. But he was a big lahnee. One of his son's became a teacher. Nother son became a doctor. This fuller went overseas and studied.

STRANGER: Yeah, you get these chaps. They battle hard from scratch and then they give their children all the things they never had in life.

SUNNY: So you don't live on the North Coast. Where you from bro?

STRANGER: From Carlisle Street.

SUNNY: Town?

STRANGER: Yes. I'm living in a flat. We used to live in Mayville. We had a big cottage, but now it's a white area.

SUNNY: Mayville was a nice place, huh? My uncle and them used to live in Blinkbonnie Road. We used to go there for porridge prayers.

STRANGER: Blinkbonnie Road? What's your Uncle's name?

SUNNY: Nagan. He used to work in the laundry.

STRANGER: Nagan?

SUNNY: He was a good soccerite—he played for Mayville—he was a fantastic player . . .

STRANGER: Wait a minute, I think I know him . . .

SUNNY: He was well known in Mayville. He was on the Temple Committee and all. He played soccer for Mayville. Hey, my Uncle was a fantastic soccerite . . .

STRANGER: His name sounds very familiar . . .

SUNNY: Wait, wait. You know Surprise Laundry?

STRANGER: Yes.

SUNNY: There by the bioscope?

STRANGER: Yes, yes.

SUNNY: Well my uncle was married to Surprise Laundry's daughter!

STRANGER: That's it! Now it all comes back. We played around there when we were kids. His house was near the river. He used to give us hints when we played ball—with a little tennis ball of course—and he'd give the winning team sweets. He was a fine man. All those memories come flooding back. What a great place Mayville was . . .

SUNNY: You-all had a big place there bro?

STRANGER: Yes, Sunny. You know, we built that house ourselves. My father was a baker's driver and he earned very little, but he always had this dream that he would one day build his own house. From the little he got he put enough together and we all pitched in. Every afternoon after school the whole family would give a hand, and we eventually built it. Our own house. We lived so happily there until the whites came and they just kicked us out . . .

SUNNY: What, they gave you-all lot money bro?

STRANGER: A lot of money, hell! They paid us peanuts—and now I'll bet they'll sell the same place for ten times the price!

SUNNY: Yeah, the wit ous can do anything and they can get away with it.

STRANGER: The trouble is we let them get away with it.

SUNNY: What can you do bro? You say anything, you're gone. Me, when my lahnee say anything I keep quiet. My job comes first. When I want anything from a wit ou I say Sir. They get very happy when you call them Sir.

STRANGER: I never call a white man sir. I don't even call my boss sir. The trouble is we're too scared.

SUNNY: But the wit ous get thrilled when you call them sir.

STRANGER: But Sunny . . .

SUNNY: I'll tell you how I got out of trouble once, through calling them sir. One day the boss told me I can take off. He put the other barman in my place and I told the wife, get dressed—I'm taking you town bioscope. I got one Morris Thousand . . .

STRANGER: Morris Thousand, now that was a good car.

SUNNY: Yeah, I painted it yellow with green stripes and all.

STRANGER: Must have been a very colorful car!

SUNNY: Yeah! I even got that long blue aerial. We all got into the car and we coming, bro. Then suddenly this big Boere cop stopped me. I pulled up one side and I told the kids, duck away in the back. I thought he gonna charge me for overloading but he reckon—What's a matter, bliksem, don't you know your tail lights are not working?—I said, sorry sir, I didn't know sir.—What you mean, you don't know? You must check these things before you drive, jong—I say, I'm sorry sir, I made a mistake sir, give me a break sir and I'll fix it up sir. He looked at me and he say—Alright, you coolie . . .

STRANGER: Coolie!

SUNNY: Yeah! Alright, you coolie—you better fix it up. Next time I'll fine you. I bet you if I didn't say sir he would have fined me.

STRANGER: I would rather have paid the fine! Nobody calls me a coolie or a bliksem—not even a cop.

SUNNY: Yeah, but sometimes it pays to act stupid. What you going to get by arguing? Look how many fullers they put in the jail when they say something about the white people. They put you in jail for nothing. They come and take you away in the night. What they call that when they take you away?

STRANGER: You mean they detain you.

SUNNY: Something like that. If they detain me who's going to buy bread for my kids, tell me that?

STRANGER: All of us don't think like that.

SUNNY: Wait, wait. Answer me that, when they . . . what you call that?

STRANGER: Detain you.

SUNNY: When they detain you who's going to pay the rent, and buy your children's food and all. Who's going to do that?

STRANGER: If we think like that things will never change.

SUNNY: But answer me that. Nobody! Not even your own brothers and sisters will help you. So why you want to break your neck? No, bro—me, I rather work hard and look after my family. Everyday I see in the paper they taking somebody away. What's going to happen to their families? You and I going to help them? No bro, I got too much trouble of my own.

STRANGER: Hold on. Hold on. You've been working here for twelve and a half years—right?

SUNNY: Right.

STRANGER: How much do you get?

SUNNY: R100 a month.

STRANGER: What does a white barman get?

SUNNY: Lot more.

STRANGER: Now tell me, why does he get more, Sunny? You are doing the same job.

SUNNY: What can you do bro? You just got to keep your mouth shut and take it. Otherwise you won't even get a job.

STRANGER: But Sunny, we've got to fight for our rights . . .

SUNNY: Bro, look at me—I got no education, nothing . . .

STRANGER: It's got nothing to do with education. It's a question of your rights. You were born in this country, why should you be treated differently . . .
(Enter MOTHIE.)

MOTHIE: Arreh, chee! Chee! Chee! I went there to make piss but number two came out. Chee, chee! The lavatory stinking. Better tell your lahnee to get us better lavatory. Everyday we come and spend our money and they give us stinking lavatory.

SUNNY: I don't know how many times I told my lahnee.

MOTHIE: Don't bluff, you never tell him. You frightened fuller, you.

SUNNY: Oh shut up, Mothie man—why I must fright to tell him thing like that? But some of our fullers too, man, they terrible, they mess the lavatory up.

MOTHIE: Hell, got one bucket there . . .

STRANGER: One bucket for all of you . . .

MOTHIE: One bucket! Everybody must use. What you expect, must get full up. I feel sorry for the fuller who must carry it. Haven't even got one chain lavatory like the white fuller got.

SUNNY: What you mean, chain lavatory?

MOTHIE: When you pull the chain, you silly fuller, the water comes out and all the shit gets washed away . . .

SUNNY: You got chain lavatory by your house?

MOTHIE: No, but . . .

SUNNY: Have you got it, yes or no?

MOTHIE: No, but you see . . .

SUNNY: No buts. If you got bucket lavatory by your house you must keep it clean, right. Then why you can't keep it clean here then?

MOTHIE: Hey, my house not bar. Lot, lot people don't use my bucket. My bucket don't get full up. You talking shit, you man. And the place where you make piss too—there too they haven't got water coming out from the pipe like automatic.

SUNNY: Like what?

MOTHIE: Like it's automatic, man—it works on its own like automatic car that change gear and all by itself. Hey, what you think I'm stupid? You think I never go to school?

SUNNY: Awright, don't shout man, I told you the lahnee's next door.

MOTHIE: You must tell your lahnee next time he want to make shit, he must make shit in our lavatory and then you see how he likes it. He'll never go there . . .

STRANGER: He most certainly won't go there, Uncle . . .

SUNNY: But some of our fullers too, man.

MOTHIE: Hey what you mean? *(Mocking)* Some of our fullers too, man! What, you think we dirty people what? Our girls don't use scent and . . . what that thing they put here?

STRANGER: Deodorant.

MOTHIE: Same thing. Our girls don't use all that. You know why? They must bathe everyday in running water when they light the god lamp. We don't eat beef and pork. We don't smell like the white people. Our girls don't smell like the white girls.

SUNNY: Hey, you saw the white girls smelling, you saw them smelling?

MOTHIE: Arreh! I'll tell you, I'll tell you. *(To* STRANGER*)* You know bhai, everyday when I'm on the tractor, my boss's daughters come and play fools with me . . . *(Mimics English accent)* Mothie! Mothie!—Me I hold my nose and run away. *(Pause)* Yeah bhai, me I taught my daughter so nicely. When her Mother died I brought her up like a gold. Not easy to bring up a girl, you know that. My sister said she must come and stay with her. I don't know why I never send her. You know me Sunny, I'm very independent fuller. I said I'll bring her up myself, I'll bring her up myself . . . gimme nother one wine Sunny!

SUNNY: No, no more Mothie.

MOTHIE: Gimme nother bloody wine, man!

SUNNY: Awright, don't shout.

MOTHIE: Wait, wait, I got no more money left.

STRANGER: It's alright Uncle, I'll pay for it.

MOTHIE: You rich fuller huh—I'm not a beggar.

STRANGER: You're definitely not a beggar.

MOTHIE: I left my money at home—I'll go bring it.

STRANGER: Don't worry, I'll pay for it.

MOTHIE: Thank you bhai—when a man got trouble what else he can do. True's God I feel like drinking so much I must drop down dead.

SUNNY: Do you know this chap who interfered with your daughter?

MOTHIE: If I catch him, I'll kill him with my bare hands. They don't know me yet. The polices don't know me yet. They laugh at me! What they think? I'm going by his house and I'm going to hit him in his own house.

SUNNY: What's his name?

MOTHIE: I'll hit him in his own house. What they think! They don't know me yet. You ask anyone here in Mount Edgecombe, bhai. Go outside and ask. Ask them about Mothie. I don't look for trouble. I mind my own business but when anyone make trouble for me, hell!

SUNNY: Who's this chap?

MOTHIE: Last time by the working place I hit one fuller . . .

SUNNY: There we go again—number one story teller!

MOTHIE: I hit this fuller, bhai. You know what he did? I'm working so nicely, I don't say nothing to nobody. This fuller go'n burn me by the Lahnee.

STRANGER: What did he do Uncle?

MOTHIE: He go'n tell the Lahnee I'm ducking work and going home lunch time. For nothing. Jealous fuller. You know, the Lahnee likes me. I hit him one shot in front of the Lahnee. He fell down. I told him, prove it. He didn't know what to say. The Lahnee started laughing. He say awright Mothie, leave him, I believe you. So good name I got in Mount Edgecombe. What you think I must keep quiet now?

SUNNY: But who's this chap interfered with your daughter, man?

MOTHIE: You know Boywa?

SUNNY: Which Boywa?

MOTHIE: Boywa Singh—that fuller fell down from the tree . . .

SUNNY: Oh that Boywa—(To STRANGER) Hey, helluva thing happened to that fuller, bro.

MOTHIE: The spook killed him.

SUNNY: That's the strangest thing happened in Mount Edgecombe.

STRANGER: Is that so?

MOTHIE: Up to today they don't know how that thing happened. There's a spook in that tree. I tell all the children twelve o'clock time don't go by the tree—but where they'll listen?

STRANGER: Where's this tree?

MOTHIE: There by the Main Road, near the school—that big gum-tree tree.

STRANGER: What happened?

MOTHIE: You see Boywa fell down by the tree . . .

SUNNY: No wait, you saying it all wrong, let me say it.

MOTHIE: Hell, what you think, I don't know? You lightie you man, you born in front of me. I know everything here in Mount Edgecombe . . .

SUNNY: (To STRANGER) You see this is what happened. Boywa was sitting by the house and then night time about nine o'clock he got up from bed . . .

MOTHIE: Not nine o'clock, 12 o'clock, man. You see you don't know nothing. Spooks don't come out nine o'clock, they come out 12 o'clock.

SUNNY: Awright, must have been 12 o'clock! Boywa got up, opened the door and went by this tree. His wife got up little later and she saw Boywa walking to this tree. He was walking like a Zombie—you saw this picture Frankenstein—hey nice picture, eh? Why they don't make picture like that now?

STRANGER: What happened to Boywa?

SUNNY: He was walking to the tree *(Demonstrates)*. His wife was running behind him and she was shouting, Boywa! Boywa! But this bloody bugger never stopped man . . .

MOTHIE: Arreh, how he can stop when the spook was making him walk . . .

SUNNY: Wait man . . .

MOTHIE: When you tell one story you must say it nicely, otherwise don't bloody say it.

SUNNY: Awright, awright. Now where I was bro?

STRANGER: Boywa's wife was shouting for him . . .

SUNNY: That's right. His wife was shouting so much, all the district people got up.

MOTHIE: Me too, I got up too. I got so frightened, with my singlet and pajamas I ran away in the yard. I went by the tree and I told all the people, now don't get excited. And I spoke to Boywa nicely. I said hey Boywa, come down reh Boywa, come down reh Boywa. Arreh mai! This fuller started climbing fast like one monkey.

STRANGER: Don't be silly!

MOTHIE: Then I got cross. I shouted, Boywa you better come down now! Then what happened?

STRANGER: Yeah, what happened?

MOTHIE: This fuller started singing.

STRANGER: Singing? He must have been drunk!

MOTHIE: No bhai, Boywa never drink . . .

SUNNY: Boywa never drink, never smoked, he never did nothing this fuller, man.

STRANGER: That's very strange. Go on, what happened next?

MOTHIE: This fuller started climbing again. He got to the top, right to the top, the branch got broken, Boywa fell down, broke his neck and died! Same Boywa Singh!

SUNNY: Not his son!

MOTHIE: No, his connection. They too live in Verulam. He got one green Anglia car.

SUNNY: You saw him?

MOTHIE: No, but my son saw him.

SUNNY: How you know he's Boywa's connection?

MOTHIE: Hell, you think I'm stupid? My son saw him by Boywa's house one day.

SUNNY: You mad. Just because he was there that means he's Boywa's connection? What's his name?

MOTHIE: Johnny.

SUNNY: Johnny? He got long hair?

MOTHIE: Same fuller, you know him?

SUNNY: You know what you do? You go to the police station and lay your complaint now before you get too drunk. Otherwise they'll lock you up.

MOTHIE: That will be the day. They must just lock me up and you'll see. I'll go straight to the magistrate, me . . .

SUNNY: Why don't you listen to me, man?

STRANGER: I think that's a good idea—you can come back after that. The important thing is to find your daughter.

(Enter the LAHNEE.*)*

LAHNEE: That's right, my friend—you'd better go to the police. See Sergeant Labuschagne—Tell him I sent you.

MOTHIE: You know my troubles, boss?

LAHNEE: Yes, I heard it loud and clear. You Indians certainly know how to use your vocal chords.

MOTHIE: I'll listen to you boss, but last time I went they was laughing at me, boss.

LAHNEE: Who laughed at you?

MOTHIE: One Indian and one African policeman. Police must take complaint, they musn't laugh—not right boss?

LAHNEE: Well the way you're carrying on—snot and tears all over the bloody floor, they must have laughed at you. They were just having a little fun I suppose. They won't laugh this time. You go see Sergeant Labuschagne.

MOTHIE: Sure boss, I'll have one more drink and I'll go.

LAHNEE: No more drinks.

MOTHIE: Please boss, one more.

LAHNEE: Look, do you want me to help you or not?

MOTHIE: Sure boss, right away boss, I'm going now boss.

LAHNEE: Okay, I'll phone Sgt. Labuschagne and tell him you're coming.

(Exit MOTHIE.*)*

(To SUNNY *after a cursory glance at the* STRANGER*)* Christ, what the hell do you people think this is—the Indian Market?

(Exit LAHNEE.*)*

SUNNY: You see, if you're nice to a white man, you see how they'll help you out.

STRANGER: Yes I suppose that's true—if you're a good little black boy and say yes boss, all the damned time . . .

SUNNY: Leave all that bro, just now that Johnny fuller is going to come here . . .

STRANGER: Which Johnny?

SUNNY: That fuller interfering with the old man's daughter, man.

STRANGER: You sure it's him, Sunny?

SUNNY: Must be him. He comes here every afternoon to pull fah-fee. If anybody interfering with girl in Mount Edgecombe it must be this Johnny fuller.

STRANGER: Then why didn't you tell the old man.

SUNNY: No bro, the old man will only mess things up. I got one plan you see . . .

STRANGER: Yeah, you're right. We've got to handle this one carefully, But I've got to deliver a parcel around here first. I've got to see Mr. M. P. Naidoo, the school principal. Do you know where he lives?

SUNNY: Oh that principal fuller? Short, bald-headed fuller? Right. You go down the Main Road. First turn left—dirt road. Next turn right. Then you take nother one turn right—Koonjebeharie Road—third house with green roof.

STRANGER: Thanks. I'll be back as soon as I deliver the parcel. Now if this Johnny chap gets here, try to keep him here. Just get him talking. When I get back we'll put the screws on him. We've got to help the old man out. I'll be back just now.

(Curtain.)

ACT TWO

(Sunny is cleaning some glasses when the phone rings.)

SUNNY: Hello! What? O, the Lahnee? Must be in his office somewhere. Put the call there man. *(Slams the phone down.)* Bloody fullers worrying me for nothing.

(Enter the STRANGER.)

STRANGER: Sorry I'm late Sunny, the principal kept me. Did Johnny come in while I was away?

SUNNY: No bro, but he must come here now to have his beer.

STRANGER: Good. This is what we'll do. We must pretend that we don't know anything.

SUNNY: That's right. We'll act like we don't know nothing. Then we'll slowly fish him out.

STRANGER: Right. We must find out where that girl is first and then . . .

(Sounds of music from outside.)

SUNNY: Ssssh, here he comes now.

(Enter JOHNNY. In his early twenties. Cool, current gear and long hair. Carrying a portable tape player, he dances his way in.)

SUNNY: *(Loudly to STRANGER)* Lot of China-guava trees in Mayville, eh?

JOHNNY: Hi Sunny! Hi there! *(Places his portable on the table and dances.)*

SUNNY: Hello Johnny. Put that damn thing slowly.

JOHNNY: What's the matter. You don't appreciate good music?

SUNNY: You call that good music?

JOHNNY: Give me a pint of ice-cold beer, dad.

SUNNY: You can't even hear what the singer is singing—good music!

JOHNNY: That's the style dad. You got to get with it.

SUNNY: Turn that thing slow Johnny, man. What my Lahnee will say, man?

JOHNNY: Awright, awright. You don't like this music. Want classic? *(Plays tape.)* How's this number from Khabi Khabi—crazy movie. You saw it?

SUNNY: Put it off man. I hear it's a good film. *(To* STRANGER*)* Did you see it?

STRANGER: No, I don't know when last I saw an Indian film. Aren't these films all alike? I mean, boy meets girl and they fall in love and dance through the trees. Then boy meets another girl and the first girl commits suicide after singing a sad song . . .

JOHNNY: Not this movie dad, it's way out and you got to see the chicks—wow, like crazy man.

STRANGER: Really? That's a welcome change.

JOHNNY: Real entertainment, and the music . . . *(Turns the tape louder.)*

SUNNY: Hey, Johnny man, I told you. *(*JOHNNY *switches it off).* What's doh-die today?

JOHNNY: Thirty-six.

SUNNY: Last night I dreamt of a lot of frogs. What number is that?

JOHNNY: Frogs? That should be fish—that's number 24.

SUNNY: There—play me sixty cents. *(To* STRANGER*)* You want to play?

STRANGER: What time are they pulling?

JOHNNY: Seven o'clock.

STRANGER: Too late for me.

JOHNNY: The Chinaman only comes here at seven-thirty.

STRANGER: You make enough money this way?

JOHNNY: It's okay.

SUNNY: Don't worry about this fuller, bro. He's a Lahnee. You want to buy a radio, tape recorder, those dirty books they keep underneath? See Johnny.

JOHNNY: Anything pal, anything. You name it, Johnny's got it.

SUNNY: Plenty of dames too, huh?

JOHNNY: Span.

SUNNY: *(Winks at* STRANGER*)* I hear you got a crazy bok in Mount Edgecombe?

JOHNNY: All over, dad, all over. I pitch my tent in one spot and if I like it I stick around for a while. Then I split. I'm like lightning—I never strike twice in the same spot.

SUNNY: Okay Lightning, who is this dame you have in Mount Edgecombe?

JOHNNY: She's lekker eksê. Crazy pair of legs, long black hair and crazy tits. Hey—who told you about this bok?

SUNNY: Everybody knows Johnny around here.

JOHNNY: But nobody saw me with her. She's a home bird—you know what I mean. Nice clean dame. It's a crazy set-up—there's no one at home during the day. She's alone.

STRANGER: Pardon me for asking, but is she in love with you?

JOHNNY: Love is for the birds.

STRANGER: That's how you feel. What about her?

JOHNNY: Yeah, she's in love with me. She wants to marry me.

STRANGER: Why don't you marry her?

JOHNNY: You know any more jokes?

SUNNY: How can you do that to a nice girl like that?

JOHNNY: She is a nice girl. She's never had a boyfriend before. She'll make some lucky guy a very nice wife.

STRANGER: Who is going to marry her after you've been messing around with her?

JOHNNY: That's not my affair. Hell, I haven't raped her.

STRANGER: That's not the point . . .

JOHNNY: Hold on, I'll tell you how I met her. I was driving down the road when I saw this chick. I slowed down and I hooted. She didn't even look at me. I said, Howzit Baby! Made like she didn't hear me. I turned my car around and I stopped. She was going to the shop. When she came out she didn't even look at me. I reckon, I'm going to get you baby. I waited for her at the same spot for three days and then she stopped one day and said—Haven't you got any work to do? So I reckon, I don't need to work, I'm my own boss. Then I asked her how she liked my tape, Khabi Khabi—I was sommer vasing it loud . . .

SUNNY: She must have been deaf like you.

JOHNNY: What you know? She smiled—but just then someone came past and she walked away. I followed her and we started talking about music—and then just like that . . . now she's in love with me.

STRANGER: You must have told her you love her a lot and want to marry her, otherwise she wouldn't have gone to bed with you.

JOHNNY: Who said she went to bed with me?

SUNNY: Come on Johnny, I know you're a shark.

JOHNNY: I told her no such thing—I just told her I smaak her a span—no promises, nothing.

SUNNY: That's the same as telling her you're in love with her.

STRANGER: Of course.

JOHNNY: Never, I made no promises.

STRANGER: That's not the point . . .

JOHNNY: Hey hold on, what are you guys getting at?

SUNNY: What you mean what we are getting at?

JOHNNY: The way you guys are asking me questions it looks as if you guys have got something up your sleeves.

STRANGER: We don't even know the girl.

SUNNY: But I got a daughter and I don't like anyone treating her like that. Look bro, if I catch any of these fullers treating her like that I kill them, me. I kill them.

JOHNNY: Your daughter may love the guy.

SUNNY: Bullshit—love only comes after you get married and have children. She wants to go out with someone, he must bring his father and mother home first. Hell, in our days if we wanted to take a girl out we had to marry her, even if we took our mother and father by the girl's house.

JOHNNY: That's your days dad, not today.

STRANGER: Girls are too free these days—that is why they get into trouble.

JOHNNY: You guys must have had a hard time. What did you do for fun—play marbles?

STRANGER: What do you think your mother and father did before they got married?

JOHNNY: *(Angrily)* There's no need to pick on my parents, okay?

STRANGER: Don't get upset, we're just having a friendly discussion.

JOHNNY: *(Picks up his portable to leave)* Watch it—you're getting too personal, the both of you. If you don't smaak the man's company, say so. *(Both protest but JOHNNY leaves in a huff.)*

STRANGER: Looks like we blew it.

SUNNY: Don't worry, he'll be back just now when all the workers come here. He'll be back before then. Good thing he left too because Mothie may be back anytime now.

STRANGER: That's good, we can still trap him. We can't allow him to abuse a girl from a good family and get away with it. He must know where the girl is—that's the most important thing. We must help the old man find his daughter. Another drink, please.

SUNNY: You know what we'll do . . .

(Enter Mothie.)

MOTHIE: Who's that fuller left here just now? He got no bloody respect that bloody swine. He walking so fast he knocked me. He didn't say sorry, nothing. He jumped in his bloody car and vroom, vroom he skidded the car. What he thinks he's a racing driver?

SUNNY: Leave all that. What happened when you went police station?

MOTHIE: Hey, they was very nice man. Hey call Mr. Simpson. I want to thank him—they was very nice man.

SUNNY: What happened?

MOTHIE: I went there. That same police fuller was there. I said I want to see Sgt. Lab . . . what the name the boss gave?

STRANGER: *(French pronunciation)* Sgt. Labuschagne.

SUNNY: Hey, what Labooshain? This is Boere fuller, eksê . . . *(Afrikaans pronunciation)* Labuschagne.

MOTHIE: Same one, same one. I said I want to see him. Hell that Hindian fuller got frightened man. He say—don't worry you can give me your complaint. He spoke so nice to me. Sgt. Labuschagne came out and he say—Moosa, take a van and go and find that girl now. I took him home and I showed him a photo of my daughter. He's looking for her now. In the van he's talking so nicely to me. He don't know all the Lahnees in Mount Edgecombe my friends. He don't know me yet.

STRANGER: Uncle, was this a recent photograph?

MOTHIE: What, bhai?

STRANGER: Sorry, was this a new picture of your daughter?

MOTHIE: Yeah, they took in the wedding. My cousin daughter got married. They took in the wedding.

SUNNY: Who's wedding was this?

MOTHIE: Kalyawathie's wedding. You forgot—you too same.

SUNNY: Oh yes, yes. I went, bro.

MOTHIE: Sunny came wearing suit, boot. So smart. So nice wedding. Boy from Chatsworth. He come from good home—made of good bricks. Gimme some more wine. Yeah, now they looking for her. That Moosa fuller don't know me yet.

STRANGER: I'll bet he knows you now.

MOTHIE: Of course. Now he knows he can't bugger around with me. Where's Mr. Simpson, I want to thank him.

SUNNY: He's busy man. He's talking to some white people.

MOTHIE: Arreh ja reh.

SUNNY: I told you he's busy man.

MOTHIE: *(As SUNNY gives him the wine and takes the money)* I brought money from the house.

What you drinking bhai? Cane eh? Give bhai nother one drink.

STRANGER: No thanks, I've had enough.

MOTHIE: Don't worry, I'm giving free.

STRANGER: That's very nice of you, but I've had enough.

MOTHIE: One more.

SUNNY: Hey what you keep asking like tape recorder? Take your drink and sit down there.

MOTHIE: I must find my daughter tonight. I must find her tonight.

STRANGER: Don't worry Uncle, the police will find her for you. *(Takes him to his table.)* They have a picture of her and it won't be long before they find her.

MOTHIE: I don't know where she is. I don't know where she is. I don't know what she done with herself.

SUNNY: Don't talk like that Mothie. She must be with one of her friends. Just because you hit her one time, you mustn't worry. You did right thing. She'll learn her lesson. She must know she comes from a good family. Don't worry, God is watching.

MOTHIE: Ram, Ram. I'm praying she don't do something funny to herself. But she haven't got sarrie.

SUNNY: What you mean she haven't got sarrie?

MOTHIE: She haven't got sarrie man. You don't know what sarrie is?

SUNNY: I know what sarrie is—but why you say she haven't got sarrie?

MOTHIE: You don't read newspapers, what?

SUNNY: What you mean man?

MOTHIE: You see in the newspapers every time girls taking sarrie from the wardrobe and they hang themselves from the mango tree.

STRANGER: Don't jump to conclusions. Mount Edgecombe is a small place. The police will find her just now. Have your wine.

MOTHIE: Wine is the best thing, eh bhai? Every day you work, you work, work, work—that's all. You don't look for trouble. Why God must do this to me?

SUNNY: That's your Karma.

MOTHIE: Everytime I go temple. I do puja—I do everything. Why God must do this to me? Wine is the best thing—gimme nother one wine.

SUNNY: Take it easy.

MOTHIE: If I want to drink, my business. You think I'm drunk what? See here I can stand one leg. *(Tries and* STRANGER *saves him from falling.)* You leave me alone. Sunny says I'm drunk. I'll prove to you I'm not drunk. *(*STRANGER *and* SUNNY *attempt to stop him but he tries again. This time he almost hits the floor and the* STRANGER *grabs him at the last moment.)*

STRANGER: You better stop this nonsense!

*(*MOTHIE *is taken and deposited on a chair by the* STRANGER *and* SUNNY.*)*

MOTHIE: Hell I'm tired, man. All I need is nother one wine and you'll see how straight I'll stand.

SUNNY: Just shut up and sit there. We are trying our best to help you and you carrying on like this.

STRANGER: Yes, we can find your daughter if you behave yourself.

MOTHIE: You know where my daughter is?

STRANGER: We think we can help you find her.

MOTHIE: How you can help me find her? You don't know where she is.

(Enter LAHNEE*)*

LAHNEE: Oh no, not you again.

MOTHIE: Oh, hello boss, thank you boss. The police was so nice to me. Thank you boss.

LAHNEE: *(Affecting Indian accent)* Don't worry Uncle, don't worry. The polices will find your daughter. Just sit down same place and catch one dop.

MOTHIE: But Sunny don't want to give me wine.

LAHNEE: *(Playfully to* SUNNY*)* Silly fuller you. Give you one shot. Give one dop to him. Otherwise I fix you up. *(Exit laughing.)* Bloody idiot!

MOTHIE: Lekker Lahnee. You see how he likes me.

STRANGER: *(Finding it difficult to control his anger)* You see how they talk to us Sunny.

SUNNY: Don't worry man.

STRANGER: They think we're a bunch of idiots.

SUNNY: Let them think what they want—You know you're not an idiot,

STRANGER: I just don't like their bloody attitude.

SUNNY: That's life—you got clever fullers one side and you got stupid fullers one side. Clever fullers don't want to act clever. If you want to get somewhere you must act stupid.

STRANGER: Just who the hell do they think they are? What makes them so damn superior? You know something, when these guys were walking around in caves wearing animal skins, our people were building temples in India. When they were hanging on to raw meat, our people were cooking their food . . . and . . . and . . . and you know something else?—Counting, numerals—where do you think they learned it from? They learned it from us! They learned it from the Indians. Now they walk all over us and you guys just sit there—yes sir, no sir. God, you make me sick!

SUNNY: Talking about Indian fullers, I remembering something. You know when that great Indian singer Pithukuli Murugudas came to this country he said, you'll laughing because I'm speaking English this way. Just imagine how I'm laughing when you-all talking Tamil.

STRANGER: I just can't understand you chaps, Sunny.

SUNNY: Look bro, I may act stupid but I know what I'm doing. Look I'm a barman, but I got my own house, I got my own car. Nothing short in my house. I give my family everything. Nothing short in my house.

MOTHIE: *(Breaking out into paroxysms of laughter)* Barmans clever fullers, bhai—when nobody looking they pour short tots.

SUNNY: When you saw me pouring short tots, eh, when you saw me pouring short tots?

MOTHIE: I never saw you. You too clever you. You got the draat. Never mine, that's your business.

SUNNY: I don't pour short tots. I work hard, me.

STRANGER: I'm sure you do.

SUNNY: I don't do things like that, I don't want to be like that Johnny fuller. I
don't want to go to jail.

MOTHIE: Which Johnny?

(Pause as SUNNY *looks at* STRANGER.*)*

STRANGER: You better tell him.

SUNNY: Same ou.

MOTHIE: What you mean same ou.

SUNNY: Same ou messing around with your daughter.

MOTHIE: You know him?

SUNNY: He was here just now.

MOTHIE: Where's he? Where's that bloody bastard. I'll kill him.

SUNNY: Same fuller knocked you before.

MOTHIE: That fuller with the long hair?

SUNNY: Same ou.

MOTHIE: Then why you never tell me?

SUNNY: We got one plan.

STRANGER: He's coming back just now.

SUNNY: First you must listen to us—we'll trap him.

MOTHIE: I don't want to trap him. I want to kill him.

SUNNY: Don't be silly, Mothie man. We're trying to help you. Just shut up and listen.

MOTHIE: Awright.

SUNNY: He's going to come back here just now. I know him—he comes and pulls
fah-fee.

MOTHIE: That's the fuller, huh? I saw him here once or twice but I don't pull
fah-fee. I don't gamble. Gambling very bad—devil's job that. How you know
same fuller that?

SUNNY: He told us.

MOTHIE: What he told you?

SUNNY: You wasting time. He's going to come back just now. Now you must
listen to us.

STRANGER: Uncle, you must listen to Sunny. We must find your daughter. To do
that we've got to play our cards right.

MOTHIE: I don't play cards—bad game that.

STRANGER: I don't mean play cards.

MOTHIE: Then what you mean? I don't play cards, I don't pull that fah-fee. I only
drink wine . . .

SUNNY: Awright, awright . . .

STRANGER: Now when Johnny comes back . . .

SUNNY: When he comes back you must act like you don't know him.

MOTHIE: Act like I don't know him? I'll take this bottle and bust it on his head!
Act like I don't know him!

STRANGER: You just go and do that . . . and if your daughter hasn't committed suicide already, then she'll definitely commit suicide, if you kill Johnny.

MOTHIE: I won't kill him . . . I'll cripple him.

SUNNY: Shut up man, and listen. You must act like you don't know him. We'll talk to him. Then we'll ask him who this girl is, what he did to her—you mustn't say one word.

STRANGER: We'll be your witnesses. What's your daughter's age?

MOTHIE: Fifteen.

STRANGER: Fifteen! You can charge him because she's underage.

SUNNY: But we won't charge him if he tells us where your daughter is and if he agrees to marry her.

MOTHIE: I don't want my daughter to marry rubbish fuller like that. What work he does?

STRANGER: He doesn't work.

MOTHIE: That's right, he only pulls fah-fee!

STRANGER: He's an intelligent chap, he can get a good job.

SUNNY: That fuller got more money than you and I put together. I know. He's not so stupid.

MOTHIE: But he's rubbish fuller . . . (*Music in the background.*)

SUNNY: Ssssh, there's he! Same ou! Now act like you don't know him. (*Enter* JOHNNY) Nice place, London—eh bro?

STRANGER: (*To* JOHNNY) Hey Johnny, I'm sorry I upset you. I didn't mean . . .

SUNNY: He was only talking, bro . . . Come on, have one beer?

JOHNNY: That's okay! How's this number. (*Puts the tape louder.*)

SUNNY: Lekker . . . but put it softly man. You know Lahnee's next door.

JOHNNY: (*Switches it off.*) Why don't you tell your Lahnee to go for a holiday?

STRANGER: Sunny, give him a beer . . .

JOHNNY: No thanks, I'll have one after fah-fee. (*Winks.*) Work comes first.

STRANGER: Aw come on, two beers won't make you drunk. (*Hands him the beer.*)

JOHNNY: Okay, thanks.

STRANGER: Johnny, I've been thinking. There's a job in my firm for a clerk. I've got plenty of say there. I can fix you up. How about it?

JOHNNY: Suddenly you like me. When must I cut my hair?

STRANGER: I'm serious. I like to see our chaps make a move in life—especially intelligent chaps like you.

JOHNNY: What's the pay?

STRANGER: I think about R120 a month.

JOHNNY: What, R120?

STRANGER: For a start . . .

JOHNNY: That's peanuts, man!

SUNNY: What you mean peanuts. I only get R100 a month here.

JOHNNY: It's okay for monkeys like you.

SUNNY: You watch your tongue you. I work honest job. I'm not ashamed of myself.

JOHNNY: Okay, okay, don't get so worked up. I also worked honest once. I left school because my parents couldn't afford to send me, like. I worked in this factory in Pinetown. Then this wit ou joined us. I had to teach him the job. He was a foreigner and he couldn't even speak English. I taught him everything and then he started pushing me around. How do you like that?

STRANGER: Same bloody scene all over!

JOHNNY: I took a good look around. Char ous were working there for years—longer than some of the wit ous, but they weren't earning more than even the lightie wit ous—even the foreigners.

STRANGER: And they just sit back and take everything!

JOHNNY: Not me, eksê! I quit. I tried to find another job . . .

SUNNY: If you don't like working for wit ous, why don't you work for char ous?

JOHNNY: They're even worse than the wit ous. They make you work in your lunchtime and all. Yeah I tell you, I looked all over for a job, looking in the newspapers, going for interviews . . . but everywhere I went they offered me peanuts, and the char ous—they offered me stale peanuts. Then I thought, why don't you be your own boss. That was it. I want to tell you something—I make more money in one month than you guys would make in three months.

STRANGER: Well I suppose that's okay in a way . . .

SUNNY: But the cops are going to get you one day.

JOHNNY: Don't tell me about cops, they're bigger crooks than I'll ever be.

STRANGER: What are you going to do with your money?

JOHNNY: I'm going to pull out of the country, man. There's no future here. Out there there's a whole lot of living. I want to go to a place where I can get the chance to live like a human being. Here you walk into a bazaar and some cheap white tit treats you like dirt.

STRANGER: But running away won't solve any problems.

JOHNNY: Who wants to solve problems? I got no time, daddio—I just want to live, man, live.

MOTHIE: You not worried about your mother and father, you!

JOHNNY: They can take care of themselves.

MOTHIE: Hey, you got no respect, you? If it wasn't for your mother and father, you won't be here . . . (*Gets up to remonstrate with* JOHNNY. *The* STRANGER *and* SUNNY *placate him.*)

JOHNNY: What's up with him?

STRANGER: Oh, don't worry about him, he's just had a hard day—that's all. You know, Johnny, I can never leave this country. I was telling Sunny here I was overseas recently. I agree with you. It's a whole new world. You can feel the freedom out there . . . and if a black guy can work half as hard as he works here he can earn himself a comfortable living. But the cost of living, now that's something else. You know Sunny, I paid one rand for a pint of beer!

SUNNY: What, one rand?

STRANGER: You'd never believe it . . .

JOHNNY: That's nothing, what about the women?

STRANGER: Is that all you think about?

SUNNY: Nothing else in your bloody head but only girls.

JOHNNY: Too much, dad, too much!

MOTHIE: Hey, where you come from, you, where you come from?

JOHNNY: Timbucktoo—where you come from?

MOTHIE: Timbucktoo! Timbucktoo. You got no respect. I'll show you! *(Gets up to tackle him.)*

STRANGER: *(Intervening—to* JOHNNY*)* He's upset over something . . .

MOTHIE: I'm not upset. What you saying I'm upset. I just want to give him one shot. I'll giving you hiding like your father never gave you . . .

JOHNNY: Old man like you.

MOTHIE: Old man? You calling me old man . . . *(Grabs a bottle.* STRANGER *wrestles it away from him.* SUNNY *also helps.)*

STRANGER: Sit down both of you.

SUNNY: Wait, Mothie, we are trying to help you. Leave it to us.

STRANGER: Just leave it to us. We will help you.

JOHNNY: What the hell is going on here?

STRANGER: You're in big trouble.

JOHNNY: Who, me?

SUNNY: Where did you take the girl to?

JOHNNY: What girl?

STRANGER: The girl you were telling us about. Come on, don't pretend like you didn't do anything. If you tell us where the girl is we'll sort this out without going to the police.

JOHNNY: You guys must be crazy. I don't know what you're talking about. If you feel like playing games, go find yourself another playmate. I'm getting sick and tired of this crap . . . *(Tries to leave but the* STRANGER *bars his way.)* Get out of my way.

STRANGER: What's the hurry?

JOHNNY: Get out of my way or you're going to get hurt. *(Whips out a knife—a fight follows.* MOTHIE*—who has grabbed a bottle at the start—is startled when he sees the knife. Shouting, "Watch out that fuller got knife!" he dodges at* *every thrust—although the thrusts are made at the* STRANGER. *Eventually the* STRANGER *gets the better of the fight. The* LAHNEE *enters.)*

LAHNEE: What the hell is going on here?

MOTHIE: That's the fuller boss, that's the fuller!

JOHNNY: Old man, just get off my bloody back!

LAHNEE: Shut up the both of you. Will somebody tell me what exactly is going on? (MOTHIE *and* JOHNNY *move to continue the fight)* If the both of you don't sit down I'll throw you out. Carrying on like a bunch of idiots . . .
(The phone rings.)

LAHNEE: *(Picks up the phone)* Hello. Yes . . . Oh hello, Sergeant . . . Yes . . . He's right here, carrying on like a bloody idiot . . . What? . . . No, that can't be, they've got the culprit right here . . . Are you sure? . . . Well that sorts out everything . . . Where? . . . I'll tell Mothie that . . . Thanks a lot. I'll see you later. Bye.

MOTHIE: Good job! The police coming to take that fuller away. *(Pointing to* JOHNNY.*)*

JOHNNY: Shit! *(Gets up to go but the* STRANGER *bars his way again.)*

LAHNEE: You got the wrong man, Mothie.

MOTHIE: Don't joke boss, this no time for jokes . . .

LAHNEE: I said you've got the wrong man, that was Sergeant Labuschagne on the line . . .

MOTHIE: What he told you?

LAHNEE: He said they've found your daughter . . .

MOTHIE: Arreh, where they found her?

LAHNEE: *(Chuckling)* They found her by one fuller's house. That fuller say he going to marry your daughter . . .

MOTHIE: Don't make jokes, boss . . .

JOHNNY: I've had enough of this. *(Wants to leave, but the* STRANGER *apologetically restrains him.)*

STRANGER: I'm sorry, but this clown made me believe . . .

LAHNEE: Your daughter is with her boyfriend's parents. They're coming to make one big proposal . . .

MOTHIE: Arreh Ram! How much I prayed. How much I prayed. I'm sorry Jonnia, I'm sorry everybody . . .

LAHNEE: Now you going to have one big, big wedding. Don't forget to bring me some curry and rice . . .

MOTHIE: I'll bring you lot boss . . .
(While this conversation is going on the STRANGER *apologizes to* JOHNNY *and in low tones reflects on the old man's undignified response to the ridicule of the* LAHNEE.*)*

LAHNEE: Hey Mothie, have one nother one wine . . . and give those chaps a drink too . . .

STRANGER: No thanks, I'm leaving . . .

LAHNEE: Aw, come on Sammy, have one on me . . .

STRANGER: *(Whirling towards the* LAHNEE *in absolute fury)* My name is not Sammy! You got no right to call me Sammy! Sammy!

(In the silence that follows, MOTHIE *tries to restrain the* STRANGER.*)*

MOTHIE: Boss only joking, bhai . . .

STRANGER: Leave me alone . . .

MOTHIE: Bhai, don't be so angry. *(Tries to hold him by the arm).*

STRANGER: *(Angrily pushing him away)* Leave me alone, you fool!

(To the LAHNEE*)* One day, white man, one day! *(Exit).*

(Shocked silence.)

LAHNEE: He's just done himself out of a drink. You get these damn agitators everywhere!

MOTHIE: Don't worry about him, boss. You want I must sing for you, boss . . .

LAHNEE: Yes, come on Mothie . . .

MOTHIE: I can dance for you too, boss.

*(*MOTHIE *sings and dances a lively number. The* LAHNEE *and* SUNNY *join in the clapping. Fade out.)*

(Curtain.)

[End]

Kessie Govender

Kessie Govender (1942–2002) was one of the pioneering voices in South African protest theatre. Govender's grandfather came to South Africa from India as an indentured laborer; and the playwright's father was a bricklayer. Kessie Govender was born in Durban, and upon leaving school after tenth grade, he, too, became a bricklayer.

Kessie's introduction to creative arts happened when he was a young Saivite devotee, who participated in local religious tableaus under Guru Subramanian Swamigal, the founder of the Saiva Sithanda Sungum in Derby Street, Durban. Later he joined his cousin, Ronnie Govender, and Muthal Naidoo in the start-up of the Shah Theatre Academy. Kessie started writing plays in the 1970s, writing *Stable Expense* and *Working Class Hero,* and working with young playwrights and actors.

Govender started his own company, the Stable Theatre, named after the aforementioned *Stable Expense.* The Stable Theatre was the first independent, black-owned theatre in South Africa. Over his thirty-year career, he wrote, produced, directed, and acted in some fifteen of his own stage productions. In addition to plays, he also wrote many poems, most of which were directed against the racist sociopolitical culture of apartheid South Africa.

First produced in 1977, *Working Class Hero* enjoyed a revival in 2001 at Durban's Natal Playhouse to coincide with the World Conference against Racism. For this conference, a special edition was published by Stable Creative Arts.

Working Class Hero

Natal Playhouse, Durban, 2001
Stable Theatre, Durban, 1977

Other Plays

Alternative Action
Black Skies
The Decision
God Made Mosquitoes Too
Herstory
I.O.D. (Injured on Duty)
Ka-goos
On the Fence
Ravanan
The Shack
Stable Expense
Tramp—you, Tramp—me
Underground

Working Class Hero

Kessie Govender

Period—1976. About three months before the Soweto uprising.
Location—A building site in a suburb close to Durban.

PEOPLE IN THE PLAY

FRANK, *Unskilled builders' laborer (African)*
JITS, *Bricklayers' chargehand (Indian)*
SIVA, *Artisan bricklayer (Indian)*
ANAND, *Third-year law student at University of Durban Westville (Siva's brother)*
GRIEVENSTIEN, *Building Industry Labor inspector (White)*

(Stage or performing area to depict a building site. Scattered about are build-ers' scaffoldings, a medium-sized ladder, a doorframe, mortar boards, bricks in piles and packed in stacks. A few empty cement bags lie crumbled. The action and props are permitted to spill outside the allowed conventional working space. Entrances and exits of characters are decided to suit chosen venues. The play is a continuous performance without scene changes. There is a short tea break for the characters on stage, during which time the audience is free to do as it pleases. Stage props are listed on the last page of this book.)

ACT ONE

(The curtains are up before the audience enters the theatre [preferably there should be no curtains]. The house lights are low. The stage or performing area is to create the impression that the place has not yet been cleared and made

ready for a performance. This is to stimulate the audience to feel as curious intruders rather than detached spectators. There is no set, and as there are no conventional chairs, actors would have to improvise their comfort needs. An incomplete raked brickwork corner of a building stands starkly out of place. Words from the song "Working Class Hero" are heard as the houselights are lowered. Performance lights to indicate early morning. In the diffused light FRANK *wheels in barrow of bricks and tips them randomly. Turning his barrow he exits. Reloads and returns. He stops close to the pile of bricks but does not empty the barrow. Leaving the barrow, he walks to an already packed stack of bricks, on top of which is a partly eaten unsliced half loaf of brown bread and a chipped mug of tea. Picking up the bread he takes a bite, pulls the cement bag over the paint container, seats himself on it, continues eating and sipping tea. At the end of the song, lights fade in gradually to normal visibility.)*

(Enter JITS. *He is carrying a kit bag in one hand and a newspaper in the other.)*

FRANK: *(as* JITS *walks past him)* Yebo Baas.

JITS: Ya. *(barely acknowledging* FRANK*) (walks to stack of bricks)* What time do you start work?

FRANK: Dala Baas, long time, must be sometimes apas six.

JITS: Then what you still sitting on your arse for? *(removes tea flask from kit bag)*

FRANK: Awa ngidila iblekfasti Jits.

JITS: Is Temba coming today?

FRANK: Angazi. I dunno. He was sick Friday.

JITS: Ya I know that story. Every Friday he's sick, and every Monday he's absent. Right then, you better mix the daka. *(pours tea into cup)*

FRANK: Ow xovile gaate. That time I'm getting up I'm mixing the daka everything.

JITS: Then come on, move it with the bricks man. What you waiting for? *(reaches into pocket for cigarettes)*

FRANK: *(empties barrow, exits) (sounds of bricks clattering into barrow is heard offstage)*

JITS: *(it's his last cigarette, he squashes the packet and flings it away, looks towards* FRANK *and calls)* Frank, *(receives no response, shouts)* Hey Frank, you bastard.

FRANK: *(above sound of bricks thrown into barrow)* Yebo Baas.

JITS: Get me a packet of cigarettes.

FRANK: *(offstage)* Ini Baas?

JITS: Lo ugwayi man, you bloody shit. You got cement in your ears what?

FRANK: *(enters with barrow load of bricks. Stops his barrow and removes the bricks by hand, after packing some of them into a stack, he walks to* JITS, *collects money, looks down at the money in his hand)* Ow Jits borrow me one rand please.

JITS: What one rand? One rand, one rand, one rand. What do you think I am? Your father or something? Do you know how much you owe me?

FRANK: Ow siza Jits, I want to tenga some inyama.[1]

JITS: Well use your own money, you got paid last week.

FRANK: Ow Jits, siza bo, hambisile mali ekhaya.

JITS: What's that?

FRANK: I'm sending the mali to the farm. I'm never going to the farm, musbe three months. I'm sending the money for my wife and my children.

JITS: Hey shit man, that's your wife and your children, and I hope you're not blaming me for any of them.

FRANK: *(walks towards barrow, takes a few steps then turns around as if a new thought has struck him, walks back to* JITS) Hey Jits, shiya zonke le zinto leaving it all that one rand everything and giving it me only one twenty cents.

JITS: Alright, take it from the rand.

FRANK: Ow Baba, wanyisiza kakhulu *(goes down on one knee in mock gratitude)*

JITS: You just give me back my money, that's all.

FRANK: Not to worley Jits. I'm giving it back your money. *(resumes packing bricks)*

JITS: Hey, how much you taking there now?

FRANK: Twenty cents.

JITS: Didn't you say that you were going to buy meat? What meat you going to buy for twenty cents? You don't take fifty cents and say you only took twenty cents. You hear?

FRANK: You mus'nt think I'm a lobber Jits. I'm getting it a inyama for the twenty cents. I'm going there by the butcher, I'm saying there by him, Hey wena, the baas he say he want the amadogbones for twenty cents. When I say that, he say, Which baas? I say the baas for the building. Ow when I say that, he pick it all the nice, nice amathambo and he gimme lot, lot inyama. *(pause, scratches his head in puzzlement)* Ow, hey Jits, I don't know why he give the baas's dog, lot, lot ama bones, goto that time I say that it is for me, he give it me leetle bit amabones, no inyama nothing.

JITS: Maybe he doesn't like you.

FRANK: How he can saying he don't like it me. He not knowing me nothing *(pause) (as if it suddenly dawns on him)* Noo. He know that the baas is a Mulungu, he get frightened. But me? I'm clever me, anything I want it, I say the Baas he want it, the baas he want it.

JITS: Alright, alright, leave all that and get my cigarettes.

FRANK: Awright. *(turns as if to walk away, stops, turns around)* We Jits, you mus speak to the foreman about my overtime mali. Awright?

---

[1] Cook some meat.

JITS: *(not looking up from his paper)* Yah, alright.

FRANK: Las week, I'm sebenzaing three hours overtime, goto fug it, I'm looking there by my volop, no overtime mali nothing.

JITS: *(looking up)* You speak to the foreman?

FRANK: Yaa, but he saying I mus putting it in the timesheet. Me? I'm telling him I'm not writing it the timesheet. It's not right that, you know, eating the 'nother munto's gazi like that.

JITS: Okay, okay. Did Siva. . . .?

FRANK: You choon the foreman alright?

JITS: What did I tell you just now? Did Siva come yet?

FRANK: No he not coming.

JITS: Go fetch the cigarettes and tell that bastard that the price of cigarettes has not gone up yet. *(resumes reading)*

FRANK: Wonke amaIndia fana nje *(going back to unpack bricks)*

JITS: What shit you talking about the Indians now?

FRANK: This tearoom ou too, he's just like the baas. The mali, hey he like it too much. Ow, the change, you forget it, it is gone, hambile. But, maar, me I'm sharp for this ou. That one time I'm going to buy the bread, what he do it. . . .

JITS: *(JITS cuts in)* Fuck all that and get my cigarettes man.

FRANK: Yaa, but I'm telling you. This amaIndia in the tea room, he thinks he's clever, but he dunno me. Hey Jits, in the jail, you learning too much things there. You can't sleeping it there. Over there they not catching me, you think this amaIndia going to catching me here, outside the jail? Ngeke.

JITS: Hey, go and get my bloody cigarettes, man.

FRANK: *(starts rolling tobacco)* That time I go to buy the bread, I give him five rands. What he do? First he give me the bread, then he talk a little bit, then he give me the loose change everything first. The amacents everything. Then what he do? He start talking some more. Leliya amaIndia uyazi ukukhuluma. Ukukhuluma, ukukhuluma, ukukhuluma, wonke ma nonsense, about the muntu children, fighting and burning it the schools everything. Ow meena I'm listening and listening. After little bit time he turn around like he got some work there, that side, there by the back. And he start to packing the amabiscuit and the lemonade everything. Ow meena I'm thinking about all the things he was telling me, I'm taking my bread everything and I'm walking it outside. Ow, I come by the road, I look by my hand, I'm only seeing it the cents only, I'm not seeing the papar money. Ow, I'm thinking where my change? I'm going back there inside by the shop, and I am saying by that amaIndia, hey mister Moosa, uphi change iyaam. What this amaIndia do? He laugh it by me, he saying I'm a stupid, I'm forgetting it my change and going. But maar meena I thinking, this one amaIndia is a big one amacrooka, this one amaIndia. Goto he not going to. . . .

JITS: Hey, how many times must I tell you to get my fucking cigarettes, man.

FRANK: *(exits)*

JITS: *(calls after* FRANK*)* . . . and make it fast.

    (slight pause SIVA *and* ANAND *enter, with* FRANK *following close behind)*

SIVA: Howzit Jits.

JITS: *(looking up)* Howzit. *(notices* FRANK*)* Hey, what you still doing here? Where's my bloody cigarettes, man?

SIVA: No man, I wanted some coke *(to* FRANK*)* Hey Frank find that bottle and make it fast. *(hands money to* FRANK*)* And tell that bastard I want a cold one, and don't stand there making your speeches.

FRANK: *(exits)*

JITS: Coke, early in the morning? You must be hanging, man..

SIVA: Hanging? Fucked, fucked, fucked. This ou's gang that *(pointing to* ANAND*)* This is my bro Anand. You remember I choon you, he wanted some graaf? These ous had a joll. Anand, this is Jits. He's the charge hand.

    (sits on brick stack)

    *(*ANAND *and* JITS *shake hands)*

JITS: Howzit.

ANAND: Hello.

JITS: You a brickie?

ANAND: *(shakes his head)* No.

SIVA: No man, I told he's studying at the university.

JITS: Aww. *(takes off his jacket).* What happened, there? Your'll burnt the place down or something?

ANAND: No, not our university, they're all too scared there. No, we've just closed up for the holidays.

SIVA: Did you speak to the foreman? Did you tell him that this ou wants a graaf for the holidays?

JITS: Ya, I spoke to him. He said that it was okay. What can you do?

ANAND: Anything.

JITS: Push daka, bricks?

ANAND: Anything.

JITS: It's hard work, and don't talk about what will happen to your hands.

ANAND: As long as I make a few rands.

JITS: You involved in that boycott business too?

ANAND: Sorry. What's that?

SIVA: He knows, he starts any of that boycott shit, my kerel will kick his arse.

ANAND: That wasn't the reason. . . .

SIVA: Where's this Frank man, I don't know why you sent that ou to the tea-room. That ou when he vies, he vies for good.

JITS: The kerels worry you.

ANAND: No, they just sit there in their cars, take down number plates and photographs. Just to show us that they are there.

SIVA: The cops got these ou's taped. Yaa, but our char lighties got no guts too.

ANAND: If you were at our university, you'll know what its like there. You can't make a move. That place is like a concentration camp. You just can't make a single move there.

JITS: But still our boys got no unity. If they had unity, they won't need guts.

SIVA: Hey Jits, whose side you're on? You chooning these ou's should burn their university too, what?

JITS: Naa, I just wanted to know how things were there, that side. Nowadays you don't know whether you are coming or going. You pick up a paper, you read one story, you listen to the radio you get another story. Then the television, that's one big box of shit.

ANAND: They are all part of the system.

JITS: What's that?

ANAND: I said they are all part of the system. The newspapers, the radio, the television. Lets face it. Who runs them? So, they are run with only one thought, and stand only for one thing That's to prop up the apartheid system.

SIVA: (cutting in) System, shit man, these ous got no work to do, that's why they start all this nonsense. (looks off stage). You know that bastard Frank, I don't know why you sent him to the tearoom.

JITS: He's the only boy this side. This Temba too, he's making it a habit nowadays, every Monday he's absent.

SIVA: I told the foreman too, fire the whole lot of the bastards, and get a new set of boys. (ANAND is staring at SIVA)

JITS: (toANAND) Have a cup of tea Anand?

ANAND: No thanks, I'll share the coke.

SIVA: He's hanging too.

JITS: Blue Monday. Shit, this is more like booze Monday, man. What were you ou's drinking?

SIVA: You name it we drank it.

JITS: Yaa, I can smell it too. How can you guys drink like that on a Sunday?

SIVA: Sunday? Friday, Saturday, and Sunday. Hey these university ou's can push, jong.

JITS: Ya, they must learn now. By the time they become qualified teachers, they'll become qualified drinkers too. (turning to ANAND) You know at one time they used to say that the ou's in the building trade were the worst drinkers, but nowadays you go into any pub and you see a ou lying on the floor, you must know that's a genuine teacher that. But why is that?

SIVA: These ou's got no limit man. (looking offstage) Hey Frank.

JITS: You going to be a teacher too?

ANAND: No.

JITS: But why do teachers drink like that?

ANAND: We talk about it at varsity too. They say it's frustration.

SIVA: Frustration, shit bloody frustration. These teachers just smaak to dop man.

ANAND: No, it's true. You can see by the number of teachers that are dying of stroke and heart failure.

SIVA: Ya, if that Frank doesn't hurry up with the coke I'll die of a bloody hangover.

JITS: If things are so bad, why don't they just give it up?

ANAND: Give up what?

JITS: Why don't they give up the teaching profession?

ANAND: Then what will they do?

SIVA: They can come and push daka here. Hey, fuck you ou's man. The man's got a heavy barbi and you ou's are chooning and chooning. *(looking out)* Hey Frank. *(turning to* JITS*)* Jits, you better get rid of this ou, man. Too much talking with him.

JITS: Then we'll end up with someone worse, besides you'll be the one to cry when he's gone. Who's going to lay bricks for you everytime you run to shit? I don't mind, I'll get rid of him tomorrow.

ANAND: Is there a toilet here?

JITS: Toilet? On a building site you don't worry about a toilet my boy. If there's a wall strong enough to stand your pee, you pee against it. As for shifting, you find the nearest bush. Why do you think the bushes are so green around here? And don't talk about the vegetables.

SIVA: Yaa, tell him, tell him. When I tell them where the vegetables are coming from they don't believe me. They think I am joking. *(*ANAND *exits)* You know the other day I was telling my ma . . . *(enter* FRANK *with coke and cigarettes).* You vied to the factory to get it what? *(opens bottle and drinks)*

FRANK: Ow you know that amaIndia. They seeing I'm a munto, they serving me last.

JITS: Where's my cigarettes? *(receives it).* How much he charged you for the packet?

FRANK: Thirty-seven cents.

JITS: With these shop ou's you must be sharp. What's the time now?

SIVA: Twenty to eight.

(enter ANAND*)*

JITS: Shit, we're chooning one way here, and we didn't even hear the bell ring. Right, come on Frank, let's move it. Where's the daka?

FRANK: Ow, I mus push the bricks, I mus mix the daka, now I mus pushing the daka futhi, what?

SIVA: You see, you see, I told you, he must start his moaning. *(passes coke to* ANAND*)* Here.

JITS: Hey, you don't want to do it? You don't want to do it?

FRANK: Ai Jits, you mustn't talking like that man.

JITS: You know what you can do if you don't like it. You can fuck off.

FRANK: Ow, hey Jits, the foreman, he hearing you just now.

JITS: Then move it then. If he comes here now and asks me why we haven't started graaf yet, I'll tell him you didn't want to bring the daka.

FRANK: But it's not right. Two amabricklayers, I'm one munto, I must giving it for the two amabricklayers.

ANAND: I'll fetch it, where's it.

JITS: No, it's all right, he'll bring it. *(*FRANK *exits with barrow)* You better watch out my boy or you'll end up doing all the work here.

SIVA: Leave him, leave him, this ou thinks this is the university here.

ANAND: I mean fair is fair.

SIVA: What fair is fair? *(turning to* JITS*).* You know Jits, you must come to my posey sometimes, one weekend or something, and listen to these ou's chooning and chooning. Me? I tell these ou's straight, they want to know anything about life they must join the building trade. They mustn't sit on their arses and think they know everything. . . .

FRANK: *(offstage)* Doomela sissy. Ow woza bo, ugifuna ukubula manje je now, now, now.

SIVA: You see? Fair is fair. The bastard wants a kiss early in the morning I don't think he even brushed his teeth yet. *(shouting out)* Bring the bloody daka here you, *(to* ANAND*)* You want to help him? Therewa, therewa.

ANAND: You don't expect him to do all the work.

JITS: Anand, sometimes it's best not bothering about what's expected and what's not expected. Right now Frank's not expecting any help from you, so lets just leave it at that. That way there'll be no arguments.

ANAND: It just doesn't seem right.

JITS: *(laughing to* SIVA*)* Hey Siva, don't bring this ou to the job tomorrow. We won't get any graaf done with him around.

ANAND: There's no point in hiding the fact that he is doing more than his fair share.

JITS: *(stopping him with his hands).* Whoa, whoa, hang on, hang on. Give me a hand with these frames. *(stands door frame upright)* Pass me one of those stays.

ANAND: What's a stay?

JITS: Sorry that long piece of wood there.

SIVA: Hey, Frank move it with the daka there.

FRANK: *(offstage)* Cabangani wena, you musn't think I'm a bongolo.

SIVA: *(to* FRANK*)* Hey, fuck you man and bring the daka here now.

ANAND: *(getting angry)* Why do you keep swearing him like that?

SIVA: What you vie to university for? Didn't they teach you about proverbs. You didn't hear this one "To swear or not to swear like a bricklayer. Now that's the fucking kweshion *(laughs).*

ANAND: They also told me a bricklayer only swears when he gets hurt. They didn't tell me anything about swearing laborers. I mean that guy is fit to be your father.

SIVA: Whose father? Whose fucking father? You think I'm a kaffir?

ANAND: Don't ever use that word again. *(spits out the words threateningly)*

SIVA: This is your first day here, you'll learn.

JITS: *(to* SIVA*)* You got any more Bros at home?

SIVA: Why?

JITS: If they are looking for graaf for the holidays, please don't bring them here, alright? *(he laughs)*

SIVA: Naa, this ou is alright. Only, sometimes his head goes a little . . . you know what I mean? *(indicates with his finger to forehead)*

JITS: Pull this one slightly to you, Anand.

ANAND: It's not right to treat a man like that.

JITS: Now pull the other one a bit, now hold it. Ya, you ou's carry on chooning, that Frank is catching a good joll there. Hey Frank. *(to* ANAND*)* If you want work from these ou's you got to push them.

ANAND: Alright, push them but you don't have to insult them. At least respect his age .

SIVA: Hey shit man, respect by the posey, not on the job.

JITS: Don't worry, you'll learn. Siva, I bet you by this afternoon this ou will be swearing too.

FRANK: *(enters with barrow of motar)* Therewa, where you want it?

SIVA: Hold it. Jits, where do you want me to start?

JITS: Get this frame right, I'll set the other one.

    *(*SIVA *starts measuring correct position of frame)*

JITS: Frank, get me two more stays and pass some bricks to Anand.

FRANK: Ubani?

JITS: To Anand man, *(points to* ANAND*)* That's Anand there.

FRANK: Aww . . . *(walks with extended hand to* ANAND*)* Xhawula mfanawami *(shakes* ANAND *by the hand)*

JITS: *(to* FRANK*)* Hey, leave all that shit, get me two stays and pass some bricks to him.

    *(*FRANK *finds two stays.* ANAND *is still holding his set of stays.* SIVA *is marking the brickwork gauge on the door frame he has set into position.* JITS *stands erect the other frame. hands* JITS *the stays)*

FRANK: Uyazi ukubamba istini.

ANAND: Sorry?

FRANK: You can catching the bricks?

ANAND: I'll try.

FRANK: *(cautiously flings brick to* ANAND*)* That the brother for you that? *(points to* SIVA*)*

ANAND: Yes.

FRANK: *(walks to* SIVA*, bends to peer into his face, walks back, resumes throwing bricks)* Goto, I can't seeing it the face. *(sings Zulu folk song)* Nibangaki?

ANAND: What?

FRANK: How many brothers you got?

ANAND: Four.

FRANK: Wena five? Ow hey Siva, the father for you, he's a inkunzi.

SIVA: Hey, you don't worry about my father, just carry on with your work.

FRANK: Ow, *(to* ANAND*)* Your brother, he's a moobi that one. Everytime he shouting, shouting. *(sings)*

JITS: Why don't you shut your mouth, man? That's enough bricks there, get me some more here.

FRANK: Jus now.

SIVA: *(placing level on frame)* Push this to me a fraction Anand, hold it, now the next one.

FRANK: *(packing bricks for* JITS*) (sings)* Ubaphetha osisi?

ANAND: Sorry?

FRANK: You got it amasisters?

ANAND: Yes.

FRANK: Ushadile?

ANAND: Eh?

FRANK: Is married?

ANAND: Yes.

   *(*FRANK *sings while packing)*

SIVA: Why don't you shut your bloody mouth man?

FRANK: Ini?

SIVA: I got a fucking headache man.

FRANK: Ow, you got it a headache Mister Nilo? *(runs off the stage)*.

JITS: *(to* FRANK*)* Hey, where you going to now? *(to* SIVA*)*. Where's that ou vying to now?

SIVA: I don't know. You know that ou, the whole day he'll run here and there, this side and that side, but when you give him a little bit of graaf to do, he'll moan and groan as if he's ready to die.

FRANK: *(runs in with bushknife held across his hands)* Therewa Mister. Pillo.

SIVA: What's that for?

FRANK: Ow, you saying you got it a headache.

SIVA: So?

FRANK: Ow the head, it is giving you trouble, you must be cutting it out. Funa ncoma. (FRANK *swings bushknife at* SIVA. ANAND *and* JITS *laugh*)

SIVA: *(steps back)* Hey you gone mad or what? *(pulls bush knife away from* FRANK, *lifts it threateningly)*

SIVA: You wait I'll fix you up tomorrow.

*(FRANK *runs off beyond* SIVA'*s reach)*

JITS: Aright, alright, lets leave all this messing around and get some work done. Right, Frank start packing these stays.

FRANK: *(sings as he packs stays)* *(to* ANAND*)* Me, I like it the amaIndia girls (ANAND *is silent.)* . . . but maar the India girls, ow, they don't like it me. *(looks out, stage left)* Hey Siva, nanku. Hey look Siva, nice one girl that. Hey Siva, size yakho numpela. That one is a right size for you. *(*SIVA *looks)* Me? I am getting one girl like that one day.

JITS: Why don't you choon her then?

FRANK: Ow, they swearing it too much.

SIVA: Frank, get me a stabe here and some daka.

FRANK: *(to* JITS*)* But maar one day, munya langa me I'm getting it one, just like that one.

SIVA: Who?

FRANK: That one, nice one amaIndia girl.

SIVA: Hey my boy, I see you with an Indian girl on the road, I'll knock you down, call the police and say it was an accident. *(*JITS *and* SIVA *laugh)*

FRANK: Aiee, whyna, you got it too much a color bar.

SIVA: Colour bar shit. If I see you with an India girl . . .

FRANK: Ya, but maar night time come you going there by the muntu girls.

SIVA: Me? You saw me? You saw me?

FRANK: Ya, in the day time you saying not going there by the muntu girls, goto night time coming, you thatha imoto, you going there looking for the muntu girls.

JITS: There's nothing wrong with that.

FRANK: Ow, I'm not saying that wrong thing that, goto this Siva, he saying that I musn't touch the amaIndia girls. Not right thing that.

SIVA: What you going to do about that? Eh? What you going to do?

FRANK: Ow whynaa Siva. Hey Jits, you must fixing me one nice amaIndia girl, alright?

*(*SIVA *sits on bricks)*

JITS: Alright

FRANK: Ngempele. You getting me one?

JITS: Yes man. What age you want?

FRANK: Eh?

JITS: How old?

FRANK: Aw, any old, any old.

JITS: Aright, I'll bring my granny tomorrow, you know my gogo. She must be any old. I don't think she even knows her own age. *(they laugh)*

FRANK: Ow, me, I want it a juniya.

(SIVA *suddenly grabs his head and leans against the door*)

SIVA: Fuck this, man.

JITS: What's wrong Siva?

SIVA: Hey I'm not drinking with these ou's anymore.

ANAND: The trouble with him is, that he doesn't eat when he drinks. He just drinks and drinks.

SIVA: Frank, get me some water.

(FRANK *unscrews the lid on* JITS' *flask, unhurriedly.*)

JITS: It's almost eight and we only got the frames standing. Siva, you better stick in some bricks. I don't like that van Niekerk squealing with me all the time. Did you know that he even counts the bricks.

SIVA: You're joking.

JITS: No, I mean it. Who do you think bombed Ram? Van Niekerk the bastard.

SIVA: Hell, that's shit you know that?

FRANK: *(looks offstage)* Aiee mana, hey Siva, therewa, there's another one. Hey Siva, this one I am telling you maar, this one is a number one mpele, *(kisses his fingers)* Hey ntombazana, look it here. This boy is a nice boy this one, He's a bricklayer this one. He got it a lot, lot mali, big one house, too much taxies, everything.

JITS: *(shouts to girl offstage)* Yes, and he's got three children and he's still paying maintenance for his first wife.

FRANK: Aiee, Jits, you musn't speaking like that, mus to giving that Siva a chance. *(looking offstage)* Aww, why you swearing like that Aiee, the amaIndia girls, tch, tch, tch, his mouth is dorty. Nanke ten cents, hamba thanga msipho. You mus washing your mouth with the soap.

SIVA: Hey Frank I got a headache, man.

JITS: *(shouts)* Yaa, he's got a hangover too.

SIVA: And where's my water?

FRANK: You must drink it a mass, that's the good one for the babalaaz.

SIVA: Fuck all that and get the bloody water. So that's why they fired Ram, eh?

JITS: Yaa. That's why. I think you must move it up too.

SIVA: What does that Van Niekerk think? He musn't come here and count my bricks.

JITS: You better not start any shit with him.

SIVA: Fuck him, man.

JITS: Jobs are hard nowadays and you know that too.

SIVA: He knows what he can do with his job. Shit man, you know how long Ram was working for this firm, and he goes and fires him just like that.

JITS: Nobody's interested in how long anymore. You don't stick in enough bricks, you go, that's all.

SIVA: What I am thinking about is how that Ram fellow must be managing now.

JITS: Yaa, Things are going from bad to worse.

SIVA: But Ram is a faster brickie than that Mitchell. You know that? Why doesn't Van Neikerk count that bastard's bricks? I don't think that shit lays more than three hundred bricks for a day. *(slight pause)* Hey, Ram was working with Mitchell. . . .

JITS: What I hear is that Van Niekerk counted the bricks in the wall Ram and Mitchell were working on . . .

SIVA: But he only fired Ram. The fucking white bastard. Doesn't he know that Ram was carrying Mitchell. Everybody knows that.

JITS: Van Niekerk knows that too, but . . .

SIVA: That Mitchell is just a waste of money to this firm. They should pension that bastard off.

ANAND: *(stands next to door frame)* That's just one of the costs of apartheid. If they did not waste so much of money protecting the white man's security, there'd be enough work for everybody. Do you know what apartheid costs this country, besides just job loses?

SIVA: Hey Jits, don't start chooning with this ou about that, just now he'll start chooning about buses, bridges, and everything.

ANAND: It's the truth isn't it? That's what is draining this country. Everywhere you look, there's got to be two of everything. Two buses instead of one, two bridges instead of one, two hospitals instead of one. In fact, anything you look at there's one for the blacks and one for whites. Do you know what these cost? Not just one or two rands but millions of rands, hundreds of millions of rands.

JITS: You mean it? Hell, I never checked it that way you know that.

ANAND: Of course, and let's not forget what about Doctor Eschel Rhoodie and the Information Scandal[2] and the millions they are spending to cover up that filth.

JITS: Ya, but you should be careful, I mean the way you are so freely using that ou's name. I was reading about that scandal thing in the papers, they said that anybody caught chooning about that ou or mentioning his name or that scandal shit will be bopaed.

ANAND: They are only trying to cover things up.

---

[2]The Secretary of Information during the 1980s presided over many scandals in the promotion of apartheid.

SIVA: I don't know what you ou's are worring about, no matter how much they fart under the water the bubbles must still come up. Where's this Frank? *(shouts offstage)* Hey Frank, make it sharp man. Bloody shit. It's all your fault this Jits. You choon nicely with these ou's, and they sit on your bloody head.

ANAND: What's wrong with them sitting on your head for a change? All their lives you sit on their heads.

SIVA: Don't start with me Anand.

ANAND: While I'm at it, I never hear you swearing like this at home.

SIVA: At home I'm Siva, on the job I'm a bricklayer.

JITS: Ya, he's like the nats, this ou. The nats too, they speak nicely to their servants, but they still make the law that fucks them up.

ANAND: Yes, but you can't compare one wrong with another and think that your wrong is better. There is no justification for treating any human being like . . . like they are nothing.

SIVA: Look, I've got a bloody hangover, and besides, he's just another . . .

ANAND: Another what?

JITS: Politics can get you into trouble, my boy.

ANAND: *(to* JITS*)* Why? You don't think you have anything to do with politics?

SIVA: *(to* FRANK*)* Get the daka everything ready you.

JITS: How can you say that, I've never been to a political meeting. I've never met any politician. The only politics I know is what I read in the newspapers. How could you say that I have anything to do with politics?

ANAND: The fact that you were born in a hospital for blacks only is politics.

SIVA: Ya, carry on, carry on. One day you'll . . .

JITS: I'll see you guys later. I've got to check on the other side *(to* SIVA*)* Push in some bricks, Siva. That wit appi comes here, ask him to come to the other side.

SIVA: OK

JITS: That bastard's getting full of shit too.

(picks up tape)

SIVA: I told Van Niekerk too, I don't want that ou on this side. He's telling me what to do.

JITS: He's starting with you too?

SIVA: Yaa, he started a little bit, I told him to find himself a nice, big pineapple, and sit on it.

JITS: Everytime he talks to Van Niekerk, he keeps on saying what he'd do if he was the foreman here. The way things are going, I'm sure he'll be the next foreman.

SIVA: He's still an appi here. By the time he gets qualified, I'll be. . . .

JITS: What, By the time? Next month he writes his trade test and he'll get through too, the damn shit.

SIVA: When that ou becomes foreman, I'll pull out me.

ANAND: Why? because you won't take any pushing around from him? Is that it?

SIVA: Of course.

ANAND: But you expect Frank to put up with all your nonsense. As I said, he feels like you and I too.

JITS: *(watching this)* Listen my boy, when a bricklayer swears, I don't think he actually means it. I swear Siva, do you think I mean it?

ANAND: But your attitude towards Siva is not the same as that to. . . .

SIVA: You know what you can do with your attitude?

ANAND: You shock me, Siva.

JITS: Anand, you can't bring your university ideas here and think they'll work.

SIVA: Hey, leave him Jits.

JITS: No, hang on.

SIVA: These ou's think we're arses.

ANAND: Well, stop behaving like one then. Do you realize that as long as you treat him like a piece of thing you are psychologically making him lose his dignity.

SIVA: Hey, shit your psycho and everything. Don't come and tell us about your yepdi psycho here. You know what you can do with it. Wait . . . . . . *(looks around, then towards* FRANK*)* Hey, Frank bring that pipe there when you coming.

FRANK: *(off stage)* Which one? This one?

SIVA: Yaa, and hurry up man. Jits, just choon this ou what that pipe is for.

JITS: Which one?

SIVA: Check that one there in Frank's hand.

JITS: Oh, that's a shit pipe, my boy.

SIVA: You know what we use it for?

JITS: Over here we got to put up with all kinds of shit.

SIVA: The inspector comes, he talks his shit. The lahnee comes, he talks his shit. The foreman comes, that's more shit. Then the chargehand, well this side, we're okay, we got Jits, it's alright.

JITS: Ya, I was a brickie too before I became a chargehand. I know how much of shit a brickie has to put up with. What about the shit the boy's give you? Then the owners of the posey will come, that's the worst shit.

SIVA: That's why we got the shit pipe. Hey, Frank, where's that pipe?

FRANK: *(offstage)* Yes, I'm coming jus now.

SIVA: You see what that ou is doing there, Jits?

JITS: Hey, sheea lo ntombi. Look, he's attacking another one there now .

FRANK: Yebo, I'm coming jus now.

SIVA: I'm sure that ou's a sex maniac. Anything goes past, he must go and choon.

(FRANK *walks in with pipe and water and hands them to* SIVA. SIVA *hands the pipe to* ANAND) You check one day he'll get V.D.

SIVA: Here, if you got any shit to talk, keep this near your mouth. Hey Jits you know when the owner of the house comes, I'm going to give him a piece of this pipe.

JITS: No, You must give it to his wife. She gives him shit at home, and he comes here and says change this and change that.

SIVA: No wait, I've got a better idea. You see these pipes, I'll cut them up into small pieces and put it on a masonite board and put a frame around it. I'll write there, nice and big at the bottom, shit pipe. Then, I'll sell it to the owner. So anytime his wife gives him shit he can take her to where he hangs it and tell her, if you got any shit to talk, you talk it in here honey.

JITS: That auntie doesn't want steel window frames.

SIVA: Tell her to come and change it herself.

JITS: I'll see you just now. Anand keep yourself busy. You don't have to do anything. Just keep yourself occupied. Siva, if the foreman wants me, tell him I'm in the next cottage. *(exits)*

SIVA: Frank, you got enough daka here?

FRANK: Ya.

SIVA: Then, come on send it then.

FRANK: Ya, now you saying that I mus sending it, goto that time Friday come, you not giving me nothing, not one ten cents, saying, therewa Frank, buying it one ijuba.

SIVA: Alright then, if you don't want to do it, you can push the bricks.

FRANK: Ow you thinking I am worried, uzosebenza meena. I can pushing it the barla I'm getting it the mali for pushing it the barla me.

SIVA: *(reaches for* FRANK) Hey, lay the fucking bricks, you. (FRANK *shrugs him off)*

FRANK: Uzokabana, you mustn't think I'm a spook spook me. I'm not a stupid. You getting the big one mali for laying it the amabricks. I'm getting the small mali for pushing the barla.

SIVA: Hey, fuck your speeches.

FRANK: Siva, maar mooya langa, uzobona, you'll be seeing one day. I'm fixing you up. Uzobona.

SIVA: So you don't want to do it? You don't want to do it? Well fuck off. Go and collect your money from the office and take all your things from the shed and get.

FRANK: You mustn't talking like that.

SIVA: Get, I'll ask Jits to get me a new set of boys. And don't forget you haven't got a dompass.

FRANK: Hey Siva. . . .

SIVA: Fuck off. You heard me? You're fired.

ANAND: Siva, you can't do that.

SIVA: You shut up, you. (FRANK *starts to push barrow*) Leave that barrow.

ANAND: This is nonsense, Siva. You can't fire him just like that.

SIVA: Who says so?

ANAND: I mean. . . . What power do you have to fire him?

SIVA: If a bricklayer is not satisfied with a boy, he must go. He must just get. Hey you, start packing your things.

ANAND: Siva, you must be crazy. He's not a bricklayer, he's a laborer.

SIVA: Then he doesn't decide what he does. He gets paid for the number of hours he puts in, not what he does.

ANAND: That does not make sense.

SIVA: Anand, you shut up. It's because of guy's like you that these ou's get so cheeky. And this ou hasn't even got his reference book. Go to that cottage there (*indicating*) and ask Jits for two boys.

ANAND: Why don't you give him a break?

SIVA: What break?

ANAND: He's got to live too, you know.

SIVA: Fuck him.

ANAND: I would never have believed it.

SIVA: This is the building trade here. When a bricklayer gives a boy an order he must do it and not get cheeky. (*to* FRANK) You want to work?

FRANK: (*quietly*) Yebo.

SIVA: Then shut your mouth and send it. Any more shit from you and I'll fire you on the spot. Get me a piece of paper first. No leave it, tear a piece from Jit's paper. Anand if anybody comes now or two hours from now, just say I went just now, you understand? Just now.

(FRANK *prepares to lay bricks*)

ANAND: What are you going to do?

SIVA: Catch a small doss. (*exits*)

(ANAND *stands uncertainly watching* FRANK)

FRANK: I think you better sitting over there. (*indicates stack of bricks*) If you see any mulungus coming you must telling me quickly.

ANAND: Sorry What's that? (ANAND *sits*)

FRANK: The inspector. If you seeing him you mus . . .

ANAND: Which inspector?

FRANK: Ow, the inspector for the building. You not knowing the muntus is not supposed to be laying the amabricks. Goto the Siva, he not listening nothing.

(FRANK *continues laying bricks*)

ANAND: Where did you learn to speak English, Frank?

FRANK: That one time I was a small boy, I was working for this one missus. That missus, she can't speaking the Zulu. I'm learning it the amaEnglish slowly, slowly. Giving me that 'alf brick, mfanawami. *(indicating)* Ya that one.

ANAND: *(handing half brick)* I'll give you some mud too.

FRANK: Aye imud le. It's the daka that one. No leaving it, I'm taking it myself. Your bro, that Siva he not liking it you giving me the daka. That time the inspector coming you must holding the trofolo shecha awright.

ANAND: Does Siva treat you like this all the time?

FRANK: Ini?

ANAND: Does he shout at you all the time?

FRANK: Ow that Siva, you not knowing which one time he going to be shouting. You got it a cigarette mfanawami?

ANAND: No. I'll get one from Siva.

FRANK: Is awright, is awright, I got it my stompi.

ANAND: *(admiring brickwork)* You're good. You know that Frank?

FRANK: Ow, I'm working by the masilan, the amabricklayers too much time. *(looking offstage)* Hey mana, meena la heepi gowe. Woza la, Ufuna quabula. Ufuna tenga inyama ne ijuba ne sweets ne cakes and lemonade. You must come to me Saturday. *(slight pause)* No, no, not on Friday. Saturday. *(turns to* ANAND*)* You see that one I'm getting her this Saturday. Ushadile?

ANAND: Sorry?

FRANK: You married?

ANAND: No, I'm not married.

FRANK: Ow three months I'm not seeing it my wife.

ANAND: Where's your wife now?

FRANK: There to the farm. Bizana.

ANAND: You should bring her here and keep her in town.

FRANK: Ngimbeke-phi?

ANAND: What?

FRANK: Where I must keeping her?

ANAND: Can't you keep her in the shed where you sleep?

FRANK: Aei, can't keeping by the job here. That one shed where I'm sleeping, got it too much the amacockloches and the goondaan, and a lot, lot nunus. 'Nother one thing, that time the amablack jacks coming here looking for me, he finding my wife here too, and he charging her too. Me and my wife sitting it by the jail. Ow the baas he not liking it all that things.

ANAND: Do they raid here often?

FRANK: By the jobs, aw ma-me. Hey, that place there by the 'spingo. The phoyisa there, they not playing there. Ima leetle bit, let me laying it some bricks. *(works)*

ANAND: So Frank, what happened there at Isipingo?

FRANK: *(after laying a few bricks)* That one time, ow, I'm chooning it this nice one girl, jus like that one girl you seeing jus now. I'm taking her there by the shed. I'm buying it a ijuba, and a inyama and everything. We eating and poozaing the juba. I'm making the bed everything nice, nice. Hey, that one amaIndian poisa, he's too good that one. One kick, the door it is opening. Ow meena, that's the time I'm sitting it there in the bushs, I'm taking it out all the inyama and the juba and everything out. That's the time they catching my girlfriend. She saying, she waiting for me. They asking her where me, she saying in the bushes. That bushes it is dark. That poisa for the amaIndia, he's too clever, ikaanyesa torch. He put it a torch, he come looking for me. Meena? I'm seeing him coming, I'm not looking this side, I'm not looking that side—kja, kja, kja,kja, I'm gone. Hambile. *(gets back to lay bricks)* I'm not looking back nothing.

ANAND: Your girlfriend? What happened to her?

FRANK: They taking her away. She haven't got it a dompass too.

ANAND: And you didn't go look for her?

FRANK: Where I mus go looking for her? I go there by the police station, they seeing me, they putting me in the jail too. Meena, I'm seeing the poias everybody gone, I'm taking my blankets and sleeping in the bushes. That girlfriend for me, she sleeping it in the jail.

ANAND: What happens if she was your wife?

FRANK: She haven't got it a dompass, she going too.

ANAND: And you still won't go and fetch her?

FRANK: You thinking I'm stupid? I must leave my graaf, everything, and sit there by the jail with my wife? Ow the baas he not liking it that.

ANAND: But she'll be in jail with other criminals.

FRANK: Aw, what I mus do? Who's going to make the mali for the food for my childrens, eh? *(continues working)*

ANAND: I'll never let my wife sleep in jail.

FRANK: Ya, but you not carrying it a dompass? How you knowing?

ANAND: Even then, I'll . . .

FRANK: Ow hey, mfanawami, you not knowing nothing about the muntus. The amaIndia, the amaColored, they is different.

ANAND: You're not different from us, we are all blacks.

FRANK: But you not carrying it a dompass.

ANAND: Yes, that's true, but we are basically blacks.

FRANK: Hey lalela mfanawami. That time you carrying it a dompass, the jail, it is like a dortyi house. You working this side, the phoyisa he a you. You working that side, the phoyisa he bopha you. What you going to doing it? You take it a chance, You take it a luck. You get caught that is a bad luck, you go it a jail. *(pause, lays a few bricks)* You haven't got it a bad luck. You not carrying a dompass. You carrying the dompass, that's a bad luck. You go jail, your wife go jail, your children go jail. Jail coming like one bad relations house, a house you not liking to visit.

ANAND: Life must be hell for you.

FRANK: Yebo, but you talking it too much kwestions. That one brother for you the Siva, he come, he starting to shouting it. Saying I am not laying it the amabricks. That time firing me, what I mus be doing.

(slight pause as ANAND *watches* FRANK *laying bricks)*

ANAND: Can't you teach me to lay bricks. Then I can help you, then we can make it faster.

FRANK: *(looks up at* ANAND, *then looks down at his trowel)* We haven't got it 'nother one trofolo.

ANAND: Oh.

FRANK: Manje futhi, nother one thing, that Siva he's not liking it the Muntu teaching the amalndia how to laying it the bricks.

ANAND: I don't think he's that bad.

FRANK: Hey, that Siva you not knowing him. That one he got it too much color bar.

ANAND: No, that's his way of speaking.

FRANK: Hey, you never seeing, he saying he knocking me down and calling the amapoisa that time he seeing me speaking to the amaIndia girls.

ANAND: He was just joking.

FRANK: Lutho wonke amaIndia ayafananje. The color bar he got it too much.

ANAND: Not all Indians. Some of them are beginning to change now.

FRANK: Lutho knyafana nje. My father saying to me, that time he was a small boy the amalndia is the same, now he's a madala, he saying the amaIndia is still the same.

ANAND: He is probably speaking about the rich ones. Do you think I'm like that? Do you think that I've got color bar?

FRANK: I dunno, how must I know? You not carrying a dompass.

ANAND: That doesn't mean anything.

FRANK: Aw, that's what you saying. You got a lot lot money, you got a big one house, shop, imoto everything. What we got it? Sheet we got it. No house, no mali, no nothing. But we must carry it a dompass. All color bar that.

ANAND: Not all the Indians are rich, besides its not the Indians that makes you carry the dompass, the white man makes the laws.

FRANK: But the amaIndia like the color bar. He saying mustn't touching the amalndia girls. But maar night time come, they going there by the muntu girls. But day time they saying the muntus mustn't staying near them. Wonka amacolorbar that.

ANAND: That doesn't mean they like color bar.

FRANK: Hey, mfanawami, you mustn't think I'm a stupid. You think I cant seeing it. That time the amaIndia wanting the same thing like the Mulungu, he
don't say nothing 'bout the colorbar. He want to stay nice, nice, house near
the Mulungu. When the Mulungu say no, then the amaIndia say he don't
like it a colorbar.

ANAND: Frank you really don't like the Indians, do you?

FRANK: *(reacting to* ANAND'*s question* FRANK *lays the next brick incorrectly, this
causes the vertical joints in the brickwork to go awry.)* Why I must liking
the amaIndia? What he doing nice by me? You tell me. You working by the
kitchen, the India missus making you like a dog. I'm knowing it was working
it in the kitchen too. They makin you sleep in the bathroom, the toilet. They
give it your food in the papar. You think my girlfriends, they not telling me.
Manje, now, now, you can going there by the house for the amaIndia, you
seeing how the amaIndia doing to the Muntus. The Muntus mus doing all
the work, clean it the house. wash the close, wash the chilrens, the izitsha,
cook it the food, everything. Goto that time that Muntu want to sheeting,
they mus go to the bushes Small one chilren for the Muntus, they bring it
from the farm and they making it them like a dog, Wonka icolor bar that.
Why I mus liking it amaIndia and the amaColored. They is the same like the
Mulungu. They all.

(tea bell rings)

*(*FRANK *lays down his trowel)*

FRANK: That's a tea time, that. Musbe you eating your tea now.

SIVA: *(enters)* Hey Frank, get me a coke.

FRANK: Aw Siva, you mustn't doing it like that. Tea time, tea time, you making
me run for the tearoom. It's not right that one.

SIVA: You starting your nonsense again?

FRANK: Ow, what time I'm going to having it my tea time?

SIVA: If you stop talking your shit and run, you'll have enough time.

FRANK: Nganyiso, One day you going to be seeing it.

*(*JITS *enters)*

SIVA: Hey Jits, I'm telling you, you must fire this ou. He don't want to listen
man.

FRANK: Siva, I'm telling munye langa uzobona, I'm telling you.

JITS: Hey. What's wrong? What's happening?

SIVA: I'm telling this bastard to go and get me a coke and he's giving me all his
shit.

JITS: Frank shut up and get the coke.

*(*FRANK *collects money from* SIVA, *picks up empty bottle and exits)*

(Tea time.)

ACT TWO

(Lights fade in on SIVA, ANAND *and* JITS. *They are in the same positions as they were, when the bell had rung for their tea break.* SIVA *sits on stack of bricks,* JITS *reaches for tea flask,* ANAND *stands awkwardly undecided.)*

JITS: You ou's want some tea?

SIVA: Naa.

ANAND: I'll have a cup.

JITS: I haven't got a spare cup. Do you want to drink now or do you want wait until I've finished?

ANAND: I'll wait. *(sits at his previous seat)*

JITS: Where's your cup, Siva?

SIVA: I had it in my toolbox and that bastard Frank started using it, so I stopped using it.

ANAND: Where is it?

JITS: Go check in the shed.

*(*ANAND *gets up and walks towards the shed)*

SIVA: Hey, don't be stupid, you can't use that cup now.

ANAND: Why?

SIVA: Frank was using that cup, it must be filthy by now.

ANAND: It can't be any more dirty than the ones you get in the tearooms or cafes.

SIVA: You wait, one day you'll learn.

ANAND: I certainly won't regret that day. *(exits)*

JITS: You ou's can't be bros man, the way you ou's fight.

SIVA: No man, these lighties think they're too big for their boots. Let them get locked up for a few days, then they'll learn.

ANAND: *(enters)* Where's the tap?

SIVA: You still going to use that cup?

ANAND: For the dirt in this cup, water is good enough, but for your kind of dirt. . . .

JITS: There's a tap there, near the drum. *(*ANAND *exits)* That bro of yours is a heavy ou man.

SIVA: Sometimes I feel sorry for him you know that. He's a sharp lighty. But when he joins up with his university chommies he goes too far with this politics shit. One day these ou's are going to get into serious trouble. They think they put their foot into a university, and they think they've changed. Fucking big mouths, that's all. My old man keeps telling him that one day he'll end up in jail.

JITS: Yaa, and once he gets involved, then the whole family's had it.

SIVA: Too much politics with these ou's.

JITS: And that, my friend, can be dangerous.

SIVA: But this fellow, he won't listen. About three weeks ago, I don't know where he comes from in the middle of the night, and he starts pulling out books and pages and posters and all kinds of shit from under the bed, on top of the wardrobe and behind the cupboards. I hear all this noise and I get up. I ask him, hey what's happening?

JITS: What did he say?

SIVA: Say? He was so scared, he couldn't even open his mouth. I can only hear ka-ka-cops.

JITS: If things are so dangerous, they should leave out all this nonsense.

ANAND: *(enters)* Thanks I'll have that tea now. *(places cup the on the newly built wall)*

JITS: *(walks to cup and pours out tea for ANAND. while pouring notices faulty brickwork)* Hey Siva, what happened here?

SIVA: Where?

JITS: Here, all these straight joints.

SIVA: That bastard Frank. I'm sure he did that on purpose.

JITS: Did he do that brickwork?

SIVA: Ya, you leave the bastard for a few minutes and he fucks everything up.

JITS: I told you man, you must keep an eye on him. All these courses with the straight joints must come down now.

SIVA: *(to ANAND)* You see, you see, treat him like a man.

ANAND: *(quietly)* I had a chat with him, a serious chat.

SIVA: *(laughing)* Ya, two mad ou's having a serious chat, that's why all the brickwork gets fucked up.

ANAND: Do you know what he thinks about you?

SIVA: You think I'm worried what he thinks about me, if he doesn't hurry up with the coke, he'll know what I think about him.

ANAND: And that's another thing, I think that was a lousy thing sending him to the tearoom during his tea break.

SIVA: What his tea break? What his tea break? Handyboys are not supposed to have tea breaks. Isn't that so Jits?

JITS: Ya, most of the other firms don't give the handyboys tea breaks. They are only entitled to lunchtimes.

SIVA: Just because we give them a chance here, they've got a lot of shit. I think that's the trouble here, Jits. Just stop all this tea time nonsense, and you'll see, the boys will wake up here.

JITS: Have a sandwich, Anand?

SIVA: I brought some too, it must be there somewhere. I don't feel like chowing, you carry on. I'm waiting for the coke. I bet you, that Frank is chooning with some dame there, Jits you must keep an eye for a good boy for me.

JITS: How's Ram's boy? I've got him digging trenches now, after Ram got fired.

SIVA: Hell, why didn't you tell me earlier? You wait, I'll fix this bastard up. There, look at him, running like he's been running all the way from the shop. I'm sure he must have started running as soon as he came around the corner. *(shouts out)* Come on you.

FRANK: Ow, ima bo. You can't see I running? Next time you must buying it the coke yourself. That shop. ou. . . . .

SIVA: That's enough, that's enough. Give me the coke.

(FRANK gives it to him and exits)

ANAND: No wonder he says all the Indians are the same.

SIVA: What shit you talking about now?

ANAND: Some times it pays to listen to people, you know.

SIVA: What you talking about?

ANAND: I asked Frank if he likes Indians. Do you know what he said? He said that the Indian is full of color bar and he's got no reason to like him and I think he's right.

SIVA: Ya, you'll think he's right, you was not there for the '49 riots.

ANAND: That's right, I was not there. If people like you treat him like this now, imagine how our grandfathers treated him in '49.

SIVA: You think the Indians caused it?

JITS: You know Anand up to now, nobody knows who caused it. Some even say that the witous caused it.

ANAND: I did not say that that the Indians caused it. But every time it comes to ill-treating an African, the Indians first defense is the '49 riots.

SIVA: Hey who got killed in '49. It was mainly the charous that died there.

JITS: You're very anti-Indian, aren't you?

SIVA: These ou's are anti-everything.

ANAND: I'm not anti-Indian, but everytime you open your mouth to an Indian about the way he treats an African the first thing he comes out with is the '49 riots.

JITS: But that is the truth, isn't it?

ANAND: Nobody is denying that it did happen, but don't blame only the African for it. We seem to be conveniently forgetting what it was like before the '49 riots. The African only gave vent to his frustration, and you don't have to look far to see who is adding to that frustration. It's bad enough being oppressed by the whitemans' laws and hatred but to also carry the Indians prejudice with it . . . . . . now that is a heavy burden.

SIVA: How can you say that?

ANAND: Well look at the way you treat Frank.

SIVA: Hey, don't talk shit man, you think only we are treating him bad?

ANAND: I didn't say that only you were doing it, and don't think Frank does not know that either. The least we can do is clean our own door step—before worrying about the others.

JITS: Anand, you keep on talking like this and you'll cause a lot of trouble.

ANAND: How can you say that? Treating Frank like an animal is causing trouble, but if I told you to treat him like a human, that's not causing trouble. As for Indians in this country. . . .

SIVA: What Indians? Why you only pick on the Indians. You think only Indians and Africans live in this country?

ANAND: For someone born in this country, you don't seem to know much about what is going on. Can't you see anything? Which other nation in the republic is draining this country besides the whites. To make matters worse the Coloreds are now joining them, no matter which side you turn, there's some Indian or the other leaving the country. They don't just leave, they convert their money into diamonds and expensive jewelry for their wives and children and sneak out like little rats.

JITS: If they are scared, what do you expect them to do?

ANAND: What are they scared of, one man one vote? All they can be scared of is all the exploiting and stealing that they are guilty of. It is their own guilt that they are scared of, that's why they are running . . . it's their own damn guilt.

FRANK: *(walking to* SIVA*)* Nangu change.

SIVA: You see the fuck-up you made with the brick work?

FRANK: Ini?

SIVA: Go and have a look there?

FRANK: Just now. *(walks away)*

SIVA: Hey, you didn't hear me?

FRANK: Ow, I'm seeing after tea time.

SIVA: You see this ou Jits, you see this ou, he don't listen.

JITS: Hey, Frank, you didn't hear him?

FRANK: Ow, funa puza tea Jits. What time I'm going to drinking my tea?

SIVA: *(to* JITS*)* Alright, leave him, tomorrow he'll see. *(to* FRANK*)* Kusasa, you're going there to the concreting gang, I'll fix you up. You full of shit eh?

FRANK: I'm just going to have my tea.

SIVA: Ya, you can have your tea, tomorrow, you'll have it there with the concreting gang.

ANAND: Siva, don't do that.

SIVA: You, shut up.

ANAND: Let him go and have his tea.

SIVA: Listen, the whole day this ou's been giving me his shit and it's all your fault. This is my graaf and I know how to get it done. *(to* FRANK*)* Where's the trowel?

FRANK: Nangu, there's it.

SIVA: Take those last two courses off.

FRANK: Manje?

SIVA: Yes.

FRANK: Ow Siva, insimbi ishaya manje.

SIVA: Fuck all that and get on with it.

ANAND: *(getting up)* I'll do it, let him have his tea. That's alright Frank I'll do it.

SIVA: You touch that trowel and this is the last time you'll come to this job. *(turns to* FRANK*)* Hamba puza your tea. *(*FRANK *exits)* (*SIVA *turns back to* ANAND*)* I'm telling you nicely now, don't interfere in my graaf.

JITS: Hey, what's wrong with you ou's? Is this how you ou's carry on in your posey too?

SIVA: No man Jits, this ou don't know anything about what happens in the building trade.

ANAND: No. *(shakes his head)* at home it is different. Even Siva is different. Besides his occasional kaffir bit, he's never like this.

SIVA: You come posey, when the old man hears of all this shit, then you'll know. Next time you ous come and choon about politics and everything, I'll phone the kerels straight away. That's the best medicine for you ou's.

JITS: Siva, you can't be serious.

ANAND: I won't be the first brother to be sold out to the police. It's happening everyday of our lives.

SIVA: Hey don't talk shit man. Don't tell me about selling out and all those things. You know what's going to happen to us when these ou's take over? Nowadays, you must be sharp. You must think ahead. You think those wit ou's and bruin ou's pulling out overseas don't know? They know, they stick around they've had it. Me, I get a graaf overseas, I'll pull out too.

JITS: You're joking.

SIVA: No. I'm serious. You think I'm going to stick around here when these ou's take over?

ANAND: Of course. What do you expect? A red carpet? You must not forget if you sow cabbages, you don't expect carrots to grow. *(tea bell rings)*

SIVA: You know what you can do with your carrots? And don't bother to take off the leaves. *(shouts to* FRANK *offstage)* Hey, what you think this is? Lunch time? Lo tea time ten minutes kupela. Come on move it.

ANAND: Don't forget time is running out.

SIVA: I think you better vie and graaf there with Jits. *(to* JITS*)* You got any graaf for this ou on the other side Jits? Seriously.

JITS: He can fill in the timesheets.

ANAND: In that case I might as well go home.

JITS: Siva is only joking.

SIVA: No man, when these ou's start chooning their shit like this, hell the man only feels like fucking them up.

JITS: *(to* FRANK *offstage)* Hey you don't yizwa the bell?

FRANK: *(offstage)* Yebo, I'm coming.

ANAND: Shall I bring my jacket too?

FRANK: *(enters, places his mug of tea and bread on brick stack)*

JITS: No leave it here. You can come here after filling in the timesheets.

SIVA: Hey Jits, give me a hand here first. I want to set the profile for the wall in the back and then you ou's can vie.

JITS: Where's the tape, Siva? *(moves behind existing brickwork)*

SIVA: Frank, get me the tape.

FRANK: *(walks to toolbox and hands the tape to* SIVA*)*

SIVA: Now move it with the brickwork. *(joins* JITS *behind the wall)*

FRANK: *(to* ANAND*)* Ow mfanawami, I'm leaving it my tea that side, ow giving it to me.

ANAND: Do you want your bread too?

FRANK: Yebo.

SIVA: Why don't you give him a saucer and tablecloth too. *(to* FRANK*)* Hey why-naa move it up with the bricks there.

ANAND: *(hands* FRANK *his tea) (to* JITS*)* Shall I wait for you in the office?

JITS: No, hang on, I won't be long. Stick around and give Frank a hand. *(flicks cigarette butt at* FRANK*)* Herewa.

FRANK: *(picks up butt)* Ngiyabonga nkosi.

SIVA: Jits, you might as well organize the window for that side where Frank is graafing.

*(*JITS *and* SIVA *remain in their positions, carrying out a low conversation in relation to their stage business of measuring brickwork positioning)*

FRANK: *(preparing to start laying bricks)* You going to be working the other side?

ANAND: *(standing undecidedly)* Yes, Jits says that I can fill in the timesheets.

FRANK: What work you was doing before you coming here?

ANAND: This is my first job. It's only part time.

FRANK: Ini?

ANAND: It's only part time. I'm on holiday now.

FRANK: Awww. . . . holiday?

ANAND: You see, I'm studying at the university.

FRANK: Oopi le indow?

ANAND: Sorry, what's that?

FRANK: Where this place? This one city?

ANAND: *(laughs)* No, no, Frank, it's not a city like that. It's a university. It's . . . it's . . . it's like a school for big people.

FRANK: Aww . . . manje he's giving it you a holiday? Ow, it's a nice place that one. Kiss-moos come they giving it you 'nother one holiday?

ANAND: Yes.

FRANK: Ow, that's a nice place that one. Me, I'm thinking I'm going that place too.

ANAND: Where?

FRANK: That place you going, that . . . that university.

ANAND: You can't go there.

FRANK: Ow ini indaba? You saying that for the big people that.

ANAND: No, it's not that, it's . . . it's . . .

FRANK: Awww. . . . It's only for the amaIndia people?

ANAND: Ours is, but there are separate ones for the African people too, but first you'll have to go to primary school, then to high school and only then can you . . .

FRANK: Kaa. Leaving it. leaving it. Shiya zonka lezinto. You must have a lot, lot mali for that things. Musbe I'm sending my children that place.

ANAND: How many children do you have?

FRANK: Amana, four. Three bafana, one girl. The girl, she's the clever one, that one. I'm thinking I'm sending my girl that one place that you going.

ANAND: To the university?

FRANK: Yebo. Then musbe she learning to speaking like you. Ow I'm seeing how you speaking to the Siva. He getting it, too much cross. They teach all the childrens to be speaking like that?

ANAND: It depends on what subject you are doing. I'm doing law.

FRANK: Aww. . . . What that thing? That thing you doing?

ANAND: Law.

FRANK: You doing it a law? How you doing it that?

ANAND: I'm studying law. You know, I'm learning law.

FRANK: Aww . . . then they teaching you how you mus speaking about all the things?

ANAND: No not about all the things. If I'm studying law, then I can speak about law.

FRANK: Ow. yini leyento? What this law thing? Not about speaking that?

ANAND: No Frank, law is not only about speaking. Law is . . . law is . . . well you see each country has it's own law, and . . . well it's like this. The government of each country makes it's own law and to understand it you . . . it's a little hard to explain, maybe if I knew the Zulu word for law then I'd be . . .

FRANK: Fanala sheeya mfanawami, leaving it.

ANAND: No, no, wait, Frank. *(slight pause)* Well it's like this, if you got caught by the police for . . . let's say stealing and you don't know anything about the law and what happens to you for stealing . . .

FRANK: Hey mfanawami, I'm not doing all that things..

ANAND: . . . or maybe you didn't steal, but the police suspect you and they arrest you . . .

FRANK: Sheeya mfanawami, leaving it. You making it too much mix-up.

ANAND: Sorry Frank, it's quite complicated to . . . *(slight pause)* Well you see Frank, if you want to become a lawyer, you must . . . er . . . er . . . you'll have to learn law. That's what I'm doing. I'm learning law. If the police catch you. . . . Did the police catch you at any time?

FRANK: Too much.

ANAND: For what?

FRANK: Ow for the dompass.

ANAND: Then I can speak for you.

FRANK: Aww . . . you is a meli.

ANAND: What's that?

FRANK: Meli. That one thing you doing it, it is a meli.

ANAND: Is that so?

FRANK: Ow hey, mfanawami, how you going to know it that time the phoyisa is going to come to catching it me? That time they coming, they not playing. They just coming one time putting it the insimbi, one ikick, pagati imoto. Zwiee you coming it the kantolo, 'nother one kick, outside the moto. Gena kantolo, faga stamp la ipaper, 'nother one two shots, I'm sitting inside the jail. Kaa mfanawami that thing you doing it, that meli thing, it is not for the Muntos. You can't speaking it for me.

ANAND: Of course I can.

FRANK: Then you must coming and staying here by me. I'm not knowing that time they coming to catch me. (FRANK *resumes laying bricks and breaks into song.)*

JITS: *(preparing to leave)(to* SIVA*)* I'll check you later. Keep a sharp eye on this ou.

SIVA: He knows what will happen to him

JITS: O.K. then. *(looks towards the wall* FRANK *is building)* Doesn't the window frame come on that course there.

SIVA: Ya. *(reaches and looks into plan, starts counting the courses and measuring the brickwork).*Yas it comes on this course. *(to* FRANK*)* Hey Frank, go and get me that frame from the shed, the makulu one kupela, only the big one.

FRANK: Hey mfanawami, you got it a room for me there by your house?

SIVA: Why? What you want a room in my house for?

FRANK: Ow Siva, the amablackjacks this side, they worling it me too much. That time I'm staying there by your house, the meli, he can speaking it for me.

SIVA: The who?

FRANK: The meli, that one thing your brother learning to do.

SIVA: Leave all those things and get that frame.

FRANK: *(exits)*

SIVA: *(to* ANAND*)* What shit is that ou talking about? You told him you going to give him a room in our posey.

ANAND: No, we were just talking about. . . .

SIVA: You bring that ou by the posey, you know what the old man will do to you.

JITS: You better watch out with these ou's, Anand. You don't know about this Frank, he's a big hustler. He didn't ask you for your old pants and shoes yet?

ANAND: I don't think you people understand much about him.

SIVA: Therewa, therewa, he's starting his politics again.

ANAND: Are you guys normally like this or are your'll trying to be funny.

SIVA: There's nothing funny about bringing Frank home.

ANAND: The man didn't even mention anything. He just wanted to be close to me.

SIVA: Why?

ANAND: I told him I was studying law.

SIVA: So?

ANAND: He felt that if I was close to him and if the blackjacks arrested him, I will be able to speak for him.

JITS: You going to be a lawyer?

ANAND: Yes. I'm in my third year.

JITS: Like I said, you don't know anything about Frank, this ou is a professional hustler.

ANAND: I think he's a very dignified man.

SIVA: Shit bloody dignified. *(shouts to* FRANK *offstage)* Hey ynaa, buisa lo dignified frame lapa. Tell you what that ou is doing there now Jits, he's catching a dignified chow. That's what he is doing. Dignified, man huh.

JITS: Hey Frank.

SIVA: That ou is not a professional hustler, he's a dignified hustler.

ANAND: Maybe if he got a better wage he won't have to hustle. You people don't seem to know anything about the man. Maybe you should take some time and find out more about him. I'm sure you don't even know how many children he's got or where he comes from or what his ambitions are. Frank never asked me for anything.

JITS: Hey Frank,

FRANK: Yebo.

JITS: Where's that frame?

FRANK: *(enters carrying window frame, his cheeks are bulging with bread)* Therewa. Nangu.

SIVA: See. Check his mouth. What did I tell you?

ANAND: He didn't have his teabreak you know that.

SIVA: You starting that tea break shit again?

JITS: Frank, bring me two stays and some bricks here.

FRANK: *(exits to fetch them)*

ANAND: How do you expect him to work, when he's got no food in his stomach?

SIVA: You see what I mean, Jits? This is what I mean. *(to* ANAND*)* You think I make the law about handyboys and their tea breaks? Go and speak to the industrial council about that. They are the ones that make the rules for the building trade.

ANAND: Those are the whiteman's rules. You're a black man like Frank, and you think what is right and what. . . .

SIVA: *(aggressively)* Hey fuck you man. I'm a fucking Indian. Don't come and tell me what's right and what's wrong. I told you, let these ou's take over then you'll fucking see.

ANAND: That doesn't in anyway justify . . .

FRANK: *(enters carrying two stays)*

SIVA: You want to come and stay in my posey?

FRANK: You got a room for me? Ow the amablackjacks is worling me too much here by job.

SIVA: Ya, I got a room for you.

FRANK: Ow, you siza me too much.

SIVA: You can sleep with my dog.

FRANK: Ow whena.

SIVA: No, no, no, first I'll take a photo of you. You know a photo? Istombe?

FRANK: Yebo, yebo.

SIVA: I'll take your photo and I'll show it to my dog, and I'll say, *(demonstrates)* Hey Rover, you see this kapri face anywhere near the house, you bite him. Now, you still want to come and stay in my house?

FRANK: Wena Siva, you're a moobi.

JITS: Siva center this frame, Anand grab the other stay.

SIVA: Frank get me the level.

FRANK: *(reaches for level and hands it to* SIVA*)*

SIVA: Push this to me a bit, not too much. Right hold it there, bopa manje. *(moves to opposite side of frame)* Pull this to you a bit, that okay. Frank bopha this side too.

JITS: Okay, I'll see you guys later. *(exits)*

SIVA: Watch the brickwork you, no more fuck-ups and no more stories.

FRANK: Ow, you can seeing I'm laying it the amabricks.

SIVA: Ya, and talking stories too and fucking up the brickwork. Just basopa.

ANAND: You going back to the bushes?

SIVA: Why you got a headache too?

ANAND: No, I'll manage.

SIVA: *(to* FRANK*)* Basopa you. *(exits)*

FRANK: Musbe you sitting back your place. *(indicating to brick stack)* *(adds water to mortar, to soften it)* Why the Siva shouting you like that?

ANAND: It's nothing. *(sits, he is free to move as he pleases during the following dialogue with* FRANK*)*

FRANK: In the house too he shouting like that?

ANAND: No.

FRANK: Musbe he not liking you speaking too much by me. Ow, I'm hearling all that things he was saying. He getting it too much cross. *(starts laying bricks)* *(slight pause)* Hey mfanawami, you must telling me all 'bout the meli. That thing you learning to do.

ANAND: Oh there's not much to tell, I study, I write exams, I'll be serving my articles under another lawyer. You know like an apprentice. After that I can practice on my own.

FRANK: Ow, then you must being my friend. You must speaking for me that time they catching me for the dompass.

ANAND: But I won't be a lawyer for long.

FRANK: Ow, ini indaba? That's a nice work that. Why you leaving it a nice one work like that?

ANAND: No, no, Frank, I won't be leaving that kind of work. It's just that I will be writing more exams.

FRANK: More futhi?

ANAND: Yes. I want to qualify as a public prosecutor.

FRANK: It's a big thing that?

ANAND: Yes, just like a lawyer, but I won't be doing any private work, you know . . . I'll be a public prosecutor. I'll be working for the government.

FRANK: Goto, what is this thing? Ini leyozinto?

ANAND: *(helplessly)* How can I explain it to you Frank? It's . . . it's . . . the kind of work where I will be reading out the charges in front of a judge or magistrate.

FRANK: You . . . you . . . you going to be learning to read out the amacharges?

ANAND: Yes. Although it won't be. . . .

FRANK: My charges futi?

ANAND: If your charges come up.

FRANK: Ow, I'm thinking you my friend.

ANAND: I am your friend.

FRANK: How you going to be my friend, you going to be reading out my charges?

ANAND: That will be my job.

FRANK: Ow inkosi yam. I must looking for 'nother one friend for speaking it for me.

ANAND: I'll still be your friend.

FRANK: You can't be. *(slight pause as he continues working)* That time you going to be my friend, you must giving it me a chance alright. You giving it me a chance? That time the amablackjack catching me for the dompass you giving it me a chance, hey mfanawami?

ANAND: Well you see Frank, if I am a lawyer or a prosecutor I am always supposed to speak the truth.

FRANK: Ow, meena nje, Frank Khuzawayo. Me, your friend?

ANAND: Even if it is my mother I must always speak the truth . . .

FRANK: Hey mfanawami, that mother for you, she not coming to that place. She not a carrying it a dompass.

ANAND: If the law says that. . . .

FRANK: Ini le law? Only the Muntos must carrying it the dompass?

ANAND: That's the law according to the government.

FRANK: Ow, I was thinking you was my friend.

ANAND: You don't understand Frank, I don't make the law.

FRANK: Then why you must coming the charges reading man?

ANAND: I do feel sorry for you Frank but . . .

FRANK: Ow, hey mfanawami, looking it here, *(pleads)* that time you seeing it that name Frank Khuzawayo, you must knowing that it is me, you seeing that name you must giving it me a chance. Alright?

ANAND: *(smiles)* Alright. If I see your name I'll . . .

FRANK: *(excited, reaches out and shakes* ANAND *by the hand)* Ow, meli wami. Shali pansi. *(dusts the bricks for* ANAND *to sit)* You coming to work tomorrow?

ANAND: I'm not too sure. You see . . . er . . . er . . . Siva

FRANK: Not to worling about the Siva. Tomorrow he haven't got it a babalaaz. He not swearing it too much.

ANAND: Alright I'll come.

FRANK: 'Nother one thing tomorrow the Temba he is coming too. He going to the farm. I'm speaking it the lies to the Jits, I'm saying he sick. Tomorrow he coming to work. Hey mfanawami, you like it a nkuku.

ANAND: Sorry, what's that?

FRANK: The nkukhu, the chicken. The Temba, he musbe bringing one nkukhu tomorrow. Next month I'm going to the farm. I'm bringing it one nice one nkukhu for you.

ANAND: You don't have to worry about all those things Frank.

FRANK: Tomorrow it is a month end, the amablackjacks, they must to coming. They not coming tomorrow, they sure, sure, coming Friday. They knowing it is a monthend and it is a Friday, they knowing that we got a mali. That time the amablackjack is coming you mus saying you my friend, my meli. You mus speak for me alright? And for the Temba too. The Temba, he too, he haven't got a dompass. He's a good one that one. Manje I mus laying it the amabricks. *(breaks into song while working)(bends down to pick up brick, notices inspector, drops the trowel and steps back)*

ANAND: *(stares, not understanding)*

INSPECTOR: *(with authority)* Hey you, what are you doing here? What's your name?

FRANK: Meena baas?

INSPECTOR: Yes you. *(to* ANAND*)* Are you a bricklayer?

ANAND: No.

FRANK: Frank, baas.

INSPECTOR: *(writing into his file)* Where's the bricklayer on this job? *(to* FRANK*)* You the bricklayer?

FRANK: Not me baas.

INSPECTOR: Then what are you doing with a trowel in your hand.

FRANK: Ow baas, nothing baas I'm not doing. . . .

INSPECTOR: Don't lie to me. I saw you laying those bricks. What's your surname?

FRANK: Ini baas?

INSPECTOR: Your spongo. I'm sure you have a surname.

FRANK: Khuzawayo, baas.

INSPECTOR: Where's your pass? Your dompass.

FRANK: La ished.

INSPECTOR: Go and fetch it. *(*FRANK *exits)(inspector writing, to* ANAND*)* What are you doing here?

ANAND: Some part-time work.

INSPECTOR: As a laborer?

ANAND: Yes.

INSPECTOR: Laborer? You are that boy's laborer? *(nods his head)* Do you know that boy is not supposed to be laying bricks and that he can lose his job?

ANAND: I did not know that he'd lose his job.

INSPECTOR: But where did you hear of an Indian being a Bantu's laborer.

ANAND: I don't see any thing wrong with that?

INSPECTOR: There's plenty wrong with that my boy, plenty wrong with that.

ANAND: Isn't there a way of saving his job? Can't there be a fine or something?

INSPECTOR: Of course there is a fine, and you can be sure that his boss is not going to pay it. It would be cheaper to fire him.

FRANK: *(enters emptyhanded)*

INSPECTOR: Where's your dompass?

FRANK: It is lost baas.

INSPECTOR: So you're working here without a dompass too?

FRANK: It is lost baas.

INSPECTOR: Never mind, I'll get everything from your boss. Right come on.

FRANK: Ow siza baas, please give it me one chance baas.

INSPECTOR: One chance and you'll do it again. You people never learn. Isn't there a bricklayer on this job?

FRANK: Yebo baas, he's going to the bushes, the toilet. He the one that telling me to lay the amabricks.

INSPECTOR: Oh . . . This is getting interesting. Very interesting. Get that bricklayer here.

FRANK: *(exits towards bushes)*

INSPECTOR: How many more Bantus on this job.

ANAND: Frank is the only laborer on this cottage.

INSPECTOR: So he's the laborer and the bricklayer here.

SIVA: *(enters with* FRANK *close behind him)* Good morning sir.

INSPECTOR: Morning, I'm from the industrial council.

SIVA: Anything wrong sir?

INSPECTOR: Yes. I saw this boy laying bricks just now. Did you ask him to lay bricks?

SIVA: Me sir? I never ask the boys to lay bricks, me.

INSPECTOR: Well, he says so.

JITS: *(enters)* What's wrong, Siva?

INSPECTOR: Who are you?

JITS: The chargehand. Is there something wrong?

INSPECTOR: Where's the boss. You people make your Bantu laborers lay bricks?

JITS: Which laborer? Who's he talking about, Siva?

SIVA: This Frank man. Hell Jits I just vied to the toilet for a few minutes, and . . .

INSPECTOR: Did you ask him to lay bricks?

SIVA: No sir, I'm a union man me, I know all the rules and regulations of the industrial council.

JITS: Frank, did you lay any bricks?

INSPECTOR: Listen, I am telling you I saw this boy lay bricks.

JITS: Well, if you saw him, he must have been messing around with the trowel You know what these boys are like?

INSPECTOR: Where is your office? Right you, come on.

FRANK: Ow Siva, tell the baas you telling me to lay the amabricks.

SIVA: Who me? When did I tell you to do that?

FRANK: Ow Jits, I'm not speaking the lies. The Siva, he the one tell me . . .

JITS: Siva can't be that stupid. You should learn to leave the tools alone, you know that you are not supposed to handle the tools.

INSPECTOR: *(to* SIVA) You sure you did not ask him to . . . . . .

SIVA: Definitely. I know the law. I know that according to the job reservations act, Africans are not allowed to do skilled work.

FRANK: Ow Siva, you must tell the baas the true.

INSPECTOR: Right you, come on, I haven't got the whole day to listen to your stories. Is your boss in his office?

JITS: Yes, he should be.

FRANK: Ow baas, I'm speaking the true. *(notices* ANAND*)* Wait baas. Eema baas. *(points to* ANAND*)* Ask that other one baas. He the brother for Siva that. He know it that the Siva he got it a babalaaz. He tell me to lay it amabricks.

INSPECTOR: *(to* ANAND*)* Did that bricklayer ask this boy to lay bricks?

ANAND: *(helplessly looks from* SIVA *to* JITS *and both avoid his eyes.* ANAND *looks at* FRANK *and* ANAND *is forced to look away)(he finally answers)* No he did not.

INSPECTOR: That's it, come on you.

    *(*FRANK *and inspector exit)*

SIVA: *(to* FRANK *offstage)* Hey Frank, come back here when you're finished. *(turns around, slight pause)* Hell that Frank is stupid you know that, I thought he was going to get all of us involved just now.

JITS: That was quick thinking Anand.

SIVA: *(proudly)* Blood is thicker that water. Jits. Thicker than water.

ANAND: What will happen to him now?

SIVA: How's this inspector Jits?

JITS: I don't know. He looks like a cheeky ou. Then again, we can't say, maybe he'll give Frank a break. First time I check this ou on this side.

ANAND: And if he charges Frank, how much will it be?

JITS: I don't know. Maybe, fifty rands or something.

SIVA: No man, that's for working weekends and holidays without a permit. I think it's about twenty or thirty rands.

ANAND: Who'll pay the fine?

SIVA: The firm will have to pay.

JITS: I don't think Van Niekerk will agree to that.

SIVA: He's just the general foreman here, he's not the lahnee.

JITS: Who runs the job? You think the lahnee? The G.F.

ANAND: If they don't pay, what happens?

SIVA: I don't know. Anyhow that Frank should have been sharp.

ANAND: But I was keeping watch.

JITS: You didn't see that wit ou coming?

ANAND: I saw him, but I didn't think he was an inspector. He looked more like a drunk.

SIVA: Hey Jits, this is the ou. I heard about this ou. He's got a funny name. This ou, you give him a bottle and all your problems are over. You must choon ou Van Niekerk to buy him a bottle. No more inspector problems after that.

JITS: Yaa, this ou looks like a big tanker.

SIVA: This ou must be collecting a span of bottles from all the contractors. Hey, if every firm gave him a bottle. . . .

FRANK: *(enters, wordlessly walks to barrow, picks up handle to wheel it out)*

JITS: What happened?

FRANK: He charging me.

SIVA: He's lying. He just doesn't want to lay bricks.

FRANK: The baas he say the papar, it's coming next week, I mus paying the fine. Otherwise he fireling me. *(starts moving the barrow)*

ANAND: *(reaching out to* FRANK's *shoulder)* We'll try and raise the money, Frank. *(*FRANK *shrugs off* ANAND's *hand)* I'm sorry Frank. I didn't know. *(*FRANK *ignores him)* Frank I didn't know that this will happen. I didn't know that. *(turns around to* JITS *and* SIVA*)* Tell him I didn't know.

(Lights fade out. Music fades in, on the words . . . "there's room at the top they're telling you still . . . ")

Kriben Pillay

Kriben Pillay, a senior lecturer in the Leadership Centre at the University of KwaZulu-Natal, is an award-winning writer, consultant, as well as playwright. His writing spans genres of theatre, poetry, essays, short stories, academic essays, and children's books. Besides *Looking for Muruga,* he has written two musicals, *Coming Home* (1993), and *Side by Side Masisizane* (1989). He has also created numerous educational theatre pieces for high school and university students.

As a consultant, Pillay has created workshops about deep learning and transformation, which he presents at schools, businesses, and government organizations. He currently edits *The Noumenon Journal,* a publication about transformation within a nondual perspective. Among his publications, his poetry and essay collection, *A Mind in Revolt* (1986), *Learning to See: Self-Discoveries through Theatre* (1988), and *Looking for Muruga* (1995) were nominated for South African literary prizes.

Pillay has written a critically acclaimed analysis of personal transformation and nonduality titled *Radical Work: Exploring Transformation in the Workplace through the Work of Byron Katie* (2001). His latest book, *The Story of the Forgetful Ice Lollies* (2003), deals with spirituality for children. In 2005, Pillay received the National Arts Council Award for Literature. His latest theatre piece, *Mindworx,* combines brain science, illusion, and philosophy.

Looking for Muruga

Indian Premiere, Hyderabad, 1999
Natal Playhouse, Durban, 1991

Grahamstown Festival, Grahamstown, South Africa, 1991
Asoka Theatre Tour, KwaZulu Natal and Gauteng, 1990–91

Other Plays

Coming Home
FM Stereotype
Mr. Bansi is Dead
Mr. O's Story
Side by Side Masisizane
The Two-Fold Tamil Rule

Looking for Muruga

Kriben Pillay

ACT ONE

(It is almost closing time when the lights come up on the set of a small hotel bar. It appears to be deserted when DANTÉ, *a Black African student, enters. He looks around, obviously looking for someone.)*

DANTÉ: *(shouts).* Coolie! Hey, coolie, where are you?

(Not really waiting for a response he begins limbering up with some dance exercises, at which point Muruga appears from behind the counter.)

MURUGA: Ever since Mandela got released you fellas got a lot buck, eh. *(Feigning mock seriousness,* DANTÉ *speaks in Zulu to which* MURUGA *replies in Tamil. The exchange happens twice).* Always nice to have a conversation with you Danté.

DANTÉ: And the same to you. You know, one day we are going to get into big trouble.

MURUGA: For what?

DANTÉ: For speaking like the way we do. They will think that we're fighting. You know how people are.

MURUGA: What people? The pekkie comrades who think every char-ou is just a white man in a dark skin, or the char-ous who think pekkies are not human beings?

DANTÉ: All of them. They wouldn't understand. All they will hear are "pekkies" and "char-ous" and think you are a racist. My varsity friends will find you and me difficult to understand.

MURUGA: *(surprised).* Even those who come here to drink?

South African Première at the Asoka Theatre, University of Durban-Westville, Wednesday, 29 August 1990

DANTÉ: Even those. People take a long time to understand.

MURUGA: So what do they think? That I only like you because I might be a pottemari and I like your body.

(Imitating a camp gay.)

Hello Danté, have I shown you my six-foot *(slight pause)* dance? It's really quite good, and it's not too hard.

DANTÉ: *(laughs).* Hey Muruga, you are too much. If anyone had to come in now, they'd really think you're queer.

MURUGA: I know. We always think others are queer if they don't behave the way we want them to behave. I got no time for that nonsense.

DANTÉ: I know. You are always giving people who have a lot to say a hard time.

MURUGA: Not everyone, just the hypocrites. But we're talking too much now, what do you think this is, an ANC conference?

DANTÉ: *(laughs).* Hey, you must be careful, one day they'll necklace you.

MURUGA: As long it's the right tire, they can do what they want. Then I can die saying I've had a Good Year.

(They both laugh at the pun.)

DANTÉ: No, Muruga, that's weak. Your jokes are much better.

MURUGA: Hey, it's no time for jokes, it's almost closing time. I must still do my practice. Big six-foot jol coming up at Motala's farm. So what can I do for you?

DANTÉ: You said I must come today to practice the dance and to try the costume. I must get ready soon for the exams. This Indian dance at the university is difficult.

MURUGA: How else you fellas going to get some culture?

(DANTÉ replies in Zulu.)

MURUGA: Very true, very true. But now you've got to practice the dance. You've got the tape?

DANTÉ: Yes, here it is.

MURUGA: *(puts the music on, and watches DANTÉ dance).* For a pekkie you learnt that very fast. Very good, very good.

DANTÉ: It's not so different from some of our African steps. Look.

(He dances.)

MURUGA: Ja, you right, you people have got some culture. Show me your steps. *(DANTÉ shows him, and they have a duel of sorts)* Right, we must stop now. *(He puts off the tape-recorder).* I must still clear up. I'll see you tomorrow.

DANTÉ: Have you forgotten?

MURUGA: What?

DANTÉ: Don't play fools with me, you said you were going to get me a costume for the dance.

MURUGA: What costume?

DANTÉ: The costume for the Indian dance exam at the university.

MURUGA: What you're worrying and fretting for, I've got it right here. *(He goes behind the counter and fetches the costume.)* Here, but look after it carefully.

DANTÉ: What costume is it?

MURUGA: Oh, just one of the gods.

DANTÉ: Which one?

MURUGA: Muruga.

DANTÉ: *(looks at him blankly).* You? You're not a god!

MURUGA: Not me stupid, the god Muruga. The boy god. That's why I chose it for you. You'll make a good boy. But don't walk around anyhow, the char-ous will give you bathies.

DANTÉ: Why, for being a god?

MURUGA: For a pekkie being an Indian god.

(DANTÉ *says something in Zulu.)*

And when you put on the costume you must only speak Tamil.

DANTÉ: Aiyayo!

MURUGA: After all I taught you that's all you know. Peri stupid nee.[1]

DANTÉ replies in Zulu.

MURUGA: And a very good night to you. Now go. Wait. Come back when you put on the costume. Put the make-up like I showed you.

(DANTÉ *leaves taking the costume and spear, but leaves the cassette behind.* MURUGA *begins clearing the tables when he notices the tape recorder. He rewinds and plays the tape. The music being played is a popular devotional song to which* MURUGA *begins dancing. The dancing is more a rehearsal with* MURUGA *furtively casting glances to see that no one is watching. He is quite absorbed in his efforts which are fairly pleasing to the eye when* SHERWIN, *a conservatively dressed teacher, walks in. In a Chaplinesque move* MURUGA *pretends that he is cleaning up.)*

MURUGA: *(irritated).* I'm sorry we're closed. Didn't you see the sign on the door?

SHERWIN: I'm sorry for coming in so late, but I'm looking for someone.

MURUGA: Well, as you can see, there's no one here.

SHERWIN: Actually, I'm looking for someone who works here; I'm looking for Muruga.

MURUGA: I'm Muruga.

SHERWIN: *(staring blankly for awhile).* Er, I'm looking for another Muruga.

MURUGA: *(facetiously).* Then you'd better try a temple. I'm the only Muruga here.

SHERWIN: But there was a waiter here by the name of Muruga. I last saw him about ten years ago. He was a thin, smallish man, about your height. I'm

---

[1] Mixed Tamil/English: you are very stupid.

sure there must be someone in this hotel who remembers him, or even knows where he is.

MURUGA: I've been here a long time now and I've never heard of any other Muruga besides myself. Maybe you've come to the wrong bar.

SHERWIN: No, this is the place. You know we'd often come here as students, and I'd come mainly because of Muruga. I could never forget him. He always did his special act for us the moment we sat down.

(SHERWIN *sees a bar tray on the counter and picks it up. It appears that he is going to start drumming on the tray. Pause. He is very uncomfortable with himself and the picture that he presents. He puts the tray down.* MURUGA *looks at him and picks the tray up. He goes into a comic routine.* SHERWIN *looks aghast at him. There is a slight pause at the end of the routine.*)

MURUGA: (*begins singing to establish routine—goes to imaginary customers*). What can I do for you madam? You want three lagers, a double cane and coke, one brandy, three plates of chips, and some fishcakes—Freddy just take the order here . . . (*he sings a snatch of a Tamil song before spotting some people*) . . . Ah, here are my varsity friends. Freddy just see to these fellas . . . (*sings*) . . . So, you all are going to become teachers. You know, my father wanted to become a teacher, but when he found out what he had to teach, he became a temple priest instead . . . (*sings*) . . . You heard the one about the teacher and the waiter. They went fishing in a boat. After some time the teacher asked the waiter if he knew anything about grammar. The waiter said no.

The teacher said, "If you don't know anything about grammar then half your life is gone." Later the boat began to sink because of a leak. The waiter asked the teacher if he could swim. The teacher said no. The waiter said, "If you can't swim then your whole life is gone."

(*Sings.*)

SHERWIN: You were just like Muruga, I can't believe it!

MURUGA: I am Muruga.

SHERWIN: I mean the other Muruga.

MURUGA: Maybe all waiters are Murugas.

SHERWIN: You must have known Muruga to do what you just did. It's impossible to be just like someone else.

(*Pause.*)

MURUGA: You're very interested to know who I am, but who are you?

SHERWIN: Excuse my bad manners. I'm Sherwin Christopher. I'm a teacher and also a bit of a writer.

MURUGA: You already know who I am. I'm Muruga and I'm a barman. And I don't know this other Muruga that you're speaking of. Tell me, why do you want to see him?

SHERWIN: It's very difficult to explain. Maybe I want to write about him.

MURUGA: You want to write about a waiter?

SHERWIN: But he wasn't just any ordinary waiter. He did what you just did. He was an entertainer. He gave us something special on those Saturday nights. He made us laugh.

MURUGA: And you want to write about that. How? Do you want to make a drama with Muruga in it?

SHERWIN: I'm not quite sure. Yes, I want to write a play about Muruga. But using Muruga is probably out of the question. If he is around he'd be too old now. No, I'd like to write a play about him. You know, write about the kind of things he did.

MURUGA: I don't know anything about writing, but all this is very interesting. Very interesting. What I want to know is why are you only looking for him now?

SHERWIN: I've been away, in and out of Durban.

MURUGA: And now you want to write a drama about Muruga.

SHERWIN: Yes.

MURUGA: Perhaps I can help you.

SHERWIN: I don't even know you. I've just met you.

MURUGA: Maybe. Maybe not.

SHERWIN: (slightly irritated). I'm sorry for wasting your time, but I came here hoping to find someone I knew.

MURUGA: That's what I'm saying. Did you know Muruga?

SHERWIN: Yes, of course. I must have come here dozens of times. I often spoke to the man . . . about his family and things like that.

MURUGA: I can tell you something about my family. I have three sons and a daughter. My wife is dead. My sons are all working but not yet married. My daughter is still schooling. Now you can write about me. One Muruga is the same as another.

SHERWIN: Please you don't understand. You can't just write a play like that.

MURUGA: Okay, so you can't write a play about me. But how were you going to write about that other Muruga? What's the difference?

SHERWIN: I don't know what you're getting at, but it's time for me to go.

MURUGA: No Mr. Big Shot Writer you can't go just yet. There are still things I want to understand, I also want to know about Muruga.

SHERWIN: Listen, I'm sorry for wasting your time, but this conversation is going nowhere. I'm not even sure that I understand you.

MURUGA: Of course you don't understand me. But maybe I understand you. You're looking for a man named Muruga. This man was a waiter and was very entertaining—and you want to write about him. You want to write a drama. But what I want to know is what drama? Can you write a drama about a man you used to see every Saturday night? Can you write about a man because you know something about his family?

SHERWIN: Yes, of course you can.

MURUGA: But you can only write about what you see and what you make up in your head, and what you make up in your head is what you want to see. I'll give you something to see. *(Goes into extended routine.)*

Now here's a little story,
I want you to hear,
It's a good, good story,
You won't even think of beer.

When people come to see me,
I give them all my time,
And they go home smiling,
Feeling everything is fine.

"Muruga," they shout,
"Muruga," they scream,
And I come dancing,
It's almost like a dream.

Now everyone asks,
What do I give,
I don't really know,
It's just the way I live.

Now here's a little story,
I want you to hear,
It's a good, good story,
You won't even think of beer.

So now you come looking,
For the perfect play,
Am I the lahnee's pleasure,
With stablexpense for pay?

Why should I care,
It's not worth a. . . . ,
The word I just left out,
Rhymes with Bombay duck.

Now here's a little story,
I want you to hear,
It's a good, good story,
You won't even think of beer.

Some words can't be said,
Pardon the omission,

But everything was kept,
In the James Commission.

We all want to laugh,
But somewhere someone's sad,
So some come to me,
While others think I'm bad.

Why that is so,
I shall never know,
Maybe it's too dangerous,
To make the stories low.

But what is low,
Are not the dirty bits,
They all love the story,
'Bout Thangachie's big . . . nits.

See what I mean,
How they laughed and cried,
But when they're home,
Will they care if I died?

I'm just a poor old joker,
Always with a song,
But making people crazy,
When I show their right is wrong.

Some say I'm at the edge,
But I think it's nice,
It certainly isn't,
Some big sacrifice.

That's what I do,
I know it's nothing new,
But it's good to give your customers,
A special kind of brew.

Now here's a little story,
I want you to hear,
It's a good, good story,
You won't even think of beer.[2]

---

[2] *The Lahnee's Pleasure, Stablexpense, Bombay Duck, The James Commission, At the Edge,* and *The Sacrifice* are plays by South African Indian playwrights and were big hits in the 1970s, 1980s, and early 1990s.

(Pause.)

Isn't this what you want to write about Mr. Big Shot Writer? You put this into your play and everybody is happy.

SHERWIN: No.

MURUGA: No?

SHERWIN: No.

MURUGA: Then what were you going to write about?

SHERWIN: About Muruga.

MURUGA: But how can you write about someone you don't know?

SHERWIN: How do you know that I don't know?

MURUGA: Oh, that's easy.

SHERWIN: It is? Then tell me.

MURUGA: Because I'm Muruga.

SHERWIN: I know you're Muruga.

MURUGA: But I'm the Muruga you're looking for, the one you want to write about.

SHERWIN: Don't talk rubbish.

MURUGA: Watch closely.

(He goes into routine. This time SHERWIN becomes part of the role-play, which is essentially a flashback. The routine becomes increasingly risqué until the alienation that SHERWIN feels leads to a verbal confrontation.)

(Sings.)

Hey, everybody Sherwin is here. Come, come Sherwin, so what's new at the varsity?

SHERWIN: *(slightly embarrassed by the attention)*. Oh, nothing new.

MURUGA: Come, come Sherwin, tell us what's new in the drama department? Not doing another play? *(Turning to imaginary customers.)* Anyone seen the plays at the varsity? *(He gets a negative reaction.)* What's wrong Sherwin, you must take all these people to see your plays. So what's the latest?

SHERWIN: We doing a play called *Waiting for Godot*.

MURUGA: Waiting for God, eh? Well I'm waiting, but nothing has happened . . . *(sings)* . . . Hey, Sherwin, why don't you show us something from the play.

SHERWIN: No, it can't be done just like that. It won't make sense.

MURUGA: Hey, kanna, nothing makes sense, so why don't you give us a little bit of drama department entertainment. Look how everyone is waiting. You waiting for God, and everyone here is waiting for Sherwin. Come, Sherwin, don't be shy.

SHERWIN: Well, there is one part I can do. But to do it properly, I need a rope, otherwise I can't do it.

MURUGA: Rope? No problem. Rope you want, rope you got. *(Goes behind bar counter and fetches the rope.)* Here's the rope. Hope you not going to hang yourself? The lahnee will get very upset. Last time they found a fella killed himself in room 201, the lahnee drank for one whole week, so upset he was. Anything else you need?

SHERWIN: No.

MURUGA: Good. Before you start you better tell us something about the play.

SHERWIN: Well, I play a character by the name of Lucky . . .

MURUGA: Hell, I knew a fella with that name. Remember him, Freddy. Every week he had a new girl with him. Everyone use to call him Lucky Fu . . . I'm sorry madam . . . sorry Sherwin, carry on.

SHERWIN: Well, the play is about . . . *(slight pause)* . . . well it's about these two men waiting for a man named Godot who never turns up . . .

MURUGA: How nice if my mother-in-law was like that.

SHERWIN: . . . and in this scene Lucky, who doesn't speak at all . . .

MURUGA: So how's he going to speak now, Sherwin?

SHERWIN: What I mean is, he doesn't speak until this point. You see, the writer is trying to show that man doesn't really communicate, that man is cut off, that he is . . .

MURUGA: Sherwin, if you don't start your play you'll be cut off.

(SHERWIN *begins.* MURUGA *is indulgent towards him for a while, until he becomes a barometer of the audience's noncomprehension of the piece. Echoing Godot,* MURUGA's *actions mirror the attempt to silence Lucky.* SHERWIN *is oblivious of the attempt to silence him, seeing* MURUGA's *actions as part of the play-acting. This section must be carefully orchestrated so that the action develops momentum with* MURUGA *running into the audience trying to get them to decipher what* SHERWIN *is doing. He is very disparaging of this kind of drama and refers to the hits of Indian theatre as the kind of drama that is worthwhile.)*

SHERWIN: "Given the existence as uttered forth in the public works of Puncher and Wattmann of a personal God quaquaquaqua with white beard quaquaquaqua outside time without extension who from the heights of divine apathia divine athambia divine aphasia loves us dearly with some exceptions for reasons unknown but time will tell and suffers like the divine Miranda with those who for reasons unknown but time will tell are plunged in torment plunged in fire whose fire flames if that continues and who can doubt it will fire the firmament that is to say blast hell to heaven so blue still and calm so calm with a calm which even though intermittent is better than nothing but not so fast and considering what is more that as a result of the labors left unfinished crowned by the Acacacacademy of Anthropopopometry of Essy-in-Possy of Testew and Cunard it is established beyond all doubt all other doubt than that which clings to the labors of men that as a result of the labors unfinished of Testew and Cunard it is established as hereinafter but not so fast for reasons unknown that as result of the public works of Puncher and Wattmann it is established beyond all doubt that in view of the labors of Fartov and Belcher

left unfinished for reasons unknown of Testew and Cunard left unfinished it is
established what many deny that man in Possy of Testew and Cunard that man
in Essay that man in short that man in brief in spite of the strides of alimenta-
tion and defecation is seen to waste and pine waste and pine and concurrently
simultaneously what is more for reasons unknown in spite of the strides of
physical culture the practice of sports such as tennis football running cycling
swimming flying floating riding gliding conating camogie skating tennis of all
kinds dying flying sports of all sorts autumn summer winter winter tennis of all
kinds hockey of all sorts penicillin and succedanea in a word I resume and concurrently simultaneously for reasons unknown to shrink and dwindle in spite
of the tennis I resume flying gliding golf over nine and eighteen holes tennis of
all sorts in a word for reasons unknown in Feckham Peckham Fulham Clapham
namely concurrently simultaneously what is more for reasons unknown but
time will tell to shrink and dwindle I resume Fulham Clapham in a word the
dead loss per caput since the death of Bishop Berkeley being to the tune of one
inch four ounce per caput approximately by and large more or less to the nearest decimal good measure round figures stark naked in the stockinged feet in
Connemara in a word for reasons unknown no matter what matter the facts
are there and considering what is more much more grave that in the light of
the labors lost of Steinweg and Peterman it appears what is more much more
grave that in the light the light the light of the labors lost of Steinweg and Peterman that in the plains in the mountains by the seas by the rivers running water
running fire the air is the same and then the earth namely the air and then the
earth in the great cold the great dark the air and the earth abode of stones in the
great cold alas alas in the year of their Lord six hundred and something the air
the earth the sea the earth abode of stones in the great deeps the great cold on
sea on land and in the air I resume for reasons unknown in spite of the tennis
the facts are there but time will tell I resume alas alas on on in short in fine on
on abode of stones who can doubt it I resume but not so fast I resume the skull
to shrink and waste and concurrently simultaneously what is more for reasons
unknown . . ." (SHERWIN *finally subsides into a panting silence.*)

MURUGA: Yes, you're right, for reasons unknown you made us all suffer. Let
me show you what real drama is. Maybe then you'll get lucky.

(*He tells a long, risqué joke with very sexist sentiments.*)

Once a fella came into the bar. He was sitting all by himself, so I went up to
talk to him. I asked him what was his name. He said his name was Mac. I asked
him for his full name. You know what he said? He said, "My name is Mac." I said,
"How can that be? My full name is Subramaniam Vadiveloo Palian, but for short
they call me Muruga, so you just can't be Mac." Then he told me his story. Long
time ago, in Scotland, he was called Willie John MacDoodle. When he was eighteen he decided to become a priest, so he went to a college for priests. After he
qualified he became a doctor of divinity and he was now Willie John MacDoodle

DD. Then he said to himself, 'What can I do with this DD that will be of any use?' He then remembered that famous doctor of divinity Albert Schweitzer who also took up medicine. So Willie John MacDoodle DD decided to take up medicine. After he finished, he was Willie John MacDoodle DD MD. He said, 'Now I'm going to go to Africa like Albert Schweitzer and become a medical missionary.' So he went to Africa. But while he was in Africa, he started messing about, and got VD. So now he was Willie John MacDoodle DD MD VD. But the college for priests heard about the VD so they took away his DD, so he was just Willie John MacDoodle MD VD. Then the medical college heard about the VD, so they took away his MD, so he was just Willie John MacDoodle VD. But the VD got hold of his Willie John, he couldn't Doodle anymore, so he became just Mac.

Here's another story.

(He tells another long, risqué joke.)

An American sailor came to the bar one day. Hell, the fella wasn't here two seconds when he come by me asking to get him a girl. I said to him, no problem, my cousin Premy stays in one room right here in the hotel. I said he must come back in half an hour while I speak to Premy. Before he goes he asked what he can do for VD. He says he's very frightened for VD and he hasn't got anything to wear. I tell him I know old Indian custom for finding out VD *(where I'm going to go get him something to wear—lahnee will fire me straightaway)*. I tell him, just take one lemon and squeeze it there. If there's any chemical reaction then the girl got VD. We got plenty of lemons in the bar, so I give him one.

Later, he went to Premy's room. Premy, too, not the first time she doing anything like this, is waiting in a pretty lingerie, you know . . . lingering for a fin- gering . . . when this sailor comes in with the lemon. So excited Premy got to see American sailor, lingerie came off straightaway. But the sailor fella, took his time cutting the lemon up into four. Then he goes to Premy and squeezes two pieces. Premy too, thought this was the American Way. The sailor fella then squeezed, and he's looking for any chemical reaction. He's looking, and Premy's looking at him. After looking like this for some time, he decides to squeeze the fourth piece. Premy got so cross, she said, "Bhai, what you think this is, puri-patha?"

(Slight pause.)

Born-again Christians put a fish on the back of their cars, right? What do born-again Hindus put? You don't know? Born-again Hindus put vaddes, you know, the one with the hole in the middle *(he makes a gesture with his fingers which has strong sexual connotations).*

What's wrong Sherwin, you not enjoying yourself?

You know what Jesus said to his followers?

SHERWIN: *(answering reluctantly).* No.

MURUGA: He said, I need just three disciples. You know why?

SHERWIN: No, why?

MURUGA: Then we can play thanni. *(While Muruga continues routine,*

SHERWIN *is noticeably quieter.)* What's wrong Sherwin, you're not enjoying yourself?

SHERWIN: I don't think you should make jokes about Jesus.

MURUGA: But you don't mind the others?

SHERWIN: No.

MURUGA: You're a hypocrite.

SHERWIN: I'm not. It's just not right to joke about someone's religion.

MURUGA: But picking on someone's privates is okay?

SHERWIN: You don't have to be so crude.

MURUGA: Only when it suits you.

SHERWIN: I didn't say that.

MURUGA: No, but that's what you mean. *(Goes into routine. Tells another religious joke.)* Three nuns died and were met by St. Peter at the Pearly Gates. "If you want to get in," said St. Peter, "you have to answer one question." He asked the first nun. "What was the name of the first man on earth?" The first nun replied, "Adam."

"Correct," said St. Peter, "you can go in. What was name of the first woman on earth?" he asked the second nun.

"Eve," replied the second nun." "Correct," said St. Peter, "you can go in." Then he asked the third nun, "What were the first words that Eve said to Adam?" The third nun thought for some time, scratched her head and said, "That's a hard one." "Correct," said St. Peter, "you can go in."

(SHERWIN is very agitated. He shouts.)

SHERWIN: What gives you the right to do this? Do you think you're God?

(SHERWIN lunges at him. There's a scuffle. SHERWIN grips MURUGA by the tie.)

MURUGA: I'm Muruga.

(Slow changeover to present time.)

MURUGA: Now you know who I am?

SHERWIN: Yes, you're Muruga. And I've come to say I'm sorry.

(Curtain)

ACT TWO

(The lights come up with MURUGA and SHERWIN walking away from each other from the positions they were in at the end of Act One. MURUGA takes his place behind the bar counter while SHERWIN sits at one of the tables.)

MURUGA: So . . . you want to write about me? What's so interesting about a poor waiter, stuck in this hotel all these years? If it was Robben Island you'd have a better story Sherwin. Want a drink?

SHERWIN: No thanks . . . no, maybe I'll have one. A Black Label please.

(MURUGA brings the beer and a glass over to SHERWIN and returns to the

counter. SHERWIN *pours the beer and takes a long sip while* MURUGA *looks on bemused.)*

MURUGA: What do you say, Sherwin, you think I'm a good story?

SHERWIN: Yes, I do. I think just being who you are makes a good story.

MURUGA: One of those plays where you laugh because we speak funny, or maybe my jokes are so dirty they make you want to see and hear more?

SHERWIN: No, nothing like that. I want to write something that's different, a story that doesn't do the same things as the others, you know . . . the cheap laughs, the coarse action, all those cheap gimmicks. I can make your story into a real story, a story that will make sense to those who want to see more than just the cheap tricks.

MURUGA: Speaking of cheap, the drink is on the house. The lahnee's not here to worry me.

SHERWIN: Er, thanks. *(Pause.)* What about you?

MURUGA: I don't touch the stuff anymore. My kidneys were giving trouble. That's why I'm looking healthy now. After I left the booze, about ten years now, the lahnee promoted me to barman.

SHERWIN: That's why I didn't recognize you. I always imagined this very thin man who was in his fifties, and this was thirteen years ago!

MURUGA: Got your facts mixed up Sherwin. I'm only about fifty-five now. But you were never sober those days.

SHERWIN: *(laughs).* That's true. What great times! And you, you were flying all the time.

MURUGA: Me flying, what about you? You remember the first time you came here? You drank then?

SHERWIN: *(hesitates).* Eh, ja.

MURUGA: Bluffing Sherwin, you bluffing. First time you came here, first time you drank. Hell, I'll never forget after the first lager how you were asking me to sing that one song over and over again.

SHERWIN: Which one? (MURUGA *sings a Tamil devotional song.*)
     Right, right!

MURUGA: Never mind right, right. You tell me, what happened after the third lager?

SHERWIN: What happened?

MURUGA: What happened? You vaandhied all over the carpet right near the toilet door. I think your varsity friends cleaned up and took you home. Your face looked like one fowl's arse. Remember?

SHERWIN: *(laughs).* You've got a good memory.

MURUGA: Can't say the same about you. And you still want to be a writer.
     Sings.

SHERWIN: So, you gave up booze just like that?

MURUGA: Had to. One day I woke up and found I was pissing blood. One thing I can't stand is blood. I gave booze up just like that.

SHERWIN: Must have been bad for business.

MURUGA: What do you mean?

SHERWIN: All those people who came to see your performance must have been disappointed to see you all quiet.

MURUGA: If I didn't stop drinking, I would have been really quiet. But, one Muruga left and another has taken his place.

SHERWIN: So, there are many Murugas?

MURUGA: Like there are many Sherwins.

SHERWIN: No, there's just me now. I've grown up, I think.

MURUGA: Even when we are grown up, there's still many of us. My right name is Subramaniam, but my calling name is Muruga. And in the Cape they know me as China.

SHERWIN: But no matter what's your name, you're still the same person.

MURUGA: I also thought that. But when I was with my mother I was always Subramaniarn. I was different, I felt different. Then the old Muruga was different. He was the joller, the fella you used to know. And China, he was for the Cape. Even spoke differently. *(He speaks a line with a Cape accent as if he is serving a patron.)* Hey ous, you heard about me and Pompies. Hell that ou is slow. He comes up to me in Adderley Street and looks at my Bruce Lee tee-shirt.

"Hey China, is that Bruce Lee?" No, I tell him, it's Mickey Mouse.

"Juslike, but he looks just like Bruce Lee, hey?" *(Slight pause.)* So, that was China.

SHERWIN: And this Muruga?

MURUGA: I can't tell you.

SHERWIN: Why not?

MURUGA: Because it's easier to see yourself when you look back. So if you write about me, which Muruga are you going to write about?

SHERWIN: All of you.

MURUGA: Is that possible? I don't think so.

SHERWIN: Perhaps not, but people like you are just as important as . . .

MURUGA: Mandela?

SHERWIN: *(laughs).* Well . . . yes, in a different sort of way. Your story is the story of all the unnoticed people who make your own contributions to our society, but are passed by as being nobodies. But you, Muruga, made . . . make so many people happy, so many have laughed, and that is why I had to find you again. But to so many who used to come to this bar you were just a another waiter with dirty jokes and some songs.

MURUGA: *(wryly).* I also told jokes about Jesus.

SHERWIN: Yes, and jokes about Jesus.

He laughs.

MURUGA: *(matter of factly).* But I am a nobody.

SHERWIN: That's because you were made to believe you're a nobody. In this country only white was right. Nothing else mattered.

MURUGA: Not true, Sherwin, not true.

SHERWIN: What do you mean?

MURUGA: Our own people make us nobodies. Never mind the Whites, our own people are just the same. You know, there have been many times when I was a waiter for weddings, twenty-first parties, and other functions. How do you think I was treated? Like royalty? Not on your life! Our Indian people, give them some money or education and their heads look like the boots of Mercedes-Benzes . . . nice and big with little, very little inside. Our high-class Indian ladies are the worst, their whole bodies look like Mercedes-Benz. Everyone is quick to laugh at Asha Rajbansi,[3] but she is just the same fancy car dressed up for a wedding. Our own people think just the same as the Whites and everybody else.

SHERWIN: You're right. But this country has made us this way.

MURUGA: I don't know about that. I don't think even the Devil could have made our high-class Indian ladies the way they are.

SHERWIN: Don't you worry, that kind of lady is all over. In Johannesburg they call them kugels.

MURUGA: Same word I use for them. Koodh . . .

SHERWIN: *(hastily interrupting him).* No, ku-gel, kugel, not the word you're thinking about.

MURUGA: I think my word fits the picture perfectly. What word is kugel?

SHERWIN: I think it's Jewish. Haven't you seen that actor Pieter Dirk Uys imitate a kugel on TV?

MURUGA: The same fella that dresses up like a woman?

SHERWIN: Yes, that's him.

MURUGA: Ja, ja, I think I've seen him like a kugel. But tell me, are kugels only White?

SHERWIN: No. For me any rich woman who has everything and is obnoxious is a kugel. There are a lot of Indian kugels, especially in Durban. Let me show you one.

(SHERWIN proceeds to mimic an Indian kugel which MURUGA obviously enjoys.)

You know, I don't know what's happening anymore. Everything is upside down. Everything. The worse thing is, you can't get good help these days. Nowadays girls and boys don't want to work like in the old days. I'm telling you, these karrias are getting too big for their boots. The other day our girl and boy were off so I asked a boy from the road to wash the BM. The car was too dirty

---

[3]The ex-wife of prominent South Indian African politician Amichand Rajbamsi, a high-profile political figure still active in the current South African government.

to go to the Lata Mangeshkar[4] show like that. I told him I'll give him two rand, you know what he told me?

"Take your two rand buy yourself a packet of jube-jubes." So much cheek they've got. And they're also getting very violent, not only the men but the women also. Look how the girl hit Mrs. Patel in Greenwood Park. The government should never have brought the ANC back into the country. We were all living so well before all this. Even Girls High got some black students now. Next year I'm sending Meena to a boarding school in India. My husband's cousin in Leeds is worrying us so much to come to England and settle down. Bhai says they going to treat us just like they treated the Indians in Kenya. But we can't just go like that, what about the business? And I don't think I can take the cold. And India is too hot. I'm so worried about all this.

But everything is going upside down, not only the karrias. Our own young girls are disgracing us. Never mind worrying about caste, they're now busy chasing Tamils and Muslims and making fools of themselves. Which nice rich boy will want to marry a girl that's been with a Madraji. A little bit better if he was Hindi, but a Madraji! Maybe I shouldn't send Meena to boarding school in India, eh? There's so much mixing happening there too.

But maybe it won't be so bad if I send her to a school for girls only. What do you think?

MURUGA: Very good Sherwin, very good. So your drama training wasn't too bad. Remember the time you came here and gave us a little show?

SHERWIN: Don't remind me, that was the last time I came here. (*Pause.*)

MURUGA: And now you've returned to write about me.

SHERWIN: Yes.

MURUGA: But I'm still not clear what you can write about.

You say you not so interested in the jokes and the songs, and all that, so what is there?

SHERWIN: There's your life, and how you came to be a waiter. Of course, writing about you as a waiter means writing about the things you did, the happiness you gave.

MURUGA: I don't know about all this . . . I can't think the way you do.

SHERWIN: Let's make it simple. Let's start from the beginning.

MURUGA: (*thinks for a moment*). Nothing is simple. I'm just Muruga and that's it. I haven't got some fancy story to tell.

SHERWIN: (*anxiously*). No, don't give up like that, you make a good story, and your story can be the story of thousands like you. In your own way you're just an important as Ahmed Kathrada . . .

MURUGA: I haven't heard of him, so he can't be that famous.

SHERWIN: He, he was on Robben Island, he was . . .

---

[4] Famous Indian singer.

MURUGA: Right, right. The same fella that was with Mandela?

SHERWIN: Yes. What was I saying?

MURUGA: How famous I am.

SHERWIN: *(laughs)*. Yes. But seriously, will you be willing to help me?

MURUGA: Okay. We can try.

SHERWIN: Good. Let's begin. Where and when were you born?

MURUGA: You're starting with the difficult questions.

SHERWIN: *(laughs)*. No, seriously.

MURUGA: Yes, seriously, you're starting with the difficult questions. I don't know. My mother said I was born in some farm area where they were staying for little while, but she only spoke Tamil and she could never give me a good idea.

SHERWIN: What about your father?

MURUGA: Oh, he died when I was about four. My eldest brother looked after us in Cato Manor. I was near the youngest out of thirteen children.

SHERWIN: Thirteen?

MURUGA: Ja, big families those days. No wonder my father died.

SHERWIN: And how old are you?

MURUGA: My papers say I was born in 1935, but it may have been two years before, that's what my eldest brother said. He's long dead now. Got killed in the '49 riots. That's how I became a waiter.

SHERWIN: That's what I want to hear. You became a waiter after the '49 riots?

MURUGA: My family couldn't keep me at school so I had to work. I started as a bellboy in a beachfront hotel, and learned the trade from the waiters there. The money wasn't too good so I took a chance and went to the Cape . . .

SHERWIN: *(beside himself)*. Wait, before you go on, I think I've got a good start with the '49 riots.

MURUGA: *(looks at him blankly)*. What's good about the '49 riots?

SHERWIN: Everything.

MURUGA: I think I'm lost.

SHERWIN: Listen. You became a waiter because you had to leave school. And you had to leave school because your brother died in the riots. And why did the riots happen?

MURUGA: Some say because the pekkies went bloody mad, that's why. Others say that the Indians caused it for themselves.

SHERWIN: No, that's not it. That's what this government wants us to believe. It happened because it was planned, so that the Indians and Africans could fight each other.

MURUGA: That's what you believe?

SHERWIN: Yes. It's obvious, isn't it?

MURUGA: I don't know, but let me tell you the story 'bout Rani.

(He begins slowly and quietly.)

You know Sherwin, when you lived the way we did in Cato Manor in those days, everyone lived his own life, but there was always that feeling for everyone else. I can't say it easily, but no matter what the troubles, we had the feeling of being a kind of family.

SHERWIN: I know what you mean. I come from a small town too.

MURUGA: Ja, that's right. You originally from Port Elizabeth, no?

SHERWIN: No, East London.

MURUGA: Funny, I always thought it was Port Elizabeth.

SHERWIN: Everyone gets it mixed up. But all small places are alike. People are more together.

MURUGA: True. That's how it was in Cato Manor. No one was really well off, everyone was struggling, but no one went hungry. Our houses were all wood and iron, and many places had Africans as tenants. In our street that's the way we lived, everyone knowing each other, fighting one day, coming to a christening the next. That's the way we carried on.

SHERWIN: I know, I grew up in that kind of community.

MURUGA: Now in our street there was this young girl called Rani. Tamil girl, but very fair—in those days people use to whisper and say she was a peri dhora's child,

SHERWIN: *(interrupting him)*. Sorry, what's "peri dhora"?

MURUGA: You know, a White lahnee. So, the people felt she was some White lahnee's child from some farm in Hillary where her mother worked. Now don't interrupt, otherwise you won't understand the story.

SHERWIN: Sorry, go ahead.

MURUGA: Now, to make matters worse, the gossipers use to say that the mother was punished for having Rani from one White man, because Rani was born with, what do you call it—a club foot—so she had a very bad limp. But she was a wonderful girl, always got a smile, but never forward. But for her parents, Bala and Saras, it was difficult, because when the time came they couldn't get her married. You know why, because of the gossip, but more, because of her foot. But her face was like a film star. I was just thirteen or fourteen then, and in the afternoon when I was coming with the baskets of vegetables and fruit that my eldest brother Sunny use to sell, I would see her sitting by the small window of their front room just looking out into the street. Sometimes I couldn't help it, I would just stand and look at her, then rush up to her with some fruit and run away. One day Sunny caught me and gave me a good hiding for trying to mix with her. This was the funny thing. Because of the stories 'bout her mother, and because of her foot, the older people felt it was bad to mix with that family. They kept to themselves, but they were also part of the street.

SHERWIN: That kind of nonsense is still happening today.

MURUGA: *(ignores the remark)*. Then one day, how it happened I don't know, we heard Rani was going to get married to one Christian boy from three streets away. Suddenly the whole street came to life. All the gossip and everything was forgotten and the street decided to have this big wedding party for her. Every family was going to give something, and slowly I went to Sunny and asked to help with the fruit and vegetables. Even Sunny who was so stern didn't think twice. The party was for the Saturday night before the wedding, and while I was very excited, I was a bit sad that my film star was not going to be at the window any more. Anyway the preparations went on for the whole week with everybody doing something.

In fact, that's how Boiling Water got his name. Now Boiling Water's real name was Morgan, and he was slightly gone, and lived three doors away from us. Never did any work, just sat around getting in his mother's way. All the children use to make fun of Morgan because he did anything you told him. One day he came visiting with his mother, and while his mother was talking with my mother in the bedroom, he came out into the yard. I decided to have some fun so I told Morgan to climb up and down the mango tree and big mangoes will come. It was July, but Morgan did just like I told him, and for one hour he went up, and came down, went up, and came down, went up, and came down, until his mother came looking for him. How I caught it from my mother that day—I couldn't sleep on my backside for one week!

Anyway for the preparations, someone playing the fool asked Morgan what he was doing for the wedding. Morgan said he wanted to boil the water. What a laugh we all had when we heard, but you know, when the time came for the cooking and the feeding, Morgan's boiling water was used by all. Since then, no one called him Morgan anymore. He had made himself useful at last, and although he didn't do any work again, the name Boiling Water stuck.

So Rani had her wedding, and the whole street was proud. No one noticed her limp. She was our film star, and more than one Tamil boy felt sorry that they listened to their parents. And during the celebrations I slipped out from the marquee and went to one quiet spot and cried. This was in 1948.

A year later Rani was expecting a child, and living very happy with her in-laws, when the riots happened. Now there was one night called the Night of Terror. Michael, Rani's husband, knew some Coloured people in Bentley Street, off Old Dutch Road in town. Some church people. He decided to take his parents and Rani there, but she refused saying she would go to her mother's place. So Michael took his parents and when he returned to the house Rani wasn't there. He quickly ran over to his in-laws but she wasn't there. They thought she was at home. The whole street came to hear about this and all the menfolk went looking. But the terrible things that were going on made it very difficult.

The next morning she was found near the African shantytown when Michael fetched the police. She was found in the road almost naked with bruise marks all over her. She had been raped many times, and she was seven months pregnant. My brother Sunny was with the search party. And he said that even though she was so bad, there was still something very beautiful in her face. Sunny was a hard man, and it was the first time that I saw him cry. Rani died later that day. It was my first death, and I still remember it like yesterday.

SHERWIN: *(taken in by the story, but still trying to assert his view).* That may have happened, but there are still the embellishments, the propaganda.

MURUGA: Propaganda? Were you there?

SHERWIN: No, of course not. But there are the facts.

MURUGA: And the violence wasn't a fact?

SHERWIN: It was a fact, except I have my doubts about how much was blown out of proportion. It's very easy to see things the way others want us to see them.

MURUGA: So Rani didn't die? So my brother, Sunny, didn't die?

SHERWIN: I'm not saying they didn't. But there's other sides to the story.

MURUGA: Like what?

SHERWIN: Like the government helped the riots get out of hand. A small human incident was turned into racial conflict.

MURUGA: *(looks at him for a long while, assimilating all that's been said).* Maybe there is propaganda like you say, but maybe we all started it.

SHERWIN: What do you mean?

MURUGA: Maybe the Indians, the Africans, the Coloureds, the Whites are all to blame. I mean look at us, even now. Are we any better than anyone else? Let me tell you about Charlie, then you'll see what I mean. Just listen, Sherwin, just listen.

Charlie was eight years old when he came to live with my family. His brother Sipho had been working with my brother Sunny, but one day he decided to become a herbalist so he left for Empangeni. But before he left, he brought his youngest brother to work for us. I was about four when he came and I can only remember calling him Charlie. Years later I found out his Zulu name, Pindani, and found it strange that he had another name.

Charlie was a fat, round fella—do you remember that photo magazine Chunky Charlie? Well our Charlie looked just liked him. Hell that fella could eat. Put anything in front of him and he'll eat it. Once the boys in the street decided to have a eating contest between Boiling Water Morgan and Charlie. Secretly we all stole some food from our houses and met in Mani's backyard. Mani's parents were fowl hawkers and they were out hawking, so we had the yard for ourselves. We brought Charlie and Boiling Water and made them sit at the broken table in the yard. Then the competition started. Aiyo! Boiling Water was still trying to work out what was happening to him when Charlie was quarter way with the food. Raghu—he later became a big-time gambler—had a bet with Mani that Boiling Water would win. No such luck. Charlie was laughing and eating his way to the bank for Mani. Raghu got so cross—ten shillings was big money in those days—he pulled Boiling Water by the ears round and round the yard until we had to stop him.

After that, even the Tamil singing contest between Charlie and Boiling Water didn't interest Raghu. Jo, Charlie could sing the Tamil numbers like a born Tamil—his favorite was Thygaraja's[5] Oru Naal.

One day I heard a big commotion in the yard. And all the noise was coming from Charlie's room. Apparently Sunny's wife Maliga was timing Charlie with the fruit, and she now decided she would catch him with all the fruit in his room. There was fruit in his room, but for me it wasn't such a big thing because we all stole when we could. But I'll never forget how something happened to me when I heard Charlie cry when Maliga threw his clothes into the yard. Maliga was very angry and shouting "kaapri, kaapri," when Charlie said, "I'm not an animal, why do you throw my clothes into the yard?"

For the first time I knew what shame was. And everytime I saw Charlie eating from his tin plate and drinking from the jam tin that Maliga kept for him, I would see the clothes lying in the yard and the hiding Sunny gave him with the sjambok for talking back to Maliga. That shame is still with me.

But I don't know which was bigger, the shame I first felt when Maliga threw the clothes, or the shock I got when I saw Charlie kissing Beauty, the next door neighbor's girl.

There was a fence separating our two yards, and on our side was a whole lot of junk including a tin bath standing upside down. We all used to stand on this when we wanted to talk to the neighbors. One day I came into the yard. It was almost dark but I could see Charlie standing on the bath. Slowly I walked up to see what he was doing when I saw him kissing Beauty. What a shock I got. Somehow we never thought of Africans kissing or doing things like that. We knew they made babies, but we never thought they felt love like we felt. That's just the way things were. And even today many of our Indians think this way. To them Africans are animals that are useful for work. People like Charlie, that live like family, are treated only slightly different. They're like the monkeys in the circus. We can laugh and play, but then they must be put into their cages.

SHERWIN: So what became of Charlie?

MURUGA: The same that happened to Rani. He was killed in the riots. They say he was trying to help my brother Sunny, when he was attacked and killed too.

We had a big funeral for Sunny, but I don't know what happened to Charlie's body. He was just forgotten. Time came when people said he killed Sunny. But it couldn't have been. But for some people it was nice to think so. Charlie's

---

[5]Reference to well-known South Indian singer and film actor of the forties, Thygaraja Bhagavathar.

story, Pindani's story, is happening even now. Many of our Indians still don't know animals from people.

(Pause.)

So, Sherwin, I think this is also part of the '49 riots story.

SHERWIN: Maybe, but looking at things like this takes us away from the real cause.

MURUGA: And this is the government, the Whites?

SHERWIN: In a way, yes. Of course, it's all got to do with capitalism, and the struggle of the classes, but yes, we can say that the government, the ruling class started the riots like they started every other fucking misery in this country.

MURUGA: (Pause). You no longer a Christian, Sherwin?

SHERWIN: I can't accept all that. It's got nothing to do with reality. I'm a Marxist now.

MURUGA: Good. Now I can start with my communist jokes.

(He goes into a routine.)

What do you call Mandela's granny?

SHERWIN: I don't know.

MURUGA: Granadilla! (He enjoys his own joke.) You know Mandela travels all over the world, even though he is quite old. How come he is so fit?

SHERWIN: (tersely). I don't know.

MURUGA: Because he has lots of vitamins ANC. (Laughs again.)

SHERWIN: (disturbed, especially by the reference to Mandela). Can't we be serious for a little while? Can't you see I'm educating you . . . I mean can't you see we're being serious for a moment?

MURUGA: (sarcastically). Oh, you're educating me now? About what Sherwin, about what?

SHERWIN: I take that back, but we are talking about the facts. About the '49 riots and everything else. About how we're all victims of the policies of this government, about . . . about oppression, and about equality in a new society.

MURUGA: You sound just like some of the pekkie students living in the hotel.

SHERWIN: (reacts). We shouldn't talk that way, that kind of racist . . .

MURUGA: (facetiously). Sorry, sorry. I meant the comrades in the hotel. (Long pause.) So you're no more writing about me. You're now educating me. Maybe you're educating me before you write about me? No?

SHERWIN: (defensively). I didn't say that.

MURUGA: It's there Sherwin, it's there. I haven't met one educated person who doesn't think he knows all the answers. But tell me, how are you going to educate all those Africans who think Indians only use them, who think Indians hate them just like the Whites? Or, how are you going to educate all those Indians who think the Africans are going to slaughter them? How?

SHERWIN: I didn't say it was going to be easy, but we can show people the lies that were given to us.

MURUGA: But lies are not lies when Africans don't think that Indians use them, they know. And lies are not lies when Indians don't just imagine the violence, they see it.

SHERWIN: What kind of argument is this?

MURUGA: It's no argument. I'm just showing you the facts which the ordinary people have. You said talk facts, so I'm talking facts. They don't understand the ruling classes and all those fancy words. They're just thinking about themselves. About how to live. Words don't mean anything; what they see and feel is real.

SHERWIN: But what they see and feel is created by society. If society changes, the people change.

MURUGA: Maybe. I don't know about all that. Maybe too many words make it too complicated. That's why I like to dance first before using words.

SHERWIN: *(incredulous at this abrupt turn.)* Dance? You mean escape from thinking about our responsibilities?

MURUGA: No. I mean dance. Dance so that we are not drowned by words. Dance so that our head is clear, so that we know what is happening: Don't you know this kind of dance?

SHERWIN: *(irritated).* Stop being foolish. There's no such dance.

MURUGA: Come I'll show you. Then you'll have something real to write about.

SHERWIN: We're wasting time on nonsense. You may have changed in some ways, but you're just as stubborn as before. I don't have the patience for all this. One must have a clear head to see things without distortion.

MURUGA: I like that.

SHERWIN: What?

MURUGA: Clear head. I know a nice story about having a clear head.

(Muruga goes into Six-Foot Dance routine as the Clown with rough make-up, singing and dancing, merging aspects of the mythological story with social commentary in such a way that we get an ambiguous sense of things. The myth could be reality, and the reality could be a myth.)

Before I begin, let me introduce the gods in the proper way. *(The typical Six Foot Dance[6] ritual is performed for the introduction of the gods. The figure of the fused Shiva and Shakti appears.)* These are the gods Shiva and Shakti, the parents of . . . *(putting on mask)* Ganesha, the elephant god, and Muruga—I don't mean me—I mean the boy god. One day Shiva and Shakti said to their sons Ganesha and Muruga—we'll see him later—that they'll give to the first son who goes around the world a most wonderful fruit—it was one of its kind—not

---

[6]Termed *therakootu*, or street dance, in Tamil, it is a long recital of religious tales mixed with song and dance on a raised platform.

an apple—but a fruit of wisdom. Without waiting to figure the easiest way to do this, Muruga impatiently sat on his peacock and traveled around the world. *(At this point the painted image turns around to reveal* DANTÉ *dressed as Lord Muruga while the backdrop suggests a peacock.* DANTÉ *dances the journey around the world.)*

But when Muruga returned to claim the fruit, he found that his parents had given it to Ganesha. You know why?

SHERWIN: Yes, Ganesha was faster than Muruga.

MURUGA: How come?

SHERWIN: I don't know, I told you before, I don't have the patience for this sort of thing.

MURUGA: That's why I'm telling you the story, kanna. Now Ganesha traveled

faster because he simply did this. *(The Shiva-Shakti image is back, and Ganesha walks around it reverentially.)*

That's how Ganesha won the fruit. Through patience he saw an easier way. That's why he's called the god of wisdom and success. Of course, Muruga's also got his good points, but in this particular story he is a bit naughty. You see, Sherwin, even the gods are not the same all the time. Ja, it's a good story with lots of meanings, especially if you look at it closely. *(*MURUGA *takes off the Ganesha mask.* DANTÉ *steps out of character.)* A good story, eh? Funny thing, the god with the clear head was an elephant. Must be some meaning there. Meet my friend Danté. Another Muruga.

*(*DANTÉ *and* SHERWIN *greet each other, with* DANTÉ *saluting in the Indian way with palms together.)*

MURUGA: Okay Danté you can clear up now.

*(*DANTÉ *clears up and returns. He shows a great interest in the ensuing conversation.)*

MURUGA: So Sherwin, what you think of our dance?

SHERWIN: It's not my cup of tea. I can't take all that symbolism. Anyway, these religious stories are accepted as the gospel by many people—they actually believe in the existence of these gods, so the symbolism has no meaning. In this day and age we can do without this kind of fantasy.

MURUGA: Fantasy? What is fantasy?

SHERWIN: Fantasy is . . . is an illusion. Like, like . . . *(looks around for something to illustrate the meaning when he hits upon an idea)* . . . do you have any cards?

MURUGA: I have a thanni pack. *(Fetches the cards. At this point* MURUGA *involves* DANTÉ *as a partner in the following magic sequence.)* Here's the cards. But two-hand thanni is no good, you must have four.

SHERWIN: We're not going to play thanni. I just want you to see something.

(SHERWIN *takes the cards and shuffles the pack. He then places* MURUGA's *dish-cloth over the cards.*) Take the top card.

    (MURUGA *takes the top card.*)

MURUGA: Like this?

SHERWIN: *(business-like throughout).* Yes. Now put the card in that jug of water, and leave the cloth over the jug. (MURUGA *complies.*) You watching carefully?

MURUGA: Of course.

SHERWIN: Abracadabra. *(He pulls the cloth away to reveal nothing in the jug.)* Now that is an illusion. Wait. May I borrow this beer mug?

MURUGA: Take it, take it.

    (SHERWIN *makes the beer disappear.* MURUGA *claps enthusiastically.*)

SHERWIN: Illusion is when what is real is made to appear unreal.

MURUGA: So illusion is when what is real is made to appear unreal. Have you got a book?

SHERWIN: What do you want a book for?

MURUGA: I want to show you something. (SHERWIN *gives him a book.*) Why such a dark book?

SHERWIN: Why do you want a light book?

MURUGA: So you can see that I'm not bluffing you. Doesn't matter, I'll use my handkerchief. *(He places two tumblers on the handkerchief which rests on the book.)* Now if I turn this over, you think the tumblers will fall?

SHERWIN: Of course. (MURUGA *turns the tumblers over. At first he holds them in place, but then removes his hand to show them suspended without any support.*) Very good. But illusion is also when what is unreal is made to appear real. What is that canister over there?

MURUGA: Oh, that's just an old gift wrap for a whiskey bottle.

SHERWIN: May I use it?

MURUGA: Use it, use it.

SHERWIN: This canister is clear, right?

DANTÉ: It's clear.

SHERWIN: I need a clean piece of paper.

MURUGA: Danté, just fetch a clean piece of paper. (DANTÉ *fetches the paper.*)

SHERWIN: *(covering the canister with the paper).* Now watch carefully.

    (He *thrusts his hand into the canister and pulls out three silk handkerchiefs—orange, white and blue—in the colors of the old South African flag.* DANTÉ *comments on this in Zulu.*)

MURUGA: So, you're quite a good magician.

SHERWIN: It's really nothing at all, just a trick.

MURUGA: *(fetching a little cloth bag).* Give me those handkerchiefs. So illusion is when what is real is made to appear unreal, also when what is unreal is made to appear real. Like this?

(He makes the South African flag turn into the ANC flag.)

SHERWIN: Not bad, not bad. So you're also a magician.

(As he says this he puts his cigarette out in what appears to be an ashtray.)

MURUGA: *(putting the bag back).* Hey, what you doing? How can you put your cigarette out in that tray? I keep my nuts in that.

SHERWIN: *(surprised).* What nuts?

MURUGA: *(takes the lid off to reveal the nuts).* Have some nuts. Have some nuts, Danté.

SHERWIN: Not a bad trick Muruga, not a bad trick.

MURUGA: But you did a better one before.

SHERWIN: When?

MURUGA: When you disappeared. And reappeared thirteen years later. Now that's a good trick. *(SHERWIN laughs.)* But what about the Kavady, is that a trick? When they put pins through their cheeks, is that not real? Like this?

(Takes a pin from his pocket and is about to push it through his cheek when SHERWIN *stops him.)*

SHERWIN: Don't.

MURUGA: But I want you to see that this is not a trick.

(Pause.)

SHERWIN: I know it's not a trick, but I don't want to see it. It makes me squirm.

MURUGA: But you know it's real.

SHERWIN: I don't know, it's something I haven't quite understood yet. *(Pause.)* You may not believe it, but about ten years ago I had an experience that some may call a trance.

MURUGA: Hard to believe you had the trance. You were always such a stiff character.

SHERWIN: This happened when my younger brother, Moses, was detained very early one morning in June 1980. He was still at varsity at the time, but he was at home when the arrest took place. It shook all of us up very badly, especially my mother. But I was most surprised at the effect it had on me. You see, we were not particularly close. Anyway, one night at my girlfriend's flat, I was suddenly seized by a strange sensation that forced me to lie down. I couldn't speak, even though I could hear the worried questions of my girlfriend, when suddenly I felt my brother—not in any kind of physical way, but emotionally. Whatever he was feeling I was feeling. And it wasn't long before I was crying because I could sense them beating him up, doing the most horrible things to him. And there wasn't anything I could do. After a while the trance faded. My mother began to lose weight and became half her size over the following eight months. The trances happened more and more, until one day, sitting in my little Volkswagen, it happened the last time. This time there were no beatings, no horrible things happening, just the fact that the trial was finally going to come up in two weeks. In two weeks the trial began, and at the end of it all, Moses was sentenced to two years for possessing and distributing banned literature. I was at the court when the sentence was passed—my mother couldn't bear to be there. As I accompanied him to his cell for the last good-bye, he suddenly turned around and held me, sobbing, and said, "I knew they would sentence me, but I thought only for six months." It's very difficult to be the composed elder brother when you have to say good-bye like this. It's hard not to cry. *(Long pause before* SHERWIN *snaps himself out of the memory.)* Anyway, how did I get to all this?

MURUGA: You were talking about trance.

SHERWIN: Yes.

MURUGA: So, you still don't believe it?

SHERWIN: I don't know.

MURUGA: Why don't you know?

SHERWIN: It doesn't seem to have anything to do with the so many real problems that people have. With all the shit that we have to put up with.

MURUGA: Maybe the shit's there because we don't have enough trance.

SHERWIN: No, that's fantasy.

MURUGA: Fantasy? But you just said you had the trance.

SHERWIN: *(testily).* Yes. Where's that book I gave you?

MURUGA: It's on the counter.

SHERWIN: *(taking a book entitled* Marx Made Easy*).* Read this, it will explain everything.

MURUGA: No, you read it.

SHERWIN: Okay, but listen carefully.

"Consciousness is from the very beginning a social product, and remains so as long as men exist at all. So, consciousness is at first, of course, merely consciousness concerning the immediate sensuous environment and consciousness, of the limited connection with other persons and things outside the individual who is growing self-conscious. At the same time it is consciousness of nature, which first appears to men as a completely alien, all-powerful and unassailable force, with which men's relations are purely animal and by which they are overawed like beasts; it is thus purely animal consciousness of nature *(that is, natural religion).*" Now you understand?

MURUGA: Sherwin, I didn't understand one word you said. Like I said, Muruga traveled around the entire world, while Ganesha took the shortcut and walked around his parents. Can't you make it simple?

SHERWIN: It's very difficult.

MURUGA: Why?

SHERWIN: Because of all the ideas.

MURUGA: Then how do you expect me to understand? The Muruga story was so simple.

SHERWIN: *(has an idea)*. Yes, the Muruga story can make it simple.

MURUGA: This I got to see.

SHERWIN: Would Danté mind joining in for a moment?

DANTÉ: Please leave me out of this. This is between you and Muruga. For the time being, I'm quite happy being a token Black in this discussion.

MURUGA: Danté, stop telling stories and come here. Sherwin wants to do the Six-Foot Dance.

DANTÉ walks over.

SHERWIN: No, I just want to show you something. Do you have a cloth and some make-up remover?

MURUGA: I'll get some.

(He fetches the items.)

SHERWIN: Now here we have a god *(pointing to* DANTÉ*)*. Right?

MURUGA: Right.

SHERWIN: Now what the writer of this book is saying—his name was Karl Marx—is that these symbols have been created by man, not by any supernatural being. See what happens when I start removing all the signs . . . *(he removes the make-up as he speaks)* and take away all the jewelry. We see that all this finery is just covering up a man. What do you have now, Muruga or Danté? God or man? That's what Marx was saying. Understand?

(Pause.)

MURUGA: So that was Karl Marx. He must have been a Hindu.

SHERWIN: What do you mean?

MURUGA: That's our Hindu belief, that man is god and god is man. I wonder if Karl Marx prayed to Muruga?

SHERWIN: I can see you still want to play games with me. In many ways you still same Muruga from thirteen years ago. How do you put up with him, Danté?

DANTÉ: Maybe Murugas don't change. It's how you look at it.

SHERWIN: You've become just like Muruga with that philosophy.

MURUGA: It's not philosophy if you can dance.

DANTÉ: Yes, you must dance.

SHERWIN: Not that again.

MURUGA: Just try. Just try. Danté will help you.

DANTÉ: Come, let me show you. Maybe you can dance at the jol at Motala's farm.

SHERWIN: I'm not in the mood.

MURUGA: Put this on. *(Gives him the bracelet taken from* DANTÉ.*)* It will give you the feeling.

(Sings Six-Foot Dance opening.)

SHERWIN: *(who is still trying to get out of it).* What has this got to do with anything?

MURUGA: Nothing. But it's just like Bombay duck, for some it's just something that stinks, but for others it's wonderful. Come join us.

SHERWIN: Okay, I'll try. *(They dance. He attempts to dance, but finds it extremely difficult.)* No, it's no good. I just get stuck.

MURUGA: That's because you think about the steps, instead of just doing them.

SHERWIN: But you must think about something first before you do it.

MURUGA: And that's why you get stuck.

SHERWIN: So how do you get unstuck?

MURUGA: You must dance.

SHERWIN: Oh no, not that argument again. You say I can't dance because I'm stuck, but to get unstuck I must first dance?

MURUGA: You understand perfectly. Simple isn't it? You see Sherwin, if you're can't dance, that means you're stuck, and to be stuck means you can't dance. One and the same thing. And if you stuck or can't dance, means you are stuck elsewhere too.

SHERWIN: What do you mean?

MURUGA: Remember the time I told the Jesus jokes and you got so angry?

SHERWIN: Yes.

MURUGA: Why?

SHERWIN: Oh, I was still young then. Thought differently, I suppose.

MURUGA: I use to watch you closely those days. Always getting worked up when your friends said something different, always getting stuck. I think you use to drink to get unstuck. Sometimes got unstuck a bit too much like when you vaandhied on the carpet. So now you won't get angry if I picked on Mandela or the communists or the Blacks?

SHERWIN: Well, no. They're just jokes.

MURUGA: Right. Now listen to this. *(Tells a non-communist joke first.)* Why did Adam have sex only six days a week? *(Slight pause.)* Because seven days would make the whole week. *(Slight pause.)* You had no problem with that?

SHERWIN: No.

MURUGA: Good. Now let's carry on.

(Muruga launches into a string of risqué Marxist and communist jokes that visibly affects SHERWIN. DANTÉ *joins in the bantering.)*

Fidel Castro was getting very worried when he heard that the Angolan soldiers the Cubans were training were losing their testicles. He urgently recalled his commandant and asked him what was going wrong.

"You see," said the commandant, "I gave very simple instructions. I said, before you throw the hand grenade, you must pull the pin and count to ten. But when I gave the hand grenades they pulled the pin *(mimes the action)*, and started counting on the one hand—one, two three, four, five—*(mimes the soldier putting the grenade between his legs as he continues counting on the other hand)*—six, seven, eight . . ."

(Pause.)

How are you feeling Sherwin? You not getting angry? Listen to this one. Why did Winnie Mandela give up smoking? (SHERWIN *makes no attempt to reply.)* Because she couldn't find anymore[7] stompies.

Come Sherwin I can see you getting angry. Good. Now listen to this one. *(Another joke.)*

You're very angry now, Sherwin?

SHERWIN: No.

MURUGA: Of course you are. *(Joke.)*

Come Sherwin, show how angry you really are. Maybe then you'll get unstuck, maybe then you'll dance. *(Joke.)*

(MURUGA *begins to taunt* SHERWIN *by slapping him lightly on his chest and shoulders.)*

Why don't you hit back, Sherwin, you so angry now you want to hit me, no?

SHERWIN: No!

MURUGA: Yes!

SHERWIN: No!

MURUGA: But you want to hit me Sherwin, I can see it. Hit me, Sherwin hit me.

Hit me and you'll change the world.

SHERWIN: *(explodes).* Yes, I'll hit you and I'll change . . . *(stops abruptly. Pause.)*

MURUGA: You still want to write about me Sherwin?

(SHERWIN *is embarrassed by his outburst, his loss of control.)*

SHERWIN: It's time for me to go. This is for the beer.

(He puts money on the counter. He notices that he still has the bracelet on. Struggling to take it off, he prefers not to make an issue and leaves.)

DANTÉ: *(noticing the book on the table).* Comrade coolie, he's left his book behind.

MURUGA: *(picking up book and going out).* Sherwin, Sherwin, your book!

---

[7]Reference to the young boy known as Stompie who was found murdered after allegedly being kidnapped on Winnie Mandela's instructions. A "stompie" is also a cigarette butt.

(He returns.)

DANTÉ: He must have been in a hurry. He walks so fast, but he can't dance
Says something in Zulu.

*(Muruga sits down at table and puts his feet up. He begins reading aloud
from the book.* DANTÉ *listens to him.)*

MURUGA: Hey, raavan, don't listen to me. Start dancing. You the one that
exams, remember. The bells are behind the counter.

DANTÉ: *(pointing to a whiskey bottle).* You mean these bells?

MURUGA: Not those bells, raavan, the dance bells.

*(*DANTÉ *begins dancing while* MURUGA *continues to read aloud.* MURUGA *soon
joins the dance while holding onto the book.* SHERWIN *returns holding the bracelet, and watches the dancing.)*

(Curtain)

Theatre of the South Asian Diaspora

Canada

Bose, Rana
    Baba Jacques Dass and Turmoil at Côte-des-Neiges Cemetery
    Blackskirt
    The Death of Abbie Hoffman
    Five or Six Characters in Search of Toronto
    Nobody Gets Laid
    On the Double
    Prairie Fire
    Some Dogs
    The Sulpician Escarpment
    Who to Please?
Cowasjee, Sowaj
    The Last of the Maharajas
Irani, Anosh
    Matka King
Parameswaran, Uma
    Meera
    Rootless but Green Are the Boulevard Trees
    Sita's Promise
    Sons Must Die
Varma, Rahul
    Bhopal
    Counter Offense
    Equal Wages
    Isolated Incident
    Job Stealer
    Land Where the Trees Talk
    No Man's Land
    Trading Injuries
    Truth and Treason

Fiji

Misra, Sudesh
    Ferringhi
    International Dateline

Malaysia

Maniam, K. S.
    The Bird and the Rod
    The Cord
    Our Own Skins
    The Sandpit
    Skinned

Singapore

Elangovan
    Dogs
    Talaq

South Africa

Gopie, Rajesh
  A Coolie Odyssey
  Marital Blitz
  Out of Bounds
Govender, Kessie
  Alternative Action
  Black Skies
  The Decision
  God Made Mosquitoes Too
  Herstory
  I.O.D. (Injured On Duty)
  Ka-goos
  On the Fence
  Ravanan
  The Shack
  Stable Expense
  Tramp—You, Tramp—Me
  Underground
  Working Class Hero
Govender, Krijay
  Women in Brown
Govender, Ronnie
  1949
  At the Edge
  Back-Side!
  Beyond Calvary
  Blossoms from the Bough
  The First Stone
  The Great R31m Robbery
  His Brother's Keeper
  In-Side!
  The Lahnee's Pleasure
  Off-Side!
  Swami
  Too Muckin' Futch
  Who or What Is Deena Naicker?
  Your Own Dog Won't Bite You
Mahomed, Ismail
  Cheaper Than Roses
  Purdah
Moodley, Vivian
  Hambha Kahle Mr. Moodley
Naidoo, Geraldine
  Chili Boy
Naidoo, Muthail
  Flight from the Mahabharata
  Ikyalethu
  Masks

The Masterplan
We 3 Kings
Naidoo, Yugan
  LATAAS FM
Narandas, Dinesh
  Inmates
Pillay, Kriben
  Coming Home
  FM Stereotype
  Looking for Muruga
  Mr. Bansi Is Dead
  Mr. O's Story
  Side by Side Masisizane
Singh, Aswhin
  Spice 'n Stuff
  To House

Trinidad and Tobago

Kissoon, Freddie
  Calabash Alley
  God and Uriah Butler
  King Cobo
Matura, Mustapha
  The Coup
  Meetings
  Playboy of the West Indies

United Kingdom

Ahmad, Rukhsana
  Black Shalwar
  The Gate-Keeper's Wife
  Last Chance
  Letting Go
  Man Who Refused to be God
  Mistaken: Annie Besant in India
  New Constitution
  Partners in Crime
  Prayer Mats
  Rags to Riches
  Recall
  River on Fire
  Sepoy's Salt, Captain's Malt
  Song for a Sanctuary
Ali, Tariq
  Consequences
  Iranian Nights
  Necklaces
  Ugly Rumors

Glossary

Aadab	greetings (Hindi, Urdu)
Achha	okay (Hindi, Urdu)
Aghya maang	May I?
aiyayo/aiyo	"Good Lord," "My, my," etc. Exclamation of continuous pain, sorrow, outrage or sympathy (Zulu)
Amathambo	bones (Zulu)
AMG	top-of-the-range Mercedes with all the accessories
Are'/Arreh'	vocative pan-South Asian term denoting exasperation
Auo Jo	"See you soon" (Gujarati)
Babalaaz	hangover (Zulu)
Bai	dear lady (Hindi)
Barbi	hangover (Zulu)
Barla	to write (Zulu)
Basopa	beware (Zulu)
Basti	locality (Hindi)
Bathies	a beating
bhai	pan-South Asian term for brother; very often used without filial associations and simply as a term of respect for any male
Bhang	a plant used in a traditional Indian drink at religious festivals, often inducing states of intoxication
Bhangra	Traditional Punjabi dance, which has been appropriated in Britain
Bhen	literally "sister" but used in general among women (Gujarati)
Biryani	rice dish, traditionally made with lamb
Bliksem	curse word (Afrikaans)
Boere	Afrikaaner
Bombay duck	a small dried-fish with a very distinctive aroma
Bongolo	donkey (Zulu)
Bopha	arrest, detain (Zulu)
Bruin-ous	Coloureds, South Africa (Afrikaans)

Chalo raasta Napo	hit the road (Hindi)
Chalo	let's go (Hindi)
Chana Bateta	chickpea and potato dish
char-ous	Indians. Not usually derogatory, except when used by some whites. Often jocular in South African Indian English (Afrikaans)
China Whites	nightclub in central London
Choon	talk, chat, South African slang
Chowkidar	security guard (Hindi)
Chunni	like a dupatta, or long scarf worn with a salwat, a long loose-fitting tunic.
CK	Calvin Klein
Coolie	term for general laborer in India, historically for indentured laborers who traveled and settled in the Pacific, southern Africa, and the West Indies
Daal	lentil dish
Dandia	folk dance from Gujarat, performed in a round with sticks
Desi	anyone hailing from South Asia, without reference to specific regional, linguistic, cultural, or religious identity
Dharma	Hindu conception of the underlying nature of the world and of humanity; Western equivalents have been duty or proper conduct
Diwali	Hindu festival of lights in the autumn; a celebration of Ram's reunification with Sita in the Ramayana story
Doh-Die	for fah-fee, the gambling racket, the number omitted from the draw
Dop	drink, shot (Afrikaans)
Eid	Muslim festival at the end of the month of Ramadan
Fah-fee	gambling racket involving dreams, visions, and numbers, originating from China
Faka	put in (Zulu)
Funa ncoma	"You want to compliment" (Zulu)
Funa puza	"Do you want to drink?" (Zulu)
Garba	Gujarati dance
Goondan	rat (Zulu)
Graaf	work, South Africa (Afrikaans)
Gujus	colloquial for the Gujaratis
Gundas	thugs
Haan haan	Yes, yes (Hindi)
Halo	let's go
Hambile	gone (Zulu)
Havan-kund	*sacrificial fire-pot*
Hindu Punjabi	a Hindu person who originates from the region of Punjab in India
Hutt, bhaag, hatt bhaag	get away, get lost (Hindi)
Impela	true (Zulu)
Ini leyozinto	"What are those things?" (Zulu)
Inkunzi	bull (Zulu)
Insimbi	steel (Zulu)

Inyama	meat (Zulu)
Iphepha	paper (Zulu)
Izitsha	bowls, plates, washbasin (Zulu)
Jol, Jolling	partying, having fun (Afrikaans)
Juba	traditional; beer
Juniya	young one (Zulu)
Kaapri	derogatory term for "blacks" in Tamil
kanna	Tamil term of affection, usually for a child
Kantolo	court (Zulu)
Karishma Kapoor	Famous Bollywood actress
karrias	Anglicization of the Gujarati word *karria* meaning black and often referring to black people.
Kathak	from the Sanskrit *katha*, or story, a classical dance form of South Asia, characterized by fast footwork, spins, and gestures that symbolize various emotions
Kavady	Festival celebrated twice a year in honor of the Hindu deity Muruga. Accompanied by prayers and acts of penance including fire-walking ceremonies
Kerala	South Indian State
Kerel	policeman (Afrikaans)
Khabi Khabi	popular Hindi film of the 1970s, starring Amitabh Bachan
Krauncha	birds in the Ramayana. The author of the Ramayana, Valmiki, allegedly saw a male krauncha bird killed by a hunter, with the female mate left alone and distraught. This compelled Valmiki to write the Ramayana, an epic Sanskrit poem about the story of Rama and Sita.
Krishna	Hindu God
Kupela	only (Zulu)
Kurtha	traditional suit
Kutch Kutch hota hai	Bollywood film, shown in mainstream British cinemas
Kutti	bitch
Ladoo	South Asian sweet
Lahnee	boss (Afrikaans)
Lekker Eksê	South African slang term meaning excellent, awesome (Afrikaans)
Lightie	youth (Afrikaans)
Louis	Lohanna, one of the three main Gujarati Hindu castes
Maa ji	mother (Hindi)
Maar	but (Zulu)
Madraji	Person of South Indian extraction, usually Tamil-speaking. Sometimes pejorative in the context of early rivalry between North and South Indians living together in Natal. The word comes from Madras, the port from which South Indian indentured workers were shipped out to the colonies.
Malayalee	people of Kerala
Mali	money (Zulu)
Malik	master or sir (Hindi)
Mana	wait (Zulu)
Mandir	temple (Hindi)

Mantri ji	Mr. Minister (Hindi)
Mapla	Muslim
Mbongolo	donkey (Zulu)
Meharban	kindness (Hindi)
Meli wami	my lawyer (Zulu)
Memsahib	South Asian term for white woman
Mfana wami	my son (Zulu)
Mlungu	white person (Zulu)
Mosis	derogatory term for Muslims
Mubi	ugly (Zulu)
Mughal ka bacha	son of a Mogul
Mughal	mogul
Mulungu	stranger, white person (Zulu)
Muntu	human (Zulu)
Muruga	boy god venerated in Tamil Hindu practices, brother of Ganesh
Mussalman	idiomatic term for Muslim in South Asia, derogatory in certain contexts
Muthachen	grandpa
Nangu	"He is" (Zulu)
Natchannia	general term for Indian dancing
Nawab	general title for Muslim nobles in pre-Mughal and Mughal Muslim India. Nawabs ruled over Awadh, Arcot, Bhopal, Hyderabad, and Bengal before the British assumption of power in the eighteenth century. Nawab forms the basis for the eighteenth-century term *nabobism,* in which European company officials would gain favor with certain nawabs over others.
NETIP	Network of Indian Professionals, U.S. organization catering to young South Asian American professionals
Ngeke	never (Zulu)
Ngena	come in (Zulu)
Ngiyabonga	"Thank you" (Zulu)
NRI	nonresident Indian
Ntombazana	girl (Zulu)
Nunus	bats (Zulu)
Pagafi imoto	inside the car (Zulu)
Pagdandi	narrow mud-path (Hindi)
Panjamridhm	ambrosia
Patel	one of the three main Gujarati Hindu castes
Penda	South Asian sweet
Phoyisa	policeman (Zulu)
Porridge prayers	Tamil prayers to the goddess Mari Amman, consisting of offerings of porridge
Pozzie	home, Indian South African English; also *posey*
Pukka	great
Pundit Ji	priest (Hindi)
Radha	Krishna's consort

Rakshasa	demon in Hindu mythology
Ram-rajya	literally, kingdom of Rama. Also refers to an ideal state of governance in which the rulers rule with the consent of the ruled. Cited in Mohandas Gandhi's *Hind Swaraj* (1908) as a form of governance that India, in the midst of colonial rule, should aspire to
Ravan	Demon-King
Ritek Roshan	Famous Bollywood actor
Roti	Indian bread
Rotli	staple flat bread in Gujarati cuisine, akin to chapattis, served smeared with ghee
Sadhu	saint
Sahib	sir (Hindi)
Samagri	ritual incense
Sandas	toilet (Hindi)
Shahs	one of the three main Gujarati Hindu castes
Shali phansi	sit down (Zulu)
Sheea lo ntombi	"leave the girl" (Zulu)
Siza	help (Zulu)
Size yakho ubani	"What's your size?" (Zulu)
Sjambok	whip (Afrikaans)
Skint	slang for having no money (British)
Slims	short for Muslims and used in a derogatory manner by British Hindus
Sloka	a poetic meter in Sanskrit in which proverbs, hymns, and prayers appear
Smaak	like a lot, as opposed to love (South African slang)
'Spingo	Isipingo, a region of KwaZulu-Natal (Zulu)
Stompi	cigarette (South African slang)
Teekhai, teekhai	"Okay, okay" (Hindi)
Tenga someinyama	buy some meat (Zulu)
Therukoothu	from Tamil Nadu and also called the Six-Foot Dance, a long, dramatic recital of tales from Tamil scriptures, mixed with comedy and song, culminating in a dance on a raised platform
Thunee	card game popular with Indian South Africans
Ufuna ukuqabula	you want a kiss (Zulu)
Ukukhluma	endless talk (Zulu)
Ukukhuluma	to speak (Zulu)
Uni	university
Uzosebenza mina	I'm going to work (Zulu)
Wit-ous	white people, South Africa (Afrikaans)
Wonke	all (Zulu)
Woza la	"Come here" (Zulu)
Yini leyonto	"What's that?" (Zulu)
Yizwa	taste; listen (Zulu)
Yudhishter	mythological prince

Notes

An Introduction to South Asian Diasporic Theatre

1. A catch-all term describing all those from South Asia, regardless of region, language, or religion. See the glossary.

2. This certainly does not imply that South Asians in North America or the United Kingdom have not faced racism at institutional or individual levels. Additionally, the treatment of Canada's South Asian population in the early nineteenth century resembled the treatment of South Asians in Natal and Mauritius in the early twentieth, when Canadian authorities tried their best to limit and eventually curtail all South Asian immigration. I am merely pointing to an important distinction between the political contexts that post-1947 migrants and indentured labor migrants (and their children) have encountered in their various locations.

3. See John D. Kelly and Martha Kaplan, "Diaspora and Swaraj, Swaraj and Diaspora," in Dipesh Chakrabarty, Rochona Majumdar, and Andrew Sartori, eds., *From the Colonial to the Postcolonial: India and Pakistan in Transition* (London: Oxford University Press, 2007) for an elaboration of this argument.

4. A few academic examinations of this topic, of course, do exist. On diasporic theatre and its relationship with India, see Aparna Dharwadker's two essays, "Diaspora and the Theatre of the Nation," *Theatre Research International* 28, no. 3 (2003): 303–325 and "Diaspora and the Failure of Home: Two Contemporary Indian Plays," *Theatre Journal* 50, no. 1 (1998): 71–94. For South Africa, see Dennis Schauffer, "In the Shadow of the Shah: The Indic Contribution to Our Developing South African Culture," *Indic Theatre Monograph Series* 2 (Durban: University of Durban-Westville Press, 1994); Suria Govender, "Interculturalism and South African Indian Fusion Dance," *Indic Theatre Monograph Series* 3 (Durban: University of Durban-Westville Press, 1996); Muthal Naidoo, "The Search for a Cultural Identity: A Personal View of South African 'Indian' Theatre," *Theatre Journal* 49, no. 1 (1997): 29–39; Neilesh Bose, "Fitting the Action to the Word: An Ethnographic Journey into South African Indian Theatre," *Indic Theatre Monograph Series* 4 (Durban: University of Durban-Westville Press, 1997); Kriben Pillay, "South African Indian Theatre—The Search for Identity," unpublished essay, 1998; and

two articles by Thomas Hansen, "Plays, Politics, and Cultural Identity among Indians in Durban," *Journal of Southern African Studies* 26, no. 2 (2000): 255–269 and "Melancholia of Freedom: Humour and Nostalgia among Indians in South Africa," *Modern Drama* 48, no. 2 (2005): 297–315. In Canada, the entire Spring 1998 issue of *Canadian Theatre Review* was devoted to South Asian Canadian theatre; the journals *alt.theatre* and *montrealserai* also publish a fair amount of material relating to South Asian diasporic theatre in Canada. For Great Britain, a multiyear research project recently completed will result in publications documenting the history and aesthetics of British Asian theatre. Two books, *British South Asian Theatre: A Documented History* and *British South Asian Theatre: Critical Essays,* will result from this research, as well as a special edition of the journal *South Asian Popular Culture.*

5. Interview with Shishir Kurup, 25 August 2005.

Part 1. The United States

1. See, Rangaswamy, 2000, chapter 2, and Karen Leonard, *The South Asian Americans* (Westport, Conn,: Greenword Press, 1997).

2. Interview with the author, 24 August 2005.

3. Ibid.

4. Ibid.

5. Ibid.

6. For overviews of the field, see Leela Gandhi, *Postcolonial Theory* (New York: Columbia University Press, 1998), Homi Bhabha, *The Location of Culture* (New York: Routledge, 1994), and Bart Moore-Gilbert, *Post Colonial Theory: Contexts, Practices, and Politics* (London: Verso, 1997). The classic work regarding postcolonial identity and literary writing is Ngugi Wa'Thiongo, *Decolonising the Mind: The Politics of Language in African Literature* (London: J. Currey, 1986). Regarding postcolonialism and theatre, see Brian Crow and Chris Banfield, *An Introduction to Post-Colonial Theatre* (New York: Cambridge University Press, 1996), Helen Gilbert and Joanne Tompkins, *Post-Colonial Drama: Theory, Practice, Politics* (New York: Routledge, 1996), and J. Ellen Gainor, ed., *Imperialism and Theatre: Essays on World Theatre, Drama, and Performance* (New York: Routledge, 1995).

7. Interview with the author, 24 August 2005.

8. Ibid.

9. Ibid.

10. Ibid.

11. Ibid.

12. Ibid.

13. Ibid.

14. Mandvi, *Sakina's Restaurant,* v.

15. Ibid, vi.

16. Ibid.

17. For example: Pushpa/Portia, I, ii, "the will of a living daughter curbed by the will of a dead father"; Sharuk/Shylock, I, iii, "Devendra/Antonio is a good man"; Sharuk/Shylock, I, iii, "The Muslim / Jew will grow Hindu / Christian he grows kind"; Pushpa/Portia, II, vi (Kurup), II, viii (Shakespeare), "Let all with his complexion choose me so"; Sharuk/Shylock, III, i, "You knew, none so well, none so well as you, of my daughter's flight"; Sharuk/Shylock, IV, i, "On what compulsion must I? Tell me that?" "I am content."

18. In Shakespeare, Portia hears of the Prince of Morocco's arrival in I, ii, and has an

interaction with him in II, i, where he makes his famous diatribe against skin-color valuation ("Mislike me not for my complexion . . ."). Then six scenes later, in II, vii, the Prince tries his hand, and fails.

19. Interview with the author, 27 August 2005.

20. Ibid.

21. II, viii in Shakespeare and II, viii in Kurup.

22. See the earlier portion of this introduction for a historical overview of this migration.

23. For a recent treatment of this subject in literary critical terms, see Aamir Mufti's *Enlightenment in the Colony: The Jewish Question and the Crisis of Postcolonial Culture* (Princeton, N.J.: Princeton University Press, 2007), particularly chapter 1.

24. Both of these incidents of violence against and stereotyping of Muslims relate to a depiction of Muslims as potentially threatening to Indian secular nationalism. In Ayodhya, the birthplace of the Hindu god Ram, Hindu nationalist forces declared that the Babri Masjid was built on the remains of a temple destroyed by a Muslim ruler, though evidence for such destruction was never found. In Gujarat in 2002, based on an altercation between Hindu pilgrims and Muslims on a train, a rampage of violence, some of which was clearly planned from beforehand, was unleashed against Muslims.

25. *Desi* simply refers to anyone from South Asia, in a way that does not pinpoint a specific geographical, linguistic, or religious identity. This catch-all South Asianness is most prominent and comprehensible in the diaspora, and especially in the United States.

26. Kurup admits that Armando functions as a device to spur the action, as he exposes and asks about *bhang* and *holi* (the equivalents of *masquing* for Kurup).

27. Ibid.

28. Ibid.

29. Ibid.

30. Chris Jones, "Bold 'Merchant' melds Bard, Bollywood," *Chicago Tribune*, 8 October 2007.

31. Ibid.

32. Barbara Vitello, "The Bard Goes Bollywood," *Daily Herald*, 10 October 2007.

33. Jones, "Bold 'Merchant' melds Bard, Bollywood."

34. Heidi Weiss, "Worldly Hindus Take on a Strict Muslim," *Chicago Sun-Times* 1 October 2007.

35. Interview with Pranidhi Varshney, 31 July 2008.

36. Ibid.

Part 2. Canada

1. See the introduction for a discussion of indentured labor migration and South Asians in the early nineteenth century. The classic work on this subject remains Hugh Tinker, *A New System of Slavery: The Export of Indian Indentured Labor Overseas, 1830–1920* (New York: Oxford University Press, 1979).

2. See Tariq Ali Khan, "Canada Sikhs," *Himal South Asian* 12, no. 12 (1999): 27.

3. As the "continuous journey" idea was the definitive issue of early South Asian migration to Canada, this phrase serves as the title for the social history by Norman Buchigani, Doreen M. Indra, and Ram Srivastava.

4. Though not represented in this volume, Parameswaran's many plays include *Sons Must Die* and *Sita's Promise*. See the list of plays for a complete listing of Parameswaran's

work. Parameswaran also edited an entire issue of *Canadian Theatre Review,* Spring 94 (1998), dedicated to South Asian Canadian theatre.

5. Interview with the author, 28 April 2006.

6. Ibid.

7. Ibid.

8. Ibid.

9. Ibid.

10. Ibid.

11. Ibid.

12. Interview with the author, 13 April 2006.

13. Ibid.

14. Ibid.

15. Ibid.

16. Ibid.

17. Ibid.

18. Quoted in the Uma Parameswaran interview with Bose, published in *The Death of Abbie Hoffman and Other Plays* (Calcutta, 1999), 113.

Part 3. United Kingdom

1. Visram's 1986 book *Ayahs, Lascars, and Princes: Indians in Britain, 1700–1947* (London: Pluto) functions as one of the first social histories of the South Asian diaspora in Britain.

2. See Parminder Bhachu, *Twice Migrants: East African Sikh Settlers in Britain* (London: Tavistock, 1985), for a discussion of the Ramgarhia Sikh migration to the U.K.

3. From 2003 to 2007, a team of researchers have documented the theatre history and anthropology of South Asians in Britain. The findings of this research were presented at the British Asian Theatre: From Past to Present conference in April 2008 at the University of Exeter. Two books and one special journal issue will result from this research. See note 3 in the introduction. In addition to this research project, the South Asian Literature and Arts Archive (SALIDAA, www.salidaa.org.uk) includes digitized archival material from South Asian theatre productions in Britain.

4. See Visram, *Ayahs, Lascars, and Princes,* 19–22, and Verma, Keynote Address to the DNAsia Conference, Watermans Arts Centre, 2003.

5. Alda Terraciano, "South Asian Diaspora Theatre in Britain," accessed 15 January 2008 from http://www.salidaa.org.uk/salidaa/docrep/docs/sectionIntro/theatre/docm_render.html.

6. On many occasions, Verma has critiqued the tendency of official British multiculturalism to focus on bounded conceptions of "Asian" or "African" or other such art forms. Though he has recognized the value in recognitions of difference, in much of his recent writing on the theatre, he favors a more holistic conception of multiculturalism in which artists are not bounded by the borders of their own cultural identities. See his thirtieth anniversary address to Tara Arts on June 11, 2007 and his March 24, 2003 speech to the DNAsia conference at the Watermans Arts Centre.

7. *Borderline* and *Birds of Passage* are the two plays by Kureishi that deal with South Asians in Britain. Both are included in his anthology titled *Hanif Kureishi: Plays* (London: Faber and Faber, 1992).

8. "The Spectre of Self-Consciousness," 81. This appears in a collection edited by

Parekh entitled *Colour, Culture, and Consciousness: Immigrant Intellectuals in Britain* (London: George Allen & Unwin, Ltd., 1974).

9. Recent books on the topic include Margaret Abraham, *Speaking the Unspeakable: Marital Violence amongst South Asian Immigrants in the United States* (Rutgers, N.J.: Rutgers University Press, 2000) and Sandhya Nankani, ed., *Breaking the Silence: Domestic Violence in the South Asian American Community* (New York: Xlibris, 2001).

10. Kureishi's famous 1981 play details the politics of young British South Asians in the context of racial and political turmoil. It tells the story of young lovers, elders, and immigrants to Britain in the 1980s.

11. Interview with the author, 14 July 2006.

12. Ibid.

13. Quoted in Katyal, Anjum, "A Dialogue with England: An Interview with Jatinder Verma," *Seagull Theatre Quarterly* 17 (March 1998), 76.

14. Ibid.

15. This is the subject of the American Anuvab Pal's *Chaos Theory,* represented in this volume.

16. Kessie Govender's *Working Class Hero* showcases these relations as central to its story, whereas all of the others in this volume include this aspect in a secondary manner.

Part 4. South Africa

1. One historian who has not presumed this is Suleiman Dangor. He examines seventeenth-century slave records from the Cape bearing Indian names in his essay, "The Expression of Islam in South Africa," *Journal of Muslim Minority Affairs* 17, no. 1 (1997). Dangor suggests that since many Cape Muslims assume the designation of "Cape Malay," their cultural origin is wrongly presumed to be Southeast, not South, Asian. He uses the slave records to argue that the Indian presence in South Africa began long before 1860.

2. Ronnie Govender's *At the Edge and Other Cato Manor Stories* (Johannesburg: Manx, 1996) shows aspects of this process.

3. For a comprehensive account of the evolution of Indian South African theatre in the late twentieth century, see Satchu Annumalai, "The Development of South African Indian Theatre from the 1950s to the 1990s," Ph.D. diss., *University of Durban-Westville,* 1999.

4. Here I am referring to the cultural movement initiated by Steve Biko, the South African Students Organization (SASO), and the Black People's Convention (BPC). This movement promoted a principle of "black" culture translating into a unified nonwhite cultural front, in opposition to apartheid.

5. Ronnie Govender has been recognized as a major figure in South African theatre as evidence by reviews of his plays appearing in mainstream newspapers such as the *Natal Mercury, The Star, The Independent,* and the *Mail and Guardian.* Although the recognition of Indian theatre practice is growing, Thomas Hansen observed that when he researched newspaper archives in the 1990s, he saw that very few plays by Indians that do not deal with "Indian" issues (an Orientalist framework of soul, redemption, spirituality, etc.) are reviewed by "white" newspapers.

6. Interview with the author, 25 May 2006. Strini Moodley and Steve Biko were student leaders of the African National Congress, the party that later gained power in post-apartheid South Africa. Biko was killed in a gruesome Special Police witch hunt in 1976. His life is the subject of Sir Richard Attenborough's film *Cry Freedom,* in which Biko is

portrayed by the American actor Denzel Washington. One of the unheralded leaders of the Indian activist community, Strini Moodley was a close associate of Biko. Moodley's famous satire of apartheid titled *Black on White* in the 1970s drew attention from the Natal authorities. Moodley worked with the Black People's Convention, the South African Student Organization, and shared a cell on Robben Island with Nelson Mandela. Moodley died in April 2006.

7. *Coloured* refers to a specific racial group created by apartheid. Though their particular genealogy defies easy characterization, they are not Black, nor are they Indian, and they are usually seen as mixes between the early Afrikaaner settlers and local Cape inhabitants, the Khoisan. Many other theories about their origins exist, however. See Ian Goldin's essay, "Coloured Identity and Coloured Politics in the Western Cape Region of South Africa," in *The Creation of Tribalism in South Africa*, ed. Leroy Vail (London: Currey, 1991) for analyses of Coloured identity and history. Natal is the former name for the province on South Africa's eastern coast. The area now is termed KwaZulu-Natal, due to the presence of the Zulu nation.

8. See Bill Freund, *Insiders and Outsiders: The Indian Working Class of Durban, 1910–1990* (London: Heinemann, 1994).

9. Interview with the author, 25 May 2006.

10. This production history is taken from the interview with the author, 25 May 2006.

11. Quoted in Hassim, Aziz, "What Makes Ronnie Run?" n.d.

12. Ibid.

13. Interview with the author, 25 May 2006.

14. Pillay's ending displays irony as Beckett's ethos and aesthetic are targets of trenchant postcolonial critique in the play.

15. This foreword was written in 1976 for its original production and was reprinted in the 2001 edition.

16. *Song for a Sanctuary* and *Sakina's Restaurant* are included in this anthology in the U.K. and U.S. sections, respectively. *Borderline* appears in Kureishi, *Hanif Kureishi: Plays,* 1992.

17. From the documentary by Junaid Ahmed titled *Act Two, Kriben Pillay,* South African Broadcasting Corporation, 1997. Hereafter *ATKP,* 1997.

18. See Thomas Hansen, "Diasporic Dispositions," 2002, for a discussion of this observation that South African South Asians are much more South African than they are South Asian. Parvathi Raman's "In Search of the Diasporic Subject? A Resting Place for the Imagination," 2003 provides a provocative rebuttal.

19. Interview with the author, 20 April 2006.

20. Ahmed Kathrada was an anti-apartheid activist who was imprisoned on Robben Island and the 1949 riots were a landmark conflict in Indo-African relations over an alleged thievery by an African boy in an Indian shop. Many Indians and Africans were killed. Indian *kugels* refers to the upper-class Indian gossiping housewives.

21. *AKTP,* 1997.

22. Ibid.

23. Interview with the author, 20 April 2006.

24. Ibid.

25. Ibid.

26. Ibid.

27. Ibid.

28. Ibid.

Bibliography

Books

Abraham, Margaret. 2000. *Speaking the Unspeakable: Marital Violence amongst South Asian Immigrants in the United States.* New Brunswick: Rutgers University Press.

Ali, N., V.S. Kalra, and S. Sayyid, eds. 2006. *A Postcolonial People: South Asians in Britain.* London: Hurst & Co.

Bhabha, Homi. 1994. *The Location of Culture.* New York: Routledge.

Bhachu, Parminder. 1985. *Twice Migrants: East African Sikh Settlers in Britain.* London: Tavistock.

Bhana, Surendra, and Bridglal Pachai. 1984. *A Documentary History of Indian South Africans.* Stanford, Calif.: Hoover Institution Press.

Bhatia, Nandi. 2004. *Acts of Authority/Acts of Resistance: Theatre and Politics in Colonial and Postcolonial India.* Ann Arbor: University of Michigan Press.

Buchignani, Norman, Doreen M. Indra, and Ram Srivastiva. 1985. *Continuous Journey: A Social History of South Asians in Canada.* Toronto: McClelland and Stewart.

Chandrasekhar, S., ed. 1986. *From India to Canada: A Brief History of Immigration, Problems of Discrimination, Admission, and Assimilation.* La Jolla, Calif.: Population Review Books.

Chatterjee, Minoti. 2004. *Theatre beyond the Threshold: Colonialism, Nationalism, and the Bengali Stage, 1905–47.* New Delhi: Indialog.

Choudhuri, K. N. 1990. *Asia Before Europe: Economy and Civilisation of the Indian Ocean from the Rise of Islam to 1750.* Cambridge: Cambridge University Press.

Crow, Brian, and Chris Banfield. 1996. *An Introduction to Postcolonial Theatre.* New York: Cambridge University Press.

Dalmia, Vasudha. 2006. *Politics, Plays, and Performances: The Politics of Modern Indian Theatre.* New York: Oxford University Press.

Dharwadker, Aparna. 2005. *Theatres of Independence: Drama, Theory, and Urban Performance in India Since 1947.* Iowa City: University of Iowa Press.

Dhupelia-Meshtrie, Uma. 2002. *From Cane Fields to Freedom.* Cape Town: Kwela Books.

Ebr.-Vally, Rehana. 2002. *Kala Pani: Caste and Colour in South Africa.* Cape Town, Kwela Books.

Freund, Bill. 1994. *Insiders and Outsiders: The Indian Working Class of Durban, 1910–1990.* London: Heinemann.

Gainor, J. Ellen, ed. 1995. *Imperialism and Theatre: Essays on World Theatre, Drama, and Performance.* New York: Routledge.

Gandhi, Leela. 1998. *Postcolonial Theory.* New York: Columbia University Press.

Ghosh, Lipi, and Ramkrishna Chatterjee, eds. 2004. *Indian Diaspora in Asian and Pacific Regions.* New Delhi: Rawat Publications.

Gilbert, Helen, ed. 2001. *Post-Colonial Plays: An Anthology.* New York: Routledge.

———, and Joanne Tompkins. 1996. *Post-Colonial Drama: Theory, Practice, Politics.* New York: Routledge.

Govender, Ronnie. 2008 *In the Manure.* Claremont, South Africa: David Philip.

———. 2006. *Song of the Atman.* Johannesburg: Jacana Press.

———. 1996. *At the Edge and Other Cato Manor Stories.* Johannesburg: Manx.

Griffin, Gabriele. 2003. *Contemporary Black and Asian Women Playwrights in Britain.* Cambridge: Cambridge University Press.

Jacobsen, Knut A., and Pratap Kumar, eds. *South Asia in the Diaspora: Histories and Religious Traditions.* Leiden: Brill, 2004.

Jayaram, N., ed. 2004. *The Indian Diaspora: Dynamics of Migration.* London: Sage Publications.

Jensen, Joan. 1988. *Passage from India: Asian Indian Immigrants in North America.* New Haven, Conn.: Yale University Press.

Johnston, Hugh. 1979. *The Voyage of the Komagata Maru: The Sikh Challenge to Canada's Colour Bar.* Delhi: Oxford University Press.

Khan, Naseem. 1976. *The Arts Britain Ignores.* London: Commission for Racial Equality.

Lahiri, Shompa. 2000. *Indians in Britain: Anglo-Indian Encounters, Race and Identity, 1880–1930.* London: Frank Cass.

Maira, Sunaina. 2002. *Desis in the House: Indian American Youth Culture in New York City.* Philadelphia: Temple University Press.

Moore-Gilbert, Bart. 1997. *Postcolonial Theory: Contexts, Practices, Politics.* London: Verso.

Mufti, Aamir. 2007. *Enlightenment in the Colony: The Jewish Question and the Crisis of Postcolonial Culture.* Princeton, N.J.: Princeton University Press.

Nankani, Sandhya, ed. 2001. *Breaking the Silence: Domestic Violence in the South Asian American Community.* New York: Xlibris.

Ngugi Wa'Thiongo. 1986. *Decolonising the Mind: The Politics of Language in African Literature.* London: J. Carney.

Parekh, Bhikhu, ed. 1974. *Colour, Culture, and Consciousness: Immigrant Intellectuals in Britain.* London: George Allen & Unwin.

Prasad, Vijay. 2000. *The Karma of Brown Folk.* Minneapolis: University of Minnesota Press.

Rajan, Gita, and Shailja Sharma. 2006. *New Cosmopolitanisms: South Asians in the US.* Stanford, Calif.: Stanford University Press.

Ramamurthi, T. G. 1995. *Apartheid and Indian South Africans: A Study in the Role of Ethnic Indians in the Struggle against Apartheid.* New York: Reliance Publishing House.

Ramdin, Ron. 1999. *Reimaging Britain: 500 Years of Black and Asian History.* London: Pluto.

Rangaswamy, Padma. 2000. *Namaste America: Indian Immigrants in an American Metropolis*. University Park: Pennsylvania State University Press.

Rustomji-Kerns, Roshni. 1995. *Living in America: Poetry and Fiction by South Asian American Writers*. Boulder, Colo.: Westview Press.

Saha, Panchanan. 2003. *Indians in Overseas Colonies*. Kolkata: K.P. Baghci & Co.

Sandhu, Sukhdev. 2003. *London Calling: How Black and Asian Writers Imagined a City*. London: Harper Collins.

Shukla, Sandhya. 2003. *India Abroad: Diasporic Cultures of Postwar America and England*. Princeton, N.J.: Princeton University Press.

Srikanth, Rajini. 2004. *The World Next Door: South Asian American Literature and the Idea of America*. Philadelphia: Temple University Press.

Talbot, Cynthia, and Catherine Asher. 2006. *India before Europe*. Cambridge: Cambridge University Press.

Tinker, Hugh. 1977. *Banyan Tree: Overseas Emigrants from India, Pakistan, and Bangladesh*. New York: Oxford University Press.

———. 1976. *Separate and Unequal: India and the Indians in the British Commonwealth, 1920–50*. Vancouver: University of British Columbia Press.

———. 1974. *A New System of Slavery: The Export of Indian Labor Overseas, 1830–1920*. New York: Oxford University Press.

Vertovec, Steven, Parekh, Bhiku, and Gurharpal Singh, eds. 2003. *Culture and Economy in the Indian Diaspora*. London: Routledge.

Visram, Rozina. 2002. *Asians in Britain: 400 Years of History*. London: Pluto.

———. 1997. *Ayahs, Lascars, and Princes: Indians in Britain, 1700–1947*. London: Pluto.

Wa'Thiongo, Ngugi. 1986. *Decolonising the Mind: The Politics of Language in African Literature*. London: J. Currey.

Articles

Ahmed, Farah, Sarah Riaz, Paula Barata, and Donna Stewart. 2004. "Patriarchal Beliefs and Perceptions of Abuse among South Asian Immigrant Women." *Violence against Women* 10, no. 3: 262–282.

Bose, Neilesh. 1997. "Fitting the Action to the Word: An Ethnographic Journey into South African Indian Theatre." *Indic Theatre Monograph Series*. No. 4. Durban: University of Durban-Westville Press.

Chatterjee, Sudipto. 1999. "The Nation Staged: Nationalist Discourse in Late Nineteenth-Century Bengali Theatre." In *(Post) Colonial Stages: Critical and Creative Views on Drama, Theatre and Performance,* ed. Helen Gilbert, 10–25. London: Dangaroo Press.

Dadswell, Sarah. 2007a. "British Asian Theatre—Community Connections Run Deep." Unpublished paper given at annual Association for Asian Performance conference.

———. 2007b. "Jugglers, Fakirs, and Jaduwallahs: Indian Magicians and the British Stage" *New Theatre Quarterly* 89: 3–24.

Daboo, Jerrie. 2005. "One under the Sun: Globalization, Culture, and Utopia in Bombay Dreams." *Contemporary Theatre Review* 15, no. 3: 330–337.

Dahl, Mary Karen. 1995. "Postcolonial British Theatre: Black Voices at the Center." In *Imperialism and Theatre: Essays on World Theatre, Drama, and Performance, 1795–1995,* ed. J. Ellen Gainor, 38–55. New York: Routledge.

Dangor, Suleiman. 1997. "The Expression of Islam in South Africa" *Journal of Muslim Minority Affairs* 17, no. 1: 141–151.

DasGupta, Samita. 2000. "Charting the Course: An Overview of Domestic Violence in the South Asian Community in the United States." *Journal of Social Distress and the Homeless* 9, no. 3: 173–185.

Dharwadker, Aparna. 2003. "Diaspora and the Theatre of the Nation." *Theatre Research International* 28, no. 3: 303–325.

———. 1998. "Diaspora and the Failure of Home: Two Contemporary Indian Plays." *Theatre Journal* 50, no. 1: 71–94.

Fuchs, Anne. 2006. "Looking at New British Heritage. Tamasha Theatre Company." In *Staging New Britain: Aspects of Black and South Asian British Theatre Practice,* ed. Anne Fuchs and Geoffrey V. Davis, 127–140. London: Peter Lang.

Goldin, Ian. 1991. "Coloured Identity and Coloured Politics in the Western Cape Region of South Africa." In *The Creation of Tribalism in South Africa*, ed. Leroy Vail, 241–254. London: Currey.

Govender, Suria. 1996. "Interculturalism and South African Indian Fusion Dance." *Indic Theatre Monograph Series.* No. 3. Durban: University of Durban-Westville Press.

Hansen, Thomas. 2005. "Melancholia of Freedom: Humour and Nostalgia among Indians in South Africa." *Modern Drama* 48, no. 2: 297–315.

———. 2002. "Diasporic Dispositions." *Himal South Asian* 15, No. 12 (December): 20–32.

———. 2000. "Plays, Politics, and Cultural Identity Among Indians in Durban." *Journal of Southern African Studies* 26, no. 2: 255–269.

Hassan, Aziz. n.d. "What Makes Ronnie Run?" Unpublished essay.

Katyal, Anjum. 1998. "A Dialogue with England: An Interview with Jatinder Verma." *Seagull Theatre Quarterly* 17 (March): 71–80.

Khan, Tarik Ali. 1999. "Canada Sikhs." *Himal South Asian* 12, no. 12 (December): 26–29.

Lal, Vinay. 1999a. "Establishing Roots, Engendering Awareness: A Political History of Asian Indians in the United States." In *Live Like the Banyan Tree: Images of the Indian American Experience*, ed. Leela Prasad, 42–48. Philadelphia: Balch Institute for Ethnic Studies, 1999.

———. 1999b. "Indentured Labor and the Indian Diaspora in the Caribbean." http://www.sscnet.ucla.edu/southasia/Diaspora/freed.html.

Ley, Graham. 1997. "Theatre of Migration and the Search for a Multicultural Aesthetic: Twenty Years of Tara Arts." *New Theatre Quarterly* 52: 349–371.

Naidoo, Muthal. 1997. "The Search for a Cultural Identity: A Personal View of South African 'Indian' Theatre." *Theatre Journal* 49, no. 1: 29–39.

Naidu, Vayu. 2006. "Vayu Naidu Company's South. New Directions in Theatre of Storytelling." In *Staging New Britain: Aspects of Black and South Asian British Theatre Practice,* ed. Anne Fuchs and Geoffrey V. Davis, 141–160. London: Peter Lang.

Pillay, Kriben. 1998. "South African Indian Theatre—The Search for Identity." Unpublished essay.

Raman, Parvathi. 2003. "In Search of the Diasporic Subject: A Resting Place for the Imagination?" *Himal South Asian* 16, no. 9: 22–30.

Richman, Paula. 2004. "Shifting Terrain: Rama and Odysseus Meet on the London Stage." *Journal of Vaishnava Studies* 12, no. 2: 33–57.

———. 2000. "A Diaspora Ramayana in Southall, Greater London." In *Questioning Ramayanas: A South Asian Tradition*, ed. Paula Richman, 35–57. Berkeley: University of California Press.

Schauffer, Dennis. 1994. "In the Shadow of the Shah: The Indic Contribution to Our Developing South African Culture." *Indic Theatre Monograph Series.* No. 2. Durban: University of Durban-Westville Press.

Schlote, Christiane. 2006a. "Either for Tragedy, Comedy, History or Musical Unlimited; South Asian Women Playwrights in Britain." In *Staging New Britain: Aspects of Black and South Asian British Theatre Practice,* ed. Anne Fuchs and Geoffrey V. Davis. 65–86. London: Peter Lang.

———. 2006b. "Finding our Own Voice," an interview with Jatinder Verma. In *Staging New Britain: Aspects of Black and South Asian British Theatre Practice,* ed. Anne Fuchs and Geoffrey V. Davis, 253–270. London: Peter Lang.

Shukla, Sandhya. 2001. "Locations for South Asian Diasporas." *Annual Review of Anthropology* 30: 551–572.

Siddiqui, Haroon. 2004. "South Asians." Lecture, Asian Heritage Month, Centre for South Asian Studies, *University of Toronto,* 18 May.

Terracciano, Alda. 2002. "Key African, Caribbean, and Asian Theatre Productions since 1975." In *Black and Asian Theatre at the Theatre Museum: A User's Guide,* ed. Susan Croft. London: Theatre Museum.

Tran, Kelly, Jennifer Kaddatz, and Paul Allard. 2005. "South Asians in Canada: Unity through Diversity" *Canadian Social Trends.* Autumn: 20–25.

Verma, Jatinder. 2003. "Asian Arts in the Twenty-First Century." Keynote Address at DNAsia Conference, Watermans Arts Centre, 24 March 2003.

———. 2001a. "Are We Visible?" Address, PUSHKAR Conference, Oldmam, UK, 12 November.

———. 2001b. "Braids and Theatre Practice." British Braids Conference, Brunel University, Middlesex, UK, 20 April.

———. 1997. "An Asian Agenda for British Public Policy?" Address, St. Catherine's Conference, The Media: Access, Roles, and Cultural Change. Windsor, UK, 11–13 April.

———. 1996a. "Binglish: A Jungli Approach to Multi-Cultural Theatre." Address, Standing Conference of University Drama Departments, Scarborough, UK, 19–21 April.

———. 1996b. "The Binglish Imperative." Address, CPR Conference, Aberswyth, Wales, UK, 5 September.

———. 1996c. "Punjabi Theatre in Britain: Context and Challenge." Unpublished essay.

———. 1994a. "Asian Theatre in Britain." Conference Paper, Historical Developments and Contemporary Identity, Asian Theatre Conference, Birmingham, UK.

———. 1994b. "The Challenge of Analysing Multi-cultural Productions." Unpublished essay.

Play Anthologies

Bose, Rana. 1999. *The Death of Abbie Hoffman and Other Plays.* Kolkata: Seagull.

Eng, Alvin, ed. 2000. *TOKENS? The New York City Asian American Experience on Stage.* Philadelphia: Temple University Press.

George, Kadija, ed. 1993. *Six Plays by Black and Asian Women Writers.* London: Aurora Metro Press.

Govender, Ronnie. 2007. *Interplay: A Collection of South African Plays.* Pretoria: Manx.

Kureishi, Hanif. 1992. *Hanif Kureishi: Plays.* London: Faber and Faber.

Parmeswaran, Uma, ed. 1996. *SACLIT Drama: Plays by South Asian Canadians.* Bangalore: IBH Prakashana.

Perkins, Kathy, ed. 1998. *Black South African Women: An Anthology of Plays.* New York: Routledge.

Robson, Cheryl, ed. 2000. *Black and Asian Plays: An Anthology.* London: Aurora Metro Press.

Theses

Alessandrini, Anthony C. 2000. "'Bombay' in Iselin: Culture, Capital and Citizens between South Asia and the South Asian Diaspora." Ph.D. diss., Rutgers University.

Annamalai, Satchu. 1999. "The Development of South African Indian Theatre from the 1950s to the 1990s." Ph.D. diss., University of Durban-Westville.

Deepak, Anne Christine. 2004. "Identity Formation and the Negotiation of Desire: Women of the South Asian Diaspora in the United States." Ph.D. diss., Columbia University.

Mani, Bakirathi. 2002. "The Imagination of South Asian America: Cultural Politics in the Making of Diaspora." Ph.D. diss., Stanford University.

Nair, Savita. 2001. "Moving Life Histories: Gujarat, East Africa, and the Indian Diaspora, 1880–2000." Ph.D. diss., University of Pennsylvania.

Rajgopal, Shoba Sharad. 2003. "From *Izzat* to *Heimat*: Ethnic Identity and Cultural Nationalism in the Cinema of the South Asian Diaspora." Ph.D. diss., University of Colorado-Boulder.

Terracciano, Alda. 2002. "Crossing Lines: An Analysis of Integration and Separatism within Black Theatre in Britain" Ph.D. diss., Istituto Universitario Orientale (IUO).

Vahed, Goolam. 1995. "The Making of Indian Identity in Durban, 1914–1949." Ph.D. diss., Indiana University.

Internet Resources

University of California-Berkeley South Asia Diaspora Bibliographic Guide, http://www .lib.berkeley.edu/SSEAL/SouthAsia/resource.html

University of Washington South Asia Diaspora Literature in English, http://www.lib .washington.edu/southasia/guides/diaspora.html#da

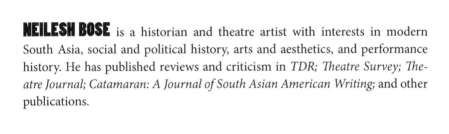

NEILESH BOSE is a historian and theatre artist with interests in modern South Asia, social and political history, arts and aesthetics, and performance history. He has published reviews and criticism in *TDR; Theatre Survey; Theatre Journal; Catamaran: A Journal of South Asian American Writing;* and other publications.

Printed and bound by CPI Group (UK) Ltd, Croydon, CR0 4YY

09/06/2025